Accounting: A Book of Readings

PAUL E. DASCHER
Drexel University

PAUL A. JANELL
Northeastern University

WILLIAM G. SHENKIR
McIntire School of Commerce
University of Virginia

1982

dame publications, inc.
P.O. Box 35556
Houston, Texas 77035

© DAME PUBLICATIONS, INC. 1982

ISBN 0-931920-30-2
Library of Congress Catalog Card No. 80-70470
Printed in the United States of America.

Preface

An effective introduction to accounting requires more than an emphasis on only accounting principles and procedures. Equally, it is important to provide exposure to the environment of the discipline and, in a broader sense, to also provide an introduction to the realities of business and the world of commerce. ACCOUNTING: A BOOK OF READINGS was prepared as a vital supplement to such introductory accounting courses.

Fundamentals of Accounting, Principles of Accounting and Financial Accounting are common identifiers for the first accounting course. In most cases, the textbook focuses on the elements of the accounting process and is restricted to functions of the accounting system. Usually, textbook structures do not provide a sufficient exposure to important factors in the accounting environment. A more comprehensive appreciation of the accounting process can be obtained when students are given the opportunity to extend their learning experience into other relevant factors drawn from the environment of the discipline. This approach tends to reinforce the basic material by addressing its development and application.

Most graduate programs make available an introductory accounting course for students coming from non-business undergraduate backgrounds. At this level, students also can benefit from expanding their view of the profession and its impact in the broader business community. The opportunity to read literature from a variety of sources which relates to current topics can provide a significant learning experience for these students. Usually, graduate students are extremely receptive to such an approach and instructors can use divergent views presented by different authors as the basis for classroom discussion.

ACCOUNTING: A BOOK OF READINGS is intended to broaden the scope of the introductory accounting course. Readings are drawn from a broad variety of sources and have been integrated into a format complementing most introductory courses. The selected articles and materials have been organized in a manner consistent with the instructional flow and they give the student a thorough appreciation of the accounting environment and its interface with other areas of business society.

Readings books are sometimes designed to reflect the editors' perspective on the issue at hand. In this case, a significant effort was made to develop a collection of materials that reflects the perspective of classroom users. In approach, this casts the materials in a light that can enhance the presentation of specific instructional concepts by permitting students to grasp and appreciate the importance and context of presented subject matter.

To approach this task, we performed the usual search of accounting and business literature. This was augmented by computer-assisted searches of significant data bases. Recognizing the usual position of the first accounting course in the curriculum, a specific effort was undertaken to identify readings which provide a general overview and approach to a subject area, rather than a detailed, in-depth commentary on a specific problem or issue. Next, materials were screened in the context of existing readings books and supplementary materials available to the instructor.

The goal of this project was to provide a compilation of reading materials that can enrich the study experience of students. The materials can be used as out-of-class readings for student assignment, as the basis for in-class discussions, or both. Sufficient selections have been provided to give the instructor maximum flexibility in making choices. Unassigned reading will also be useful reference materials for students in the course.

It should be noted that the intent of ACCOUNTING: A BOOK OF READINGS is to address current issues in the context of intellectual curiosity. In this sense, the assembled materials do not merely restate contents traditionally found in accounting textbooks. Rather, they present alternative views, challenges to current practice, and interpretations of professional developments on a selected basis to enhance the student's awareness of the environment, opportunities and conflicts inherent in the practice of professional accounting.

The editors appreciate the cooperation of publishers of the many sources used in compiling this collection. Also, the helpful comments and assistance of colleagues at our institutions and at colleges throughout the country is appreciated. Of particular note were suggestions offered by the following:

James Benjamin, Texas A&M University
Vincent Brenner, Louisiana State University
Ronald Copeland, University of South Carolina
Joseph Ford, Drexel University
Art Francia, University of Houston
Stan Kligman, Jesco International
Robert Landry, Massasoit Community College
Michael Lane, Northeastern University
David Rothfuss, Coopers & Lybrand
Bill Sabatino, Community Accountants
Robert Schuster, Drexel University

Many of the readings included in this book were written in a style which uses the masculine pronoun. Such construction reflects individual style and some historic insensitivity to current social issues. All students of accounting should recognize that the profession is practiced by both men and women and that any description, discussion or illustration involving a male will apply equally to a female. Most current accounting publications include references to both sexes. Likewise, readers of these articles should recognize that pronoun utilization is not intended to be restrictive, but illustrative.

Paul E. Dascher
Paul A. Janell
William G. Shenkir

Contents

SECTION I

The Accounting Environment

Like most important professions, accounting exists as an integral part of a complex environment. Environmental factors include formal influences such as legal constraints, regulatory policies and legislative mandates. Less formal influences encompass the societal, interpersonal and institutional constraints which have an impact on the profession.

The accounting profession may be viewed from two distinct positions — that of the preparer of accounting information and that of the user of accounting information. In this sense, accounting either impacts or has the potential to impact on all members of our society. Economic factors have a significant effect on the conduct of our lives, the practice of our professions and on the growth and development of our country. Accounting is the basic information source available to all individuals in addressing these economic factors.

From the view of a prospective accountant, it is important for the individual to grasp the full extent of the environment of the profession. Only by recognizing the position and importance of the discipline and the constraints and responsibilities accompanying its practice can one develop as an effective accountant. Too narrow a view or too limited a perception of its position can hamper the effectiveness of an accountant.

Non-accountants also have a vital need for accounting information. This is true if one contemplates movement into any sort of managerial career or, in a more restricted scope, as an individual. Consider, for example, the impact of Internal Revenue Service regulations on all citizens of the United States and the inherent accounting requirements specified or implied in these regulations. Again, an understanding and appreciation of the scope of accounting can enhance the individual's ability to access and utilize the information and service available.

This section is divided into five parts which present a broad selection of readings addressing the accounting environment. Materials relate to the societal role of the profession, the interrelationships of accounting with other business disciplines, organizational influences on accounting, career opportunities and the scope of present accounting services. This perspective can place the profession in the context of our society, economy and environment.

The Accounting Review

VOL. XVIII JULY, 1943 No. 3

THE NATURE OF THE FINANCIAL ACCOUNTING PROCESS*

GEORGE O. MAY

ccounting has been defined by a committee of the American Institute of Accountants as "the art of recording, classifying and summarizing, in a significant manner and in terms of money, transactions and events which are, in part at least, of a financial character, and interpreting the results thereof." It is an art, not a science, but an art of wide and varied usefulness. The purely recording function of accounting, though indispensable, concerns only technicians. Its analytical and interpretive functions are of two kinds. One type of analysis is intended to afford aid to management in the conduct of business and is of interest mainly to executives. The other type leads to the presentation of statements relating to the financial position and results of operations of a business for the guidance of directors, stockholders, credit grantors, and others. This process of financial accounting, therefore, possesses a wide importance for persons who are neither accountants nor executives.

Many accountants are reluctant to admit that accounting is based on nothing of a higher order of sanctity than conventions. However, it is apparent that this is necessarily true of accounting as it is, for instance, of business law. In these fields there are no principles, in the fundamental sense of that word, on which we can build;

and the distinctions among laws, rules, standards, and conventions lie not in their nature but in the kind of sanctions by which they are enforced. Accounting procedures have in the main been the result of common agreement among accountants, although they have to some extent, and particularly in recent years, been influenced by laws or regulations.

Conventions, to have authority, must be well conceived. Accounting conventions should be well conceived in relation to at least three things: first, the uses of accounts; second, the social and economic concepts of the time and place; and, third, the modes of thought of the people. It follows that as economic and social concepts or modes of thought change, accounting concepts may have to change with them.

The first point for consideration is, therefore, the major uses of financial statements. We can recognize at least ten distinguishable uses:

1. As a report of stewardship
2. As a basis for fiscal policy
3. As a criterion of the legality of dividends
4. As a guide to wise dividend action
5. As a basis for the granting of credit
6. As information for prospective investors in an enterprise
7. As a guide to the value of investments already made
8. As an aid to government supervision

---

* Adapted from materials prepared for a forthcoming book by the same author.

The Accounting Review

9. As a basis for price or rate regulation
10. As a basis for taxation

General-purpose statements are not suitable in all of these cases; in some instances, special-purpose statements are called for. This has become increasingly recognized in respect of rate or price control and taxation, and it should also be recognized, for reasons which I shall indicate later, in respect of information for new investors—or, in other words, for the prospectus—and also in some cases for the determination of the legality of a dividend. But even if these purposes are eliminated, there remain at least six which are expected to be served by general-purpose statements.

It is immediately apparent that any general-purpose statements cannot be expected to serve all the purposes equally well—indeed, if they are to be appropriate for the major uses, it is likely that they will not serve some other purposes even reasonably well. It becomes necessary, therefore, to consider which are to be regarded as the controlling objectives, and to view the possibility of changes therein.

Accounting conventions must take cognizance of the social and economic concepts of the time and place. Conventions which are acceptable in a pioneer, free-enterprise economy may not be equally appropriate in a more mature, free-enterprise economy, and may lose their validity entirely in a controlled economy. Some existing accounting conventions seem to assume implicitly the existence of *laissez faire* and may require reconsideration as prices, interest rates, and other vital elements become the subject of conscious government control. Under this head must be considered, also, the forms of business organization and changes either in the nature of the dominant type or types or in the laws governing them. Systems of taxation and legal decisions growing out of them also influence accounting concepts.

The third and last consideration which has been mentioned as affecting accounting conventions is the modes of thought of the people. The extent and the nature of legal influence in business affairs will affect the conventions; those developed in the atmosphere of the common law will differ from those evolved under a civil code system. So, too, a people thinking in terms of capital value and a people thinking in terms of annual value will naturally reach different conclusions on some points, as is evidenced by the American and British attitudes towards capital gains and losses in taxation and accounting.

The relevance and importance of such considerations as these have been borne in on me by the events of the forty-five years of my experience in American accounting. Within this time we have moved from what might be called the last days of a pioneer, free-enterprise economy to a period in which a large and growing segment of enterprise is under a substantial measure of government control. The major part of the development of the corporation as the typical form of business organization has occurred within the same period; there has been a marked movement toward the separation of beneficial ownership from management.

Beginning with the control over railroad accounting given to the Interstate Commerce Commission in 1907, we have seen a steady growth of accounting by prescription, and a shift from the common-law mode of thought towards that of the civil code.

The laxness of our corporation laws and the ease of reincorporation have impaired the significance of the corporation as an accounting unit. The extension of intercorporate holdings has increased the importance of accounting for interest, dividends, and other forms of transferred income; manifestly, such accounting involves different problems from those

The Nature of the Financial Accounting Process

encountered in dealing with primary income, such as that from manufacturing. The creation of a wide variety of forms of capital obligations has raised questions as to the accounting significance of legal distinctions, often highly artificial, between bonds and stocks and between interest and dividends.

Perhaps the most significant change of all is the shift of emphasis from the balance sheet to the income statement, and particularly to the income statement as a guide to earning capacity rather than as an indication of accretions to disposable income.

It is appropriate, next, to consider what alternative approaches to the problem of formulating or revising the conventions of financial accounting are open to us. First of all, there is a choice between the value and the cost approach, or perhaps rather a question as to how the two can best be combined. This combination is illustrated in the custom of carrying inventories at cost or market value, whichever is lower—one of the oldest of accounting practices.

There is a choice between different concepts of income and between different theories of allocation of income to periods. We have the concept according to which income arises gradually, and the concept which treats income as arising at a moment when realization is deemed to have occurred. Here again, both concepts in practice are adopted to some, but not to an unchanging, extent. Today, the interesting question is presented whether accounting is likely to move in the direction of a more complete adherence to the realization concept of income or towards wider application of the doctrine of gradual accrual.

There is also a choice between the enterprise as the accounting unit and the legal entity that carries on the enterprise as the accounting unit. The system of consolidated accounts, freely employed in cor-

porate reporting, is a departure from the strict separate-entity theory. In recent years, the adoption by public service commissions of the concept of cost to the first person who devoted property to the public service, as the basis of property accounting of the present owners, has created a new interest in enterprise accounting, of which it is a crude and inadequate variant, and along with it a new series of problems.

The range of possible choice of conventions might be extended if some postulates, commonly adopted, were discarded. It is, for instance, generally assumed that financial statements must be in a continuous, related series, but it may be argued that there is no absolute compulsion that they should be. The problem of continuity presents difficulties when a substantial change of conventions occurs—as, for instance, when public utility corporations are required for financial accounting purposes (and not merely for rate purposes) to account for property on the basis of the cost to the first purchaser who devoted the property to public service, instead of on the traditional basis of cost to themselves; or when straight-line depreciation accounting is substituted for other methods of dealing with property consumption which have been employed and sanctioned for decades.

Again, the monetary unit is generally assumed to be substantially constant in value, but at times this assumption of stability has to be abandoned, with the result that accounting conventions have to be modified.

The choice of conventions in financial accounting, as in cost accounting, is to some extent affected by the conflict among considerations of speed, accuracy, and expense. The accountant is called upon to produce general-purpose statements within a few weeks of the completion of the fiscal period to which they relate. These reports are expected to be final and to serve a

The Accounting Review

great diversity of purposes. Delay in preparation might permit of greater refinement but might impair the usefulness of the statements; hence conventions must be such as to be capable of prompt application.

In a pioneer economy, the great opportunity for making profits is likely to lie in participating in the growth of the country and in the accompanying increase of values. At such a time capital will be relatively scarce, whereas labor—particularly if there is free immigration—may be plentiful. These causes will contribute to make capital investment relatively small; and the proportion of assets that are readily salable, and may be expected to be realized in a short time, will be comparatively high.

In such circumstances, the value approach to accounting has a strong appeal. In reading American accounting literature, it is surprising to find how generally accounting has been described as a process of valuation, how this view has been maintained down to a rather recent date, and how pronounced and rapid the change of view has been. In a more mature economy, when greater capital resources, and, perhaps, changes in labor conditions also, tend to produce constantly increasing capital investment, business units become larger and enterprises more complex. Then the valuation approach becomes impracticable and resort to cost as the primary line of approach becomes almost inevitable.

The change from a value basis to a cost basis is of great importance in relation to such questions as the rate base and the "surplus assets" theory of limitation of dividends. It is undeniable, though not fully recognized outside the profession, that books of large enterprises are kept predominantly on a cost basis and do not, therefore, constitute evidence of the value of either the enterprise as a whole or of the separate assets thereof, particularly the

capital assets. This might be deemed to be a serious defect of accounting procedures except for two considerations—first, that the value of the enterprise is seldom a material fact for consideration; and, second, that when it is, it can be measured only by looking ahead. For this purpose, the sole relevance of accounts of the past is as a means of throwing light on the prospects for the future. These considerations have additional force if the implicit assumption that the monetary unit remains stable is widely at variance with reality—as, for instance, in the case of property acquired before a substantial decline in the purchasing power of the monetary unit such as occurred between 1913 and 1920.

Forty-five years ago the external influence acting on accounting with the greatest effect was that of the credit grantor. In recent years there has been a marked shift of emphasis, and the use of accounting statements as a guide in the purchase or sale of securities has been more heavily stressed as a result of the efforts to impart liquidity to investments in long-term enterprises. In the early days, conservatism was the cardinal virtue of accounting; now, the virtue of conservatism is questioned, and the greater emphasis is on consistency. At that time, also, uniform classifications that were binding on particular forms of enterprises were practically unknown. Today, they are numerous and increasing in number and scope.

In this article the only objects have been to bring out the true nature of the accounting process and to advance the thought that accounting conventions are not something fixed and unalterable, but something that, like the law, should have elements of stability and of flexibility. Times are changing and accounting conventions will change with them. Today, a study of the historical development of accounting conventions and of the causes which have brought about change may be more useful *than a* description of present practice. It *has* frequently been said that the changes *revealed* by successive balance sheets are *more* significant than the individual balance sheets themselves. The same may be true of the conventions upon which balance sheets are based.

Governmental accounting past, present and future

An adaptation of an address by Robert H. White, *CPA, Lester Witte & Company, Chicago, general chairman of the Illinois Society of Certified Public Accountants Governmental Accounting Committee, presented at a technical session sponsored by the ISCPA, April 26 and 27, 1974.*

Certified public accountants involved in financial audits of local governmental units are learning much about our society from a new vantage point: the political environment of government in the arena of public affairs.

The educational experience is both exciting and frustrating. The auditor who expects to find accounting and reporting systems comparable to those in use in the private sector will do well if, as a minimum, he or she can maintain an optimistic view for the future.

If he is a product of the protestant ethic, which is considered naïve today, he will be disappointed to find very little of the reverence for hard work that was considered necessary for success in private industry in the past.

If he is a product of the post-World War II society, which is fast becoming a more service-oriented and so-called "post-industrial" environment, he will recognize the great need for accounting improvements in both sectors of society.

While society's values and objectives have been changing at a relentless rate in the last 30 years, it's become increasingly obvious that society hasn't been able to keep pace with necessary accounting, auditing, budgeting and reporting improvements to meet these changing objectives, especially in government at the local level.

Traditionally, the profession has been expected to make a sacrifice or contribution to society, for the common good, in governmental audits. This means that we cannot expect to invoice the governmental client at rates applicable for similar services to private clients. This is interesting in light of government's increased competition with industry and the profession in acquiring ac-counting personnel. It is especially interesting in terms of the "best use of resources," if we consider the effects of alleged government waste and the ineffectiveness of its programs.

The primary duty of governmental management has traditionally been "to comply with the law." We are told that the same is true today. Problems arise, however, because of the narrow construction and application of this principle. For example, it is often very difficult to get any real action on suggestions for improvements resulting from an audit. We are told that "the real purpose of an audit is to comply with the law—nothing else is really necessary—all that's important is that the audit provide a 'clean bill of health.' "

The implementation of a "management letter" recommendation too often depends on the evaluation of the issue in terms of political considerations—Can it be used as a campaign issue? Will it make us look good? How do the proposed issues and related costs rank in terms of "important" political considerations?

It has been exceptionally difficult

to communicate effectively with state and local government management (either at the executive, legislative or administrative level) in terms of the need for proper priority rankings and needed appropriations for bookkeeping and accounting controls, management information systems or necessary improvements in reporting. While necessary expenditures are often made for these programs, it is seldom that such programs are properly or completely implemented and followed.

Government traditionally has been more interested in political issues, not accounting issues—an unfortunate emphasis which obscures the fact that good accounting can also be "good politics." Today, however, we see value changes taking place that eventually will result in priority reevaluations and more and better accountability. However, progress (or "reform," to use a more familiar governmental term) has been disappointing. We have yet to produce an accepted body of accounting theory generally applied in local government. This is not to say that much thought hasn't been given to the problem. Numerous textbooks, articles, publications of the Municipal Finance Officers Association and others, and the recently released AICPA audit guide, *Audits of State and Local Governmental Units*, are available. Of special interest, however, is the large body of studies and other material consisting of insistent and critical commentary which, for reasons which are difficult to determine, has been largely ignored.

It is difficult if not impossible to identify a basic or coherent overall frame of reference. Available principles are fragmented, impossible to apply on any consistent basis in practice because of what are often called "environmental" or "legal" constraints.

Theory is unproductive and of little use unless it is applied. Most local governments still follow cash-basis budgeting, accounting and reporting practices and/or various modifications of accrual accounting. Few maintain the fund–entity integrities called for by the National Committee on Governmental Accounting and also endorsed by the recently released AICPA audit guide. Even fewer use cost accounting or performance measurement

techniques suggested (but not required) by both the NCGA and the AICPA.

A major fault of the "authoritative" texts, in my opinion, is that many of the generally accepted accounting principles which are intended for use in the multifaceted structure of suggested systems are of minimum value in terms of relevancy to current needs. The insistent emphasis on "legalistic" dollar accountability, the complex fund structure, object-of-expenditure accounting and the failure to recognize the need for "operational" accountability on a function or program basis are prime examples of institutionalized inertia of a high order.

Perhaps an attempt to gain a new perspective would be timely and of some value. A fresh look at governmental accounting in terms of current needs might be fruitful.

Definitions

Accountants and others have produced a variety of definitions of what accounting is and isn't and how the development of accounting principles should or should not proceed. Consideration also has been given to the question of whether or not it is possible or desirable to develop a basic structure or "mainstream" of accounting theory that would be broad enough for our expanding needs.

Webster's Dictionary defines accounting as "the system, science, or art of keeping, analyzing and explaining commercial accounts." The *American Heritage Dictionary* definition is "the bookkeeping methods involved in recording the business transactions and preparing the financial statements of a business." These definitions reflect our traditional preoccupation with profit-motivated industry and would, therefore, be inappropriate for our discussion. This traditional preoccupation with profit, at least as implied in the above definitions, may partially explain the reluctance of public officials and the general public to recognize accounting as a necessary and important service activity in government.

Nevertheless, these definitions are more likely to be available for general use than a definition from our technical literature. To the extent, therefore, that a "technical" defini-

tion would significantly vary from one in common use, we can expect public misunderstandings.

Accounting Principles Board Statement No. 4 (October 1970) defines accounting as a "service activity" which "is to provide quantitative information, primarily financial in nature, about economic entities that is intended to be useful in making economic decisions—in making reasoned choices among alternative courses of action" (para. 40). Accounting is also described as consisting of three branches: financial, managerial and governmental.

Because the Statement is concerned basically with accounting for business enterprises, explanations are not given for the breakdown of the three branches. Does the separate category of governmental accounting suggest the need for or acknowledgment of a preoccupation with private sector needs? Or does it imply that the not-for-profit characteristics of government are so different from industry that separation into a special category is necessary?

Financial and managerial accounting are equally important to society today in both government and industry. Differences between government and industry accounting needs are minimal and overemphasized to the extent that the development of governmental accounting systems has been unnecessarily and unfortunately impeded.

It would be appropriate to add at least two more branches of accounting to the list, social (socioeconomic) accounting and macro-accounting. The former is concerned with the impact on society of activities of organizations and individuals in all sectors of our economy, and the latter, with our national accounts in a macro sense.

Statement No. 4's definition, for purposes of our discussion, is too limited in scope for today's general use. Expansion to include *qualitative* information which may be *nonfinancial* in nature about *noneconomic* activities intended to be useful in making economic *and* other *social decisions* is in order.

The APB's definition places emphasis on financial information and economic matters but does not provide for information on qualitative data and noneconomic activities which relate to the common purpose of both industry and government in providing services to all of society. While it is important for industry to generate profits (an activity which is itself a service to society) and for government and other public not-for-profit entities to provide services primarily at cost, these organizations are also concerned with noneconomic matters, many of which broadly defined can be described as "quality of life," and other social issues that depend on qualitative measurements for evaluation.

Not all activities and their impacts on the organization and society can be measured in dollars. The effectiveness of government programs in areas of health, public aid, crime control and education, and industry's programs for employee satisfaction and welfare, pollution control, consumerism, product quality, community relations and minority issues are prime examples.

The Report of the AICPA Study Group on the Objectives of Financial Statements (chaired by the late Robert Trueblood) states that "accounting is a social system much like language and law. As such, it tends to evolve by adapting to its environment; but evolutionary changes may occur which are incompatible or even in conflict with current notions of what the objectives of this system ought to be" (page 13).

The report also acknowledges that there have been substantial changes in the types of users and the kinds of information users have sought. However, the report goes on to say (page 16) that "it should be remembered that accounting is a social system based largely on conventions or traditions. Many of these conventions are now being challenged. Official pronouncements of the profession have not, to date, provided a framework for meeting these challenges."

These remarks of the Trueblood Study Group are as germane to governmental accounting as they are to accounting in private industry, perhaps more so. Governmental accounting practices have not changed significantly since the turn of the century. The profession has generally maintained an indifferent attitude in the whole not-for-profit area and still has made no significant contributions to the literature (except for the current AICPA guide), or an accepted theoretical frame-

work on which to build accounting systems for government to meet current needs.

Developments to date

Since the turn of the century developments in governmental accounting have been left generally to the laity—such organizations as the Municipal Finance Officers Association, Association of School Business Officials, federal and state governments and the American Hospital Association — with representation from the profession on only a liaison basis. With all due regard for the efforts of these organizations, governmental accounting has been unable to keep up with necessary improvements required by a changing society.

We are still totally concerned with dollar accountability to the neglect of operational accountability. We are still overly concerned with maintaining an inflexible and complex legalistic fund accounting system to the extent that accounting for government as an entity is not only ignored but is also generally prohibited as acceptable practice. Such generally recognized accounting conventions and procedures as full accrual accounting and budgeting; full cost-based accounting and budgeting; standard costing techniques; proper fixed asset and depreciation accounting; and systems designed to justify the existence of units and their activities on the basis of efficiency, effectiveness and needs by society are still not in use.

The new AICPA audit guide does make contributions in the area of reporting in recognition of the need for full disclosure of legal compliance matters and budget data for comparison with actual transactions (a procedure that has been commonly followed in the past). However, the auditor's responsibility is restricted to a determination that a budget has been formally approved and adopted. Neglected is a requirement that the budget incorporate acceptable accounting principles to insure the comparability of such budget data with actual transactions and a recognition that the auditor's responsibility is to satisfy himself that the financial statements overall present both budgeted and actual financial information on a comparable basis.

Of particular significance to those

states where the counties are the assessing, extending and collection agencies for local government is the failure of the guide to recognize the need to apply a "matching principle" to the overall relationships of planned costs and required funding and actual costs and actual funding on the bases of the benefit (budget) year and nonprofit (balanced budget) operational concepts. An example is the guide's requirement for cash-basis accounting for property taxes where all the payments are not due within the budget year. Usually a significant item, property taxes become a lien on the property and are substantially measurable when levied. The receivable and the revenue should be recognized when the levy is made to finance planned expenditures, regardless of due dates on the tax bills or their timely mailing by the counties.

What appears to be a curious contradiction is the statement that "the primary responsibility of governmental officials is to comply with the law" and the accounting principle established by the guide that where there is a variation between the law and a recommended accounting principle, the accounting principle prevails. Do we suggest noncompliance with the law?

A more accurate—or less confusing—statement would be that responsibilities of public officials include the necessary executive, legislative, policy and operational (or administrative) functions in connection with providing required services to the public on the bases of custodial and trust relationships. Of course public officials have a responsibility to comply with the law, as we all do. Distinctions can be drawn, however, in that law making is itself a public service activity and that governmental officials have exceptional opportunities to make laws for their own convenience or political expediency in the absence of (and sometimes in spite of) public pressure to the contrary.

Because law making is a public service activity, it would appear to be in the public interest, as well as in the officials' interest, to provide legislation on accounting matters that is responsive to society's needs. So that a full accounting could be made with integrity and responsibility in terms of the custodial and trust relationships established.

The obvious question becomes, Why pass audit laws at all? It would seem to be equally obvious that public officials in the discharge of their duties would be well aware of the need to utilize generally recognized good business practices which include the application of appropriate accounting procedures as well as independent audits. The answer is that without such laws we would have few audits, as we know from experience.

Equally perplexing is the tendency to construct laws dealing with accounting, auditing, budgeting and reporting matters that fall far short of the need. An example is the Illinois municipal audit law requiring the application of generally accepted accounting principles and audit standards. Under pressure from public officials, the law was eventually amended to include the provision that audits "may be made upon either an accrual or cash basis of accounting depending upon the system followed." I hasten to compliment Illinois, however, for at least providing audit legislation.

State attorneys general are often asked to give legal opinions on such legislation. I recall an instance where an attorney general's opinion was requested involving the meaning of the phrase "generally accepted accounting principles." The opinion given relied on the *Black's Law Dictionary* definition of "generally accepted" which was at variance with accounting technical literature and consequently offered little in the way of clarification of the issues involved.

Resistance
Historically, suggestions for improvements in governmental accounting have been met with resistance from the profession and the laity alike, as well as from those bureaucracies bent on grinding out accounting rules by legislative fiat: our general assemblies and their related rule making groups and regulatory agencies.

Accounting issues, even for professionals, are sometimes complex and difficult to communicate, especially to officials and management who do not feel the pressure from shareholders to make a profit. Nevertheless, accountants must bear a large part of the blame as citizens and as professionals for the failure

to update governmental accounting practices to meet the needs of a rapidly changing environment and a better educated and more demanding public.

On this point I am reminded of Dr. Paul McCracken's article entitled "1974's Basic Problem—Inflation" in the February 21, 1974, *Wall Street Journal* in which he described this kind of inertia as "a certain establishmentarian resistance by the accounting profession to new thinking." With respect to governmental accounting, it could be added: there is the same kind of resistance to the application of already available and appropriate principles and necessary procedures awaiting authoritative support.

To explain, last February I delivered a paper to a prestigious group of legislators, accountants and others in which the following suggestions were made for improvements in accounting in local governmental units: (1) use "program" accounting in addition to dollar accountability on fund and "object of expenditure" bases, (2) use full accrual and full cost-based accounting concepts and (3) produce full accrual-based data that will allow determination of (a) total expenses of the governmental unit, (b) costs (including depreciation) by functions or activities and (c) unit costs of measurable units of output.

Comments from the group ran the gamut from "I'm opposed to the accrual basis" to "There is an avant-garde of accountants who propose improvements that may not now be feasible."

To be a member of such an "avant-garde" group may be flattering indeed, but it is necessary that I disqualify myself on the basis that such suggestions were not expressions of a vanguard. Identical suggestions can be traced back at least to 1914 when the *Handbook of Municipal Accounting* was produced by the Bureau of Municipal Research in New York City. This handbook was one of a series of handbooks of city business methods developed by the Metz Fund which dates back to about 1910.

Some of the recommendations for acceptable "city business practice" of over 60 years ago might be of historical interest as an indication of how far we have progressed to 1974. Quotations are directly from the

Metz Fund handbook:

☐ A purpose of the manual was described as "to establish a procedure which will make available to the public a definite test of economy, efficiency and fidelity of service."

☐ "The differences between private and public accounting are not differences in purpose or differences in method; they are differences in the subjects concerning which information is needed.

"In each case the purpose of accounting and reporting is to provide the information which is needed to carry on the business; in each case the method must be one which will protect the officer and the beneficiary against incompleteness, inaccuracy of reports and delay in making facts available. For both private and public institutions the principles which govern the technique of accounting are the same."

☐ "The citizen and the officer of the public corporation are entitled to the same completeness, the same accuracy, the same lucidness of statement about public affairs as are the shareholder and officer of the private enterprise. In each case the persons to whom the facts are to be made known are those who hold a beneficial interest or a position of trust and responsibility."

☐ "The historic reason for the statement that the accounting of a city is 'entirely different' from that of a private corporation is this: that heretofore few cities have maintained any accounts other than those of appropriations—accounts which are required in order to keep the officer out of jail. Practically no accounts have been kept pertaining to subjects in which the officer as administrator and the citizen as beneficiary are interested. Few cities have kept accounts of property, stores, equipment. Few cities have a complete account of their liabilities. Few cities keep operation or cost accounts. Few cities attempt to keep operating data which will enable the citizen or the officer to know what results are being obtained or to obtain information by means of which the efficiency or economy of management may be measured. For this reason many persons who have grown up in the municipal service have thought that the occupation of the municipal bookkeeper has nothing in common with what has been too often called 'commercial book-keeping.' The fact is that everything of interest to the community has been left out of the picture and upon the dull gray background of institutional inhibition they have been painting pictures for the information of the few members who are interested in the technical and legal requirements of appropriations.

". . . it may be said that there are 10 general subjects concerning which complete, accurate and prompt information is needed as a basis for thinking about the business of the city, or, to put it in other terms, about the business of the citizen:

1 Expenditures and the revenues or other means provided for meeting them.
2 What the city owns and what the city owes.
3 What fund authorizations have been made by the legislature or by the board and what are the limitations placed on the officer with reference to expenditures.
4 Permanent properties and bonded debt incurred in providing them.
5 Sinking funds for retirement of bonded debt.
6 Trust funds.
7 Functional expenses and unit costs.
8 Control over the accrual and collection of revenues.
9 Control over the city's purchasing and contracting relations.
10 Control over the fidelity of custodians."

Does this sound familiar? Such recommended standards may have been made by an "avant-garde" group over 60 years ago, but today such suggestions are not creative, innovative or forward-looking—rather, they're ideas long past due. In the meantime, our changing environment and the "rising expectations" that the late Bob Trueblood and others have talked about are demanding more accountability from both sectors of our economy.

With respect to the cash-basis/accrual-basis controversy, and thus the need for reliable budgets and necessary references to financial statements in the development of budgets, the handbook says:

"Questions pertaining to last year's operations must be answered by a statement of revenues and expenses, showing
1 The revenue that has accrued to

the city by virtue of its right to levy taxes and to charge for privileges and services.
2 The operation and maintenance cost of the city.
3 The excess of revenue over cost or the excess of cost over revenues.

"The amount to be recorded under the first head would not be determined by the cash collected, for this would invariably include revenue which had accrued or fallen due in previous periods, as, for example, cash from taxes levied in a previous year, and would leave out revenues due for which cash had not yet been received. Consequently, we are forced to conclude that *revenue accrued* is something entirely different from *cash received* and that, if we are going to record the facts which will tell us how our financial program has worked, we must enter under the head of revenue the full amount due the city regardless of whether it has been received in cash or not, proper allowance being made for the amount which from experience might be regarded as uncollectible.

"On the other hand, the amounts to be recorded under the second head would not be determined by the cash paid out, for this would in many cases include payments of cost incurred in, and for the benefit of, prior periods; it would also omit expenses properly chargeable to the period which perchance had not yet been paid. Consequently, if we are to get a clear picture of *costs incurred* we must have something different from a record of *cash payments*. If a city is to record the facts which will show how the financial program entered upon at the beginning of the period has worked, it must enter under the head of expenses all of the liabilities incurred during the year, regardless of whether they have been paid in cash or whether it still owes for them.

"With these facts available, the city may also have before it the data to show what liabilities are outstanding that must be met and the cash and other assets, such as accounts receivable, to meet them.

"Simply because each person in a municipality has only a small financial interest in the public business is no reason why all principles of business economy and common sense should be cast to the winds.

"A municipality's financial state-

ments, to be truthful reflections of what has taken place in its finances, should be based upon accretions to and depletions of wealth. A statement of revenues and expenses should explain the changes in assets and liabilities which have taken place in a period. This means that all financial transactions whether based on cash or credit must be taken into account."

In retrospect, it is difficult to understand why, 60 years later, the vast majority of local governmental units are still budgeting and reporting on the cash basis and municipal officials (many of whom are businessmen) and organizations of governmental officials are opposed to the accrual basis. Many accountants prefer cash-basis accounting, budgeting and reporting for local government, and legislators continue to pass laws requiring far less than what would be necessary for adequate custodial reporting of the allocation and use of local governmental resources.

The economic and accounting sense of the logic expressed in the Metz Fund handbook is as valid and relevant today as it was 60 years ago. The argument that a tiny municipality should not be required to assume the cost for such "complex accounting" begs the question, misses the point and shows a lack of understanding (or desire to understand) what's involved. Only rudimentary bookkeeping, in most cases, is involved! A local government with annual gross revenues of $1,000 would most likely have no more than a few entries (other than cash transactions) for a full year. The volume and complexity of transactions bear a close relationship in most cases to the size of the budget. The fact that statutory tax ceilings often encourage the formation of numerous small units does not negate the necessity for proper accountability of the taxpayers' dollars. If there is a need for the governmental unit at all, there is a concomitant need for meaningful accounting.

On August 28, 1973, the General Assembly of Illinois passed an amendment to the Park District Code, which now requires a combined annual budget and appropriation ordinance. Certain provisions of this recent law (which are not peculiar to Illinois) might be of interest in light of our discussion thus far:

"The budget included in such ordinance shall contain a statement of the cash on hand at the beginning of the fiscal year, an estimate of the cash expected to be received during such fiscal year from all sources, an estimate of the expenditures contemplated for such fiscal year and a statement of the estimated cash expected to be on hand at the end of such year. The estimate of taxes to be received may be based upon the amount of actual cash receipts that may reasonably be expected by the Park District during such fiscal year, estimated from the experience of the Park District in prior years and with due regard for other circumstances that may substantially affect such receipts. However, nothing in this Act shall be construed as requiring any Park District to change or preventing any Park District from changing from a cash basis of financing to a surplus or deficit basis of financing; or as requiring any Park District to change or preventing any Park District from changing its system of accounting."

It is this kind of legislation in the various states which creates real problems in attempts to establish uniform accounting systems in local government and which contributes very little toward an understanding of local government accounting, reporting and budgeting needs. Local officials who would otherwise be responsive to suggestions for improved systems are understandably confused by such legislation.

Amitai Etzioni, in an article entitled "There Oughta Be a Law—Or Should There Be?" in the Winter 1973-74 issue of *Business and Society Review/Innovation* is right on point when he says, "True, a good part of the laws passed are not meant to be implemented, at least not systematically and effectively. Passing laws is part of the make-believe or theater of politics in which politicians try to placate two (or more) opposing camps. They give one faction the law (saying, in effect, 'You see, I took care of it') while the other faction more or less retains the freedom to pursue activities which violate the law. It's a politician's way of eating his cake and having it. Take, as an example, laws against gambling. They are very sporadically enforced throughout most American metropolitan

centers; this allows the moralistic parts of the community to feel they had their day, and the gambler to gamble. Similarly, tough but rarely enforced laws against pollution both please the ecology movement and fail to deter most polluters.

"Concerned citizens should be able to distinguish between laws which are unauthentic gestures and laws which are instruments of societal change."

"Concerned citizens" should include accountants in government and in professional practice as well. The producers of the AICPA audit guide recognized, implicitly at least, the multiplicity of conflicting and irresponsible laws in the various states as a problem area when they included the standard that generally accepted accounting principles should prevail when there is a variation between such principles and the law.

Whether or not the application of this principle will hold up in practice remains to be seen. I have strong evidence to indicate that our firm's recent loss of an old and valued client was directly related to our attempts to convince the client of the need to maintain the integrity of an enterprise fund in accordance with generally accepted accounting principles. In this case, both state and local laws were silent on the matter and the local attorney chose to take the position that even though the enterprise fund was entirely self-sustaining, it could and should be combined with operations of the general fund of the unit. Home rule provisions will result in a rash of similar cases unless controls are provided.

Environmental changes

If you agree that accounting principles evolve from and should be responsive to environmental changes, it follows that such changes must be considered in response to society's accounting and reporting needs. We don't have to read the voluminous amount of literature today to recognize that profound changes have taken place in the transitions from an agricultural society to an industrial state, and now to what many call a "post-industrial" society.

The Trueblood Study Group reminds us (page 14 of the report) that "in the United States, where the economic system emphasizes private

enterprise, individuals and enterprises generally attempt to maximize their own wealth. Financial information helps them make sound economic decisions. This process is assumed to lead to the broader social goal of the efficient allocation of resources throughout the economy."

While we owe much to our free enterprise system, it should be obvious that the system has changed considerably in the 200 years since Adam Smith in *The Wealth of Nations* proposed that the marketplace (through self-interest) provided the form of provident control necessary to keep the activities of a business in the best interests of society.

Edward H. Bowman (*Technology Review,* October/November 1973) argues that a "neo-invisible hand" is present in contemporary western society which constrains the activities of business in a manner not unlike the markets of Adam Smith. Others would point out that today there is a considerable amount of evidence to indicate that society no longer relies entirely on private economic decisions to best serve the public interest and that increased government participation is necessary.

One thing is certain, the role of government in society's affairs has been increasing dramatically since World War II. We know that today our society is more service-oriented, that economic success has brought environmental problems with it, that a better balance must be obtained between the public and private sectors' involvement in programs of social concern and "quality of life" issues and that the public sector must be more responsive to pressures exerted by society to use available modern business technologies, managerial capability, and efficiency, economy and program effectiveness techniques that can improve the bases for resource allocation such as program planning and budgeting systems (PPBS).

To complicate the problem is the seldom-recognized impact of our present strong inflationary trend on state and local governments. The prices of goods and services purchased by state and local governments have increased at twice the rate of the private sector over the last fifteen years, according to the "Revenue Sharing Bulletin" of February 1974.

Expenditures in the public sector have grown by well over $200 billion per year, on a 1950-1973 comparative basis. Coupled with such increases in expenditures are taxpayer resistance and legislative demands for public accountability. Public accountability is now defined by the General Accounting Office as the evaluation of the economy and efficiency with which a government has used its allocated resources and the effectiveness of its programs.

Prospective views

Governmental accounting and auditing are no longer functions concerned primarily with financial operations and compliance matters. The major concern now is whether governmental organizations are achieving the purposes for which programs are authorized and funds are made available, whether they are doing so economically and efficiently and whether they are complying with applicable laws and regulations.

The critical issues are not hard to find. Hundreds of articles and studies have been produced in the last 10 to 20 years that zero in on the same issues over and over again—many of the same matters discussed in the Metz Fund books in the early 1900s.

□ Fund accounting—Because of state and federal law and local administrative action, we are saddled with fund structures that are complex, not generally understood and difficult for local governments to properly maintain. Reporting is therefore overly focused on individual funds to the exclusion of the operating entity as a whole.

Consideration should be given to the development of accounting, budgeting and reporting systems that will cross fund lines and develop material for proper planning and control on the bases of programs, activities and functions. Developed data should include qualitative and nonmonetary quantitative data and descriptive material where necessary.

The legalistic fund data requirements (which are not uniform in the various states or even within a particular state) should be maintained in subsidiary records and reports as is necessary to show compliance with the law.

Basic financial statements should be on a consolidated basis, with the exception of certain trust funds, i.e., a pension fund.

□ Budgets—Present budget practices are largely limited to "legalistic" dollar stewardship on a fund and year-by-year basis. Budgeting for the governmental entity as a whole over longer periods of time is not generally considered, and operational accountability for the *total entity* is rarely encountered.

Available cost accounting techniques used in private industry should be used in the public sector. Modernization of local government budgeting practices would include the use of full cost-based budgetary data, standard cost systems and cost-based standards of performance. Cost centers and responsibilities should be established and controllable cost analyses used where appropriate. Planning-programing-budgeting systems that cover longer time spans (five or six years) for the total organization should be considered as an improvement over present practice because of their adaptability to legalistic dollar accountability needs, but full cost-based budgets should be the objective.

□ Basis of accounting—Practice in this area is far from uniform among the states or within a state. Legislation and standards developed by the laity have so muddied the waters that we even have trouble in arriving at a consensus in definitions of such terms as accrual or modified accrual, modified cash-basis accounting, etc. The generally accepted definition of the term "accrual" as used in industry and the full-accrual basis of accounting should be considered as required practice in local government.

□ Depreciation accounting—The premise that accounting for "enterprise funds" in government should be the same as similar operations in industry and that the so-called "budgetary" or general government funds are of a different character is difficult to reconcile with the overall objective of local government to provide services to society at cost. The primary difference between general government funds and enterprise funds is that the former provide services at cost which are financed by general tax levies and other revenues and the latter, services at cost which are financed by

direct charges to users of the services.

The rationale that enterprise funds somehow fall outside the realm of general governmental services and that the accounting should be on an accrual basis, whereas general funds should be on a modified basis and not include depreciation, appears to be inconsistent with acceptable cost accounting methodologies. Therefore, full accrual-based and full cost-based accounting (including depreciation on fixed assets) is recommended, except for certain trust funds where this accounting would not be appropriate.

These suggestions are by no means a complete inventory of needed improvements in governmental accounting. Obviously, in the area of performance accountability, audit standards, procedures and the degree of responsibility to be assumed by independent auditors are all matters that need attention.

Needed, also, is local legislation which in fact is responsive to current needs, many of which are discussed above. Legislation must not be produced in a vacuum by governmental fiat or on an "as-usual" basis but, instead, should be based on the best thinking of available professionals with expertise in the specialized areas. The usual exceptions based on local constraints should be examined critically and objectively in terms of required accountability needs instead of on the basis of political or local expediency issues.

Accountants, with their discipline of measurement used as a basis for effective communication, as well as those in other disciplines can contribute to the management (and perhaps direction) of change in our private and public institutions which is so evident today.

We can start by putting governmental accounting in a frame of reference that relates to today's world and by using necessary expertise, much of which is already acquired, to provide accounting and information systems to meet the challenges of our coming post-industrial society. ■

Thomas C. Taylor, CPA, Ph.D.

The Illusions of Social Accounting

The author questions the emperor's new clothes, represented by this widely called-for new responsibility of corporate reporting. In raising these questions, the author states where he thinks true social responsibility lies.

Thomas C. Taylor, CPA, Ph.D., has been associated with Arthur Andersen & Co. and Price Waterhouse & Co., as well as being a cost accountant with Western Electric Company, Inc. He is presently in the Department of Business and Accountancy at Wake Forest University.

Introduction

Financial and business literature in recent years has been replete with claims that business enterprises have responsibilities beyond the so-called *economic* realm and that accountants have a concomitant responsibility to provide leadership in measuring and reporting the extent to which these enterprises have met these noneconomic responsibilities. Thus, businesses are said to be socially responsible and the accountability in this area is commonly referred to as social accounting. The term *socioeconomic accounting* also has emerged to reflect the idea that both social and economic results are to be measured and reported.

Most advocates of social or socioeconomic accounting assert that it represents a great and inescapable challenge for the accounting profession. Their zeal and enthusiasm for this new direction are conspicuous. And their intentions are worthy and commendable. Most of us would be happy indeed to see significant strides toward the elimination of illness, ignorance, crime and poverty, to see a rise in the general standard of living in our society, to help shape a world better for future generations and to enhance the overall quality of life.

It is not, then, the ultimate aims or intentions of those who subscribe to the concepts of social responsibility and social accounting that must be called into question. The problem lies with the concepts themselves and the prospect that these ideas call for actions which will prove to be ineffective and even detrimental to the success of the goals sought. Actions and ideas, no matter how well-intentioned, are doomed to failure if grounded in faulty reasoning.

Social Goals

Undefined Social Goals

At present the whole concept of corporate social responsibility and accountability lacks a critical element: a clear delineation of social goals to be pursued by business enterprises. Most published discussion of corporate social responsibility has been couched in vague and general terms. The lack of definitive purposes is a serious deficiency and can only result in frustration and ineptitude on the part of business management in any attempt to be socially responsible.

The nebulousness of social goals is in sharp contrast to the clarity of the economic or profit goal which business decision makers have recognized traditionally as primary. Business managers' indecision and confusion about courses of actions have not been due to a lack of clarity of their ultimate purpose. Now they are being told that they must "consciously and deliberately act to improve our social environment and the quality of life as well as continuing to add to our quantity of goods."[1] This quotation characterizes the vagueness of the admonitions concerning social responsibility in recent accounting and business literature.

The accountability of business activity must pertain to its purposes and responsibilities. Traditional recognition by business managers of monetary profit as their primary purpose and responsibility has had its impact upon accounting theory and practice. Conventional accounting theory relating to the private sector of society views the role of accounting as in the economic or monetary sphere, and accounting output is generally in the nature of financial reports designed to assist decision makers in the economic realm.

With the advent of claims of corporate social responsibility has emerged quite logically the concept of social accounting. If business managers are to pursue social goals

[1] S. Kerry Cooper, Mitchell H. Raiborn, Accounting for Corporate Social Responsibility," *MSU Business Topics,* Spring 1974.

THE ILLUSIONS OF SOCIAL ACCOUNTING /

in addition to economic goals, then they must account for their performance in the social as well as economic realm. What is so astonishing is the suggestion that accountants can no longer delay in effecting a measurement process to accommodate the task of social accountability[2], in view of the fact that the socially desired goals are still conspicuously undefined. To say that businesses should act upon problems of health, education, minorities, ecology and the quality of life in no way provides individual decision makers with concrete objectives to pursue. To contend that the clear definition of social goals is unnecessary for effective action is sheer nonsense. And without clear objectives in the area of social performance, on what reasonable basis can accountants be implored to "let's get on with the social audit"? One sees the dilemma this creates for accountants. Where do they begin in preparing social performance reports when companies have little understanding of their specific social goals? Measurement of performance relating to undefined goals is an unrealistic and illogical expectation.

A workable definition of social goals entails far more than a list of general areas of social concern. Ultimately what is needed is a blueprint of particular goals for each specific business separately or in conjunction with other businesses, detailed in terms of priorities and timing of fulfillment. Only by coordinating the efforts of all businesses can duplication of social performances and failure to attend to serious social concerns be avoided. Actions taken to achieve social aims must be undertaken in specific and discrete steps by specific individuals or groups of individuals acting in concert. It is simplistic and unrealistic to admonish the corporate business world in general and to expect satisfactory performances to result from a "willy-nilly" approach on the part of the separate entities.

Determining Social Goals

How shall the social goals of

corporations be determined? The published pleas for social accounting have given little attention to this question. It is not clear if their authors see each corporation's social goals being set by its managers at their own discretion or whether they view influences external to the corporation as the source of the direction for corporate social actions.

Most proponents of corporate social responsibility hasten to state the general social concerns in which corporations should become involved, but it is not clear how the general public has communicated this information to them. One can hardly avoid concluding that these concerns reflect the proponent's own personal value judgments or emanate from special pressure groups.

The idea of social goals is usually put forward in terms of the goals or interests of "society as a whole." Yet, it is never really clear just who comprises this whole. People act in different roles, and benefits to one group can cause detrimental effects upon others. What may benefit people as employees, such as the goal of "reasonable" or "fair" wages, may not be considered "fair" to consumers who are unable to pay the prices necessary for the business to recoup such employee remuneration. The decision not to relocate a plant and capitalize upon reduced production costs, because of a sense of social responsibility to the company's employees, is harmful to the investors and customers and to the interests of those living in the area of the proposed relocation.

The problem with the concept of social goals is that society is not some kind of integral whole or organism with its own objectives or values. Only individuals have goals and act to achieve them. Collectives like clubs, unions and even corporations are cooperative associations of individuals whose actions have been joined to achieve certain goals set by individuals.

The ultimate traceability of human goals and actions to individuals is important in order to avoid a futile search for social goals that exist apart from the aims of the individual members of society. Further, the determination of the interests or goals of society as a

whole must lie in a process of consensus about the preferences of the millions of individual members of society.

There appear to be serious shortcomings in corporate managers deciding upon socially desirable actions to be taken by their companies.

First, the aforementioned need for coordinating the efforts made by numerous separate companies in all probability would go unfulfilled.

Second, the belief that corporate managers will perceive with even a minimum degree of accuracy a public consensus about social concerns *and their priorities* is without basis.

Third, as Hayek has pointed out[3], to charge corporate managers with this task places in their hands power that could be excessive and detrimental. In the pursuit of profits, corporate managers do not establish or choose values but rather act in the service of the values of others. To encourage them to pursue values they deem important is to place the members of society in a position dangerously subservient to the wishes of corporate managers.

Fourth, there is serious question whether corporate managers can be counted on to act voluntarily in a sufficiently socially responsible manner, particularly in difficult economic periods.

Fifth, the logical extension of the concept that corporate managers are to serve the interests of society as a whole is that they must ultimately come under the control of the protector of the public interest, the government. Without control over business managers by the appointed representatives of the public interest, to whom are corporations accountable to act in a socially responsible way? Who will have authority to assure that corporate social responsibilities are met? The power of corporate managers to decide on socially desirable ends can only be transitory and ephemeral.

Thus, it follows that the social

[2] David F. Linowes, "Let's Get on with the Social Audit: A Specific Proposal," *Business and Society Review/Innovation*, Winter 1972–73, pp. 39–42.

[3] Friedrich A. Hayek, "The Corporation in a Democratic Society: In Whose Interest Ought It and Will It Be Run?" in *Management and Corporation—1985.* (New York: McGraw-Hill, 1960), pp. 99–117.

The cpa JOURNAL / JANUARY 1976

goals to be sought by corporations should be (and eventually must be) established through the channels of government. Such an approach is consistent with the traditional roles of government and business. Through government there is established a framework of rules, vital to society as a whole, within which businesses are permitted to operate in performing the central task of putting economic resources to the most profitable use. Legislation and regulation, representative of the public interest, provide the indispensable means to assure that actions deemed essential to society are taken. Recognizing governmental responsibility here is totally consistent with its familiar role in dealing with entrenched social concerns in business, such as minimum wages, air and water pollution, advertising, factory and product safety, fair employment practices, subsidized industries and pricing.

The Chimera of Social Measurement

The rationale of corporate social responsibility has as its corollary the proposition that corporations must be held accountable for their performance in the social area. This type of accounting has been called by a variety of terms including *social accounting, socioeconomic measurement, social measurement, accounting for corporate social responsibility* and *arithmetic of quality.*

The advocates of social accounting lament the failure of traditional financial accounting to provide the basis for evaluating the social performance of corporate businesses. While present practice effectively fills the need for useful information on the economic performance of corporate managers, the boundaries of accounting allegedly must be extended to enable the reporting of corporate performance in social concerns. Conventional statements are deemed inadequate in failing to reflect the social good or bad a company effects through action or inaction relating to societal matters.

Despite some enthusiasts urging immediate implementation of some form of corporate social accounting, there is a conspicuous lack of even a semblance of a measurement system. The only ideas they generally agree on are that the effectiveness of corporate social performance must be measured and reported, that this system would entail the measurement of social costs and social benefits, and that standards of measurement must be designed to achieve these aims. Passing references are made to puzzling terms like *qualitative measurements, nonmetric scales* and *relative weights,* but no elaboration offers any real understanding of what these mean.

Devoid of any measurement system, the notion of a social audit as the outcome of efforts to account for corporate social performance nevertheless is posed as the new path of accounting. Bewilderment is indicated when a prominent proponent asserts that measurement indicators will necessarily be varied and will depend upon the views of each particular organization reporting.[4] Interestingly, the measurement puzzle has not deterred most proponents from providing lengthy lists of areas they feel are subject to quantification and measurement.

The Socioeconomic Operating Statement

Patterned somewhat after the conventional income statement, one proposal for reporting corporate social performance has received widespread exposure. This is the Socioeconomic Operating Statement (SEOS) through which the results of the social audit for the recent year of operations would be reported along with the conventional audited financial statements.[5] The SEOS would show as benefits of social actions the money costs incurred in undertaking and/or maintaining certain social projects. The specific projects and related costs would be disclosed by cate-

gory or area, i.e., people, environment, product. The total cost of each area represents total improvements in that category. Note that *money costs* are proposed as a measure of *benefits.* The benefits are matched against the recognized *detriments* for each category. Detriments refer to certain projects (and their related costs) which should have been undertaken and were not. These are listed and the total dollar cost is subtracted from total improvements to yield a net improvements or net deficit for each category. The net results of all categories are then summarized to provide a bottom-line dollar result for the year that is added to the net cumulative result of all previous years reported on to provide a "grand total net socioeconomic actions" to date.

The fallacy in the contention that this plan provides an effective means of measuring and reporting upon corporate social performance lies in errors in the underlying reasoning. And despite the author's argument that the need for measurement improvements and refinements should not delay the immediate application of this plan, accounting practice has no business employing a faulty approach in its attempt to yield useful information.

The dollar cost of undertaking or maintaining social projects has nothing to do with the benefits of such activities. It is fallacious to suggest that such monetary determinations are a measure of the benefits, if any, of such actions. The continuous debate in the public arena about the desirability of expenditures in such areas as defense, education and welfare attests to the immeasurability of benefits relating to societal matters. One cannot overstate the importance of meaningfully evaluating benefits; rational decisions and actions hinge upon the evaluation of both benefits and costs.

There are two fundamental problems connected with disclosing the detriments as a deduction from the benefits. First, because the cost of projects not undertaken has no relation to the cost of projects undertaken, there is no compatibility between the benefits area and the detriments area and thereby no

[4] Norton M. Bedford, "Corporate Accountability," *Management Accounting,* November 1973, p. 43.

[5] David F. Linowes, "Let's Get on with the Social Audit: A Specific Proposal," *Business and Society Review/Innovation,* Winter 1972–73, pp. 40–42. Also see "The Accounting Profession and Social Progress," *Journal of Accountancy,* July 1973, pp. 38–40.

THE ILLUSIONS OF SOCIAL ACCOUNTING /

basis exists for matching the two.

Second, the proposal that the cost of social projects not undertaken be disclosed as detriments is untenable due to the totally subjective question of which projects should have been undertaken. Because there is no provision in this process for screening and ranking proposals based on a benefit-cost analysis, how does the accountant or others concerned decide which projects should not have been left undone? The answer to this question calls for an analysis that grapples not only with project priorities but also with the question of money otherwise available for use or actually used in nonsocial purposes, i.e., generating profitable operations.

The Essential Task of Accounting

Proponents of social accounting characteristically credit financial accounting with reporting how well the corporation has performed in the economic realm. This implies that: (1) Dollar revenues reflect benefits and dollar expenses reflect costs and the matching of the two provides a net profit or loss significantly indicative of economic performance and (2) The determination of corporate performance in the "social" realm is not served by the conventional financial accounting model. The second implication is undeniably true but the first is partially open to question.

There is no parallel between the accounting for a corporation's financial affairs and accounting for the social effects of a business. There is no pretense that money profits or losses represent an excess of benefits over costs. Dollar revenues do not measure benefits for customers or for the participants in the corporate enterprise. Profits and losses are the culmination of market prices that signal what the consuming public deems to be the preferred uses of scarce resources. *It is essential to understand that signals concerning the preferred allocation of resources do not measure the benefits or costliness of such uses.* The indications provided by monetary profits and losses are of the nature of guiding which lines of resource use are more urgently

desired by the public. Any ultimate measurement of the net *value* of such uses is impossible.

The indispensable role of financial accounting is its contribution toward the rational allocation of scarce resources among countless and competing uses. While real benefits and real costs are not being measured and reported, valuable monetary indicators are produced to help reveal the preferences of the members of the society. Contributing to the solution of the allocation question is a far greater accomplishment than the usually narrowly pictured role of reporting financial position and results to investors and creditors. In this sense, one can properly ascribe to conventional accounting a societal impact. Although crucial accounting results are in the nature of monetary profits and losses and are of primary interest to investors, their overriding effect is to induce actions which reflect the more urgent wants of the members of society.

Subjectivity of Ultimate Valuations

The market process and the system of financial accounting facilitate the complex decisions about resource use *without measuring real costs and real benefits to anyone.* The ultimate valuation of any object or service rests in the mind of the person making the value judgment.

Because all valuations ultimately must be personal and dependent upon individual preferences, there is no means by which corporate managers or accountants, public or private, can measure the benefits of corporate social projects. Any valuation on their part can only manifest their own personal value judgments and can only be subjective. At best they can arrive at an approximation of the dollar costs of such projects. No meaningful determination of the excess of benefits over costs is possible without a common unit of measure. There is no way to compare the inflow of social utility against the sacrifice of social utility for particular actions taken. Consequently, no meaningful determination of overall corporate social performance can take place.

Corporate social projects are meant to benefit society as a whole, while products and services produced and sold in the market are meant to benefit the specific purchasers. The market affords a workable system for solving which products and services are preferred by the public. But there is no market for determining socially desirable undertakings by corporations. The large aggregates of services devoted to the general public are not separable into small quantities to be accepted or rejected by individual persons. For this reason a means of communicating the wishes of the general public is necessary and must be effected through the political process.

By relegating social concerns to the domain of government within our legal framework, the accounting records of corporations would reflect the dollar costs of any corporate social projects which the political process has determined to be desirable. The question of real benefits and costs would have to be resolved, if democratically, at the polls or, if dictatorially, through the value judgments of centralized planning authorities of some sort.

The reporting of corporate social performance would then take the form already pervasive today: fulfilling requirements of filing reports with government agencies and being subject to governmental or private audits. To the extent that the accounting profession can contribute meaningfully to the satisfaction of these requirements, one could speak of social accounting. Thus, auditing to attest to the investment in required pollution-control equipment or minority-employment programs is conceivable. But it is important to emphasize that such accounting falls far short of measuring benefits or overall corporate social performance. Its nature would be essentially that of attesting to the extent of conformity with governmental or legal regulations. Even attesting to reported surrogate measures like the number of minority employees hired during the year would not involve a measurement of benefits.

Conclusions

Good intentions are not enough

THE CPA JOURNAL / JANUARY 1976

to bring about satisfactory results. The euphoric appeals to social responsibility and social accounting ascribe superior knowledge to corporate managers and practicing accountants not supported by objective evidence. Social concerns by definition are concerns of the general public and the determination of these concerns necessitates a process of discerning which specific matters are of greatest interest to the general public.

The notion of social measurement as an accounting function is untenable because the quality of life and the valuations of specific social projects are necessarily personal and subjective value judgments. The ultimate role of accounting as it pertains to corporate social action is in the nature of reporting upon and attesting to the compliance with legal requirements. This role is not new. Corporate accountants and independent auditors have long concerned themselves with the cost aspects of societal problems such as financing the Social Security program through payroll deductions, corporate adherence to wage-price controls and providing monopoly services at an allowed rate of return.

The appropriate channel for communicating public concerns is provided by government and the political process. Through the legal framework, public policy and governmental regulations, the task of determining the proper balance between corporate profit-seeking activities and social goals can be achieved. Ω

statements in quotes

The changing face of financial reporting*

This paper by John C. Burton, *chief accountant of the Securities and Exchange Commission, is based on a talk he gave for the DR Scott Memorial Lectures in Accountancy at the University of Missouri's College of Administration and Public Affairs, Columbia, Missouri, last year.*

In a rapidly changing world such as we have today the standard by which financial reporting must be judged cannot imply static goals; rather, it must serve as a constantly moving target which must be pursued.

The basic standard may be articulated as follows: Financial reporting must reliably communicate the results of business activities to various interested parties on a timely basis.

This standard has several elements, the implications of which are

significant in trying to develop a reporting structure that will meet the needs of users of the reports. A careful analysis of the various components of this standard will indicate some of the problems of achieving it in today's world. The implications of these elements are significant in trying to develop a reporting structure that will meet the needs of the users of the reports.

Various interested parties

The standard first indicates that reporting must communicate to various interested parties. This leads to an analysis of who the users of financial information are. Broadly, it can be said that financial information is used principally by economic decision makers. The first group of economic decision makers with interest in financial information are the managers of a business. Since this group can control the information which they receive on the basis of their perceived needs, however, it is not necessary to give them primary consideration in the development of a framework for public financial reporting. Nevertheless, it is important to recognize that to the extent public reporting requires information not felt to be needed internally, the incremental cost of developing these data are likely to be higher and the resistance of managements to reporting it will similarly increase

Even if our concern is primarily with decision makers external to the business firm, we find many different types with legitimate interests. In the first place there are investors making decisions for their own account either as owners or lenders of capital to an enterprise. This is the group to which the disclosure framework of the securities laws has traditionally been addressed, but it certainly does not comprise the whole market for data.

In recent years the needs of fiduciaries who are investors on behalf of others has become increasingly important as the role of investing institutions, both in the trading market and in the process of capital formation in this country, has expanded. The investment decisions of fiduciaries carry a burden of responsibility which differs from decisions made by many of those who invest for their own account, since fiduciaries have a direct responsibility to their clients and must bear the risk of being called to account legally if they fail to exercise it.

Other potential users in addition to users who are concerned with investments must also be considered. Macroeconomic decision makers, including both the executive and legislative branches of government, must be viewed as users of this information. To the extent that the business community wishes to communicate effectively to this group, and it is essential that they do so, the financial reporting system of business must contemplate the needs of such policy makers. We cannot have, for example, a system of accounting which overstates economic earnings, and expect government personnel to recognize this and adjust for it in determining tax policies and in evaluating the adequacy of profits for purposes of capital formation.

Finally, of course, there are specialized interests that must be considered in developing a reporting framework. While every possible user of information cannot be identified and satisfied within conventional financial reporting, significant users should be considered. Employees are certainly one such group. Business must be concerned with how it communicates its activities to its employees as individuals and to its employee organizations.

Another group which the SEC has recently been directed by a court to consider is environmentalists. Hearings have been held on the subject of whether the commission should require certain data in regard to environmental protection and employee safety and employment policy as part of its disclosure system. While it is easy to see how reaction to all possible highly specialized information needs could unduly clutter a reporting system, needs of significant groups cannot be overlooked if the system is to achieve its objective. In a recent release, the commission proposed rules which would make available to investors information regarding the extent to which corporations have failed to satisfy environmental standards under federal law.

As we look at these varying types of interested parties it is evident that the different types have different information needs. Furthermore, some decision makers with similar objectives may perceive their information needs differently. We have discovered, for example, that there are many different approaches to investment decision making. Some believe that financial analysis of corporate results is a vital tool which plays a major role in selecting good investments. Others view this as much less important and have adopted investment approaches varying from those based upon market indicators to those which contemplate communication with the occult (if that is different from market indicators).

In addition, there are broad differences in the training and capacity of decision makers and substantial variations in the time they have available or wish to devote to studying economic information. Some revel in detail, while others abhor it.

The SEC has attempted to take at least a first step in the direction of meeting diverse needs by articulating a policy of differential disclosure under which varying levels of summarization are presented in different documents so that users can find information consistent with their perceived needs.

The communication process

The second major element of the standard is that reporting must communicate. The process of communication is not well understood or simple. Even the mechanical problem of getting public information to users is a major one when users are dispersed and data channels are limited. A magnificent short wave transmitter is not of much use unless there are radios around.

Beyond this, the problem of how to structure the communication so that it can be received by a user is a major one. Even if you have transmitters and radio receivers, the receiver will not be of much use if a foreign language is being used.

In summary then, we must have a good transmitter, good receivers and programs that people can understand. To achieve this, both the preparer and the users of financial reports must have a common frame of reference. This means that the education of users is critical and it has been a matter that has been too long neglected in financial reporting. . . .

Measuring the results of business activities

The third element of the standard is that reporting must communicate "the results of business activities." While this sounds simple, it has certainly not proven so in the development of accounting principles.

Three basic characteristics of business activities are that they are continuous, usually complex and that decisions regarding them are based primarily on expectations. As we contrast this with the characteristics of the accounting model which deals with discrete periods, which is simplistically based on a simple trading enterprise for which it was initially developed, and which has traditionally downgraded expectations, it is not surprising that measurement problems arise.

Reliability

A fourth element of the standard requires that reporting should communicate "reliably." This implies the absence of bias and the absence of error together with some congruence between the reporting and the business reality. It suggests the need for adequate controls over the reporting process and for the application of professional expertise and detachment in the reporting environment.

Timeliness

Finally the standard suggests that reporting must meet the test of being timely. If reporting is to be useful, it must occur in time to enable a decision maker to utilize it in reaching sound decisions. While prompt after-the-fact reporting may achieve this goal in many cases, in some circumstances this objective may necessitate reporting prior to an event, based upon expectations. In all circumstances, it implies reporting promptly so that users can access current activities before they become irrelevant.

Changes in the reporting environment

If the financial reporting environment is going to move toward this standard, and I believe it essential that it do so, a number of significant changes in the face of reporting are likely to take place. These will not suddenly appear, but should come about through an evolutionary process.

A continuous reporting framework

First, it seems inevitable that there will be a move toward a continuous reporting framework for public financial reporting. Continuous reporting does not mean that every transaction will be publicly reported when it occurs but rather it implies the development of a reporting attitude. Management must think of its public reporting responsibilities throughout the year and not simply when annual or quarterly statements are due.

One element of this will be more frequent and more comprehensive reports covering shorter periods. As shorter periods are reported, the nature of the business continuum should become more apparent. The objective of such reporting is not to report the short period as such, but better communication of the business continuum. In such reporting, imprecision must be recognized. The shorter the period, the more it will be necessary to make estimates and to recognize that exactitude is not needed to assure accuracy.

The commission has recently taken a significant step in this direction by its broad expansion of Form 10-Q, which will require registrants to file income statements, balance sheets and source-and-application-of-funds statements quarterly rather than simply to produce the abbreviated income data which was previously required.

In addition to more frequent and more comprehensive reports, this new framework of continuous reporting will require a greater focus on key periods in the case of a seasonal or cyclical business. Where a growing season or a selling season is key to operating results, disclosure of relevant facts during that period should not await particular calendar dates. Any data which may reflect a significant change in trend should be reported promptly. In some industries this is done today. Automobile sales, for example are reported for 10-day periods and these reports are of considerable importance to economic and financial analysts.

Continuous reporting also implies prompt reporting of significant or unusual events outside the normal course of business. While it is sometimes difficult to define what is significant or unusual, it is important that such attempts be made. The commission, in early 1973, adopted a reporting requirement associated with Form 8-K which requires companies to make full and complete disclosure, on a timely basis, of material unusual charges and credits to income and to associate their independent public accountants with the accounting procedures followed in connection with these items.

A significant element of a continuous reporting framework requires that data be reported within the context of an appropriate perspective. This suggests the need for a forecasting system. I have little doubt that forecasting will be an integral part of financial reporting within 10 years, even though the SEC has no plans to mandate it in the near future. We have issued proposed rules which we had hoped would contribute to the orderly development of the forecasting area but which seem to have aroused substantial criticism, suggesting that these rules may prove to be counterproductive. This is an area that will require careful consideration before any final commission action is taken.

It should be emphasized, however, that much of the discussion about forecasting seems to have focused on the wrong elements. The purpose of forecasting in a reporting system is not to tell users what next year's earnings per share will be, but rather to provide better information about operations. An ongoing forecasting system will set current period results in better perspective based upon management expectations. Such an ongoing forecasting system may in fact eliminate the need for some interim data as long as business results do not change expectations. A forecasting system as part of the total financial reporting package will be of great value in enabling investors to understand why results deviate from forecasts. This analysis will make historical reporting far more meaningful.

The requirement that data be reported within the context of an appropriate perspective also suggests the need for a system which offers an alternative to historical monetary costs. The proposals of the commission that financial statements be supplemented with replacement cost data and the proposal of the Financial Accounting Standards Board for financial reporting in units of general purchasing power are movements in this direction.

Improvements in communications technology
A second major change that may be expected in financial reporting will be the development of improvements in communications technology. Systems must be developed to get data more efficiently into the

hands of those who need it. As a first step, some means must be found of achieving more channels of communications. Traditionally the two channels that have existed are the financial press, which provides for general communications between preparers of information and all users, and direct channels where the preparer communicates directly to specific users. We need to find additional channels whereby specialized users can be reached more readily with information that is of particular relevance to their needs. At the same time, some system should be developed whereby various parties are given reasonable safeguards against liabilities which may arise from any selective distribution of financial information in the absence of legal protective provisions.

Improvements in communications technology should also include better receivers of information. This would suggest improved education for users of financial information and perhaps development of increased professionalization in the use of data. The Financial Analysts Federation is now beginning the process of developing professional standards for that group, and this is a significant step forward.

Development of various levels of detail
Another major change in financial reporting will be the development of reporting at various levels of detail, rather than an emphasis on a single set of data for all. Inevitably as financial reporting evolves in the direction of this standard, there will have to be much more data publicly available. When a multimillion dollar entity operates for 12 months with thousands of employees and many different business activities, one cannot expect to describe it in a few pages for someone who is interested in developing an in-depth understanding of its operations.

At the same time as we see multiple levels of detail, there will also be an obligation placed upon preparers of data for better and more analytical summaries of the key factors in business performance to meet the needs of investors who do not wish to or are unable to perform detailed analysis of highly complex financial data. The commission took an initial step in this regard by requiring management's analysis of the summary of earnings, and it seems likely that this type of obligation will increasingly be placed upon management.

Broader role for public accountants

Another major change which is occurring and seems likely to continue is the greater involvement of independent public accountants in financial reporting. Auditors are partners in the reporting process with public responsibility to assure an appropriate result. They will increasingly be viewed as "auditors of record" with some continuing responsibility for all public financial reporting of their clients. This seems a logical corollary to the idea of continuous reporting.

It should be emphasized that auditors are not, and should not be viewed as, policemen conducting adversary audits. The auditor serves as a detached professional whose reporting expertise is of value both to the reporting company and to the users of information. The basic auditing approach must continue to be based on the assumption of good faith on the part of all, since to assume otherwise is to suggest the total destruction of the entire underpinning of our current business system.

The commission has recently adopted rules which we believe will encourage the development of the concept of auditor of record and the continuing involvement of the auditor in financial reporting. Our new rules require association of the auditor on a retrospective basis with certain limited quarterly data which will be included in an unaudited footnote in audited annual financial statements. We believe this requirement will encourage management to involve public accountants on an ongoing basis, and we hope that it will lead the accounting profession to view the audit as a continuous obligation rather than an annual exercise.

I should reemphasize that this limited auditor involvement is not primarily designed to catch gross abuse, but rather to improve interim reporting. We feel that it will encourage greater attention to the measurement principles involved in quarterly reporting and will result in improved disclosure and analysis of quarterly results. In addition, it should reduce the likelihood of undetected error and it will create a greater behavioral incentive for management to produce meaningful quarterly reports. This is not to suggest that management today does not do a conscientious job. But we recognize that most of us do a little better and are a little more careful when someone is reviewing our work. The procedures that will be established do not constitute an audit and are not designed to catch intentional misrepresentations or other frauds.

The new rules, therefore, are part of a changing audit approach. They should lead to increased audit knowledge about the company, a more analytical and continuous audit and ultimately a situation in which the auditor will view his job as auditing the company, not just the financial statements. It should follow that the auditor must feel some responsibility for the entire financial reporting system of his client; annual financial statements are only one part of this system. This approach should not increase audit fact-finding work. There should be no increase in the observation of inventories, the confirmation of receivables, the counting of petty cash. Rather, it will increase the amount of analytical auditing work and probably increase the auditor's alertness to problems.

Ultimately, this may mean that the auditor's reporting responsibility will be increased as well. The president of the American Institute of Certified Public Accountants has recently suggested that auditors may some day become interpreters of financial statements for investors.

The process of increasing auditor involvement will be an evolutionary one, not one mandated overnight by the commission, although we are willing to encourage the process as our recently adopted rules should do. Our new rules, however, do not in themselves require continuous involvement and the development of such an approach will ultimately depend upon the willingness of the accounting profession to move in this direction.

Summary

A careful analysis of the demands of society suggests that a substantially changing face of financial reporting will be one of the realities that all who are involved in the process must recognize. Investors and other consumers of information will see their needs met with more information that is more effectively communicated. Hopefully, the result of these changes will be a more efficient capital market where scarce resources are allocated to their most productive use. ■

John Paul Dalsimer, CPA, Paul E. Dascher, Ph.D. and
James J. Benjamin, CPA, DBA

An Aspect of the Profession's Social Commitment

Every profession has an obligation to serve the public interest. The authors describe how an important and successful service effort has been accomplished in Philadelphia.†

THE decade of the 60s was characterized by a changing social awareness throughout the United States. Some have identified this as the dawn of an era of volunteerism, in which individuals seek to share their talents, energies and abilities with those in need. Accountants have become part of this process.

Many sources document a developing social role for the accounting profession. Historically, this involvement has included commitments to nonprofit organizations. Participation tended to focus on maintaining records and providing regular audit examinations of an organization. Recently, this role has expanded to meet the needs of the times and the profession.

Individual commitment and professional interest led to formalization of direct assistance programs. Direct service for disadvantaged businesses and certain community agencies was a logical extension of volunteer accounting service. Nationally, the AICPA and the National Association of Accountants established pioneering programs which formalized channels of assistance. While generally beneficial and always well-intentioned, many times accounting services were not available where most needed and at other times organizations competed to serve a single client.

From such a background, Community Accountants in Philadelphia emerged as a viable regional service force, active in the neighborhoods of the city and the surrounding area and ready to address important social issues requiring an accounting perspective. After five years of service, a comprehensive study of the organization was undertaken. The process provided information which confirmed some expectations, altered others and supported the continuation of the project. These results are not without parallel in other parts of the country. They add a dimension to the profile of the accountant as an involved citizen and support the developing social base of the profession.

Community Accountants

In 1973, several members of the Philadelphia accounting community began discussing the focus of volunteer professional involvement. Specifically, some concern existed about the delivery of services to disadvantaged businesses and nonprofit organizations in the metropolitan area. Support programs seemed to lack effectiveness because of poor coordination, inadequate publicity to attract applications for service and a lack of follow-up or evaluations. A decision was made to create a coordinating agency to facilitate the delivery of these important services. Community Accountants was incorporated as, "a nonprofit organization of accountants, CPAs and community leaders dedicated to assisting disadvantaged businesspeople and nonprofit organizations with their internal accounting and financial problems and to offering unbiased and independent financial and accounting expertise to groups acting in the public interest."[1]

Initial funding was sought from a variety of sources, including accounting firms, accounting organizations, individual accountants, corporations and foundations. Support for the concept and financial contributions enabled the organization to begin service in February 1975. From

John Paul Dalsimer, CPA, is Executive Vice President of F. A. Davis Company. Mr. Dalsimer serves as President of Community Accountants. Paul E. Dascher, Ph.D., is Professor of Accounting and Dean of the College of Business and Administration at Drexel University. Dr. Dascher is a member of the Board of Community Accountants and is Vice President of the organization. James J. Benjamin, CPA, DBA, is presently Professor of Accounting at Texas A&M University. His involvement with Community Accountants developed during his appointment at Drexel University.

† See also these articles in The CPA Journal: "Social Responsiveness of the Accounting Profession," Linda C. Bowen, June 1978; and "The Ascending Profession of Accounting," Thomas J. Burns and Edward N. Coffman, March 1977.

[1] Policy Statement of Community Accountants.

its inception, quality and professionalism have been hall-marks of Community Accountants' activities.

Volunteers were sought from all major accounting organizations: CPA firms, large industrial organizations and colleges and universities. Clients were solicited through business development centers, banking institutions, direct publicity on radio, television, newspapers and through community leaders. The importance of service was emphasized by an early decision to include community and client representation on the Board of Directors of Community Accountants. Care was taken to insure that the organization was not insulated from its client base.

> '**Support programs seemed to lack effectiveness because of poor coordination, inadequate publicity to attract applications for service and a lack of follow-up or evaluations.**'

Organizationally, a structure was prepared to provide an interface between volunteers and clients needing accounting services. Because services were provided without cost, specific screening criteria were established to insure that a need was real, that the ability to pay was truly missing and that the organization was at least marginally viable with a potential for survival. Community Accountants was not viewed as a vehicle for staving off inevitable bankruptcy, but rather as a genuine service to assist businesses and nonprofit organizations through formative years or trying times. Neither was Community Accountants intended to divert fees from valid providers of accounting services. For instance, no auditing services were offered. By focusing on marginal operations, an effort was made to share accounting talent, help individuals and assist in the development of viable businesses for the future.

Another dimension of the organization's service base relates to the public interest. Many community problems have a financial aspect. While maintaining a solid nonadvocacy position, Community Accountants has been prepared to lend the skills and abilities of its volunteers to analyze and interpret financial data, reports and presentations. Regardless of the organization initially requesting the service, Community Accountants retains and exercises the right to publicize its findings on a public interest issue. In addressing a community problem or public controversy, objectivity is an essential quality. This quality is deeply inherent in the professional accountant.

Service Opportunities

Over the years, Community Accountants has been presented with many important and challenging opportuni-

ties for service. Significant effort has been devoted to nonprofit organizations. Volunteer accountants have provided assistance in establishing and installing bookkeeping systems, training personnel to operate the systems and preparing budgets and financial reports. A regular series of workshops has been developed to address the accounting needs of nonprofit entities.

> '*Initial funding was sought from. . .accounting firms, accounting organizations, individual accountants, corporations and foundations.*'

Disadvantaged and developing businesses have also benefited significantly from Community Accountants' service. Volunteers have worked with these businesses to develop accounting systems, prepare reports necessary to secure financing, complete and file tax returns and analyze operation with a managerial view. Typical clients have included home remodeling contractors, neighborhood stores, small wholesale operations and service concerns.

Issue-oriented cases have broadened in perspective over the years. Teams of accountants and support personnel joined to investigate broader issues of public concern. Cases have included an analysis of financial reports supporting rent increases at HUD financed housing projects, *amicus curiae* testimony relative to control procedures used by a state and an investigation of the funding and budgetary procedures of a major school district. All of these cases resulted from public concern supported by a specific request from a bona fide organization with specific interest and expertise in the issue under consideration. The results of Community Accountants' investigations are made public regardless of the wishes or position of the requesting organization. Thus, volunteer assistance supports the public's right to know and be informed.

The resources drawn together through Community Accountants' coordination have been formidable and are growing. Last year, the organization served slightly more than 200 new clients (individuals or organizations) of varying size and delivered in excess of 4,000 hours of volunteer time. Facilities for workshops of up to 300 people were prepared and developed along with a variety of materials to support the organization's effort.

An Evaluation

In some respects, Community Accountants could be evaluated in strictly quantitative terms; new clients counted, hours tabulated and reports accumulated. However, a meaningful evaluation must address those issues that reflect the purpose of the organization. This is tied to the social role of the accounting profession.

AN ASPECT OF THE PROFESSION'S SOCIAL COMMITMENT

An early contributor to current accounting thought, William A. Paton, recognized the breadth of the profession and its scope of interest and responsibility. In discussing the role of accounting, Paton focuses on the social role and asks, "What is the function of accounting from the standpoint of the community. . ."[2] In this sense, assistance in promoting and elevating the general economic well-being of an individual or of a segment of society is consistent with the purpose of the profession. Practically, such a goal will also enhance the community and provide additional business opportunities as new firms are able to become viable.

> ### 'Care was taken to insure that the organization was not insulated from its client base.'

To address these aspects of Community Accountants, a study was undertaken to assess the attitudes of its clients. Opinions, impressions and reactions were sought in assessing the concept and implementation of a community-based organization providing access to accounting services. The results suggest lessons for other communities and other members of the profession.

The Study and Its Findings

The study sought to assess the attitudes of clients regarding several issues relating to the services of the organization. Questionnaires were sent to 70 individuals, businesses and organizations which received assistance from Community Accountants. Usable replies were received from 42 of the 70, a response rate of 60 percent; this level of response suggests an interest in the purpose of the study and the organization being studied.

The initial section of the questionnaire focused on the services of Community Accountants. Responses are summarized in Table 1.

All respondents agreed with the importance of the service provided by Community Accountants for their business or organization. This was consistent with their responses to Item 2, where, again, there was total agreement that volunteer accounting services were important to the community. It should be noted that in this sense, the "community" extends beyond the neighborhood and embraces the world of minority business, nonprofit organizations and groups working in the public interest. From this base, it was interesting to note that a "halo effect" did not result in Item 3. Opinion seemed to be spread out about whether accountants as individuals shared the community interest of the organization. It may be interpreted that respondents were unwilling to generalize the community interest away from Community Accountants. How-

ever, it would be interesting to contrast this level of feeling against that held by a similar group not exposed to a volunteer accounting organization.

The next three items relate to operations of the organization itself. Most of the respondents found it easy to get in contact with Community Accountants. About 10 percent of the participants did not agree with the positive nature of the statement and this has been a continuing area of concern. Exposure in the neighborhood and awareness by the potential client base is a concern of both accounting firms and volunteer accounting organizations. Some respondents offered viable suggestions in this area.

> ### 'Neither was Community Accountants intended to divert fees from valid providers of accounting services. For instance, no auditing services were offered.'

In Item 5, all respondents expressed agreement with the statement that the Community Accountants' staff was cooperative. Again, while reassuring, this is expected because of the nature of the organization—cooperation and interest are hallmarks of the involved individual. Item 6 presented a challenge for future effort. A small number of the respondents (about 15 percent) seemed to feel that they received a lower quality service than would be provided if they had paid a fee. While organizational quality control, feedback and evaluation techniques are aimed at preventing this, the attitude nevertheless exists. It is an area of concern and effort on the part of the staff and volunteers.

The next three items are closely related in completing the profile of attitudes about the organization. Some individuals felt that the services provided were limited. This is a fact. The organization does not attempt to exceed or even approach the margins of its expertise. Services are limited to those essential to the existence of an organization and they have the end goal of enabling the client to become self-sufficient. Item 8 builds on the previous question and adds the halo effect of satisfaction. Clients pleased with the service probably wish the organization would provide more. This leads into the last item, where all of the respondents recognized the importance of accounting services.

Two open-ended questions related to the service provided were also included in the questionnaire. While the comments varied considerably, the most frequent response used the opportunity to compliment the organization and praise its services. In response to the direct question of how can the service of Community Accountants be improved, one respondent indicated that, "We

TABLE 1
Percentage Responses to Statements Regarding Community Accountants Services

Item No.	Statement	Strongly Agree	Agree	Undecided	Disagree	Strongly Disagree
1	The service provided by Community Accountants is important for a business or organization like ours.	90.5	9.5	0	0	0
2	Community Accountant renders an important service to the community.	88.11	11.9	0	0	0
3	Accountants, as individual people, are interested in their community.	4.8	21.4	59.5	9.5	4.8
4	It is easy to get in contact with Community Accountants.	81.0	9.5	4.8	4.8	0
5	The staff of Community Accountants is cooperative.	83.3	16.7	0	0	0
6	The quality of service received from Community Accountant is lower than what would be provided if we paid a fee.	4.8	9.5	11.9	31.0	42.9
7	Community Accountants provides only a limited amount of accounting service.	4.8	35.7	11.9	31.0	16.7
8	Community Accountants should provide more services to businesses or organizations like ours.	14.3	45.2	40.5	0	0
9	Accounting services are not really necessary for most small businesses and community organizations.	0	0	0	11.9	88.1

found their service to be so excellent that nothing could be improved—believe it or not!''

One further observation must be made. In response to a question which asked if the organization had *hired* a professional accountant or *contracted* for accounting services since dealing with Community Accountants, one-third of the respondents said yes. This is from a group which was evaluated to be marginal for survival and unable to pay for such services when first accepted as a client. In a short time, the interest of a professional and the service provided enabled the organization to rise to a level where it could acquire accounting services in the marketplace.

In Conclusion—A Beginning

The formative years are vital for any organization. Community Accountants has proven itself to be of value to its clients, its community and the profession it represents. Through the coordination and communication of this organization, hundreds of professional accountants are able to add a dimension to themselves and help fellow man with their own talents and abilities. Each day brings new challenges and new opportunities. Accountants have responded to these and will continue to do so. After several years of successful operation in Phila-

delphia, Community Accountants joined with a few similar organizations from other parts of the country in forming what was to become Accountants for the Public Interest. The need for such service and such concern extends beyond geographic boundaries and reflects concern of the profession on a national basis. The thrust of Accountants for the Public Interest is to provide accounting resources to respond to appropriate problems and issues affecting broad segments of society on a regional and a national basis.

. . .the interest of a professional and the service provided enabled the organization to rise to a level where it could acquire accounting services in the marketplace.'

The needs, the resources and the concerns which characterize Community Accountants exist elsewhere. As in Philadelphia, what is needed is for individuals to step forward and commit themselves to fulfill the potential of

AN ASPECT OF THE PROFESSION'S SOCIAL COMMITMENT

their profession. The challenge and importance of this opportunity was recently highlighted in remarks made by Wallace Olson, President of the AICPA.

In the past, we laid claim to be a profession on the grounds of having all the trappings traditionally identified with those of other professions. However, our preoccupations have been largely with matters within the profession. Our understanding of the true public interest nature of our role has not been as clear as it is now becoming. It has been all too easy to expose in our literature our dedication to serving the public. Now, however, we are being pressed to make our actions correspond more fully with the ideals that we have articulated in the past.[3] Ω

---

[3] Wallace E. Olson, "Is Professionalism Dead?" *Journal of Accountancy*, July 1978, p. 82.

Corporate taxation and accounting in an era of chronic inflation

At the Conference Board's meeting on "New Directions for Taxation" in New York City on November 20, Michael O. Alexander, director of research and technical activities of the Financial Accounting Standards Board, discussed the impact of inflation on income measurement. He also explained that, although an objective of the recent FASB statement on changing prices is to help investors and creditors assess a company's performance and future cash flow, it is also intended to provide decision-makers in government with information on the implications of inflation when they propose changes in economic policy and taxation. Following is an adaptation of his address.

The word "income" sends a powerful message to each of us. The way we measure income is basic to the way we manage our wealth. It affects how much we consume as individuals, how corporations are taxed and how much our society spends and saves. From the concept of income, the corporate taxation pendulum swings.

Sir John Hicks wrote that "the purpose of income calculations in practical affairs is to give people an indication of the amount they can consume without impoverishing themselves. Following this idea, it would seem that we ought to define a man's income as the maximum value which he can consume during a week and still expect to be as well-off at the end of the week as he was at the beginning."[1]

This definition of income seems straightforward and is easily applied to corporations. Why, then, have accountants, businessmen, economists and others been embroiled in a heated debate over what constitutes income?

The meaning of "well-off"

Corporations are taxed on their income—which is assumed to reflect how "well-off" they are. The taxation debate revolves around what we mean by well-off. Basically, there are two ways to interpret well-off.

One view describes well-off in a purely financial sense: the amount of dollars a company has or the money invested. This is the basis for conventional accounting as we know it today. The other view describes well-off as what a company is able to do with its dollars in physically productive terms. Each view has a fundamentally different meaning, and the income figure resulting from the use of each concept will be very different. The distinction becomes particularly important during times of rising costs and prices. By applying a concept that is incompatible with the underlying assumption of what we have in mind by well-off, the message derived from the resulting income numbers may be quite misleading.

Let me use a brief anecdote to show what happens when costs and prices rise: Two merchants had an identical item in their shops; each had paid $1 for it. One sunny morning, one of the merchants opened his shop for business while the other closed his shop and went fishing. The merchant who opened his shop sold his item for $2, making a profit of $1. On this profit, he paid a tax of $.50. During the day, the wholesale cost of the item

rose to $2. The hard-working merchant who had sold his item for $2 and had paid $.50 in taxes now had only $1.50 with which to replace the same item of inventory. He was forced to go to the bank to borrow the additional $.50 he needed. At the end of the day, he assessed his results. He had made a profit of $1, he had the same item in stock and he owed the bank $.50. Meanwhile, the other merchant had thoroughly enjoyed his day fishing, had done no work and made no profit—but he had the same item in stock and owed the bank nothing.

Apart from the obvious social message on work ethics, this little anecdote demonstrates the important and basic dilemma in deciding what is income during times of inflation.

Table 1, this page, shows how the merchant's income is derived under each assumption of the meaning of well-off.

Well-off: the amount of money

The income derived from this assumption is the conventional accounting income of today. It is the amount that the merchant was told by his accountant that he had earned during the day. It is also the current method used by corporations in financial reporting, and it is the basis from which governments determine income to be taxed. While differences exist between accounting income as disclosed in financial statements and

Table 1 "Well-off"?	Conventional accounting	Current cost
Sales	$2.00	$2.00
Cost	− 1.00	− 2.00
	1.00	0
Tax	− .50	− .50
Income (loss)	$ .50	$(.50)

---

[1] J. R. Hicks, *Value and Capital*, 2d ed. (Oxford, England: Oxford University Press. 1946), p.172.

the income used for taxation purposes, the conceptual basis for determining income is the same and is based on the matching of original historical cost with current selling prices. Differences arise in the calculations of taxable income and reported income because of practical problems or fiscal policies.

The merchant's income under this method is $.50. This figure is based on the assumption that capital or well-offness at the beginning of the day is the historical cost of the inventory in terms of the number of dollars spent. This notion of profit—the difference between the amount originally paid for an item and the amount received when it is sold—is the one with which most people intuitively associate.

Well-off: the capacity to produce

This assumption views well-offness as the physical capacity to produce a certain number of units—often referred to as productive capacity. Under this assumption, income is the amount that is available for distribution (reinvestment or repayment of debt) after maintaining the productive capacity (meaning well-offness) at the beginning of the year.

This concept of income is not used in conventional accounting and financial reports. Financial Accounting Standards Board Statement no. 33, *Financial Reporting and Changing Prices,* issued last September, requires supplementary disclosure of this income number for the first time.

For the merchant, this concept of well-off is equated with his ability to continue to produce or to maintain the number of units of inventory on hand at the beginning of the day. This means that before declaring a profit, the merchant must ensure that he replaces the unit of inventory he sold during the day (this assumes that he is a going concern and does not intend to liquidate his business). To do this, the merchant must spend $2 to replace his item in inventory at the increased wholesale cost. Income is determined by matching current costs with current revenues. Because the current cost of the item is $2 and current revenues are $2, the net income before tax of $.50 is nil. Because the

merchant ended the day with a bank loan of $.50, it could be said that he borrowed to pay his taxes.

Assumptions for taxation

The tax predicament of the merchant illustrates what happens when taxation policy assumes the conventional accounting definition of income during a period of rising prices. The problem is similar for most industries; as with the merchant, not only is the incentive discouraged but the combination of higher costs and the impact of taxation can also make it difficult for a business to grow or to even survive. Additional cash may be borrowed to fill the gap, but there is a limit to the merchant's borrowing ability or recovery through selling price increases alone.

Because present tax policies are based on "the amount of money" concept rather than the productive capacity concept, the effects of tax policies may unknowingly devastate the well-being of certain industries. For example, oil is being taxed in the same way as the little merchant; so, too, are steel and other manufacturing industries. They will suffer similar effects on their capacities to produce. The choice of underlying assumptions in determining income is the key to the right tax policy. If it is a national objective to maintain or increase productive capability in certain industries, then a taxation method based on the conventional accounting concept of income may have serious consequences for those industries and for society in meeting its goals. Income based on the conventional accounting concept will overstate how well-off a company is during inflation in terms of its capacity to produce.

As businessmen know, productive capital investment requires that the expected return on that investment exceed the cost of the outlay. However, conventional accounting shows only the relationship of past costs to current prices. The resulting income may have

little relationship to the current margins between costs of new plant and equipment and expected returns. Conventional income may indicate that all is well when it is not. If this is to be a continued basis for public understanding, then it is unlikely that the appropriate tax changes will be made. Accelerated depreciation allowances are only possible in political terms with a better public understanding of the investment formula required to increase productive capacity, yet the facts about productive capacity are not evident from the conventional accounting and financial reports of business. When they are, there is reason to hope for a change. An objective of accounting should be to clarify such issues and thereby increase the level of economic literacy.

Recent editorials in the *Wall Street Journal*[2] have illustrated what happens to the effective rate of corporate taxes. Based on Department of Commerce adjusted data, these rates are as high as 70 percent of an income that is based on maintaining industry's capacity to produce (see table 2, page 78).

The weight of inflation falls unevenly on industries. Those with inventory and substantial investment in capital assets generally suffer the most. Their conventional income is more overstated than other industries during inflation; as a result, their tax burden is also heavier in relative terms. A heavier tax burden means that additional capital is necessary to maintain present levels of capacity. This problem is especially acute for smaller businesses because of the difficulties they may have in financing such additional capital.

---

[2] *Wall Street Journal*, August 23, 1979.

Table 2

Inflation and effective taxes

Year	Consumer Price Index increase	Effective rate of corporate taxes
1975	7.0	73%
1976	4.8	67
1977	6.8	66

The overall impact of inflation may be reflected in the market price of corporation stock. (Indeed, it has been demonstrated that the path of stock market prices has more closely followed the pattern of adjusted income based on maintaining capacity to produce rather than the path of conventional accounting income as reported.) While the market in the aggregate seems to understand the general impact, individual investors may not have been able to assess the impact of inflation on specific industries or individual corporations. Nor can we be confident that the effect of inflation and taxation levels on these different industries is clearly known to those responsible for formulating tax policies.

Business management has called on government to recognize the impact of rising costs on capital formation by changes in taxation. But governmental policymakers find it difficult to face the politics of making tax changes that benefit business when those same corporations are reporting increases in profit.

Management, of course, has been reluctant to voluntarily disclose the effects of inflation on reported earnings—in the absence of an accounting requirement, it would have little impact unless such reporting were widespread. In addition, management has, understandably, hesitated because of the perceived risk of such disclosure on its competitive ability in the financial markets. FASB Statement no. 33 helps both management and government by making information available to policy decisionmakers and minimizing the risks to management by ensuring that the effects of inflation will be reported on a widespread basis.

Statement no. 33—accounting for changing prices

Statement no. 33 meets an urgent need for information about the effects of changing prices on a corporation. Not only is Statement no. 33 intended to help investors and creditors understand the performance of business and assess its future cash flows but it is also intended to help people in government who participate in decisions on economic policy and who may lack important information about the implications of their decisions in taxation and other matters. An important objective of Statement no. 33 is to promote a better understanding by the general public of the problems facing a business during inflation.

Statement no. 33 addresses the concept of income based on capacity to produce. It requires the disclosure of income from continuing operations on a current cost basis as supplementary information to the financial statements. This provides a broad measure of the relationship between current costs and current revenues and thereby sheds insight into the reality of today's capital formation environment and the ability of a business to maintain its productive capacity.

In 1980 and 1981, we can expect to see 1,200 of the largest U.S. corporations begin to report the information called for in that statement. It is not possible to predict what the results will be on an individual company basis, but it is safe to say that, in the aggregate, the supplementary income from continuing operations on a current cost basis will demonstrate what is currently happening to the productive capacity of business, along with the effective taxation rate on an income determined on that basis.

A recent editorial in the *Wall Street Journal* expressed the belief that Statement no. 33 will help to dramatize the problems of taxation and give those who care about capital formation some more sophisticated ammunition. Statement no. 33 incorporates the effects of inflation in the business scorecard on a formal basis. This should increase the credibility of statements by business managers, by providing quantitative information about the effects of inflation in their financial reports. The actual message, however—that is, how business presents and explains the information about taxation and capital formation—is up to business.

Statement no. 33 is a major step forward in accounting, but, like all accounting, it must be neutral in its measurement and description of the facts. To be useful, it cannot advocate a particular policy or position. Accounting by itself cannot prevent or remove inflation, but, with better information, we improve the chances of making better decisions and of taking the right actions. ∎

Accounting in an Expanding Environment

BY FRANK S. CAPON

Future economic and social pressures will bring new concepts of accounting, fiscal, and monetary policies for the measurement and distribution of national wealth

Like all types of men through the ages, the accountant of tomorrow will be a creature of his environment. Thus, to get any feel for his opportunities, his responsibilities, or his problems, it is necessary first to consider the environment in which he will operate. Since accountants collect, analyze, evaluate, interpret, and report on the myriad transactions that take place daily between individuals, corporations, and institutions, the environment in which we are interested is that of the total economy—its basic nature, its fiscal policies and tools, its political orientation, and even the economic relationships between nations.

It would be both easy and reassuring to assume that we shall continue to follow the comfortable gradual economic development of the past, with the free enterprise system secure in the developed nations and rapidly spreading its proven blessings into the underdeveloped nations. But in

Frank S. Capon is a director and vice president of Du Pont of Canada. Born in Britain, he came to Canada in 1930, attaining his Chartered Accountant degree in 1938. He has served successively as assistant treasurer, treasurer, secretary and treasurer, and vice president of his company. He is a past president of Financial Executives Institute and a member of the Board of Overseers of the Amos Tuck School of Business Administration of Dartmouth College.

a world of constant change, the one thing we can be sure of is that the environment of tomorrow will be vastly different from that of today. The very speed of change itself is increasing on an exponential curve. The discernible trends which will determine our economic future—population, technology, productivity, and so on—are all in the early phase of a steep upward curve after gradually gathering momentum through the ages. The challenge to our leaders—business, political, professional, and academic—will be to maintain enough control to prevent the entire system from disintegrating through the force of its gathering momentum. And because control will depend upon ever more accurate, ever faster information, the accountant of tomorrow will be a key figure as the increasing momentum of change brings fateful decisions within the range of our generation.

Our basic assumption is that the

FINANCIAL EXECUTIVE December 1967

first objective of any community is to achieve the highest possible average living standard for its people. While there have always been differences of opinion on how this should be achieved, it seems safe to assume that it will continue to be the aim of all peoples. Regardless of its political or social system, the average living standard of any community must depend upon the amount of wealth it creates and the manner in which that wealth is distributed. If wealth generation is low, average living standards will be low. If wealth generation is high, average living standards will be high unless too much wealth is retained by a few wealthy groups.

Geometric Rate of Growth

Wealth is generated by the application of man's faculties to the natural resources placed at his disposal. Apart from the limitations of raw materials, the amount of wealth generated depends both on man's ingenuity and on the degree of effort he is prepared to devote to improving his living standard.

For the earliest man, mere maintenance of life called for constant, brutally hard labor with bare hands. Such discoveries as the shovel, the axe, the wheel, and metals, spaced thousands of years apart, made possible fantastic leaps forward in man's fight to improve his way of life. And naturally one development led to another, so that progress fed upon itself.

It is, of course, this last fact which accounts for the geometric rate of growth in technology. For the great technological discoveries, which at first came painfully slowly, developed with increasing rapidity as the total body of technical knowledge accumulated. The developments of the present generation—computers, television, the jet engine, atomic power, space travel, antibiotics, lasers, masers, and so forth—have probably been greater than the sum of all prior human accomplishments in technology. This explosive increase in our ability to create wealth threatens to outpace our social ability to distribute wealth under our existing systems.

Living with Automation

Already technology exists for rev-

olutionizing the management process and particularly the information collection and dissemination system which is at the heart of the accounting function. Since 1945 we have seen in North America a sharp drop in the proportion of workers employed directly in production and a sharp rise in the proportion of so-called white-collar workers. This phenomenon is due largely to the fact that we were able to introduce new technology very quickly into production operations, whereas sharply higher output processed by the old clerical and marketing methods resulted in huge increases in employment in these tasks. Machine systems exist for the automation of much of this work, permitting a totally new concept of management with far fewer people,

---

"The human effort needed to produce wealth is decreasing, the productivity of men is being replaced by productivity of machines."

---

more delegation of authority, and vastly improved control. The new standards of efficiency can become effective only when accountants make the fullest use of the new machine systems to collect business information automatically, to process it on predetermined programs, and to provide the figures and explanations needed for planning and control through a small but highly skilled staff backed up by the new hardware. There are, of course, frightening social and emotional problems involved in the sudden utilization of these new machines. But the machines exist, they will be used, and we will have to learn to live with them and realize to the fullest the tremendous benefits they offer us.

The accountant's responsibilities relating to the production of wealth are primarily concerned with the collection, processing, and interpretation of the information needed to ensure that optimum output and efficiency are maintained. But the distribution of wealth may be of

much greater concern to accountants than its production. The accountant of tomorrow can have vast responsibilities in this area if he has the vision, the courage, and the ability to reach out for them.

New Definition of Wealth

Up to the present, generation of wealth has been directly related to human effort, and it has been possible to distribute our wealth very largely in the form of wages for work done. Capital—the implements and machines used to increase human productivity—has slowly gained in importance, and some wealth has been distributed in the form of dividends and interest for the use of capital. As long as the rate of technological development was gradual, bringing rising wealth generation, we could pay increasing wages for fewer working hours and at the same time pay the slowly growing amount necessary to attract capital. Thus, there has been justification for maintaining our job-oriented social and economic structure.

But suddenly technology permits steeply rising wealth generation by machines using little or no human effort. The traditional basis of wealth distribution is no longer valid; justice will soon demand that wealth be distributed primarily as payment for the use of capital and only secondarily as wages for work done. The human effort needed to produce wealth is decreasing, the productivity of men is being replaced by productivity of machines. Labor becomes increasingly obsolete as we enter into the era of which man has dreamed through the centuries—a life of ease and luxury while machines do the work. But under such a system high average living standards are possible only if there is a wide distribution of the ownership of capital among the households. For accountants, such a total change in the economic and social structure can only mean a radical new concept of accounting, fiscal, and monetary policies affecting the measurement and distribution of national wealth. The calculation, payment, and taxation of wage income have been easy in comparison with tomorrow's complex problems of redistribution of the ownership of capital and of distribution of national income through the capital channel.

Prosperity Dependent on Others

But there are other major environmental changes to concern our accountant of tomorrow. Most technological developments have favored very large manufacturing units supplying huge markets. This trend has had its impact on international trade and on the development of the international community. In the first place, nations are building productive capacity well beyond their domestic needs, seeking to export the surplus in order to achieve the economies of large-scale output. In the second place, as a defensive measure against the rapidly growing economic power of the great nations, smaller nations are banding together into groupings such as the European Common Market in order to achieve the large domestic markets needed to justify production units of an economical size. Thus the nations of the world are becoming rapidly more interdependent, the prosperity of each depends on that of the others, disaster in one damages the economy of the others. No longer can we cut ourselves off from one another.

That three-quarters of the people on earth have submarginal living standards can no longer be regarded with equanimity by the wealthy few. Thanks to our publicity and our tourists, they know what we have and they can be stirred to want what we have. Unless we can devise the means for them to raise their living standards, how can we hope to live at peace with them? While our technological development from their level was painfully slow, theirs can be fast because the knowledge now exists. They have the natural resources, but we must help them to develop the abilities and management skills and to accumulate the capital necessary to convert resources into wealth. And, above all, this wealth must be theirs to use for raising living standards and for new capital formation by their households. The branch-plant subsidiary-company form of exploitation of underdeveloped countries will not answer their needs.

Fearsome Lack of Capital

Two phenomena are threatening our free enterprise way of life. In the poorer nations, which comprise three-quarters of the world's population,

the fearsome lack of capital pushes men towards socialist totalitarianism because they see the state as the only institution capable of putting together the capital formations needed to finance productive enterprises. In the wealthy nations, the displacement of human effort by machines combines with the relatively narrow distribution of capital ownership to increase the pressure for socialism. Even though the incentives of the free enterprise system have proven their effectiveness in generating the highest average living standard ever known to man, the fundamental change needed in our wealth distribution system is being resisted by labor because it signifies the end of the labor-dominated wages system of wealth distribution and by capital because present owners of capital strive to maintain their tight control of equity capital. In a democracy, the majority vote counts, and present trends indicate a majority move towards socialist totalitarianism.

But let us take a quick look at the chief financial effect of these trends. The socialistic approach to wealth distribution now evidenced in a rapidly increasing variety and amount of government social security payments is in fact no different from the classical inflations which destroyed economies in the past. Initial steps in payment of old-age pensions, unemployment relief, universal medical care, and so forth are always justified on the basis of need and covered by direct taxation on those who produce the nation's wealth. But as politicians continue to follow this easy route to win elections, social security payments rise beyond the level that acceptable tax rates can bear. Governments start incurring deficits, which pushes up costs, brings on demands for higher wages, forces up prices, and increases the need for still more social security. Governments, in this process, are merely printing money to hand out to old, unemployed, or sick voters. Once the process begins it will gather momentum.

The printing of money without sound backing can only cause inflation, as it has always done. While inflations of tomorrow may stem from a cause different from those of yesterday, the accountant of tomorrow will have substantially the same problems as his ancestor in trying to rebuild a sound money system out of the rubble.

Erosion of Money Value

The almost universal trend towards socialist totalitarianism—except, of course, in the communist countries, which are now beginning the long climb back towards capitalism—brings on substantial and increasing abuse of our private corporations. Although attainment of the world's highest living standards would have been impossible without

---

". . . the stubborn refusal of accountants to reflect changing money values in financial statements causes even greater overstatement of profits."

---

these inanimate entities, the great mass of our people seem ready to crucify them with excessive taxation, unfair labor demands enforced by crippling strikes, total refusal to understand the incentive effect of profit, and outright abuse of corporations and managements alike. A very great share of the blame for the public misunderstanding of profits, for the popular belief in the fallacy that corporations can in fact be taxed, and particularly for the totally erroneous picture of rising and excessive profits, must be laid on the accounting profession. Its willingness to deal with "profit before taxes" and even "profit before depreciation" hands to the critics of freedom a high "profit" figure to criticize, whereas in truth there can be no true profit until all costs, expenses, and taxes are paid. And then the stubborn refusal by accountants to reflect changing money values in financial statements causes even greater overstatement of profits. The accountant of today must accept the responsibility for adverse trends which are eroding our freedoms, and thus it will be up to the accountant of tomorrow to save our system by developing financial statements that are truly informative.

A challenging responsibility for the accountant of tomorrow is that of measuring the results of government operations and interpreting these results to the community. This duty is becoming significant because government operations of one type or another affect or involve a large and growing portion of the total national wealth generation and distribution. By its policies and actions, government is the greatest single determinant of living standards, even though government produces nothing. Because those who govern are politicians usually more motivated by being in power and staying in power than by the best ultimate interests of the people, it becomes imperative that the people be provided with some disinterested, objective analysis and interpretation of the immediate effects and ultimate results of government policies. As the impact of government actions on the community increases, we cannot rely solely on the reporting of accountants employed by government. Mechanisms are needed whereby the people can obtain objective and informative reports from independent sources such as the professional accounting bodies.

Distributing Wealth by Votes

Governments do not produce wealth, but through their taxation, social security, and other laws they have a major impact on the distribution of wealth. Because the incentive of politicians is to obtain the support of the largest number of voters, the tendency will be to redistribute income so as to give as much as possible to the largest number of voters regardless of their contribution to the generation of that wealth. Such policies invariably contravene the incentives towards the maximum generation of wealth and thus tend to be damaging to the true welfare of the community. The imposition of steeply graduated taxes upon the most productive people necessarily results in a drop in productivity. Furthermore, attempts to shift the tax burden onto inanimate corporations serves only to increase costs and to damage productivity. Only people can earn income or pay taxes, and the taxation of corporations, popular as it is politically, is merely a means of taxing people indirectly rather than directly. Recognition of the true impact of taxation and simplification of the tax structure—which requires extensive effort by the finest accounting minds—would make an immeasurable contribution to our productivity and prosperity.

Another great factor that will determine the kind of tomorrow in which accountants will find themselves is the morality, the moral standards, that will be observed by nations and by men. Casual observation indicates that moral standards and living standards may well follow opposite trends. The moral standards that will be determining are those of business and social ethics, of enactment and observance of sound laws, of honesty, of true charity, and of equity in all human relationships. It was the establishment and observance of moral standards that permitted man to develop from the animal brutality of the jungle; the present apparent tendency for moral standards to be pushed aside, particularly by youth, could quickly send us back into a kind of economic jungle in which might would be right.

The professional bodies, such as the corporations of accountants, lawyers, doctors, and scientists, are responsible for the development of moral standards as well as of knowledge in those areas in which they profess to be expert. It is to such bodies that mankind must look for the safeguarding of our future morality as well as the development of the knowledge which can ensure peace and prosperity.

And so the economic environment in which the accountant of tomorrow will work will be one of rapidly developing and fast-spreading technology, with vast increases in the production of wealth through greater reliance on capital and decreasing contribution by human effort. Population will continue to expand exponentially, and, unless very drastic and sudden action is taken to reverse present trends, the wealthy nations will become rapidly wealthier and the poor poorer. The social pressures arising from such growth curves will build up with the speed and force of an explosion. There will be ever more interdependence between nations, with a fast-growing volume of international trade and communications, resulting in complex international relationships. The economy of size will cause a growing proportion of production and distribution to be centered in giant international corporations, accompanied by conflict between those people who favor state ownership and those who favor private ownership. This world will be deeply affected by the pressures to bring about the economic development of the poor nations and the education of their people within a period infinitely shorter than that in which the developed world achieved its present position. And it will be constantly haunted by the threat of total annihilation now that man has the technical knowledge with which to destroy life on earth.

Figuring in the Future

So much for the environment in which the accountant of tomorrow will work. What will be his responsibilities and how will he train himself to meet them?

For ease of discussion we can divide the total work of the accountant into two parts, which I will label bookkeeping and accounting. The first is the routine recording of transactions of every type, so that information will be available. The second is the verification of the accuracy and objectivity of the information and the analysis, interpretation, and employment of that information in the management process.

The development of computers has made possible the automation of the bookkeeping system. Information must be reduced to the simplest terms for mechanization, but once fed into the computer, it can be processed in an infinite number of ways with virtually no human effort. The programming of information will call for both accounting and mathematical skills of a high order because such work can be done effectively only by those with a concept of the total operation, the total information needs of management, and the capabilities of alternative machine systems available. But the bookkeeping work will be done mainly by machines fed by workers on production lines or payroll, stores, and sales order clerks. There will always be small operations which do not justify mechanization, but we can predict a drop in the need for bookkeepers.

While the accountant will always need to have the basic knowledge of bookkeeping or information recording, he is essentially a highly skilled, and often highly specialized, professional expert. Just as the complexity of technology has caused scientists to become highly specialized, so also the complexity of economic affairs will call for new degrees of advanced specialization by accountants. They will have to understand the total economic and social system, recognize what information is necessary for its management, planning, and control, and also have a sound concept of all aspects of the collection, analysis, and interpretation of that information. They will aid in, or be responsible for, planning and implementing fiscal policies, particularly those which influence the distribution of income and the flow of international trade and payments. They will put together and report on the information needed by governments, businesses, and institutions for their operations which, in total, determine the living standards of all mankind. And they will check at all levels to ensure that policies and plans are executed properly, that honesty prevails, and that stewardship is carried out in a trustworthy and efficient manner.

Because our businesses and our institutions primarily generate and distribute the total national wealth, all citizens are concerned with their operations, not only as employees, consumers, or suppliers, but as citizens whose way of life depends upon the most effective exploitation of the nation's total resources. Thus, those accountants recording the transactions of business and those checking and reporting on the honesty and effectiveness of management have a duty not only to owners of the company but also to the people as a whole. If such analysis and reporting is to be of value, it must obviously be of heroic objectivity. Any deviation from ethics, from objectivity, not only makes the accountant valueless, it actually renders him harmful to the community.

Recognizing the overpowering importance of ethics and objectivity in the complex work of the accountant of tomorrow, we cannot help but be conscious of the need for the vast degree of judgment he will have to exercise at all times. Seldom is there one right and one wrong way to record or report on any transaction. Certainly the routine transactions can be mechanized according to rigid manuals, but the analysis of information and the reporting on results calls for extensive interpretation and the exercise of a great deal of judgment. Moreover, the degree of judgment required, and thus the effect of this judgment, increases rapidly with the complexity of our economy, the changing value of money, and the growing interrelationships of business and government at national and international levels. As long as this judgment is exercised on the basis of expert skill and according to the strictest ethics, the community will be well served even though standardization in accounting may have to give way to great flexibility in financial statements and reports.

Our history has been that of nations slowly coming to know one an-

---

" . . . must train accountants to be highly selective in the information they produce."

---

other better, becoming more dependent upon one another and finally consolidating their interests. With the existence of ultimate weapons, and with the technological developments which will be fully effective only if they are allowed to serve the entire world population in one heterogeneous system, we are now emerging into an era in which all nations and all men will become so interdependent, so inextricably intertwined in their economic and social life, that national boundaries will come to lose their significance. The implications of such a course for accountants are obvious and overwhelming. The need to overcome differences between nations in monetary systems, fiscal policies, accounting practices, commercial law, and so on will become increasingly apparent if we are to avoid distortions in the production and flow of wealth and in the information needed to record, to analyze, and to plan the maximization of this production and flow.

Free enterprise corporations re-spond readily to market forces, and we have already seen the rapid development of huge international corporations dedicated to taking advantage of local situations anywhere. The task of the accounting officer forming part of top management of such corporations is clearly different from that of the average accountant of today, since his sphere of influence extends into many countries, each with its own laws, customs, and policies. He is the forerunner of the accountant of tomorrow, for his is the task of measuring the needs of each area and the effectiveness of its policies, the task of influencing the adoption by each nation of those fiscal and economic policies designed to bring about the optimum exploitation of its total resources. In the interdependent world of tomorrow, most accountants will be so engaged. The first real steps in this direction must surely be the establishment of internationally accepted standards of recording and reporting, an increase of international coordination and standardization of information, and rapid improvement of international information on the production and distribution of wealth.

Clearly, accountants will continue to function in two broad groupings. The first group comprises those who will form part of management in all types of operations, and who are thus actively involved in the production and distribution system. The second covers those who, as practicing professionals, will be responsible for auditing to ensure that businesses, institutions, and governments operate with honesty and efficiency. The constant development of the art or science of accounting must be a duty of all accountants of both groups, for new knowledge should come just as much from those engaged in management as from the practicing professionals.

Finally, what about the training of the accountant of tomorrow? Here we must be prepared to talk with a considerable degree of certainty, because the accountant of tomorrow must in fact be trained today.

Bookkeeping can, and should, be taught at the high school and undergraduate level in university. But each science or art has its special impact on all community life. To be fully effective, accountants must have a sound knowledge of all those basic elements which together make up the life of the community—its history, its traditions, its customs, its values, its laws, its aspirations. Thus, to be a whole man and to make his greatest contribution, the accountant must be well versed in the humanities. Such knowledge will best result from constant study of these subjects from earliest school days throughout the formal education system. Those who reach the top will as always be those who devote much personal time throughout their lives to the continual study of the humanities.

An immense challenge for accounting training comes from the new potential to employ machine systems to automate the recording, collating, and processing of financial information. Not only is it now necessary for accountants to understand how to use a totally new tool for processing information on an integrated and instant basis, but more particularly, it is necessary for us to understand how to use this information in the management process. It is now practical to produce information of types, in volumes, and at speeds hitherto undreamed of. But if we are to make our maximum contribution to management, and thus to higher living standards, we must train accountants to be highly selective in the information they produce. They must concentrate on those matters that are truly significant and avoid producing a mass of useless data just because it can be produced. This is a new area of accounting, but one which will be of increasing importance and which will require highly specialized training courses.

Training or education in data processing systems and computers is becoming so necessary for all types of employment that it is generally taught in the senior years of secondary education and throughout college or university education. Advanced training in this special field will be essential for the accountant of tomorrow since he will either have to operate or manage information systems or be expert in using their output in the management process. To a greater extent than in the past, tomorrow's accountant must be trained in mathematics, for computers have made it possible to apply mathematics to the solution of accounting or financial problems as never before. In fact, the computer potentiality for simulation of all types of management problems permits a new approach to problem solving which replaces obsolete accounting techniques and vastly increases the possible value of the accountant to management.

A vital factor in the training of the accountant of tomorrow will be the advanced education in the special fields which will make of many of them highly skilled experts in relatively narrow spheres. Just as medical men now specialize in the treatment of portions of the body and as scientists specialize in polymer chemistry, the physics of light or the electronics of sound transmission, so accounting will have to develop its highly qualified specialists in automated information processing, fiscal policy and tax law formulation, international financial reporting, money management, and so forth. The complexity of economic life can only increase. This complexity must surely result in an ever-growing need for expert skills of a depth that will call for the concentration of training of specialists in these areas, possibly—and unfortunately—to the exclusion of broader training. Special training of this order can come only after an accountant has finished basic training and has become a seasoned practitioner. There will, therefore, be a need for extensive post-graduate education in specialized accounting and financial subjects.

The accountant's horizons have broadened immeasurably. His service to the community of tomorrow will be of a new order of significance. The potentiality for contribution, for service, and for reward was never greater, and it can only increase as the world of tomorrow unfolds. But potential rewards will materialize only if the contribution is in fact made, the service actually rendered. Accounting has a right to be a profession only if it fulfills its professional responsibilities to the utmost. For only if all accountants live and work as true professionals, maintaining absolute integrity in their work at all times, insisting always on thorough competence, and keeping up-to-date the body of technical knowledge and science on which their contribution depends, can they make their greatest possible contribution to world progress.

It is, of course, always possible that our world will fall apart, that our civilization will crumble. We can only proceed, however, on the assumption that we will be able to control the forces tending to overthrow us, that we will avoid total destruction, and that we will make the best use of the vast technological gains and our natural resources to raise the living standards of all mankind. But we now know that we can survive only if nations can live and work together for common ends, overcoming their differences and distrust, probably coming eventually to common citizenship and to the surrender of national prerogatives in favor of a single world community.

Such fusion cannot happen suddenly, but it may have to happen very, very quickly if the awesome alternative is to be avoided. Economic considerations will be crucial to such decisions, and these will depend upon objective and illuminating financial information. The accountant of tomorrow will therefore be at the center of the decision-making process of mankind. E

In the past, financial accounting standards were primarily based on technical considerations. This emphasis on technical aspects was understandable because the analysis of accounting issues and the development of related standards was done almost exclusively by accountants. More recently, a broader based Financial Accounting Standards Board (the "FASB") has been giving increasing attention to potential economic effects in its deliberations.

OPINION

THE ECONOMIC IMPACT OF FINANCIAL ACCOUNTING STANDARDS

Consistency with established principles should be paramount in setting accounting standards, but conclusions must be reconcilable with real or perceived economic effects.

Victor H. Brown
Vice President & Controller
Standard Oil Company—Indiana

"Reprinted from *Financial Executive*, September 1979, with permission of the publisher."

Because accounting and reporting pronouncements are being made more frequently and the issues dealt with by these statements are more complex, there is much discussion about how much emphasis should be given to economic consequences by the standard setters. This issue is complex and does not seem to have a simple solution.

POTENTIAL ECONOMIC IMPACT

Financial accounting standards can affect not only the primary financial statements but also the form and extent of supplementary disclosures such as those contained in statement footnotes or in Securities and Exchange Commission (the "SEC") filings. Both measurement and disclosure dimensions can have potential economic consequences. One of the principal effects is the impact which a standard is likely to have on reported earnings, shareholders' equity, and other significant accounts and ratios of affected companies. Most corporate managements are extremely interested in the effects of such standards on their financial reports because such reports are a primary way to measure management performance.

Management's interest in reported amounts is also related to the extensive use of statement data for a number of business purposes—both externally and internally. Financial results are used to determine, among other things, the extent of compliance with restrictive convenants in loan agreements, payments to be made under contractual arrangements, amounts available for executive bonuses, budget targets for divisions of an organization, etc. Changes in accounting which affect these relationships can have a significant economic impact on the operations of a company and on those companies with which it does business. As a result, it is natural for corporate managements to be concerned with the impact of accounting standards, particularly changes that have a potentially negative or confusing effect on reported results. While this concern may be obvious, it has several implications.

First, management may be prompted to take action to prevent what is thought to be a harmful proposal from becoming effective. Depending upon the possible extent of the financial statements' effects, a new standard could be modified—or in extreme cases—eliminated altogether. One example is FAS 15, which dealt with troubled debt restructuring. The banking industry testified that extremely adverse economic consequences would result if the procedures specified in the exposure draft were adopted. Whatever the economic consequences may have been, the final rules were modified considerably. This is one example of how an affected industry's perception of economic impact could have influenced the final standard. While the FASB has acknowledged the need to consider economic impact, in this particular situation it might have avoided the modifications if the industry's reactions had been more fully assessed at an earlier stage.

In addition, management actions may be changed to minimize or to offer alternatives to what it sees as adverse changes in reported results. It is not always easy, of course, to predict changes in behavior but such changes may occur. For example, during the period that the accounting standards for oil and gas producing companies were under consideration, a number of companies stated that their exploration programs would be cut back—in some cases by up to 50 per cent—if they were forced to change from the full-cost to the successful-efforts method of accounting. It may well be argued that the wisdom of doing this is questionable because the underlying cash flows and economics are unaffected by the accounting method. Some firms, however, may attach such importance to a stable pattern of reported earnings that they may program their activities to minimize fluctuations. It can be expected that companies which must modify their oper-

> **"The objectives of accounting are themselves a function of perceived social purposes, and it would seem unrealistic to view them as immutable. Accounting is ultimately based on social need and must be flexible."**

ations to fit new accounting standards are likely to resist the rules in question. Those responsible for setting the rules need to consider that reaction.

Another factor is the impact of accounting changes on capital markets. A great deal of research has been directed at determining whether the market is efficient or not. Although some aspects of this question are unanswered, the market appears to be relatively efficient. This suggests that market prices should not be significantly affected by accounting standards or by changes which merely give information already available to the market in some other form. Accordingly, many accounting changes, such as the elimination of certain accounting alternatives, should have little effect on prices because the market in many cases already has enough information to adjust prices to suit different bookkeeping practices. It is important, therefore, to distinguish accounting and reporting changes which provide new information from those which do not. New requirements which convey information not otherwise available may well have a price impact. They could affect the distribution of wealth among investors and the cost of capital to business. Those who believe they are affected can also

be expected to actively protect their interests.

In addition to the potential economic impact of accounting changes from the standpoint of corporate management, reported information may also have an impact on a wide variety of other groups. These groups include labor unions, competitors, government regulatory agencies, those responsible for macroeconomic policies, various social groups, and so forth. To the extent that the behavior of these groups is influenced by what they know about a particular firm, there is the potential for additional economic effects.

Financial information can have very diverse ramifications on many business interests and social groups. Those providing financial information and those receiving it can be significantly affected. Consequently, it is not surprising that proposed rules are scrutinized very carefully to evaluate their possible economic consequences.

THE INSTITUTIONAL SETTING

One helpful way of viewing the present institutional setup for establishing accounting standards is to look at where the power to establish such standards

lies. Under our system of government, that power is vested in Congress. Congress itself, at least until very recently, has been quite restrained in using its power over accounting. By delegating responsibility to the SEC, it has—with few exceptions—largely removed itself from direct involvement in standard setting. The SEC in turn has delegated some of its authority to the private sector. Indeed, the present relationship between the FASB and the SEC is similar to any decentralized organization. The SEC acts as top management, while the FASB analyzes, formulates, and implements accounting standards subject to review by the SEC.

For the most part, this system has worked efficiently. There are highly technical elements in the complex process of setting accounting standards, but the FASB has been able to call upon and utilize the skills and talents of the private sector to deal with the involved issues. Many believe a government agency would not be able to attract and motivate highly competent professional people such as those now at the FASB. This certainly is one of the key reasons why the SEC has generally relied on the private sector.

The present system, however, is not without its problems. One which appears particularly relevant is the attitude of accountants as a group. It is not clear that accounting professionals alone, however technically qualified, bring to bear the perspective needed to balance broader economic considerations against technical accounting considerations. Accountants can lose their policy-making ability if they fail to analyze the economic impact of their rulings.

This criticism may be overstated, but is does deserve careful consideration. In fact, the FASB has taken a number of steps responding to those concerns. Without mentioning all of the changes, there are several which are especially significant. These include the selection of board members with more diverse backgrounds, a corresponding widening in the composition of the Financial Accounting Standards Advisory Council, and the conduct of formal activities under sunshine rules that compare favorably with procedures followed by governmental agencies.

In its operations, the FASB now shows many similarities to a legislative body, with its elaborate system of task forces, discussion memoranda, and the encouragement of wide public participation in its activities. As a result, from a structural point of view, the FASB already has the capability to gather and evaluate information from many sources and review the impact that rulings might have on various interests and groups. A more unsettled area is striking a balance between technical considerations and political consequences.

The FASB has no power of its own to make judgments having an impact on the distribution of wealth. The amount of authority which it does have derived from a Congress which itself is answerable to the electorate. Therefore, one can justifiably point to the undesirable consequences which would result if accounting decisions were made primarily on the basis of their popularity, or based on the way they promote whatever political goals are popular at the time. If setting standards depended primarily on political criteria, it is clear that the FASB itself would be redundant. Politicians can make political decisions better than accountants.

The present institutional arrangements recognize that technical considerations are essential to the standard-setting process. However, technology cannot be the only consideration. It must be applied along with general social awareness and sensitivity to the political realities of a pluralistic society.

The record of the FASB in balancing technical criteria with political necessities has been encouraging but by no means perfect. At this point, it seems premature to say that there is a satisfactory accommodation that is good for the long run. While the FASB appears to have a structure that is broadly compatible with the environment in which it operates, there are a number of actions which could be taken or emphasized to ensure long-run success.

RECOGNITION OF ECONOMIC IMPACT

To begin with, the FASB should monitor the environment very closely to identify emerging problems in accounting practice in the earliest stages. This would allow prompt action to eliminate undesirable practices before they come entrenched. Such a program could be particularly useful in cutting off the growth of new, undesirable accounting alternatives. This would seem to have high priority with both the FASB and the SEC. An example is the controversy surrounding the oil and gas accounting project. The full-cost method was virtually unused until the early 1960's. It could have been eliminated with little resistance at that time. Because of the delay, however, what could have been accomplished quite simply turned out to be impracticable.

A second area is the selection of items for the FASB agenda. No item should be added until its potential economic impact has been carefully assessed. The agenda should also reflect an appropriate mix of controversial and relatively more innocuous items. It is important that the FASB be very conscious of what is likely to be involved in the resolution of each potential agenda topic. Relevant questions at this stage should include such matters as:

- Identification of existing practices.

- Identification of the extent to which each of the existing practices is used.

- Assessment of the significance of the practices to the financial statements of the companies concerned.

- Evaluation of the extent to which a new ruling may change behavior by management and others and how it might affect resource allocations.

- Conclusions on the extent that a mandated change may arouse opposition.

- The political support which might be sought by those who feel adversely affected.

Following such a review, the FASB would then be in a better position to assess the degree of controversy likely to surround a particular issue.

Actual agenda selection should reflect the results of this preliminary assessment and recognize that the FASB simply does not have the resources to take on too many highly controversial issues at the same time. The FASB also has to be aware of how its support in the business community may be eroded if a large number of controversial projects are considered in a short time. While the FASB obviously cannot and should not avoid all highly controversial projects, the mix of issues should be balanced. That balance depends significantly on potential economic impact.

Selection of task forces and preparation of discussion memoranda should also recognize economic impact. Representatives of groups likely to be affected should be included on the task force. Additionally, the discussion memorandum itself should clearly state and identify the anticipated economic consequences of the measurement and disclosure alternatives under consideration. Such a procedure should minimize the probability that the FASB would issue a controversial exposure draft that threatens the FASB continued viability.

When deliberating on an exposure draft, the FASB should assess the entire spectrum of potential solutions so as to note the economic impact of each option. Technical accounting considerations are certainly highly important at this stage; however, the FASB may sometimes find it desirable to choose an answer that is less favorable from a theoretical viewpoint but potentially more acceptable. Such a pragmatic approach is opposed by some who believe that the goal should be only to pursue truth. The latter concept is elusive. In accounting, it often is just not apparent that one option is technically better than any other. As a result, it becomes even more important that the answer adopted should be acceptable.

The FASB should continue to sponsor additional research in several areas. For example, it would be particularly useful to assess in more detail the way managements react to accounting changes. The studies which have been conducted on ways in which companies may have altered their foreign exchange hedging policies in response to FAS 8 are a good illustration of useful, application oriented research. Since many of those opposed to new rulings cite capital market effects, either real or alleged, it would also be beneficial to see additional research which might permit firmer conclusions to be drawn on the efficient market theory. The more the market can be proven to be efficient, and the more that view becomes accepted, the more freedom the FASB will have to act on controversial issues.

Also valuable would be further research into the needs of users of financial statements. Effecting changes in accounting and reporting practices entails cost—measured not only in terms of implementation but also in terms of the potential behavioral impact these changes can have. Research into user information needs can lead to more informed assessments of whether the benefits from accounting changes outweigh these attendant costs.

The manner in which the FASB calls for implementing accounting changes is also important. Financial statement information is used for many business purposes, and it is understandable that there is resistance when a sudden transformation of those statements is ordered. In some cases, problems could be substantially eased by phasing in major new rules and procedures gradually. In this regard, it is particularly noteworthy that in certain situations the SEC supports such an approach.

A final point implicit in many of the areas discussed is that the FASB needs to view its task of improving financial accounting and reporting standards as an evolutionary process. Improving and updating current accounting practices is a task which can only be accomplished by steady progress over an extended period.

A FRAMEWORK FOR CONCLUSIONS

There is no simple answer to the question what weight should be given to economic impact in formulating accounting standards. While it is clear that economic consequences cannot be ignored, accounting is in many respects a technical subject. Professional expertise and direction are essential to maintaining and improving existing standards. The real issue, therefore, is not whether one factor should prevail to the exclusion of the other, but whether a balance can be struck between the two.

At one end of the range of possible outcomes is the conclusion that standard setting should be directed towards purity of accounting truth alone. In such a case, the objectives of accounting would ideally be defined in terms of a comprehensive conceptual framework. Given clearly outlined objectives, the approach to be taken on specific accounting questions and issues should be apparent. The result would ideally be an internally consistent structure of principles, logically interrelated, and in harmony with the defined goals.

The difficulty with this concept lies not so much with the production of results as with the definition of objectives. If the objectives are misdirected, disputed, or incomplete, the results are likely to be deficient. Therefore, the value of such an approach depends on the degree of unanimity and comprehensiveness with which objectives can be identified. Experience suggests that unanimity is unlikely. The best that can be expected is consensus.

Moreover, there is no assurance that any consensus will be permanent. The objectives of accounting are themselves a function of perceived social purposes, and it would seem unrealistic to view them as immutable. Accounting is ultimately based on social need and must be flexible. Consequently, if one concludes that the purpose should be to pursue truth alone, that truth can be identified only in the context of the times.

At the other end of the spectrum is the notion that only conse-quences matter. On this basis, each accounting issue would be decided by attempting to reflect the majority view on each particular question, without reference to any other guiding principles or theoretical objectives. The result of this would be an eclectic jumble of the principles in effect at any particular moment. New rules would be established to meet the current need. Other rules, established when different needs or priorities were predominant, would likely be counterproductive. The outcome would be a continual change in practices and quite probably a collapse of confidence in reported financial information.

Between these two extremes, there is, of course, a wide range of possible compromises. One approach would be to give primary consideration to economic impact, except when it is grossly inconsistent with established accounting concepts. The process would have two steps: first, the standard setters would identify the desired economic result and its compatible accounting alternative; next, they would try to assure that the indicated accounting practice was not entirely incompatible with existing accounting principles.

The complementary case would reverse the emphasis. The merits of issues would first be assessed in terms of their relation to guiding concepts. This process would seek to find the answer most compatible with present theory. The indicated solution would be implemented, absent compelling evidence that its economic consequences would be unacceptable. This approach reflects a basic assumption that it is indeed possible to identify objectives of accounting that are durable. It further implies that it is practicable to build an integrated set of principles on such a foundation. However, it would also recognize both the progressive change of objectives and the fact that worthy concepts must sometimes give precedence to economic considerations. An approach along these lines would seem best to reflect an appropriate emphasis on economic consequences in the standard setting process.

The FASB itself appears to be setting a course that is similar to that just described. It is very encouraging that the FASB is also focusing more attention on the issue of the economic impact of accounting standards. Many people in corporate management recognize the difficulty of the issues facing the FASB and the pressures to which it is subject. These pressures have many roots, but are mostly caused by economic effects, real or imagined. To balance these often conflicting pressures on each issue, and at the same time to keep accounting principles logically consistent, will continue to be a challenging task.□

RELIANCE ON INTERNAL AUDITORS

Can independent auditors use more extensively the work of their internal counterparts?

by D. Dewey Ward and Jack C. Robertson

For a long time, independent auditors have relied on the work of internal auditors and other client personnel. Five years ago, Statement on Auditing Standards no. 9, *The Effect of an Internal Audit Function on the Scope of the Independent Auditor's Examination,*[1] superseded a single paragraph on the topic in earlier professional literature and, by codifying current practice, became a standard for cooperative audit performance.

Today, no one needs to be convinced that reliance on internal auditors can be vital. The economics of auditing and the increasing demands for new and different services signal a clear need for cost efficiencies at all levels and in all forms of auditing. The rise in stature of internal auditors thus comes at the right time; auditing resources are indeed scarce and costly, and much is demanded of all auditors. Many organizations—the Institute of Internal Auditors (IIA), the EDP Auditors' Association, several international accounting firms and one or two universities, to name a few—have created or augmented educational programs for internal auditors.

But the independent auditor, challenged to join forces with his internal counterpart to accomplish all that is demanded, wants to know "How do we stand now?" and "How do we do it?" By attacking these two questions, the research reported in this article may help independent auditors improve their practices.

What We Hoped to Learn

Our survey of 42 independent and 47 internal auditors aimed to

☐ Determine the extent to and manner in which independent auditors already rely on the internal audit function.

☐ Determine whether both groups of auditors believe this extent and manner of reliance is sufficient.

☐ Elicit predictions of how the extent and manner of reliance may change.

Participants, chosen carefully from experts we deemed most up to date, included partners in large accounting firms, independent auditors with personal experience in relying on internal auditors' work, other independent auditors who had served on the auditing standards executive committee (replaced in 1978 by the auditing standards board) of the American Institute of CPAs when SAS no. 9 was under consideration, internal auditors employed by large corporations with well-developed internal audit functions and 10 former members of the IIA's international research committee.

The expertise of this group notwithstanding, we do not claim that their collective opinions constitute the "final policy" answers to the questions we posed. However, our research tools—including two questionnaires, with the second summarizing responses to the first and allowing a

---

[1]Statement on Auditing Standards no. 9, *The Effect of an Internal Audit Function on the Scope of the Independent Auditor's Examination* (New York: AICPA, 1975). See also *AICPA Professional Standards* (Chicago, Ill.: Commerce Clearing House, Inc. 1977), AU section 322.

Journal of Accountancy, October 1980

D. DEWEY WARD, Ph.D., is assistant professor of accounting at Michigan State University, East Lansing. He was the coauthor of a monthly column in the *Chartered Accountant in Australia* on current developments in accounting and auditing in the United States. **JACK C. ROBERTSON,** CPA, Ph.D., is Price Waterhouse Auditing Professor at the University of Texas at Austin. He is a member of the American Institute of CPAs accounting standards executive committee task force on the conceptual framework for accounting and reporting and a member of the American Accounting Association, the Texas Society of CPAs and the EDP Auditors' Association.

participant to amend any earlier response if suitably convinced by this "feedback"— were specially designed to highlight areas of agreement and disagreement, narrow the range of problems and reach well-considered conclusions.

Reliance Is Alive and Well

The survey showed that virtually all independent auditors rely on internal auditors to some extent, the degree of reliance varying with each internal audit department, each audit engagement and each independent auditor. However, 50% of the independent auditors and 45% of the internal auditors queried said that internal auditors are not relied on to the fullest extent possible. Reasons cited were a lack of initiative and a lack of understanding on the part of the auditors involved and insufficient training in methods, procedures and the limits of reliance.

Theoretically, another factor is the unwillingness of internal auditors to participate in the financial audit. However, the survey data indicated that there are relatively few internal audit departments unwilling to assist independent auditors; usually, internal auditors are unavailable only because of other pressing duties.

Because reliance decisions, under SAS no. 9, are made on a case-by-case basis by individuals considering the competence and objectivity of other individuals and evaluating their work, it is difficult to determine the general level of reliance with statistical precision. Let it suffice to say that independent auditors rely on their internal counterparts to a substantial degree during financial audits.

Respondents also were asked their views on what the extent of reliance should be, assuming that an internal audit department is found to be competent and objective. Independent and internal auditors' views were almost exactly alike—about 75% agreed that internal auditors should be relied on in most (but not all) audit areas, while 15% disagreed and 10% were neutral. Similarly, both groups basically agreed that reliance generally should increase (62% of independent auditors and 71% of internal auditors). The findings, simply put, are not surprising: A majority of experts

want to strengthen and extend the reliance relationship under proper conditions.

What Reliance Means

Two general areas of reliance are available to independent auditors: first, internal auditors' contribution to the client company's system of internal accounting control and, second, internal auditors' performance of substantive audit procedures under the supervision of and review by independent auditors. Respondents gave emphatic "yes" answers when asked whether reliance is frequently placed on the internal auditor's role in the internal accounting control system. However, independent and internal auditors had dissimilar perceptions about the latter group's performance of substantive audit procedures. Internal auditors perceive themselves as doing considerable substantive work, as shown in exhibit 1, below.

Exhibit 1

Perceptions of substantive audit procedure performance

	Yes	No	Not appli-cable
When independent auditors use or rely on internal auditors, is it frequently to perform such substantive audit procedures as account balance verification? IND*	53%	33%	14%
INT*	66	19	15

*IND = independent auditor responses; INT = internal auditor responses.

Exhibit 2, page 65, lists areas where independent auditors rely on the work of internal auditors. The list probably is not exhaustive, and one other caution is in order: The survey data do not suggest that internal auditors perform all the substantive work in the listed areas. The percentages of acknowledgment of reliance simply indicate that cooperation takes place. SAS no. 9 obligates independent auditors to reserve final judgments and decisions affecting the report on financial statements. The interesting information in exhibit 2 is that independent auditors show a general tendency to perceive more internal auditor involvement in all areas than do internal auditors.

Perhaps this is so because independent auditors are familiar with how internal auditors may be deployed to varying degrees in many audit engagements, while most internal auditors are familiar only with the independent audits of their own companies.

Competence and Objectivity

Paragraph 4 of SAS no. 9 requires an independent auditor to acquire an understanding of the internal audit function as it relates to the study and evaluation of internal accounting control, and, if the work performed by internal auditors may have a bearing on the nature, timing and extent of his procedures, the independent auditor should consider the competence and objectivity of internal auditors and evaluate their work. Considering the competence of internal auditors involves making inquiries about the qualifications of the staff. The examples cited in SAS no. 9 are inquiries about hiring, training and supervision. In considering objectivity, the independent auditor investigates the organizational level to which internal auditors report. This level indicates their ability to act independently of the managers responsible for the functions being audited.

SAS no. 9, in paragraph 7, suggests judging internal auditors' objectivity by reviewing the recommendations made in their reports. Also, the standard contains a few suggestions for evaluating the technical quality of work performed by internal auditors; these mainly involve reviews of audit programs, working papers and reports and actual tests of some of the work performed.

However, as a brief, universal standard which can only go so far without programming all the judgment out of a professional activity, SAS no. 9 leaves to individual auditing firms the task of devising detailed technical programs for reliance on internal auditors. Nevertheless, the standard does lead one to suspect that an accountant who can perform a peer review of another accountant or firm also can "consider the competence and objectivity of internal auditors and evaluate their work."[2] In effect, then, reliance on internal auditors' work demands a type of informal peer review by the independent auditor. In

this light, competence and objectivity have two characteristics. First, they are "terms of art" and not susceptible to precise definition; second, to consider these qualities, independent auditors must be able to perceive them and conduct an objective review without arousing resentment on the part of the internal auditors. In short, the independent auditors must be perceptive and tactful.

The survey data show that 90% of the internal auditor respondents consider their departments to be independent. Likewise, 90% of the independent auditors reported that they review internal auditors' competence and objectivity and consider them-

Exhibit 2

Areas in which independent auditors rely on internal auditors

	Independent auditors responding "yes"	Internal auditors responding "yes"
Preparation of schedules, clerical work	89%	49%
Analysis of accounts	86	68
Inventory observation at branches	86	62
Counting cash	79	53
Audits of entire branches, divisions, subsidiaries	74	66
Inventory pricing	72	39
Test of internal accounting control	72	57
Accounts receivable confirmation	67	57
Audit of account balances	62	60
Inventory observation at major locations	57	64
Audit of cost accumulation on internally manufactured assets	57	21
Review of EDP systems	48	43
Evaluation of internal accounting control	38	40
Audit of long-term debt	26	15
Review of unaudited interim financial statements	26	15
Planning the independent audit program and scope	12	40
Examination of corporate minutes	7	15

[2]Ibid., par. 4 and AU sec. 322.04.

selves qualified to do it. None of the independent auditors thought himself unqualified; the other 10% responded "not applicable." However, this rosy outlook was not shared by the internal auditors, only 59% of whom agreed that independent auditors are qualified to determine their competence, with 76% agreeing that independent auditors are qualified to determine their objectivity.

One might expect that these different views could lead to conflicts when a review is conducted. Indeed, 26% of the independent auditors reported that their reviews sometimes created resentment on the part of the internal auditors. Needless to say, an expectation of one conflict situation in every four reviews is not very appealing when cooperation among auditors is the goal. Nevertheless, internal auditors turned out to be more charitable; only 11% reported resentment of independent auditors' evaluating their competence, and only 4% reported having resented evaluations of their objectivity. These views, however, were reported by internal audit executives and may not truly reflect the attitudes of their staff auditors. In any case, the data and their possible implications suggest that independent auditors should work closely with internal audit executives to assure smooth working relationships.

Because generally accepted auditing standards give no extensive list of procedures to perform when considering competence and objectivity, independent auditors have created their own programs. The procedures commonly performed by the survey respondents are shown in exhibit 3, this page. (As expressed by the respondents, these procedures tell independent auditors what to do but not how to make a final decision about competence or objectivity; this is left to judgment.)

These evaluations are not easy, and independent auditors must decide whether to apply them to individual internal auditors or to the entire internal audit department. On this point the survey data gave mixed signals, as shown in exhibit 4, page 68. Respondents' extra comments indicated that evaluations should be on both an individual and a collective basis. No doubt each reliance situation may differ to some extent, sometimes involving individual internal auditors, other times involving more extensive work done under the aegis of the entire department.

Exhibit 3

Independent auditors' procedures for considering the competence and objectivity of internal auditors

Steps in considering competence

1 Review the education and experience of the internal auditors.
2 Evaluate the performance of internal auditors as evidenced by documentation in workpapers and reports.*
3 Review the quality of the work, including procedures employed, coverage of procedures, performance of procedures and accomplishments.*
4 Evaluate personal contacts and prior experience with individuals.*
5 Review the professionalism of the internal audit department. Evaluate such factors as continuing professional development, staff training, experience in public accounting (CPA certificate) and performance evaluations.
6 Review the company's emphasis on the role and status of the internal audit function as reflected in hiring, training and promotion policies of the company.
7 Review job descriptions, audit programs, time budgets and work schedules.
8 Review the personnel files.

Steps in considering objectivity

1 Review internal audit reporting responsibilities and levels within the company.
2 Review content, quality and distribution of internal audit reports, noting recommendations made.*
3 Review the way internal audit recommendations are received by management, including management's initial reaction and follow-up.*
4 Observe the attitude of objectivity in discussions and interviews with internal auditors. Also, look for an attitude of objectivity in written reports.*
5 Review the internal auditors' freedom from operational responsibilities. Determine whether the internal audit department functions as a special-project staff.
6 Review the quality, type and significance of audit programs and areas audited.*
7 Evaluate stated and de facto organizational independence.

*These responses indicate that competence can be evaluated as part of the evaluation of performance. A separate evaluation of competence need not be undertaken.

One final matter involved in considerations of competence and objectivity is the standard used for an evaluation. How competent and how objective must an internal auditor be to justify reliance? (This question, of course, is equally applicable to independent auditors.) Herein lies a problem: Independent auditors apparently believe that internal auditors need be only as competent and objective as the complexity and difficulty of the work require. Because most work on which reliance is planned is not very complex or difficult in independent auditors' opinions, two-thirds of them believe that internal auditors' competence need not be comparable to their own. On the other hand, two-thirds of the internal audit executives—perhaps as a matter of professional pride—responded that internal auditor competence should be comparable to that of independent auditors in a reliance relationship. This difference of opinion spilled over into responses to a similar assertion about internal auditor objectivity. Two-thirds of the internal audit executives believe that internal auditors' objectivity should be comparable to that of independent auditors; only about one-third of the independent auditors held this view.

One need not exercise much insight to realize that internal auditors are expressing their desires—perhaps frustrated ones—to be perceived by the business world at a higher professional plane than they have enjoyed to date. They show a strong belief in their own independence and objectivity; they see many relatively inexperienced independent audit staff people and conclude their own competence is equal or greater; and they voice legitimate views that in all respects they should be seen as technical equals of independent auditors.

Based perhaps on having observed many internal audit departments of varying capabilities, independent auditors generalize freely that internal auditors do not have to be very good because the work thats relied on is not all that hard and because independent auditors supervise them closely anyway. Needless to say, in-

---

Exhibit 4

Views on individual or collective evaluation

		Agree	Neu-tral	Dis-agree
The competence of each internal auditor should be evaluated separately rather than the department as a whole.	IND*	41%	16%	43%
	INT*	12	23	66
The objectivity of the internal audit department as a whole should be evaluated rather than that of each internal auditor separately.	IND	65	14	21
	INT	75	6	20

*IND=independent auditor responses; INT=internal auditor responses.

---

dependent auditors should not carry such stereotypical images into each new audit engagement.

Testing Internal Auditors' Work

When independent auditors intend to rely on internal auditors' work, some tests of that work should be performed in addition to the initial consideration of competence and objectivity. These tests may include procedures designed to consider the competence and objectivity of the internal auditors; as indicated, the procedures listed in exhibit 3 include several that appear to be tests of the work as well as means of initial evaluation.

In one sense, detail tests of internal auditors' work are analogous to compliance tests. The independent auditor may select a portion of the details audited by internal auditors and reperform the audit work or audit a sample of similar details to confirm the internal auditors' findings. Survey responses from independent and internal auditors suggest strongly that independent auditors' tests should be based on both reperformance and selection of similar details. This is stronger than the SAS no. 9 guidance in paragraph 8 indicating that either way of testing is acceptable.

However, as the survey respondents indicated, the actual testing has the potential to produce behavioral conflicts and resentments similar to those that may occur with respect to evaluations of competence and objectivity. Compounding the potential for conflict is the tendency of independent auditors to review and test an internal auditor's work more extensively than similar work performed by their own staff members. One can understand the independent auditor's skepticism about the internal auditor's work product; in fact, one respondent likened it to "management's unsupported representations about elements of financial statements." Nevertheless, it seems that the initial work

"Most auditors believe that audit costs can be reduced—or their increase slowed—by cooperative audit performance."

on competence and objectivity may be at least partially wasted. If internal auditors are found to be both competent and objective, cannot the actual tests of their work conform to those performed on the work of the independent auditor's own staff? Such questions of efficiency notwithstanding, 67% of the independent auditor respondents would apply a stricter standard to supervision and testing of internal auditors' direct assistance work. In contrast, 57% of the internal auditor respondents would observe the same standard for both internal and independent staff work.

Both respondent groups believe strongly that independent auditors should apply a stricter supervision and testing standard to work done by client personnel who are not internal auditors. Thus, independent auditors are skeptical of internal auditors' work product, and both are skeptical of work done by clerical personnel.

Survey data on testing internal auditors' work yielded observations that independent auditors should

☐ Perform at least a minimal amount of testing in each area of internal auditors' work on which reliance is planned.

☐ Audit not only some of the details audited by the internal auditors but also some details not audited by them.

☐ Ensure that supervision and testing procedures for the work of their own staff members are different from those for internal auditors' work. (Internal audit executives do not agree wholeheartedly.)

☐ Supervise and test the work of other client personnel who are not internal auditors more extensively than the work of internal auditors themselves.

Training for Reliance

Organizational policies for cooperative audit performance are not especially widespread. Survey data indicate that a little more than half the independent auditors have firm-wide policy statements regarding reliance on internal auditors. However, about three-fourths of those without such policies permit individual practice offices and individual auditors to develop their own; unfortunately, the extent of such local policies is not known. Less than one-half of the internal audit organizations have adopted a formal policy statement concerning cooperation with independent auditors. Obviously, there is room at the policy level for more attention to cooperation.

Similarly, independent auditors have not devoted extensive training resources to the subject of reliance on internal auditors. From 60% to 80% of the independent auditor respondents reported that they or their firms had not provided staff members with formal guidelines, held general sessions on the benefits and problems of reliance or held technical sessions on procedures and methods for accomplishing reliance. To a great extent, operational reliance on internal auditors appears to be proceeding on an almost ad hoc basis, largely dependent on the interest and capability of auditors in the field.

This phenomenon is itself interesting. In many technical areas, independent auditing firms have produced detailed policy statements, programs, manuals, questionnaires and training programs to make functional the general guidance in official statements on auditing standards. But this natural inclination to program and systematize has not really taken hold in the reliance area. Even so, the survey prompted the respondents to think about a new audit guide. Independent auditors were not wildly enthusiastic that the AICPA should produce a detailed guide; 46% agreed the effort should be undertaken, 16% were neutral and 38% disagreed. Internal auditors thought differently: 74% agreed that the

AICPA should produce such a guide, and several mentioned the possibility of a joint AICPA-IIA project. Apparently, the independent auditors are relatively satisfied with the state of the art, but internal auditors see considerable room for improvement.

Benefits of Reliance

Most auditors believe that audit costs can be reduced—or their increase slowed—by cooperative audit performance. The logic underlying this belief is sound, but the extent of cost efficiency realized depends on the capabilities of the internal auditors and the reliance placed on their work by the independent auditors. Recognizing this, and realizing also that work done by internal auditors can result in cost-savings per se, at least two international accounting firms are actively promoting professional training programs for internal auditors.

But cost savings and better audit coverage are not the only possible benefits. Several others were mentioned by survey respondents. Those mentioned by independent auditors included the following:

☐ Independent auditors can obtain better insight into client operations in specialized areas through the experience and knowledge of the internal auditors.

☐ Client relations are improved because of a feeling of involvement through cooperation and coordination of effort.

☐ Independent auditors are allowed to concentrate on more significant areas and to rotate audit emphasis.

☐ Independent auditors receive beneficial training from coordinating and managing an audit team of internal auditors.

Internal auditors mentioned the following benefits of reliance:

☐ Training for the internal audit staff is enhanced through the interchange of new and different audit techniques, procedures, ideas and information.

☐ Areas for further internal audit work and procedures for accomplishing that work are identified.

☐ Internal auditors obtain a better understanding of independent audit standards and objectives and are encouraged to become more professional.

☐ Independent auditors' appraisals of the effectiveness of internal audit functions are useful.

What Does the Future Hold?

Predictions of the survey participants about the manner and extent of reliance on internal auditors during the next 10 years were consistent with their beliefs about what current reliance should be. Furthermore, because all participants were audit practitioners, their predictions could become self-fulfilling prophecies.

In the next decade, reliance on internal auditors and their work should increase, according to 81% of the independent auditors and 83% of the internal auditors. The following reasons were cited:

☐ Because of their widening legal responsibilities, managements and audit committees seem more committed to increasing the quality, quantity and objectivity of personnel in internal audit departments.

☐ Clients are increasing the pressure for more audit efficiency to reduce or stabilize audit fees. The need to be competitive and timely will cause independent auditors to use whatever resources are available to them.

☐ As governmental regulation of industry increases and business systems grow larger and more complex, independent auditors will increase their reliance on internal auditors, who should have a better knowledge of company systems.

☐ With increasing demand by audit committees and regulatory agencies for "continuous" auditing, independent auditors will need to rely extensively on internal auditors to make the process cost-effective.

☐ Independent auditors have difficulty obtaining and retaining enough qualified entry-level accountants to handle their needs. Thus, increased reliance on internal auditors will become necessary to achieve adequate audit coverage.

However, the extent to which reliance on internal auditors can increase is limited. Independent auditor respondents to the survey identified the following as possible future problems:

☐ Excessive reliance on internal auditors. Without substantive guidance on the limits of reliance, the use of internal auditors' work may become so excessive that it virtually substitutes for that of the independent auditors. (SAS no. 9 expressly forbids this condition.)

☐ Definition of responsibilities for internal

and independent auditors. SAS no. 9 reserves certain audit decisions to independent auditors, but the degree of internal auditor participation may become so great that the integrity of these restrictions is jeopardized.

Either of these two conditions could cause a loss of independence by independent auditors. A majority of respondents indicated, however, that by exercising due care, auditors can avoid these problems— at least during the next decade.

Conclusions

The authors of this article surveyed each other on the subject of whether a detailed audit guide should be produced on cooperative audit performance. One believed such a guide would be very beneficial and would contribute to greater uniformity of practice and greater reliance on internal auditors; the other believed that a guide could not be made specific enough both to fulfill those noble ends and to satisfy the individual technical preferences of the majority of auditors.

Such differences of viewpoint as this can be settled only by experimenting with guides already published and determining whether the benefits of reliance have been realized. As noted, several auditing organizations have guides and programs for reliance on internal auditors. To the extent these can be shared, auditor cooperation can be improved and many audits made more efficient. ∎

A Description of Public Accounting

Accounting is a discipline which provides financial and other information essential to the efficient conduct and evaluation of the activities of any organization. It includes the development and analysis of data, the testing of their validity and relevance, and the interpretation and communication of the resulting information in quantitative terms, or in symbolic or verbal forms.

The Organization

The American Institute of Certified Public Accountants is the national professional society of CPAs devoted to organizing the body of accounting knowledge, conducting research, and enforcing the technical and ethical standards of the profession. Its purpose is to guide the profession's development along lines that serve the broadest public interest. Since its origin in 1887, the Institute has grown steadily, increasing its membership at an annual rate of 10 percent. At present, the Institute membership is approaching 150,000 in public practice, industry, government, and education.

The chairman of the Institute is elected from the membership for a one-year term, along with a vice chairman, three vice presidents, and a treasurer. Heading the staff in New York is Wallace E. Olson, president. From this headquarters, the Institute conducts national programs on continuing professional education, technical and professional standards, regulation, research, state legislation, public relations, and other activities. Its Washington office is a two-way information source, providing CPAs with current information on government programs and furnishing officials in the executive and legislative branches with data and analyses useful in the development of legislation and agency regulations.

Institute programs and policies are determined by a governing Council, consisting of 250 members from the 50 states, the District of Columbia, Puerto Rico, the Virgin Islands, and Guam. The Council meets twice yearly.

One hundred sixty boards, committees, and task forces comprising more than 1,500 volunteer CPAs carry on Institute activities, supported by a full-time staff of nearly 500. In the course of a typical year, the Institute sponsors 650 meetings, held at various locations around the country, ranging from an annual meeting attended by more than 3,000 members and guests to small committee sessions. The Institute also answers more than 90,000 phone calls, receives over 700,000 pieces of mail, greets more than 25,000 visitors, and has yearly sales of publications amounting to nearly

$3 million. Annually, the Institute issues to members and the public 40 million items of information—periodicals, courses, books, brochures, technical pieces, and other materials.

Objectives

The main objectives of the Institute are (1) to provide the U.S. accounting profession with a broad series of programs designed to maintain and improve the quality of its services, (2) to promote and maintain high professional standards of practice, and (3) to enable the profession to make its most effective contribution with other organizations active in accounting and related fields.

Accounting, Auditing, and Consulting Services

Major emphasis is placed on developing technical guidance for CPAs and on presenting the Institute's views to other standards-setting bodies.

The accounting standards division, consisting of an executive committee, subcommittees, task forces, and staff, presents the Institute's position on current accounting matters to the Financial Accounting Standards Board, the Securities and Exchange Commission, the Cost Accounting Standards Board, and other groups concerned with accounting and financial reporting. The division's statements of position on accounting matters serve as guidelines for CPAs until pronouncements are put forth by the FASB.

The accounting and review services committee, a senior technical committee, is charged with developing standards for the services a CPA may render in connection with the unaudited financial statements or other unaudited financial information of a privately held company.

The auditing standards division is the Institute's policy-setting body on auditing matters. Consisting of an auditing standards board, subcommittees, task forces, and staff, it issues statements

on auditing standards, auditing interpretations, and industry audit guides. Activities of the auditing standards board are monitored by an independent auditing standards advisory council. Institute pronouncements on auditing have provided authoritative guidance for independent auditors since 1939, when the first statement on auditing was issued. Since then, more than seventy-five auditing pronouncements have been issued. The Institute's code of ethics requires adherence by the membership to generally accepted auditing standards, recognizes statements on auditing standards as interpretations of the basic auditing standards, and requires that members be prepared to justify any departure from them.

The management advisory services division, with an executive committee, subcommittees, task forces, and staff, provides assistance to members engaged in MAS practice—the task of helping management solve operating and policy problems. It issues guidelines and standards on what are considered to be the best professional practices and publishes technical studies on a variety of specialized subjects.

The technical information services division conducts research in accounting and financial reporting. It also provides a continuing consultation service for members inquiring about technical matters.

Practice Services

The computer services division develops standards and techniques for the auditing of computer-based financial systems. It monitors developments in data processing and provides information to the members about the impact of EDP on auditing, client services, and the internal management of accounting firms. Libraries of time-sharing programs are made available to members through the facilities of two international data processing service organizations. The division also develops training materials on EDP topics. Every year, the division sponsors a four-day computer conference in a major city. In addition, it is responsible for the Institute's internal computer processing.

The financial and practice management division develops and distributes programs, information, published documents, and consultative reviews on administrative and technical aspects of accounting practice. These include studies and programs to meet the professional needs of CPAs in industry, finance, and government. An information retrieval group administers a computerized information retrieval system, which provides access to data on many thousands of corporate financial statements and to accounting literature. With computer terminals located throughout the United States, the system is a cooperative effort on the part of a number of CPA firms and the AICPA. Nonparticipating firms can use the system through the Institute's facilities. The retrieval system also produces a series of financial report surveys on matters of current interest.

International accounting and auditing standards. The Institute maintains cooperative relations with professional accounting bodies in other countries and is represented on the fifty-four-nation International Federation of Accountants, which seeks to develop compatible international auditing, ethical, and educational guidelines, and on the ten-nation International Accounting Standards Committee, which formulates world-wide standards for financial reporting.

Professional Regulation and Review

The professional ethics division interprets and administers the Institute's code of professional ethics, which defines members' responsibilities with regard to independence, integrity and objectivity, competence, adherence to technical standards, and responsibilities to clients, colleagues, and the public. It investigates complaints and, if justified, disciplines members administratively or summons them before the profession's joint trial board, which has the power to acquit, admonish, suspend, or expel a member and, if warranted, to seek revocation of his right to practice. It also provides a continuing consultation service for members' inquiries on application of the rules of conduct.

The state legislation department works closely with the state societies on accountancy legislation and regulation that protects the interests of all practitioners and the general public. The monthly newsletter, *Legislative Report*, provides information on noteworthy legislative and regulatory events. The legislative reference service acts as a central information exchange for dissemination of information on state accountancy legislation, regulation, court cases, and generally useful background information. Among its other publications, the department publishes guides for the development of the Key Man program and the CPA/Political Action Committee.

Practice reviews are arranged as a special Institute service. The program is designed to assist firms of all sizes to maintain standards of practice through reviews of their audit reports. An Institute service group assists the practice review committee in evaluations of reports submitted to the committee.

Professional Education and Qualification

The uniform CPA examination, prepared by the Institute and used by each state, together with the advisory grading service, is the qualifying test for CPA candidates. The rigorous two-and-one-half-day examination is given in May and November at ninety-eight locations in all the fifty states, the District of Columbia, Puerto Rico, the Virgin Islands, and Guam. Approximately 100,000 candidates now take the exam each year.

Continuing professional education is carried out by a staff division, guided by an executive committee. The division prepares and conducts courses on professional subjects and assists state societies in using these courses and in implementing their own programs. More than 80,000 persons currently participate in approximately 3,000 seminars, training programs, or courses held each year.

The relations with educators division encourages the improvement of educational standards for CPAs through a close liaison with colleges and universities. Its activities include development of Institute policy on personnel testing, recruiting for the profession, and professional accounting education.

A CRITICAL LOOK AT PROFESSIONALISM AND SCOPE OF SERVICES

The SEC's former chief accountant suggests a new framework for viewing auditing and MAS.

by John C. Burton

During the last decade, the accounting profession has been subject to a variety of attacks challenging its independence both in fact and in appearance as a result of the scope of its services to clients. These attacks do not seem to be abating despite vigorous defense, and, accordingly, it seems to be time for a new look by the profession at the meaning of auditor independence. This is necessary because the current approach may result in a substantial dilution of the efficiency and effectiveness of auditing as well as the economic function and prosperity of the public accounting profession. An effective initiative by the profession is required to supplement its stout defense of its role in management advisory services.

The Attack

While for many years some critics of the profession have raised questions concerning the compatibility of performing consulting and auditing services simultaneously for a client, it is only in recent years that these concerns have been expressed by official bodies responsible for the oversight of the profession.

Several congressional initiatives have been undertaken—by the late Senator Lee Metcalf's (D-Mont.) Subcommittee on Reports, Accounting and Management, by Congressman John E. Moss's (D-Calif.) Subcommittee on Oversight and Investigations and by the Subcommittee on Governmental Efficiency, chaired by Senator Thomas F. Eagleton (D-Mo.), who assumed an oversight role over the profession after Senator Metcalf died.[1]

The Securities and Exchange Commission, which has direct responsibility for the oversight of accounting matters under the securities laws, has a long history of concern about auditor independence and traditionally has taken a more restrictive view than has the accounting profession. It has, for example, prohibited accountants from auditing books and records which they have maintained for the client, although the profession's own standards do not contain any such prohibition. The commission stated in Accounting Series Release no. 234, *Independence of Accountants,*[2] that the "major value" of an outside audit of financial statements is that an "independent" viewpoint "not connected with management" is obtained. ASR no. 234 adds: "The application of an independent viewpoint is particularly important with respect to judgments exercised in the determination of appropriate principles and meth-

---

JOHN C. BURTON, CPA, Ph.D., is Arthur Young Professor of Accounting and Finance at the Graduate School of Business of Columbia University. He is former deputy mayor for finance of New York City and a former chief accountant of the Securities and Exchange Commission. Dr. Burton is the author of numerous books and articles on accounting and finance.

[1] Reports generated by these initiatives are as follows: Subcommittee on Reports, Accounting and Management of the U.S. Senate Committee on Government Operations, *The Accounting Establishment: A Staff Study,* December 1976; Subcommittee on Reports, Accounting and Management of the U.S. Senate Committee on Governmental Affairs, *Improving the Accountability of Publicly Owned Corporations and Their Auditors,* November 1977; Subcommittee on Oversight and Investigations of the House of Representatives Committee on Interstate and Foreign Commerce, hearings, 95th Cong., 2d sess., *Reform and Self-Regulation Efforts of the Accounting Profession* (Committee print, 1978); and Subcommittee on Governmental Efficiency of the U.S. Senate Committee on Governmental Affairs, hearings, 96th Cong., 1st sess., *Securities and Exchange Commission's Report to Congress on the Accounting Profession and the Commission's Role* (Committee print, 1979).

[2] SEC Accounting Series Release no. 234, *Independence of Accountants,* December 13, 1977.

ods applicable to the recording, classification and presentation of financial data. By their nature such judgments cannot subsequently be evaluated on an impartial and objective basis by the same accountant who made them."

At the same time, however, the commission has not expressed concern about the adverse effect of nonaudit services as long as "managerial and decision-making functions are the responsibility of the client and not of the independent accountant."[3] In ASR no. 126, *Independence of Accountants—Guidelines and Examples of Situations Involving the Independence of Accountants*,[4] the SEC noted that "it is the role of the accountant to advise management and to offer professional advice on their problems" while it cautioned that accountants must be careful not to pass the "point where advice ends and managerial responsibility begins."

In ASR no. 250, *Disclosure of Relationships With Independent Public Accountants*,[5] however, the commission raised a red flag regarding a possible change of view with regard to scope of services. In this release, rules were adopted which required a registrant to disclose in proxy statements filed with the SEC a description of any nonaudit services provided by its public accountant, together with the cost of these services expressed as a percentage of the audit fee. Perhaps more significantly, nonaudit services were singled out for special consideration by the client's board of directors through a requirement that disclosure be made "whether, before each professional service provided by the principal accountant was rendered, it was approved by, and the possible effect on the independence of the accountant was considered by, (1) any audit or similar committee of the Board of Directors and, (2) for any service not approved by an audit or similar committee, the Board of Directors." In addition to adopting these rules, the commission went further to note that the public oversight board of the SEC practice section of the AICPA division for CPA firms was considering the problem of scope of services and added that such consideration should be completed before the commission determined "whether it should propose rules to prohibit public accountants from rendering certain

types of services to their publicly held audit clients because they might impact on independence."

In March 1979, after holding hearings and receiving comments, the POB reported on its examination of the scope of services issue and concluded that it was not necessary or desirable to impose any new rules limiting the scope of services.[6] This report clearly did not satisfy the SEC, which in June 1979 issued an "interpretation" in ASR no. 264, *Scope of Services by Independent Accountants*.[7] The release, which was issued without prior exposure for comment and did not propose any specific rules, stated that it was necessary to "sensitize the profession and its clients to the potential effects on the independence of accountants of performance of non-audit services for audit clients." While the release did describe the potential benefit of nonaudit services by CPAs, its emphasis was clearly on the dangers to independence inherent in such services.

The release elicited a fiery response from the AICPA and from a number of individual firms on both substantive and procedural grounds, and the commission and the profession have growled at each other since about this issue.

What Is the Problem?

Since this issue has been generating much heat, it is perhaps desirable to try to isolate

---

[3] SEC ASR no. 126, *Independence of Accountants—Guidelines and Examples of Situations Involving the Independence of Accountants*, July 5, 1972.
[4] Ibid.
[5] SEC ASR no. 250, *Disclosure of Relationships With Independent Public Accountants*, June 29, 1978.

[6] See *Public Oversight Board Report: Scope of Services by CPA Firms* (New York: AICPA, 1979).
[7] SEC ASR no. 264, *Scope of Services by Independent Accountants*, June 14, 1979.

the nature of the problem and the reasons that such disagreements about it exist.

Independence in fact. The arguments offered by those who express concern normally are divided into problems of independence in fact and problems relating to the appearance of independence. Problems in fact are alleged to arise when the auditor becomes so involved with the consulting role that he in effect supplants management and his audit thus becomes a review of his own work. In addition, it is suggested that if consulting services become sufficiently important to a firm, either in the aggregate or in serving a particular client, the firm's economic dependence on the client will be such that it cannot retain its objectivity.

These concerns are seldom buttressed by empirical data of either a systematic or anecdotal nature. Several groups have studied with considerable care the major examples of audit failure uncovered in the 1960s and 1970s, and the relationship of nonaudit activities to any of these occurrences seemed very limited. This author served as "chief pathologist" for most of the failures that occurred during his years at the SEC, and in only one case can any relationship between a nonaudit activity and the audit failure be discerned. This occurred in a case where it appeared that the auditor's involvement in the merger and acquisitions activity of his client did affect the quality of audit judgments rendered in connection with reporting these combinations, although management fraud was also involved. In the overwhelming majority of situations, however, the problem in these cases arose from too little involvement by auditors in the activities of their clients rather than too much. A significant proportion of the cases arose in initial audits where the pattern was normally one of the client misleading the auditor rather than conspiring with him.

It is difficult to develop evidence of any circumstances in which economic incentives arising out of nonaudit work created problems of independence in fact for the accounting firms involved. Data filed with the AICPA suggest that two-thirds of the practices of the largest public accounting firms still arise from audit service. At the same time, it is clear that there are a few cases in which auditing firms derive a significant proportion of their revenue from a given client from nonaudit activities. A recent survey of 4,300 proxy statements filed subsequent to the effective date of ASR no. 250 in October 1978 determined that 10 percent of the surveyed companies reported fees for nonaudit services amounting to more than 50 percent of the audit fees.[8] In such cases, the audit fee would be less than two-thirds of the fees paid by the company. In a few cases, very high percentages were reported.

These data, however, merely suggest that there are situations in which a large proportion of the auditor's fees in serving a particular client for a particular year come from nonaudit services. They do not deal with the question of independence in fact, which could presumably only be demonstrated by comparing the behavior of the auditors on these engagements with their behavior in other situations with different fee relationships. In the final analysis, then, all that can be said about the questions of independence in fact is based on the perceived potential for problems rather than on the existence of demonstrated problems. The absence of demonstrated problems does not mean that none exists as both the Commission on Auditors' Responsibilities (the Cohen commission) and the POB have pointed out in their reports dealing with this issue.[9] Nevertheless, until some factual situations are developed, it is difficult to propose a massive regulative initiative as an appropriate solution to deal with the possible emergence of a problem that has not yet surfaced, despite considerable scrutiny by critics as well as by friends.

The appearance of independence. The more significant question raised by those concerned about the scope of services relates to the appearance of independence. The AICPA, the POB and the SEC have long emphasized the importance of the appearance of independence as well as its fact.* Generally accepted auditing standards require the maintenance of an independence in mental attitude; in explaining this, the AICPA auditing procedure committee in November 1972 noted that "independent auditors should not only be independent in fact; they should avoid situations that may

[8] Private survey conducted by Ernst & Whinney, Cleveland, Ohio, 1979.
[9] Commission on Auditors' Responsibilities, *Report, Conclusions, and Recommendations* (New York: CAR, 1978), and supra, note 6.
* Ed. note: For an analysis of auditor independence, by Wallace E. Olson, see page 80.

lead outsiders to doubt their independence."[10]

The SEC in ASR no. 264 quotes with approval the report of the POB which states that "it is also important that the auditor *appear* independent to all users of the financial information he provides. This latter concept is a key ingredient to the value of the audit function, since users of audit reports must be able to rely on the independent auditor. If they perceive that there is a lack of independence, whether or not such a deficiency exists, much of that value is lost."[11] Since appearance is in the eye of the beholder, and there are many beholders of the practice of public accounting, it is not surprising that the appearance issue has proved to be the key one in the discussion of auditor independence.

The basic question to be resolved in dealing with an appearance criterion is whether appearance should be examined on the basis of that which would be perceived by an informed person with a knowledge of the facts or by a person with no understanding of the audit process or the nature of relationships that conventionally exist. Most reported surveys of perceptions of independence indicated that the greater the degree of knowledge about the profession and auditing, the less concern there is about threats to independence emerging from the scope of services performed. On the other hand, those without information or background of this sort are inclined to perceive a problem.

If the pursuit of the appearance of independence is to continue and is to be expressed in terms of the suspicions of uninformed persons, there seems to be no way in which the current structure of auditing and the accounting profession can be sustained. No uninformed and suspicious citizen who views the world through skeptical eyes could be expected to be convinced of an auditor's independence when the auditor is paid for his services by the client. This issue dominates the appearance-of-independence problem and is impossible to cure within today's system. This issue is ignored by the SEC in its analysis of the independence problem, and yet further discussion of independence as it will be perceived by the uninformed must necessarily fall into the "aside from that, Mrs. Lincoln, how was the show?" kind of

analysis. If fees can be ignored, the second problem—where the CPA is serving as an advocate for his client in tax planning matters—will clearly emerge. Surely it would be difficult to suggest to someone who is not fairly well informed about the nature of tax and financial reporting practice that the auditor is independent in regard to financial statements but can dutifully aid his client as an advocate in the tax field. Yet the commission in ASR no. 264 notes that tax services are those in which the benefits of using the service may outweigh the costs of possible reduced independence.

In the management consulting area, logic dictates that it is once again those services which are most closely associated with accounting and auditing that are the most suspect. The accountant who advises his client on the installation of a management information system and the internal controls associated with it surely appears less independent in reporting on the financial statements, which are one of the system's outputs,

> "While audits can help prevent fraud or errors, this results more often from the auditor's presence rather than from specific discoveries."

than does the accountant who may perform executive search, psychological testing, employee benefit consulting or plant layout services, which have only a peripheral influence on financial statements. Yet, in ASR no. 264, the commission notes with approval the benefits which the accountant's knowledge and expertise bring to providing consulting services of the MIS sort while condemning certain peripheral services as having little benefit.

If the appearance of independence to the uninformed lay person is to be the key for evaluating scope of service issues, the cost-benefit argument will not play. The commission cannot sustain with any logic a position that accepts as appropriate those services with which the auditor's involvement is most suspicious from an outsider's viewpoint while criticizing and perhaps ultimately forbidding those services where the independence problem is limited at best. The commission may make a political decision that certain ritual sacrifices be demanded from accounting firms in order to solve its problems with Congress,

10 Statement on Auditing Standards no. 1, *Codification of Auditing Standards and Procedures* (New York: AICPA, 1973), section 220.03. See also *AICPA Professional Standards* (Chicago, Ill.: Commerce Clearing House, 1979), AU sec. 220.03.
11 *Public Oversight Board Report*, p.27.

but it cannot build a logical argument supporting this view while accepting the basic institutional framework of auditing that now exists. To sustain the concept of independence in its generic sense to the uninformed, major changes will have to be made in fundamental relationships that exist today.

If, on the other hand, the appearance-of-independence issue is to be dealt with on the basis of the appearance as seen by an informed individual, the scope of services problem is satisfactorily dealt with by present professional literature.

The audit. In order to justify a criterion based on the views of an informed citizen, it is essential that more persons be educated to understand what an audit is. Many outside the profession, particularly attorneys who are often the most active critics of the current auditing system, misperceive it as an adversarial or prosecutorial investigation, based on a search for error. While audits can help prevent fraud or errors, this results more often from the auditor's presence rather than from specific discoveries. The audit process is designed to bring material fraud and error to light, but it is far from perfect. The auditor does not start with the assumption that management is covering up the facts. Professional skepticism does not imply a phi-

> **"... it would be [an] economic waste if the auditor was not permitted to employ his insights to improve the efficiency ... of the client's operation.... This does not make [him] a manager but, rather, an adviser to management."**

losophy of distrust. When an auditor ceases to trust a client, it is fundamental that he should withdraw from an engagement.

From the viewpoint of the accounting profession, an audit is a cooperative venture between management, whose primary responsibility is to the economic success of the enterprise, and the public accountant, who is an outside third party possessing training and expertise in communicating economic results and whose primary professional responsibility is to fair reporting. Since the

objectives of auditor and manager do not conflict except in unusual cases, the audit need not be conducted in an adversary framework.

Auditing is the examination of information by a third party other than the preparer or user with the intent of establishing its reliability and the reporting of the results of this examination with the expectation of increasing the usefulness of the information to the user. To achieve this result, the auditor should develop an understanding of the information requirements of a company and be able to evaluate whether the company's information system meets these requirements. The auditor must therefore have a comprehensive knowledge of the business being audited, a knowledge of information systems and needs of the client's operations and an understanding of the economic measuring techniques conventionally used to measure aggregate results. He also must have a full technical knowledge of the disclosure requirements of regulatory agencies and the needs of users who require the data for decision-making purposes.

While the auditor's principal professional commitment must be to full and fair disclosure and his technical competence focused on accounting information and control, the auditor also must be sensitive to the economic success of the client and should be prepared to contribute to that success. If the auditor is to perform his fundamental reporting function satisfactorily and marshals adequate talent to do this, it would be a great economic waste if the auditor was not permitted to employ his insights to improve the efficiency and effectiveness of the client's operation as well as to comment on its reporting to outsiders. This does not make the accountant a manager but, rather, an adviser to management.

The auditor cannot achieve any of these objectives if he is totally independent—i.e., without dependence. He cannot obtain information without depending on the client's records and personnel. He cannot form judgments about the business without depending extensively on the client's descriptions of it and of its strategies for meeting material business problems. He cannot exist economically without the fee the client pays for his services. Given these necessary dependencies, the use of the term "independent" perhaps was ill chosen to describe the auditor's relationship to his client. Serious consideration should be given to changing the emphasis from "independence," which tends to be used in its narrow sense by the unsophisticated person in evaluating the process, to "unbiased professionalism from a third-party perspective," which appears to describe the auditor's relationship with his client in the proper context.

Within this context, there must be an understanding of the purpose of the audit and why it warrants substantial costs. What are the procedural protections that exist in the absence of total independence in an adversarial sense? Fundamentally, there are three protections on which the public can rely. The first is the primary allegiance which the accountant owes to matters of economic measurement and reporting. Public accountants must retain their professional commitment, transcending a commitment to the profitability of their clients. This commitment must be instilled in accountants early in their professional lives, and it must be tested by rigorous quality controls throughout their practices.

Second, the public is protected by the quality and competence of the persons licensed to practice public accounting. This is essential if the audit is to be of any social usefulness. Auditors must be knowledgeable and well trained, and the profession must continue to attract talented people into its ranks and to maintain their expertise through continuing education as well as through training and experience on the job.

The final elements that offer protection to the public are the countervailing economic pressures which provide the economic incentive for unbiased professionalism and for audit efficiency. An auditor's revenues in the long run depend on his reputation. Were he to opt for short-run maximization and in so doing damage his reputation, the long-run cost could be high indeed. Society imposes a substantial cost on an auditor who does deficient work, either through inadvertence or in response to short-run economic pressures brought by the client. The costs of litigation today are extremely high and promise to grow higher, and an investigation by the SEC or a U.S. attorney can require enormous commitments of time and resources as well as threatening a professional firm's ability to practice. Awards to third parties have been very large, and it is likely that one of the great incentives for the im-

proved quality control evident today in the accounting profession has been the substantial increase in auditor liability imposed by the courts in the past two decades.

It is also important, however, that audit fees not grow without limit. Quality controls cannot be imposed without regard to cost. Incentives must exist for enhanced efficiency in auditing procedures. This is the role of

> "The auditor should perhaps become an investigator, starting with the assumption that his responsibility is to find errors rather than to participate in a cooperative process designed to report in the most meaningful fashion."

competition, which currently exists to a heightened extent as a result of the elimination of ethical bans on promotion, advertising and solicitation.

At present, countervailing economic pressures in the accounting profession seem to be in a reasonable if delicate balance. The forces of competition fuel the effort to achieve audit efficiency so that audit fees do not grow without limit. At the same time, the risk of liability provides a powerful deterrent to inadequate work.

A Reexamination of the Basic Approach

Before accepting the basic institutional structure employed today and seeking to improve it, it is perhaps appropriate to look once again at alternatives to that structure to determine whether they would provide an improvement. It may be, for example, that an audit should be approached from a more adversary posture. The auditor should perhaps become an investigator, starting with the assumption that his responsibility is to find errors rather than to participate in a cooperative process designed to report in the most meaningful fashion. This would require auditors to adopt much higher standards of proof while essentially eliminating reliance on representations of management.

Another approach would be to give the auditor primary responsibility for financial statements. The independent accountant could have the responsibility of satisfying himself as to the adequacy of the client's information system and then report from the data produced in the fashion he found most appropriate to describe the company's economic activities. In other words, the auditor's role could become that of the professional reporter digging after the facts and presenting them in the fashion he thought best.

If either of these approaches was to be adopted, it would seem necessary to deviate from the traditional approach in which the client pays his independent accountant. A

" ...consulting practice has enabled the profession to hire and develop experts in a number of specialized areas... who are of great value to an audit."

reporter or an investigator cannot reasonably be expected to be paid by the object of his reporting or investigation if the process is to be credible. A new device would have to be developed to provide for compensation by outside parties. This might be achieved by a statutorily mandated fee paid by all public companies to a governmental or an independent agency. This agency, be it akin to the SEC or to the stock exchange, could then take on the responsibility for selecting and paying auditors.

While it is conceptually possible to devise such a system, and this would presumably represent the ultimate solution to the independence problem, there would also be very substantial costs involved. In the first place, the removal of the economic relationship between auditor and client would remove one of the most direct sources of pressure for audit efficiency. This would mean that, on the one hand, the auditor would have little incentive to minimize his work while, on the other, the audited firm would have little incentive to assist the auditor in his process. In addition, communication between auditor and auditee would presumably be reduced, and the social productivity of the audit function would decline. This would imply a less satisfying work environment for auditors and a far more difficult task in recruiting audit staff.

In general, the record of third-party auditors has not been such as to engender great enthusiasm for the substantial expansion of the process. It is widely thought that both tax auditors and auditors of cost and compliance fall far short of general success in their roles. There seems little reason to think that the

incentives for fair financial presentation would be enhanced by adversary auditors, particularly when financial statement auditors would presumably lack the ability to assess immediate economic penalties which tax auditors possess. The cases of abuse that cause critics to suggest a change in the current system therefore seem less likely to be avoided under a system of audit "purity" which would sever the relationship between the auditor and his client.

In addition, it is quite clear that the ability of the accounting profession to attract qualified people is in part a function of the productivity of the role which they can play. Nonaudit advisory services today are a major source of this productivity. In many years as a business school professor, the author has observed that the consulting practices of accounting firms attract the highest quality students to the profession. Although a number of these persons ultimately wind up in audit practice, they would not have entered the profession without the attraction of consulting. In addition, consulting practice has enabled the profession to hire and develop experts in a number of specialized areas, such as electronic data processing and actuarial science, who are of great value to an audit.

An additional cost of sharply reducing nonaudit services would be a lack of knowledge about the client's business and information systems currently obtained from such services. Since a major element of auditing is obtaining information about the client's business, the elimination of consulting would certainly reduce the information available to the auditor.

While the adoption of a fundamentally new approach to auditing would have the benefit of increased independence in fact and appearance, it would be a benefit bought at substantial cost. It seems unlikely that the trade-offs would meet normal cost-benefit tests. What should be emphasized, however, is that it is not feasible to achieve any significant benefits from a limited patchwork approach to prohibiting the provision of public accounting services; indeed, such an approach would run a substantial risk of incurring significant social costs without achieving the fundamental purpose of enhancing the appearance of auditor independence in any significant way.

Accordingly, it seems that the process currently being entered into by Congress and the SEC is one which will not resolve the basic problem of independence but, rather, will simply reduce the quality of audits without substantially enhancing their independence. In addition, the process will remove from the business community a significant resource for improvement in financial controls, although presumably organizations other than accounting firms could move into this area if it was so proscribed or firms could perform such services for nonaudit clients. Finally, of course, there is the philosophical question of whether economic activity by professionals should be circumscribed in the absence of evidence of social costs when this activity is being performed.

A Program for the Profession

If the profession is to demonstrate to the public and the regulators that it is operating currently in the public interest and that a scope of services limitation would not enhance but in fact reduce the quality of its social service, it is necessary to adopt a comprehensive program that will emphasize the positive aspects of a broad scope of services both to the public and to the profession. Such a program also should show that the need for dramatic changes in the basic audit framework does not exist. A suggested program is presented below. Some elements of this program are already in existence, while others require development and implementation.

☐ An adequate self-policing mechanism. It is of primary importance that the profession continue to maintain a strong commitment to professional audit quality and to the self-policing of that quality. Certainly, the actions of the AICPA to date in the creation of an SEC practice section, a POB and a peer review process are significant steps forward in this respect. The profession must be certain, however, that this process has not only the form of oversight and quality control but also the substance. This means that there must be a viable, visible disciplinary process that identifies and penalizes those who do not meet the standards. To date, the oversight and peer review process has not been conspicuous for effective discipline. As peer reviews are conducted, deficient work must be identified and brought to the attention of disciplinary bodies for action. Otherwise, the process will not remain credible.

☐ Education of outsiders about the nature of an audit. The profession must continue the process of educating the public and regulators as to the nature of an audit and what it accomplishes. The cooperative nature of the activity should be emphasized, but so also should the primary commitment of professional accountants to measurement accuracy. The profession should be careful in this connection not to express its role in negative terms or to be apologetic or appear to be primarily concerned with the avoidance of liability in identifying its responsibilities.

☐ Gradual reduction of the emphasis on the term "independence" in professional literature. Serious thought should be given to the possibility of emphasizing the words "professional," "unbiased" and "objective" in place of the word "independence" in the professional literature. It would also be desirable to emphasize the significance of the third-party nature of the accountant's role and his external responsibilities.

☐ Increased emphasis on accounting firms' primary commitment to accounting measurement, reporting and control. The profession should take steps to ascertain that accounting firms continue to have their primary professional commitment to accounting measurement, disclosure and control. This has been furthered by the SEC practice section requirement that a majority of partners of member firms be CPAs. Beyond this, steps might be taken to provide that accounting and auditing services make up more than half of a firm's practice. Other specific requirements might be imposed, but the essence

> "Accounting firms should undertake further integration of auditing and consulting services to emphasize the synergy which exists between them."

of them all should be to sustain both the image and the fact of the public accountant's primary commitment to his accounting expertise.

☐ Further integration of audit and nonaudit services to emphasize the totality of audit service. Accounting firms should undertake further integration of auditing and consulting services to emphasize the synergy which exists between them. This would require a firm to define an audit more broadly and to provide a variety of services as a legitimate part of audit outputs. The approach suggested by some of building a "Chinese Wall" between consulting and auditing practice will lose the benefits to auditing of consulting and will also simplify the process of dismemberment of the firms involved.

☐ Develop auditing standards that require the use of information gained through non-audit services for audit purposes. It is important that the profession develop auditing standards that specifically reflect the responsibility of audit personnel to review the information gathered in connection with all services to the client so as to be fully aware of its possible implications for an audit. It would be most inappropriate for an audit partner to be unaware of significant information gathered in connection with consulting. It is useful in this regard to assign the audit partner primary responsibility for any consulting or tax engagement and to cross-assign audit and MAS staff when possible. To cite a particular case in which the author was involved, an accounting firm was asked to do a study of the client's system of credit granting and control as a consulting engagement. The insights gained from this engagement, which was staffed by both consultants and audit personnel, substantially enhanced the auditor's ability to assess the collectibility of the receivable portfolio and to make adequate provision in the financial statements. If audit personnel had not been involved, it would have been unlikely that as full an understanding would have been achieved.

☐ Encompass all parts of the firm, including tax and consulting, in the peer review process. The MAS and tax aspects of professional practice should be included in the peer review framework. At present, peer reviews extend only to the audit process and do not consider the quality of other professional services rendered. If firms are to be increasingly integrated and if the consulting function is to be seen as an assistance to audit, there seems little reason for excluding this part of the business from the peer review process. It is the firm that is being "peer reviewed," and it is the firm as a whole that must withstand the scrutiny of its peers and the public.

☐ Full disclosure of all aspects of the relationship between auditor and client. It is important that the profession adopt a new outlook toward the disclosure of all elements of the auditor-client relationship. The auditor has a special relationship which requires public trust, and this can only be damaged by confidentiality concerning the nature of the relationship. Accordingly, the process which the SEC has begun of requiring disclosure of all services provided by the independent accountant to the client should be extended to include disclosure of auditing fees as well as all other fees paid. Full disclosure that lays out all the facts lessens suspicions which may arise about undescribed relationships. It is encouraging that Lewis Gilbert, a widely known ombudsman for shareholders, is currently proposing to many corporations the voluntary disclosure of audit fees, and a significant number have agreed to do so. The profession should step forward in this respect to advocate such disclosure and to require it either through its rules or by requesting the SEC to restore its previously proposed rule which was not adopted because of the profession's concerns.

Conclusion

If the profession is able to develop a positive program that supports the current approach to auditing, there is substantial likelihood that it can sustain this approach. Many years of history support the relationship of client and auditor and the rendering of consulting services. Such an approach enhances substantially the economic value of an audit, both by increasing audit outputs and enhancing efficiency. Cooperation in the audit process is both efficient and more effective than confrontation. With adequate protections for the public, this case can be made and the interests of society will be better served if it is sustained. ∎

ANALYZING THE EFFECT OF CASB STANDARDS ON BUSINESS

Has the profession yet recognized CASB standards? The author thinks not and offers a blueprint for future action.

by James P. Bedingfield

The Cost Accounting Standards Board has been in existence for nearly a decade. During this period, it has not had a significant impact on the financial disclosures of the companies that it affects. In a 1976 survey, an international CPA firm stated

"All fifty of the companies in this survey must comply with the pronouncements of the CASB. Nevertheless, none of the companies mentioned the CASB or its standards in their annual reports. . . .

"We might expect some disclosure of the impact of the CASB in the future, when certain of its standards, such as depreciation and allocation of general and administrative expenses, become effective and result in changes in accounting methods utilized for pricing and costing contracts. . . ."[1]

Due to its pervasive impact on companies subject to its standards, the time has come to consider accommodating the CASB in our auditing procedures and accounting disclosures.

The federal government is the most influential purchaser of goods and services in our economy. Government-oriented companies or segments of companies witness this influence on at least two levels. One is in the materiality of the government's purchases—it is their major customer. The second is the federal government's ability to affect the accounting practices—and thereby the profits —of its suppliers through the provisions of its contracts. The impact of the federal government's control of its contractors is changing. In this article, the CASB's impact on companies is examined, and recommendations are presented for recognizing the increasing influence of the CASB on business.

Exit Renegotiation

The U.S. Renegotiation Board ceased operations on March 31, 1979. This ended the board's prospective impact on companies that sell to the federal government under contracts subject to the Renegotiation Act of 1951. Companies no longer have to worry about their profits on governmental business being "renegotiated," i.e., reviewed and, if found to be excessive, a refund being required by the board.[2]

Of more specific interest to CPAs is the fact that the expiration of the board will eliminate the need for financial statement disclosure of the renegotiation environment affecting a particular company. This disclosure was controlled by chapter 11, "Government Contracts, Section B—Renegotiation," of Accounting Research Bulletin no. 43, *Restatement and Revision of Accounting Research Bulletins*. The basic disclosure re-

JAMES P. BEDINGFIELD, CPA, D.B.A., is associate professor of accounting at the College of Business and Management at the University of Maryland. He is the author of numerous articles and the coauthor of a book on cost accounting standards entitled *Government Contract Accounting*. A member of the Maryland Association of Certified Public Accountants, he is also a member of the American Accounting Association, the Association of Government Accountants and the American Institute of CPAs.

The Journal of Accountancy, April 1980

---

[1] Price Waterhouse & Co., *1976 Survey of Financial Reporting and Accounting Practices of Government Contractors* (New York: Price Waterhouse & Co., 1976), p.47.

[2] The expiration of the Renegotiation Act reactivates the Vinson-Trammell Act which limits profits on contracts for naval vessels (to 10 percent of cost) and on contracts for aircraft (to 12 percent of cost). However, these absolute limits eliminate the reporting problems associated with excess profit determinations made long after the fact as was the case with renegotiation.

quired by ARB no. 43 was footnote coverage of the renegotiation environment and provision in the financial statements when the amounts to be refunded were reasonably determinable. Since its effective date for fiscal years beginning on or after July 1, 1975, Statement of Financial Accounting Standards no. 5, *Accounting for Contingencies,* affected the use of provision for refunds (i.e., the amount would have to be reasonably estimated and information available prior to the issuance of the financial statements would have to support the conclusion that a liability had been incurred).

Enter Cost Accounting Standards

Coinciding with the eclipse of the renegotiation board has been the rise to prominence of the CASB, which was established by Congress in 1970. Its charge was to promulgate cost accounting standards to be used in the pricing, administration and settlement of negotiated national defense contracts and subcontracts in excess of $100,000. In 1972, by administrative action, the standards were made applicable to nondefense contracts in excess of $100,000.[3] To date, 17 standards have been promulgated and 4 others are in the proposal stage. Appendix A, page 65, lists these standards.

Before detailing the recommended audit procedures and accounting disclosures for companies subject to cost accounting standards, the nature of the standards and the impact that they have on these companies should be explained.

First of all, what are these standards? In the law that established the CASB, Congress called for the CASB to ". . . promulgate cost accounting standards designed to achieve uniformity and consistency in the cost accounting principles followed by defense contractors and subcontractors. . . ."[4] In interpreting its charge from Congress, the

CASB has not adhered to the traditional demarcation between financial accounting (dealing with the measurement and assignment of cost to a particular accounting period) and cost accounting (dealing with the assignment of a period's cost to that period's cost objectives, e.g., divisions, product lines, job orders, contracts). Rather, the CASB has taken a rather broad view of cost accounting. This can be seen in its definition of a "cost accounting practice": ". . . any accounting method or technique which is used for measurement of cost, assignment of cost to cost accounting periods, or allocation of cost to cost objectives."[5]

Indeed, several of the CASB's standards deal almost exclusively with cost measurement and assignment to a period. Several others are similarly more financial-accounting-oriented than cost-accounting-oriented.

Cost accounting standards do not always conform to generally accepted accounting principles. For example, CAS no. 414, *Cost of Money as an Element of the Cost of Facilities Capital,* allows companies to recognize an imputed cost based on their investment in fixed assets, regardless of the source of the funds so invested. Likewise, CAS no. 416, *Accounting for Insurance Costs,* has a company recognize a "self-insurance" charge for potential losses against which either it elects not to purchase insurance, or for which it cannot purchase insurance. This is not to say that the CASB has abrogated its charge from Congress. For example, in the case of the standard on insurance costs, the alternatives to the CASB's position (of normalizing anticipated losses through purchased or "self-insurance") would be either not to consider losses in costing contracts or to charge actual losses to the contracts being performed in the period that the loss is incurred. The first alternative would be inequitable to the company; the second alternative would make the negotiation and forward pricing of fixed price contracts rather difficult and the cost accumulation under cost-type contracts

---

[3] The regulation controlling civilian agencies' procurement—the federal procurement regulation (FPR)—was recently modified to make a company's CAS-coverage of its civilian agency contracts contingent, in part, on its having CAS-covered national defense contracts.
[4] U.S., Congress, PL 91-379, 2d sess., p.2.

[5] U.S., Cost Accounting Standards Board, 4 CFR 331.20(h).

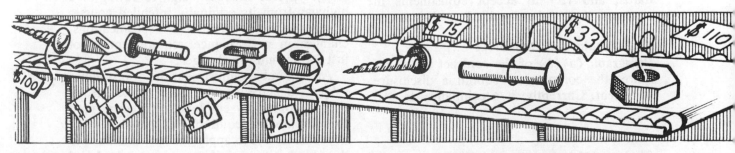

subject to the vagaries of experienced losses. What the CASB has done is equitable. However, it falls outside of the traditional purview of cost accounting. So the substance of cost accounting standards is more than meets the eye in the title of the CASB.

Who Is Subject to CAS?

Not all companies who do business with the federal government are subject to cost accounting standards. The basic provision of the law is that negotiated national defense contracts and subcontracts in excess of $100,000 are subject to the standards:

☐ For an overall perspective, it should be realized that about 90 percent of defense procurement and about 50 percent of civilian agency procurement are negotiated (as opposed to a bidding procedure).

☐ A company only becomes subject to the standards (on all contracts in excess of $100,000) after having received a CAS-covered contract in excess of $500,000.

☐ There is modified CAS coverage under which qualified companies (based on volume of total sales and volume of CAS-covered sales) can elect to comply only with CAS nos. 401 and 402.

☐ A provision was recently adopted by civilian agencies that makes the full CAS coverage of their contracts contingent on the company's already being subject to CAS under military contracts.

While there is no definitive list of companies that are subject to the standards, it is clear that all major defense contractors must comply with them.

CAS Contract Clause

Contractors are subjected to cost accounting standards by signing a contract that contains the standards' contract clause. A portion of this clause is reproduced in appendix B, page 65.

In the clause, companies agree (1) to disclose and consistently follow their established cost accounting practices; (2) to follow the provisions of the various cost accounting standards; and (3) to accept adjustments in contract price under specified conditions.

CAS Disclosure Statement

Paragraph (a)(1) of the contract clause requires the company to submit a disclosure statement. Currently, if a company has $10 million or more of CAS-covered contracts in its prior cost accounting period or receives a single CAS-covered contract of $10 million or more, it must file a disclosure statement. The statement, 40 pages in length, is a detailed documentation of the company's cost accounting practices—as broadly defined by the CASB. Currently over two hundred companies have disclosure statements on file with the CASB and the procurement agencies.

New Standards

In paragraph (a)(3) of the contract clause, the company agrees to apply to this contract any new standards that are issued after the contract is signed (and which the company becomes subject to by reason of signing another contract incorporating the new standards).

For example, assume that a company signed a CAS-covered contract A on June 30, 1979; this contract is to be performed over the next two years. On January 1, 1980, a new standard becomes effective; at this time the company does not have to apply the new standard to contract A. However, on May 1, 1980, contract B, incorporating the CAS contract clause, is signed. The company must apply the new standard to both contract B and contract A. Large companies that annually enter into hundreds of governmental contracts are subject virtually to all new standards from the effective date of the new standards.

Note two things: First, the company is agreeing to comply with an as-yet-unseen standard(s). Second, under paragraph (a)(4)(A) of the contract clause, the company agrees to an "equitable adjustment" in applying the new standard(s) to the existing contracts.

Equitable Adjustment

The term "equitable adjustment" refers to a legal concept of returning both parties to the contract to the same relative position that they were in prior to the change under the contract. Equitable adjustments are made for many types of changes—e.g., rerouting of a highway from its originally intended course; changes in architectural specifications; changes in performance requirements—not just for accounting changes.

An equitable adjustment is a procedure subject to agreement by both parties. However, a commonly employed procedure used to compute the equitable adjustment for a new standard is to apply the new standard to the old contracts as if the new standard had been used in their negotiation. For example, if contract C had been negotiated for a firm fixed price of $1 million (i.e., $900,000 in anticipated cost and $100,000 in anticipated fee), and the application of a new standard indicated that the cost allocated to this contract would be $100,000 less, this contract would be adjusted downward by $100,000 *plus* an adjustment in the fee provision.

Where does the $100,000 in costs not allocated in this contract go? It will be allocated to other contracts (or other work not under contract). If these other contracts are CAS-covered, their prices will be adjusted upward. But what if these other contracts are not governmental contracts? The cost siphoned from contract C (and resulting in reduced revenue under that contract) will be allocated to nongovernmental contracts.

With no change in the absolute level of cost needed to complete these contracts (both governmental and nongovernmental), and with a decrease in their revenue, it is obvious that there has been a reduction in the profit potential of the company. Just how much of such equitable adjustment a contractor can absorb before being severely affected is open to question. However, two sources indicate that the answer is "not very much":

☐ In the *Defense Industry Profit Study* conducted by the U.S. General Accounting Office, it was reported that the average profit *before* income taxes on defense contracts studied for the period 1966 through 1969 was 4.3 percent of sales (compared with 9.9 percent on commercial work).

☐ More recently, *Profit 76,* a study conducted by the Department of Defense in 1976, found that the average profit *before* income taxes for defense profit centers of companies studied for the period 1970 through 1974 was 4.7 percent of sales (compared with 17.7 percent for commercial profit centers of those companies).

These studies certainly indicate that there are not very large profit margins on governmental contracts.

Voluntary Changes

Any change that a company makes in its cost accounting practices (other than a change mandated by a new standard) is referred to as a voluntary change. The concepts of cost accounting practice (as defined above) and change-in-cost-accounting practice can best be appreciated by reviewing examples of changes (and "nonchanges") given by the

CASB. Appendix C, page 66, gives illustrations of changes that meet the definition of "change to either a disclosed cost accounting practice or an established cost accounting practice." A review of these illustrations leads one to the conclusion that the concept of "change in cost accounting practice" is quite pervasive.

What is the impact of a voluntary change? Before March 10, 1978, the answer was unequivocal: Such a change could result in no increased cost being paid by the federal government. This meant that if, under the new cost accounting practice, less cost was allocated to CAS-covered contracts than under the former practice, the prices of these contracts would be reduced. If, under the new

> "Prior to agreeing to an equitable adjustment for a voluntary change, the contracting officer must '... make a finding that the change is desirable and not detrimental to the interests of the Government.'"

cost accounting practice, more costs were allocated to CAS-covered contracts than under the former practice, none of these costs would be passed on to the government (i.e., result in increased prices being paid).[6]

Due to the downward-only adjustment permitted for voluntary changes, companies claimed that they were, in effect, discouraged from making changes in their cost accounting practices which were needed to accommodate changing circumstances and which, in the long run, would be to the benefit of all parties concerned.

For example, if a department of a company was previously labor-intensive and employed a direct labor base in allocating its overhead, and if at some time or over a length of time the department was automated and became capital-intensive, a change in base (e.g., to machine hours) might be warranted. If the company made such a

---

[6] The determination of "increased costs" is applied on a net basis of all CAS-covered contracts. That is, increases or decreases on individual contracts are offset to determine whether there is a net increase in cost to the government.

change, however, it would be subject to the downward-only adjustment on its existing CAS-covered contracts.

The CASB recognized such problems and changed its regulations, effective March 10, 1978, to permit the government (i.e., the government's contracting officer) to agree to an equitable adjustment for certain voluntary changes. This is provided in paragraph (a) (4)(C) of the contract clause. Prior to agreeing to an equitable adjustment for a voluntary change, the contracting officer must ". . . make a finding that the change is desirable and not detrimental to the interests of the Government."[7] Any voluntary change for which the contracting officer does not permit an equitable adjustment is still subject to the downward-only adjustment (paragraph (a)(4)(B) of the contract clause).

The term "voluntary change" is somewhat misleading in that it implies that the company, on its own, initiates a change in its cost accounting practices. Actually, there can be so-called voluntary changes that are initiated by others:

1 A new financial accounting standard from the Financial Accounting Standards Board affecting cost measurement, cost assignment to cost accounting periods or the allocation of cost to cost objectives.

2 A new law enacted by the U.S. Congress requiring a change in the measurement of

"If the noncompliance is judged to be deliberate, cost increases on some contracts cannot be offset against cost decreases on other contracts, and the company is liable for the total of cost increases on all contracts...."

cost, assignment of cost to cost accounting periods or the allocation of cost to cost objectives.

3 A change in the procurement regulation's cost principles. There are two procurement regulations, the defense acquisition regulation (formerly armed services procurement regulation) for military contracts and the federal procurement regulation for civilian agency contracts.[8] Each regulation includes

a set of cost principles affecting the measurement of cost, assignment of cost to cost accounting periods and the allocation of cost to cost objectives. These cost principles are periodically changed.

A change in any one of these areas could cause a company to make a voluntary change. Further, other "voluntary" changes are sometimes actually initiated at the urging of governmental auditors. Regardless of their origin, all such changes must be approved for an equitable adjustment by the government's contracting officer. Otherwise, the change would result in a downward-only adjustment.

The CASB is, of course, aware of the potential problems for companies that are required to make a less-than-voluntary change. Therefore, it has always worked closely with the organizations responsible for changing the procurement regulation's cost principles. Here is a CASB comment on its working with bodies such as the FASB:

"The legislative history leading to creation of the Cost Accounting Standards Board shows that standards and principles issued for financial accounting purposes were not deemed suitable for cost accounting for negotiated Government contracts. The Cost Accounting Standards Board views its own work as relating directly to the preparation, use and review of cost accounting data in the negotiation, administration and settlement of negotiated defense contracts. The Board is the only body established by law with the specific responsibility to promulgate Cost Accounting Standards and these Standards have the force and effect of law in the negotiation, administration and settlement of defense contracts.

"The Board seeks to avoid conflict with similar organizations having other responsibilities in the area of Accounting Standards and through continuous liaison makes every reasonable effort to do so. The Board will give careful consideration to the pronouncements affecting financial reporting and in the formulation of Cost Accounting Standards it will take these pronouncements into account to the extent it can do so in accomplishing its objectives. Nevertheless, the nature of the Board's statutory authority and its mission

---

[7] U.S., Cost Accounting Standards Board, 4 CFR 331.51.
[8] A new procurement regulation—the federal acquisition regulation (FAR)—is currently being developed to replace both DAR and FPR.

to establish Cost Accounting Standards for negotiated defense contracts is such that it must retain full responsibility for meeting its objectives."[9]

And here is the CASB philosophy on dealing with procurement regulations and acts of Congress:

"A contractor desiring to make a change in cost accounting practice for any reason must negotiate with the contracting officer under the appropriate subparagraph of the CAS contract clause.

"Should a situation arise where major changes in cost accounting practices would be required by contractors to comply with express provisions of a law or regulation, the Board would seek to accommodate any such requirement by a change in its standards, rules or regulations."[10]

Noncompliance

Paragraph (a)(5) of the CAS contract clause gives the consequences of a company's failure to comply with a cost accounting standard or to follow its disclosed cost accounting practices. The company must repay (or have its contract prices adjusted) for any increased costs paid by the government as a result of the noncompliance *plus* interest accrued from the time the payment was made. It should be noted that while the adjustments discussed above (i.e., for new standards and voluntary changes) were prospective, in cases of noncompliance, the company's prior period(s) are reopened to the point where noncompliance originated.

Another feature of cases of noncompliance is that the determination of "increased costs" varies depending on the nature of noncompliance: (1) If the noncompliance is judged to be inadvertent, cost increases on some contracts are offset against cost decreases on other contracts, and the company is liable only for any net increased cost paid by the government (plus interest on the net amount). (2) If the noncompliance is judged to be deliberate, cost increases on some contracts cannot be offset against cost decreases on other contracts, and the company is liable for the total of cost increases on all contracts (plus interest).[11]

The determinations of whether there has been noncompliance and the type of noncompliance is made by the government's contracting officer. Both issues are subject to appeal if the company disagrees.

Because of the effect that the CASB has on companies subject to its standards, it would seem necessary to identify the probable impact on the audit procedures and accounting disclosures with respect to these companies. The following recommendations are offered for consideration.

Recommended Audit Procedures

In 1975 the AICPA issued an industry audit guide titled *Audits of Government Contractors*. The guide makes only brief mention of the CASB. Based on the maturity of

"Unsettled noncompliance issues, when discovered by the government, entail adjustments from the date that the noncompliance began."

the CASB, the number of standards that it has promulgated and the impact of its contract clause on the profit potential of companies, the following procedures warrant consideration by auditors of governmental contractors:

Review the company's disclosure statement(s). Many companies subject to cost accounting standards have disclosure statements on file with the CASB and agency procurement offices. If a client has a disclosure statement on file, it should be reviewed. This review will be useful to the auditor in understanding the client's cost accounting practices. An additional review at the end of the audit will help the auditor draw conclusions on the client's compliance in practice (as observed in the audit) with the disclosed practices. Any apparent variance should be brought to the client's attention. A verifiable variance could trigger the noncompliance provisions of the contract clause. Instances of noncompliance that are discovered and corrected by the client would appear to be more readily explained as inadvertent noncompliance. Unsettled noncompliance issues, when discovered by the government, entail adjustments from the date that the noncompliance began.

---

[9] U.S., *Federal Register*, vol. 43, no. 48, March 10, 1978, pp.9776-7.

[10] Ibid.

[11] A recent proposal of the CASB would eliminate the distinction in adjustments for inadvertent versus deliberate noncompliance. Both would be subject to the right of offset.

For companies that hold CAS-covered contracts but do not as yet have to file a disclosure statement, a pro forma review and application of the disclosure statement format will help to highlight the company's established cost accounting practices. In effect, the disclosure statement can be used to document the client's cost accounting system.

Review CAS matters with the client. This, of course, entails discussions with key client personnel involved in the negotiation and accounting for governmental contracts. It also involves reviewing correspondence between the client and the governmental procurement staff (e.g., contracting officers, auditors). The independent auditor must understand the team of governmental personnel with whom the client must deal and its members' various roles. For example, the conclusion of the governmental auditor may or may not be adopted by the contracting officer. It is the decision of the contracting officer that is binding on the company and subject to appeal.

In these discussions and correspondence, incipient disagreements will be discovered that could affect past, present and future contracts. Otherwise, they are unlikely to be discovered in the normal course of correspondence with the client's legal counsel.

Review the effect that new CAS and proposed voluntary changes will have on existing contracts. Since existing contracts will have to conform to new cost accounting standards as they become effective (and applicable to the client), the profit potential of existing contracts could be impaired. Voluntary changes can have a similar effect. The independent auditor should investigate the prospective impact of new standards and voluntary changes on existing contracts. This is particularly significant since many governmental contractors have backlogs of contracts running into the hundreds of millions of dollars (and in some cases into the billions). In some cases, this information will be available in the form of "cost impact statements," i.e., estimates of the impact on existing contracts prepared by the company for the contracting officer.

The adjustments mandated by new standards or voluntary changes could affect the computation of revenue recognition where the percentage-of-completion method is employed. The auditor must ascertain that the

client has made the appropriate adjustment in its computations.

Recommended Financial Statement Disclosure

Where the following matters are material to a company's overall operation, their disclosure should be considered:

Disclosure of CAS coverage. Companies subject to cost accounting standards should disclose this in the footnotes to the financial statements. Also, the volume of sales subject to the standards should be disclosed. If the company discloses governmental sales as a segment or major customer, the percentage subject to the standards should be noted. If governmental sales cut across segments or lines-of-business, the percentage of the sales and CAS-covered governmental sales should be disclosed.

Backlog. Some governmental contractors currently disclose their backlog of sales in their annual reports.[12] (The Securities and Exchange Commission requires backlog disclosure when it is needed to properly understand the company's business.) This disclosure is not typically an integral part of the audited financial statements. It should be made an integral part of the statements through footnote disclosure. In particular, the CAS-covered portion of the backlog should be disclosed.

Impact of new standards. The effect of implementing new standards on the current period's work, and, more important, on backlog work, should be noted. We have seen that equitable adjustments of existing CAS-covered contracts can involve shifts in costs from those contracts (whose prices are adjusted downward) to other contracts (e.g., nongovernmental contracts) whose prices are not adjusted upward. This leaves the company in a less favorable position for the future. The opposite situation also could occur when costs are shifted and prices increased for governmental contracts. When such an effect is material, it should be disclosed. It might also help explain the results for the current period and anticipate changes in the profit potential of the backlog work. The same disclosure would be required for material adjustments caused by voluntary changes and noncompliance. ■

---

[12] In *1976 Survey of Financial Reporting and Accounting Practices of Government Contractors,* Price Waterhouse & Co. reported that 29 of 50 governmental contractors disclosed information about their backlogs in their annual reports but typically not as part of their audited financial statements.

Appendix A

Promulgated and proposed cost accounting standards

CAS no.	Promulgated Standards
401	*Consistency in Estimating, Accumulating and Reporting Costs*
402	*Consistency in Allocating Costs Incurred for the Same Purpose*
403	*Allocation of Home Office Expenses to Segments*
404	*Capitalization of Tangible Capital Assets*
405	*Accounting for Unallowable Costs*
406	*Cost Accounting Period*
407	*Use of Standard Costs for Direct Material and Direct Labor*
408	*Accounting for Costs of Compensated Personal Absence*
409	*Depreciation of Tangible Capital Assets*
410	*Allocation of Business Unit General and Administrative Expense to Final Cost Objectives*
411	*Accounting for Acquisition Costs of Material*
412	*Composition and Measurement of Pension Costs*
413	*Adjustment and Allocation of Pension Costs*
414	*Cost of Money as an Element of the Cost of Facilities Capital*
415	*Accounting for the Cost of Deferred Compensation*
416	*Accounting for Insurance Costs*
420	*Accounting for Independent Research and Development and Bid and Proposal Costs*

	Proposed Standards
417	*Distinguishing Between Direct and Indirect Costs*
418	*Allocation of Indirect Cost Pools*
419	*Allocation of Overhead Costs of Productive Functions and Activities*
421	*Cost of Money as an Element of Cost of Facilities Under Construction*

Appendix B

CAS contract clause

Contractors are subjected to CAS by signing a contract that contains the CAS contract clause which reads in part:

"(a) Unless the Cost Accounting Standards Board has prescribed rules or regulations exempting the contractor or this contract from standards, rules and regulations promulgated pursuant to 50 U.S.C. App. 2168 (Pub. L. 91-379, August 15, 1970), the contractor, in connection with this contract shall:

"(1) By submission of a Disclosure Statement, disclose in writing his cost accounting practices as required by regulations of the Cost Accounting Standards Board. The required disclosures must be made prior to contract award unless the Contracting Officer provides a written notice to the contractor authorizing post-award submission in accordance with regulations of the Cost Accounting Standards Board. The practices disclosed for this contract shall be the same as the practices currently disclosed and applied on all other contracts and subcontracts being performed by the contractor and which contain this Cost Accounting Standards clause. If the contractor has notified the Contracting Office that the Disclosure Statement contains trade secrets and commercial or financial information which is privileged and confidential, the Disclosure Statement will be protected and will not be released outside of the Government.

"(2) Follow consistently the cost accounting practices disclosed pursuant to (1) above in accumulating and reporting contract performance cost data concerning this contract. If any change in disclosed practices is made for purposes of any contract or subcontract subject to Cost Accounting Standards Board requirements, the change must be applied prospectively to this contract, and the Disclosure Statement must be amended accordingly. If the contract price or cost allowance of this contract is affected by such changes, adjustment shall be made in accordance with subparagraph (a)(4) or (a)(5) below, as appropriate.

"(3) Comply with all Cost Accounting Standards in effect on the date of award of this contract or if the contractor has submitted cost or pricing data, on the date of final agreement on price as shown on the contractor's signed certificate of current cost or pricing data. The contractor shall also comply with any Cost Accounting Standard which hereafter becomes applicable to a contract or subcontract of the contractor. Such compliance shall be required prospectively from the date of applicability to such contract or subcontract.

"(4)(A) Agree to an equitable adjustment as provided in the changes clause of this contract if the contract cost is affected by a change which, pursuant to (3) above, the contractor is required to make to his established cost accounting practices whether such practices are covered by a Disclosure Statement or not.

"(4)(B) Negotiate with the contracting officer to determine the terms and conditions under which a change may be made to either a disclosed cost accounting practice or an established cost accounting practice, other than a change made under other provisions of this subparagraph (4): *Provided* that no agreement may be made under this provision that will increase costs paid by the United States.

"(4)(C) When the parties agree to a change to either a disclosed cost accounting practice or an established cost accounting practice, other than a change under (4)(A) above, negotiate an equitable adjustment as provided in the changes clause of this contract.

"(5) Agree to an adjustment of the contract price or cost allowance, as appropriate, if he or a subcontractor fails to comply with an applicable Cost Accounting Standard or to follow any practice disclosed pursuant to subparagraphs (a)(1) and (a)(2) above and such failure results in any increased costs paid by the United States. Such adjustment shall provide for recovery of the increased costs to the United States together with interest thereon computed at the rate determined by the Secretary of the Treasury pursuant to Public Law 92-41, 85 Stat. 97, or 7 percent per annum, whichever is less, from the time the payment by the United States was made to the time the adjustment is effected."

(Source: Code of Federal Regulations, title 4, section 331.50)

Appendix C

Illustrations of changes (and nonchanges) in cost accounting practices

The following are illustrations of changes which meet the definition of "change to either a disclosed cost accounting practice or an established cost accounting practice" because:

I. The method or technique used for measuring costs has been changed.

Description of change

Contractor changes his actuarial cost method for computing pension costs.

Accounting treatment

Before change: The contractor computed pension costs using the aggregate cost method.

After change: The contractor computes pension costs using the unit credit method.

II. The method or technique used for assignment of cost to cost accounting periods has been changed.

Description of change

Contractor changes his established criteria for capitalizing certain classes of tangible capital assets whose acquisition costs totaled $1 million per cost accounting period.

Accounting treatment

Before change: Items having acquisition costs of between $200 and $400 per unit were capitalized and depreciated over a number of cost accounting periods.

After change: The contractor charges the value of assets costing between $200 and $400 per unit to an indirect expense pool which is allocated to the cost objectives of the cost accounting period in which the cost was incurred.

Appendix C continued

III. The method or technique used for allocating cost has been changed.

Description of change

Contractor changes his method of allocating G&A expenses under the requirements of Cost Accounting Standard no. 410.

Accounting treatment

Before change: The contractor operating under Cost Accounting Standard no. 410 has been allocating his general and administrative expense pool to final cost objectives on a total cost input base in compliance with the standard. The contractor's business changes substantially such that there are significant new projects which have only insignificant quantities of material.

After change: After the addition of the new work, an evaluation of changed circumstances reveals that the continued use of a total cost input base would result in a significant distortion in the allocation of the G&A expense pool in relation to the benefits received. To remain in compliance with Standard no. 410, the contractor alters his G&A allocation base from a total cost input base to a value added base.

The following are illustrations of changes which do not meet the definition of "change to either a disclosed cost accounting practice or an established cost accounting practice," and accordingly do not require price adjustments under subparagraphs (a)(4) and (a)(5) of the CAS contract clause.

Description of change

Changes in the interest rate levels in the national economy have invalidated the prior actuarial assumption with respect to anticipated investment earnings. The pension plan administrators adopted an increased (decreased) interest rate actuarial assumption. The company allocated the resulting pension costs to all final cost objectives.

Accounting treatment

Adopting the increase (decrease) in the interest rate actuarial assumption is not a change in cost accounting practice.

The basic benefit amount for a company's pension plan is increased from $8 to $10 per year of credited service. The change increases the dollar amount of pension cost allocated to all final cost objectives.

The increase in the amount of the benefits is not a change in cost accounting practice.

(Source: 4 CFR 331.20(j))

THE CHALLENGE OF CULTIVATING ACCOUNTING FIRM EXECUTIVES

Existing management development practices are inadequate, say the authors, especially in today's turbulent environment.

by Larry E. Greiner and Alan Scharff

Yesterday's ways of managing a public accounting firm, which may have been satisfactory under the more stable conditions of the past, will prove inadequate in today's world of tough competition, demanding clients, pressures from regulatory agencies and self-regulation. Skilled accounting firm executives are needed who can manage a complex organization and also meet the needs of clients for diverse services in a turbulent environment. Unfortunately, many firms are ill-equipped managerially at this time—although some are awakening and seeking solutions.

This article discusses existing practices and problems involving executive development in accounting firms. It also makes specific recommendations for improvement. These changes would affect everyone, from junior accountants aspiring to managerial positions to firm partners attempting to cope with their executive responsibilities.

A typical example based on our experiences of what can occur in career development in a CPA firm follows.

A Traditional Management Progression

An accountant, recruited out of college, generally stays with the same CPA firm for as long as he or she remains in public accounting. The firm's staff training heavily emphasizes the technical aspects of accounting and occasionally the supervisory aspects—but it does not contain any preparation for senior management responsibilities.

When an opening occurs for promotion to a supervisory position, the young staff member is selected for the spot, based on his high level of technical competence along with good personal characteristics such as reliability. Now the accountant is a manager—at least in title. However, he hasn't yet been taught how to manage. Maybe that skill can be learned on the job—or can it?

The new manager often supervises assignments for more than one partner. In fact, it is not unusual for the manager to move about so much that he does not really report to one supervisor in the traditional sense. These reporting relationships emphasize the audit's requirements and rarely address the personal development of the manager (everyone is too busy meeting the quality, schedule and cost requirements of the project).

The manager attends additional training sessions given by the firm, but these are still oriented toward technical matters—although a more enlightened firm may include material aimed at improving project manager skills in handling audits. In some local firms, a manager may not receive any internal training and is too busy, or not motivated enough, to use external outlets

LARRY E. GREINER, D.B.A., is professor of organizational behavior at the Graduate School of Business Administration, University of Southern California, Los Angeles. He is a member of the Academy of Management, the American Psychological Association and the American Sociological Association. Dr. Greiner is author of several articles in professional publications. **ALAN L. SCHARFF** is president of Management Associates, a management consulting firm in Palos Verdes Estates, California. He is currently a guest lecturer on management at the University of Southern California, Los Angeles.

for self-improvement that are not directly connected with technical issues. Therefore, the manager often learns how to manage by trial and error.

At last there is an opening in the partnership ranks. What factors will be the most important in selecting a manager for promotion to partner? In order of importance (which we have found varies little from firm to firm), the selection criteria are

☐ Technical competence.
☐ Good client relationships.
☐ A history of completing projects within budget at satisfactory quality levels.
☐ Practice development abilities.

The manager has become a partner with only questionable management skills and without any formal management training for performing as a senior executive. The

"Developing good executives is like growing a garden that flourishes through cross-fertilization from the outside world."

new partner reports directly to a managing partner. In the typical firm structure, he may be one of 15 to 20 partners reporting to the same person in a medium-sized office of an international firm or in a large national firm.

What about management development for the new partner? We have found that few firms offer any formal management training for new partners, nor will there be time to seek this education from outside sources. Instead, the new partner is oriented toward client service and marketing activities; he delegates the management of audits to the junior staff, and there is little opportunity for contact with the overburdened managing partner. Can the new partner improve his management skills by trial and error alone?

If the partner progresses still further in management to become the managing partner of an office or a director of a functional specialization, the scenario is repeated. This time, however, there are further complications because the new executive partner is usually more managerially iso-

lated from peers and supervision because of functional or geographical separation. He is still learning management by trial and error—a hard and expensive way to learn when experienced at a senior level.

Existing Practices—The Problems

Developing good executives is like growing a garden that flourishes through cross-fertilization from the outside world. An accounting firm can grow its own in a closed, greenhouse environment, ignoring new ideas and the rooting of new management talent. But this inbreeding can stifle management ideas, concepts, practices and policies. From a management standpoint, each firm should not be an island unto itself, feeding on its own mistakes. Such isolation, for example, can cripple a multi-office firm if mistakes are repeated at the regional and office levels, as well as in functional and industry specializations.

The existing practices that can cause some CPA firms to overlook management training follow:

☐ *Emphasis on technical expertise.* Although continuing education in the technical aspects of accounting is important—especially with the rising number of recent pronouncements affecting CPAs—the exclusive emphasis some accounting firms place on this area can result in insufficient attention to management development.

☐ *Inadequate supervision.* The absence of fixed superior-subordinate relationships among partners, managers and the staff minimizes the opportunities for coaching in management. For example, handling a variety of assignments enables a manager to learn new technical skills and enhances flexible scheduling of engagements to meet client needs. However, the manager's supervisor can find it difficult to measure and assess the accountant's management strengths and weaknesses. Management evaluations are difficult enough in private industries with structured organizations where output is more visible. They are even more difficult when supervisory relationships are infrequent and are centered largely on paperwork outside the firm. How can supervisors be expected to spend time on management development when their working relationships are so ephemeral and are tuned to the completion of numerous assignments?

A strong "project orientation" can easily cause a manager or partner to feel a closer association with clients than with his changing subordinates. This project orientation also can contribute to an overemphasis on billable time, which makes it difficult to assign personnel to management development—which is, of course, a nonbillable function.

☐ *Partners' separation from management function.* In some firms, partners divorce themselves from typical management functions and delegate these activities to subordinates. For example, a partner may allow the engagement manager to prepare all the planning and scheduling for an audit. The partner may not become involved in the monitoring and control of the engagement until close to the scheduled completion date or even later when signing the management letter.

☐ *All partners are created equal.* The legal concept that all partners are created equal can be reflected in the reluctance to install an organizational hierarchy of partners. From a management viewpoint, this practice becomes untenable when a large number of partners are involved. There are accounting firms, and offices of larger firms, where as many as 30 partners report to the same managing partner. This may preclude coaching of subordinate partners by the managing partner. Moreover, the managing partner is usually required to spend considerable time and energy outside the office in practice development activities. As a result, this key executive may have little time available to handle meetings with subordinates regarding daily operating problems, including individual management development.

Plan of Action

A concerted effort is required if accounting firms are to develop their accountants into executives capable of dealing with the complex problems and opportunities facing the accounting profession. Our plan of action encompasses a dozen steps:

1 Recognize that management is a separate discipline from accounting with its own principles and skills and is a critical factor in the success or failure of the firm. Technical expertise is only one leg of a three-legged stool that also involves practice development and management skills.

2 Modify the criteria for partner and manager selection to include consideration of who will be the best manager rather than just who is the best accountant (technical expertise should, of course, be required). Private industry discovered long ago that

the best scientist doesn't necessarily make the best research director, nor does the best salesman make the best sales manager.

3 Establish policies and practices that require the measurement of managerial performance. Partners should be held accountable for profit responsibilities—not just for client service or billed hours. They will become more managerially oriented when the full costs of an engagement are counted against billings on a profit and loss statement. Each partner should be treated like an executive who must develop goals, plans, budgets and people.

4 Design a reward system that establishes a closer correlation between performance and compensation. For example, a problem in this area may be rectified by a combination of (a) removing shares in the firm from low performing partners, (b) establishing a percentage of the firm's share value to be determined by local office performance and (c) setting aside a portion of firm income for annual cash bonuses to be awarded for exceptional performance.

5 Arrange for each staff member to have one superior who is responsible for his or her development. This does not mean that it is necessary to adopt a pyramidal organizational structure with rigid staff assignments but, rather, that everyone should have a "mentor," regardless of other reporting relationships. It would be more natural if staff members could pick their own mentors or at least change them easily if the personal chemistry is not right. Firms should be aware that mentors are important in a professional organization where staff members are concerned about their careers and where there is little consistency in supervisor-subordinate relationships.

6 Provide regular forums for the discussion of management problems. For larger firms, this should include frequent interchanges among functional groups (e.g., audit, tax and management advisory services), among partners and the managing partner at each office and among the managing partners of several offices. This will enable all levels of management to learn from each other. In addition, these meetings can expose a broader group to the management problems that are too often confined to the managing partner.

7 Evaluate all management personnel and those identified as having management potential. Prepare personally tailored development programs for both groups, including training programs. Many courses on management skills (both group and individual study courses) are available, for example, from the American Institute of CPAs and the state CPA societies. Group courses have the advantage of giving participants an opportunity to learn from and cooperate with management personnel in other companies and industries. On the other hand, internal programs allow for a freer exchange of confidential client and firm information. Smaller firms may find external programs more economically feasible.

8 Introduce an intensive management training program for managing partners of firms or offices and national directors of audit, tax and management advisory services. These key executives are the persons who must provide guidance and a role model for other staff members to emulate. (At present, we are aware of only one such ongoing program.) The focus of the program should be on such topics as strategic planning, marketing in a profession, management control and evaluation, matrix organization, team building, communication and career development.

9 Free managing partners in larger offices of direct client responsibilities. We find too many firms that still require their managing partners to carry a heavy client load while also holding them accountable for numerous management activities.

10 Reduce the managing partner's span of control by establishing a limited hierarchy of partners so that managing partners can devote more time to management and personnel development. In our experience, hierarchies are already common in tax and management advisory services and can be established in the audit area by appointing executive-level partners over groups of other audit partners. Large audit operations can also be subdivided into profit centers with their own staffs and sets of clients.

11 Appoint a limited number of new partners directly from the outside who have outstanding managerial skills. It will take years to develop sufficient managerial talent from within the firm. Outside partner-managers can accelerate this process, and their appointment will symbolize management's commitment to improved managerial performance.

12 Obtain the best qualified person available (considering both staff members and outsiders) to head the personnel function and give the position stature by having it report directly to the managing partner. Since accounting is a people business, the need for attracting high-quality personnel is obvious. In larger firms and offices, the personnel director should be a qualified personnel executive—not an accountant who is working as a personnel trainee.

However, the firm can't do it all; what can the individual employee do? He or she can take full advantage of management training offered by the firm, enroll in outside training courses, establish a personal development program and ask for assistance from those in the firm with the highest degree of managerial skill.

Lack of understanding and knowledge of management principles and practices precludes accounting firm executives from giving sound advice and assistance to clients in these areas. Therefore, an important opportunity to enhance client rapport and further practice development can be lost. We are aware of many clients that changed firms because the accountant "did not understand our business." CPAs who have developed broad management skills can attest to how valuable such skills have been in achieving a high level of client satisfaction as well as in opening doors to additional client work.

A void in management development carries a high cost to the firm because it not only inhibits effective management within the firm but it also limits new opportunities for practice development. ∎

Thomas J. Burns, CPA, Ph.D., and Edward N. Coffman, DBA

The Ascending Profession of Accounting*

Rule-Making Agencies

Currently for U.S. accountants there are at least three primary rule-making groups and a host of others including at least three which often have a major impact on practice. This does not include the legislatures and the courts, both at the state and the national level, whose newly enacted laws and court decisions frequently cause changes in accounting.

The three primary rule-making groups for U.S. accounting are two in the public sector, the Securities and Exchange Commission (SEC) and the Cost Accounting Standards Board (CASB), and one in the private sector, the Financial Accounting Standards Board (FASB).

The CASB has begun issuing rules in the last six years. It is a five-member Board created by and responsible to Congress. Although its original mission was to enact cost accounting standards to achieve uniformity and consistency in the cost accounting for defense contractors, the CASB is coming to set cost accounting standards for all organizations selling goods and services to the federal government.

The chief statutory authority for establishing accounting rules is vested in the SEC which was established in 1933. Unlike in any other country in the world, this governmental rule-making agency has largely permitted the private sector to make the rules governing accounting practices. Nevertheless, the SEC has long issued its own rules (Accounting Series Releases) controlling accounting practice and in recent years has substantially accelerated these releases. It also continually informally reviews and evaluates the rules issued by the FASB. Although the SEC sometimes argues that its chief concern in establishing its own rules is with *accounting disclosure* issues, whereas those of the private sector rule-making group should be with *accounting measurement,* these two functions may overlap. Although the SEC commissioners have statutory authority over accounting matters, the SEC Chief Accountant actually exercises their power and because of this he is widely regarded as the most powerful accountant in the world.

The current chief rule-making group in the private sector is the seven-member FASB established in mid-1973, as a successor to the American Institute of Certified Public Accountants' Accounting Principles Board (established in 1959) and the earlier AICPA Committee on Accounting Procedure. The authority for this group rests on its acceptance not only by the SEC but also by the private sector of the economy, most notably by professional and business interests. The structure of the private sector rule-making group has evolved into a full-time activity and one whose membership has broadened to include others besides former practicing CPAs. If a CPA does not follow a pronouncement of the FASB, this must be explained in the report.

Three other agencies that have a major impact on accounting practice are the Internal Revenue Service (IRS), the American Institute of Certified Public Accountants (AICPA) and probably in the years to come, the International Accounting Standards Committee (IASC).

The first of these has influence due to the authority of the IRS. Although its power is directly based on its authority to require tax units, individual or group, to file tax returns, it often influences general

---

* This is the second part of a two-part article. The first section was presented in our February issue.

THE CPA JOURNAL / MARCH 1977

accounting practice. Millions of individuals and small organizations, whose tax returns are their chief accounting report, fundamentally keep their books to prepare tax returns. The IRS sometimes requires, for specific items, that the accounting for the tax return must be the same as it is for the financial statement. Where the tax savings are important, this situation can exert powerful pressure on the reporting organization to prepare its general statements so as to be able to realize tax savings. Even when this is not required, the allowance of a certain accounting practice by the IRS on tax returns (i.e., accelerated depreciation) sometimes provides the impetus for using it in the financial statements.

The AICPA, although it has relinquished to the FASB its authority for the establishment of financial reporting standards, still exerts a powerful influence on professional standards. CPAs, as explained elsewhere, exercise much influence over how financial statements are prepared since it is customary to have such statements reported on by them.

Still only largely a potential rule-making group is the IASC, started in 1973, whose announced function is to develop and gain worldwide acceptance for basic accounting standards. The accounting profession is the first profession in the world which has undertaken not only to lay down international standards of practice but also to consider disciplining those members who do not comply. The IASC has already issued ten standards. Although the IASC is now composed of Western countries, it is expected to be superseded in 1977 by the International Federation of Accountants (IFA) whose membership will be open to Communist countries.

In addition to the six groups named, there is a myriad of other institutions which have more than an occasional impact on the practice of accounting.

Allied Professions: Law, Actuarial Science, Economics

Although accounting historically has been related to many professions, contemporary accounting is probably closest to these three — law, actuarial science and, of course, economics.

The FBI has long required its personnel to qualify in either law or accounting. Much of accounting practice, perhaps most notably accounting for equities, has to do with the law. Certainly the courts and the rule-making agencies such as the SEC are major determinants in how accounting is practiced. Probably the area of tax practice is the one most dominated by the law. College students majoring in accounting find their tax accounting courses to be largely legally-oriented. CPAs or other accountants are expected to have a good understanding of the relationships between the parties in a business, the concepts involved and the special terminology. Also the accountant needs a general knowledge of the concept of law in society. On the other hand, a lawyer needs considerable understanding of accounting, particularly in a society that is raising its standards of accountability. Accounting has come to be regarded in recent years as a highly desirable pre-law school major.

Not much is known by the general public about the profession of actuarial science. Actuaries are statisticians who assess the probabilities of human mortalities and other phenomena. Traditionally, they have devoted their mathematical skills to computing premiums for insurance companies and designing and pricing pension programs. The latter use of their training is availed of by a number of public accounting firms in their management consulting services.

Probably the professional group most closely linked to accountancy is that of economists, at least theoretically. Both groups deal with similar problems with consistently complementary approaches. The accountant has chiefly dealt with financial data in a historical setting, the economist in a future-oriented setting. The economist relies on accounting data for economic data, the accountant relies on economic data in developing accounting data. In practice, of course, in the past, the economist has chiefly practiced in the governmental or public sector, while the accountant has chiefly practiced in the business or private sector. With the increased emphasis on accounting for decision-aiding purposes and prediction, the new accountant's orientation will likely become even closer to that of the economist.

There is at least one other emerging group, the specialists in computer technology, that accountants are closely associated with. Although not yet possessing professional status, this group of computer programmers and information systems or data processing specialists occupy a key business sector.

The Formal Education of Accountants

Dean Georges of Ohio State University indicates that accounting is the most rapidly growing major in his institution. The number of accounting majors has doubled over the past five years and he notes that many of the brightest students have been attracted to accounting. One reason for their interest is, of course, job opportunities; another, he indicated, is increased awareness that accounting is a broadly-based discipline. Many students, planning to go to law school, are now majoring in accounting rather than in the traditional pre-law school majors, political science or history. Accounting is also considered an excellent pragmatic major for anyone going into a business career. "Compared to earlier student generations," Dean Georges reports, "the present one is highly pragmatic with a much stronger orientation to business and the marketplace."

But majoring in accounting does not automatically qualify one for a successful career. What should the formal education of accountants encompass? It should be conceptually-oriented, rather than manipulatively-oriented, according to the AICPA's Committee on Education and Experience Requirements for CPAs. Courses in the area of general education that the Committee recommends are of two types. First are those that provide the prospective accountant with a rounded exposure (i.e., courses in humanities, physical and social sciences and the arts). Second are those that provide a foundation in areas that are more related to the practice of accounting. This would include written and oral communication skills, economics, computer programming, mathematics, statistics and behavioral science. A partner of Ernst & Ernst points out, "A complete professional has many roles to play. As an auditor, the professional must be able to maintain unwavering independence, but do it with a charm and grace that, as much as possible, avoids offense to client personnel. He must relate well to his associates within the firm. Training in the behavorial sciences should help in this area."

Courses in the area of general business are also recommended — to provide understanding of the major functions of organizations in society and of social forces that influence organizations. Courses should include: economics (theory and monetary system), social environment of business, business law, marketing, finance, organization, group and individual behavior, quantitative applications in business, written communication and policy.

Besides elementary accounting, courses should be required in financial and managerial accounting, taxation, auditing and computer information systems. These courses should provide an understanding of the functions of accounting, the concepts of accounting theory and their application to accounting business situations. At Ohio State, for example, accounting majors are encouraged to spend the winter quarter of their senior year on a public accounting internship. Industrial accounting internships are often available to accounting majors during the summer between their junior and senior years.

While formal accounting education has been traditionally a four-year program, the AICPA Committee advocated that a post-baccalaureate program be established to convey the common body of knowledge. About 10 percent of accounting majors at Ohio State now take a fifth year and a master's degree either at Ohio State or elsewhere. There has been considerable discussion about whether the educational requirements of the beginning professional accountant can be obtained in the conventional four-year program. Impetus for a post-baccalaureate program has been added by the recommendations of the AICPA Board on Standards for Programs and Schools of Professional Accounting created in July 1974 to identify standards that, when satisfied by a school, would justify its recognition by the accounting profession. The Board favors establishment of professional accounting schools and programs of study that lead to a post-baccalaureate accounting degree as the minimum necessary to graduate an entry level professional accountant.

Whether the common body of knowledge for the entry into the accounting profession is taught in a five-year or a four-year program will necessarily have a bearing on the depth of coverage. However, the educational requirements in either case should approximate that recommended as a common body of knowledge for the beginning accountant: about half for general education; about a fourth for general business; and about a fourth for accounting.

While it is important that the new accountant possess the common body of accounting knowledge, it is equally important that the candidate's academic performance be high. Overall grade-point averages of "B" as well as "B" averages in the accounting courses are minimum acceptable averages for those considering employment in many public accounting firms. Involvement in extracurricular activities (i.e., president of student government) which might indicate leadership abilities is also a desirable trait in prospective accountants.

The Certification of Accountants

Besides obtaining the common body of accounting knowledge, the new accountant should plan to become certified. Certification is *required* to practice public accounting on the highest level; it is *desirable* in the other two career areas.

The CPA certificate is awarded by the state or other jurisdiction in which the accountant desires to practice accounting. (Most states have a "dying class" of licensed public accountants but grant admission to public accountancy only to those who have passed the uniform CPA examination.) Certification is obtained by passing the CPA examination (offered twice a year) and by meeting experience and other requirements of the particular jurisdiction. The two and one-half day uniform CPA examination is divided into four sections: auditing, accounting practice, accounting theory and business law; these examinations are at the level of a college graduate from an accredited institution with a major in accounting.

The Certificate of Management Accounting (CMA) is granted by the Institute of Management Accounting of the National Association of Accountants on passing the CMA examination and completing related professional experience in management accounting. Such a credential is desirable for a young accountant who anticipates a career in managerial accounting.

The Institute of Internal Auditors, Inc. confers the Certificate of Internal Auditor (CIA) to those who meet certain education requirements and pass a CIA examination. This credential is desirable for young accountants practicing internal auditing.

The Continuing Education of Accountants

As in the case of other leading professions, the education and development of accountants does not cease on being graduated from the university. The practicing accountant must continually update his or her education in order to meet technical changes and increasing demands on the profession; education becomes a life-long process. This means returning to the campus from time to time to attend formal workshops or technical courses, participating in in-house professional development programs, and attending seminars and workshops on accounting and related topics offered by professional accounting organizations such as the AICPA, NAA and state and local organizations of certified public accountants.

Continual self-improvement is a timely and costly process in terms of out-of-pocket cost and opportunity cost for both the accountant

THE CPA JOURNAL / MARCH 1977

and the firm. Therefore, it is important that the practicing accountant accept continuing professional development as part of the responsibility of being a professional.

A number of states have adopted the requirement that practicing accountants holding the CPA certificate complete a certain number of hours of continuing education within specified time intervals in order to maintain their certification.

Most public accounting firms provide remarkably extensive and rigorous formal training for their professionals throughout their entire career. Soon after they are hired, staff men and women are sent to a firm-wide audit-training school for a one or two-week program. At every stage of their development, they continue to be enrolled in firm-wide or local office training courses; these courses are sometimes a few hours or a day in length, sometimes a week or longer. Such courses are developed and taught by firm personnel. The customary ratio of instruction is one instructor to six or seven participants. In larger firms, the programs of these courses are supervised by a Director of Education and his or her staff. The superior quality of such training, truly comparable in many aspects to that of a first-class and well-endowed institution of higher education, has long been an important factor in the profession's ability to recruit outstanding college graduates. Even graduates who are uncertain about public accounting careers are strongly attracted by the quality of the training offered which is generally held to be superior to the training offered in both industry and government. To supplement the training programs of firms, particularly those of the smaller firms, the AICPA and the state societies have conducted for many years an extensive program of courses throughout the country. A CPA in a public accounting firm can expect that his or her formal education will never be completed. Even after becoming a partner, he or she will regularly attend courses.

Professional Organizations

Accountants are expected to be active in professional organizations throughout their career. Such organizations regularly publish periodicals and other publications including research studies, hold meetings at which professional programs are conducted, and frequently sponsor professional education courses. These organizations elect officers annually both at the local and national level and appoint committees to study professional problems. Each organization holds an annual convention. Memberships are often open to students at a reduced price. Those starting professional careers as accountants are expected to join one or more of these organizations. Many public accounting firms expect one or more staff members to be active in prominent professional organizations operating in their community. Those holding office in the local chapters are regarded as the leading accountants of their community. Those holding such posts on a state or national level are considered to be the country's leading accountants.

Largest and most powerful of the U.S. organizations is the AICPA with a membership of over 125,000. It is concerned with public accounting and auditing issues, and exerts great influence over its membership, industry, business and government. It prepares and grades the professional examination for those wishing to become CPAs, and conducts an extensive continuing professional education program as well as a variety of other programs including, for example, seminars for financial reporters and week-long meetings for minority race accounting educators. The Institute also publishes the *Journal of Accountancy* which is widely recognized as an authoritative journal throughout the business world.

In addition to the organizations that are national in scope, each of the 54 jurisdictions has a "state" CPA society, many of which have chapters for the various regions within the states. Membership in a state society is usually limited to certified public accountants who reside or are employed in the state. The societies conduct research projects and publish the results, encourage improvement and offer programs of advanced accountancy education—many through their own educational foundations—and generally promote closer professional and social relationships among members of the profession. Although the state societies are entities separate from the AICPA, the state bodies and the national body cooperate in the development and maintenance of programs offered to members of the profession.

In addition, many state societies publish their own professional journals, of which the *CPA Journal* is probably the most widely-known.

A relatively small organization but a very influential one by the position of its members is the Financial Executives Institute. Its approximately 9,000 membership is limited to the top financial manager of (mostly) business organizations. It publishes reports of its sponsored research projects. It has chapters in most of the larger cities and most industrialized areas of the country.

The leading academic accounting organization is the American Accounting Association which is chiefly concerned with the teaching of accounting. Yet of its 14,000 membership (including 2,000 students) only several thousand of its members are actually engaged in teaching. This organization sponsors research projects and publishes the results; it also publishes extensive committee reports. Annually it cosponsors with Haskins & Sells a several-day research workshop for the leading doctoral students in accounting. It also conducts short educational programs for professors including currently, with the support of Touche Ross & Co., a series of faculty seminars.

The National Association of Accountants is the second largest accounting organization in the U.S.; it has over 73,000 members. It is chiefly concerned with accounting within companies. Its Institute of Management Accounting supervises the certificate management accounting program. It sponsors research projects and publishes the results.

The Association of Government Accountants consists of accountants employed by the federal, state or local government. It has about 9,000 members. Other specialized and relatively small organizations are the: American Society of

Women Accountants (5,000 members) and the American Woman's Society of Certified Public Accountants (2,000 members); the Institute of Internal Auditors (whose 10,000 members, auditors and controllers within firms, conduct the certified internal auditor program); the National Association of Black Accountants (grown to 1,500 members since 1970); and the National Association of Accountants for the Public Interest (whose 100 members provide accounting counsel without fees to other nonprofit public interest organizations). There are many other accounting organizations usually with specialized interests.

Community and Governmental Involvements

The practicing accountant is looked on by members of society not only as one rendering valued professional service but also as one deeply involved in civic and public activities. Accountants in public accounting and in all areas of practice are expected to assume community and social leadership particularly as they gain experience. Accountants have traditionally devoted their time and effort to serving on boards of trustees of philanthropic organizations—hospitals, colleges and universities, churches, cultural organizations, research and scientific organizations. Serving in various capacities with the Chamber of Commerce, charitable fund raising organizations, Junior Achievement, Big Brother programs for children without fathers, and Boy Scouts are but a few of the many community involvements where accountants fully participate.

Many accountants have served government at the local level in such capacity as members of the Board of Education, at the state level as Auditor of Public Accounts, and at the federal level as Commissioner of the IRS, Chief Accountant of the SEC, Director of the Budget, and as members of special committees appointed by the President of the United States. Yet few accountants have ever become full-time politicians. In 1956, a prominent accountant, T. Coleman Andrews, was the Independent Democratic Party's candidate for the United States Presidency, but that is unu-

sual. The background of almost all U.S. politicians is law and, given how overcrowded the legal profession is, this is likely to continue.

The Monetary Rewards

In an accounting career, what can one expect in salaries, promotions and fringe benefits? Salaries, policies on promotions and fringe benefits vary for the new accountant. But starting salaries in public accounting are higher than in industry and industry's are higher than in government. Ohio State University figures for 1975 show that a graduate starting in public accounting is paid $100 more a month on the average than starting in industry and $200 more than starting in government. Fringe benefits are generally comparable to those in other professions.

Those holding the bachelor's degree in accounting and starting a career with a national public accounting firm (in 1976) could expect beginning monthly salaries to average $1,100; those holding a master's degree could expect an average monthly salary of over $150 more. In public accounting, firms may compensate staff members for a stipulated amount based on ability and other factors such as work habits, relationships with clients and fellow colleagues and general attitude. In 1975, the two largest Big Eight firms reported average partner compensation of $90,000 and $95,000. The top several partners in the largest public accounting firms may earn around $500,000 annually.

While many public accounting firms do not reimburse employees for the cost of formal advanced education programs such as a master's or law degree, they do provide at least two weeks of participation in formal courses annually and do reimburse expenses incurred. Reimbursement may include the cost of CPA coaching courses and the CPA examination fee. In industry, large companies sometimes do reimburse employees for the cost of advanced degree programs. Public accounting firms and industry sometimes reimburse employees for license fees, annual dues and meeting expenses of professional organizations and, where the employer

has requested membership, expenses for civic and business organizations. For an accountant employed by government, these benefits are more restricted.

While it is understandable that retirement plans are not ordinarily of interest to those just entering the profession, future benefits do become important as the years pass and one reaches management levels. Benefits offered vary considerably between the many public accounting firms. Formerly, industry was ahead of public accounting in the retirement benefits it offered, mostly because of the tax law structure. However, the new tax laws, allowing partnerships better retirement benefits, are having an important effect in this area. Now retirement plans are becoming increasingly common and there are benefits equivalent to industry's in public accounting firms.

The Nonmonetary Rewards

While increased remuneration and promotions are the more common and immediate rewards, there are other means by which individual accountants may be rewarded or honored. Honors might come in the form of awards of recognition from state or local chapters of accounting organizations, from branches or agencies of the federal government such as the annual service award granted by the CASB, or from national professional organizations such as the NAA, AAA or AICPA.

Two prominent national awards are administered by the AICPA. For accountants starting their careers who pass all four sections of the CPA examination at one time, the Elijah Watt Sells Award of either a gold or silver medal is given by the AICPA to those receiving the highest grades. This award was established in 1923 to recognize a founder of the public accounting firm, Haskins & Sells. Awards for excellence in the CPA exam are given in many states. For those "elder statesmen" completing their accounting careers, the AICPA presents its Gold Medal Award annually for outstanding contributions to the profession. Similar awards are given at the state or local level.

As an ultimate recognition, the national accounting leader may be

THE CPA JOURNAL / MARCH 1977

elected to the Accounting Hall of Fame. The Hall of Fame was established in 1950 at Ohio State University to honor accountants making significant contributions to the advancement of accounting. Through 1976, 36 U.S. accountants have been elected to the Hall of Fame. These honors to individual accountants are likely to increase as the profession matures and expands and its accomplishments become better understood and more highly valued.

But the most valued rewards of accountants are not in public recognition. When asked about their greatest satisfactions in practicing public accounting, the answers of leading public accountants varied. But each reported that providing professional service to their clients was fulfilling. As one partner put it, "I enjoy most the satisfaction that comes from developing a long-time professional relationship with a client not unlike that of a family doctor or a family lawyer." Several reported that they found developing young professionals to be most gratifying.

The challenge of leadership in a changing profession was mentioned frequently. For, "the world . . . is changing," as the senior partner of Peat, Marwick, Mitchell & Co., Walter E. Hanson, puts it, "and, in so doing, has generated a subtle and significant new focus on the accounting profession. *Accounting* is changing. It is being changed by the demands of business, the demands of society, and domestic and international considerations and value shifts. The profession itself is changing from within, adapting to new emerging priorities. And last, but far from least, there is a new vigor in accounting nowadays which stems from the vitality and contemporary outlook and skills of the new accountant." Ω

environmental management opportunities for the CPA

by William G. Gaede

In the mid-1960's, new words were introduced into the vocabulary of the American public. Terms like "pollution abatement," "biodegradable" and "environmental impact statement" were seen and heard with increasing regularity as the nation became more concerned about the stewardship of its environment. The recent emergence of the energy crisis has forced us to think even harder about environmental goals now that we realize some of the sacrifices and conflicts they entail. Energy problems may postpone some environmental achievements, but there is no undoing the basic awakening we have experienced with respect to the importance of managing correctly our relationship with our environment.

As part of that awakening, the American Institute of CPAs in 1970 established a committee on

environmental accounting to monitor the involvement of CPAs in environmental management activities and to assess new opportunities for expansion of the profession's services in that area. The committee was charged with implementing the following objective:

"To compile information on the work being performed by CPAs in the area of environmental management and to recommend methods by which the resources of the accounting profession can be used effectively in resolving the ecological crisis."

Since that time the committee worked toward this objective. This article is one in a series to be produced by the committee which will furnish the profession with information concerning the professional opportunities in environmental management and how certain accounting firms are taking advantage of them.

Background of environmental management

Very simply, the environmental management opportunity is created because industries, governments and citizens create wastes that are introduced into the environment and cause harmful effects on

William G. Gaede, *CPA, is with Touche, Ross & Co. in Washington, D.C. He is currently chairman of the committee on environmental accounting of the American Institute of CPAs. Mr. Gaede is also a member of the Institute of Management Consultants.*

The Journal of Accountancy, May 1974

The AICPA environmental accounting committee believes the accounting profession can be successful in expanding its practice into new areas.

health, safety and the quality of life. The combined impact of these by-products has finally exceeded the ability of the environment to combat or absorb them.

Environmental management is the process of regulating man-made pollution with the goal of reducing and eventually eliminating it. Environmental management is a shared responsibility of federal, state and local government, working together with private industry and the public.

Conceptually, environmental management falls into two major categories. The first deals with the legislation and programs designed to reduce or eliminate the effects of existing pollutants on the environment. These programs can be divided into three major subcategories:

☐ Air—Cleansing the atmosphere of such pollutants as gases and tiny particles.

☐ Water—Removing such pollutants as chemicals, animal waste and heated material from streams, rivers and lakes.

☐ Land—Disposing of such solid waste as garbage and car bodies that pollute land space.

The second category covers those activities designed to keep new ventures from becoming polluters. This aspect of environmental management is known as "impact analysis." Impact analysis is a formal process of forecasting the air, water and land pollution implications of such major actions as the construction of new facilities. In essence, this category provides a system for avoiding recourse to the first category of legislation and programs designed to reduce or eliminate existing pollution.

Major legislation

Four major pieces of federal legislation correspond to the previously mentioned categories. These are significant in terms of national impact; however, many state and local laws deal with the same or similar subject matter. In some cases, federal law has preempted state and local rules; in others, there is the interweaving of responsibilities characteristic of so many areas in the American federal system. These are the four federal laws:

☐ Air—Clean Air Act of 1963, as last amended in 1970.

☐ Water—Federal Water Quality Act of 1965, as

last amended by the Federal Water Pollution Control Act of 1972.

☐ Land—Solid Waste Disposal Act of 1965, as last amended by the Resource Recovery Act of 1970.

☐ Environmental impact analysis—National Environmental Policy Act of 1969, Section 102 (c) (2).

Economics and environmental management

Typically, environmental management costs may be subdivided into these four categories:

☐ *Damage costs*—Those resulting directly from a polluting activity, such as personal illness or property damage from air pollution.

☐ *Avoidance costs*—Those incurred in order to avoid or reduce damage costs, such as driving farther to find an unpolluted beach.

☐ *Transaction costs*—The resources consumed in making and enforcing policies, such as air pollution monitoring costs.

☐ *Abatement costs*—Those associated with reducing the amount of environmental degradation, such as building and operating sewage treatment plants.

In its fourth annual report, the Council on Environmental Quality estimated that abatement costs during 1972-81 will be $274.2 billion. The major components of this figure are (a) $105.6 billion for air pollution, (b) $121.3 billion for water pollution and (c) $41.8 billion for solid wastes.

The report points out that in the past the capital investment requirements for pollution abatement have been overemphasized in relation to operating costs. In fact, over the 10-year period, operating and maintenance costs will account for 40 percent of cumulative total costs for water pollution abatement, 70 percent for air pollution and over 90 percent for solid wastes. After the economy passes through the initial period of heavy environmental investment requirements, operating costs will probably outweigh investment requirements even more.

The Council estimates that incremental pollution control costs (i.e., expenditures beyond those which would have occurred without recent federal environmental initiatives) will total $152.7 billion by 1981. Eighty percent of this amount will be borne by the private sector in response to new requirements for air and water pollution control. The public sector's share is small, because a large portion of public expenditure for solid waste collection and water pollution treatment plant operation would have occurred in any event.

The CEQ report also examines the incidence of environmental costs—the extent to which various income groups experience damages from pollution and pay for its abatement. In 1976, the report estimates, a medium-income family with earnings of $13,500 can expect to pay about 1.8 percent of its income, or about $250, for the incremental costs of abating air and water pollution and for improving solid waste disposal. About one-fourth of this amount will represent higher costs of owning and operating automobiles, and the remainder will represent generally higher prices for all consumption items.

Responsibility of the CPA to his client

Since the passage of these laws, a new body of knowledge has been created which the CPA must be familiar with in order to properly serve his clients. Today, most businesses, utilities and governmental entities are subject to or affected by some provision of one or more of the four federal statutes or a state or local pollution control law. As a result, the CPA must now know what they say and require. He must be able to assess the financial impact of these statutes on the client's business in order to properly determine the cost or pricing consequences for the products or services produced. He must know the administrative and reporting requirements attached to grants-in-aid received by local governments and sewer districts. This knowledge is important whether the CPA is serving his client as auditor, tax adviser or management consultant.

Some specific examples illustrate the new dimensions confronting the CPA. In the area of taxation, the federal Tax Reform Act of 1969 allows an individual or corporate taxpayer to amortize the cost of a certified pollution control facility over a 16-month period. This facility must be certified by both the state and federal agencies. Some state and local statutes also allow the purchaser to accelerate the depreciation writeoff value over a period of from one to five years of income tax and/or franchise tax purposes, or exempt the purchase of pollution abatement equipment from sales and in-use taxes, or exempt pollution abatement installations from property taxes.

Another area in which knowledge of the environmental requirements is important concerns filings with the Securities and Exchange Commission for publicly held companies. Under the terms of SEC Release 33-5386, adopted amendments for Forms S-1, S-7 and S-9 and Forms 10-K and 8-K require the disclosure of the effects of compliance

> In 1976, the report estimates, a medium-income family with earnings of $13,500 can expect to pay about 1.8 percent of its income, or about $250, for the incremental costs of abating air and water pollution and for improving solid waste disposal.

with federal, state or local environmental requirements upon capital expenditures, earnings and competitive position. The release also requires disclosure of administrative or judicial proceedings arising from such requirements and modifies certain disclosure requirements for litigation and the basis for determining when claims for damages are material. This release is effective for reports and registration statements filed on or after July 3, 1973.

Environmental accounting committee surveys

To develop a better understanding of how these new federal statutes and related state and local ordinances were affecting the opportunities for the CPA, the AICPA's environmental accounting committee conducted surveys in 1972 and 1973 to determine what services CPAs were providing in the areas of environmental management. The committee selected 45 CPA firms for inclusion in the 1972 study. All of the larger firms were included based upon the known management services capabilities of these organizations. In addition, a representative sample of smaller firms was included. Of the 45 firms, 15 responded. Seven of these indicated that they had performed work in the environmental management area. In 1973, the same questionnaire was sent to these 15 and one additional firm to see whether there was an increase in the number of environmental management engagements since the previous year.

The initial questionnaire attempted to determine to what degree engagements performed by the firms over the past three years included work directed in some way toward improving the environment. It was emphasized that the nature of the engagement, not the type of client, was of primary interest.

> [One successful] firm adopted the basic strategy of accepting only those engagements that could be performed with traditional accounting skills or where such skills were a key part of the engagement.

interest. So, installation of a payroll system for a department of sanitation, for example, was not to be reported. However, a study to recommend sewage rate adjustments to cover the additional costs for a municipality to treat industrial wastes was considered relevant.

The questionnaire was designed to elicit information of four general types:

☐ General data relating to the revenue contributed from environmental management engagements.

☐ Problems encountered in providing services during the engagements.

☐ Future opportunities for the profession based on the engagements to date.

☐ Basic accounting skills that were required to perform the engagements satisfactorily.

> During the next 10 years, environmental management engagements will afford perhaps the major new field for client service in which all practitioners can participate.

In addition to the general information, specific information relative to individual engagements was requested.

While the results could not be considered statistically precise, they did give some indication of the types of services being provided and also identified other areas for services where respondents believed the CPA had something to offer.[1] From the survey the committee reached some basic conclusions:

1 Although the number of engagements in environmental management was small, the figure appears to be growing. Only 16 engagements were reported in the 1972 survey for the previous three-year period; 24 engagements were reported for the subsequent year in the 1973 survey.

2 Firms need not be among the largest to serve clients successfully in this emerging area of practice.

3 Many engagements can be performed using normal, basic accounting skills. However, the accountant must know the pertinent statutes. Also, he may need to consult with members of other professional disciplines on certain points involving engineering concepts, etc.

4 Successful development of a practice in this area requires planning. The CPA must make a special effort to enlarge his reading list, learn new information and add to his circle of professional acquaintances.

5 While CPA skills are sufficient for many assignments, there are others in which additional resources are needed. The practitioner must learn to recognize the limits of his professional competence. This means understanding federal, state and local

---

[1] Gratis copies of the survey may be obtained in reasonable numbers from John R. Mitchell, Director, Management Advisory Services Division, AICPA, 666 Fifth Avenue, New York, N.Y. 10019.

statutes and developing working relationships with civil engineers, microbiologists and landscape architects, all of whom can provide complementary skills.

The survey results also identified many different opportunities for performing engagements in environmental management. The following were among the opportunities mentioned:

1 Assistance to commercial and industrial concerns

☐ Performing economic studies to determine the feasibility of installing pollution control and recovery systems.

☐ Evaluating the impact of new construction projects on the ecological balance of the environment.

☐ Determining the impact on operating costs of installing new pollution control equipment.

☐ Analyzing the cost impact on product profit margins for businesses meeting new environmental control requirements.

☐ Performing studies to determine the appropriate treatment of corporate expenditures devoted to environmental preservation or improvement.

☐ Expanding the scope of traditional financial audits to evaluate compliance with pollution control standards or regulations and determining the associated costs.

2 Assistance to governmental units

☐ Developing new methods of public financing for pollution abatement programs.

☐ Designing new environmental information systems that statistically monitor pollution incidence and other quantitative data.

☐ Developing new standards and regulations for waste and water controls.

☐ Estimating the financial or economic effects of implementing various alternative pollution control or abatement programs.

☐ Forecasting the impact of new environmental policies on a specific enterprise, industry or geographic area.

☐ Performing compliance audits for recipients of federal grants.

☐ Designing procedures for measuring the benefits derived for implementing antipollution regulations.

A successful firm

In order to illustrate the applicability of this type of work to firms of all sizes in the profession, the committee explored in depth the characteristics of one of the smaller firms that had been successful in developing new work related to the area of environmental management. At the time of the 1972 survey, this firm had approximately 30 professional associates. In excess of 10 percent of its total gross services was being obtained in connection with environmental management.

This firm adopted the basic strategy of accepting only those engagements that could be performed with traditional accounting skills or where such skills were a key part of the engagement. Engagements not meeting this test would be referred to firms in other professional disciplines. The firm would maintain an active relationship with selected firms in these related professions. As a result of this relationship, it could employ these specialist skills needed to supplement those of the firm on a specific engagement. The firm employed the following procedures in implementing this basic strategy:

1 Subscribed to environmental reporting services and periodicals which enabled the firm to become familiar with the basic subject matter and the changes taking place through new laws and regulations.[2]

2 Became involved in community affairs of an environmental nature, such as citizens' boards and commissions, where an accountant's expertise can be productively applied and demonstrated.

3 Attended related professional programs and participated in conferences on environmental matters, such as those conducted by the local university or college.

4 Developed and maintained an active relationship with other firms in related professions possessing interdisciplinary skills which might be required in performing environmental management projects. Examples of such firms are engineers, landscape architects, investment bankers, lawyers and civil engineers.

5 Studied various state and local statutes covering environmental practices and controls and determined where they were applicable to local problems.

6 Began talking to clients about the financial implications of the new laws and regulations on the client's business, especially in the area of capital investment, operating costs and product pricing.

Through following such a strategy, the firm has significantly expanded its practice in a new area, which it had not previously considered possible. Similar types of efforts have been undertaken by other firms. The environmental accounting committee believes that successes of this type can be generated almost anywhere today, since the laws and regulations which have created this opportunity are so widely applicable. During the next 10 years, environmental management engagements will afford perhaps the major new field for client service in which all practitioners can participate. All they have to do is seize the opportunity. ■

---

[2] For a list of the resources available to expand a CPA's knowledge in the environmental area, see JofA, July73, pp.75-79.

PERSONAL FINANCIAL COUNSELING BY CPAs— A NEGLECTED SERVICE

An efficient program can put financial counseling within the grasp of many of the CPA's individual tax return clients.

by Rudolph J. Bergwerk

In the early 1970s financial counseling became a fashionable fringe benefit for executives. The need for financial counseling had always existed, but widespread recognition of that need came as a result of aggressive promotion by consulting firms, banks and insurance agents. Because the cost is high, company-sponsored financial counseling is normally restricted to senior executives. A survey conducted by the Conference Board[1] shows that the cost per executive ranges from $3,000 to $5,000 for the first year and $1,000 to $2,000 per annum thereafter.

However, senior executives are not the only ones who need financial counseling. Every CPA who prepares individual income tax returns knows many clients who could benefit from systematic financial planning. Even financially sophisticated people have gaps in their knowledge, and there are many who simply never get around to putting their own houses in order.*

Financial counseling has a tremendous potential for the CPA if it is properly promoted and priced. Promotion may consist of an explanation of a program when it becomes apparent that a client needs more guidance than a few remarks made incidental to the preparation of the income tax return.

Free Financial Counseling

Financial counseling has many facets. For instance, selling life insurance is, in effect, a form of such counseling. As part of the selling job, the insurance agent will depict the prospect's exposure to various contingencies and the need for prompt action, i.e., buying insurance that will mitigate or even nullify the financial impact of death, illness, accident

RUDOLPH J. BERGWERK, CPA, is a sole practitioner in East Orange, New Jersey. He is a member of the AICPA and the New York and New Jersey state CPA societies. He is the author of "Effective Communication of Financial Data," which appeared in the February 1970 *Journal*.

The Journal of Accountancy, May 1978

[1] Burton W. Teague, Conference Board Report no. 608, *Financial Planning for Executives* (New York: Conference Board, 1973).
* Ed. note: Information on how an individual might include members of his family in the tax planning aspect of financial counseling can be found in Stanley H. Breitbard's article in this issue's Statements in Quotes department, page 80.

or other casualty. The pitch of a life insurance agent is the only source of financial planning for many people.

Of course, insurance agents must concentrate their efforts where they can write new business. The client never knows if he really needs that much insurance (or a new policy) or if the agent has made these recommendations merely to earn a commission.

Insurance agents are not the only ones who offer free financial counseling; salespersons of all kinds use financial advice as a selling tool. The quality of this advice varies a great deal, since some salespersons really know what they are selling and can give expert advice, while others offer as technical advice a thinly veiled sales pitch.

The Need for Objectivity

There is an obvious need for disinterested advice that will help the prospective investor evaluate the counseling proffered by persons who make their living selling insurance, pension plans, securities, tax shelters and other investment opportunities. The first requirement for objectivity is financial independence, i.e., the counselor should not derive any profit from the investment decisions of his client.

An objective evaluation of the quality of a particular investment is not enough; what is a good investment for one person may be unsuitable for another. Therefore, the second requirement for objective advice is a thorough analysis of all relevant facts. Financial counseling on a piecemeal basis without adequate background information is usually unsatisfactory.

The third requirement for objectivity is the state of mind of the counselor, who must try to suppress his personal preferences. This is far from easy. For instance, CPAs and other tax advisers must banish from their minds the notion that the value of their advice is contingent upon the amount of taxes that will be saved. At times it may be preferable to pay more taxes in order to avoid the consequences of transactions designed to reduce tax liability.

While objective advice is a desirable goal, usefulness is more important than abstract objectivity. A long dissertation detailing the pros and cons is of no use to a client who wants his question answered with a simple yes or no. Even though most problems do not lend themselves to such a solution, many clients feel let down when their advisers are unable to present findings in a usable form.

The Scope of Financial Counseling

Financial counseling includes all aspects of an individual's finances, such as advice on budgets, debt management, income tax planning, investments (including tax shelters), insurance programs, employment contracts, retirement plans and estate planning.

Complete financial counseling requires the services of more than one professional adviser, and best results are obtained through a team effort by an accountant, an attorney and an insurance expert. A bank trust officer and investment advisers may also be part of the team. When costs are not of critical importance, the team can meet as a committee; otherwise a coordinator is needed to make sure that all other consultants base their recommendations on adequate background information.

The services of an attorney are essential because nobody else can draw up wills and other legal documents. The degree of the attorney's participation in financial counseling will depend on both the personal relationship between lawyer and client and the willingness of the client to pay for legal services.

The services of a well-qualified insurance broker are necessary in order to achieve a sound and well-balanced insurance program at minimum cost. Costs can be reduced by avoiding duplication and unnecessary coverage and by obtaining insurance from the best source.

A trust officer can give advice based on his experience with problems arising during the administration of trusts. Whether a bank should be a trustee under a "living" or under a testamentary trust will depend on the size of the trust and the availability of relatives or friends capable of acting as trustees.

The Role of CPAs

A CPA is the obvious person to act as coordinator of the financial counseling team because he is most likely to have the necessary qualifications by training and experience. Furthermore, the fact that CPAs are bound by a code of ethics ensures that there will be no conflict of interest. Clients know that the advice given by CPAs is not influenced by the prospect of earning commissions or finders' fees.

The Journal of Accountancy, May 1978

Accounting has been defined as the organization and presentation of financial data in a form suitable for decision making. This is, in effect, the foundation of financial counseling. After reviewing all of the "what ifs," the coordinator has to prepare, at least mentally, a series of pro forma personal financial statements giving effect to all options. Some of these pro formas will be so unrealistic that they can be rejected outright—some options or certain combinations of options simply are not feasible. Through a process of elimination the counselor will come up with options worthy of further consideration.

Personal financial planning is similar to the preparation of budgets for commercial enterprises. In few cases can a financial counselor come up with solutions that are so obvious that they can be presented to the

"A realistic financial plan should use as a starting point the cost of maintaining the present standard of living."

client in the form of instructions. Nearly every solution will have its drawbacks so that the decision will have to be made by the client.

Insurance is a typical example. Some people want to be fully insured against all risks; others find the resulting premium cost too high and are willing to take their chances with a lower level of coverage. There are many other decisions which cannot be made by the counselor. Unless the client is actively involved in the decision-making process, the financial plan becomes nothing but a useless, albeit expensive, piece of paper.

Establishing a Financial Counseling Program

A formal program for a financial counseling engagement may be compared to a program for an audit engagement. Both are indispensable, but there is an important difference. For financial counseling the program is not a mandatory work schedule but a comprehensive checklist of what might be needed. The counselor has to decide which information requests are relevant and which are unnecessary.

Every audit involves a considerable amount of cost and inconvenience, but when an unqualified opinion is essential, the client has no choice. Collecting data for financial counseling is more difficult, since clients will

balk at what they consider unnecessary cost and inconvenience, particularly when they personally will have to dig up information, fill in questionnaires and look for papers. The counselor should, therefore, be prepared to explain why each request for details is appropriate and necessary.

Assuming that the client has already been "sold," we divide our financial counseling program into 10 segments. Willingness to pay the fee is not enough; the client has to know exactly what financial counseling involves and has to be willing to give sufficient thought to the questions to be answered.

1—Preparation of Personal Balance Sheets

At least two balance sheets are required, one for the beginning of the year and one for the yearend. These balance sheets have to be in sufficient detail to serve the following purposes:

☐ Determining net savings for the year. For this purpose assets must be shown at cost. Savings will, of course, include increase in cash value of life insurance, amortization of home mortgage and changes in other indebtedness. Net savings will be a negative figure when the net worth at yearend is less than at the beginning of the year.

☐ Relating assets to future needs. For this purpose assets must be shown at market value.

☐ Review of investment mix. This review pertains to adequate liquidity, diversification, yield, safety and appreciation potential.

☐ Estate planning. Present net worth plus life insurance and other death benefits are the basis of a realistic estate plan.

Estimates and approximations can be used initially if the client cannot retrieve the papers relating to the acquisition of assets. Financial counseling requires an annual follow-up and updating; eventually the balance sheet and supporting schedules (if needed) should show the cost and date of acquisition of every asset because this information will be needed sooner or later.

2—Preparation of a Cash Flow Statement

A realistic financial plan should use as a starting point the cost of maintaining the present standard of living. The most painless way to arrive at this figure is to determine the total cash available by adding tax-free income and other cash receipts to the income shown on the tax return. The residue after deducting taxes, insurance premiums, nonrecurring expenditures and net savings (obtained at step 1) represents the basis for preparing a budget.

It is always advisable to keep work at a minimum; at least initially, it is sufficient to break down expenditures into five categories: taxes, insurance, savings, nonrecurring expenses and normal living expenses. After a review of savings and insurance needs, a client may decide to reduce his standard of living.

3—Review of Insurance Coverage

Most agents provide an insurance analysis as a free service, but insurance is important enough to warrant an independent review of the analysis and recommendations furnished by the agents.

☐ Property insurance. The review will ascertain whether insurance valuations are realistic. Since insurance companies have to charge premiums that exceed their actuarial risk, it pays to have large deductibles.

☐ Liability insurance. Jury awards become larger every year and adequate coverage may, in the span of a few years, become inadequate.

☐ Health insurance. Most policies have a dollar limit and a time limit for any one disease. Sometimes the dollar limit may be adequate, yet people who contract a chronic disease may find themselves without coverage after the expiration of the time limit of as little as two years.

☐ Disability insurance. Full coverage includes income replacement until normal retirement age, the value of homemaker services and the additional cost of caring for a person who is disabled but does not require enough treatment to be covered under a medical policy. Such a comprehensive coverage will probably be too costly, particularly since only the social security portion of the disability income will go up automatically with inflation. The affordable amount of disability income insurance needs to be calculated as part of the financial plan.

☐ Life insurance. A great deal of thought should be given to the amount and the type of life insurance needed. Strictly from an insurance point of view, the coverage should be equivalent to the potential financial loss, i.e., the after-tax income less the living expenses of the insured. In most cases this full coverage will be beyond the means of the insured. Furthermore, since the insurance in-

dustry must meet overhead and make a profit, the premiums will be considerably more than the risk covered.

An alternative approach is to carry the minimum amount of insurance needed to prevent excessive hardship in the event of untimely death. There are tables which show that insurance amounting to three to eight times the annual gross income is necessary for the family to maintain the accustomed standard of living. These tables are based on the assumption that the widow will not remarry and remains a full-time homemaker. Usually, the first impulse is to provide generous insurance protection, but this creates the problem of fitting the required premiums into the budget. Varying the assumptions which determine the amount of insurance needed is, therefore, part of the financial budgeting process.

The cost of life insurance is an important item; however, so few buyers are able to make meaningful cost comparisons that there appears to be no price competition among companies. An important function of financial counseling is to ensure that interest-adjusted cost comparisons are available for life insurance decisions. Agents can supply these figures, and, to be on the safe side, more than one agent should be consulted. The Denenberg report[2] is also helpful in ranking life insurance companies.

The comparison between straight life and renewable term insurance should be based on the length of time the coverage will be needed. Straight life insurance has the advantage of doubling as a forced savings plan. Although the yield may not be very exciting, life insurance is the only asset for many people.

4—Estate Planning

Everybody likes the idea of saving taxes, and the tax aspect of estate planning is generally emphasized because it shows the need for and the benefit of professional advice. However, tax planning cannot come until after the difficult decisions of who should get how much and when.

Although small estates may not present any estate tax problems, they do require as much thought and planning as a large estate —perhaps even more so when there are not enough assets to provide fully for all needs. The testator should weigh the actual and potential needs of dependents and of others

[2] A Shopper's Guide to Life Insurance (Harrisburg, Pa.: Pennsylvania Insurance Department, 1972).

under consideration as heirs. Sound estate planning requires the contemplation of a premature death of one or more designated heirs, extraordinary needs due to illness and other causes as well as the rest of life's vicissitudes.

A "sprinkling" trust may be the best solution when the estate is too small to take care of all the potential needs of the designated heirs. It would then be up to the trustees to apportion the estate. Before this type of trust is considered, the testator must find persons in whose judgment he has enough confidence to entrust them with such discretionary powers.

The parent of a minor child also needs to decide who should be guardian in case both parents die.

Larger estates present an opportunity for tax planning, but planning cannot take place until the testator has come to grips with the problem of distribution. Too large an inheritance could cause more harm than the hardship of not having enough money.

The testator should know how much his estate would be worth were he to die suddenly. Although this information is not essential for drafting a will, it is important that the testator and all professional advisers know the value of the estate because it can affect many options and decisions.

Some assets will bypass the probate estate (pass without the will), often distorting the intended distribution among heirs. Because many life insurance policies have been in force for a long time, the client may have

> "Personal financial counseling is concerned with balancing the budget primarily through control of expenditures."

forgotten assignments or changes in beneficiaries made years ago. There is no assurance that all assignments and changes in beneficiaries have been attached to the policies. It is, therefore, important to verify ownership and beneficiaries of all life insurance policies by directly communicating with the insurance companies concerned. Similarly, employers should be contacted for verification of beneficiary designations under company benefit plans.

Before seeing an attorney about making out a will, the testator should give a good deal of thought to the following points to make the consultation more productive:

☐ Who should get what, taking into consideration that one or several intended heirs could die prematurely, either before or soon after the death of the testator.

☐ Whether the estate should be distributed as soon as possible or whether assets should be held in trust.

☐ Whether the share of each heir should be determined in the will or whether trustees should have discretionary powers to make distribution in light of changing needs and circumstances.

☐ Who should be the executor(s).

☐ Who should be the trustee(s).

☐ Who should be the guardian of a minor child.

These decisions may take time, but there should be no delay when no valid will exists. Absence of a will does not confer immortality but merely wastes assets of the estate. An important function of financial counseling is to ensure that there are valid and up-to-date wills for both spouses.

5—Future Needs and Plans

Assigning a present dollar cost is the first step in planning for future needs, which might include such items as a down payment on a first home, education of children or eventual retirement. Uncertainty over the future rate of inflation makes computation of total eventual needs difficult. One way to approach this problem is to disregard anticipated investment income; in other words, we assume that investment income will just about equal the erosion of the principal due to inflation. By comparing the savings presently available with today's cost we can get the amount still needed in current dollars.

As far as retirement income needs are concerned, life expectancy for males at age 65 (based on U.S. mortality experience 1969-71) is 15 years. Life insurance companies use the individual annuity table for 1971, which shows a life expectancy for a 65-year-old male as 17 years. (The discrepancy in life expectancy is designed to generate reserves for the insurance companies.) We recommend that, in order to take care of continued inflation, savings available at retirement should be about 200 times the monthly retirement income desired.

Annuities are an ideal investment for retired people of limited means who want to enjoy their savings during their lifetime. The guaranteed monthly income means that they don't have to worry that they will outlive their savings.

Evaluation of future needs and plans is also important for investment decisions. In order to avoid liquidation losses, investment should be designed to mature when funds will be needed.

6—Budget Preparation

Personal financial counseling is concerned with balancing the budget primarily through control of expenditures. Keeping a record of all monies spent is not often a workable suggestion; most people have an intense dislike of personal bookkeeping that is aggravated every time they have to prepare an expense reimbursement voucher.

An overall approach has a better chance of success. We compare anticipated income with current expenditures (step 2), insurance needs (step 3) and the need for saving (step 5). More often than not, the total of needs will exceed the available income. If this is the case, the client will have to decide whether to save less, to carry less insurance or to lower his standard of living. Experience has shown that presentation to the client of options within this type of framework is all that can be achieved initially by the financial counseling process. However, it would be unwise to make insurance or saving commitments based solely on the client's intention to cut expenses drastically. Only an annual follow-up can show to what extent expenses can be controlled.

7—Debt Management

There are three aspects of debt management: interest costs, maturities and the reasons for borrowing.

Every tax return preparer is aware that many people pay too much interest. Sometimes the cause is pure negligence, such as missing the deadline shown on credit card statements. More frequently, we find that people borrow from the more expensive sources because of the attractiveness of privacy and the convenience of "loans-by-phone" or mail order loans. Another cause of excessive interest is human nature and the dominance of hope over facts. Passbook loans which are continued year after year are a relatively harmless example. Much more costly are credit card purchases, which incur an 18 percent finance charge, when the buyer could have withdrawn the amount from a savings account earning over 5 percent interest. Auto loans can present the fi-

nancial counselor with a dilemma. It is easy to demonstrate on paper the advantages of withdrawing from a savings account the amount needed for the purchase of a new car, but many car buyers consider it wiser to take out a loan which forces them to make regular monthly payments.

Financial counseling seeks to explore all sources of credit, including life insurance policy loans, margin accounts, automatic checking account overdraft facilities and first mortgages. The ultimate decision will have to rest with the client, who may feel that certain types of loans threaten his sense of financial security. However, it cannot be disputed that good debt management means borrowing from the cheapest source while at the same time leaving open an adequate borrowing capacity as reserve for emergencies.

Watching maturities is essential for a good credit rating. Rollovers of demand loans should be discussed with the lender well in advance of the due date. Payments on installment type loans should be made within the grace period since late charges are detrimental both to the credit rating and the pocketbook. Incurring late charges can be accurately described as paying interest at an annual rate of 60 percent. Every financial counseling program ought to include an explanation of the importance of avoiding late charges.

Examination of the reason for the indebtedness is another function of financial counseling. When debt is incurred to acquire or hold investments, the carrying costs should be compared with the yield and appreciation potential of the investments. People who go into debt by living beyond their means certainly need financial counseling, but before accepting such an engagement, a CPA should remember that neither training nor experience will automatically qualify him to help compulsive spenders.

8—Tax Planning

Tax planning falls into three categories: timing of transactions which could take place either late in the year or early in the next, using all tax-free fringe benefits and tax-favored investments.

The timing of income, deduction, capital gains and losses can be important even though many events do not lend themselves to advance planning, e.g., few people know in summer whether they will have substantial medical expenses in December. Similarly, the timing of sales of investments is governed mainly by the market, or by the opportunity to find a buyer willing to pay the right price. When advance planning is not practical, financial counseling still has an educational value through its explanation of which events or proposed transactions warrant an evaluation of the tax effect—and a fee for the service.

Tax-free fringe benefits are worth more than the same amount paid out as taxable salary. It is in the interest of the employer to get the most employee satisfaction from each compensation dollar, but it is up to the executive to state his preference and initiate negotiations for an alternative compensation plan. Whenever there is the slightest chance that the employer is amenable to change, a review of the present compensation package is indicated.

The tax saving resulting from employee fringe benefits, including qualified retirement plans, should be carefully examined when a client wants to know the advantages and dis-

> "Unlike professional investment advisers, whose living depends on creating the impression that they can do better than the market, CPAs do not have to pretend that they know which investments will prove superior."

advantages of incorporating a proprietorship or a partnership. Not surprisingly, insurance agents and retirement plan specialists who stand to benefit from such a move will tend to base the comparison on assumptions skewed toward incorporation.

The most productive tax planning revolves around investments. The Tax Reform Act of 1976 has, for all practical purposes, put an end to highly leveraged shelters that could yield immediate tax savings in excess of the investment. Furthermore, since it is likely that the assault on tax shelters will continue, it becomes necessary to evaluate the merits of each proposed tax shelter on the basis of its anticipated cash flow and the tax consequences over its entire life without having to rely on rollovers later on.

Qualified retirement plans are a superior tax shelter because they permit the deduction of the investment from the taxable income

without having to participate in a venture that shows losses.

Deferred compensation can also be considered as an investment and should be so evaluated. When the employee has a choice between current and deferred compensation, the present after-tax value should be compared with the future after-tax value to arrive at its yield. If the employee does not have a choice, the adviser should compute the present value of deferred compensation by using an appropriate interest factor.

9—Investment Strategy

Portfolio review and the planning of an investment strategy constitute an important part of financial counseling. Most clients would prefer to receive specific investment advice, but a CPA should not really be thought of as a professional investment adviser.

Few professional investment advisers can honestly claim that they outperformed the market over the long run. Portfolio managers of mutual funds, whose performance can easily be gauged against the various market indexes, have lately been singled out for criticism. The poor performance, as a group, of even the most highly qualified security analysts has given rise to the index funds, which are based on the concept that, over the long haul, nobody can beat the market.

Unlike professional investment advisers, whose living depends on creating the impression that they can do better than the market, CPAs do not have to pretend that they know which investments will prove superior. The function of the CPA as adviser is to assist in the formulation of an investment strategy by concentrating on such essential areas as tax consequences, liquidity, appropriate risk and suitable investment media.

Tax consequences are an important factor in the selection of investments. Politicians continually woo voters with promises that all tax shelters will be abolished, but by no stretch of the imagination can our present tax system be so modified that tax aspects will have no bearing on investment decisions. The yield on tax-favored investments tends to be lower than the yield on investments of similar duration with comparable risk that are taxable as ordinary income. Sellers of tax-favored investments stress the tax advantages, but it is up to the buyer's adviser to come up with a meaningful comparison based on the actual tax situation of the client. A typical example is municipal bonds. Comparison of their yields with the after-tax yield of corporate bonds can be misleading when the purchase of municipals has an effect on the interest deduction allowed.

The need for liquidity has to be determined on the basis of various factors such as job security, health insurance coverage, investment needs and available credit facilities. Anybody who holds securities on margin has to weigh the possibility of margin calls and sudden cash needs in order to guard against being hurt by a temporary decline.

The degree of risk which an investor is willing to accept is his personal decision. It should be governed by the age, income, resources and temperament of the investor— in other words, by how badly he can afford to get hurt when an investment turns sour.

Present investments reflect the preference of the investor even in the absence of a formal strategy. Consequently, all plans should use as a starting point the existing investments and resultant mix of securities, real estate and rare objects. When the holdings of securities are substantial, the services of a bank trust department should be considered. Important points which influence this decision are whether the client enjoys selecting his own investments and related activities as well as his past performance.

A portfolio review by a financial counselor should concentrate on the quality of each stock in terms of institutional acceptance, on the choice between growth and income stocks and on adequate diversification. Finally, there should be an evaluation of the advantages and disadvantages of mutual funds as an alternative to direct investments.

Real estate has desirable investment features such as protection against inflation and a tax-favored treatment of income, but owning rental property should be regarded as a business rather than as a passive investment. It should be recommended only when the client has the time, the inclination and the ability to manage rental property.

The rapid increase in the price of collector's items—ranging from paintings to classic cars—has blurred the distinction between hobby and investment. The purpose of an investment is resale at a profit. Since dealers work on a healthy margin, it is a good rule of thumb that articles bought from dealers and resold through dealers have to appreciate at least 50 percent before the investor can break even. The investor in rare objects has to keep abreast of the market both to buy

right and to be able to unload before tastes and demands change; the only way to get a realistic idea of currently obtainable prices is to keep trading. Sales should amount to at least 25 percent of purchases, and, needless to say, they should be independent sales because trade-in values are no real indication of prices which cash buyers are willing to pay. Concomitantly, disposing of less desirable items leads to a better collection.

10—Written Report

At the conclusion of every financial counseling engagement, a written report should be prepared summarizing the work done and listing in detail recommendations and unresolved issues. The report should contain the following:

☐ Balance sheets with supporting schedules listing in detail all available information.

☐ Cash flow statements giving a breakdown of the prior year's expenditures.

☐ The budget.

☐ Comments on property insurance that state on what information the conclusions are based (for instance, on a review of original insurance policies and replacement costs or merely on a review of an analysis prepared by an insurance agent).

☐ A statement whether potential personal property insurance claims can be adequately supported by an inventory or photographs.

☐ Comments on whether liability insurance appears to be adequate.

☐ Comments on hospitalization and major medical insurance coverage.

☐ Comments on disability insurance coverage.

☐ Comments on life insurance coverage.

☐ An estimate of the value of each beneficiary's share if the testator were to die tomorrow (if there is no valid will, the financial counseling engagement is incomplete).

☐ A schedule of assets that will bypass the probate estate, such as life insurance proceeds and jointly held property.

☐ An estimate of social security benefits available to survivors.

☐ An estimate of benefits available to survivors under a company benefit program.

☐ Comments on unresolved problems in connection with the will, such as provisions for various contingencies or intended reappraisal of executors, trustees or guardians.

☐ Comments on amounts which need to be saved to meet future needs.

☐ Comments on debt management.

☐ Suggestions for tax-saving changes in the compensation package.

The Journal of Accountancy, May 1978

☐ Comments on whether liquidity of investments is adequate for emergencies.

☐ Comments on current investment strategy or the absence of any discernible plan.

☐ Suggestions for strategy which will improve the investment mix in accordance with the needs, desires and goals of the client.

The preparation of the written report is the culmination of the engagement. It involves a considerable amount of work and may contain many important recommendations and suggestions, yet experience has shown that a written report delivered by mail is worthless because somehow clients never seem to get around to acting on any of the suggestions. A problem can be discussed orally at great length until each party is satisfied that all grounds have been covered. Not until the discussion has been reduced to writing does it become clear whether anything has been accomplished. In addition, a written report is essential to enforce discipline. The written report may not have too much value on its own, but it is extremely useful as a memorandum of the recommendations and suggestions discussed orally.

All statements and schedules should be submitted, even if they are based on incomplete information and estimates (any deficiencies must be clearly indicated). In the absence of a proper audit, a review by the client is the next best thing. It will bring to light misunderstandings or missing information, such as the disposition of assets, as well as act as an incentive for the client to dig up the required information.

The Benefits of Financial Counseling

In many cases a financial counseling engagement will lead to specific recommendations that have value which can be measured in dollars. In these instances, the tangible benefits will probably far outweigh the cost of financial counseling. No dollar value can be assigned to recommendations dealing with contingencies, but, in any case, specific recommendations are merely a by-product of the engagement.

The main purpose of financial counseling is educational. The economics of a professional service do not leave much room for handholding; in the absence of any specific problem, a client who is not in business should meet with a CPA only twice a year: once for tax return preparation and once for a financial counseling follow-up. Most clients would prefer to combine both, but CPAs are generally too busy during the tax season for nonemergency financial counseling.

The annual follow-up is needed to nail down the benefits of the initial engagement. In addition to updating the work done previously, the follow-up ensures that there is a definite date for a reconsideration of unresolved issues and a reappraisal of all plans.

After a few years, financial counseling becomes comparable to an annual audit or to an annual physical checkup. All are undertaken primarily as precautionary measures and everyone involved is just as happy when nothing remarkable is found.

In conclusion, personal financial counseling represents a market for professional services that is waiting to be tapped. Every CPA who prepares individual income tax returns has clients who need counseling. Translating this need into fees requires an appropriate program, first to explain to the client what financial counseling involves and then to perform these services in a thorough, competent manner. An efficient program can bring the cost down and put financial counseling within the reach of many more people as well as apply the CPA's professional expertise to a broader range of client needs. ■

SECTION II

The Accounting Model

An information system must rely on a formal set of concepts, principles and procedures to insure the orderly processing of all relevant data. The accounting information system is built upon the accounting model which expands to specify procedures, options and choices consistent with the goal of the reporting process. Its importance traces through the entire system and is manifest in the final product or published financial statements prepared for users.

In this section, divided into six parts, a selection of readings addresses the full scope of the accounting model. Starting with fundamental issues relating to the accounting cycle, the readings move through treatments of specific types of events to issues relating to the importance of the final product and the impact of computerization and electronic data processing on the system.

As an accountant or as a user of accounting information, it is vital to understand the issues inherent in the accounting model. As a preparer of accounting information, these issues effect the very nature of the accountant's work. Wise choices can only follow a thorough understanding of relevant issues and an openness to grasp new ideas and concepts.

The user of accounting information must appreciate all of the ramifications inherent in the accounting process. Effects of alternative accounting principles will appear in the final product of the profession — the published financial statements. A total grasp of their magnitude and meaning requires an appreciation of the underlying structure. While it is possible to precisely state the accounting model, applications will be influenced by current developments. Many times, accountants face unique situations which require judgment-type decisions relative to processing data. The implications and propriety of these decisions should be explored in a broader context.

The readings in this section include graphic explanations of parts of the accounting process, current material which deals with the impact of choices made and projections as to the future effects of current decisions. They cover a broad range and present a spectrum of views relative to this important area.

THE CRITICAL EVENT AND RECOGNITION
OF NET PROFIT

John H. Myers
Professor, Northwestern University

THE matching of cost and revenue has grown during the past fifteen or twenty years into a cardinal principle of accounting. We have learned to postpone or accelerate either cost or revenue, as the case might require, in order to get all the elements of a single transaction into the same period. In spite of such problems as price level fluctuations and requirements of governmental regulatory bodies, we have made considerable headway in sharpening the determination of net income. However, in this effort to sharpen the determination of net income we have given very little attention to the timing of income recognition. We have relied on a variety of rules for specific situations, not on an over-all principle. In this paper I review both the economic concept of net income and the accounting procedure in a number of specific business situations, and then suggest a principle which is compatible with economic theory and at the same time coordinates most current accounting practice. I hope this discussion will provoke further thought on the subject leading to the ultimate refinement and acceptance of a principle which is both (1) as clear and uniform in its applicability as that of matching cost and revenue and (2) sound from an economics standpoint.

Economic theorists since the days of Adam Smith have spoken of land, labor, and capital as the three factors of production. Compensation to these factors has been known as rent, wages, and interest. Under a perfectly functioning system, these three factors receive all the income. Any residual that remains in an actual case is due to the imperfections of the system in the individual case at the particular moment of time. Later economists acknowledged a fourth factor of production: entrepreneurship. Its compensation is known as profit. Profit is the reward for bearing risk—the risk of enterprise, the risk of venturing in business, the risk of owning something in hope of selling it later. This profit may be positive or negative depending upon the entrepreneur's decisions as to the directions in which to risk his capital, his labor, and his land. This profit is very close to what the accountant calls profit.[1]

Let us assume for accounting purposes that profit is the same as the profit of the economist, a reward for having taken the risks of enterprise. This being the case, profit is earned by the operating cycle, the round trip from one balance sheet position back to that position, whether the starting point be cash or inventory or any other factor. Even in a simple merchandising business several steps occur: buying, selling, collecting. The question arises as to when during that cycle any profit should be recognized. Should the profit be recognized when a specific point on the cycle is reached, or should it be spread over that

---

[1] The accountant's profit includes, in addition to the economist's reward for bearing the risks of enterprise, "interest" on the owner's investment and, in some cases, "wages" to the owner of an unincorporated enterprise. However, these two variations do not negate the basic relationship between the profit of the accountant and of the economist. The wage element may be omitted for it is pertinent only in the unincorporated business, and even in such businesses there is a growing tendency to include a fair wage to the owner among the expenses. Interest is seldom if ever set out separately but in profitable corporations it may well be a minor part of the profit.

"Reprinted from *The Accounting Review*, October 1959, with permission of the publisher."

Recognition of Net Profit

cycle in some manner? If it should be recognized at a point, what is that point? If it should be spread, what criterion should be used? In order to set some limits on this article, I have assumed that profit should be recognized at a single moment of time. This article will be devoted, therefore, to a consideration of the moment of time at which to recognize the profit. Perhaps after considering carefully the implications of the assumption we shall be in a better position to consider the question we have by-passed.

If profit is to be recognized at a moment of time, we must select that moment. The economist gives a clue in the function of entrepreneurship as the function of directing a business, bearing the pain of the risks, and reaping the rewards of astute decisions. This suggests that profit is earned at the moment of making the most critical decision or of performing the most difficult task in the cycle of a complete transaction. Just what event this is may not be easy to distinguish in many cases. Although in most types of business we recognize profit at the moment inventory is converted into accounts receivable, such timing is far from universal.[2]

Let us examine a number of different types of businesses (1) to determine what is done and the apparent theory behind such action and (2) to test the applicability of the critical function theory in that business. In so testing the theory, we must remember that it must not fall merely because the critical function is difficult to determine. A proposed accounting theory must provide the basic objective and leave room for developing means of implementing that theory. Objectivity is one of the desiderata of any means of achieving a goal, but it in itself must not be allowed to be the goal.

Merchandising is one of the most common businesses. The merchant generally performs three steps: (1) wise buying, (2) effective selling, and (3) efficient collecting. If "wise," "effective," and "efficient" permit, there is a profit. We recognize the profit at the time the second step, selling, is performed. Two reasons commonly are given for recognizing profit at this time: (1) an asset has been transferred for a valid claim (transfer); (2) the merchant's opinion as to value is not needed (objectivity). To claim that any profit was realized at the time of purchase would be contrary to our past heritage, but to defer profit until cash has been collected is not uncommon. Major reasons for deferring profit realization until receipt of cash are the risk of collecting in full and the possibility of incurring additional expense. Bad debt and collection expenses are common, but most businesses feel that they can set up adequate reserves for the estimated expense. Thus, it sounds as if the real principle behind current practice were certainty, but that cannot be so for we do prepare income statements in spite of such major uncertainties as unaudited income tax returns and renegotiable contracts.

The principle of the critical event seems to fit the situation of the merchant very well. Where collection is a critical problem (and I doubt if there are many cases where it is), profit may be taken up at collection time. For most businesses, most of us would agree that selling is the critical event and that profit should be recognized at that time. In rare cases buying might be critical, as where an extremely good price is paid for some rapid-turnover, staple item.

A manufacturer's business is much like that of a merchant except that an extra step is added, converting the purchased raw materials into salable units. This gives

---

[2] One clue to the most difficult or crucial task in the operating cycle may be the function of the business from which the president was selected. Was he in sales, manufacturing, collection or something else? A background in sales would tend to confirm most present accounting practice.

The Accounting Review

an extra point at which profit might be recognized, i.e. time of efficient manufacture. In general we do not use this time because of uncertainty as to eventual sale price. However, in the case of gold refining where the market is assured, profit is recognized at the time of manufacture. The same reasoning as in the case of the merchant seems to apply; again it is the certainty principle. The critical event principle also is pertinent. Selling is very important in most cases; in gold mining it is a mere clerical detail, for the market and the price are assured by the government.

However, in contracting and manufacturing goods to order, especially if the manufacturing time will extend over several fiscal periods, the situation is quite different. In many cases there is no assurance the goods can be made at the contracted price. Therefore, profit is recognized when it becomes certain, when the goods have been made. The critical event theory, if applied to this situation, might be construed to come to the same answer as the certainty theory. In many cases it probably will. However, there may well be cases when profit should be recognized at sale date before the goods are manufactured. If a manufacturer regularly makes standard items for stock, it does not seem right to defer profit recognition beyond sale date merely because the item is temporarily out of stock. Somewhere between these two extremes there will be a twilight zone in which determination of the critical event will be difficult, but knowing that such an event is the determining factor would clarify thinking considerably.

Some people argue that profit can be recognized only when a transaction has been completed, when both purchase and sale have taken place. They argue that both of these elements are necessary and that the sequence of the two is immaterial. This almost assumes that the normal position is to have nothing but cash and that any other position is one of risk. A merchant would consider himself on dangerous ground, assuming he plans to stay in business, if he did not have a stock of merchandise. Anyone who has maintained a heavy cash position in the last decade or so has been assuming a position in which risk (of price level change) has been high. Consider an individual who has accumulated more funds than needed for current living and for an emergency cushion. The normal position for him is to have an investment in stocks or bonds. When he is out of the market, he is assuming substantial risk until he reinvests. There is a real question if he is to measure profit from purchase to sale of a security or to measure from the time he gets out of the market until he again assumes his normal position with respect to the market. Point of view seems all important. What is the critical function in making a profit? This question may be a most useful over-all guide.

Profit is recognized by magazine publishers in the period when the magazines are distributed. In most cases sale occurs and cash is received at the time the subscription is booked. Manufacturing costs are incurred shortly before distribution date. Advertising revenue as well as sale price are considered earned at the time of publication. There is serious question if this routine is correct even using the theory of certainty typically followed by manufacturers. Long in advance of publication date, the sales of magazines (by subscription) and of advertising are known. Printing costs are usually incurred under long-term contracts, so no element of uncertainty appears here. The only other element is the editorial one. Since most or all of the editorial staff will be paid fixed salaries, no uncertainty exists here. If the certainty theory is to be used, profit should be recognized at the time the subscription is sold. Among the currently

Recognition of Net Profit

used theories, only the completed contract theory explains the present practice.

Under the critical function theory we must determine whether sales of magazines, sales of advertising, or production of the magazines is the critical function. Without good advertising contracts, the firm cannot prosper. Since advertising rates are based on circulation, sales of magazines seems all important. However, unless the editorial work pleases the subscriber, he soon will fail to renew his subscription. The readers' response will be felt much more quickly in newsstand sales. Choice as to which of these functions is the critical one may well not be unanimous. If it is agreed that editorial work is critical and that editorial work culminates in publication, then the current practice is appropriate.

Lending agencies (banks, small loan companies, etc.) generally recognize profit over the period a loan is outstanding. When the note is discounted at the inception of the loan, the banker has, in a sense, collected the fee in advance. The fact that this fee is called interest might lead the unwary to assume that it should be spread over the period, because the payment is based on time. However, closer inspection shows that the theory behind the lending agency's recognition of gross income over the period of the loan is that many expenses (particularly interest paid on money loaned out and collection and bookkeeping expenses) are spread fairly evenly over the loan period. If expenses of setting up the loan are also spread over the collection period or are minor, the matching of revenue and expenses is well done. The resulting net income is spread over the loan period. In a sense the situation is somewhat comparable to the contractor and magazine publisher in that the customer has been "sold" at the beginning and only rendering of service is left to be performed. Profit is taken up as each piece of the service contract is com-

pleted. However, a fundamental difference exists, the manufacturer and banker have different responsibilities after "sale." The manufacturer or publisher must incur many costs to complete the service to the buyers. The banker's role is much more passive; he has only to wait for payments in the normal order of business.

The current practice of recognizing income during the period the loan is outstanding does not seem to agree with the critical function idea. The only things happening while the loan is outstanding are (1) the money borrowed to lend is incurring interest charges and (2) the economic situation is changing, especially as regards the borrower and his ability to pay. If the loan requires periodic payments there is an additional bookkeeping function. Perhaps in individual cases the critical function is the decision to loan or not to loan. If that is so, profit probably is earned at that time even though collection and exact determination of the amount might be delayed quite some time. This delay is, I am sure, one of the reasons profit is measured over the life of a loan. The service-rendered concept might be another reason for accruing profit over the life of a loan, but my experience is that the borrower receives the greatest service at the time he gets the money. Many merchants selling on the installment plan recognize all profit at time of sale of the merchandise and set up adequate reserves for loss. Their situation is only slightly different from that of a lending agency. The goods are sold and the loan is made in a single transaction. In the merchant's case, more rests upon this event than does in the case of merely making a loan. Nevertheless, a satisfactory or unsatisfactory lending policy, it seems to me, is the one thing that makes loans profitable or unprofitable.

A company owning and renting real estate presents an interesting case. Typically, rents are taken into income in the

The Accounting Review

period to which the rent applies. Expenses are recognized as incurred. A major function of such a firm is providing various building services through payment of taxes, insurance, and the costs of maintenance, heat, and elevator operation. Rental of small dwelling units on a month-to-month basis is very different from rental of large areas for manufacturing or office use. Not only may more service be required for commercial purposes, but also the term of the lease will probably be considerably longer so that the tenant may feel justified in making many improvements to suit his operations. Even though the lease term may be short, there will be a strong presumption to renew because of the large expenses of moving. Under these circumstances, is profit really earned merely by serving the present tenants? When a major tenant occupying a whole floor or two is secured or lost, it would seem a renting firm would have real cause for a feeling of profitability or loss thereof. I would suspect the agent securing a long-term tenant would be well paid in recognition of his great service to the real estate company. The critical function theory would seem to demand that all profit for the term of the lease be recognized at this time. Practical difficulties of determining the ultimate profit from such a contract are large. The basic cause of the problem is the custom of determining profit at least annually. Although this custom is the root of the whole problem discussed in this paper, the problem is larger here because of the length of term of the contract. The practical difficulties of applying the theory in this case must not be the cause of rejecting the theory. If the critical function theory should be correct theoretically, then we must strive to find a way to apply it to the practical situation.

The theory of the critical event as the moment at which to recognize profit or loss on a transaction seems very useful. In the types of business which we have considered, it rather closely matches current practice and gives insight into the true nature of the business. It is a theory based on a fundamental economic process rather than upon such frequently used rationalizations as convenience, conservatism, certainty, tax timing, and legal passage of title. This theory may, at first, seem a radical departure from current practice. Upon further thought it does not seem so different. Perhaps this critical event theory will be rejected in favor of another, but the present status of relying upon many different theories of when to match revenue and expense cannot long stand in a profession. We need to give special attention to the development of a single theory for the timing of profit recognition.

Get it off the balance sheet! More and more frequently that appears to be the demand of corporate treasurers facing financing alternatives. Find a way to do the financing, they say, but do it so that resulting obligations do not have to be recorded. Ingenuity in structuring financing arrangements is a quality that they seek. Whereas the coup of the '60s was to pull off a pooling-of-interests business combination in purchase and sale circumstances, the coup of the '70s was to arrange

GET IT OFF THE BALANCE SHEET!

Various methods have been devised to remove debt from the balance sheet. These deletions can distort financial reporting results.

RICHARD DIETER
Partner

ARTHUR R. WYATT
Partner
Arthur Andersen & Co.

long-term financings that need not be recorded in liability incurrence situations.

METHODS THAT CAN BE USED

A number of vehicles have been developed to enable companies to obtain needed financing without including it in the balance sheet:

Finance subsidiaries. The accounting literature guiding preparation of consolidated financial statements helps by permitting the nonconsolidation of finance subsidiaries. The American Institute of Certified Public Accountants' (AICPA) Accounting Research Bulletin No. 51, "Consolidated Financial Statements," specifies that:

" . . . For example, separate statements may be required for a subsidiary which is a bank or an insurance company and may be preferable for a finance company where the parent and the other subsidiaries are engaged in manufacturing operations."

This permits nonconsolidation of finance subsidiaries, and increasingly, companies have established captive finance subsidiaries. In many cases, roughly equal amounts of receivables and debt are transferred to the subsidiary and are thereby eliminated from the consolidated balance sheet. In this era of diversified operations, however, the basis for nonconsolidation of finance subsidiaries is increasingly suspect.

Sales of receivables with recourse. Some view such transactions as the same as a secured borrowing, that is, a loan secured by the pledge of accounts receivables. Because the lender has recourse to the "seller" of the receivables in case of noncollection, this view has considerable merit; the borrowing is reported as a liability and the receivables remain on the balance sheet. Others regard such transactions as a sale of receivables, with the proceeds being applied to reduce existing borrowings. The effect on a consolidated balance sheet is similar to the creation of a finance subsidiary: Receivables and liabilities are eliminated from the balance sheet.

Product financing agreements. There has been little specific guidance on accounting for transactions involving the sale of a product accompanied by a seller's agreement to repurchase the product at a later date. In late 1978, the Accounting Standards Executive Committee (AcSEC) of the AICPA issued Statement of Position 78-8, "Accounting for Product Financing Arrangements," indicating that sales of a product with an agreement to repurchase should be recognized as a borrowing and not as a sale when certain specified charac-

tion made in the accounts of the agreement to repurchase. The effect was similar to a borrowing with the pledge of inventory, except that neither the borrowing nor the inventory was reported in the balance sheet of the borrower.

Leases. Financial Accounting Standards Board (FASB) Statement No. 13 provides guidance on accounting for leases. Unfortunately, the objectives sought to be achieved in this Statement will not be attained by application of its criteria for lease classification. While definitive statements about practice under the standard await full implementation in 1980 (when compliance becomes mandatory), early indications are that no significant increase in lease capitalization over prior practice has resulted from its application. Significant numbers of long-term leases that pass substantially all the risks and rewards of ownership of property to the lessee

an operating lease for the lessee for a given lease, but such matters are negotiated daily.

Project financing arrangements. In recent years, a number of financing arrangements have been devised for large construction and operating projects. For example, a joint venture is formed by two or more entities, with no one entity owning more than 50 percent of the venture. It is thinly capitalized and highly leveraged, generally with the debt guaranteed by the venturers. Under current accounting practice, as specified by Accounting Principles Board (APB) Opinion No. 18, "The Equity Method of Accounting for Investments in Common Stock," investments in such ventures are accounted for on the equity method, that is, no portion of the debt incurred is reported in the balance sheet of any venturer. Thus, the debt is off the balance sheet. The use of a trust to handle the financing, generally during the construction period of large capital assets, is another device to keep the borrowing off an entity's balance sheet. In late 1978, the Securities and Exchange Commission (SEC), which appears to be increasingly concerned by the spread of off-balance-sheet financing, issued Staff Accounting Bulletin No. 28, which required electric utility companies to include in their balance sheets the assets and liabilities of construction period trusts. The equity method of accounting for investments was developed to achieve improved

"By getting debt off the balance sheet, the character, or quality, of the balance sheet is improved. Ratios that have stood the test of usefulness for generations will therefore appear more favorable to the borrower."

teristics are present. Under prior practice, however, the sale of the product was often recognized (with profit recognized currently or deferred), the proceeds used to reduce existing indebtedness, and no recogni-

continue to be negotiated and accounted for as operating leases. Those who structure leases may have to work harder (and give up something of value in the process) to achieve a finance lease for the lessor and recognition of income from the investment and improved reflection of the economic earning capacity of the investor.

Additional examples of these arrangements are presented in the following section, but each method has one common characteristic: an arrangement whereby some believe—or hope—that the incurred indebtedness need not be reported in the balance sheet of the entity or entities benefiting from the borrowing. Some of the examples presented have been accounted for as off-balance-sheet financings, some as incurred indebtedness, and some were rejected for accounting or other reasons.

Timber Financing. An entity sells its standing timber at cost to a newly created thin-equity company whose sole purpose is to handle this transaction. The entity also enters into a timber-cutting contract with the newly created company, giving the entity the right to harvest certain quantities over a specified period at specified rates. The entity agrees to make certain payments at future dates should the minimum specified timber harvest not be achieved. The newly created thin-equity company finances the purchase of the timber through bank financing secured by the timber and the cutting contracts. The entity proposes to remove the timber from its balance sheet and account for the payments under the cutting contract as they are made. It would disclose the aggregate commitment under the cutting contract in the notes to the financial statements.

Through-Put Arrangement. Company A forms a partnership with Company B, a customer, to own a project and service Company B's product requirements with a through-put contract. Financing, on a nonrecourse basis, is obtained for 80 percent of the project's cost. Company A is the general partner and invests 10 percent of the partnership equity. Company B is a limited partner, owns 90 percent of the partnership equity and accounts for its limited partnership interest on the equity method of accounting, since it has no control (not being the general partner) and is not at risk on the project except to the extent of its equity investment. Company A accounts for its general partnership interest on the equity method because it has only a 10 percent equity interest. Neither company includes any of the 80 percent borrowed funds in its balance sheet.

Take-or-Pay Contract. Several utilities enter into an agreement to construct a synthetic natural gas facility. A contract is signed with an independent party for the construction of the facility. The several utilities guarantee the debt during construction. The utilities also create a new entity to own the facility upon completion. Each utility enters into a take-or-pay contract for the entire output of the facility. None of the individual utilities will own over a 50 percent interest in the new entity. Each utility will guarantee the debt of the facility and pay amounts that will cover all operating costs and debt service requirements. Because this agreement has many similarities to a joint venture, the individual utilities propose to account for it by using the one-line equity method.

Land Option. A developer buys an option on a land parcel and concurrently agrees to spend a significant amount on the development of the land under option. The option requires an initial down payment, with a continuing option payment that equates to interest. The developer proposes to defer recognition of the acquisition of the asset (land) and the related obligation under the option, even though significant amounts of development funds have been capitalized as a part of the cost of the option. In other circumstances, the developer has "sold" lots to customers while the land and related obligation is still under option and not reported on the balance sheet.

Limited Partnership. A company forms a limited partnership to finance acquisition of a property. The company is the general partner and puts in no investment. The limited partners provide 100 percent financing. The general partner guarantees the limited partnership debt and agrees to manage the property for a fee. The payments committed to by the general partner or a third party user will cover all debt service as well as the management fee. The general partner shares profits and losses with the limited partners equally until the borrowed funds are paid. At that point the general partner would receive 90 percent of any partnership profit, including proceeds from sale of the property. The general partner contends no accounting is required because he has no investment in the limited partnership and even if he did, it is improper to apply accounting to investments in corporations and to investments in partnerships.

whether or not services are actually rendered, and includes other terms that protect and provide a return to F on its investment in the committed facilities. E does not propose to account for its obligations under the servicing agreement until services are rendered and payments are made.

WHY REMOVE DEBT FROM THE BALANCE SHEET?

Many motivations exist to encourage entities to get debt off the balance sheet. While they may fall in a range from praiseworthy to suspect, the

generations will therefore appear more favorable to the borrower. The ratio of debt to equity is decreased, and such decrease is viewed positively by many who evaluate balance sheets. More frequently, however, the motive is to prevent an adverse ratio from evolving. The entity may be near a danger point in its debt-to-equity relationship based on historical standards. Additional debt could so impair the ratio that it would trigger other, more adverse, developments. Credit ratings could be altered. Borrowing costs could increase. Future expansion, replacement, or research plans could be imperiled. With all these potential adversities, it is somewhat surprising that few seem to question whether historical relationships for the debt-to-equity ratio continue to be useful to evaluate financial liquidity under current conditions. Some may feel that such questioning is for academics to pursue; why struggle with such an issue when the matter can be solved more simply by removing it from the balance sheet.

"One rather apparent explanation [for the expansion of off-balance sheet financing methods] is that existing accounting concepts of a liability are so ill-defined that they are inadequate to deal with the increasingly sophisticated financing methods being practiced today."

Servicing Agreement. E arranges for services to be rendered by F. The service involves a form of processing of a commodity owned by E. The processing is performed in a facility owned by F, and located near E's operations. The service agreement generally runs for a period approximating either the estimated useful life of the facility or the period of repayment of debt used to finance the facility. The service agreement provides for E to pay F specified fees

methods described previously rely heavily on accounting for the form of the arrangements, not for their substance. Frequently the transaction form is soundly motivated, but even more frequently, the form flows from pressures over which the borrower has little, if any, control.

By getting debt off the balance sheet, the character, or quality, of the balance sheet is improved. Ratios that have stood the test of usefulness for

Loan covenants pose even more significant stumbling blocks to accounting for financing arrangements according to their substance. Loan covenants often impose specific restrictions on the amount of additional debt a company can incur. Sometimes they specify a debt-to-equity ratio that must be maintained to prevent an existing loan from being placed in default. Loan covenants that were prepared in less-complicated times may not preclude the borrower from incurring additional obligations, such as those arising from leases, captive finance subsidiaries, or any of the project financing vehicles commonly found today. As loan covenants drafters become more sophisticated, however, they require that certain types of off-balance sheet obligations be considered the equivalent of balance sheet debt to meet the loan covenant. Consequently, new and more innovative methods are being developed. Thus, some long-used procedures for getting debt off the balance sheet (e.g., leases) no longer escape loan covenant requirements.

Other motivations may be somewhat less criticial, yet of some practical significance. Corporate planning may indicate a level of borrowing over the next several years that will press projected historical debt-to-equity ratios. While a current project may not lead to a critical problem in this area, the goal may be to get the financing for the current project off the balance sheet to provide room for future borrowing. Thus, some entities that today appear to have no real debt-to-equity problems may be using off-balance sheet methods as part of a longer-range financing strategy.

Interest cost reductions are sometimes a motivation, too. The use of a trust method by rate-regulated entities for financing projects during the construction period was principally aimed at removing the interest costs from the regulated entity's accounts during the construction period. Because interest incurred and capitalized by an entity is viewed by some analysts with suspicion, the motivation is not spurious. Likewise, some merchandisers attempt to get non-interest bearing receivables off the balance sheet in order to reduce interest costs and to improve a key ratio in the merchandising industry, the ratio of interest charges to earnings. In other industries, return on assets is considered important. Thus, removal of an equal amount of assets and debt is favorably viewed.

WHY IS OFF-BALANCE SHEET FINANCING PROMOTED?

Why has the trend of eliminating debt from the balance sheet become so pronounced, and what can be done by accounting professionals to find optimum solutions to the inherent business problems of this trend?

One rather apparent explanation is that existing accounting concepts of a liability are so ill-defined that they are inadequate to deal with the increasingly sophisticated financing methods being practiced today. The concept of a liability under historical-cost accounting relies much more on legal notions than on economic notions. If the financing arrangement does not result in legal debt to the reporting entity, that is, if that entity is only a guarantor or is only secondarily liable, a strong argument can be made to exclude the financing from the entity's balance sheet. If financial statements are expected to reveal the economic effects of transactions and other events in which the enterprise engages, reliance on the legal notion of a liability for accounting purposes needs a critical reevaluation. Accountants need to decide if their reporting is to be principally governed by legal notions (and thus by transaction forms) or by economic notions (and thus more often by transaction substance).

Another plausible explanation is that off-balance-sheet financing is a consequence of the inability of historical-cost accounting to deal effectively with inflation. Under historical-cost accounting, the effects of inflation on the economic activities of the enterprise are neither reported nor well understood: One effect is that the balance-sheet carrying amounts of many assets are currently far below their current value, whether measured on a current-cost basis, a discounted cash-flow basis, or some other measure of current value. For example, many companies have adopted the LIFO method of accounting for inventory costs, both to lower taxes and to eliminate the effect of price fluctuations on "inventory profits." Under LIFO, the carrying amounts for inventories during periods of inflation increasingly diverge from the current values of those inventories. The carrying amount of depreciable property often shows a similar disparity.

As this divergence becomes more pronounced, the pressures for getting new financing arrangements off the balance sheet increase markedly. If asset-carrying amounts were reported on their higher current-value basis, a significant portion of the increased basis (generally the amount of increase less the related tax effect) would be added to the shareholders' equity on the entity's balance sheet. Consequently, using traditional debt-to-equity relationships, entities would have additional capacity to carry increased liabilities. Similarly, to the extent that loan covenant restrictions relate to debt-to-equity relationships, such covenants would be more easily met on a current-cost basis and would thereby tend to permit companies to embark on new capital replacement or expansion programs by using traditional financing arrangements.

Thus, what we have today under the historical-cost accounting basis that underlies current practice is a failure to recognize in balance sheets the current value of assets and a consequent pressure to eliminate from the balance sheet liabilities associated with financing arrangements. In effect, accounting compensates for the understatement of asset-carrying amounts by also understating liabilities. The latter understatement is achieved through acceptance of a wide range of off-balance-sheet financing vehicles. For example, one defect in historical-cost basis of accounting during periods of inflation— the understatement of asset-carrying amounts—is partially alleviated by omitting a more or less compensating amount of liabilities. Surely, neither the business community nor the accounting profession can expect that financial statements can long retain any semblance of credibility if users come to understand the extent to which current balance sheets are being misstated. FASB Statement No. 33, "Financial Reporting and Changing Prices," is a first step in achieving greater awareness of how badly inflation distorts the balance sheet and indirectly promotes creation of novel financing vehicles.

GET IT ON THE BALANCE SHEET

Of the various methods used to get debt off the balance sheet, the FASB has dealt only with the subject of accounting for leases, and many view the conclusions of that Statement as ineffective. AcSEC has made recommendations to the FASB concerning various kinds of project financing arrangements. AcSEC has also requested the FASB to amend Accounting Research Bulletin No. 51 by requiring the consolidation of certain finance subsidiaries. The issues involved in the accounting for sales of receivables with recourse are also under active consideration by AcSEC. These AcSEC projects have been well over two years in development, a period that has seen acceleration in the use of off-balance-sheet financings.

All of these approaches, however, are likely to have only minimal long-run effectiveness. The only sound basis for achieving proper accounting for liabilities is to address the underlying concepts involved. It is hoped that the project of the FASB on the conceptual framework of financial accounting will move along more rapidly and will provide suitable bases for achieving more effective accounting for liabilities (as well as for assets, revenues, and expenses). Preparers and users of financial statements will be better served if financial statements reflect the economic—rather than legal—effects of the transactions of the enterprise. Users should no longer be expected to understand that the understatement of assets in times of inflation is partially offset by omitting substantive liabilities.

Getting debt off the balance sheet is only a symptom of a more fundamental problem in financial accounting, which is giving adequate recognition in financial statements to the varied effects that inflation can have. Getting debt back on the balance sheet will not solve all the shortcomings of the current framework of financial accounting, but it will give users a much more complete and dependable basis for evaluating financial position. □

By *Maurice Moonitz*

The Changing Concept of Liabilities

"If we compare various definitions of liabilities, some surprising results emerge, enough so to reinforce our hunch that the concept is neither simple nor well-understood."

APPARENTLY the concept of liabilities is undergoing a change. We have seen a great deal of activity recently involving the credit side of the balance sheet. For example, recent years have seen a great deal of discussion concerning the reflection of deferred taxes, the proper disclosure of pension costs, and the short but significant life of "reserves for estimated expenses" in the 1954 Internal Revenue Code. In the discussions of these and related topics, there seems to be a lack of rigorous separation between the debit and credit aspects of the transaction under scrutiny. The impression remains that most of the thought and analysis has gone into the determination of the debit, the charge to income, with the credit introduced as an afterthought. Some indication is also at hand of "bootstrap lifting," that is to say, the practice of introducing expenses or other charges into the determination of income without first analyzing the situation to determine whether or not an asset has been used up, or a liability incurred. As a result, we see fairly frequently the spectacle of expenses paired off with credits to some element of proprietary interest.

Problems of this type are not new, of course, since they are merely one aspect of the continuing problem of the relationship between the balance sheet and the income statement. But the number of examples appears to be increasing, and their importance is definitely on the upgrade. The problem of definition is explored at some length later, but here we note that current usage is clearly not able to cope with the situation. For example, we cannot agree as to whether a "deferred tax" is a real tax or not, and if it is, whether it is to be shown as a liability or "netted" against an asset. All liabilities are indeed "credits" in the balance sheet, but some credits (e.g., allowance for depreciation, allowance for bad debts) are not liabilities. As a result, we need some way to tell us which credits belong under liabilities and which do not.

These reasons seem sufficient to justify an inquiry into the nature of that which we call liabilities. Of even more importance, however, is the question as to whether we are prepared to cope with new problems as they arise, problems which will involve, among other things, some answer to the question of the presence or absence of a liability.

The diversity of liabilities

As reported in *Accounting Trends and Techniques,* the following items have appeared as liabilities, so labeled, in recent published financial statements, under a caption which clearly excluded them from proprietary elements. I am responsible for the classification employed below; it is clearly designed with an eye to the discussion which follows. The specific examples under each class are taken from recent editions of *Accounting Trends and Techniques;* I have merely paraphrased the account titles reproduced literally in that source:

(A) cases involving an outlay of cash in the near future: (1) estimated collection costs on receivables; (2) additional costs on completed contracts; (3) estimated additional costs under a performance-guarantee clause; (4) estimated costs of product or service guarantee

(B) cases involving part of an outlay in the near future: estimated loss on purchase commitments

(C) cases involving a future outlay under certain conditions: estimated sales returns and allowances

(D) cases involving future outlays, current and noncurrent: payments under a leasehold contract

(E) cases involving a possible future outlay: deferred Federal tax on income including the case of the deferred tax on installment sales

(F) cases involving financing arrangements: billings on uncompleted contracts

(G) cases involving items that are probably not liabilities at all: (1) reserve for self-insurance; (2) minority interest in a consolidated balance-sheet; (3) reserve for furnace rebuilding and relining; (4) reserve for repairs

The diversity and variety of "liabilities" listed above raise a real question as to the common thread or threads which hold them together. Later in this article we submit a framework to hold most of them.

We are not directly concerned with the question of whether liabilities include some forms of capital stock. Most of the issues involved in this inquiry would still exist even if we included all proprietorship in the liability category. We will assume, however, that a distinction between liabilities and proprietorship is made, as in fact it is in most published statements. Whether or not preferred stock is better treated as a liability than as a proprietary element becomes a secondary matter. The only necessary condition for our purposes is that someone outside the entity itself owns the residual interest.

We may decide that some of the items listed above are not really liabilities under any acceptable definition of liabilities. Certainly a revenue agent would take this position. The following propositions may help as a point of departure in discussion of the reasons for lack of agreement on what constitutes a liability. (These propositions are based on some material in Dohr, Thompson, and Warren, *Accounting and the Law*):

1. Based upon experience, accountants for the most part assume "normal" developments in the future in assessing the presence and magnitude of debts. For example, accountants assume ordinarily that contracts entered into will be honored by the participants, as in fact they are in most cases. Breach of contract is not contemplated as normal or usual. The "allowance for bad debts" measures our estimate of the extent to which this assumption is inaccurate.

2. Lawyers, in the nature of their profession, must be concerned primarily with what happens if participants do *not* live up to their agreements or, what amounts to the same thing analytically, disagree as to the meaning of the contracts made. As a consequence, the law (to the extent that it is influenced by this attitude) tends to recognize debts only when a rather rigorous set of conditions has been satisfied.

3. The income tax is influenced greatly by both law and accounting but, in addition, must recognize the demands of administration. For example, certainty and accuracy of income and of deductions may be more important than the equity of the results. Also, income tax rules and regulations must always be influenced by the Treasury's interest in protection of the revenues.

Weaknesses in present definitions

If we compare various definitions of liabilities, some surprising results emerge, enough so to reinforce our hunch that the concept is neither simple nor well-understood.

Accounting Terminology Bulletins, Review and Resume, published by the American Institute of Certified Public Accountants in 1953, covers the topic as follows:

Similarly, in relation to a balance sheet, *liability* may be defined as follows:
"Something represented by a credit balance that is or would be properly carried forward upon a closing of books of account according to the rules or principles of accounting, provided such credit balance is not in effect a negative balance applica-

ble to an asset. Thus the word is used broadly to comprise not only items which constitute liabilities in the popular sense of debts or obligations (including provision for those that are unascertained), but also credit balances to be accounted for which do not involve the debtor and creditor relation. For example, capital stock and related or similar elements of proprietorship are balance-sheet liabilities in that they represent balances to be accounted for, though these are not liabilities in the ordinary sense of debts owed to legal creditors."

Consideration of the facts noted in the last sentence of this definition has led some accountants to the view that the aggregate of *liabilities* as contemplated in this definition should be referred to as the aggregate of *liabilities and capital,* and that the balance sheet consists of an asset section, a liability section, and a proprietary or capital section, with the monetary amounts represented by the first shown as equal to the sum of those represented by the other two. The committee feels that there is no inconsistency between this view and the suggested definition (pages 13-14).

This definition says in effect that if you want to know what a liability is, ask an accountant. But I am an accountant, and you are an accountant. Whom do we ask?

Kohler (*A Dictionary for Accountants,* 1952) defines "liability" as:

1. An amount owing by one person (a debtor) to another (a creditor), payable in money, or in goods or services; the consequence of an asset or service received or a loss incurred; particularly, any debt (a) due or past due (current liability), (b) due at a specified time in the future (e.g., funded debt, accrued liability), or (c) due only on failure to perform a future act (deferred income; contingent liability).

The Committee on Concepts and Standards of the American Accounting Association, in its 1957 Revision discusses liabilities under the general category of "equities":

The interests or equities of creditors (liabilities) are claims against the entity arising from past activities, or events which, in the usual case, require for their satisfaction the expenditure of corporate resources. . . . Equities should be accorded accounting recognition in the period in which money, goods, or services are received or obligations incurred, and should be measured initially by the agreed cash consideration or its equivalent. The elimination of an equity should be recognized in the period in which it ceases to exist.

This definition is fairly loose. The one point worthy of comment at this time is that the Committee apparently identifies "liabilities" with "creditors." Since the determination of who is a creditor and who is a debtor is entirely a legal matter, the Committee apparently clings closely to

the law to determine what should and what shouldn't go into the liability section of the balance sheet.

Corpus Juris Secundum summarizes the legal attitude in Vol. 53, p. 17:

The term (liability) has been variously defined as meaning amenability, or responsibility to law; . . . the state of being bound or obliged in law or justice to do, pay, or make good something; . . . the state or condition of one who is under obligation to do at once or at some future time something which may be enforced by action. (*White* v. *Green,* 105 Iowa 181, 74 N.W. 929 adds: "It may exist without the right of immediate enforcement.") It is a condition which creates a duty to perform an act.

In a restricted sense, liability is that which one is under obligation to pay to another, that for which one is responsible or liable; that which one is under obligation to pay, or for which one is liable; one's pecuniary obligations, or debts collectively.

The first paragraph of this legal definition is surprisingly broad. If, however, we look for a legal definition of "debt," the picture changes.

. . . debt may generally be identified as an obligation to pay a fixed sum of money on a definite determinable date (with the right to enforce payment by some appropriate legal remedy) plus interest even when not earned. ("Not earned" by the debtor, I presume.) George S. Hills, *The Law of Accounting and Financial Statements* (Boston, 1957) pages 119-20.

The "restricted" definition of *Corpus Juris Secundum* and the "debt" of Hills are close in tenor to Kohler. Apparently most accountants have used "debt" as a synonym for "liability" and have therefore been constrained by the legal tests necessary to establish a debt. Not all accountants, obviously; among the examples cited at the outset, liability under leasehold contracts is clearly a "debt" in the legal sense. And yet this is the one case where most accountants will ordinarily not reflect the item at all in a balance sheet.

Vatter's definition is clearly an "accounting" definition and far from the legal concept of "debt."

As distinct from the notions of obligation or legal liability, equities are restrictions upon, or reservations that apply to the assets of the fund; they may arise from legal, equitable, economic, or even managerial considerations. Although some equities are removed by the process of disbursement, they may be discharged or they may disappear for a considerable number of reasons. . . . (Vatter, *Fund Theory of Accounting,* page 95.)

This excursion into the world of definition leaves us with a tentative conclusion—as a minimum, all items which meet the legal tests for "debt" qualify without further ado also as "liabilities." But the legal test does not establish the outer limits of the concept for accountants, either in theory or in practice. We need agreement on the area we do wish to include in the notion of liability. Ideally a definition of "liabilities" should enable us to do several things. For one thing, we should be able, by its use, to tell (a) whether all items labeled as "liabilities" in financial statements really deserve that label, (b) which of two or more alternative practices with respect to a liability is the correct one, and (c) whether financial events described in footnotes or elsewhere really should be reflected in the balance sheet itself. Of equal importance, a definition should enable us to analyze new situations as they arise in the future to determine if a liability element is present. We need this predictive feature to give continuity to what we do, and to reduce our need for and reliance on authoritative pronouncements issued after two or more alternative treatments have already been adopted.

Characteristics of a liability

The following four characteristics will serve as a starter to establish an accounting definition of liabilities:

1. A liability involves a future outlay of money, or an equivalent acceptable to the recipient.

2. A liability is the result of a transaction of the past, not of the future. "Transaction" is used here in its primary sense of an event involving at least two accounting entities—an "external transaction."

   "Transactions" encompass the following types of financial events: (a) The receipt of money from someone outside the enterprise; (b) the payment of money to someone outside the enterprise; (c) the acquisition of goods or services —materials, supplies, power, services of human beings of all types and grades, equipment, land, mineral deposits, leaseholds, etc.; (d) sales of goods or services of all types; (e) lending and borrowing of money on a short- or long-term basis; (f) the imposition and collection of taxes.

   Accruals of all sorts are omitted from this list; so are the amortization of costs, as well as all "internal transactions" such as the transfer of work in process to finished goods. These accruals, amortizations, and transfers, however, are all consequences of the transactions listed above, and hence fit into the picture neatly as arising from past events. What does not fit in so neatly are events that have not yet occurred, e.g., next month's payroll, next year's purchase of fixed assets, next quarter's borrowings against a bond issue, etc. Therefore, none of these future events will qualify as a liability under this second characteristic.

3. The amount of the liability must be the subject of calculation or of close estimation. This condition is true generally of all accounting entries and is not restricted to liabilities. Accounting Research Bulletin No. 47, issued in September, 1956, presents excellent material in this connection. After some introductory remarks, the committee states in paragraph 4 that "because of these factors, the total cost of the pensions that will be paid ultimately to the present participants in a plan cannot be determined precisely in advance, but, by the use of actuarial techniques, reasonably accurate estimates can be made. There are other business costs for which it is necessary to make periodic provisions in the accounts based upon assumptions and estimates. The committee believes that the uncertainties relating to the determination of pension costs are not so pronounced as to preclude similar treatment."

   And in paragraph 5: "In the view of many, the accrual of costs under a pension plan should not necessarily be dependent on the funding arrangements provided for in the plan or governed by a strict legal interpretation of the obligations under the plan." In other words, let the pension costs be a function of the operating factors to which they relate. Use of the legal definition of debt, however, is relied on in one recommendation of the committee (paragraph 7): ". . . for the present, the committee believes that, as a minimum, the accounts and financial statements should reflect accruals which equal the present worth, actuarially calculated, of pension commitments to employees to the extent that pension rights have vested in the employees, reduced, in the case of the balance sheet, by any accumulated trusteed funds or annuity contracts purchased."

4. Double-entry is taken for granted. If, for example, we do wish to consider the presence and influence of *future* purchases of depreciable assets, for any reason, we should consider the obligation to pay for the blamed things.

Reliance on income effect

One feature both of accounting practice and of accounting theory at the present time is the heavy reliance on the "income effect" to decide whether an item is admissible to the liability section or not. Items which apparently clearly qualify as *debts* are often omitted because their presence or absence will not affect current profits or retained earnings. The leading example here is the case of executory contracts, e.g., leaseholds. Ray Dein comments approvingly on this practice of making the balance sheet dance to the tune of the income statement in the July, 1958 issue of the *Accounting Review* ("The Future Development of Accounting Theory"). Dein quotes Pixley's 1908 book on this point (see page 391 of the *Accounting Review*).

Fragmentation in statements

One interesting manifestation in present-day accounting of this reliance on the "income effect" is the presence of fragments in the statements. Take, for example, the "reserve for estimated loss on purchase commitments." The "loss" is not the debt—presumably we owe the full amount contracted for. Literally the "loss" is the estimated amount of damages to be paid if we breach the contract. But we don't need this type of fragmentation. If we introduce into our double-entry system both the asset (goods on order) and the liability (accounts payable for goods on order), we have no problem with respect to the liability. The asset problem then becomes a problem in inventory valuation and might be solved, for example, by application of the cost-or-market rule. Under this type of analysis, the exceptional nature of the purchase commitment case disappears.

Profit calculation is certainly an important function of present-day accounting, perhaps even the most important single function it can perform. But we shouldn't concentrate exclusively on that aspect to the detriment of everything we do or could do.

Remaining examples. Let us now discuss the specific examples listed at the beginning of this article. We will use the four characteristics previously set up to test each example. These four characteristics are as follows: (1) future outlay of money or its equivalent; (2) result of a transaction of the past; (3) subject to reliable estimation; and (4) part of a double-entry system.

All of the cases involving an outlay of cash in the near future qualify as liabilities under the tests laid down. Estimates of collection costs, of additional costs on completed contracts, and of costs under various types of guarantees involve future outlays of money, clearly result from past transactions, are the subject of close estimation, and are parts of a double-entry system. The case of the estimated loss on purchase commitments

has been discussed already, under the heading of "reliance on income effect."

The case of estimated sales returns and allowances is an interesting one. If a refund is to be made, the item is clearly a liability of the sort we are talking about. If instead the allowance merely reduces the amount to be collected from the customer, it is analogous to the allowance for bad debts, and should be so classified in a balance sheet.

The outlays under leasehold contracts clearly qualify as a liability not only under the definition developed in this article, but also under the legal definitions. As a matter of fact, an old case (1903) in Kentucky states the legal principle quite well. A tenant leased a storehouse for a term of five years at a fixed rental per month. After eighteen months, the tenant failed. The court was asked to decide if the rent for the remaining forty-two months was a debt of the tenant at the date it failed. The court held that the contract was a liability. (*Hyatt* v. *Anderson's Trustee*, Ct. of Appeals of Ky., 1903. 74 S.W. 1094.) In recent years warnings have been sounded from many quarters concerning the omission of a substantial debt from the balance sheets of companies leasing properties. But accountants blithely move on, with no trace of the leasehold in the statement of financial position itself.

Deferred taxes

The wisdom of reflecting "deferred taxes" in our financial statements has been widely debated recently in THE JOURNAL OF ACCOUNTANCY and the *Accounting Review,* among other journals, although the practice itself is becoming more firmly imbedded in published statements as time moves on. Based on our own criteria, we arrive at the conclusion that if they exist at all, these deferred taxes involve a future outlay of money. They also definitely arise out of transactions of the past engaged in by a going concern; they fit into the framework of double-entry. On the basis of reliability of estimate, however, we must walk circumspectly. The strongest case for the allocation of taxes is made in situations such as the ones discussed in ARB 43, page 92, on "disclosure of certain differences between taxable and ordinary income."

If, because of differences between accounting for tax and accounting for financial purposes, no income tax has been paid or provided as to certain significant amounts credited to surplus or to income, disclosure should be made. However, if a tax is likely to be paid thereon, provision should be made on the basis of an estimate of the amount of such tax. This rule applies, for instance, to profits on installment sales or long-term contracts which are deferred for tax purposes, and to cases where unrealized appreciation of securities is taken into the accounts by certain types of investment companies.

These cases are strong because the probability is high that revenues already realized or recognized in the accounts will be taxed in some year or years. If they have not been declared for tax purposes, but deferred, then the tax on that amount of revenue is almost certain to be paid. The probabilities are somewhat less where we have taken a deduction for tax purposes greater than that shown on our financial statements. We have thereby received the benefit under the law; whether we ever will suffer a corresponding burden later on depends, among other things, on the generation of revenues in the future. To forecast future revenues is riskier than to forecast a tax payment on revenues already in hand.

"Billings on uncompleted contracts" meets the tests laid down for a liability if we interpret these billings as advances by the customer to finance the contract. In such a case, the liability will be worked off by refund of cash, or, more usually, by delivery of the completed product to the customer. Furthermore, under this interpretation, the liability consists of the total amount billed or billable; any costs incurred to date are analogous to work in process, and belong among the assets of the enterprise. If, however, this amount of billings is an excess of billings over related costs, it is an "unrealized profit" less applicable income taxes and hence belongs with the proprietary elements, not with the liabilities. Traditionally, with the possible exception of appraisal surplus, we have put only "realized" gains in proprietorship; this has forced us to put the "unrealized" elements somewhere else. But they don't fit anywhere else in the statement of financial position. Observe that this analysis indicated that the net amount of the excess of billings over related costs does not belong among liabilities, whatever the interpretation of the credit balance may be. If the customer has advanced funds, the gross amount is the liability; if the customer has made partial payment against work which has been completed, the net amount is a proprietary element.

We now come to the group which will not meet the tests for a liability. A "reserve for self-insurance" represents a possible future transaction which may never take place; it is not the result of a past one. The fact that I own a building does not doom me to suffer a loss by fire in whole or in part in any year or succession of years. My failure to make an outlay last year for insurance premiums does not create an obligation to pay out anything to anyone this year or next or the year after that. If a "reserve for self-insurance" has to exist in the statements, it should not be booked through income at all, but only through an earmarking of retained earnings.

The minority interest in a consolidated balance sheet reflects the interest of a group of proprietors, the owners of a piece of one of the constituent elements of the consolidated group. No one is obligated to pay anything to anyone at any time for this alleged liability. To whom are the checks to be issued? By whom will the money be paid? Who sues whom if the payments are not forthcoming? This minority interest is clearly a proprietary element and should not be forced into the liability category.

Reserves for furnace rebuilding and relining, or for repairs of any type do not qualify either. True, they represent outlays in the future which can be estimated with a high degree of accuracy, but they represent a future transaction, not one of the past. When we rebuild or reline a furnace, we have incurred a cost to be amortized against the subsequent periods of use; we have not paid off an obligation accumulating from past periods. The real problem here is the proper classification of the asset involved, not the determination of a liability. If, for example, we set up the lining of the furnace as a separate asset, amortize it over its useful life, then retire it and show its replacement as a new asset, we have no problem with respect to liabilities. This procedure will probably give us the same effect on income as the "liability reserve" technique, but a better balance sheet will emerge if we treat these cases as involving assets. Instead of fighting to get the "reserve for repairs" recognized as a liability item, which it is not, we should fight for better classification on the asset side and better amortization procedure with respect to the related costs.

Conclusion

Relatively speaking, the problems relating to liabilities are simpler than those relating to assets. But the growth of situations in which future obligations loom more and more important in financial position and the underlying acceptance of accrual accounting have increased the importance and the difficulty of the liability section of the balance sheet. By a more rigorous use of double-entry reasoning, and by less reliance on short-term expediency, we can make progress to improve the balance sheet and move it away from its technical function as a post-closing trial balance to its more significant function as a statement of financial position.

The Accounting Review

VOL. XXXVII   JULY, 1962   No. 3

ASSET RECOGNITION AND ECONOMIC ATTRIBUTES—THE RELEVANT COSTING APPROACH

GEORGE H. SORTER* AND CHARLES T. HORNGREN*

INTRODUCTION

SOME of the most controversial areas in accounting—direct costing, selection of inventory valuation methods, lower of cost or market, capitalization of research and other non-manufacturing costs—revolve around a central problem that permeates theory and practice. It is the asset versus expense problem that must be resolved on a most fundamental level before hoping to find answers to specific accounting controversies. In this paper we will (1) define the problem (2) examine the assumptions that have been made by accountants in dealing with this problem (3) compare and evaluate the assumptions in detail and (4) illustrate how our suggested approach—the relevant costing approach—is distinct from other commonly used approaches.

THE PROBLEM

The central issue of expiration. The central problem we must examine is found within the asset-expense dichotomy. If we accept the notion that original acquisitions always represent assets (why acquire expenses?), the central problem narrows to the expiration problem. Should the original asset be carried forward as an asset in some form, or should it be recorded as an expiration (an expense or loss)?

Basic definitions and concepts. Before analyzing the expiration problem, we should define a basic term—asset. Although many definitions of assets have been advanced, there seems to be wide acceptance of the concept of assets as service potential:

"Assets are economic resources devoted to business purposes within a specific accounting entity; they are aggregates of service-potential available for or beneficial to expected operations. The significance of some assets may be uniquely related to the objectives of the business entity and will depend upon enterprise continuity."[1]

---

* George H. Sorter is Assistant Professor in the Graduate School of Business Administration, University of Chicago. He is the author of several articles on accounting. Charles T. Horngren is Associate Professor of Accounting in the same school, is the author of a cost accounting text and co-author of a CPA problem book. He was chairman of the 1961 AAA committee on the CPA examination and was a member of the AICPA Project Advisory Committee on Cash Flow Analysis and the Funds Statement.
The authors are indebted to the members of the Workshop in Accounting Research of the Institute of Professional Accountancy of the Graduate School of Business, University of Chicago—especially Professors Sidney Davidson and David Green, Jr.—for constructive criticism.
[1] Committee on Concepts and Standards Underlying Corporate Financial Statements, "Accounting and Reporting Standards for Corporate Financial Statements, 1957 Revision," THE ACCOUNTING REVIEW, October, 1957, p. 538.

The Accounting Review

When assets have "no discernible benefit to future operations" they are expired and "may be classified as 'expense' or 'loss'."[2]

Working with these basic definitions and with the widely accepted concept of enterprise continuity, accountants have adopted two concepts to deal with the expiration decisions: (1) costs attach and (2) match costs and revenue. Certain qualifying assumptions are needed to make these concepts operational. These qualifying assumptions are basic sources of disagreement among accountants.

Costs attach. Paton and Littleton have stated:

" . . . it is a basic concept of accounting that costs can be marshaled into new groups that possess real *significance*. It is as if costs had a power of cohesion when *properly* brought into contact.

" . . . accounting assumes that acquisition costs are mobile and may be reapportioned or regrouped, and that costs reassembled have a natural affinity for each other which identifies them with the group. . . . Some costs, like manufacturing overhead, in which an affinity with a product can be detected, are allocated directly to a product . . . "

" . . . the purpose of reassembling is to trace the *efforts* made to give materials and other components additional utility."[3]

The "costs attach to product" proposition has been widely misinterpreted. For example, accounting literature is peppered with the notion that manufacturing costs somehow cling, adhere, stick, or fuse to the physical product to be sold. Although such picturesque thinking may be helpful for certain purposes, this is a good example of how Paton and Littleton's fundamental ideas can be misinterpreted. As they point out:

"In a broad sense, all costs of factors which contribute to the grand total of objects and conditions making up the economic structure of the enterprise are represented in the physical structure of the enterprise, even though it may not be expedient to assign all of them to specific sections or elements of such physical structure. Accountants have undoubtedly been unduly preoccupied with the view that assets are properly recognizable only in terms of definite units. Accounting is concerned *with economic attributes and measurements*, not with the physical layout as such."[4]

Matching costs and revenue. Paton and Littleton describe the matching concept as follows:

"Costs are traced carefully from the first acquisition of goods and services through various regroupings for the specific object of having available at the time of sale of the product information regarding *relevant* costs—that is, those costs related to a specific segment of revenue because they are *technically* or *economically* associated with the corresponding segment of product. . . .

"The ideal is to match costs incurred with the effects *attributable* to or *significantly related* to such costs."[5]

THE ASSUMPTIONS

Clearly, to make these concepts operational, accountants need workable assumptions about the italicized portions of the above quotations. When do new groups of cost possess *real significance?* When are costs *relevant?* What is *proper* contact? How are costs *technically* or *economically* associated with product? How are costs *significantly related?* To us, the formulation of convincing answers to these questions is not at all as clear-cut as many accountants maintain.

As a point of departure, let us examine and evaluate the assumptions or rules that are usually followed by three groups labeled as follows: conventional costers, variable costers, and relevant costers. We have included variable costers because the "direct" costing controversy highlights the fundamental issues. These three groups agree on the basic concepts just discussed. The question in dispute is which working assumptions or rules are most

[2] *Ibid.*, p. 541.

[3] W. A. Paton and A. C. Littleton, *An Introduction to Corporate Accounting Standards* (American Accounting Association, 1940), pp. 13–14. (Emphasis supplied.)

[4] *Ibid.*, p. 32. (Emphasis supplied.)

[5] *Ibid.*, p. 15. (Emphasis supplied.)

Asset Recognition and Economic Attributes

likely to result in a *valid* application of the basic accounting concepts to the realities of our economic world.

A. Conventional costing. Conventional accounting has followed a physical interpretation of attach and match. Two general implicit rules have been adopted, one negative and one positive:

(1) *If a cost cannot be associated with a physical object or a contractual right, it cannot be considered as an asset.*[6]

This rule leads to current write-off of such costs as research, employee training programs, advertising, sales promotion, and so forth. In general, all selling and administrative expenses are accorded such treatment. Manufacturing costs receive elaborate treatment for asset-expense determination purposes, while the other costs continue to be expensed with little ado.

(2) *A cost that is necessary for a class of physical product must be allocated to each member of that class.*

For example, the cost of a machine is obviously a part of the cost of the *total output* of that machine. It seems obvious that the cost of the machine is "relevant" and "technically or economically associated with" its total output. What is not so obvious, and where the differences arise, is whether this cost must also be relevant for each specific unit of output. By adopting rule (2), conventional costers have decided that generally what is relevant to the whole must also be relevant to each part.[7]

B. Variable costing. Proponents of variable costing seem to have either accepted rule (1) or else remained silent on that point. However, they have adopted a totally different and conflicting rule (2).

(2) *A cost is relevant to (and allocable to) a unit of product if, and only if, the cost varies with the number of units produced.*

This rule has been challenged and discussed repeatedly in the profuse anti-direct costing literature. It also is too narrow and too shallow to meet head on the broad issue of asset recognition which must be confronted.

C. Relevant costing. Under relevant costing, only one basic assumption is needed: *Any cost is carried forward as an asset if, and only if, it has a favorable economic effect on expected future costs or future revenues.*[8] Under relevant costing this rule is completely general; no disitinction is made between physical product and economic attributes because *only* the economic attributes are important and governing.

A prime task of the accountant is to report financial results in the historical sense. But the asset-expense measurement problem is inextricably linked to future expectations as well as to past performance. Here is where the concept of relevancy appears. To have a bearing on the future,

---

[6] Accounting for goodwill is an exception to this rule.
[7] Practically, in some instances undcrutilization of a machine or plant will be recognized as a loss and will not be allocated to inventory.
[8] In a previous article (Horngren and Sorter, " 'Direct' Costing for External Reporting," ACCOUNTING REVIEW, January, 1961, pp. 84–93) we advocated this same assumption (pp. 86, 88–89) as a proper criterion for asset valuation. However, our preoccupation with direct costing per se evidently obscured our arguments for relevant costing as a principle distinct from both conventional and direct costing. For example, two recent articles critical of our earlier paper are heavily aimed against variable costing rather than against relevant costing as a concept. Furthermore, we considered future revenue as an important aspect of our relevant costing approach. Yet we apparently failed to make the breadth of our cost concept (it included opportunity cost!) clear because James F. Fremgen ("Variable Costing for External Reporting—A Reconsideration, THE ACCOUNTING REVIEW, January, 1962, pp. 76–77) and Phillip E. Fess and William L. Ferrara ("The Period Cost Concept for Income Measurement—Can It be Defended?" THE ACCOUNTING REVIEW, October, 1961, p. 601) mistakenly asserted that our position confined itself to future outlays and ignored future revenues.
Our colleague, David Green, Jr., uses the coinage "cost obviation" in his discussion of these issues. See his "A Moral to The Direct Costing Controversy?" *Journal of Business* (July, 1960), pp. 218–226.

The Accounting Review

to represent service potential, a given cost must be an index of future economic benefit in the form of a reduction of *total* expected future costs or an addition to *total* expected future revenue in the ordinary course of business.[9] Expressed another way, if the total expected future costs or revenue of an enterprise will be changed favorably because of the presence of a given cost, that cost is relevant to the future and is an asset; if not, that cost is irrelevant and is expired.

In contrast, the conventional view is that future cost recoupment is the general criterion for asset measurement. But our goal, within the limits of historical cost, is to reflect economic realities. Then no cost can represent a future benefit if its absence will not influence the obtaining of future revenues or the incurrence of future costs. For example, if an item can be replaced and used in normal operations at zero incremental explicit or opportunity cost, its presence or its physical amount does not represent service potential; in other words, its absence would have no impact on total future costs or revenues.

In sum, the test for asset recognition under relevant costing is quite simple. If a given cost will not influence either *total* future revenue or *total* future costs, it is not an asset. We maintain that this is completely consistent with the attach-match concepts. We cannot see how a "significant relationship," how "relevance" or "economic association," can be said to exist between two attributes (historical cost and future results) if the absence of one will not affect the other.

COMPARISONS OF ASSUMPTIONS
Relevant Costing and Conventional Costing

Emphasis on economic benefit rather than physical form. A major weakness in the conventional costing approach to asset recognition is its emphasis on physical form rather than economic substance. The working rules used in applying the concepts described so lucidly by Paton and Littleton have been too concerned for too long with appearances—with physical objects or contractual rights—instead of the underlying fundamental reality of economic benefits.

This preoccupation with physical evidence often results in expensing expenditures that should be capitalized. Thus, expenditures for research, advertising, employee training and the like are usually expensed, although it seems clear that in an economic sense these expenditures represent future benefit.[10] The difficulty of measuring future benefits is the argument usually advanced for expensing these items. Although the measurement problems are admittedly imposing, predictions as to future benefits are explicitly or implicitly made to warrant these spending decisions. There is some justification for using these predictions as a basis for measuring unexpired costs.

Of course, one ostensible reason for immediate expensing is that any capitalization of these expenditures is arbitrary. But

---

[9] An expenditure for a machine is an asset because it has impact on future revenue and/or costs. This impact could be quantified in two ways: (a) by the earnings lost if the machine were absent or (b) by the alternative costs that would have to be incurred to produce these earnings if the machine were absent. Thus the cost of the machine can be viewed as the present value of the revenue attributable to the machine, or, as Canning stated (*Economics of Accountancy*, The Ronald Press Company, 1929, pp. 187–188) as "the present worth of future outlays necessary to obtain like services in like amounts by the best available alternative means." These two concepts would give identical results in a world of perfect knowledge. Ideally, assets should represent present values of future streams of income (future rents, cost savings, net earnings). However, translating this economic notion into meaningful, objective measurements is too difficult, so accountants have used historical costs as a maximum limit of these present values. Working within this historical cost framework, the question becomes one of deciding when costs represent future economic benefit and when they do not.

[10] This seems especially obvious in the case of employee training programs. The expensing of these costs implies that they represent no future benefit. This means that training costs benefit the training period i.e. make the employee a better trainee rather than a more effective employee in the future.

Asset Recognition and Economic Attributes

it is not more arbitrary and more erroneous to favor immediate write-offs? By doing so these assets are shown, implicitly if not explicitly, as assets with zero valuation. Is a classification of an expenditure as asset 0% and expense 100% any less arbitrary than, say, as asset 20% and expense 80%, or as asset 60% and expense 40%? Immediate write-off is in fact more arbitrary and in many cases much further from economic reality than some positive asset figure obtained through the principle of relevant costing.

Another practical reason for immediate expensing is that the resulting effects on net income are undistorted because most non-manufacturing costs are recurring in nature. Besides having no conceptual merit, this argument frequently fails on practical grounds. For example, immediate expensing can seriously distort the reported incomes of growing companies.

The conventional emphasis on physical form also often results in capitalizing costs that should be expensed. For example, consider a paper manufacturing company, a going concern. Assume that Batch A-1 of inventory is carried on the balance sheet at $100,000, consisting of $40,000 of variable production costs and $60,000 of fixed factory overhead. Also assume the following:

1. If Batch A-1 were not on hand, a similar batch, Batch A-2, could be produced next period by utilizing otherwise idle capacity. Therefore, no additional fixed costs would have to be incurred and the total expected incremental cost of Batch A-2 would be the $40,000 of variable production costs.
2. Batches A-1 and A-2 cannot both be sold. The outlook is such that only one batch can be sold.

The conventional approach maintains that the production of physical Batch A-1 results in a valuable asset. The full cost of A-1 is an asset as long as it can be recaptured in the form of future revenue. This asset-expense technique is dependent

on a physical rather than an economic identification of Batch A-1 and the forthcoming revenue.

The relevant costing approach would recognize only $40,000 as representing economic benefit. Under the circumstances described, the $60,000 fixed cost is a cost incurrence that cannot qualify as an economic good. If Batch A-1 can be replaced in normal operations at variable cost, its presence or its physical amount represents economic benefit only in the amount of the variable costs that will *not* have to be incurred in the future. In other words, if Batch A-1 were not on hand, $40,000 would be the only future outlay necessary to restore the enterprise to an equivalent *economic* position.

Indeed, we need only ask ourselves, "What is the maximum price that a purchaser of this business would be willing to pay for the inventory?" It seems obvious that he would be willing to pay a maximum equal to the present value of the inventory's expected impact on future cash flows—no more than $40,000 in this instance.

Conventional costers may severely doubt the proposition that Batches A-1 and A-2 cannot both be sold. Then no quarrel exists. If there is a strong probability that the presence of A-1 will really have a favorable impact on *total* future revenue, then the fixed cost relating to A-1 should also be carried forward as an asset measure.

Emphasis on future. The relevant costers take the position that future sales outlooks, future availability of capacity, and future expected costs have a bearing on asset valuation. Conventional costers, however, maintain that it is irrelevant whether Batch A-2 can be produced next period, whether Batch A-2 can be produced at certain specified costs, whether A-1 and A-2 can both be sold. Assertions such as the following are made frequently:

"Future benefits have nothing to do with the

The Accounting Review

valuation of inventories. Inventories are simply an expression of all costs used up in the process of acquiring revenue which has not yet been recognized."[11]

In other words, even if the suppositions made above concerning A-1 and A-2 were accepted by conventional costers as valid and accurate, the conventional approach would nevertheless treat the full cost of object A-1 as an asset.

Fess and Ferrara also state, "If the service potential has been used in the production of income the recognition of which is delayed, the cost must be delayed. . . . If the service potential has been wasted . . . the cost must be treated as a loss. . . ."[12] The relevant coster agrees with every word in the last quotation. But the relevant coster and the conventional coster do not agree on the meaning of "production of income [revenue]." Fess and Ferrara maintain that production of income is delayed if a physical object is produced now and sold later. The corollary to this position is their assumption that waste of fixed facilities can be avoided by producing objects that can later be sold. To the relevant coster, "production of income" is delayed if, and only if, income is different in the future because of the decision today. He would maintain that "waste of fixed facilities" cannot be avoided merely by physical production. The waste can be avoided only if production today means more revenue or less costs tomorrow. If production today fails to change revenue or costs tomorrow, then economically the production is meaningless—regardless of how many units are produced.

Effort and accomplishment. The attempts to match costs and revenue is said to be an attempt to match "effort" and "accomplishment." The relevant coster maintains that no rational relationship exists between effort and accomplishment if the amount of accomplishment (revenue) is independent of and unaffected by the amount of effort (cost). Proper matching prohibits the linking of costs that have no *economic* effect on future revenues with such revenues. Proper matching calls for the deferral of all costs that have an economic impact on future events. Conceptually, such deferrals should be measured by the present value of the necessary alternative expenditures that would be needed to maintain the projected level of income.

Furthermore, it seems to us that the relevant costing approach makes "value added" operational. Only costs representing scarce resources add value to the product. Utilization of fixed facilities in one period to accumulate inventories does not represent the utilization of "scarce resources" if the fixed facilities will stand idle during the subsequent period.

Comparisons of asset measurements. How does the application of relevant costing affect asset measurement for the "average" company? Asset measures will not necessarily be different. Let us make a tabular comparison:

	Approach to Measuring Unexpired Cost	
	Recoverability	Relevancy
Merchandise inventory	✓	✓ (1)
Prepaid rent, taxes, etc.	✓	✓ (1)
Patents	✓	✓ (1)
Fixed assets	✓	✓ (1)
Inventories carried at market when lower than cost	✓	✓ (2)
Manufactured goods:		
Direct material (variable)	✓	✓
Direct labor (variable)	✓	✓
Variable indirect manufacturing costs	✓	✓
Fixed indirect manufacturing costs	(3)	(3)
Selling costs	(4)	(4)
Research costs	(4)	(4)

Note: Where check marks are shown, the results of both approaches should generally coincide; but the logic applied in measurement is different.

(1) Merchandise inventory, prepaid rent, patents, and fixed assets all represent valuable rights to future services. These rights are assets because their absence would require new acquisitions of the same kinds of

---

[11] Fess and Ferrara, *op. cit.*, p. 601.
[12] *Ibid.*, p. 602.

Asset Recognition and Economic Attributes

rights in order to sustain operations as a going concern.

(2) In the case of the lower of cost or market inventory method, our maximum cost will be historical dollar outlay. Write-downs are justified where events subsequent to acquisition show an opportunity cost to be lower than historical cost. Unless written down, the historical cost overstates the expected economic benefit. If the cost were reincurred at the balance sheet date, it would be less than the historical cost. Current market quotations on inventory provide an objective means of measurement.

(3) Relevant costing would often lead to expensing more quickly.

(4) Relevant costing would often lead to expensing less quickly.

Relevant Costing and Variable Costing

As our analysis in the previous section indicated, the relevant costing approach often will lead to asset and income measurements that coincide with results under the controversial direct costing approach. However, the relevant costing approach to fixed factory overhead is distinct from both the conventional and the direct costing approaches. While conventional costers will say that fixed factory overhead is an asset, and direct costers will say that it is a period cost, the relevant coster will say, "It depends."

For example, let us examine the relevant coster's approach to depreciation on machinery.

If depreciation is most closely related to production rather than time, it is properly treated as an asset because the decision to produce a unit in period 1 rather than in period 2 affects the service potential of the fixed asset. Each decision of this kind affects the asset's useful life, while in the former case such a decision has no effect on useful life.

In summary, if production today will in no way affect either the number of units to be sold in the future or the cost (including opportunity cost) of those units, the relevant coster would maintain that the depreciation conventionally allocated to such units is not an asset.[13] Of course, in many practical situations, it is nearly impossible to measure with assurance what portion of depreciation is related to time expiration and what portion is related to physical use. The point is that, depending on the circumstances, the evidence of economic realities should dictate the accounting treatment of depreciation.

ILLUSTRATION OF THE RELEVANT COSTING APPROACH

The B.E. Company. The following is the B.E. Company income statement for the year 1961:

Sales (17,000,000 units @ $2.00)		$34,000,000
Cost of goods sold (no opening or closing inventories):		
Variable (17,000,000 units @ $1.00)	$17,000,000	
Fixed	8,400,000	25,400,000
Gross margin		$ 8,600,000
Selling and administrative expenses:		
Variable (17,000,000 units @ $.50)	$ 8,500,000	
Fixed	600,000	9,100,000
Net Operating loss		$ —500,000

The "normal capacity" per year (based on three to five-year demand) is 30,000,000 units. Maximum production capacity is 40,000,000 units per year.

time expiration (due to obsolescence, supersession, technological change, etc.), it is not an asset unless the utilization of the machine in a particular period will make possible future sales that would otherwise be lost forever.

If depreciation is most closely related

[13] This is similar to the Keynesian concept of user cost, which is the expected change in the value of an asset due to use from the beginning to the end of some time span. See Myron H. Ross, "Depreciation and User Cost," ACCOUNTING REVIEW (July, 1960), pp. 422–428, and J. M. Keynes, *The General Theory of Employment, Interest and Money,* (New York: Harcourt Brace and Company, 1936), p. 53.

The Accounting Review

The board of directors has approached a competent outside executive to take over the company. He is an optimistic soul, and so he agrees to become president at a token salary; but his contract provides for a year-end bonus amounting to ten per cent of net operating profit (before considering the bonus or income taxes). The annual profit was to be verified by a huge public accounting firm.

The new president, filled with rosy expectations, promptly raised the advertising budget by $3,500,000 and stepped up production to an annual rate of 30,000,000 units. As soon as all outlets had sufficient stock, the advertising campaign was launched, and sales for 1962 increased—but only to a level of 25,000,000 units.

The verified income statement for 1962 contained the following data:

ing the most recent income statement?
2. Would you change your remarks in (1) if (consider each part independently):
   a) Sales outlook for the coming three years is 20,000,000 units per year?
   b) Sales outlook for the coming three years is 30,000,000 units per year?
   c) Sales outlook for the coming three years is 40,000,000 units per year?
   d) The company is to be liquidated immediately, so that the only sales in 1963 will be the 5,000,000 units still in inventory?
   e) Maximum production capacity is 40,000,000 units per year, and the sales outlook for 1963 is 45,000,000 units?

Analysis of the illustration. Our analysis should help show how the relevant costing approach differs from both conventional costing and direct costing.

Answer 1. Depending on the business outlook, we would object strenuously to the

Sales, 25,000,000×$2.00		$50,000,000
Production costs:		
Variable, 30,000,000×$1.00	$30,000,000	
Fixed	8,400,000	
Total	$38,400,000	
Inventory, 5,000,000 units, (⅙ of $38,400,000)	6,400,000	
Cost of goods sold		32,000,000
Gross margin		$18,000,000
Selling and administrative expenses:		
Variable	$12,500,000	
Fixed	4,100,000	16,600,000
Net operating profit		$ 1,400,000

The day after the statement was verified, the president resigned to take a job with another corporation having difficulties similar to those that B.E. Company had a year ago. The president remarked, "I enjoy challenges. Now that B.E. Company is in the black, I'd prefer tackling another knotty difficulty." His contract with his new employer is similar to the one he had with B.E. Company.

Let us consider the following questions:

1. As a member of the board, what comments would you make at the next meeting regard-

most recent income statement because the $1,400,000 profit is represented by $1,400,000 share of fixed production costs (5/30×$8,400,000). The $1,400,000 which was plowed into inventory is an asset only if it represents a future economic benefit in the form of added sales that would otherwise be lost or decreases in future production costs.

Under relevant costing, the $1,400,000 profit could easily be zero because $1,400,000 of fixed production costs might be written off immediately instead of being

Asset Recognition and Economic Attributes

held back as an asset.

On the other hand, the profit may be some other figure because some of the selling and administrative expenses might properly be capitalized.

Fixed indirect manufacturing costs are unexpired only when the utilization of these costs in production this period will reduce total future costs or enhance total future revenue. When will the latter situation occur? Only if failure to produce now would lead to additional costs (or lost sales) in the future in order to conduct contemplated operations.

What assumptions are necessary to justify treating fixed indirect manufacturing costs as unexpired? (a) Future production must be at maximum capacity with future sales in excess of capacity by the amount of increase in ending inventory; or (b) variable production costs are expected to increase; or (c) future sales will be lost forever because of lack of inventory.[14] That is, the absence of inventory at a certain place at a certain time will result in a permanent loss of certain sales.

Note that this approach to whether fixed indirect manufacturing costs are expired or unexpired may yield answers in favor of treatment as assets in some cases (for example, seasonal businesses, building base stocks of new products) or as expenses in other cases (for example, operations of a seasoned company at less than maximum capacity, increases in inventory stocks because of a slow-down in sales).

Answer 2. (a) (b) (c) No. As long as the sales outlook is 40,000,000 units per year or less, the company can meet its sales needs out of current production. The fixed costs do not represent assets because no future economic benefits are forthcoming unless either condition (b) or (c) specified

in our Answer 1 above is met.

(d) If the fixed costs must continue to be incurred during liquidation, and selling prices remain the same, the answer would be "No." If the fixed costs do not continue and the regular selling price can be attained, the answer would be "Yes."

(e) Yes. If the 5,000,000 units were not held in stock, the future sales would be only 40,000,000 units. Therefore, the case for recognizing $1,400,000 of fixed production costs as an asset is strong because condition (a) in our answer (1) is fulfilled.

Further, the case may also be strong for recognizing some advertising and other selling costs as an asset.

CONCLUSION

The controversial issues in accounting have led us to quest for a workable assumption about asset valuation that will bring convincing and universally applicable answers to the problem of asset expiration. We believe that the relevant costing approach is more likely to result in a *valid* application to accounting practice of the basic accounting concepts (enterprise continuity, attach, match). Conventional accounting rules are too often preoccupied with physical form instead of economic substance. In contrast, the relevant costing rule emphasizes the "economic attributes and measurements" with which, according to Paton and Littleton, accounting is primarily concerned. The implementation of relevant costing will often result in expensing certain costs that are conventionally capitalized and capitalizing certain costs that are conventionally expensed.

[14] For an expanded discussion, see Horngren and Sorter, *op. cit.*, pp. 88–90.

An Enquiry Into the Nature of Assets

By R. M. LALL, M.Com., LL.B., D.Litt., F.C.A., F.C.C.S.

The theoretical question (which is sometimes a pragmatic one) — what is an asset? — is here discussed briefly, interestingly and with readily evident erudition.

Strangely enough, without adequately vouching the conceptual veracity of assets, writers have taken great pains in dealing with their classification and valuation at considerable length. They seem to have taken for granted what the term 'assets' stands for. Practically all writers, whether old or new, have developed the nature of assets implicitly rather than explicitly, and in doing so, some of them have conceived the subject matter in their own way. It would perhaps be not incorrect to say that today there is no general acceptance of a definition of assets or of the basic common characteristics of assets. The main object of this paper is to bring out the homogeneous pattern of salient ingredients of assets that we account for.

DISTINCTION BETWEEN ASSET AND NONASSET

In practice it is generally implied that "assets are simply all those items which are listed on the left side (in certain countries, on the right side) of the balance sheet." This view, how-ever, fails to explain how one can distinguish an asset from a nonasset. Obviously this view is open to a serious criticism that although the relevant side of the balance sheet bears the caption 'assets', yet on that very side certain items are displayed, as for example, debit balance of profit and loss account, preliminary expenses, deferred revenue expenditure, discount on issue of shares and debentures, and so on, the items which can, by no stretch of imagination, be called 'assets.' Thus this view is too vague and unscientific for common acceptance.

VARIOUS DEFINITIONS

Acquisition Basis. Some authors prescribe the specific method of acquisition of an item as a pre-condition to its being christened an asset. Sanders, Hatfield and Moore opine that items can be treated as assets only when "the business has acquired them at a cost."[1] Perhaps no special efforts are needed to rebut this contention, for there is no denying the fact that accountants do record assets which have come in just as a gift or by discovery, and in the acquisition of which no cost was incurred. To a similar charge is exposed the definition of an asset as given by W. A. Paton who identifies an asset with "any consideration, material or otherwise, owned by a specific busi-

DR. R. M. LALL is Senior Lecturer at the School of Accountancy, Singapore Polytechnic, and previously lectured at Lucknow University (India). Dr. Lall has been a member of the Central Council of the Institute of Chartered Accountants of India.

THE NEW YORK CERTIFIED PUBLIC ACCOUNTANT   NOVEMBER 1968   •

ness enterprise and of value to that enterprise."[2] Furthermore, Paton's definition does not provide any tests by which an asset can be differentiated from a nonasset; nor does it not state what specific operations must be performed to constitute a consideration so as to bring about the existence of an asset.

Transaction Basis. There are well-known writers who hold that assets cannot be acquired except as a result of a transaction. To quote Mautz, Zimmerman, DeMaris, Fess, Moyer, and Perry: "They (assets) are the result of enterprise transactions."[3] In the same way Sprouse and Moonitz maintain that rights to assets must "have been acquired by the enterprise as a result of some current or past transaction."[4] Such qualifications to the definition of assets are of little significance.

A transaction need not necessarily precede the acquisition of an asset Unless used in some special sense, a transaction implies a transfer of goods or services from one person to another. One can cite a number of instances where no transfer of goods or services takes place from one enterprise to another, nevertheless assets are acquired, as for example on certain changes in personnel, finances, materials etc. occurring within an enterprise itself. In the same manner, amendments to laws, enactment of new laws, completion of a phase of a programme for expansion, or occurrence of natural causes, hardly have the colour of transactions, yet all the same they may add new assets or diminish the existing assets of an enterprise. In evolving a definition of assets, the factor of how they were acquired is not relevant.

Unamortized Cost. Some writers have defined assets in terms of 'unamortized costs.' According to Paton and Littleton, "Assets are those factors acquired for production which have not reached the point in the business process where they may be treated as 'costs of sales' or 'expenses'. Under this usage, assets or costs incurred would clearly mean charges awaiting future revenue, whereas expenses or costs applied would mean charges against present revenue."[5]

In a sense this definition has a decisive merit in as much as it precisely states how in the accounting process assets come into being and what they are held for. All the same it too does not provide any indicator by which assets can be distinguished from nonassets. Further, the definition is not comprehensive enough. There is little doubt that bank balances, bills receivables and such other financial claims are well-recognized examples of assets. They would, however, be excluded from assets under this definition, for the simple reason that they are neither 'charges awaiting future revenue' nor are they 'charges against present revenue'. Moreover, this definition excludes all items from assets, which are not represented by 'costs' or which are not subject to amortization.

AICPA Position. The American Institute of Certified Public Accountants offers a comparatively better definition of assets in these words: "Something represented by a debit balance that is or would be properly carried forward upon a closing of books of account according to the rules or principles of accounting (provided such debit balance is not in effect a negative balance applicable to a liability), on the basis that it represents either a property right or value acquired, or an expenditure made which has created a property right or is properly applicable to the future."[6]

It highlights the importance of trial balance and specifies the point of time when assets are shown in the process of income determination. Further it so defines assets as to exclude a loss. It does not, however, bring out very clearly the homogeneity of substance of assets, nor does it state expressly for whom the assets represent rights. According to this definition, an expenditure which creates a property right *ipso facto* qualifies as an asset, but the fact is that howsoever valuable the property right so created, it should not be regarded as an asset unless it is of current or future benefit to the enterprise. This definition therefore needs a further restatement.[7]

MISCONCEPTIONS ABOUT ASSETS

At times a few misconceptions about the concept of assets seem to be prevalent. The first misunderstanding is that all assets are legal rights. As a matter of fact, legal title is no determinant of the existence of an asset. A mortgaged property or a leasehold is as good as an asset as land with absolute right of ownership. Likewise with ample justification special advertising campaign, research expenditure or deferred charges in certain cases are treated as unquestionable examples of assets notwithstanding the fact that none of them is evidenced by a legal title.

A second misconception is that assets are necessarily physical or material in the sense that they can be seen, touched or felt. Physical characteristic like the one in question is not relevent to asset determination. This phenomenon is not common to all assets. Tangible assets like building, plant and fixtures are as good assets as intangible assets like goodwill.

A third misunderstanding is that assets are but money values. Often assets are referred as plant is $50,000, building is $35,000 or cash, Rs. 25,000, and so on. Assets are what they are made of, that is, the usefulness they promise to bring in to the enterprise which holds them. Monetary unit is a convenient though not necessarily a sound yardstick in terms of which assets are expressed. Logically it is wrong to identify a measure with the object measured.

COMMON PROPERTIES OF ASSETS BASIC TO DEFINITION

In coining a definition of assets, the underlying approach should be to pinpoint the common properties of assets. It appears that an item to be called an asset must possess the following characteristics:

Future Benefits—Service Potential. First, the item must ensure some specific future benefits or service potentials to an enterprise. In fact it is its usefulness to the enterprise that makes the subject-matter of an asset. To the extent an item ceases to be useful, it ceases to be recognized as an asset. This statement has two implications.

First implication is that an item does not have usefulness in general. The issue of its being useful can be answered only by reference to the question: useful to whom?, because nothing can be useful to all persons at the same time generally. The answer to this question is 'useful to the enterprise or the person who possesses the item.'

The second implication is that usefulness means some positive benefit or service potential. For example, a machine with a negative value in the sense that it has been rendered obsolete and its cost of removal would exceed its residual value, cannot be considered as an asset. Again, expired capital outlay is not an asset. No doubt, in certain cases formidable difficulties may be experienced in determining the quantum of usefulness or service potential of an item, but this factor would affect the valuation without changing the nature of the asset.

On a deeper reflection it would be apparent that what accountants actually account for is usefulness or service potential, and not the forms in which these attributes are embodied. These forms are designated as land, building, plant, machinery, fixtures, receivables, advances, bank balances and so on. When a certain form ceases to be of economic benefit to the enterprise, it is excluded from assets.

It is aptly remarked by Paton and Littleton: "Behind accounting's array of figures, . . . lie the tangible and intangible embodiments of services."[8] The concept of assets favoured herein is in keeping with the basic approach of accounting theory. Incidentally it may be stated that the service potential nature of assets has not been emphasized as much as it deserves. Happily enough during recent years there has been a growing realization that assets are essentially in the nature of "aggregates of service potentials,"[9] "future economic benefits,"[10] or "rights to prospective benefits."[11]

Legal Rights. Secondly, assets must necessarily have the protection of law in the sense that the enterprise to which they belong should have a legal claim to their enjoyment. An asset is not worth its name unless it is in the nature of a legal right. Rights to assets are not confined to property rights;[12] they may as well arise under the law of obligation. They may represent rights in personam (those rights which avail against certain person or persons), or rights in rem (those rights which avail against persons generally). They may arise from ownership or from possession, or *nemo dat mod non habet.* They may be right to real prop-erty or personal property, corporeal or incorporeal. They may just be 'profits a prendre'.

It is immaterial whether these legal claims to enjoyment or ownership are evidenced by contracts, written agreements or legal title. If the legal claims are liable to be withdrawn at any time without any compensation by other parties, they should not be called assets. What is important is that the enterprise must have a reasonable chance of the enjoyment of the legal claims, whether at present or in the future.

Other Aspects. Incidentally it may be stated that a concept of assets must possess two qualifications. First, the economic potentials or legal claims constituting assets must arise from some economic event. Economic events is a broader term than 'transactions,' and includes all significant economic changes concerning an enterprise which must be recognized in the accounting process in order to make accounting reports not misleading to their users.

Second, economic potentials or legal claims are considered only in reference to an enterprise. Items not meeting any of these qualifications are not the concern of the accountant. Perhaps an explicit statement of these qualifications is not warranted for the simple reason that Accounting records data arising from economic events relating to an enterprise.

Thus assets may be defined as embodiments of present or future economic benefits or service potentials measurable in terms of monetary units, accruing to an enterprise as a result of economic events, the enjoyment of which by the enterprise is secured by the law.

REFERENCES

1 Thomas Henry Sanders, Henry Rand Hatfield, and Underhill Moore, A Statement of Accounting Principles, A.A.A., 1959, p. 58.

2 W. A. Paton, Accounting, 1924, p. 28; Essentials of Accounting, 1938, p. 23.

3 Group Study at the University of Illinois, A Statement of Basic Accounting Postulates and Principles, Center for International Education and Research in Accounting, 1964, p. 16.

4 Robert T. Sprouse and Maurice Moonitz. A Tentative Set of Broad Accounting Principles for Business Enterprises, Accounting Research Study No. 3. AICPA, 1962.

5 W. A. Paton and A. C. Littleton, An Introduction to Corporate Accounting Standards, 1940, pp. 25 and 26.

6 The Committee on Terminology, AICPA, Review and Resume, Accounting Terminology Bulletin No. 1, 1953, p. 13.

7 The Committee on Terminology originally gave the definition in 1941 and then restated it in 1953.

8 Paton and Littleton, op. cit., p. 13.

9 AAA Committee on Concepts and Standards, Accounting and Reporting Standards for Corporate Statements and Preceding Statements and Supplements, 1957, p. 3.

10 Sprouse and Moonitz, op. cit.

11 Moonitz and Jordon, Accounting, An Analysis of Its Problems, rev. ed., 1963, vol. I, p. 163.

12 More often than not, assets are stated to represent at best property right excluding other legal claims.

By *Charles T. Horngren*

Increasing the Utility of Financial Statements

A survey conducted by the author among security analysts reveals that an overwhelming majority use funds statements in their work and find such statements valuable.

A combination of income and funds statements is suggested which might help to resolve some of the problems of dealing in both historical and current dollars, without the application of index numbers to dollars of original investment.

In the author's opinion, the concepts of net income and funds provided by operations, taken together, "reveal a story that neither divulges separately."

PUBLISHED financial information must be judged by its usefulness in facilitating analysis and interpretation. The pragmatic test must prevail; that is, what improvements in published reports will meet the need for more functional data.

Private reports, drafted in various informative ways, may be prepared for special parties, such as management, trade associations, and lending agencies. But published reports properly are oriented toward the investor group. A weighty and vocal representative of this group is the professional security analyst. His opinions and his analytical methods deserve recognition and consideration in the development of corporate reporting. This article considers the wants of the analyst in relation to possible improvements in financial reporting.

QUESTIONNAIRE ON FUNDS STATEMENT

In the last few years analysts have shown greater interest in the statement of sources and applications of funds (funds statement). To discover more views on the funds statement, this writer circulated a fairly detailed and technical questionnaire to a random selection of 350 security analysts. One hundred twenty replies (34 per cent) were received. Exhibit I presents the answers to a few important questions.

Exhibit I

Questions and Answers on Uses of Funds Statement
120 Security Analysts

1. Do you ever use funds statements in your work?
   Yes 114; No 6.
2. Do you find a funds statement useful?
   Almost always 63; Frequently 42; Seldom 5; Rarely 4; No reply 6.
3. If a company-prepared funds statement is not available, do you generally try to prepare your own funds flow analysis (either a word summary or a condensed, "make-shift" schedule)?
   Yes 96; No 18; No reply 6.

The Journal of Accountancy, July 1959

4. Do you attempt to project fund flows (either via pro forma statements or a similar type of analysis)?

Almost always 10; Frequently 60; Seldom 29; Rarely 15; No reply 6.

5. Do you feel that annual reports should include funds statements as well as the customary balance sheet and income statements?

Yes 108; No 6; No reply 6.

The answers in Exhibit I clearly show that many analysts feel that a statement of sources and applications of funds is a helpful analytical device. Analysts cited the following information as being revealed by a funds statement:

1. Major sources from which funds were obtained (i.e., profits, borrowings, stockholder investment)

2. Financial management "habits" of the company (i.e., managerial attitudes toward spending and financing)

3. Proportion of funds applied to plant, dividends, debt retirement, etc.

4. Determination of the disposition of profits

5. Impact of spending upon working capital position

6. Indication of the trend of general financial strength or weakness of the company

7. Indication of impact of sources and uses of funds upon future dividend-paying probabilities

The following specific comments by analysts in their answering of the questionnaire may clarify the uses cited above:

1. There is probably no more useful analytical tool in statement analysis than the flow of funds, and we incorporate it in all our financial reports, whether for loan or investment purposes. In very concise terms, it manages to blend balance sheet and profit and loss together into meaningful terms and gives a quick bird's-eye view of what happened to a business in the period under review. There is no doubt in my mind that its use will increase, and it will emerge, if it has not already, as an absolutely essential financial schedule, included in all audit and annual reports.

2. Its importance ranks with balance sheet and income statement. It reveals [all uses cited above], plus the fact that if its usage became commonplace or universal in annual reports it would be a common tool of intra- and inter-industry analysis.

3. Use to judge whether the company (1) is likely to increase or cut dividend, (2) is likely to have to do financing, and (3) is expanding vigorously.

4. In evaluating common stocks we frequently consider "funds flow" as exceeding in importance reported profits—particularly where large capital expenditure programs are under way.

5. Use the funds flow statistics as a means of judging whether company can finance further additions without additional financing and/or increase dividends or retire debt.

6. Not only to determine the manager's past ideas but to project possible policies into the future, the funds statement is vital to me.

7. The funds statement is essential to equate earnings statements by adjusting for partially discretionary noncash charges (policy differences, etc.) and to attempt to predict financing (outside sources).

In recent years many analysts have tended to use a "working capital earnings" (funds provided by operations) basis as well as a "reported earnings" basis in the valuation of stocks in certain industries (i.e., oils, chemicals, aluminum). Evidence of this trend is found in the 1957 annual report of the Standard Oil Company, New Jersey. The report presents a summary of working capital earnings (adapted) as shown by the table on page 41.

The "working capital earnings" notion does not replace the usefulness or significance of the net income concept, but it does aid in the interpretation of reported income. This approach has been adopted because of the widespread variations in depreciation and amortization policies and because of the difficulty of comparing similar firms which have invested in a large proportion of fixed assets at different price levels. In these cases a statement of funds should be especially helpful because it gives many answers *directly*, thus minimizing the necessity for probing other statements for the information sought.

	(In Millions) 1957
Revenue:	
Sales	$7,830
Income from investments	148
	$7,978
Less Expenses:	
Amount spent for oil, materials, and services	$5,103
Wages	993
Income taxes	554
	$6,650
Working capital earnings	$1,328

The results of the questionnaire certainly indicate that a funds statement, which now appears in a few annual reports, should be universally adopted as a required financial report. Further, the funds flow concept should be recognized explicitly in the income statement.

PRICE-LEVEL CHANGES

The intention here is not to dwell upon the controversial impact on conventional accounting of the many very real problems which have been raised or complicated by the dancing dollar. While index-number applications to conventional statements may be helpful in interpreting income, funds flow analysis also offers aid in this task.

Depreciation and fund flows

The analyst's fund flow approach to the interpretation of income is tied in with his attitude toward depreciation.[1] Depreciation may be viewed in at least two different ways. Accountants view it as the allocation of original fixed asset costs to operations in a systematic, rational manner. But a financial analyst looks upon depreciation as that portion of incoming funds from customers which is, or should be, devoted to spending on fixed assets or to retirements of long-term debt which arose from past fixed asset outlays. If the latter view of depreciation is an important analytical

concept, then the information required for this type of analysis should appear in corporate reports.

The fund flow approach to the income statement may be briefly described as follows. Revenue from customers represents total current dollars provided by operations. Current expenses represent outlays in current dollars (with some exceptions in the case of wildly fluctuating raw material prices coupled with Fifo inventory methods). After the current expenses are met, the difference is "what's left" of revenue (current dollars). The "what's left" is commonly called *funds provided by operations* or, less accurately, *cash flow*. A part (depreciation) of funds provided by operations is considered to be the recovery of past fixed asset outlays. This recovery is (or should be) devoted to paying off the long-term debt which arose from prior expenditures, or else it is applied to maintaining or enhancing physical capacity. Thus depreciation is "something special" which is related to fixed asset outlays. The final difference (residual) may be used in a variety of ways, such as dividends, plant expansion, more working capital and payment of long-term debts.

The analyst's approach does emphasize *current* dollars, and the analytical problems of the price level do not appear ominous to him. Surely, however, this fund flow approach to the income statement does not mean that the analyst ignores the value of the dollar in terms of the economic backdrop. The intelligent investor realizes that reported earnings are not distributable earnings. He is aware that simple "replacement" of productive facilities requires more dollars than are being "generated" by depreciation charges. He deems depreciation to be inadequate if the price level has changed so that the depreciation amounts being charged are now insufficient to meet capital replacement demands.[2] The analyst considers price-level changes by relating capital expenditure requirements—past and future—to funds available.

An intelligent analysis of the flow of funds may be as enlightening as index-number adjustments. Such an analysis is much more objective and readily understood than any index-number approach. Just how does the analysis of the flow of funds help in interpreting price-level effects?

1. It offers, with few exceptions, a report of

---

[1] Conclusions from author's prior survey of existing investment literature plus interviews with 51 security analysts in New York and Chicago and scrutiny of 123 of their written analytical reports: Charles T. Horngren, "Security Analysts and the Price Level," *Accounting Review*, October 1955, pp. 573-582.

[2] This is not simple. Replacement in kind assumes no technological progress. It is doubtful that American industry replaces in kind except on rare occasions. See "How Industry Modernizes—And How it Does its Job," *Business Week*, September 27, 1958, pp. 76-121. In effect, "replacement" is a new commitment—the results of which must await future happenings.

dollar flows in terms of current purchasing power.

2. It is a useful way of dealing with widespread variations in depreciation policies and with the difficulty of comparing similar firms which have invested in a large proportion of fixed assets at different price levels.

3. Management must deal with *assets*, not with the net income abstraction. Net income reflects increments in net assets. Income may be interpreted as to its realism in terms of its impact upon dividend possibilities, capital replacement needs, long-term debt retirement, and plans for diversification and expansion.

ANALYTICAL TECHNIQUES

Analysts' major interest in long-term analysis centers about the income statement. What are future earnings per share going to be? Such interest is justifiable because long-run stock prices are probably influenced by earnings per share more than by any other single factor.

An intelligent analyst will not be satisfied with a mere earnings per share figure. He is interested in interpreting that figure, in extracting the full story which points toward that figure. He does not have a fiery desire for an index-number application to the figure because the result is not specific, is not crystal-clear, and is difficult to relate to other companies. His major task, that of comparison between companies, must not be overlooked. He is concerned with estimating *future* figures. What "correct" index number should be applied to the latter?

The overemphasis upon a single net income figure breeds wide misunderstanding. Modern business operations are too complex to be portrayed by a single figure that might provide the golden key which will unlock the door, and free the analyst from his chamber of horrible financial data. The analyst must interpret *any* net income figure, whether conventional or the product of some scrupulous index-number applications, in the light of the outlook for each of its determinants and with a view to company plans and obligations.

Character of income

Specifically, what does the analyst want to know or struggle to project? He wants to know the *character* of the future income, both as to the revenue and expenses which yield the dollar income and as to the latter's probable disposition. No matter what we accountants want to think about it, the investor regards income as everyday money which management can use or misuse in a variety of ways.

In studying revenue the analyst considers the following factors for each product line: capital investment needs, pricing changes, stability, research productivity, competitive situation, general business conditions. In studying expenses the analyst considers the following: What are the cost behavior patterns? Are some expenses postponable? Which types vary with volume? Which types do not? Which types may be eliminated in cases of drastic decreases in revenue? What are the expense-sales ratios on various product lines? What about labor conditions and cost-control consciousness? What about research outlays and attitudes?

If the above factors can be estimated with some degree of confidence, the income residual may be projected. (Such work is admittedly an imposing undertaking.) But what of the disposition of the income? The analyst will isolate depreciation, where it is relatively important, and compare it with planned or needed capital expenditures and debt retirement arising from past capital expenditures. He will wonder if depreciation is adequate with respect to the outlays just mentioned. He will also try to determine the return on additional dollars being committed to plant and equipment through comparisons of recent (five to seven years) additions with recent changes in revenue and income. That is, he will try to see if there is a lag correlation between dollars spent and increased revenues and income.

This kind of analysis requires a firm command of the facts and seasoned judgment in interpreting figures. One technique which is used, when the facts are available, is to compare the return on investment in new plant with the return on investment in old plant restated at insurable values. This sometimes helps the analyst to estimate returns on projected plant expansion.

The balance sheet comes in for attention because of possible changes in capitalization structure and its effect on income and dividends. Are there any long-term debt maturities in the near future? Will the debt be paid? Will it be refunded? How?

The answers to all of the above questions lead the analyst to a final question. What is going to be left of the dollar income after plant, long-term debt, and working capital needs have been met? In short, what is the outlook for dividends? Thus the analyst does more than grasp for a future earnings per share figure. He interprets income. His thoughts as to the future possibilities for earnings and dividends are heavily influenced by such interpretation of *dollar flows as they affect the earnings, dividends, and capital structure of a specific company.*

IMPROVING FINANCIAL REPORTS

How may an intelligent analysis of a corporation be facilitated through more informative financial reports? Index numbers may provide one interpretative device, especially with respect to an approximation of so-called "economic" or "real" income. But other means of presentation also deserve attention.[3] Exhibit II is this writer's view of how financial reports may be improved; it is submitted as only one of a number of possibilities.[4] It is over-simplified and condensed in order to bring out certain points.

The reports in Exhibit II contain the following features:

1. The combined statement of income and retained earnings *(Report 1)* distinguishes between postponable and nonpostponable charges and also between variable and nonvariable charges. The

---

[3] For examples, see William J. Vatter, *The Fund Theory of Accounting and its Implications for Financial Reports,* Chicago, University of Chicago Press, 1947, Chapters V-VII. Also see R. K. Mautz, "Accounting for Enterprise Growth," *Accounting Review,* January 1950, pp. 81-88.

[4] The author is grateful to Professor George H. Sorter, University of Chicago, for his suggestions concerning Exhibit II.

evolution of the income statement should follow this direction. Admittedly, the difficulties of classification and of terminology are imposing. But the conventional income statement also has difficult problems of classification and terminology.

Report 1 is not particularly superior to a number of other feasible arrangements. The point is that the income statement of the future ought to stress the various patterns of cost behavior through the use of appropriate cost classifications.

2. *Report 1* has two major figures: funds provided by operations and net income. The statement properly de-emphasizes the net income figure. Partial or full index-number applications (e.g., to depreciation) may be applied to the statement. For instance, a variety of adjusted depreciation charges may be used. But the figure for funds provided by operations is not affected by the choice.

The figure representing funds provided by operations is more verifiable and objectively determinable than net income. In any given situation, a dozen independent accountants who individually compute funds provided by operations are more likely to obtain a narrower range of variation in the funds figure than if they independently attempt to compute a net income figure.

3. The conventional funds statement causes much confusion with respect to "adding back" depreciation in the computation of funds provided by operations. The presentation and cross-

---

Exhibit II

Report 1 — Statement of Income and Reconciliation of Retained Earnings for Year Ending Dec. 31, 1958

Sales			$1,180,000
Less: Charges requiring working capital			
Nonpostponable charges:			
Variable expenses (materials, direct labor, etc.)			500,000
Variable operating margin			$ 680,000
Nonvariable expenses (insurance, property taxes, etc.)		$200,000	
Postponable charges:			
Research	$50,000		
Maintenance	50,000	100,000	
Income taxes (based upon net taxable income of $270,000)		135,000	435,000
FUNDS PROVIDED BY OPERATIONS (to *Report 2*)			$ 245,000
Less: Other charges (credits) to operations not affecting working capital:			
Depreciation		$ 90,000	
Provision for deferred income taxes		10,000	100,000
NET INCOME			$ 145,000
Less: Dividends			40,000
			$ 105,000
Add: Retained earnings, December 31, 1957			1,700,000
Retained earnings, December 31, 1958			$1,805,000

referencing of the latter in *Reports 1* and *2* should avoid this awkward problem by integrating the calculation of funds provided by operations in the income statement rather than in the funds statement.

The suggested format for the statement of funds is only one of a number of possibilities. Various sub-totals and descriptive breakdowns may be employed. Recent suggestions to use more precise terminology (such as "Statement Explaining Change in Working Capital") have merit.

4. The problem facing the investor is future performance. A study of past performance may be used as a guide in predicting future funds to be generated as well as future net income. *Report 3* contains ingredients which should facilitate such analysis.

Report 3 recognizes the analytical view of depreciation as that portion of the revenue dollar which should be devoted to plant outlays or to long-term debt retirement. It permits a direct size-up of company performance over a span of years with respect to replacement, expansion, financial management, depreciation policies and funds provided by operations. Such information should aid in the interpretation of the meaning of conventional net income as it is reflected in the financial behavior of the firm.

The original costs of assets retired are restated by applying a price-index specific to the particular kind of assets retired. Thus an approximation may be made of what proportion of current purchases of fixed assets is being applied merely to maintaining gross dollar investment in fixed assets. The author included this column of figures with some misgivings, but he still believes the column offers some useful clues for distinguishing between expansion and replacement of *dollars* invested in fixed assets. As pointed out in the footnote to *Report 3*, the fact that assets are retired does not mean that they are or ought to be replaced. Nor does the index apply as technological changes and shifts in product lines or markets occur.

Some observers may be inclined to center their attention on funds provided by operations rather than on depreciation amounts. *Report 3* shows the fixed asset dollar needs for replacement, for expansion, and for long-term debt retirement. These needs may be compared with funds provided by operations. A sort of lag correlation between increases in funds provided by operations and fixed asset purchases over a span of years may provide some useful information for inter-company comparisons, especially since individual company depreciation estimates do not influence the results except for income tax effects. *Report 3* highlights the expansion and diversification which do influence the inter-company comparisons.

Reports 1 and *3* emphasize the capriciousness of depreciation in analysis. For example, assume that each of two companies spends $100,000 on a fixed asset; the expected average annual return over a five-year life is 30 per cent on original cost:

Increase in funds provided by operations	$ 50,000 per year x 5 years
Total funds flow	$250,000
Less cost of asset	100,000
Margin	$150,000
Average margin for one year ($150,000 ÷ 5)	$ 30,000

Now compare the net income effects using two methods of depreciation over a five-year period:

Sum-of-the-Years' Digits

Year	Funds Flow	Depreciation	Net Income Effect
1	$50,000	$33,333	$16,667
2	50,000	26,667	23,333
3	50,000	20,000	30,000
4	50,000	13,333	36,667
5	50,000	6,667	43,333

Report 2 — Statement of Sources and Applications of Funds for the Year Ending December 31, 1958

Sources:

Funds provided by operations (from *Report 1*)		$245,000
Proceeds of long-term debt		35,000
		$280,000

Applications:

Purchases of fixed assets (see *Report 3*)	$170,000	
Retirement of long-term debt	10,000	
Dividends	40,000	220,000
NET INCREASE IN WORKING CAPITAL (see *Schedule of Changes in Working Capital*—not reproduced here)		$ 60,000

Straight Line

Year	Funds Flow	Depreciation	Net Income Effect
1	$50,000	$20,000	$30,000
2	50,000	20,000	30,000
3	50,000	20,000	30,000
4	50,000	20,000	30,000
5	50,000	20,000	30,000

These two companies show radically different earnings performances; yet both firms basically have the same pre-tax earning power under these assumed conditions. The only real difference would be in the financial impact of the timing of income tax payments and changes in income tax rates over a five-year period. The latter problem is beyond the scope of this article.

Increased emphasis on funds provided by operations will aid in the interpretation of reported net income. Both concepts of net income and funds provided by operations are important; taken together, they reveal a story that neither divulges separately.

5. A study of these financial reports in conjunction with knowledge of the operating characteristics of the company, its place in the industry, the status of the economy, the administrative attitude toward financial management, over-all policies, and expansion opportunities, will often explain more of a company's operations than any mere income tabulation.

Management works with current dollars. They obtain current dollars and whatever they spend immediately is also in current dollars. The only real meaning of purchasing power is reflected in what is acquired with what is spent at the time of spending. If management delays spending (e.g., Montgomery Ward) then the analyst may judge, using industry performance comparisons, the wisdom of those delays by conjecturing on the opportunity costs of not spending. The real test of spending decisions must wait until the future becomes the past.

Funds flow analysis is not the panacea for the very real problems which have been raised by

---

Report 3 — Comparison of Fund Flows, Depreciation, and Outlays for Fixed Assets

	Retirement of Fixed Assets		Purchases of Fixed Assets		
	Original Cost	Restated in Terms of Current Year's Price Level*	Gross Cost	Long-term Debt	Operating Funds Used
1952	$20,000	$ 30,000	$ 30,000		$ 30,000
1953	32,000	50,000	120,000	—	120,000
1954	28,000	40,000	100,000	$30,000	70,000
1955	31,000	40,000	140,000	30,000	110,000
1956	62,000	90,000	90,000	20,000	70,000
1957	75,000	100,000	130,000	10,000	120,000
1958	90,000	120,000	170,000	35,000	135,000

	Funds Used for Retirement of Debt which Arose from Prior Fixed Asset Purchases	Total Operating Funds Used	Funds Provided by Operations	Depreciation Per Financial Reports	Depreciation Per Federal Income Tax Return
1952	—	$ 30,000	$100,000	$30,000	$ 30,000
1953	—	120,000	170,000	40,000	40,000
1954	$10,000	80,000	185,000	50,000	60,000
1955	—	110,000	195,000	60,000	75,000
1956	10,000	80,000	210,000	65,000	80,000
1957	20,000	140,000	230,000	75,000	90,000
1958	10,000	145,000	245,000	90,000	110,000

*Restatement of original cost of assets retired by applying a price index specific to the particular kind of assets retired. This figure would give some indication of what proportion of current purchases of fixed assets is being devoted to replacement rather than to expansion. This figure needs qualitative interpretation because replacement often involves the acquisition of new assets which are technologically superior to the old.

the eroding dollar. But then neither is index-number analysis. Coupled with index-number applications, funds flow analysis may be a definite aid in the interpretation of income and in the analysis of the entire enterprise.

Conclusion

Conventional financial statements should be recast in order to meet today's analytical needs. The suggested changes for financial statements in this article: (1) continue to offer information which is usually available in conventional statements; (2) stress fund flow effects of operations; (3) may be used with desired index-number applications; (4) facilitate interpretation of reported net income in the light of managerial plans, future earning power, and future dividend possibilities.

Much accounting research has recently been directed toward various attacks on the problem of changing price levels. Suggested changes in financial reporting most often have entailed index-number applications. While useful in many instances, perhaps the latter approach has been over-emphasized. Accounting research should probe more thoroughly into alternate means of presenting useful historical dollar information which will aid financial analysis.

achieving the objectives of APB Opinion No. 19

by J. W. Giese and T. P. Klammer

Accounting is and should be a dynamic process. The measuring and reporting of economic events must evolve with the changing needs and activities of users. The rapid changes which have taken place in our productive processes have, however, outpaced the process of accounting evolution. Thus, pressures for improvements in measuring and reporting economic activity have intensified.

In response to these demands, the American Institute of CPAs has issued numerous professional pronouncements suggesting improvements in the accounting process. The Financial Accounting Standards Board provides a new structure for the development and implementation of improvements. Effective progress depends upon how well public accounting and the financial community interpret

and implement these pronouncements in light of our social responsibility.

Our purpose in this article is to analyze the application of APB Opinion No. 19, "Reporting Changes in Financial Position"; to indicate how practice has implemented it; to provide an analytical critique of its implementation; and to offer suggestions for improvement.

Opinion No. 19 provides a unique opportunity to analyze the application and interpretation of an evolutionary accounting change for the following reasons:

1 The Opinion is relatively uncontroversial.
2 The objectives of reporting changes in financial position are specifically stated.
3 The reporting format suggested provides flexibility.
4 The change is evolutionary—designed to update and improve existing practice.
5 Analysis is facilitated by the existence of a separate statement.

Opinion No. 19

The Accounting Principles Board issued the Opinion in March 1971. The Opinion specified the objectives and purposes of reporting changes in financial position and elevated the statement of changes

J. W. Giese, *CPA, Ph.D., is professor of business administration at North Texas State University, Denton. He is a member of the AICPA, the American Accounting Association and the Texas Society of CPAs and is a trustee and past president of the society's Education Foundation.* **T. P. Klammer,** *CPA, Ph.D., is an assistant professor at North Texas State University, Denton. He is a member of the AICPA, the American Accounting Association, the National Association of Accountants, the Texas Society of CPAs and the American Institute of Decision Sciences.*

The Journal of Accountancy, March 1974

An analysis of how corporations and the accounting profession are complying with the APB's requirements for reporting changes in financial position

in·financial position to a status equal to that of the income statement and balance sheet. The requirement has been in effect for all periods ending after September 30, 1971.

Statement objectives

The objectives of a funds statement are as follows:

"1 To summarize the financing and investing activities of the entity, including the extent to which the enterprise has generated funds from operations during the period.

"2 To complete the disclosure of changes in financial position during the period."[1]

Principal financing activities include the issuance and retirement of owners' equity securities and the issuance and retirement of debt securities.

Operational activity is the net inflow of resources from operations. Investing activity is the allocation of available resources to productive activity. A firm's allocation of available resources to the improvement of current operations and expansion into new activities is an indication of management's future expectations. For example, if the firm is expanding capacity, this is an indication that management anticipates future growth and profitability.

The APB recognized that disclosure of financing and investing activities was not adequate. Guidelines are therefore set out in Opinion No. 19 that allow completion of the disclosure process. The section below lists these criteria and comments briefly on why each is necessary.

Statement format

Opinion No. 19 requires that all financing and investing activities be disclosed regardless of whether cash or working capital is affected.

Each corporation may adopt the disclosure format that is most informative in the circumstances as long as the presentation complies with the following general guidelines:

1 Cash or working capital provided from or used in operations should be prominently disclosed.
2 The effects of extraordinary items should be reported separately from the effects of normal items.
3 The effects of other financing and investing activities should be individually disclosed.[2]

Other specific disclosure requirements are:

[1] Accounting Principles Board Opinion No. 19, "Reporting Changes in Financial Position," par. 4 (New York: AICPA, 1971).

[2] *Ibid.*, pars. 10, 13.

Exhibit I
Principal statement components

ILLO Company
Statement of changes in financial position
year ended December 31, 19__

Resources provided:	Resources used:
From operations (cash or working capital)	Investing activities (plant equipment, new lines of business, debt retirement and dividends)
Extraordinary items	
Financing activities (debt and ownership securities)	Financing activities
	Total resources used
Total resources provided	

"In addition to working capital or cash provided from operations (see paragraph 10) and changes in elements of working capital (see paragraph 12), the statement should clearly disclose

"**a** Outlays for purchase of long-term assets (identifying separately such items as investments, property and intangibles).

"**b** Proceeds from sale (or working capital or cash provided by sale) of long-term assets (identifying separately such items as investments, property and intangibles) not in the normal course of business, less related expenses involving the current use of working capital or cash.

"**c** Conversion of long-term debt or preferred stock to common stock.

"**d** Issuance, assumption, redemption and repayment of long-term debt.

"**e** Issuance, redemption or purchase of capital stock for cash or for assets other than cash.

"**f** Dividends in cash or in kind or other distributions to shareholders (except stock dividends and stock split-ups as defined in ARB No. 43, Chapter 7B, 'Stock Dividends and Stock Split-Ups')."[3]

The general guidelines improve the informational content of the statement. The separation of operational items from extraordinary items enables the user to better identify continuing influences on cash or working capital. Individual disclosure of financing and investing inflows and net inflows from operations may be related to outflows for investing and financing activities. The statement data should enable the user to better evaluate the trend of resource flows and thus provide one more insight into possible future results. Exhibit I, above, provides a skeleton outline of the statement.

We believe the requirements of Opinion No. 19 have strengthened financial reporting. However,

there is still much room for improvement. The remaining sections of this article examine current practices and suggest additional improvements.

Current practices
A sample of 50 firms was randomly selected from the "Fortune 500." The statement of changes in financial position appearing in the 1971 annual report of each selected firm was examined. The results are reported below.[4]

The APB concluded that a statement of changes in financial position based on an all financial resources concept was essential. Although all sample firms included the statement in their reports, two of the 50 firms did not adopt the name change suggested as a better description of the broadened concept of the statement.

In addition to recommending a name change, the APB suggested that the terminology used in the statement be more explicit. It did not, however, specify or recommend any one set of terms for major headings within the statement.

The Opinion does imply quite strongly that the term "funds" is too ambiguous to be used effectively principally because its meaning has varied over the years. Twenty-one of the statements examined used terminology such as "funds provided." The continued use of this vague term does not improve the process of communication.

Eighteen of the 50 firms continued to use the major headings "working capital provided" and "working capital used (or applied)." The use of these captions when all changes in the financial resources are to be reported is misleading. Six firms used the innocuous captions "sources" and "uses." Thus, 45 of the 50 sample firms used terminology in their major internal statement headings that is far too easy to misinterpret.

Only 5 firms used what we view as preferred terminology, "resources provided" and "resources used." It is also more understandable to the layman and less subject to misinterpretation. This minor modification in terminology could substantially improve our reporting process. The professional accountant needs to exert effort to eliminate the carelessness and casualness exemplified by the reporting of 45 of our sample firms.

Opinion No. 19 specified that working capital or cash provided by operations be prominently disclosed. Forty-one firms specifically labeled the total. The other nine provided an unlabeled total within a section labeled operations.

The Opinion provides for flexibility in determining cash or working capital from operations. The conventional method which begins with income (loss) before extraordinary items and adds back (or deducts) items not requiring working capital or

[3] *Ibid.*, par. 14.

[4] An examination of the majority of 1972 statements shows little if any change in the format or content of the statement.

Exhibit II
Working capital provided by operations

Illustration of add-back format working capital approach

	1972	1971
Operations:		
Net income	$18,990	$11,905
Add (deduct) items not involving use of working capital		
Equity in earnings of related companies	(2,255)	(3,803)
Depreciation	10,225	8,921
Deferred income tax	1,040	2,892
Working capital provided by operations	$28,000	$19,915

rationally assumes a homogenous pool of resources and is, therefore, less informative.

The use of the all financial resources concept as required by Opinion No. 19 is better served by the cash approach. Short-term investing and financing activities are shown as either resources provided or used, or both, in the formal statement. Using the working capital approach, changes in the components of working capital can only be shown net. Generally these changes are excluded from the statement and shown separately. Financing and investing activities not affecting cash or working capital are, of course, disclosed in the same manner under either approach.

Flow through vs. add back

The presentation format adopted is critical for informative disclosure. Improper presentation will eliminate the advantages of any approach.

The presentation format adopted in the development stage was the add-back technique. This method starts with net income and adds back items not requiring the current use of working capital or cash. This short cut in computation has caused confusion. (Many "experts" still believe that depreciation is a direct source of funds).

The add-back technique remains the conventional approach. All 50 sample firms used this method. The classic argument for this approach as a simple and direct presentation has broken down. As our economy and financial reporting has become more complex, operational items not requiring or providing resources have expanded. Even using the working capital approach, the typical statement in our sample contained three or four items, either

added to or subtracted from income. Typical items included depreciation, depletion and amortization; deferred income taxes; equity in earnings of unconsolidated companies; installment accounts due after one year; dry hole cost; losses on discontinued operations; and minority interest.

Looking at Exhibit II, this page, can you expect the reader to understand why undistributed net earnings of unconsolidated subsidiaries is subtracted from operations or why deferred income taxes presents an addition to "from operations"? As a professional accountant how easily could you explain these items to an investor? When the cash approach is coupled with the add-back technique, the complexities and ambiguities increase in number because more items are involved.

The flow-through approach segregates the separate but related inflows and outflows from operations before arriving at a net number from operations. Exhibit III, page 59, clearly shows that revenues provided over $766,000 of working capital in 1972 while expenses required an outflow of over $739,000 in arriving at the $27,000 of working capital provided by operations. This format explicitly shows the inflows and outflows from operations. Sales are readily seen as a source of working capital (or cash) and expenses as a use of working capital (or cash). The adjustments for items not affecting working capital are presented in a straightforward manner. The explanation of why depreciation is omitted as an expense not requiring working capital is substantially easier than explaining why depreciation is added to net income.

For the reasons explained earlier, the cash approach is more useful than the working capital approach. Exhibit III is a schedule analyzing the net cash provided from operations using a flow-through

> In all cases changes in items such as inventories, accounts receivable and payable were treated as nonoperational. It appears as if the operations section is computed using a working capital approach while the statement professes to be cash.

approach. Note that the revenue and expense flows are adjusted for items not resulting in a current inflow or outflow of cash. This presentation parallels the normal operating cycle. Cash is expended for goods and services (i.e., inventory). These goods and services are then converted into a marketable product or service which is generally sold for credit. Cash is returned only to the business when collec-

Exhibit III

Working capital provided by operations illustration of flow-through format

	1972	1971
Operations:		
Revenues:	$769,314	$703,560
Less: Revenues not resulting in increase in working capital		
Equity in earnings of unconsolidated companies (net of dividends)	3,255	3,803
Working capital inflow from operations	$766,059	$699,757
Expenses:	$750,324	$691,655
Less: Expenses not requiring current outflow, working capital		
Depreciation	10,225	8,921
Deferred income taxes	1,040	2,892
	739,059	679,842
Working capital provided by operations	$ 27,000	$ 19,915

Exhibit IV

ILLO Company

Analysis of cash flow from operations for year ended December 31, 1972

Schedule I

Analysis of revenue flows:		
Revenue as reported on income statement		$4,600,000
Less: Increase in accounts and notes receivable that have no effect on cash inflow		54,000
Net cash inflow from operations		$4,546,000
Analysis of expense flows:		
Expense as reported on income statement		4,530,000
Plus: Increase in inventory which caused an increase in cash outflow		17,000
		4,547,000
Less: Changes in items that have no effect on cash outflow		
Amortization of intangibles	$10,000	
Depreciation	52,000	
Decrease in prepaid expenses	6,000	
Increase in accounts payable	19,000	
Increase in income tax	2,000	
Increase in accrued liabilities	4,000	
Increase in deferred income taxes	5,000	
Net changes not requiring cash outflow	98,000	
Net cash outflow from operations		4,449,000
Net cash flow from operations		$ 97,000

tions are made. The approach shown in Exhibit IV, page 59, allows analysis of the leads and lags in operational cash flows.

Exhibit IV, a separate schedule showing only the operational activities, displays the formal statement of changes in financial position. Exhibit IV and Exhibit V, this page, could be combined into a single statement. Showing the operational activities as a single figure and combining this amount with the financing and investing activities does present a more concise and clearer picture of the overall changes in financial position. The information in Exhibit IV is necessary to meet the disclosure guide-

---

. . . it is our recommendation that the cash approach using a flow-through format be adopted as a standard for presenting the statement of changes in financial position.

---

lines of Opinion No. 19.

The add-back technique is not readily adaptable to informative disclosure using the cash approach. There would be nine items added back or subtracted from net income using the facts in Exhibit IV. This greatly compounds the possibilities for confusion.

Each of the 5 sample firms that indicated they were accounting for a change in cash did not properly compute cash provided by operations. Exhibit VI, page 61, is typical of the presentation used. In all cases changes in items such as inventories, accounts receivable and payable were treated as non-operational. It appears as if the operations section is computed using a working capital approach while the statement professes to be cash. The result is a mixing of the working capital and cash approaches. This approach to cash from operations is a throw-back to the discredited idea that net income plus depreciation represents cash flow. This is clearly not what is meant by cash flow. Cash flow as described in Opinion No. 19 and as illustrated in Exhibits III and IV is an analysis of total cash inflows and cash outflows from operations. Operational activities do include changes in current operational assets such as accounts receivable and inventories.

In summary, it is our recommendation that the cash approach using a flow-through format be adopted as a standard for presenting the statement of changes in financial position.

Conclusions

With the issuance of Opinion No. 19 the profession recognized a third major financial statement, a statement of changes in financial position. Certainly the profession and the APB should be lauded for this major step forward.

The Journal of Accountancy, March 1974

The effectiveness of the statement has been limited because of the approach and presentation formats that have evolved. The traditional approach has been working capital with an add-back presentation format. This presentation may have been reasonably satisfactory in a less mature economy, but in our present environment it creates confusion and errors in interpretation (for example, the common belief that depreciation is a source of funds).

The add-back technique evolved as a short cut in the computation of operational flows and does not necessarily provide the most informative format. It is our belief that the flow-through approach does provide a disclosure that is more comprehensive and easier to understand. For these reasons it better meets the objectives of Opinion No. 19. This technique reveals all basic flows. It enables an investor to evaluate the trend of resource flows and thus gives him more insight into possible future results.

The determination of cash provided (or used) from operations is generally superior to working capital from operations. Cash represents a single resource rather than a pool; also, cash is the only completely discretionary resource available to management. In addition, the changes in current assets

---

Exhibit V

ILLO Company

Statement of changes in financial position for year ended December 31, 1972

Resources provided:		
Cash from operations (Schedule 1)		$ 97,000
Extraordinary gain from income statement	$2,000	
Book value of plant	6,000	8,000
Sale of investments		38,000
Increase in short-term notes payable		47,000
Increase in current portion of long-term debt		2,000
Increase in long-term debt		16,000
Total resources provided		$208,000
Resources applied:		
Short-term investments		$30,000
Plant and equipment investment		104,000
Payment of long-term debt		20,000
Treasury stock acquired		5,000
Dividends paid		40,000
Increase in cash		9,000
Total resources applied		$208,000

Exhibit VI

Consolidated statements of changes in financial position*
for the years ended December 31, 1972 and 1971

	1972	1971
Source of funds:		
From operations—		
Net earnings	$34,806	$25,665
Adjustments for noncash items:		
Equity in undistributed net earnings of 50 percent owned foreign affiliate	(8,336)	(4,013)
Minority shareholders' equity in net earnings	1,282	1,317
Depreciation	16,859	14,242
Provision for possible losses on receivables	600	600
Funds provided from operations	45,211	37,811
Borrowings—		
Notes payable to banks, due 1982	12,000	
Notes payable to banks, short-term	6,368	
Long-term, secured	1,171	591
Common stock sold under stock option plans	1,292	1,072
Reduction in notes and accounts receivable	2,585	17,444
Increase in accounts payable, accrued expenses and income taxes, etc.	11,560	13,729
	$80,187	$70,647
Disposition of funds:		
Reduction of debt—		
5¾ % notes payable to banks and insurance companies	$16,555	$14,170
Revolving credit	2,000	20,000
Debentures	4,200	2,188
Other	1,526	3,464
	$24,281	$39,822
Purchases of treasury stock	11,627	
Cash dividends paid	3,009	2,251
Additions to plant and equipment, less sales, retirements, etc., of $3,354,000 in 1972 and $7,083,000 in 1971	28,357	23,147
Increase in inventories	15,391	10,657
Increase (decrease) in other assets	(15)	4,190
	$82,650	$80,067
Reduction in funds for the year	(2,463)	(9,420)
Cash and marketable securities, beginning of year	22,505	31,925
Cash and marketable securities, end of year	$20,042	$22,505

*These tabulations are taken from an actual financial statement.

---

and current liabilities are properly related to operations, investing and financing activities.

Our sample survey shows that in general the profession has attempted to comply with the requirements of Opinion No. 19. Unfortunately, the terminology and formats selected often do not provide the most informative statements. We have pointed out some of these weaknesses that can be easily cor-

rected and thereby provide statements that better achieve the objectives of the Opinion.

It is our recommendation that the profession move to the adoption of the cash approach with a flow-through format. Certainly we should always be aware that financial statements are a one-to-many communication and that terminology and format are crucial. ∎

LET'S SCRAP THE "FUNDS" STATEMENT

The profession should identify the objectives of the funds statement and then design new statements that achieve those objectives.

by Loyd C. Heath

Funds statements found in practice today are a hodgepodge of miscellaneous information presented in a confusing and misleading way.

Many accountants see the problem as one of defining "funds." They attribute the confusion over the funds statement to confusion over what is meant by the term "funds." R. A. Rayman, for example, argued:

"The fact that funds analysis has not made more headway may be attributable to the absence of a definition of funds which is generally accepted. There is, in fact, a variety of definitions ranging over the whole spectrum of liquidity, from cash at one extreme to total resources at the other, with compromises like working capital somewhere in between."[1]

In my opinion, the fundamental problem is not a definitional one. Confusion over what is meant by the term funds is merely a symptom of a more basic problem: confusion over the objectives of the funds statement. The solution does not lie in redefining

funds; it lies in scrapping the funds statement, identifying the objectives it tries but fails to meet and designing statements that achieve those objectives.[2]

Specious Objectives

The stated objectives of funds statements in Accounting Principles Board Opinion no. 19, *Reporting Changes in Financial Position*, are specious. Superficially they appear to be reasonable but when analyzed and applied in practice they are unclear, misleading and unattainable. According to the opinion, the objectives are "(1) to summarize the financing and investing activities of the entity, including the extent to which the enterprise has generated funds from operations during the period, and (2) to complete the disclosure of changes in financial position during the period."

The meaning of the first objective is unclear. It begs the question of what effects of financing and investing activities should be summarized. Financing and investing activities, like all business activities, have many different effects. A single transaction may affect cash, working capital, total assets, capital structure, net assets and so forth. Obviously not all of those effects can be portrayed in a single statement, but the opinion is silent as to which one or ones are the object or objects of attention in the statement. Paragraph 8 says only that the statement "should be based on a broad concept embracing all changes in financial position" without even saying a broad concept of what! The problem reflects more than just poor draftsmanship; it reflects the absence of an underlying concept.

The second objective is unattainable. As noted, business activities have many effects. No statement can possibly "complete the disclosure of changes in financial position" (par. 4) or "disclose all important changes in financial position for the period covered" (par. 11). A meaningful statement must focus on

---

[1] R. A. Rayman, "Is Conventional Accounting Obsolete?" *Accountancy*, June 1970, p.423.

LOYD C. HEATH, Ph.D., is associate professor of accounting at the University of Washington, Seattle, Washington. He is a member of the American Accounting Association and the author of several articles that have appeared in professional publications.

The Journal of Accountancy, October 1978

---

[2] The analysis and recommendations that follow are based on my forthcoming research monograph, *Financial Reporting and the Evaluation of Solvency*, to be published by the accounting standards division of the American Institute of Certified Public Accountants.

a specific aspect or dimension of financial position such as cash, working capital, net assets, monetary assets and so forth. The possibilities are almost limitless. No statement can portray in an understandable way all effects of all activities on all possible measures of financial position. As Arthur Stone Dewing observed:

"But no representation of anything in this world can be perfect. It must portray one or more aspects or attributes of the thing represented and neglect or throw into insignificance the other aspects or attributes. This observation is conspicuously true when we are dealing with . . . accounting statements. Such statements must select one or at most a very few aspects of the objects represented and neglect all others—as vital statistics consider only the length of years of a man, neglecting every other aspect of his life or characteristics as a human being."[3]

Many of the alleged objectives of funds statements described in accounting literature are even more confusing than those in Opinion no. 19. For example, one widespread belief is that fund statements are somehow supposed to show what "happened" to a company's profits or "where its profits went."[4]

Profits are not a physical "thing" that can be disposed of, retained or paid out. Profit is

simply the name given to the change in a company's net assets that results from selected operating, financing and investing activities during a period of time, or, as the APB defined it, "the net increase (net decrease) in owners' equity (assets minus liabilities) of an enterprise for an accounting period from profit-directed activities. . . ."[5] It is a *change* in net assets, not an asset. It is measured in money but it is not money. One could, of course, show what became of a company's *cash*—part of which may have been received as a result of its profit-directed

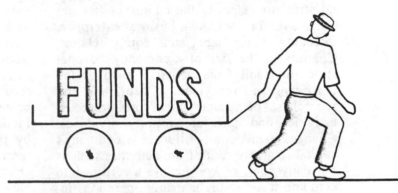

activities. A statement of cash receipts and payments would show that. Similarly, one could also prepare a statement that explains changes in some group of assets, say, its quick assets, part of which may have been received as a result of its profit-directed activities. But to try to show what "happened" to a company's profits is a meaningless objective; no statement can possibly show that.

Implicit Objectives

Although the APB's stated objectives in Opinion no. 19 are unclear, a careful reading of the opinion suggests that the board was concerned with reporting the effects of *all* business activities (not just financing and investing activities) on at least two and perhaps three different measures of financial position.

The first was to report changes in some measure of the cash or near-cash resources of a company, that is, changes in some measure of its debt-paying ability. A number of specific provisions of the opinion support that view. Paragraph 10 requires that "the Statement should prominently disclose working capital or cash provided from or used in

[3] Arthur Stone Dewing, *The Financial Policy of Corporations*, 5th ed., vol. 1 (New York: The Ronald Press Co., 1953), p.517.

[4] Perry Mason stated that a funds statement "contributes materially to . . . the answers to such questions as . . . Where did the profits go?" (Perry Mason, *"Cash Flow" Analysis and the Funds Statement*, Accounting Research Study no. 2 [New York: AICPA, 1961], p.49). Paton and Paton stated that a funds statement "is designed to . . . indicate what disposition has been made of earnings." (William A. Paton and William A. Paton, Jr., *Corporation Accounts and Statements* [New York: Macmillan Co., 1955], p.440). A. B. Carson maintains that "among other things it supplies an answer to the question: 'What happened to the profit?'" (A. B. Carson, "A Source and Application of Funds' Philosophy of Financial Accounting," *Accounting Review*, April 1949, p.160). Roy A. Foulke argues that it "gives a clear answer to the question of what has become of the net profits." (Roy A. Foulke, *Practical Financial Statement Analysis*, 6th ed. [New York: McGraw-Hill Book Co., Inc., 1968], p.474).

For other similar examples, see Donald A. Corbin, "Proposals for Improving Funds Statements," *Accounting Review*, July 1961, p.398; National Association of Accountants Research Report no. 38, *Cash Flow Analysis for Managerial Control*, (New York: NAA, 1961), p.58; David F. Hawkins, *Corporate Financial Reporting*, rev. ed. (Homewood, Ill.; Richard D. Irwin, Inc., 1977), p.125; Donald E. Kieso and Jerry J. Weygandt, *Intermediate Accounting*, 2nd ed. (New York: John Wiley & Sons, 1977), p. 983; and Jay M. Smith, Jr., and K. Fred Skousen, *Intermediate Accounting*, 6th ed. (Englewood Cliffs, N.J.: Prentice-Hall, Inc., 1977), p.682.

[5] APB Statement no. 4, *Basic Concepts and Accounting Principles* (New York: AICPA, 1971), par. 134.

operations for the period." Paragraph 11 states, "The Statement may be in balanced form or in a form expressing the changes in financial position in terms of cash, or cash and temporary investments combined, of all quick assets, or of working capital." Paragraph 14 further specifically requires that "outlays for purchase of long-term assets . . . proceeds from sale (or working capital or cash provided by sale) of long-term assets" and "dividends in cash" all be disclosed.

The second type of change that the board appears to have been concerned with having reported was capital structure changes. Capital structure refers to the claims on the resources used to operate a business enterprise, including both debt and equity claims. Changes in the size of a company's capital structure result from activities such as the borrowing and repayment of debt, sale and repurchase of capital stock, profit-directed activities and cash or property dividends. Changes in the composition of a company's capital structure result from activities such as the conversion of convertible securities into common stock and refinancing operations including the "swapping" of one type of financial instrument for another in a financial reorganization.

Many changes in the size and composition of a company's capital structure also affect its cash, it working capital and other measures of debt-paying ability, but some of them do not. Evidence that the board was concerned with having changes in the size and composition of a company's capital structure as well as changes in its debt-paying ability reported is found in the requirement in paragraph 14 that "the Statement should clearly disclose" activities such as "conversion of long-term debt or preferred stock to common stock . . . issuance, redemption, or purchase of capital stock . . . for assets other than cash" and "dividends . . . in kind or other distributions to shareholders." Other evidence of the board's concern with changes in a company's capital structure is found in paragraph 6:

"However, a funds statement based on either the cash or the working capital concept of funds sometimes excludes certain financing and investing activities because they do not directly affect cash or working capital during the period. For example, issuing equity securities to acquire a building is both a financing and investing transaction but does not affect either cash or working capital. To meet all of its objectives, a funds statement should disclose separately the fi-

nancing and investing aspects of all significant transactions that affect financial position during a period. These transactions include acquisition or disposal of property in exchange for debt or equity securities and conversion of long-term debt or preferred stock to common stock."

The third type of change that the board seems to have been concerned with having reported is changes in a company's long-term assets such as plant and equipment and long-term investments. Many of the increases in those assets would, of course, be revealed by a statement that shows only changes in cash or working capital. Some, however, such as those resulting from the issuance of debt or equity securities, would be excluded from that type of statement.

The requirement to show the issuance of securities for consideration other than cash or working capital as sources and uses of funds appears to have been motivated in part by the desire to disclose changes in long-term assets as well as the desire to disclose changes in a company's capital structure. However, the opinion does not contain similar requirements for transactions that increase long-term assets but do not either decrease working capital (or other measure of debt-paying ability) or increase total capital. Such transactions are undoubtedly unusual but do occur. The exchange of a long-term investment in securities for plant and equipment or the exchange of land for securities are examples. The opinion requires that outlays for the purchase of long-term assets be disclosed but whether the term "outlays" embraces or excludes exchanges of the kind mentioned is not clear.

In summary, the APB may have intended to require the disclosure of all increases in long-term assets, but its intentions are not clear. It certainly gave no indication of any desire to show decreases in long-term assets; only the "proceeds from sale (or working capital or cash provided by sale) of long-term assets," not the book value of assets sold, is required to be disclosed.

Relevant Objectives

Changes in all three of the measures of financial position discussed in the last section are clearly of interest to investors, creditors and other external users of financial statements. Changes in debt-paying ability are of such obvious interest to creditors and investors that the matter hardly requires comment; the only real issue is which measure of debt-paying ability is likely to be most useful. Changes in the size and composition of a company's capital structure are also clearly of interest. One of the most widely used financial ratios in credit analysis is the ratio of debt to equity. That ratio would obviously be affected by changes in the composition of a company's capital structure such as the conversion of debentures into common stock and various kinds of refinancing operations. The nature of those activities and a report of how they affect a company's capital structure would, therefore, also be of interest. Changes in the amount or composition of long-term assets are likely to signal changes in a company's future profits and future cash needs so that they, too, are likely to be of interest to investors and creditors.

Conflicting Objectives

The basic problem with Opinion no. 19 is not, therefore, that it requires disclosure of unimportant or irrelevant information but that it requires too many different types of information to be disclosed on the same statement. The result is a confusing statement.

Financial statements are maps of economic territory; they portray the financial characteristic of business enterprises. Different maps are needed for different purposes because only a limited amount of information can be portrayed on a single map. A single geographic map designed to portray changes in annual rainfall, changes in educational level of the population, changes in agricultural crops and changes in unemployment is not likely to portray any of that information clearly. Similarly, a single financial statement designed to portray many different types of changes in the financial position of a business enterprise is not likely to portray any of that information clearly. That, however, is exactly what Opinion no. 19 requires of the funds statement. To achieve the multiple and disparate objectives of that statement, the term funds was defined so broadly that it has become meaningless, and

a funds statement based on a meaningless concept of funds does not communicate information effectively. That is the heart of the problem of the confusing funds statements found in practice today.

Recommendation

Once the basis of the confusion over the funds statement is diagnosed, the general nature of a solution becomes obvious; several different statements are needed to communicate clearly the information now crammed into a single statement. Specifically, three

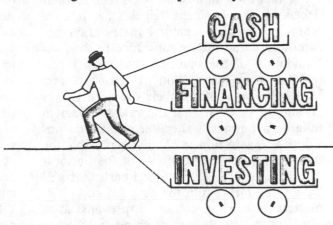

statements are needed to replace the funds statement and achieve its objectives: a statement of cash receipts and payments, a statement of financing activities and a statement of investing activities.

Statement of Cash Receipts and Payments

One of the relevant objectives of funds statements is to report changes in some measure of debt-paying ability. Both historically and currently the measure of debt-paying ability used most frequently in funds statements has been working capital. That measure is rejected here in favor of cash.

The principal reason for recommending a change from working capital as a measure of debt-paying ability to cash is that the approach to evaluation of a company's solvency, or "credit analysis" as it is often called, has changed and the information needs of financial statement users have therefore also changed. During the 1920s when funds statements based on working capital changes were developed, the adequacy of a company's working capital position, particularly as measured by its current ratio, was considered the "alpha and omega" of credit analysis.[6] It was argued that current liabilities are paid with current assets and current

---

[6] Foulke, p.178.

assets must therefore exceed current liabilities by an "adequate margin."

During the 1950s there was a searching reappraisal of working capital as a measure of debt-paying ability. Arthur Stone Dewing wrote in 1953 that "bankers learned by tragic experience that there was no mystical significance in the two-to-one ratio. They observed that in many types of business, under the stress of general disaster, inventories could not be sold, and if such an attempt should be made, not a two-to-one or even a three- or four-to-one ratio would bring them the immediate payment of their debts. If the business failed, the relative amounts of current capital in the days before failure had little significance in the final liquidation of the bankrupt business."[7]

That same year Bion B. Howard and Miller Upton wrote in their classic text that "it should be clear that the real problem in judging a business's short-term financial position is to ascertain as closely as possible the future cash-generating ability of the business in relation to the claims upon cash that will have to be met within the near future. . . . It matters not what condition prevails at a given time; the important thing is whether the business in performing its regular operating functions can continue to generate cash in sufficient quantity and in satisfactory time to meet all operating and financial obligations."[8]

More recently, John B. Coughlan observed ironically that "working capital has been thought of as a 'pool' of resources available to satisfy the claims of short-term creditors. But it is unlikely that any banker or creditor will slake his thirst from any part of the pool other than the cash portion. Many a firm has been known to pay its debts with cash, but not one has drawn a check on working capital. Working capital, *per se*, has no bearing on short-term credit standing and it is only useful for whatever implications it may have for cash and cash flow."[9]

Those views are widely accepted by financial analysts today. The emphasis in credit analysis has shifted from analysis of current working capital position to dynamic analysis of future cash receipts and payments in much the same way that the emphasis in security analysis shifted from static analysis of balance sheet values to dynamic analysis of net income some thirty or forty years earlier.[10]

The central question in credit analysis today is not whether a company's working capital is "adequate" but whether the cash expected to be received within a given time period will equal or exceed required cash payments within that same period. Analysis of working capital position does not provide that information. A company's principal sources of cash are from sale of its products or services to its customers, from borrowing and from issuance of stock to investors. Its principal uses are payments to employees, suppliers and governments, repayment of debt and purchase of plant and equipment. Most of the cash a company will receive within the following year is not represented by assets classified as current, and most of the obligations it will have to pay are not represented by liabilities classified as current.

The old concept of current assets as the source from which current liabilities will be paid is meaningless under this framework of analysis. Current liabilities are not paid with current assets; they are paid with cash. Whether a company's current or its noncurrent assets were the source of its cash is an unanswerable question. One can no more determine whether current or noncurrent assets provided the cash generated by a company's operations than he can determine which blade of the scissors cut the cloth, because both were clearly necessary.[11]

The rationale for recommending a statement of cash receipts and payments as one of the statements to replace the funds statement is implicit in the above discussion. If a financial statement user's primary object of attention is the future cash receipts and payments of a company, then it follows that a statement of past cash receipts and payments would be useful for the same reason that historical income statements are useful in predicting the future income of a company: both provide a basis for predicting future performance.

[7] Dewing, pp.708-09.

[8] Bion B. Howard and Miller Upton, *Introduction to Business Finance* (New York: McGraw-Hill Book Co., Inc., 1953), p.135.

[9] John W. Coughlan, "Funds and Income," *NAA Bulletin*, September 1964, p.25.

[10] For a discussion of this shift in security analysis, see Benjamin Graham, David L. Dodd and Sidney Cottle, *Security Analysis: Principles and Technique*, 4th ed. (New York: McGraw-Hill Book Co., Inc., 1962), p.214.

[11] The role of current–noncurrent classification of assets and liabilities in the evaluation of a company's solvency is discussed more fully in the monograph referred to in footnote 1. That study concludes that the present practice of identifying certain assets and liabilities as current on a company's balance sheet is misleading and recommends that it be discontinued.

Reporting cash receipts and payments is widely advocated today by many financial statement users, particularly bankers. For example, Walter B. Wriston, chairman of the board of Citibank, N.A., stated in a recent speech before Peat, Marwick, Mitchell & Co. personnel, "When I came into the banking business, we were asset-conscious and we loaned money on that basis. Well, assets give you a warm feeling, but they don't generate cash. The first question I would ask any borrower these days is, 'What is your break-even cash flow?' That's the one thing we can't find out from your audit reports and it's the single most important question we ask. It's important that you figure out a way to present the difference between real cash flow and accrual cash flow."[12]

An example of the form of cash receipts and payments statement recommended, together with a recommended supporting schedule showing details of cash provided by operations, is presented for Example, Inc., in exhibit 1, page 100.

Only business activities that affected cash are shown on the statement of cash receipts and payments. If financing and investing activities that did not affect cash are shown on statements of cash receipts and payments as if they did, users will become confused over the purpose of the statement and what it shows. Financing transactions that did not affect cash are shown on the recommended statement of financing activities; investing transactions that did not affect cash are shown on the recommended statement of investing activities.

For the purpose of clarity of presentation, details of cash provided by profit-directed activities or what are called operations (to simplify terminology on the statement) are shown on a separate schedule rather than on the face of the statement of cash receipts and payments. Both the absolute magnitude of many of the cash receipts and payments from operations (such as the amount of cash collected from customers and the amount paid for merchandise) as well as the many types of cash payments would tend to overshadow some of the other items on the statement of cash receipts and payments (such as cash borrowed and fixed assets purchased), which may be of greater significance to the financial statement user in estimating future cash receipts and payments.

The schedule of the cash provided by

operations illustrates the direct (as opposed to the indirect) method of calculating that amount. When the direct method is used, the schedule shows the actual sources and uses of cash. If the indirect method was used, the schedule would start with net income and adjust that figure for all revenues and expenses that did not affect cash. Those are the two alternative methods of presenting funds provided by operations in statements of changes in financial position that the APB described as acceptable in Opinion no. 19.

The indirect method is basically a set of worksheet adjustments rather than an explanation of how operating activities affected cash. It is analogous to calculating income by subtracting stockholders' equity at the beginning of the year from stockholders' equity at the end of the year and then adjusting the

"A statement of cash receipts and payments alone would not accomplish all of the objectives of Opinion no. 19."

difference for nonincome items, such as dividends and purchases and sales of capital stock. This method, of course, will always "work" if the proper adjustments are made, but if accountants were to prepare income statements in this way, many financial statement users would be confused. They would begin to describe dividends, for example, as a "source" of income in the same way they now describe depreciation as a "source" of funds because they are both "add-backs" when the indirect method of calculation is used. The indirect method of calculating cash provided by operations is pernicious because it is almost certain to continue to confuse financial statement users by reinforcing the incredible belief that profits and depreciation are sources of cash. The direct method, on the other hand, is likely to be useful in dispelling some of the confusion that now exists over the relationship between business activities and cash receipts and payments because it shows clearly that profits are neither cash nor a source of cash, that cash comes from customers, that it is paid for merchan-

12 *World* (Peat, Marwick, Mitchell & Co.), Spring 1974, p.49.

Exhibit 1

Example, Inc.
Cash receipts and payments statement
Year ending December 31, 1977

Cash balance December 31, 1976		$15,666
Sources of cash:		
Cash provided by operations (schedule 1)	$27,537	
Sale of marketable securities	3,062	
Sale of land, buildings and equipment	12,793	
Net amount borrowed	31,092	
Received from sale of common stock	7,495	81,979
Cash available		97,645
Uses of cash:		
Land, buildings and equipment purchased	62,119	
Dividends paid	13,558	75,677
Cash balance December 31, 1977		$21,968

Schedule 1

Calculation of cash provided by operations

Cash collected from customers		$783,545
Interest and dividends received		1,417
Total cash receipts from operations		784,962
Cash payments:		
For merchandise inventories	$457,681	
For administrative and selling expenses	264,577	
For interest	6,941	
For other expenses	14,953	
For taxes	13,273	757,425
Cash provided by operations		$ 27,537

---

dise, administrative and selling expenses, taxes and so forth and that depreciation is neither a source nor a use of cash.

Statement of Financing Activities

A statement of cash receipts and payments alone would not accomplish all of the objectives of Opinion no. 19. The APB was concerned with the effects of business activities on the size and composition of a company's capital structure and on its long-term assets as well as how those activities affected its debt-paying ability. The second statement recommended in this article, the statement of financing activities, is designed to achieve the second of those objectives: disclosure of the effects of business activities on the capital structure of a firm.

Before describing and discussing the recommended form of the statement of financing activities, it is necessary to clarify what is meant by the term "capital structure." As noted earlier, that term is used to refer to the claims on a company's resources. Typically,

however, only equity and long-term debt are considered parts of a company's capital structure; short-term debt is excluded. Some short-term debt, however, such as bank loans and commercial paper, is analogous to long-term debt in the sense that it requires conscious effort or specific negotiation on the part of owners or managers to obtain. Other short-term debt does not require conscious effort or negotiation to obtain; it is "spontaneous" or "self-generating" and grows "out of normal patterns of profitable operations without especial effort or conscious decision on the part of owners or managers."[13] Examples of spontaneous debt include trade accounts payable, wages payable and taxes payable. Debt that requires negotiation, whether short or long term, may be referred

[13] Pearson Hunt, Charles M. Williams and Gordon Donaldson, *Basic Business Finance*, rev. ed. (Homewood, Ill.: Richard D. Irwin, Inc., 1961), p.116.

to as financing liabilities. Debt that does not require negotiation may be referred to as spontaneous liabilities.[14]

Although both short-term financing liabilities and spontaneous liabilities are usually classified as current, the distinction is useful in preparing a statement of financing activities because different underlying considerations affect the amount of credit available from those two different sources. The amount available from spontaneous sources depends on considerations such as the volume of purchases of inventories and supplies, normal credit terms of a company's suppliers and conventional practices as to frequency of payment of salaries and wages. Credit available from spontaneous sources tends to increase as sales rise and fall when sales decline. Credit available from short-term financing sources, on the other hand, depends on the same basic consideration as credit available from long-term sources, that is, lenders' evaluations of a company's ability to repay a loan when due. Furthermore, financial statement users tend to regard commercial paper and short-term bank loans (which may, in fact, be short term in name only) as financing sources in the same sense that bonds and long-term bank loans are financing sources. Consequently, the term "capital structure" as used in this article refers to both equity capital and financing liabilities regardless of whether those financing liabilities are short or long term.[15] A statement such as the current form of funds statement that purports to report financing activities but excludes by definition a class of financing activities that most businessmen regard as major sources of financing is misleading.

[14] R. K. Mautz made a similar distinction. He referred to "primary financing interests" and "incidental financing interests." He argued that incidental financing interests including, for example, trade creditors and employees "provide financing, but this is neither the primary intent of the particular interest nor the basic reason for the transaction." (R. K. Mautz, *An Accounting Technique for Reporting Financial Transactions*, Special Bulletin no. 7 [Urbana, Ill.: University of Illinois, Bureau of Economic and Business Research, 1951], pp.21-22.)
[15] Other implications of the distinction between financing and spontaneous liabilities are discussed in the monograph referred to in footnote 1. That study recommends that liabilities be classified as financing, operating and tax. Operating and tax liabilities are two types of spontaneous liabilities.

A statement of financing activities for Example, Inc., is shown in exhibit 2, page 102. This statement is similar in form to the recommended statement of cash receipts and payments. It explains changes in a company's capital structure in much the same way that a statement of cash receipts and payments explains changes in its cash position. However, it includes changes in the composition of a company's capital structure (conversion of securities into common stock) as well as changes in its size. Profits and dividends as well as financing activities more narrowly defined, such as borrowing and repayment of debt and purchase and sale of capital stock, all affect a company's capital structure and should therefore be shown on the statement of financing activities.

Many business activities that affect a company's capital structure, such as borrowing money, repayment of debt, sale of capital stock and payment of dividends, also affect its cash position and should therefore appear on its statement of cash receipts and payments as receipts and payments of cash as well as on its statement of financing activities. While this might appear to be duplicate reporting of those activities, it really is not. Different effects of them are reported on each of the two statements. The statement of cash receipts and payments reports their effects on cash, whereas the statement of financing activities reports their effects on capital structure. That is necessary to keep both statements clear, simple and understandable. The alternative, of course, is to design a statement that reports both types of effects on a single statement. That is what the APB tried to do in Opinion no. 19. It cannot be done in such a way that both the objectives of the statement as well as the information reported on it are clear and understandable to financial statement users.

Both increases and decreases in each type of debt instrument are shown on the recommended statement of financing activities rather than only net changes. The fact that a company engaged in extensive short-term financing, for example, during the year may be regarded as significant by some financial statement users even though there was little or no net change in that liability. It indicates a dependence on credit that, if jeopardized, could have important implications. Although not illustrated in exhibit 2, the rate of interest and other significant terms of any new financing might usefully be described briefly either on the face of the statement or in notes to the statement. Other details of financing might also be usefully shown. Divorcing the statement from cash or working capital changes allows both the preparer and user to focus attention on financing activities and may open the door to several additional types of disclosure not illustrated in exhibit 2.

Statement of Investing Activities

A statement of investing activities is the third of the three statements recommended to replace the funds statement. The rationale for such a statement is that long-term investment in plant and in securities acquired for the purpose of control have special significance to financial statement users because they represent relatively inflexible long-term commitments and all changes in those assets should therefore be reported.

A statement of investing activities for Example, Inc., is presented in exhibit 3, page 103.

The statement of investing activities should disclose all acquisitions of long-term investments (including plant and equipment, investments in other controlled companies and deferred charges of various types) re-

gardless of whether they were acquired for cash, for debt or equity securities or in exchange for other real assets. The statement of cash receipts and payments, of course, would show the cash paid for long-term investments, and the statement of financing activities would show the securities issued, but only the statement of investing activities would disclose all acquisitions. Retirements and other decreases of long-term investments, on the other hand, would appear only on the statement of cash receipts and payments to the extent they were sold for cash, and they would rarely appear on the statement of financing activities, but they would appear on the statement of investing activities.

Conclusion

In 1964 John B. Coughlan observed that the funds statement based on working capital changes has "baffled a generation of accounting students" and "it is therefore hardly conceivable that it has enlightened stockholders and other lay readers."[16] In the years since Coughlan wrote, two APB opinions on the

---

[16] Coughlan, p.24.

Exhibit 2

Example, Inc.
Statement of financing activities
Year ending December 31, 1977

	Increase or (decrease)
Debt financing	
Notes payable to banks	
Borrowed	$ 50,000
Repaid	(16,908)
Net amount borrowed	33,092
Mortgage repaid	(2,000)
Net increase in debt financing	31,092
Equity financing	
Convertible preferred	
Conversion of 300 shares $100 par value 5% convertible	
preferred for 1,500 shares $10 par value common stock	(30,000)
Common stock and capital in excess of par	
Issued 1,500 shares on conversion of 300 shares	
5% convertible preferred	30,000
Issued 500 shares for $7,495 cash	7,495
Retained earnings	
Net increase	3,983
Net increase in equity financing	$11,478

Exhibit 3

Example, Inc.
Statement of investing activities
Year ending December 31, 1977

Plant and equipment

Land, buildings and equipment, December 31, 1976	$319,101
Plus purchases	62,119
	381,220
Less cost of properties disposed of	31,595
Land, buildings and equipment, December 31, 1977	$349,625

subject of funds statements have been issued. They have baffled another generation of accountants by casting the funds statement in the role of a statement with no clear goal or purpose but merely as a dumping ground for reporting heterogeneous transactions not reported elsewhere. The result should have been predictable: these statements do not enlighten either lay or sophisticated users.

The solution to the problem of the enigmatic funds statement does not lie in searching for a new definition of funds that will enable all of the objectives of the statements to be achieved. It lies in identifying clearly the financial reporting objectives that need to be achieved but are not achieved by the balance sheet and income statement and designing new statements that achieve those objectives. ∎

Although accounting systems are accepted as the financial information intermediaries of the business community, some of their information gathering, processing and dissemination techniques have been criticized as major obstacles to management decision-making. Part of this criticism is aimed at the amount of data that must be aggregated by the traditional accounting systems in order for it to perform its recording and processing duties. Critics have

INVENTORY CONTROL: USING A SYSTEM OF DATA BASE MANAGEMENT

Data base management is an innovative system of information storage and retrieval that holds benefits for the executive concerned with inventory control, operations and planning. The system is an important building block in a total management information approach to decision-making.

WILLIAM E. BLOUCH
Assistant Professor of Accounting
Shippensburg State College

felt that valuable information is lost to a firm almost in proportion to the degree of its data aggregation; under traditional information-gathering systems such information could have been useful for decision-making.

DATA BASE MANAGEMENT

Since the early seventies, the concepts of data bases and data base management systems (DBMS), operating within a total management information system (MIS), have received much attention as possible remedies to this problem. Perhaps the most important characteristic of a DBMS is the way it operates with respect to information flows. Functioning as part of a total management information system, the data base approach creates a reservoir of business information within the company, available to all although specific data still may be retained by one group or department in the organization.

Data base management has been defined as an attempt to develop a corporate management information system that cuts across various corporate functional areas. Therefore, a data base is a structured, integrated collection of files and records stored on computer-based, direct access storage devices. This data base provides information required in the decision-making process at all management levels.

Due to the free flowing nature of the data base system, raw data is randomly entered and stored. Utilizing the computer's capabilities and a software application program, the system is designed to use raw data and construct needed information in any type of summary report that might be desired. Of course, this assumes management really knows what information it needs. Although a

FINANCIAL EXECUTIVE September 1980

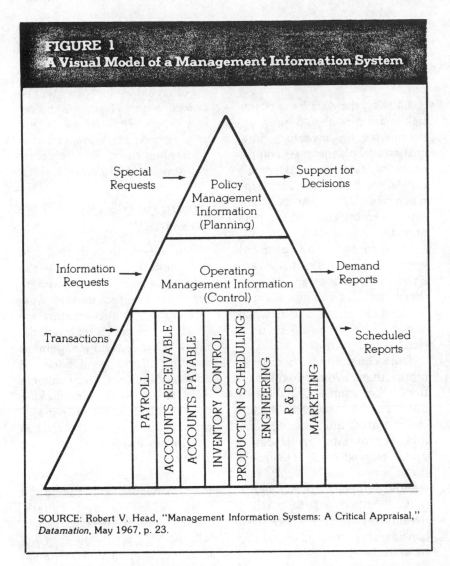

FIGURE 1
A Visual Model of a Management Information System

Special Requests →

Policy Management Information (Planning)

→ Support for Decisions

Information Requests →

Operating Management Information (Control)

→ Demand Reports

Transactions →

PAYROLL

ACCOUNTS RECEIVABLE

ACCOUNTS PAYABLE

INVENTORY CONTROL

PRODUCTION SCHEDULING

ENGINEERING

R & D

MARKETING

→ Scheduled Reports

SOURCE: Robert V. Head, "Management Information Systems: A Critical Appraisal," *Datamation*, May 1967, p. 23.

a management information system is constructed of three parts:

■ A standard, integrated data base.

■ A system design that provides for data base input to be used in the efficient and timely development of required information.

■ The facility or plan to utilize such data for projecting future activity and for planning management action.

And, when attempting to define a management information system, it is evident how important the role of data base management really can be. One acceptable definition, of many, is that a management information system is the set of human and capital resources within an organization. It is responsible for collecting and processing data that yields useful information for management planning and control activities.

A model of how a management information system functions is presented in **Figure 1.** Functional business areas are represented horizontally, while the upper two vertical levels represent the basic management information needs. Request and transaction information enter the system, as does input from the various departments. Such information might be stored in the data base, which would provide information for use in scheduled reports, i.e. those used in payroll processing or inventory control, and for demand reports and would be useful in controlling and possibly directing operations. Of equal importance, the data base

direct-access, on-line, computer-based system might be desirable to use with a DBMS, batch processing also is possible. And, many business organizations utilizing the batch mode easily could adapt to an on-line DBMS.

People from all departments of a firm using the system would be able to enter, retrieve and monitor the data, using reference categories, passwords, or other types of access keys. Compared to the traditional financial accounting system, a management information system which utilizes the data base concept could provide decision-makers with more timely and accurate information, enabling them to make better corporate judgments.

MANAGEMENT INFORMATION SYSTEMS

As indicated earlier, a DBMS is only one part of a firm's total management information system, however, it is an important part of that system. It is a building block for the MIS. Generally, would supply information useful in supporting decisions made in the planning function of the organization. Of course, different levels of management may utilize different pieces of data. The data base subsystem serves as the link that joins the entire MIS into an integrated whole, by providing the means for gathering and communicating data.

DBS INVENTORY CONTROL

Utilizing a DBMS within a complete management information system, managers will be able to minimize total inventory costs while maintaining sufficient and proper inventory levels. These costs include carrying costs, reordering costs, costs associated with backorders, as well as costs experienced from lost sales when inventory is depleted.

At the functional level, various inventory models exist to determine optimum levels of inventories and optimum reorder quantities (and times). Firms can perform cost/benefit analyses to determine what models best suit their needs. While, most of these models depend on data availability, as management information systems become more sophisticated, more timely and accurate information will be available.

INVENTORY FORECASTING

Management planning decisions are equally as important as

any decisions made at the control and operational level. In fact, it has been suggested that planning decisions are the most critical.

Utilizing the data base potential, managers should seek opportunities for inventory forecasting and planning. As competition increases, it is extremely critical for both small and large businesses to minimize their total inventory costs and to plan ahead.

Assuming management knows and has defined the variables to be forecasted, data on these variables can be collected so that it is available when needed for forecasting or decision-making purposes.

Data can come from sources other than ordinary transactions. For example, published data can be purchased and incorporated into the system, and original data can be developed or collected. However, these steps usually incur substantial additional costs. Quantitative methods of forecasting inventories generally require considerable amounts of data to be collected before they can be used in preparing a forecast. Frequently, a lack of historical data is a big problem. Use of the data base concept could help alleviate this problem, since the system acts both as an information clearing house and repository of data.

Also, as varied data are collected, a data pool is created. More varied demand reports and information requests could be generated for those controlling inventory levels and costs. Moreover, those managers involved with planning would have data available that could be used to analyze alternative decisions. In the future, the quality of inventory forecasts will be crucial in minimizing total inventory costs. But, forecasts are only as good as the data used in generating them. Bad forecasts increase inventory costs.

CONCLUSION AND SUMMARY

Innovations in gathering and communicating data, outside the traditional role of the accounting function, are required to adequately fulfill the information needs of all levels of management. Data base management systems offer a good basis for collecting and utilizing available data, to aid the decision-making process at all levels of management. This is especially true in controlling inventory levels and costs.

At the functional level, inventory managers are concerned with the use of historic data. Using a DBMS, these managers will be able to obtain specific, updated summary information about inventories from the data base as needed.

For managers of smaller firms, as well as those of larger corporations, the major advantages of DBMS for inventory control, operations and planning lie in utilizing information taken from the data base, in their decision-making process. Data base management, as part of an overall management information system, offers vast opportunities for the more effective managing of inventories. □

The Hammer of "Thor"

The potential penalties for noncompliance with *Thor Power* could be substantial.

By Carolyn J. Benner-Dale

Carolyn J. Benner-Dale is a senior assistant accountant with the tax department of Charlotte, N.C., office of Deloitte Haskins & Sells. She has a Juris Doctor degree from the University of South Carolina Law School. She is a member of Charlotte Gold Chapter, through which she submitted this article.

Effective for taxable years ending on or after December 25, 1979, the IRS is providing a mandatory procedure for restoring write-downs for "excess" inventory in accordance with the unanimous Supreme Court decision in *Thor Power Tool Co. v. IRS Commissioner,* 439 U.S. 522 (1979).

The *Thor Power* case involved a taxpayer using the lower-of-cost-or-market method of valuing inventory on a consistent basis. Facing the problem of predicting future demand for its tools, Thor decided to produce liberal quantities of the parts to ensure timely, adequate supply and to prevent costly additional production runs. The result was "excess" inventory, a common problem of many manufacturers.

In 1964, Thor's principal stockholder entered into an agreement with Thor to buy most of its assets. A subsequent audit revealed that Thor's assets were overstated and the stockholder rescinded the agreement, deciding to provide Thor with management assistance. Under new management, Thor made substantial write-downs of obsolete goods which were to be scrapped shortly thereafter. In addition, Thor decided to write down inventory held in excess of any reasonably foreseeable future demand to net realizable value (which, in most instances, was scrap value). This write-down was, and is, in accordance with generally accepted accounting principles (GAAP).

The measure of the write-down was based on management's estimates of the ultimate salability of the goods. Thor's estimate of future demand was determined by an aging schedule that the Court found to be subjective in nature. For example, if only 20% of the units on hand at the end of the year of any item were sold during the year, that item would be arbitrarily written down by 72.5%. This write-down was based upon anticipated demand for such item over a period of two years. If a certain number of units of an item was not expected to be sold or used in production within a two-year period, the item would be written down completely to scrap value. Despite the "excess" inventory write-down, Thor continued to hold the items for sale at original prices.

Table 1 shows inventory valuation under the lower-of-cost-or-market method. This valuation method, according to the Court's decision in *Thor,* requires objective evidence substantiating write-downs in accordance with the regulations.

As Table 1 shows, "excess" inventory is not segregated into a separate category to alleviate the otherwise stringent evidential standards of the Regulations. As a general rule, a taxpayer must

0025-1690/80/6205-3468/$01.00/0

value its "excess" inventory at replacement cost, if lower than actual cost. To substantiate a loss due to lack of foreseeable demand, a taxpayer must show, at a minimum, that it offered the goods for sale within 30 days of the inventory date. In such a case, the taxpayer is allowed to value goods at net realizable value, if lower than both replacement cost and original cost.

Thor has been widely criticized for not affording "excess" inventory special treatment. The Supreme Court held that the taxpayer could not write down its parts inventory to scrap unless it actually scrapped the parts. In addition, it confirmed the broad discretion of the Commissioner in determining whether an accounting method clearly reflects income.

The task of identifying slow or nonmoving goods and actually offering them for sale within 30 days at lower prices will be onerous. Companies using either a percentage write-down or an aging formula write-down almost assuredly will face disallowance under Thor Power. It has been suggested that actual scrapping of otherwise normal "excess" goods is not only unsound from a business point of view, but would cause a widespread lack of availability of parts to meet consumer needs. On the other hand, if spare parts were kept in inventory to meet consumer demand, the additional taxes imposed would be passed on to the consumer in the form of increased prices, thereby promoting inflation.

GAAP Vs. Tax Accounting

Generally accepted accounting principles define "market" as the median of:
- current replacement cost
- net realizable value (i.e., the estimated selling price in the ordinary course of business, less reasonably predictable costs of completion and disposal), and
- net realizable value less an allowance for an approximately normal profit margin.

For example, an item that cost $23 can be replaced at inventory date at a cost of $25. The estimated selling price is $28 and the costs of completion and disposal are $8. The approximately normal profit margin is 15%.

Cost		=$23
Market:		
Replacement cost	$25	
NRV $28-8	$20	
NRV-normal profit		
$20-.15 ($20)	=17	
median (middle figure)		=$20
Lower-of-cost-or-market under GAAP		=$20

For comparison, let's look at tax methods of accounting. Internal Revenue Code Section 446 provides that a method of accounting used for books must be used for tax purposes unless it does not clearly reflect income. The regulations thereunder state that if the method used is in accordance with GAAP applied on a consistent basis, the method will "ordinarily" be regarded as clearly reflecting income.

Although the Supreme Court in Thor conceded that the write-down of "excess" inventory by Thor is in accordance with GAAP, the Court does not attempt to rationalize inequivalency between financial and tax accounting. It firmly concludes that application of a GAAP method will be acceptable for tax purposes only if it clearly reflects income. In such regard, a tax deduction will be deferred until all events have occurred which will make it fixed and certain. Reasonable estimates are inadequate for tax purposes. Therefore, use of an estimated selling price for computing net realizable value is not sufficient.

The selling price must be supported by some evidence: a sale, compensation for a contract cancellation for purchase commitments, or an actual offering for sale. It is unclear, however, what would qualify as an "actual offering." An advertisement in a trade journal, although considered by contract law to be an "invitation to offer" and not an "offer," may still satisfy the evidential stan-

Table 1

Description	Definition of "Market" under lower of cost or market method	Objective evidence of valuation required
Normal goods are all goods not classified as subnormal goods	Replacement cost	Current bid price prevailing on the date of valuation for goods in volume normally bought by the taxpayer (amount required to replace merchandise)
Subnormal goods are: For sale under inactive market conditions. Unsalable in the ordinary course of business. Unusable in the ordinary course of production.	Net realizable value (bona fide selling price less cost of disposal)	• Actual sales • Actual contract cancellations, or • Actual offering for sale of merchandise within 30 days of inventory date and at prices lower than than replacement cost.
Damaged, imperfect, shopworn, in odd or broken lots, obsolete due to style changes or similar causes.		Records of actual dispositions must be kept.

dards. In any case, the regulations provide that a determination of selling price with an offering as evidence takes into consideration actual sales during a reasonable period of time before and after the inventory date.

The Post-Thor Dilemma

Following the Supreme Court's decision in Thor, taxpayers who had written down "excess" inventory found themselves in a peculiar position. A taxpayer is confronted by the Code and regulations with two tests in substantiating its inventory method write-down:

1. The inventory method must conform to the best accounting practice (i.e., GAAP), and
2. The inventory method must clearly reflect income (i.e., be in accordance with specific regulations).

The Supreme Court, in effect, makes the first requirement merely a factor in satisfying the second requirement. Since *Thor,* any taxpayer who has written down "excess" inventory using a percentage or aging formula will be found by the IRS to be using an inventory method not in accordance with the regulations. Also, the courts are not likely to provide taxpayers any assistance. The Supreme Court has confirmed the Commissioner's wide discretion in determining whether a method clearly reflects income.

To compound the problem, Section 446(e) and the regulations pertaining to this section do not allow taxpayers to change from an incorrect method to a correct method without first obtaining permission from the IRS. Generally, permission is requested by filing an application on Form 3115 within 180 days after the beginning of the taxable year in which the taxpayer desires to make the change.

Since it would be difficult, if not impossible, for taxpayers to apply on a timely basis, the IRS decided to provide a remedy in accordance with Section 1.446-1(e)(3)(ii) of the regulations. This section permits the 180-day rule to be waived by prescribing administrative procedures to obtain IRS consent.

Implementation of Thor Power

The IRS concurrently released Revenue Ruling 80-60 and Revenue Procedure 80-5 on March 10. Revenue Ruling 80-60 requires all taxpayers using an "excess" inventory valuation that is not in accordance with specific IRS regulations to change its method of accounting to the "prescribed method." The "prescribed method" is a method permitted by the regulations under Section 471 of the Code. The required change in method must be made for the first taxable year ended on or after December 25, 1979. One who fails to use the "prescribed method" in preparing and filing a federal tax return will have filed a return "not in accordance with the law."

In order to implement this ruling in accordance with *Thor Power* and the regulations, the Commissioner issued Revenue Procedure 80-5. This procedure grants immediate permission to taxpayers to change their accounting methods to comply with the applicable regulations. It provides a

The courts are not likely to provide taxpayers any assistance in the writedown of excess inventory.

waiver of the 180-day rule for filing the Form 3115 with the IRS. The procedure requires that the form be filed in duplicate with the federal income tax return no later than the extended time for filing such tax return. A copy of Form 3115 must be simultaneously sent to the IRS.

The procedure requires that certain adjustments be made in accordance with Section 481(a) to prevent amounts from being duplicated or omitted as a result of the method change. The taxpayer has the option of treating the change as one "initiated by the taxpayer" or as one "not initiated by the taxpayer." If the first option is chosen, the net adjustment may be spread ratably over a period not to exceed ten years. The number of years over which the spread may be taken is equal to the number of years during which the taxpayer used an improper method of inventory valuation. For example, if a taxpayer has used the impermissible write-down method for seven years, it must spread the net adjustment ratably over the next seven years, beginning with the year of change.

If the taxpayer has used the incorrect method for three or more taxable years, the amount of the net adjustment to be spread over each of the applicable years is determined as follows:

- An "as if" amount, equal to the Section 481(a) adjustment attributable to each of the three preceding taxable year periods, is computed.
- The lowest of the three "adjustments" is then subtracted from the entire net adjustment.
- If the resulting amount is at least 67% of the net adjustment, then such resulting amount is spread equally over the next three taxable years, including the year of change.
- The lowest adjustment is then spread equally over the remaining taxable years of the maximum spread period allowed.

As an example, let us assume a company has been using the impermissible write-down method for 12 years. If an adjustment had been made in any one of the three preceding taxable periods, such adjustment would have been $40,000 for 1978, $45,000 for 1977 and $30,000 for 1976. It has a taxable year end of December 31, 1979, and the net adjustment on that date is $100,000. The computation is shown in Table 2.

Because the resulting amount is at least 67% of the net adjustment, the $70,000 is spread equally over the 1979, 1980 and 1981 taxable year periods. The remaining $30,000 of the total $100,000 net adjustment is spread equally over the rest of the spread period. In this case, the remaining number of periods is seven since the maximum number of spread periods is ten.

If the net adjustment is wholly attributable to the taxable year preceding the year of change, then the entire adjustment is required to be taken into account in the year of change.

If the taxpayer elects to treat the change as one "not initiated by the taxpayer," then the entire net adjustment under Section 481—less the portion of

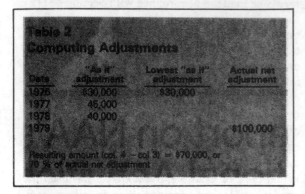

Table 2
Computing Adjustments

Date	"As if" adjustment	Lowest "as if" adjustment	Actual net adjustment
1976	$30,000	$30,000	
1977	45,000		
1978	40,000		
1979			$100,000

Resulting amount (col. 4 − col 3) = $70,000, or 70 % of actual net adjustment

the adjustment attributable to years prior to 1954—must be taken into account in the year of change. For example, assume a company has been using the improper method for 30 years. The adjustment would have been $10,000 if the company had changed its method of accounting in or before 1954. The amount of the net adjustment is $100,000 on December 31, 1979. Under this alternative, $90,000 ($100,000-$10,000) must be taken into account in full as an item of ordinary income for the taxable year ended December 31, 1979.

If at any time during the spread period, the value of the inventory is reduced by more than one-third of the value of inventory at the beginning of the first taxable year ended on or after December 25, 1979, the unamortized portion of the net adjustment under Section 481(a) must be taken into account in full as an item of ordinary income. For example, if the value of inventory at the beginning of the taxable year ended December 31, 1979, is $75,000, the inventory value must not go below $25,000 at any time during the spread period. If it does, the balance of the net adjustment not previously taken into income must be taken into income at that time. This provision does not apply, however, if the liquidation is due to strike or involuntary conversion.

If at any time during the spread period, the taxpayer adopts the last-in, first-out (LIFO) method of inventory valuation, the unamortized portion of the net adjustment under Section 481(a) must be taken into account in full as an item of ordinary income in the year LIFO is adopted. Also, if at any time during the spread period the taxpayer ceases to engage in the trade or business to which the Section 481(a) net adjustment relates, the unamortized portion of the adjustment must be accounted for in full as an item of ordinary income.

The potential ramifications of the *Thor* decision and anticipated IRS action are far-reaching for many businesses using the lower-of-cost-or-market method. Many companies will become subject to substantial increases in taxes.

One of the more disturbing implications of the IRS action is the imposition of penalties on both the taxpayer and the tax return preparer for negligence or intentional disregard of the IRS rules and regulations. The penalty that can be imposed on the preparer is $100 and placement on the IRS list of negligent preparers. The penalty imposed on the taxpayer is 5% of the total tax underpayment assessed, *including* unrelated adjustments. Thus, the potential penalties for noncompliance with *Thor Power* could be quite substantial. ☐

As a result of the Thor decision, many companies will become subject to substantial increases in taxes.

INVENTORY VALUATION—THE ACCOUNTANT'S ACHILLES HEEL*

CHARLES E. JOHNSON
Associate Professor, University of Oregon

MOST of the everyday problems which plague practicing accountants in the realm of inventory accounting are somewhat divorced from the theory of inventory valuation and its inevitable relationship to income determination. With the practical inventory problems of verification, accountability, and control, you as practitioners are far more familiar than am I, and I shall not presume to burden you this morning with any ivory tower advice on the subject. Instead I should like to entice you to stand back and take a bird's-eye look at some questions currently at issue in the field of inventory valuation—and in particular to look at them in their perspective against the background of some fundamental theoretical concepts in accounting.

Any accountant worth his salt has learned long ago to shy away from the word "value." The "value" of something implies its worth, and you don't have to be a timid soul to shudder at the insuperable problems which surround an attempt to determine the worth of anything.

In part this is because value, like beauty, lies in the eyes of the beholder. Examine the horrible abstract painting which adorns a friend's living room and then note the obvious satisfaction he gets from owning it. Remind yourselves of the times you have seen a seller and a buyer walk away from a transaction—each feeling that he has stolen the other blind.

In the business world, however, this individualistic viewpoint plays a lesser role in making value a treacherous concept than does the fact that determining the money-worth of an asset—its value is essentially a speculation about the future. This is a lesson you all learned early in your training or experience—that essentially the monetary value of any productive asset is the present discounted worth of the *future* net returns to be expected from its use. Cost, replacement cost, physical quantities, operating characteristics—all are secondary to a careful, well reasoned forecast of future earning power.

Looking at the asset side of a balance sheet, we are reminded that in this sense the accountant does come pretty close to valuing some assets. Cash, for example, causes us almost no trouble, given a confidence in the banking system. We view receivables clearly as the present right to receive money at some future date, after discounting the ability of some debtors to pay. We could come even closer to the correct value of receivables were we to apply a discount factor to allow for the fact that $1 due in 30 days is not now worth $1, and if we adjusted for prospective shrinkage through the taking of sales discounts. In most cases these factors are not material, and we are thus justified in saying that accountants *value* receivables.

Turn now to the question of inventories —product, partially completed product, raw materials, and supplies—all awaiting the ultimate fruition of the sales transaction. Value theory tells us that such inventories must be worth the present discounted amount of the net receipts which will ultimately flow into the business as a

* This paper was given at the Second Northwest Graduate Accounting Study Conference sponsored by the Washington Society of Certified Public Accountants, the School of Business Administration of the University of Washington, and the American Institute of Accountants, held at Harrison Hot Springs, September 24–26, 1953.

The Accounting Review

result of their sale. Roughly, this is what Accounting Research Bulletin #29 refers to as "net realizable value," but it is discussed only as one element of the "lower of cost or market" rule. Accountants do not normally "value" inventories on a net realizable basis. Why?

The barrier which stands between value theory and the accounting treatment of inventories is essentially the *realization* convention. Let's take a brief look at just what is involved in this concept of realization. Realization, as I understand it, is a set of rules devised as a guide in determining when the *quality* of the evidence with respect to prospective net revenues is such that they may be directly valued as an element of the firm's financial position. In support of this position it is argued that the primary operational problem facing a firm holding an inventory of goods is to find a buyer at an acceptable price. The mere existence of an inventory and of past transactions is thus not considered good enough evidence to warrant estimating the ultimate net selling price and discounting that back to an inventory value—there are too many slips 'twixt the cup and the lip. The accountant's position is to remain neutral with respect to these prospects until better evidence is available. Now, when a sale takes place, or where production under a fixed contract occurs, or where production of goods which sell on an organized market at given prices is completed—in all these cases the accountant is willing to grant that the evidence is satisfactory. Uncertainty has been reduced to a point where the value of the prospect of future net receipts warrants recognition as an asset on the records. To put it another way—these events are deemed to constitute realization.

Now if the rule is to postpone valuing inventories until realization takes place (and they are transformed in essence into receivables), what course do accountants follow in the meantime? The answer might be that we establish a *valuation* for inventories. This, you say, is the academic mind playing with words. I think the distinction between value and valuation is, however, a useful one. By valuation I mean only that a useful relationship has been established between the monetary unit and some element of property or property rights. Valuation in this context must be judged primarily on the basis of its usefulness—if it serves well the purpose for which it is intended, and everyone understands that purpose, it is a useful valuation. The relationship between physical inventories and the monetary outlay necessary to bring them to their present status is a useful valuation, to be compared with a later selling price to establish a gain or loss. If the selling price turns out to be greater than expected, it may also be useful to determine that a speculative price gain has been realized as well as the normal operating margin. Thus a whole series of valuations may be used in accounting for economic events to furnish information to those concerned. The choice among methods of *valuation* rests not on any proof of the correctness of one valuation over another—but on questions of logic, usefulness, and measurability.

This gives us only a highly subjective basis for judging various methods of inventory valuation. If we wish to estimate what inventories are worth—it seems evident that the best evidence is the discounted estimated future net selling price. If we agree not to do this until realization occurs, then the primary issue must be the purpose to be served by inventory valuation. The answer seems evident: we are interested in attaching a valuation to inventories in order to determine periodic realized monetary income—and we must then ask ourselves, what do we mean by income?

An English economist, J. R. Hicks, pub-

Inventory Valuation

lished in 1946 a highly theoretical treatise called *Value and Capital*.[1] He would no doubt have been surprised had he known that his discussion therein of the nature of income would receive a great deal af attention by accountants and others who were giving renewed attention to various possible concepts of business income. No doubt you have all stumbled across Hick's definition of income in the recent literature. As applied to a business enterprise it runs something like this: *Business income is the maximum amount a company could distribute during a given period of time and remain as well off at the end of that period as at the beginning.*

Now, that definition is not operational in the sense that if we were all to agree upon it this would solve all our problems in income determination. I think as a definition it is useful because it expresses the essence of what is meant by business income. The element with which I am particularly concerned here, however, is this basic assumption that the process of arriving at income involves determining whether the business unit at the end of any period is better off, worse off, or as well off as at the beginning. Note that the definition does not say—"The maximum amount the firm could distribute without forgoing expansion, selling assets, or borrowing money. Merely could dispose of and remain as well off—in a comparable position."

There are, of course, many different meanings which could be attached to the phrase "as well off"—each involves essentially a different concept of income—but we are here concerned with the meaning inherent in the *accounting* concept of income.

Accounting income is based on what I would call a "recovery of monetary investment" concept of income. The income

[1] Second Edition (London: Oxford University Press, 1946).

earning activities of a business are viewed as a series of overlapping investment and realization cycles in which available funds are committed by management in the expectation of realizing future net receipts having a present value equal to or greater than the outlay. The success of these expectations is tested periodically by comparing realized receipts with that portion of the past investment which is deemed to be related thereto. Those investments which have not reached fruition are carried forward from one period to the next to be tested for recovery against future revenues. And—a firm is generally considered as well off as before when it has recovered its monetary investment in any particular turnover of assets.

The major conceptual weakness of this approach to income is that there exists no provable theoretical basis for determining the portion of any given investment which has expired during any period. Strictly speaking the revenues of any period are a joint product of the entire resources of the firm—and there is thus no immutable principle which may be applied in determining what portion of any given revenue dollar represents a recovery of past investment and what portion is realized gain.

This does not mean that we must accept *any* arbitrary write-off of past investments. There are two major reference points available for testing the logic and usefulness of various "flow" assumptions. The first is the fact that the essence of any asset is that it represents a future service potential. Every business expenditure presumably results in the acquisition of some useful service. If at any point in time some portion of this service remains as a source of future advantage to the business, the monetary outlay involved in its acquisition, it would appear, should be a reasonable representation of the asset which exists, prior to realization. The second reference point is this underlying assump-

The Accounting Review

tion that the firm is as well off when it has recovered—in some sense—its past monetary investment. There is no point to matching revenues and costs in a vacuum —these points of reference constitute the basis for a reasoned preference for one method over another.

All this is pretty fundamental. At the risk of belaboring the obvious, I have been trying to make the point that questions of inventory valuation go back ultimately to some very basic assumptions behind the accounting process.

In the time remaining I should like to examine, in the light of the groundwork just laid, two currently significant problems in the area of inventory valuation— first the variable cost assumption which has been given a great deal of recent attention under the title of "direct costing"; and secondly, the LIFO assumption in inventory pricing, which is once more in the spotlight as a result of current attempts to gain acceptance for "lower of LIFO cost or market" for tax purposes.

Variable Costing

The term "direct costing" is actually a misnomer—"variable costing" would be a more accurate and descriptive name for the idea. But, as is the case with many pieces of terminology, an ill-fitting handle originally attached by Jonathan Harris in 1936, has somehow stuck. The idea of distinguishing between fixed and variable costs is not a new one. Professor Dohr claimed, in a recent *Journal of Accountancy* article, to have discussed the idea in a 1924 edition of his text, and economists would probably claim much earlier antecedents. The assence of the system being referred to currently as "direct costing" is that this distinction between fixed and variable costs should be built into the accounting records. The system itself is quite simple—it goes something like this:

All cost and expense accounts are divided into their two elements: those which are fixed or "period" costs and those which vary directly with changes in volume of output or operations, i.e. variable costs. This distinction is maintained in the records, and only variable costs are assigned to the product and carried through the various inventory accounts—work in process, finished product, and eventually into cost of sales. The difference between Sales and "direct" cost of sales for any period is labeled "marginal income," which replaces gross profit on the income statement. (The same classification between fixed and variable may be maintained in selling and administrative expenses and a marginal income computed after the variable portion of such costs is deducted.)

From marginal income so computed is deducted fixed costs of operations to arrive at operating income. The net effect is that all fixed costs are charged off in the period in which they are incurred, as a function of time rather than as a function of sales volume or revenues.

It should be carefully noted that, in theory at least, the distinction between fixed and variable costs differs from the distinction between *direct* and *indirect* costs. Direct costs, defined as those costs which may be associated directly with a given product or process, will be largely variable, but not entirely. There are important costs directly and solely attributable to the output of a particular product or process which are *fixed* within wide ranges of volume of operation. Likewise there are numerous elements of indirect cost which change with variations in volume over fairly narrow ranges of operation. It must be remembered that the use of direct costing involves the assumption that it is possible to distinguish objectively from among both direct and indirect costs, those costs which are fixed and those which are

Inventory Valuation

variable—as a function of *volume of operation.*

The advantages claimed for such a method of costing are numerous. Cost-volume-profit relationship data needed by management for profit planning are readily available from the accounts. Marginal income figures facilitate the relative appraisal of products, territories, and departments. Variable costing ties in nicely with standard cost systems and flexible budgets. In general, the effect on income will be to reduce reported income during periods when physical inventories are being increased (i.e. production is outrunning sales) and to increase income during periods when physical inventories are being depleted (i.e. sales are outrunning production)—this reduction and increase being in comparison with the effect of *"absorption costing,"* the term now given to conventional costing methods.

In considering variable costing in its relationship to inventory valuation and thus to income determination I should like to focus attention on two points. The first is the problem of establishing some reasonably objective meaning of the concepts of fixed and variable. The separation of all costs into their fixed and variable elements is not as simple and straightforward a task as it sounds. Depreciation, for example, when charged on a straightline basis appears to be a fixed charge; yet for the most part only the obsolescence element of depreciation is truly fixed. With modern methods of "mothballing" almost the entire wear and tear element of depreciation may well be considered variable. In some industries wear and tear may be a negligible factor in useful life, in others it will be highly significant. On the other hand restrictions in current wage contracts make large portions of direct labor cost fixed in nature. If the guaranteed annual wage becomes widespread, a substantial portion of direct labor cost may in effect become a fixed charge which does not vary with volume. Are these costs to be excluded from inventory?

Some consistent assumption must be made as to the range of volume variation within which the fixed and variable assumption is framed. In the range from 0–100% of capacity, only standby costs are truly fixed. On the other hand in the 80–100% range, a large number of salary and service department costs become essentially fixed. It is obvious that if each firm makes different assumptions in this respect the results will vary widely. Another element for decision is the time factor. What is fixed with respect to monthly variations in volume may be variable with respect to annual volume variations.

Workable assumptions are being made on these points for internal accounting today, and any assumption which satisfied management is satisfactory for managerial accounting. In order to accept the results for corporate reporting, however, the public accountant must be satisfied that some standard can be derived which can be objectively verified and consistently applied. If not we may find we are approaching the *"sayso"* inventory method—inventories are what the company says they are.

There remains the question whether variable costing produces meaningful and useful financial statements for the use of outsiders. This question must ultimately revolve around the relationship between inventory valuation and income determination—and we are back to the reference points described earlier in this discussion.

Absorption costing involves the assumption that all cost traceable to the existence of inventoriable goods and services should be allocated thereto and carried forward as a representation of the future services inherent in its ownership. Variable costing

The Accounting Review

involves the assumption that only those costs which vary with volume shall be carried forward. This requires the assumption that period costs are associated entirely with the passage of time and not with the existence of inventories; i.e. fixed costs are somehow the cost of providing production facilities of a given capacity and thus unrelated to the amount of product turned out. The corollary assumption is that the firm must recover these fixed costs from the revenues of any period before it is better off—or conversely that a failure to recover them makes the firm worse off, without regard to the amount of saleable product which is on hand at the end of any given period.

This, it seems to me is regression not progress in inventory valuation. If the essence of an asset is that it represents service potential to the company, there is no logical reason which can be deduced why that service potential is best or even adequately represented by only that portion of the past investment which will vary with volume of output. Were that particular assumption to become the basis for the decision between capital expenditure and revenue charge, we should approach the cash basis of accounting in a hurry. What we are asked to do, it would seem, is to transfer what is a highly desirable idea from one basic purpose to another. As a managerial device I have nothing but acclaim for variable costing. It can be devised to fit whatever assumptions management cares to make—and these assumptions not only can but perhaps should be inconsistent from year to year as the problems facing management change. For most managerial decisions are matters of alternatives, and the fixed costs which have a tendency to be irrelevant to such decisions change with the alternative, while different kinds of variable costs come into the ascendency. In reporting progress over time however we should keep our methods

of asset valuation firmly rooted in the idea that an asset represents a future service potential and that a firm which has invested in such future services is not worse off for having done so as long as the prospect exists that net realizable receipts will exceed that investment.

LIFO

Now lets turn to a method of inventory valuation designed to cope, not with fixed and variable costs, but with changing prices. LIFO, which is essentially a variation on the older base-stock method of inventory accounting, has been rationalized under a whole series of arguments in the past, and we should perhaps first clear away the deadwood to get down to current issues.

The idea of LIFO as some approximation to the actual flow of inventories from stock into production or sales has long since been abandoned. The idea that the investment in inventories is somehow irrevocably fixed is inconsistent with its classification as a current asset on the balance sheet. In tax legislation dealing with the "involuntary liquidation" of inventories during 1941–47 it was assumed that taxpayers could replace such liquidated inventory before the end of 1952—a not unreasonable presumption. Yet in the June, 1953 *Taxes*, Ray Hoffman of Price Waterhouse points out "taxpayers have not only been unable to obtain goods to replace *wartime* liquidations but have suffered further involuntary liquidations."[2] The ability to maintain an expanded volume of business while remaining in a state of "involuntarily liquidated inventories" would seem to indicate that the so-called fixed quantity of inventory necessary for operations is a very elastic concept, and certainly bears no relation to the

[2] R. A. Hoffman, "Tax Shortcomings of the LIFO Provisions," *Taxes*, June, 1953, p. 407.

Inventory Valuation

quantity of inventories on hand at LIFO adoption date.

The idea that LIFO is some sort of evolution away from the use of historical costs may appear at first glance plausible, since under "dollar value" LIFO the result may be to price the inventory at costs which were never in fact actually incurred by the firm. Nevertheless LIFO *is* a *cost* method, in the sense that it involves an allocation of the actual past investment in goods and services between inventories and cost of sales—no more and no less than actual monetary outlay is allocated.

A more persistent line of argument is that LIFO is somehow a part of an evolutionary movement from monetary income to *real* income. This argument has a distinct advantage in that it puts your adversary on the defensive—if *you* are dealing with reality, *he* must be arguing for something unreal and non-genuine.

In examining this argument, however, we must remind ourselves that the distinction between monetary and real is a distinction between a measuring unit and what is being measured. Changes in the general level of prices are evidence of changes in the size of the measuring unit— the value of money—and it is *this* which produces the divergence between *monetary* and *real*. Looked at in these terms it seems clear that LIFO has no strong claim to reality. In the first place LIFO results in neutralizing only those price changes affecting some given quantity of inventory which happened coincidentally to be on hand at the time the adoption was made. But even more important—those who argue for LIFO as reality fall into the well populated pitfall of confusing *any and all* price changes with changes in the *general* price level. To say that a company should price its 1953 inventories at 1938 prices because they represent approximately the same physical quantities and therefore the company is no better or worse off than

before, ignores the possibility that this collection of goods almost certainly has a different significance in the economy in 1953 than in 1938. The divergence in the movement of *specific* prices in relation to the over-all average is a well known phenomenon. If the price of copper has tripled while the general level of prices has doubled, something has happened to the significance of copper in the economy. To ignore this possibility is like telling the fellow who owned a uranium mine in 1929 and still has it today that his position has not changed and therefore he is no better off in "real" terms. Something may have happened to uranium in the meantime!

Take a close look at this inherent assumption behind the decision to freeze prices as of LIFO adoption date, and you begin to see that the argument that LIFO is *realistic* has some gaping holes in it. Fortunately, many respected authorities have abandoned it.

That leaves two major strongholds left for supporters of LIFO. The first is a highly practical one. If adopted at the right time and under certain conditions the use of LIFO will almost certainly reduce total income taxes paid over a period of time. The possibility of reducing *property* taxes also exists. If an unsophisticated assessor grabs for book values, the LIFO user may find an extra incentive for its use when he examines his property tax bill. The only answer to this, I suppose, is educating tax assessors.

In advising businesses within the present structure of our tax laws the accountant is derelict in his duty if he does not advise his clients to use LIFO whenever conditions are such that it will produce a probable tax advantage. Since at present the law requires that tax-LIFO must likewise be used in corporate reporting this automatically puts LIFO on the books. Arthur Cannon has effectively battered one-half of this position by pointing out that ques-

The Accounting Review

tions of equity, and governmental fiscal policy which govern taxable income have no counterpart in questions of business accounting, and he therefore urged a clearer delineation between taxable and business income.[3] If the inference is drawn from this, however, that the solution then is to *remove* the requirement that tax-LIFO must be accompanied by the use of book-LIFO, it should be pointed out that arguments for the use of LIFO for *tax purposes alone* are weak.

Several recent studies on the problem of business taxation have reached the conclusion that LIFO as a tax device is undesirable.[4] I am not going to speculate as to how many staunch LIFO advocates would fall by the wayside were its use denied for tax purposes. Nor do I have time to fully develop the position that it *should* be denied. Briefly the conclusion rests on two major considerations. The first is intertaxpayer equity. LIFO is not a device to reduce the total tax load—therefore it must necessarily shift the burden from one class of taxpayers to another. Since some businesses and most individuals have no compensating device to reduce taxes in times of rising prices, it appears inequitable to allow such a device to one group of taxpayers. To quote Moonitz on this point "the accounting profession should be wary, now and in the future, of new 'principles' of accounting whose major objective is to shift the burden of income tax from one group of clients to another."[5]

But an even stronger argument against LIFO for tax purposes is that its use produces results which are at odds with the presumed desirability of counter cyclical fiscal policy. The desirability of increasing the tax load and running a government surplus during periods of prosperity and inflation, and conversely decreasing the tax load promptly and incurring deficits in periods of deflation and recession is, I think, well agreed upon in principle, however inept we have been in putting it into practice. The use of LIFO operates in the *opposite* direction—by decreasing taxable income in periods of rising prices and increasing taxable income in periods of declining prices. Thus it may well be argued that as professional advisors we should inform clients of the tax advantages inherent in the use of the LIFO device; but as well informed citizens, accountants should take the lead in opposing that particular element of the tax law.

Instead through our official representatives we find ourselves urging the adoption of lower of LIFO cost or market for tax purposes.

It is interesting to note the line of argument being used. In the very nature of the proposition it is possible to transfer the debate away from the merits of LIFO as good or bad tax policy and to base the case on questions of *equity*. Some companies were able to adopt LIFO at a low point in the price cycle, while others through legal barriers, lack of foresight, or pure inertia failed to do so. Now these companies are barred from getting on the bandwagon by the thought that if prices fall below the LIFO inventory price, such price losses cannot be deducted under present rulings.

At the time the original extension of the use of LIFO was being argued before Congress there were those who said that its supporters would never face the logic of their arguments when prices turned downward. They may now wear a satisfied "I

[3] A. M. Cannon, "Tax Pressures on Accounting Principles and Accountants' Independence," ACCOUNTING REVIEW, October, 1952, p. 423.

[4] Richard Goode, *The Corporation Income Tax* (New York: John Wiley & Sons, 1951), p. 171. E. C. Brown, *Effects of Taxation: Depreciation Adjustments for Price Changes*," Boston: Division of Research, Harvard Graduate School of Business Administration, 1952). "The equity considerations for LIFO are nearly the same as for replacement-cost depreciation" (p. 76). "Our general conclusions are that historic-cost depreciation is more desirable than replacement-cost depreciation for tax determination" (p. 17).

[5] M. Moonitz, "The Case Against LIFO," *Journal of Accountancy*, June, 1953, p. 687.

Inventory Valuation

told you so" smirk—but they've been out-smarted. The inevitable retreat in the face of the implications of falling prices is being handled with tactical genius. Instead of retreating over the terrain by which they advanced the beleaguered advocates of LIFO are being flown out over the ruins of their arguments in an equity helicopter.

In my opinion the real solution to the lower of LIFO cost or market argument is to eliminate the LIFO device for everyone for tax purposes. I have no real hope that this will be done—I'm merely exercising my inalienable right to fight a hopeless rear guard action. This is one of the ever present dangers facing program chairmen —whenever you give a number of people a platform, one darned fool among them is almost certain to start exercising his in-alienable rights.

To those who argue for LIFO as a matter of accounting principle without regard to tax questions—the final stronghold is the question of *realization*.

This was the cornerstone of Mr. McAnly's case for LIFO in a recent issue of *The Journal of Accountancy*.[6] I think I state his position fairly, if briefly, as follows: LIFO is a device to keep unrealized income out of the accounts. As prices rise it costs more to maintain the same inventory of goods on hand. To the extent that funds are used for this purpose they do not represent realized income, for "certainly no realized profit *or loss* results from mere fluctuations in the value of things we must continue to own in order to be a going concern." Because under LIFO we do not recognize income to the extent it is represented by a gain in inventory prices, we thus do not have to report a loss when it is represented by a fall in inventory prices. Thus LIFO stabilizes earnings as they should be. Anyone who can't see this

—————
[6] H. T. McAnly, "The Case for LIFO," *Journal of Accountancy*, June 1953, p. 691.

doesn't understand the realization principle in accounting.

Let's examine this reasoning in the case of a price decline. The firm has made a commitment in inventory at $1 a unit, let us say, expecting to sell for $2. Current cost is 60¢ and the selling price has fallen to $1.20. Following through on Mr. McAnly's argument, the inventory should be carried at $1 rather than at 60¢ since this decline in the investment in inventory is an unrealized loss. The firm must always carry this basic investment in inventory— which it can buy now for 60¢ per unit. Therefore the difference between its original investment ($1) and current cost (60¢), or 40¢ is freely available as disposable income without the necessity of reducing the scale of operations.

If this argument sounds somehow strange it is because I have deliberately reversed its usual direction—the case of rising prices. But if gains which must be reinvested in inventories are unrealized, it follows that losses which need not be reinvested in inventory are likewise unrealized. And if the balance sheet inventory figure is to be a meaningless residual incapable of interpretation, there seems no reason why it cannot as well be meaninglessly high as meaninglessly low. And if the problem can be solved by showing current cost parenthetically on the balance sheet, this seems as true if current cost is *below* LIFO cost as above. Furthermore there is no good reason in logic why LIFO for accounting purposes should not be adopted at the top of the price cycle as at the bottom. Inventory price losses will then not be reported and this will relieve the company of the necessity of reporting inventory price gains when they occur. In past history there is more support for the statement that pricewise what goes down must come up than for the converse that what goes up must come down—the trend of

The Accounting Review

prices throughout history has been in an upward direction.

If proponents of LIFO would argue along these lines, I would still not be won over, but I would have a great deal more respect for their position as a valid difference of opinion as to whether *earned* income or *disposable* income should be used in business reporting. Looked at from this direction, however, the argument loses much of its flavor. Mr. McAnly in particular abandons this unpalatable hot (if not burned) potato and moves over to sample the equity argument for dessert. When prices decline, he argues, it is inequitable to deprive the firm of a deduction for these unrealized losses.

The basic flaw, in all this, it seems to me, is the assumption that we can produce *meaningless* balance sheets and *meaningful income* statements at the same time. One of the motivations behind the development of accrual and inventory accounting was to get away from the idea of income as a disposable cash balance—yet we are again and again, in the name of progress, referred back to this idea that if a dollar of revenues must be reinvested in more valuable assets it somehow should be removed from realized monetary income.

Let's start with the premise that the most recent costs are the most relevant *cost* figures which can be attached to any given collection of goods and services on the balance sheet, until such time as evidence that a reasonably certain sum of money will be realized from their disposal warrants revaluation and recognition of income or loss.

Now what is the effect of price changes on the results which will follow in the income statement? First off we should recognize that because of the time lag between an investment in resources and their ultimate disposal a business is always in a position to gain from a rise in prices and suffer from a fall, unless this risk can be hedged. For most firms there exists no futures market through which any substantial hedge can be made. Now if prices do in fact change between the time the commitment is made and the time that the ultimate sale restores the liquidity of the original investment in inventories, the monetary margin between cost and selling price will be composed of two elements: An operating margin consisting of the difference between current cost and current selling price, and a price gain or loss consisting of the difference between actual costs and current costs—i.e. costs as they are at the time the sale takes place.

I reject the assumption that this price gain or loss is not realized, since once the firm's liquidity is restored any new commitment in inventory must be made primarily because management expects net realizable value to be equal to or greater than cost. The concept of periodic realization through turnover seems to me a more useful one than the assumption of a fixed dollar investment to be congealed at some nominal figure picked out of the past, largely by accident, providing it is low enough.

But it may well be that it would be useful to disclose separately these two elements of monetary profit—the operating margin and the price gain or loss. A proforma statement illustrating how such a separation might be presented (not only for inventories but for all elements of operating cost) is shown in Exhibit I. This is not a new idea—it has been in the literature for some time—but I think this is a good time to give it serious consideration.

Such a statement will show that during rising prices most firms will make an operating gain and a price gain. During price declines the operating gain will be offset to some extent by a price loss. Whether these price gains and losses will offset each other over the long run thus remains clearly to be seen by all who read financial

Inventory Valuation

EXHIBIT I

An illustration of the separation of "operating margin" from price gains and losses

STATEMENT OF OPERATIONS
Year Ended December 31, 19XX

Total Revenues	
Sales (Net of Sales Discounts, $XX; Sales Returns & Allowances, $XX)...........................	$XXX
Miscellaneous Revenues..	XXX
Interest Earned...	XXX
Total Revenues..	$XXX
Contemporaneous Costs (Actual Goods & Services Used Stated at Current Period's Prices):	
Materials and Supplies..	$XXX
Employees' Compensation Including Contributions Toward Retirement, Unemployment & Accident	
Insurance...	XXX
Depreciation...	XXX
Purchased Services...	XXX
Taxes Other Than Income...	XXX
Interest on Borrowed Funds...	XXX
Total Contemporaneous Costs...	$XXX
Current Operating Margin...	$XXX

Estimated Monetary Gain or Loss Due to Price Changes		
Excess of Contemporaneous Costs Over Actual Costs		
Depreciation...	$XXX	
Purchased Services...	XXX	
Excess of Actual Costs Over Contemporaneous Costs		
Materials and Supplies..	(XXX)	
Add Net Price Gain...		XXX

Net Income Before Taxes..		$XXX
Deduct Taxes on Income...		XXX
Net Income for the Year		$XXX
Deduct: Dividends to Preferred Shareholders..............................	$XXX	
Dividends to Common Shareholders................................	XXX	XXX
Amount of This Year's Income Retained in Business...........................		$XXX
Balance of Retained Income at Jan. 1, 19XX.................................		XXX
Total Retained Income Dec. 31, 19XX..		$XXX

statements. The management which shows foresight in adjusting its position to the vicissitudes of the price cycle will receive their credit when it is evident that price gains are maximized and price losses minimized. But even if it is shown that price gains and losses tend to cancel out in the long run, this does not warrant a failure to disclose them. Corporations may go on forever but the outsider's interest in their financial affairs is often ephemeral. Persons who read financial statements have a right to information concerning the impact of *all current* operating conditions on the corporation's position.

By adopting this approach the account-

ant is placed in the defensible position of having made a full discolsure of all information available to him. For those who believe that price gains and losses are unrealized—the data on disposable income is available to them for whatever use they wish to make of it. Those who reject this position likewise have the kind of information they desire in forming their judgement of corporate affairs. Those who wish to derive supplemental computations of "real" income have a solid foundation on which to build such analysis through the use of an index of the general price level.

I think the outstanding results of adopting this kind of disclosure would be the

The Accounting Review

impact in restoring or building (depending on how pessimistic one is) public confidence in financial statements. Management, which is deeply and personally concerned with the need for additional funds to finance replacements and expansion, is understandably enamored with any accounting device which will result in lowering income during price rises. It is entirely understandable why—pressed with higher costs, higher taxes, and demands for increased wages and dividends,—corporate management should feel strongly that a dollar which must be reinvested in more valuable inventory is not available for distribution—and thus, somehow not income. It is not quite so understandable why the dollar which need not be invested in lower priced inventories is apparently still not available for distribution.

Nevertheless, if the word independent has real meaning, the public accountant should balance this position against that of investors and other public users of accounting information. I doubt seriously whether any real service is done by acceding to management's demands and failing to disclose the amount of inventory price gains and losses. The comparability of financial statements is to a material extent destroyed, since even those companies using LIFO have adopted at different dates and therefore their base prices have been set at different points in time. Furthermore sophisticated users of financial statements will often attempt a rough adjustment of income to add back the unstated price gains—and if they are prejudiced in the opposite direction from management the result will be misinfor-

mation. Finally the omission of this information cannot help but stimulate cries of subterfuge—which appear only too plausible to the layman who sees an inventory valuation of 8¢ per pound which "fairly presents the financial position" on an item currently being exchanged on an organized market at 26¢.

On these grounds I believe the case for LIFO falls. If you tell me you are for LIFO because it reduced taxes, and Lord only knows taxes are too high—I will respect that for an honest opinion. If you tell me you are for LIFO because it is an income smoothing device, and anything which knocks off the peaks and valleys of reported income is a good thing—I recognize the usefulness of averages. I cannot respect the logic of the argument that LIFO results in a more realistic, more accurate, more truthful, or more factual presentation of periodic business financial information.

We have been presenting income statements in which price gains and losses and operational gains and losses are lumped together. To the extent that LIFO has gained a foothold, we are currently in the position of omitting some portion of inventory price gains and losses from the financial picture altogether. Rather than encourage this device even further by allowing its users to have their cake and eat it both—now may well be the time to carry the evolution to its logical conclusion, and to fully disclose both *price* and *operational* gains and losses as elements of the most useful measure of *monetary* income we can at present devise.

The Numbers Game

When Goodwill Is Bad News

ONE of the big problems of the accounting profession is that it must lay down general principles to deal with specific cases. The general principles, however, like ready-made suits, do not fit every specific case. That, in essence, explains the excitement now going on over the accounting requirement that intangible assets, especially goodwill, must be amortized.

Such intangible assets are a queer breed. Accountants define them as what you buy in a company if you pay more than the fair market value of the company's tangible assets—plant, machinery, inventory, land, receivables and the like. When high-stepping conglomerators

of the 1960s paid outrageously inflated prices for companies, the excess was called "goodwill." Using goodwill, hustlers created huge, often fictional asset growth with no corresponding penalty, since in those days the accountants did not require that goodwill be written off. It could sit on the asset sheet forever, looking impressive, but often worth nothing or less than nothing.

That abuse was finally outlawed in October 1970 when the accounting profession adopted Accounting Principles Board Opinion 17. It said no asset has an eternal life; therefore all intangibles, including goodwill, must be amortized. The amortization period set was 40 years.

A decent general principle, but it apparently does not fit all the specific cases. There has been an increasing outcry against it from a variety of companies—truckers, for instance, whose most essential possession is the Interstate Commerce Commission license (an intangible asset) that permits them to haul freight across state lines. And newspaper publishers, who insist that the most important things they buy, when they acquire a new paper, are the intangibles of an established name and circulation base.

Most seriously affected are the broadcasters. Here's why:

Take the case of New York-based Lin Broadcasting Corp. (1974 revenues: $26.5 million). In November 1974 Lin acquired KXAS-TV in the lush Fort Worth-Dallas market. Lin paid $35 million. Of that, only $11 million was assigned to KXAS's tangible assets. The other $24 million was paid for the station's Federal Communications Commission license and its lucrative NBC network affiliation, both intangibles.

This is common practice in broadcasting. When another broadcast company, Metromedia, bought a Chicago FM station for $2.8 million, a trivial $20,000 was assigned to tangible assets. The rest went for the FCC license and other intangibles.

Under Opinion 17, those intangibles must be charged to profits within the next 40 years. So the KXAS-TV deal will cost Lin some $600,000, or 26 cents per share, annually. Considering that Lin's 1974 per-share net was only 95 cents, that charge hurts plenty.

On top of it all, the Internal Revenue Service gen-

erally will not allow amortization of the intangibles as a deductible item for tax purposes. So, the penalty to earnings is equivalent to $1.2 million pretax, rather than just $600,000. "Put another way," says Arthur Andersen & Co. partner Charles Johnson, "a 40-year amortization period with no tax benefit is really only a 20-year write-off. That's what really hurts these companies."

The broadcasters agree that Opinion 17 is a good thing for stopping the abuses of conglomerators. But they argue that the broadcast industry is in a different class. Its intangibles are almost certain to increase in value, since the licensing system limits market entry. Michael O'Sullivan, Lin's controller, puts it this way: "These intangibles have continuing value, and I don't see why we should have to amortize them."

He has a point. Back in 1962 Lin bought three radio stations for $2.5 million, of which $1.8 million was for intangibles. Last May Lin sold the same three stations for $8.7 million to Multimedia Broadcasting Corp. Of that $8.7 million, Multimedia figures it paid $5 million for intangibles. So Lin's intangibles *increased* some 200% in value.

The industry also argues that Opinion 17 affects it far worse than other industries, since typically 60% of a broadcast company's assets will be intangibles. "One-fortieth of very little is very little," says Ron Irion of the National Association of Broadcasters. "But one-fortieth of a hell of a lot can be a hell of a lot."

Another inequity, claim some, is that the young and growing broadcast companies are penalized more than the industry giants like CBS or NBC, which purchased most of their stations before the rule went into effect. Thus, their amortization burden is much less than it is for the younger companies.

The companies apparently do have the support of many accountants. A special entertainment companies task force of the American Institute of Certified Public Accountants recently wrote an opinion reaffirming the applicability of Opinion 17 to the broadcast companies. But according to Charles Johnson, an author of the draft, "When we got to the intangible assets, most of us were sympathetic with the industry."

Why, then, doesn't the AICPA provide some relief? No power, says Johnson, pointing out that only the Financial Accounting Standards Board can do that.

The FASB does have the whole matter of accounting for business combinations on its agenda. Michael Pinto, FASB member, agrees that the board feels the rules need re-evaluation. But when an opinion will come from the already overburdened FASB is anybody's guess.

The sooner the better. You can make the case that accounting should be aimed at ending abuses. But it should also reflect an accurate economic picture. For broadcast companies at least, Opinion 17 gives a faulty image. ∎

FORBES, NOVEMBER 1, 1975

Convertible Bonds and Financial Reality

The approach required by APB Opinion No. 14 not only fails to depict financial reality but also causes net earnings and earnings-per-share to be overstated.

By Boyd Collier and Curtis Carnes

Accounting practice should be as descriptive of economic and financial reality as the state of quantitative measurement and information costs allows. Unfortunately, some procedures unnecessarily move us away from this objective. Currently, APB Opinion No. 14 requires that convertible bonds, in the absence of detachable stock warrants, be treated solely as debt instruments.[1] As yet, the Financial Accounting Standards Board has not reconsidered this requirement.

Consider briefly the history of APB actions on this matter. In 1966, APB Opinion No. 10 required that convertible bonds be treated as having both a debt and an equity portion. During the following year, APB Opinion No. 12 suspended this requirement. Three years later, the APB reversed itself in APB No. 14 requiring that convertible bonds be accounted for as if they are debt only. The principal reasons given for reversing its position in such a short time are that (1) in the absence of detachable stock warrants, the debt and equity portions are not separable, and (2) because of this inseparability, the portions to be assigned to debt and equity cannot be derived from the markets.[2]

Thus, the classic theory-versus-practice syndrome emerges again. In principle, accounting for convertible bonds upon issuance should involve an allocation between debt and equity because investors impute a value to the conversion privilege, but in practice it is assumed that accountants are not able to measure adequately the respective portions.

Approach to Convertible Bond Allocation

We dispute this notion and think that the approach we propose is superior both analytically and practically to that required by the APB. The approach is based on the contention that the marginal cost of debt does not vary as a result of the way the firm packages its bonds. The difference in rates between a firm's convertible bonds and nonconvertible bonds is due solely to the perception of the investor that he is purchasing not only a debt instrument but also a right to ownership equity.

There are, of course, many variables that can affect the cost of money capital to a firm. Nonetheless, if the only variable that changes is the issuance of bonds with a conversion feature, then any change in the effective rate of interest must be due to the investors' evaluation of the value of the right to convert to equity.

Therefore, the accounting problem becomes

what is the present value of the debt portion and what is the present value of right to the owner's equity portion? The present value of the debt portion is unchanged from what it would have been if no convertible feature were offered. For instance, suppose a corporation could issue $100,000, 10%, ten-year, nonconvertible bonds for $94,110 (market rate 11%). The accounting entry for this issue, exclusive of bond issue cost, is:

Cash	$94,110	
Discount on bonds payable	5,890	
Bonds payable (non-		
convertible) 10%		$100,000

The market rate of 11% is the firm's cost of capital whether debt or equity-financed.[3] In well-articulated and competitive financial markets the costs of debt capital and equity capital should be equal with all identified risks being adequately discounted.

Now suppose instead that the firm chooses to issue convertible bonds, and it is able to sell $100,000, 8% convertible bonds for $105,000. Accounting for the debt and equity portion should be accomplished as follows. Note the cost of debt remains at 11%. The present value of the right to convert debt to owner's equity is the sum of two results. First, there is a lump-sum receipt of cash of $10,890 greater than if the bonds were nonconvertible ($105,000 − $94,110). Next, there is also a difference in the amount of interest paid per annum. Without conversion the firm will pay $10,000 per year but with conversion the firm only pays $8,000 per year. The present value of the conversion right is the sum of the present values of these two differences because these differences are due solely to the introduction of the conversion feature.

The present value of $10,890 received today is $10,890. The present value of the annual interest saving of $2,000 is $11,778. Therefore, the present value of the right to convert to an equity position in this case totals $22,668. This is computed by subtracting the present value of the bonds from the cash received ($105,000 − $82,332).

The current bond price (nonconvertibility) is determined by calculating the present value of the future principal and the present value of future annual interest payments. From the present value tables we derive the present value of the bonds, $82,332, which is the sum of the annual interest payments of $8,000 discounted at the market rate of 11% ($47,114) plus the principal to be paid in ten years discounted at 11% ($35,218).

Since the face value of the bonds in question is $100,000, the discount on the bonds is $17,668 ($100,000 − $82,332). However, the premium on the convertible bonds is $5,000, so that $17,668 plus $5,000 is the $22,668 that is caused by the introduction of the conversion feature. This result can be summarized as follows:

Cash received	$105,000
Less PV of bonds	82,332
PV of conversion right	22,668
Less lump-sum received	10,890
PV of annual interest saving	$11,778

The present value of annual interest saving includes an 11% rate of interest. This rate represents the alternative cost of acquiring equity by the firm and is defined as the minimum rate of return that must be earned on equity-financed investments to keep unchanged the value of existing common equity.[4] The accounting entry is:

Cash	$105,000	
Discount on bonds payable	17,668	
Contributed capital-bond		
conversion option		22,668
Bonds payable		
(convertible) 8%		100,000

Financial Reality Achieved

This approach is reflective of financial reality while the approach required by APB No. 14 not only fails to depict the reality of this type of financing event but also causes net earnings-per-share to be overstated. Treating the convertible issue solely as debt understates interest expense thereby overstating net income.

In summary, the contention is that the cost of debt is unchanged whether the financing method chosen is debt or debt/equity instruments. Accordingly, the cost of debt instruments is unchanged by the introduction of a conversion feature. Capturing the financial reality of such a financing event affects both the balance sheet and income statement and reduces income tax expense.

By accounting for convertible bonds in the manner presented, we achieve a number of desirable results. First, an imputation of the cost of equity capital is available. Since the cost of debt remains unchanged, the marketing of a conversion feature establishes the current cost of equity capital. Second, this method seeks to eliminate the overstatement of earnings resulting from understatement of interest expense, while more correctly presenting an accounting for financial reality. Thirdly, the taxing of equity as income is eliminated. If we treat convertible bonds solely as debt, the accounting entry would be:

Cash	$105,000	
Bonds Payable		$100,000
Premium on Bonds Payable		5,000

CONVERTIBLE BONDS AND FINANCIAL REALITY

The difference between the discount on bonds using our method and the premium on bonds using the APB method is the $22,668 attributable to equity capital. By amortizing the premium over the life of the issue, rather than the discount, we overstate taxable income by $22,668. If this amount truly is equity capital, capital contributions are being taxed instead of earnings from operations. □

[1] APB Opinion No. 14, *Accounting For Convertible Debt and Debt Issued with Stock Purchase Warrants,* AICPA New York, N.Y., March 1969.

[2] Glenn A. Welsch, Charles T. Zlatkovitch and John Archwhite, *Intermediate Accounting,* 4th Ed., Richard D. Irwin, Inc., Homewood, Ill., 1976.

[3] Eugene F. Brighan and James L. Pappas, *Managerial Economics,* 2nd Ed., The Dryden Press, Hinsdale, Ill. 1976.

[4] J. Fred Weston and Maurice B. Goudzwaard, (Editors), *The Treasurer's Handbook,* Dow Jones-Irwin, Homewood, Ill., 1976.

MANAGEMENT ACCOUNTING/FEBRUARY 1979

Computers have had an unparallelled impact upon the nature and conduct of American business during this century, and the continuing development of smaller, faster, and less expensive computer systems is making them more and more accessible to small companies as well as to large ones.

PEOPLE PROBLEMS BEHIND MIS FAILURES

Confusion, and a little awe, still surrounds the operation of the computer. But, by placing it in its proper perspective, managers can reconcile the people with the system.

LEROY G. FAERBER
Associate Professor of Accounting

RICHARD L. RATLIFF
Assistant Professor of Accounting

University of Utah

Over the past 25 years, countless systems have been successfully implemented in business, industry, government, and not-for-profit organizations. The list of typical improvements computers make in management information systems includes more timely reporting, greater accuracy in the reports, better budget control, reduced clerical effort, improved cost analysis, and simplified production of non-routine reports. The emphasis has consistently been on improved information for better decisions.

Some managers, however, have become somewhat disillusioned with the computer revolution. They often complain of too much of the wrong kind of data, too little of the right kind of information, and excessive costs to acquire, staff, and maintain the computer installation. Some say that their computer systems even cause something akin to mass confusion. For example, MIS specialists of one major CPA firm recommended that two of its clients scrap their computer systems altogether and return to manual accounting systems. In another case, a western state government installed a major computerized fund accounting control system, which after a full year is still inoperative.

The dramatic contrast between the successful and unsuccessful computerized MIS applications raises some questions: Why are some applications apparently so much more satisfactory than others? Why do some seem to fail so miserably?

While numerous factors can affect the success or failure of a system, four major reasons have become apparent for many failures of computer applications: unrealistic expectations of computer capabilities, inadequate systems design and implementation, the resistance of some employees to computer-induced change, and invalid cost/benefit analyses. These problems are closely interrelated. Difficulty in one area can trigger difficulties in other areas. Note, too, that these are not computer technology problems; they are people-related problems.

UNREALISTIC EXPECTATIONS

Descriptions of the computer as an "intelligent, thinking machine" (as if it has a mind of its own) may have caused some managers to acquire unrealistic expectations of computer capabilities. Many routine decisions, such as may be found in various inventory control systems, have been computerized so that it may appear as if the computer were the sole manager of the system—ordering, locating, issuing, and paying for the inventory. Perhaps some managers have forgotten that people make the systems function, and poor inventory management can be computerized as easily as good inventory management.

"If the computer generated this information, it must be correct," is a widely accepted notion. A common misconception is that the computer itself will make the decisions necessary to solve management problems. But, while the computer can be a valuable resource for effective management, it cannot operate the business by itself. A better understanding of this problem is possible by considering the computer's capabilities and the inappropriate demands that can be placed upon the computer system.

Computer Capabilities

Some managers assume that computers have almost magical powers. In reality, the computer possesses only a few simple capabilities, as important as they may be. One computer specialist suggested the key attribute of the computer:

"The computer is only a machine. It will do only what you tell it to, but it will do exactly what you tell it to do."

Several other capabilities are also important:

■ Computational speed,

■ High degree of accuracy,

■ Large, compact storage area,

■ Convenient organization of data for different purposes, and

■ Rapid access to stored data.

The important contributions these special capabilities can make will be considered in a later section.

Inappropriate Demands

A major function of information systems is the development, design, and preparation of information and reports to facilitate management decision making. The computer is merely a vehicle for the processing and delivery of information, and can play an important role by preparing information to help the people who use the system to make better decisions. The computer should serve management, not the other way around.

Unrealistic expectations of computer capabilities will lead to user disenchantment as actual results fail to match expected performance. In contrast, realistic expectations establish a climate conducive to successful systems applications because the computer can be viewed as a management tool rather than as a miracle worker.

INADEQUATE SYSTEMS DESIGN

Major factors causing inadequate systems design include the unsuitability of certain computer systems for particular tasks and the failure to coordinate user needs and qualifications with computer capabilities.

Unsuitability

Some computer aficionados display more enthusiasm than understanding of computer applications. They often promote large, powerful, and expensive systems for all tasks, stressing the notion that "more has to be better." Certainly this is not the case. Important considerations in determining the nature of the system application include the size of the task, the required frequency of execution, and the amount of flexibility required to meet changing input and output requirements.

Applications well suited to the large, centralized computer installation will not require extensive reprogramming, and generally will require a large number of frequently performed computations. In contrast, small scale applications requiring frequent program revisions or new programming and infrequent execution may be best suited to mini-computers, service centers, or even manual systems. If this latter type of application were done on a multimillion dollar main-frame system, the cost of system design, programming, and computer time could far exceed the benefits.

For example, one computer service center that could use its own computers at essentially no cost has found manual preparation of some reports more economical than designing an additional computer preparation. In another case, a large bank corporation began using a time-sharing service center for its management reports instead of employing its central computer facilities, which would have required costly interruption of the company's high volume of transactional record-keeping. The reports are now provided on a more timely basis than the previous manual system could produce, and they are prepared with only a fraction of the resources required by the

larger system. In fact, the cost of the small computer application is comparable to the cost of preparing the reports manually.

Working with Users

Because the computer can generate output so rapidly, it is easy to inundate management with superfluous and useless data and reports. A small firm with 150 employees computerized its general ledger accounts and divided and subdivided its accounts into such detail that it soon had 400,000 accounts in the system. A mountain of detailed performance reports bewildered its management, which was paying a staggering computer processing bill. Considering such a situation, one systems analyst confided that he begins his analysis under the premise that at least 50 percent of all computer output is neither needed nor wanted by any decision maker using the information system. Careful planning and coordination between the designers and users of the information and reports is vital to avoid this type of problem.

The skills of the user's staff must also be considered in designing computer systems. A computerized system may require the staff to work at a more sophisticated, analytical level than otherwise would be re-

quired. Inability or refusal to do so will greatly reduce any realized benefits from the system. One firm developed a very sophisticated forecasting model which is now unused, because the only person in the company qualified to operate it left. For a systems application to fully achieve its objectives, management and staff may require additional training so that they may use the system effectively.

Good computer systems design is a matter of effectively combining user needs and qualifications with the special capabilities of the computer. There are five areas in which the special capabilities of the computer can significantly contribute to management information systems:

Timeliness. Monthly and year-end reports that required days or weeks to prepare by manual processing may be made available within hours using computer processing. For example, the annual revision of cost standards, which by manual methods required a major manufacturer two months to complete, is now computer processed and completed in three days. On-line terminal file-inquiry capabilities can make information instantaneously available to management.

Detail. Computer processing makes it possible for a soft-goods retailer, for example, to maintain a perpetual, real-time inventory control record of individual items stocked by vendor, style, class, color, season, store, size, and price. This cross-classi-

> "Computers . . . with their associated jargon, still bear a mystique which tends to frighten, or at least discourage, many people."

fication facilitates report preparation and summarization in many forms and degrees of detail to meet the information needs of different levels and areas of management. Proper summarization can help solve the problem of superfluous and useless data.

Convenience. A well-designed automated system not only retains source data accessibility, but also tends to make it more accessible as data accumulates. More source data require summarization and reorganization to maximize their usefulness.

For example, a large, non-profit organization recently developed a new chart of general-ledger accounts. By use of a computer's cross-reference table of old and new account numbers, meaningful historical comparisons between current activity and historical activity (before account changes) can easily be made. These comparisons would be prohibitively costly and time-consuming to obtain manually.

Validation checks. By having the computer perform a series of logic checks, such as the range in which input data should fall and a check for correct coding by comparing the code with a table of descriptions, the number of input errors can be significantly reduced. Generally, the amount of checking the computer can do far exceeds the capabilities of a manual system. If errors occur, the computer may facilitate correction by rapidly going through the transaction chain and making all necessary changes.

Flexibility. One large multinational organization requires financial data in U.S. dollars for consolidated reports and information in more than 40 foreign currencies for local management and report purposes. The data are entered into the computer in the currency of the transaction, then converted by the computer to U.S. dollars for consolidated report preparation (using currency exchange rates at the transaction date). For local reports, they are still carried in the foreign currency.

Good systems design requires consideration of whether the task is appropriate for the particular computer system. If so, it must use the computer's capabilities to meet user needs.

RESISTANCE TO CHANGE

No matter how potentially effective a system might be, if the users oppose it, the system will fail. One service center analyst stated that it is much easier for dissatisfied employees to subvert a computer system than a manual system. Much of the resistance people have comes from a fear of the computer, or from poor communication between the information user and the systems designers and programmers.

Fear of the Computer

Computers, data processing, and management information systems, with their associated jargon, still bear a mystique which tends to frighten, or at least discourage, many people. This concern, coupled with visions of having their jobs replaced or downgraded by the computer, provides ample motivation for resistance and opposition to the computer. A 58-year old paymaster maintained his manual accounting system for two years after installation of a new computer system to prove to his superiors that he was as good as the "electronic wonder" and less expensive. The efficiency of his department suffered significantly while costs increased.

Interface Problems

The problem of developing effective communication and understanding between the users and the systems designers and programmers is often difficult to solve. The lack of familiarity of some users with the specialized vocabulary makes communication difficult. A software service center found that communication between its systems design specialists and its customers deteriorated so badly that it discontinued systems design work. In a similar case, customers of another service center said the center's systems did not meet their expectations or requirements. After a careful analysis of the problem, the second computer service center's management concluded that the design work was satisfactory. But, the communication between its systems specialists and the customers was so poor that the systems were not properly understood. This firm's solution to the problem was to request that the customers play an active role in the planning and design of the system, thus insuring improved understanding. This strategy worked, and customer satisfaction improved markedly.

Sometimes the problem of resistance to computer-induced change requires either the computer system or the users (personnel) to change. Either change can be difficult. Unfortunately, a solution to this type of problem is difficult to prescribe. With care, however, the impact of this problem can be minimized. First, the employees affected by the computerized information system need to know how the computer will affect their jobs. An honest appraisal of these effects, emphasizing the computer's benefits to their job, can help avoid disappointment. Also, as the employees are asked to participate in the planning, design, and implementation of the new computerized information system, they can feel more a part of it, and can strive for its success.

Realistically, the computer does cause some job displacement, requiring either the release or relocation of some of the firm's employees. Many companies have found that the least unpleasant solution to this problem is to make needed personnel changes quickly, assisting any displaced personnel either to acquire needed training for other positions within the firm or to locate acceptable employment elsewhere. Occasionally, when a particular employee is near retirement, it may be expedient simply to retain him or her without either of these measures. Finally, be patient. A new generation of workers is now entering the labor market. They are more comfortable and familiar with computer applications.

COST/BENEFIT ANALYSIS

Sometime ago, a cartoon depicted two hobos lounging beside a freight train as one explained to the other, "We acquired all the data, programmed it, analyzed it, used it to control production and marketing, then went broke paying for the computer." These managers failed to take advantage of a good cost/benefit analysis.

On the surface, determining whether to install a computerized accounting system might appear simple. Consider the alternative systems, manual, computerized, or some combination of the two, add up their respective costs, divide by their associated benefits, and choose the alternative with the best cost/benefit ratio. Three problems arise, however, with this procedure: Some costs and benefits are often overlooked or miscalculated, other costs and benefits are difficult to quantify, and some predicted costs and benefits fail to materialize.

Oversights and Miscalculations

Assume that a small growing retail chain decided to expand its MIS to incorporate centralized inventory control. An examination of the various costs and benefits persuades top management to adopt a newly developed software package provided by its hardware manufacturer, quite different from the business's current control system. Suppose, however, that the estimate of the costs to convert to the new system fails to account for the three to eight months required for the employees to learn to use the system efficiently. It is easy to envision management's disappointment when, six months after the conversion to the new system, $50,000 worth of perishables are never delivered out of a central warehouse.

Suppose, on the other hand, that such learning costs were anticipated but were estimated at a maximum of $10,000 over a six-month period. Management may be as distraught as if the cost had been completely overlooked.

Major factors contributing to omission or miscalculation of costs include unrealistic expectations of the system, poor design or implementation of the system, and internal opposition to the system, all discussed

"Some managers have forgotten that people make the systems function. . . ."

"The computer is only a machine. It will do only what you tell it to, but it will do exactly what you tell it to do."

previously. Other reasons could be simply bad guesses, misinformation, or a lack of information.

Non-Quantifiable Costs

Most managers as well as computer specialists and management accountants are well aware of the difficulty in measuring and quantifying some of the costs and benefits. Unfortunately, too many then ignore these non-quantifiable factors in their analyses as if they have absolutely no impact on the system. Failure to at least recognize costs and benefits, even though they may be non-quantifiable and do not fit nicely into a ratio analysis, can result in gross errors. The goal of analysis is to provide guidance for a better investment decision, not merely to use sophisticated, quantitative decision techniques.

The publishing industry has most recently been highly involved in computerization of many of its accounting and production systems. One of its major factors in making the conversion to computerized systems has been the effect on labor union relations. Although this is a complicated issue and difficult to express in terms of dollars, any cost/benefit study should consider this factor.

Other important costs and benefits that are difficult to quantify might include opportu-nity costs, customer goodwill, risks of litigation, public image, and work atmosphere.

Failure of Benefits to Materialize

Any time the decision-maker tries to anticipate the future he runs the risk of error, because the future is uncertain regarding the development of the system's costs and the benefits. Most analytical attention has been given to costs, but the benefits, too, require analysis. Often, the very reasons for a new systems application fail to materialize. Careful attention to the benefits at the beginning of the decision process can help in assessing risks and in anticipating potential hurdles.

How to Improve Cost/Benefit Analyses

By anticipating and avoiding the three problems of unrealistic expectations, inadequate design, and resistance to change, the cost/benefits analysis can be simplified and improved. Three other steps should also help:

- Prepare an exhaustive listing of both the quantifiable and non-quantifiable costs and benefits of the system,

- Examine each one for potential errors, and

- Subject the cost/benefit analysis and results to periodic review.

The first two of these can be accomplished by using some readily available sources of information. Computer sales representatives, eager to see their products work successfully, can provide valuable insight into the different costs and benefits and can show how to minimize one and maximize the other. Owners of similar systems are also generally quite willing to discuss their experiences with the systems, identifying factors that affect costs and benefits. Industrial and professional associations maintain close contact with many similar businesses, and strive to stay abreast of technological developments in their respective industries. These associations offer information about the experiences of many managers with various computer applications. Additionally, individuals within the firm at different levels of organization may have experience or otherwise be in positions to help assess the costs and benefits arising from the computerized accounting system.

After the cost/benefit analysis has been completed, it should be subjected to a review process throughout the planning, design, and implementation of the system. A formal reexamination of the projected costs and benefits should be undertaken to take full advantage of the added knowledge gained from the development process. A few months after the system is operating, another examination of both the quantifiable and non-quantifiable costs and benefits can help evaluate the performance of the new system. At this point, some of the earlier non-quantifiable costs may then be more easily measured to give an even better perspective of the performance. Finally, as trouble spots are overcome, a general monitoring of the system with appropriate control and performance reports is helpful for effective management of the new computerized system.

CONCLUSIONS

The problem of disappointing or unsatisfactory computerized management information systems applications is often one of human error. We have considered this problem by examining the four major reasons for failure: unrealistic expectations of computer capabilities, inadequate systems design, the resistance of people to computer-induced change, and invalid cost/benefit analysis. **Figure I** (at right) summarizes the suggested measures for dealing with these problems. An increasing number of successful MIS applications will result from reducing or eliminating these problems.

Recognition and understanding of these problems are important steps in resolving them. In addition, a few significant changes are now occurring that should reduce the impact of these problems.

The fear of the computer and unrealistic expectations should diminish with the rising generation of young managers and staff personnel who have grown up in the computer age. This generation should better comprehend

that, rather than being a threat to meaningful employment, the computer may be a useful tool to increase its significance and value.

Strides are being made in computer hardware cost reductions. This alone should improve the results of cost/benefit analysis. Technological progress as reflected in computer service centers, time-sharing, remote terminals, and the macro-computers and mini-computers have opened the computer world to even the very small business. Perhaps most significant are the changes and progress that are being made in the area of computer languages and soft-

ware which can greatly increase the flexibility and ease of designing systems and making systems changes. This will also decrease the communications problems between the information user and the systems designer. These benefits arise because computer languages are evolving toward the point where the user is able to communicate with the computer at a level more closely approximating common spoken and written languages.

The coming decade should see the computer contributing increasingly to the MIS's role of providing timely, accurate, and relevant information for decision-making. □

FIGURE I
How to Avoid Computer Application Failures in Managerial Accounting Systems

Causes of Failure	Proposed Solutions
I. Unrealistic expectations of computer systems	Realize the computer has limited, though powerful capabilities. Realign demands on computer to best use its capabilities.
II. Inadequate systems design	Determine most appropriate MIS application: large, centralized installation; mini-computer; service center; manual system. Fit the system to the skills and needs of its users.
III. Resistance of personnel to computer system	Emphasize the computer's benefit to the affected personnel and their job performance. Encourage the affected personnel to participate in the planning, design and implementation, as well as the use of the system. Make needed personnel changes quickly, assisting displaced personnel either to acquire needed training for other positions within the firm or to locate acceptable employment elsewhere.
IV. Invalid cost/benefit analysis	Incorporate both quantifiable and non-quantifiable factors into the analysis. Examine each cost and benefit identified in the analysis for potential inaccuracies. Subject the analysis and results to a periodic review process.

SECTION III

Financial Reporting and Its Importance

This section is divided into four parts and addresses issues related to the importance of financial reports. Initially, a selection of articles discusses accounting principles and basic concepts used in report preparation. The final product will reflect the principles and concepts employed in its construction, and thus, the impact of these alternatives should be considered. Also, students must recognize that the quest for an optimal set of concepts continues as the profession develops. Comprehensive constructs of the past, thorough analyses of the present and ideas for the future are manifest in these readings.

Moving from the basic reporting process, consideration can be given to the relationship between income taxes and financial statements. In some sense, this relationship is one of mutual dependency as the tax position of the firm reflects its financial position and in turn, impacts on the ultimate earning ability of the organization.

Users of financial statements have a point of view also, which can be addressed and should be recognized by students of the subject. One method of formalizing this approach is to view financial statement analysis and its progress and procedures. Finally, corporate financial reporting itself is addressed.

An understanding of financial reporting is fundamental to all accountants. Students of accounting must deal not only with the fundamentals and concepts underlying the reporting process, but also with the effects of their applications. Consequently, financial statement analysis can provide the accountant with the perspective of an ultimate user and create an awareness as to the vitality of the end result.

Alternatively, non-accountants will eventually be placed in the position of users of financial accounting statements. A grasp of principles and concepts underlying accounting is generally not sufficient to appreciate subtleties of published financial reports. An awareness of alternative views and unsettled issues in accounting which ultimately impact on the financial reports can broaden the scope of the user and enable him or her to deal more intelligently with the results.

Overall, all students of accounting should recognize that the profession continually is confronted with repeating issues; alternative views and controversies relative to these issues exist within the profession itself and have been observed by others. Effectiveness warrants due deliberation of these important areas.

Generally Accepted Accounting Principles
in the United States

by WELDON POWELL
Partner, Executive Office

** Published in Die Wirtschaftsprüfung, the Journal of the German Institute of
Certified Public Accountants—February 1964*

THE STANDARD independent certified public accountant's opinion on
financial statements issued in the United States reads as follows:

We have examined the balance sheet of X Company as of
December 31, 19— and the related statements of income and
retained earnings for the year then ended. Our examination was
made in accordance with generally accepted auditing standards,
and accordingly included such tests of the accounting records
and such other auditing procedures as we considered necessary
in the circumstances.

In our opinion, the accompanying balance sheet and statements of income and retained earnings present fairly the financial
position of X Company at December 31, 19—, and the results of
its operations for the year then ended, in conformity with generally accepted accounting principles applied on a basis consistent
with that of the preceding year.

The first paragraph of the standard opinion deals with the nature
and extent of the audit examination. The second paragraph contains
the expression of the accountant's opinion on the financial statements
examined. The essence of this opinion is that the financial statements
are a fair presentation "in conformity with *generally accepted accounting principles.*"

The term "generally accepted accounting principles" is required
as the frame of reference in accountants' opinions by generally accepted auditing standards as set forth in a special report† by the
Committee on Auditing Procedure of the American Institute of
Certified Public Accountants, the national professional organization
of certified public accountants in the United States. Moreover, the
Code of Professional Ethics of the Institute provides that a member
or associate may be held guilty of an act discreditable to the profession if "he fails to direct attention to any material departure from
generally accepted accounting principles . . . ."

---

* Reprinted by permission.
† Footnote, p. 14.

In view of the significance attached to this term in the accountant's opinion, it may be surprising to the practitioner outside the United States to learn that "generally accepted accounting principles" have never been officially defined by any governmental authority or professional organization. Although the Director of Accounting Research of the American Institute of Certified Public Accountants has recently undertaken a project to prepare a catalogue of these principles, at present no such catalogue exists.

It should not be inferred from this that generally accepted accounting principles do not exist. Rather, it reflects the fact that they have evolved through years of practice, not unlike the evolution of the common law. The term "generally accepted accounting principles" first appeared as a frame of reference in the accountant's opinion in the 1930s (as accepted principles of accounting) as a result of the joint efforts of the New York Stock Exchange and the American Institute of Certified Public Accountants (then known as the American Institute of Accountants) to develop ways to educate the public concerning the significance, as well as limitations, of financial statements, and to make published corporate reports more informative and authoritative.

In this connection the Institute dealt with such matters as the nature and importance of financial statements, considered the nature of accounting principles underlying their preparation, and recommended that corporations be required to apply,

"... certain broad principles of accounting which have won fairly *general acceptance,* and within the limits of such broad principles to make no attempt to restrict the right of corporations to select detailed methods of accounting deemed by them to be

---

† Generally Accepted Auditing Standards, a special report by the Committee on Auditing Procedure, published in 1954, sets forth (1) General Standards, as to training, independence, and due care in the performance of work; (2) Standards of Field Work, which relate to planning the audit, evaluation of internal control, and the competence of evidential matter; and (3) Standards of Reporting which require that,
1) "The report shall state whether the financial statements are presented in accordance with generally accepted principles of accounting.
2) "The report shall state whether such principles have been consistently observed in the current period in relation to the preceding period.
3) "Informative disclosures in the financial statements are to be regarded as reasonably adequate unless otherwise stated in the report.
4) "The report shall either contain an expression of opinion regarding the financial statements, taken as a whole, or an assertion to the effect that an opinion cannot be expressed. When an over-all opinion cannot be expressed, the reasons therefor should be stated. In all cases where an auditor's name is associated with financial statements the report should contain a clear-cut indication of the character of the auditor's examination, if any, and the degree of responsibility he is taking."

best adapted to the requirements of their business" (emphasis added).

In addition, the Institute recommended and the Exchange agreed to a change in the form of the accountant's opinion so that the accountant would specifically report to the shareholders whether the accounts were presented in accordance with "accepted principles of accounting."

Thus, the desire to achieve more informative and authoritative reports led to the concept that accounting principles be judged by their general acceptance; hence the term "generally accepted accounting principles."

DEVELOPMENT OF GENERALLY ACCEPTED ACCOUNTING PRINCIPLES

"Generally accepted accounting principles" in the United States have evolved through years of practice, and their development has been influenced primarily by the business and financial communities and the accounting profession. As a principle has become commonly applied it has acquired the stamp of "general" acceptability and has been recognized as such by the various elements of the United States economy concerned with financial statements. It is important to stress that the development of principles and their application has been voluntary on the part of business, rather than enforced by law, regulation, or other fiat.

The development of generally accepted accounting principles has also been greatly influenced by the accounting requirements of the United States Securities and Exchange Commission and the stock exchanges, primarily the New York Stock Exchange. Furthermore, the influence of these organizations has resulted in greater adherence to generally accepted accounting principles.

New York Stock Exchange

The New York Stock Exchange was one of the first to call for financial reporting to stockholders in an era when few companies published financial data. Since about the year 1900, the Exchange has required that a company issue financial reports to stockholders in order to list its stock on the Exchange. Moreover these financial reports must comply with generally accepted accounting principles.

In the area of reporting financial data the Exchange has long required the publication of comparative consolidated financial statements, the disclosure of the method of inventory valuation and depreciation policy, and the segregation of operating costs in the income statement.

United States Securities and Exchange Commission

The Securities and Exchange Commission is an administrative agency of the United States Government, established by the Congress to administer various statutes relating to the issuance and sale of securities to the public. The SEC, however, is also quasi-legislative in nature: It promulgates rules and regulations and prescribes registration and report forms. It is also quasi-judicial in nature: It conducts investigations, holds hearings, and issues orders and opinions, some of which are of a disciplinary character. Many of the Commission's actions are subject to judicial review.

The Securities Act of 1933 and the Securities Exchange Act of 1934, two of the basic acts administered by the SEC, have had great influence on the widespread application of "generally accepted accounting principles."

These acts require, with some exceptions, that new offerings of securities be registered with the SEC by the issuing corporation. In addition, these corporations and corporations having securities listed for trading on national securities exchanges are required to file annual financial reports with the Commission.

The SEC has established accounting requirements that govern the form and content of financial statements and provide that dependable, informative financial statements that disclose fully and fairly the financial position and results of operations be filed with it and furnished to prospective investors. The acts contain civil and criminal penalties where untrue statements of a material fact are made, or where material facts necessary to make the statements not misleading are omitted.

The SEC generally has not asserted control over annual reports to stockholders. In practice, however, stockholder reports are essentially the same as those filed with the SEC except that some of the supplementary information required by the Commission is usually omitted in stockholder reports.

In establishing its accounting requirements, the SEC issued Regulation S-X in 1940 to deal primarily with the form and content of financial statements filed with it. In addition, from time to time the Commission has rendered decisions in cases before it and its staff has issued Accounting Series Releases expressing views and requirements as to specific applications of accounting principles.

In this manner the SEC has dealt with such matters as asset valuation, accounting for stockholders' equities, income determination, financial statement footnotes, all-inclusive versus current operating concept of the income statement, interaction of financial accounting and the income tax, consolidated statements, pension plans, depreciation and replacement cost, and price-level adjustments.

However, in the broad area of accounting principles, the Commission's reliance for full and fair disclosure in corporate reports has been on the application of generally accepted accounting principles. Moreover, the Commission stated in Accounting Series Release No. 4 in 1938 that reports prepared in accordance with accounting principles for which there is no authoritative support would be presumed misleading or inaccurate despite disclosures contained in the footnotes, or opinion, if the matters are material.

The influence of the SEC on the development of generally accepted accounting principles has for the most part been indirect. In setting high standards to obtain full and fair disclosure in reports filed with the Commission, and in insisting on compliance with generally accepted accounting principles, the Commission has influenced corporations to report to their stockholders in no less an informative manner.

Internal Revenue Service and the Federal Income Tax

Income-tax laws in the United States, with some exceptions, have not had a major influence on the development of generally accepted accounting principles. In fact, the gap between tax laws and accounting principles seems to be widening to the extent that the income tax is becoming more of an excise tax. In general, tax accounting and financial accounting need not be the same. The outstanding exception to this generalization, however, is the general acceptance of the LIFO (last-in, first-out) method of inventory valuation. The method has gained widespread adoption for tax purposes because it results in the postponement of income taxes. Its appearance in financial statements stems primarily from the requirement that it be used in the books of the taxpayer in order to be acceptable for tax purposes.

Depreciation accounting has also been greatly influenced by the income-tax laws and the majority of companies record the same depreciation they are allowed for tax purposes. This is not required by the income-tax laws, however, and many companies have substantial differences between tax and book depreciation. In general, where this difference results from tax depreciation's being greater than book depreciation, a provision for deferred taxes is recorded. Where book depreciation exceeds tax depreciation, no accounting recognition is given to the tax effect of the difference.

Of course, the income-tax laws have had a tremendous impact on the profession of accountancy through the expansion of the role of the accountant in the business and financial community. Nevertheless, the income-tax laws have not contributed substantially to the development of generally accepted accounting principles.

American Institute of Certified Public Accountants

Perhaps the greatest contribution to the development of accounting principles has come from the members of the profession through the American Institute of Certified Public Accountants.

The early interest of the AICPA, and the profession, in the development of generally accepted accounting principles is shown by the publication of "Approved Methods for the Preparation of Balance Sheet Statements." Prepared by the Institute in 1917 at the request of the United States Federal Trade Commission for the purpose of achieving greater uniformity in accounting practices, especially with respect to financial statements submitted for bank credit purposes, the publication dealt with auditing procedures, financial statement presentation, and the application of principles to specific accounts and transactions. This work was revised and reissued in 1929 under the title, "Verification of Financial Statements."

The major contribution of the Institute during this early period was the 1934 publication, "Audits of Corporate Accounts." An outgrowth of the joint efforts of the AICPA and the New York Stock Exchange, discussed previously, this publication examined the nature and importance of financial statements, considered the nature of accounting principles underlying their preparation, recommended that corporations be required to apply certain broad principles of accounting which had gained general acceptance, advocated a change in the auditor's opinion, and set forth five principles which were later adopted by the membership of the Institute.

1) "Unrealized profit should not be credited to income account of the corporation either directly or indirectly, through the medium of charging against such unrealized profits amounts

which would ordinarily fall to be charged against income account. Profit is deemed to be realized when a sale in the ordinary course of business is effected, unless the circumstances are such that the collection of the sale price is not reasonably assured. An exception to the general rule may be made in respect of inventories in industries (such as the packing-house industry) in which, owing to the impossibility of determining costs, it is a trade custom to take inventories at net selling prices, which may exceed cost.

2) "Capital surplus, however created, should not be used to relieve the income account of the current future years of charges which would otherwise fall to be made thereagainst. This rule might be subject to the exception that where, upon reorganization, a reorganized company would be relieved of charges which would require to be made against income if the existing corporation were continued, it might be regarded as permissible to accomplish the same result without reorganization provided the facts were as fully revealed to and the action as formally approved by the shareholders as in reorganization.

3) "Earned surplus of a subsidiary company created prior to acquisition does not form a part of the consolidated earned surplus of the parent company and subsidiaries; nor can any dividend declared out of such surplus properly be credited to the income account of the parent company.

4) "While it is perhaps in some circumstances permissible to show stock of a corporation held in its own treasury as an asset, if adequately disclosed, the dividends on stock so held should not be treated as a credit to the income account of the company.

5) "Notes or accounts receivable due from officers, employees or affiliated companies must be shown separately and not included under a general heading such as Notes Receivable or Accounts Receivable."

Accounting Research Bulletins

From 1938 to 1959, the principal voice of the public accounting profession concerned with the continued evolution of accounting principles was that of the Committee of Accounting Procedure of the AICPA. Formed in the Fall of 1938, the Committee in its first report concluded that it would not be practical or desirable to formulate comprehensive rules covering the whole field of accounting. Rather, the report stated that its plan was,

> ". . . to consider specific topics, first of all in relation to the existing state of practice, and to recommend, wherever possible, one or more alternative procedures as being definitely superior in its opinion to other procedures which have received a certain measure of recognition and, at the same time, to express itself adversely in regard to procedures which should in its opinion be regarded as unacceptable."

> "In considering each case, particularly where alternative methods seems to possess substantial merit, it will aim to consider the conflict of considerations which make such a situation possible and thus gradually to prepare the way for further narrowing of choices."

Issuance of an opinion required the approval of two-thirds of the twenty-one-member Committee.

The authority of the pronouncements issued by the Committee rested on their general acceptability, rather than on any compulsion. Indeed, each opinion reiterated that,

> "Except in cases in which formal adoption by the Institute membership has been asked and secured, the authority of opinions reached by the committee rests upon their general acceptability. The committee recognizes that in extraordinary cases fair presentation and justice to all parties at interest may require exceptional treatment. But the burden of justifying departure from accepted procedures, to the extent that they are evidenced in committee opinions, must be assumed by those who adopt another treatment."

From 1939 to 1959 the Committee issued 51 Accounting Research Bulletins dealing with such topics as:

Business combinations
Consolidated financial statements
Contingencies
Depreciation
Foreign operations
Intangibles
Income taxes
Inventory pricing
Leases

Presentation of income and retained earnings
Stock dividends
Stock options
Working capital

The influence of the Committee is evident in the fact that its Accounting Research Bulletins are generally regarded as authoritative statements on the application of accounting principles. The SEC has, with rare exceptions, accepted the Accounting Research Bulletins as guides to accepted accounting practices.

Accounting Principles Board

In 1959 the Committee on Accounting Procedure was superseded by the Accounting Principles Board. The formation of the Board reflected a change in emphasis of the AICPA from the issuance of pronouncements on specific accounting problems as they arose to the development and codification of accounting principles as a basis for dealing with such problems. The broad problems of financial accounting are visualized as requiring attention at four levels: first, postulates; second, principles; third, rules or other guides for the application of principles in specific situations; and fourth, research.

To carry out the research phase of the project, an accounting research staff was formed under a Director of Accounting Research. When a research project is undertaken, a project advisory committee, composed of Institute members and qualified individuals from industry and other sources, is formed under the chairmanship of a member of the Board to consult and work with the staff in the conduct of the project. Research studies published upon completion of research projects are intended to be informative, but tentative and not highly authoritative. Their function is to explore problems under review, giving pro and con arguments and offering conclusions and recommendations. Before the formulation of any conclusions by the APB, the research studies are widely distributed so that members of the profession, the business and financial communities, and others can have an opportunity to express their views. In this manner the APB hopes to obtain a consensus and be in a position to issue statements on generally accepted accounting principles. To date, five research studies have been published and seven other research projects are in progress.

Statements of the position of the AICPA concerning generally accepted accounting principles can be issued only by the Board and must be approved by two-thirds of its twenty-one members. To date, two statements, not related to research studies, have been issued. In the usual case, it is expected that statements of the Board will result from research studies. As was true with the former Committee on Accounting Procedure, the authority of the pronouncements of the Board in the absence of formal membership approval rests upon their general acceptability. It is expected, however, that these statements will be regarded as authoritative expressions of what constitutes generally accepted accounting principles.

Other Accounting Organizations

Among the other accounting organizations that have contributed to the development of generally accepted accounting principles, is the American Accounting Association, an organization consisting primarily of educators. Its publication, "Accounting and Reporting Standards for Corporate Financial Statements," sets forth the views of the organization on the framework of accounting principles underlying corporate reports.

In addition, important contributions have been made by individual practitioners and educators through personal contributions to accounting literature and text books.

DESCRIPTION OF GENERALLY ACCEPTED ACCOUNTING PRINCIPLES

Against the background of the foregoing discussion, and emphasizing again that generally accepted accounting principles in the United States have evolved through practice and have not been codified or catalogued, I shall describe what I consider some of these principles to be. In doing so, I shall use "principles" in a broad sense to include assumptions, doctrines and conventions, as well as postulates and practices.

Accounting entities. Accounting is conducted for specific entities. An entity represents a group of assets subject to common control and may be legal (corporation, trust) or non-legal (single proprietorship, partnership). The entity is viewed as the owner of the assets and the recipient of the income.

Accrual accounting. Accounting under the accrual basis requires that income be recorded in the period earned or realized and that expenses be recorded in the period incurred.

Conservatism. Conservatism represents a policy of caution, a desire to avoid positive error and to lean to the safe side. Conservatism may be illustrated by the phrase "record no gains till realized, but record losses when recognized." Conservatism, however, does not countenance the accumulation of secret or hidden reserves.

Consistency. The principle requires the consistent application of accounting practices and methods by a given company through periods of time. An inconsistency must be disclosed in financial statements and in the accountant's opinion. For example, a change from the straight-line to an accelerated method of depreciation or from the FIFO to the LIFO method of inventory cost would be an inconsistency requiring disclosure.

A change in conditions necessitating an accounting change, such as a change in the estimated useful life of property, does not create an inconsistency in accounting principles.

Cost. In general, assets are accounted for on the basis of acquisition cost measured in cash or its equivalent. Whenever assets are acquired in exchange for non-cash assets, cost may be considered either the fair market value of the consideration given or the fair market value of the property received, whichever is more clearly evident.

Going concern. The accounting for the transactions of a going concern is conducted under the assumption that it will continue in operation indefinitely.

Informative disclosure. Financial statements should disclose all information necessary to make the statements not misleading. This doctrine relates to such things as form, content, parenthetical comments, and notes to the financial statements.

Matching cost against revenue. This principle requires that costs incurred (or to be incurred) to produce revenues be recorded as expenses in the same period that the revenues are recorded. The application of this principle can result in the accrual of costs in periods preceding that in which incurred (future expenses under a product warranty) or the deferral of costs to a period subsequent to that in which incurred (research and development expenditures).

Materiality. Inherently a part of the application of accounting principles, the doctrine of materiality specifies that items of little or no consequence may be dealt with as expediency may suggest.

Objectivity. To the extent practicable accounting should be based on facts as shown by completed transactions. When estimation is required (depreciation, bad debts, etc.), the accountant should be objective in the required determinations.

Realization. Income should not be recorded until it is realized. In general, income is realized when a sale or exchange is made or when services are rendered and a collectible receivable (or equivalent) results.

Stable measuring unit. The dollar, which is the unit of account, is assumed to be a stable measuring unit. This assumption and its questionable validity are discussed later.

Uniform accounting period. Comparability in reporting requires that accounting reports be prepared for uniform periodic intervals.

The foregoing principles, assumptions, conventions or doctrines have served as the base from which accounting practices have grown. Many of the practices are self-evident from the description of the principles. Other practices and matters of interest are discussed under the following headings:

Financial statements
Inventories
Fixed assets
Intangible assets
Net income
Price-level adjustments

Financial statements

The basic financial statements in the United States considered necessary for the fair presentation of financial position and results of operations are the statement of financial position (balance sheet), the statement of income and the statement of earnings retained in the business (earned surplus). Frequently, the last two statements are combined. The statement of funds is becoming increasingly popular and is included in many reports to stockholders; it is not, however, considered one of the basic financial statements.

In the statement of financial position, assets and liabilities are usually divided between current and non-current. One year is the normal dividing point between current and non-current although the time length of the normal operating cycle may be the dividing point if it is clearly defined and exceeds one year.

Reasonable detail is given under each balance sheet caption, including disclosure of receivables from officers, employees and affiliates. The valuation basis of assets is stated. Stockholders' equity is divided into its major components: capital stock, other paid-in capital, and earnings retained in the business.

The income statement generally reveals sales, cost of goods sold, selling and administrative expenses, operating profit, Federal income taxes, and net income. Depreciation and depletion charges are separately stated.

Notes to financial statements usually disclose such matters as:
Assets subject to lien
Changes in accounting practices
Consolidation practices
Contingent liabilities
Commitments
Long-term lease agreements
Pension and retirement plans
Post balance sheet disclosures
Preferred stock data—call, conversion, or preference features
Restrictions on the availability of retained earnings for dividends
Retroactive adjustments
Stock options and stock purchase plans

Inventories

The primary basis of accounting for inventory is cost, and the major objective thereof is to match costs with revenues for purposes of income determination.

Only those costs which are necessary in bringing an article to its final condition and location are included in the inventory. For example, normal manufacturing overhead is included but costs arising from idle capacity, excessive spoilage, and other abnormal costs may be excluded. General and administrative expenses may be included in inventory to the extent applicable to the manufacturing process; selling costs are not included.

Accounting for the flow of cost (expired vs. unexpired) may be accomplished by specific identification, or, as is more common, by an assumption as to cost flow—first-in, first-out; last-in, first-out; average. The objective under these methods is a reasonable assignment of costs to the physical inventory on hand without the need for specific identification.

With few exceptions, inventories are valued at the lower of cost or market value. As used in inventory valuation, market value means the current cost to replace the article by purchase or reproduction. There is, however, both a floor and a ceiling to the market value thus established; it should not exceed the net realizable value (normal selling price less costs of completion and disposal) and it should not be less than net realizable value reduced by a normal profit margin.

Fixed assets

The common basis of accounting for fixed assets is acquisition cost. As in the case of inventories, accounting for the flow of cost may proceed under different methods, each of which will result in a different periodic cost allocation. The most frequently used depreciation method is the straight-line, age-life method although the so-called accelerated methods, double-declining balances and sum-of-the-years-digits methods have become increasingly popular since 1954 when they became allowable for income tax purposes (see page 17). The unit of production methods are also widely used by the sinking fund, annuity or other interest methods are used only rarely in special situations.

Over the last two decades the cost of replacing fixed assets in the United States has increased considerably. Because of this, consideration has been given from time to time to the desirability of writing up fixed assets to reflect these higher values on the balance sheet and in depreciation charges. The advocates of this procedure maintain that it would reflect periodic income on a more realistic basis and would result in accumulated depreciation provisions more nearly equal to the replacement values. The more conventional view that it is not the function of depreciation to provide for the replacement of property has prevailed, however, and depreciation based on the cost of property remains the generally accepted method.

Intangible assets

Intangible assets are carried at cost or cost less amortization. Those intangible assets having a limited life, whether by law or by their nature, are amortized by systematic charges to income over the period of their useful lives. Intangibles falling within this category are patents, copyrights, leases, licenses, franchises, and some forms of goodwill.

Intangible assets that do not have a limited life, such as perpetual franchises, trade names, secret processes, and most goodwill, may be carried at cost or amortized by charges to income over a reasonable period of time. If it becomes evident that the benefit period of such intangibles has become limited, then the intangibles should be amortized by charges to income.

It is not considered acceptable to write-off intangibles in a lump sum immediately after acquisition.

Net income

In reporting net income for the year, it is generally accepted that all items of profit and loss recognized during the year are to be included. The only exceptions to this practice relate to material items that are unrelated to the typical business operations of the period and that if included in the determination of net income might tend to impair the significance of net income and lead to misleading inferences.

According to Research Bulletin No. 43 issued by the Committee on Accounting Procedure of the AICPA, only the following items may be excluded from the determination of net income:

a) Material charges or credits related to operations of prior years.
b) Material charges or credits arising from unusual sales of assets not acquired for resale.
c) Material losses resulting from events not usually insured against.
d) Material charges arising from the write-off of intangible assets that have become worthless.
e) Material charges arising from the write-off of bond discount or premium and bond issue expenses at the time of the retirement or refunding of the debt before maturity.

The items excluded from the determination of net income may either be shown as charges or credits to surplus in a separate statement of retained earnings or be shown in the income statement below net income under the caption "special items" with the final figure in the income statement being designated "Net income and special items."

Price-level adjustments

The assumption of a stable measuring unit, fundamental to accounting, has been subject to question over the past two decades because of the inflation the economy has experienced.* The position taken by the accounting profession over the years, and reflected in accounting practice, has been to adhere to historical cost and the

---

* U.S. Dept. of Labor Wholesale price index, 1947-1949 = 100, August 1963 = 119.
U.S. Dept. of Labor Consumer price index, 1947-1949 = 100, July 1963 = 131.
U.S. Dept. of Commerce, Construction cost index, 1947-1949 = 100, August 1963 = 152.

stable dollar assumption. Despite suggestions that supplementary statements reflecting price-level adjustments would be valuable to users of financial statements, few companies have presented such information.

The accounting profession and the business community in the United States are well aware of the changes that have taken place in the purchasing power of the dollar. Moreover, the stable dollar assumption never envisioned a rigid inflexible price structure. Rather, it was assumed that fluctuations in the value of the dollar, such as they were, would not have a materially significant impact on the financial statements.

In recent years, members of the profession and the American Institute of Certified Public Accountants have expressed the opinion that with the prospect of a continued lack of price stability it would be unrealistic to ignore fluctuations in the value of the dollar.

Although the stable dollar assumption continued to underlie the preparation of conventional statements, the Accounting Principles Board expressed the opinion that it would be wise to explore ways and means of presenting separate financial statements in terms of "common dollars"; such common dollars would explicitly reveal gains and losses in purchasing power resulting from the monetary position of the firm, and reveal the composition of long-term assets in terms of current purchasing power.

To that end, there has been under way since 1961 a research project, the results of which may be published shortly* for purposes of exposure and comment by members of the profession and the business community. The ultimate goal is to achieve some acceptable methods for dealing with the problem.

SUMMARY

The objectives of this article have been to acquaint the practitioner outside the United States with the generally accepted accounting principles that provide the framework of accounting and reporting practice in the United States. To aid in an understanding of these principles, I have discussed the evolutionary and voluntary nature of their development and have described some of the major forces that have contributed to their development.

Generally accepted accounting principles are the basic frame

---

* Since published as Accounting Research Study No. 6, "Reporting the Financial Effects of Price-Level Changes."

of reference in the auditor's opinion; they have gained the respect and confidence of financial statement users. This development, however, is not complete; it likely never will be. Many difficult and controversial problems remain. The research studies and the research projects of the Director of Accounting Research of the American Institute of Certified Public Accountants deal with some of these problems, others will be dealt with in due course. It is my earnest hope that our accounting problems will continue to be resolved in the manner I have described in this paper.

GUEST EDITORIAL

Financial Reporting—What Course Is It On?

The course of financial reporting necessarily grows out of the objectives of the reporting. To serve its purpose, financial reporting must be useful to those considering a financial commitment with an enterprise. For most of the early years of financial reporting, the objective was perceived to be limited to custodianship. In a money society, custodianship refers to money entrusted to those responsible for company affairs: money earned, money spent, money distributed and money in custody. That notion may have been useful in a society with little reliance on credit or capital goods, but certainly not in a complex one. Accrual accounting evolved to better measure custodial performance of enterprises. Perceptions of stewardship changed at the same time to comprehend the notion of operating perfomance, as well as custodial performance.

The drift from custodial performance to operating performance probably started with the blossoming of a capital market in which an investor without an inside association could transfer his ownership to another investor. That kind of investor is concerned about custodial integrity, to be sure, but also is concerned about operating performance. He seeks indicators of performance. Unfortunately, financial statements serving well to report custodial performance may serve poorly to report operating performance.

Hunger for simplicity of reporting followed proliferation of corporate share ownership. There was a craving for simple measures to impound complex variables of return and risk. In due course, earnings per share became the indicator—a barometer intended to give a reading of present financial health of an enterprise, as well as prospects for future health. That was too much to ask of any single periodic figure. Indeed, that role asks too much of financial accounting itself. It confuses earnings with earning power—that is, with sustainable earnings potential.

Earnings are for accountants to measure and report in financial statements. Earning power is for users of financial statements to assess. Objectives of financial reporting that mix those notions will misdirect the course of reporting, as they have led to confusion about things for which financial accounting can competently account.

Oscar S. Gellein, CPA, is a retired partner of Deloitte Haskins & Sells and a former member of the Financial Accounting Standards Board. He was an AICPA gold medal winner for distinguished service.

The drift to concern about earning power was accompanied by adoption of accounting policies that stressed normality and nondistortion, instead of things in the real world—assets and liabilities. At the same time, normality and nondistortion went largely undefined, as if they could be sensed. There was inconsistency and a barrier to evenhandedness and the narrowing of alternatives, both of which have been long-standing goals of standard setting. The result has been damaging to the capital market because of investor skepticism about financial reporting. Capital seekers, capital providers and the general public have been harmed by the attending impediments to a healthy capital market.

The objectives of financial reporting pronounced in FASB Statement on Financial Accounting Concepts No. 1 assume that investors have a common concern: return on and of investment, the timing of the return and the attendant risks.

Those assumptions lay the basis for concluding that investors wish to compare enterprises' returns and risks to decide where to place their funds. Those assumptions also provide the basis for seeking evenhanded treatment of enterprises needing capital and a healthy capital market in which interests in enterprises may be exchanged. Enterprises are treated evenhandedly if their peculiar returns and risks are reported.

The unique competence of financial accounting is preserved if its results are tested by reference to events that have occurred. If that line is broken, the door is open for admission of the effects of anticipated events that could transform the principal focus of financial accounting from real things in the business world—that is assets, liabilities and earnings—to statistical measures—indicators and extrapolations.

This is not to downgrade the need for financial data helpful to those assessing earning power. Indeed, that kind of data and related displays are an important part of financial reporting. The point is that an effort to focus on earning power, instead of earnings, takes financial accounting beyond what it can be expected to do competently and sustain a belief in its results.

A limit that bears on the future course of financial reporting is the timing of issuance of financial statements. They cannot with our present state of the art be issued concurrently with events. To date, at least, there is no ticker tape reading that comprehends up-to-the minute financial effects, nor is it likely to be available soon, if ever. For that reason, observers have said that financial statements report stale news. That feature, however, does not destroy their significance. But it does put in focus their role of being maximally useful for assessing the significance of current and later happenings.

The assumptions, constraints and objectives that will determine the future course of financial reporting can be summed up as follows:

• Financial reporting's role is to contribute all it can within its competence to an equitable and efficient use of available resources.

• Its competence concerns measuring and reporting an enterprise's resources and obligations and changes therein. Others use the data reported to make assessments of earning power and prospects.

• Investors (including creditors) are interested in cash flows to themselves and have varying preferences of return on investment and attendant risk. They wish to compare returns and risks of enterprises before investing.

• Investors look to cash receipts directly from an enterprise in some cases and indirectly through market transactions in others.

• Prices of an enterprise's securities are influenced by assessments of enterprise cash flows. Therefore, investors are interested in enterprise cash flows, whether they expect to realize cash directly from the enterprise or through a market transaction.

• Earnings based on accrual accounting are the best credible data that financial accounting can provide for assessing prospective enterprise cash flows.

• Earnings based on accrual accounting, disaggregated to display characteristics of earnings, also are the best credible data for assessing the performance of an enterprise, which is largely inseparable from the performance of its management.

• Objectives of financial statements are subject to change because they manifest perceptions of usefulness, which in turn may be changed by the data reported. Perceptions steeped in tradition are slow to change, but they do change.

• There is no ultimate, absolute economic reality to be reported in financial statements.

• Financial statements cannot report events as soon as they happen. They serve a significant role as a credible reference point from which current developments can be assessed.

• Financial reporting developments may be hastened, slowed or thwarted by political forces. Standard setting lives in a political environment and must accommodate itself thereto as long as the accommodation does not sidetrack or unduly deter advance of financial reporting for the public good.

Those factors set the course of future financial reporting, at least they determine a general direction. Certain matters are clearly candidates for increasing attention, such as: the nature of accounting income; measurements other than historical cost; cost variability; rate of return; and financial statement display.

There are many notions of income. Its determination

and measurement stand at the center of financial reporting, and are the essence of financial accounting. A first step, therefore, is to identify the notion of income that financial accounting chooses to measure and report. How is the choice made? The ultimate test is usefulness to those contemplating an economic association with an enterprise. Usefulness comprehends relevance to the decisions involved and sufficient objectivity for users to perceive sufficient reliability for their purpose.

A concept of income compatible with the objectives of financial reporting can be highlighted as follows:

• The income of a business enterprise for its lifetime is measured from cash to cash. Income so determined can be measured by various scales, two of which have had recurring attention; units of money (the prevailing scale) and units of purchasing power.

• An enterprise's income for a period (year or quarter and the like) has the same nature as income for its lifetime. There is a dilemma in measuring the same kind of income for a period because cash-to-cash cycles in business operations are not separately identifiable and many are longer than the reporting period.

• The dilemma is overcome by looking to the things in a business that have potential for future cash inflows—that is, its assets; and to things that represent demands on cash—that is, liabilities. A notion of income that focuses on revenue and expense transactions and allocations, each aspect of which is tested by reference to changes in assets and liabilities, will have credence because it concerns the very essence of a business: its assets, its liabilities and its people. Accrual accounting serves better than cash-basis accounting to measure cash potential or economic benefits inherent in an existing business based on past transactions and events.

• If the foregoing conditions and tests are met, it reasonably can be said that the nature of periodic business income is the same as the nature of income for the life of the business.

The system of measurements currently applied in financial statements will, in my opinion, continue indefinitely. An abrupt change to another system would be disruptive, even more so than a change in the custom of driving on the right side of the road, or a change from the present systems of measures to the metric system. Conventional measures alone, however, are not enough. Persistent inflation for extended periods has brought about a need for supplemental measures.

Various efforts have been made around the world to recognize the effects of price changes in financial statements. Those efforts have had fruition in some Latin American countries and are stalled in other countries. The FASB recently issued a statement requiring larger companies to show in their financial reports certain information about the effects of changing prices both specific and general. Considerable flexibility is permitted in the measure of costs that would be incurred if the assets owned were acquired now. Companies are encouraged to experiment with display and explanation, as long as specified requirements are met. The statement sidesteps the issues of the kind of enterprise capital that is to be maintained before the enterprise can be said to have had income or earnings. Those interdependent issues need early resolution.

This author predicts that, as to capital maintenance, only a financial capital notion is meaningful or workable. A physical capital approach requires an impossible foreseeing of changes in technology. How many companies today are making and selling products by processes or with tools and equipment reasonably similar to those of fifty years ago, or even twenty-five years ago? Income and capital are susceptible only to monetary measurements in today's society. Perhaps physical capital is meaningful in a barter society, but it defies interpretation in a money society.

Except for the shortcoming of not coming to grips with the kind of income and capital that should be central to financial accounting, the FASB statement on changing prices is about right for its time. Companies in different industries are affected differently by changing prices. Some managements cope better with changing prices than others. Financial accounting can be helpful in identifying those differences.

Costs are variable in several respects: (1) by level of production (or sale), (2) by time of incurrence (discretionary variability), and (3) in relation to changing prices.

Investors who assess prospects in relation to the most recently issued financial statements need information about expense variability. How better can an investor assess earnings prospects than to adjust the financial statements for changes in expenses attending expected changes in revenue? Data about expense variability is needed to do that. Allocations of costs, which are indispensable for periodic income determinations, work against the objective of assisting those who wish to assess earnings prospects. That is why data concerning cost variability is a useful supplement to financial statements. Segment information of the kind required in FASB Statement No. 14, for example, is especially helpful for estimating changes in levels of expenses for assumed changes in level of revenue; a profit contribution notion is central in that context.

The near future of financial reporting should see a growing interest in reporting of expense variability.

Emphasis on earnings per share as an indicator of

performance will begin to fade; some rate of return measure gradually will supplant it. Earnings per share lacks a denominator to be a good comparative indicator. As the objectives of financial reporting expand to meet needs for enterprise-by-enterprise measures, a common denominator is needed. Rate of return can provide it. Much work yet is to be done to identify the denominator: total assets and net assets are candidates, but the matter needs considerable study. The mixture of measures in conventional financial statements has been a deterrent to rate of return developments. Supplemental disclosures of the effects of changing prices furnish data that can be used to experiment with rate of return.

Display of financial data concerns more than the packaging of a communication. Packaging in one sense implies a tight bundle. Perhaps that has been a fault of financial reporting in the past.

The long-standing philosophy of aggregating, combining or consolidating to the maximum extent may have been overdone. As a result, some widely disparate things have been grouped under common captions or headings. This has led to considerable sentiment for unbundling. The unbundling of the income statement has focused on the characteristics of extraordinary, unusual, infrequent, rare and the like, and more recently, segmentation. It may be that characteristics focusing on abnormality cannot be defined satisfactorily for display under general captions; perhaps they should be dealt with only by narrative. That might also have the salutary effect of diffusing the focus on single-figure measures that otherwise are perceived in some omnipotent way to communicate all that needs to be known about the financial progress of an enterprise.

Liquidity is a characteristic that deserves some fresh thinking. An income statement conventionally shows little about liquidity—it could show a great deal. The balance sheet and the funds statement show an aspect of liquidity—but there are other aspects that could be shown. The classification of working capital at times aggregates too many unlikes.

The future course of financial reporting will derive mainly from objectives that are evenhanded to issuers and fair to users. Those objectives will change as perceptions of usefulness change and, therefore, the course of financial reporting will alter from time to time. Only one thing is certain about the future—an accounting millenium is not in the offing. Ω

THE POLITICIZATIUN OF ACCOUNTING

The impact of politics on accounting standards.

by David Solomons

There was once a time, not so many years ago, when accounting could be thought of as an essentially nonpolitical subject. If it was not as far removed from politics as was mathematics or astronomy, it was at least no more political than psychology or surveying or computer technology or statistics. Even in areas of accounting such as taxation, which might be thought to be most relevant to questions of public policy, practitioners were generally content to confine themselves to technical issues without getting involved as accountants in the discussion of tax policy.

Today, to judge from current discussions of the standard-setting process, accounting can no longer be thought of as nonpolitical. The numbers that accountants report have, or at least are widely thought to have, a significant impact on economic behavior. Accounting rules therefore affect human behavior. Hence, the process by which they are made is said to be political. It is then only a short step to the assertion that such rules are properly to be made in the political arena, by counting heads and deciding accounting issues by some voting mechanism.

There are several articulate spokesmen for this point of view. Dale Gerboth writes that "a politicization of accounting rule-making [is] not only inevitable, but just. In a society committed to democratic legitimization of authority, only politically responsive institutions have the right to command others to obey their rules."[1] And, in another passage from the same article, Gerboth says, "When a decision-making process depends for its success on public confidence, the critical issues are not technical; they are political. . . . In the face of conflict between competing in-terests, rationality as well as prudence lies not in seeking final answers, but rather in compromise—essentially a political process."[2]

In the same vein, Charles Horngren writes that "the setting of accounting standards is as much a product of political action as of flawless logic or empirical findings. Why? Because the setting of standards is a social decision. Standards place restrictions on behavior; therefore, they must be accepted by the affected parties. Acceptance may be forced or voluntary or some of both. In a democratic society, getting acceptance is an exceedingly complicated process that requires skillful marketing in a political arena."[3]

Robert May and Gary Sundem take a similar position: "In practice as well as in theory, the social welfare impact of accounting reports apparently is recognized. Therefore it is no surprise that the [Financial Accounting Standards Board] is a political body and, consequently, that the process of selecting an acceptable accounting alternative is a political process. If the social welfare impact of accounting policy decisions were ignored, the basis for the existence of a regulatory body would disappear. Therefore, the FASB must consider explicitly political (i.e., social

---

[2] Ibid, p.479.
[3] Charles T. Horngren, "The Marketing of Accounting Standards," JofA, Oct.73, p.61.

DAVID SOLOMONS, FCA, is Arthur Young Professor of Accounting at the Wharton School, the University of Pennsylvania. A consultant to the special committee of the AICPA to study the structure of the auditing standards executive committee, he was a member of the AICPA's study group on the establishment of accounting principles (the Wheat committee). Dr. Solomons is a fellow of the Institute of Chartered Accountants in England and Wales and a member of the National Association of Accountants. He also is the immediate past president of the American Accounting Association and former AAA director of research. The author of several books on accounting, Dr. Solomons received an AICPA award in 1970 for notable contribution to accounting literature for *Divisional Performance: Measurement and Control* (New York: Financial Executives Research Foundation, 1965; later published by Richard D. Irwin, Inc.). This article is adapted from a paper appearing in *Essays in Honor of William A. Paton—Pioneer Accounting Theorist,* edited by Stephen A. Zeff, Joel Demski and Nicholas Dopuch (Ann Arbor, Mich.: Division of Research, Graduate School of Business Administration, University of Michigan, 1978).

---

[1] Dale L. Gerboth, "Research, Intuition, and Politics in Accounting Inquiry," *Accounting Review,* July 1973, p.481.

welfare) aspects as well as accounting theory and research in its decisions."[4]

Other voices that call for an explicit recognition of the probable economic and social impact of a new accounting standard are not always easily distinguished from those asserting that political considerations should determine what the standard should be.[5] However, these two views should not be confused.

The structure committee of the Financial Accounting Foundation grappled with the question of the political nature of the standard-setting task in *The Structure of Establishing Financial Accounting Standards*. On the nature of the standard-setting process, it says: "The process of setting accounting standards can be described as democratic because like all rule-making bodies the Board's right to make rules depends ultimately on the consent of the ruled. But because standard setting requires some perspective it would not be appropriate to establish a standard based solely on a canvass of the constituents. Similarly, the process can be described as legislative because it must be deliberative and because all views must be heard. But the standard setters are expected to represent the entire constituency as a whole and not be representatives of a specific constituent group. The process can be described as political because there is an educational effort involved in getting a new standard accepted. But it is not political in the sense that an accommodation is required to get a statement issued."[6]

There is something here to please everyone. Yet the committee does finally come out on the side of the angels: "We have used the word constituency to indicate that the FASB is accountable to everyone who has an interest. We are not suggesting that the Board members are in place to represent them or that the standards must necessarily be based on a numerical consensus."[7]

That accounting influences human behavior, if only because it conveys information, is obvious enough, though research into the workings of "the efficient market" has cast doubt on some of the supposed results of accounting choices. There are, without question, political aspects of accounting. There are similarly political aspects of physics, which result in enormous expenditures on research into nuclear energy and weaponry. Geology, in its concern with the world's reserves of fossil fuels, obviously has political implications. Research into sickle cell anemia became a political question when the heavy incidence of this disease among black Americans came to light. There are very few areas of human knowledge which are devoid of political significance. But that does not mean that the processes by which knowledge is advanced or by which new applications are found for old knowledge are themselves political processes in the sense in which that term is usually understood. Political motives for asking a question may be entirely appropriate. A politically motivated answer may or may not be appropriate. It obviously depends on the nature of the question.

It may be useful to look more carefully at the part which politics should and should not play in accounting standard setting. The future of the FASB may depend on a better understanding of that issue. Indeed, the very credibility of accounting itself may be at stake.

Accounting and National Goals

The most extreme expression, so far as I am aware, of the view that political considerations should enter into the formulation of accounting standards—not merely into the choice of accounting questions to be studied but also into the formulation of the standards themselves—is to be found in a lecture given in New York in November 1973 by Professor David Hawkins. He noted that Congress and the executive branch of the federal government were "becoming more and more aware of the behavioral aspects of corporate reporting and its macro economic implications. Increasingly, I believe, these policy makers will demand . . . that the decisions of those charged with determining what constitutes approved corporate reporting standards result in corporate reporting standards that will lead to individual economic behavior that is consistent with the nation's macro economic objectives. . . . This awareness on the part of economic planners

[4] Robert G. May and Gary L. Sundem, "Research for Accounting Policy: An Overview," *Accounting Review*, October 1976, p.750.
[5] John Buckley (in "FASB and Impact Analysis," *Management Accounting*, April 1976, p.13) straddles this line most uncomfortably. His article has been thought to support politically slanted standards although he nowhere explicitly says that he does.
[6] Structure committee, *The Structure of Establishing Financial Accounting Standards* (Stamford, Conn.: FAF, April 1977), p.19.
[7] Ibid.

The Bettmann Archive

brings accounting standards setting into the realm of political economics."[8]

Events since 1973 have not shown any diminution in this awareness. The question is whether this is to be regarded as a threat to the integrity of accounting or as an opportunity, perhaps even an obligation, on the part of accountants to cooperate with government in furthering its economic policy. Hawkins left us in no doubt where he stood in this matter: "The [FASB's] objectives must be responsive to many more considerations than accounting theory or our notions of economically useful data. . . . Corporate reporting standards should result in data that are useful for economic decisions *provided that the standard is consistent with the national macro economic objectives and the economic programs designed to reach these goals."[9]* And, as if that were not enough, he added that "because the [FASB] has the power to influence economic behavior it has an obligation to support the government's economic plans."[10]

In that last passage, the word "because" is noteworthy, implying as it does that the power to influence economic behavior always carries with it an obligation to support the government's plans. Even if the matter under discussion were, say, pricing policy or wage policy or some aspect of environmental protection, the assertion would be open to argument. In relation to accounting, where the end product is a system of measurement, the position which Hawkins urges on the FASB could, I believe, threaten the integrity of financial reporting and deprive it of whatever credibility it now has.

There is no question as to the sensitivity of some, indeed most, of the issues that have been or are now on the agenda of the FASB or its predecessors, and of course this sensitivity stems from the fact that standards dealing with those issues have influenced or will influence behavior. This can only mean that there is widespread skepticism about the "efficient market" hypothesis. The financial community is not indifferent to the accounting rules imposed on it by the FASB. It is not the purpose of this article to explore the nature of this concern.[11] It will be enough to recognize that the FASB's constituents think it matters whether leases are capitalized or

---

[8] David M. Hawkins, "Financial Accounting, the Standards Board and Economic Development," one of the 1973-74 Emanuel Saxe Distinguished Lectures in Accounting, published by the Bernard M. Baruch College, City University of New York, April 1975, pp.7-8.
[9] Ibid., pp.17, 9-10.
[10] Ibid., p.11.

[11] Yet one cannot ignore the troublesome paradox posed by the numerous empirical studies which have shown "that the capital market does distinguish between [accounting] changes that appear to be reporting changes of no economic importance and those that appear to have substantive economic implications." (Nicholas J. Gonedes and Nicholas Dopuch, "Capital Market Equilibrium, Information Production, and Selecting Accounting Techniques: Theoretical Framework and Review of Empirical Work," *Studies on Financial Accounting Objectives: 1974*, supplement to vol. 12 of the *Journal of Accounting Research.*) If the market can "see through" accounting changes that result from changes in standards, why do they generate so much heat?

not, whether foreign currency transactions are accounted for by one method or another, whether contingencies are provided for by charges against income or by allowing retained earnings to accumulate. These questions do not affect the amount of information that is disclosed but simply the way in which these economic phenomena are reported; yet this fact does not desensitize them. Perhaps investors *are* naive. Only on the basis of such an assumption (and on the assumption that no new information will be disclosed by a politically motivated standard) is the impact of politics on accounting standards worth discussing at all.

The Economic Impact of Accounting Standards

Few if any accounting standards are without some economic impact. The requirement that U.S. companies write off purchased goodwill is said to give an advantage to foreign companies in bidding for American businesses because, not being subject to the same accounting requirement, they can afford to offer a higher price. FASB Statement no. 2, *Accounting for Research and Development Costs,* which requires that R&D be expensed as incurred, has been said to constitute a threat to technological progress, especially by smaller companies that may be contemplating seeking access to the capital market and will therefore want to show good profits before doing so.[12] FASB Statement no. 5, *Accounting for Contingencies,* by greatly restricting the circumstances in which an estimated loss from a loss contingency can be accrued by a charge to income, is said to have caused U.S. insurance companies to reinsure risks for which previously they would have relied on self-insurance.

One of the most sensitive standards has been that dealing with foreign currency translation (Statement no. 8, *Accounting for the Translation of Foreign Currency Transactions and Foreign Currency Financial Statements).* Under the so-called temporal method mandated by the board, monetary assets and liabilities of a foreign subsidiary of a U.S. corporation have to be translated, for consolidation purposes, at the rate of exchange current at the balance sheet date. Assets which, in accordance with generally accepted accounting principles, are carried

at cost or cost less depreciation have to be translated at the rate current at the time they were acquired. Exchange gains and losses, realized and unrealized, have to be brought into the income statement. For companies that formerly used a current/noncurrent classification, the important changes lie in the treatment of inventories and of long-term debt. Inventories, as current assets, were formerly carried at the current rate and are now carried at the historical rate; long-term debt, as a noncurrent liability, was formerly carried at the historical rate and now, as a monetary item, is carried at the current rate. Moreover, unrealized translation gains, formerly kept out of the income statement, now have to be brought in. The result has been greatly to increase the volatility of the reported earnings of companies with important foreign operations. Criticism of Statement no. 8 has focused on this increased volatility rather than on whether the new rules result in a better or worse representation of financial performance.

Whatever one may think about the merits of FASB Statement no. 19, *Financial Accounting and Reporting by Oil and Gas Producing Companies,* there can be little doubt that the Securities and Exchange Commission would not have acted as it did at the end of August to overrule this standard if there had not been political pressure from certain oil and gas companies which felt that they would be injured by the mandatory use of the "successful efforts" method of costing. It will be some time before the full effect of this action on the standard-setting process can be seen in its true light.

Numerous other politically sensitive accounting issues could be cited, but none has received as much attention as accounting for inflation, for none has such widespread potential repercussions throughout the business world. Each method which has been proposed to replace or to modify traditional methods would affect different companies differently, making some look more prosperous than they are under present methods and others less prosperous. For example, current purchasing power adjustments to historical cost accounting (general price level accounting) tend to make utilities with heavy debt capital look better off; replacement cost accounting tends to make companies with a large investment in depreciable assets, such as steel companies, look relatively less profitable. A system using exit values (e.g., continuously contemporary accounting, or

---

12 This argument, when the treatment of R&D was still on the FASB's agenda, led Hawkins to say, in his 1973 Emanuel Saxe Lecture (p.14), "I do not believe the Board can eliminate the alternative capitalization." Events proved him wrong.

COCOA) would make firms using assets that are not readily salable look bad. Though the protracted arguments about the relative merits of these and other rival systems have not generally overtly recognized the vested interests that stand to gain or lose by the way the argument goes, the political implications of inflation accounting have probably had as much responsibility for the difficulty in reaching agreement on the direction in which to move as have the technical problems involved.

In some of these instances, notably those concerning contingency reserves and foreign currency translations, critics of the FASB are asserting that economic behavior, such as reinsurance or hedging, which would not have been rational under the old accounting rules becomes rational under the new ones. Such an assertion is difficult to defend because the new rules have not changed the underlying cash flows or the risks attached to them. Only if significance is attached exclusively to "the bottom line," rather than to the present value of the enterprise, can the change in behavior be defended.

Measurement and Politics

The above examples will serve to illustrate some of the points of contact between accounting and politics. Many more could be cited. Indeed, because standards need to be set mainly in areas where there is controversy, it is highly probable that in every case someone will find the new treatment less favorable than the status quo and there is constantly a temptation for such people to rush off to their legislative representatives to get the government to interfere.[13] That sort of initiative represents the gravest threat on the horizon to the private control of standard setting.

If we are looking for ways to achieve political ends by tinkering with methods of measurement, there is plenty of scope outside the accounting field. Indeed, the danger has already been observed in other areas. For instance, the index of retail prices has a powerful effect on wage settlements in many industries. There is nothing absolute about a price index. The number obtained depends on the choice of base year, the items chosen

for inclusion in the market basket and the weights attached to the items in constructing the index. A statistician who agreed with Hawkins about the responsibilities of those concerned with measurement could easily construct an index which would damp down price changes and could take credit for aiding in the fight against inflation.[14]

I have suggested elsewhere[15] that one way of reducing the traffic accident rate would be for highway authorities to lower the average speed by arranging to have all speedometers consistently overstate speeds so that drivers would think they were driving faster than they actually were. Speedometers influence behavior. Why not influence it in a beneficent direction?

This last example will serve to lay bare the

> "Information cannot be neutral—it cannot therefore be reliable—if it is selected or presented for the purpose of producing some chosen effect on human behavior."

profound threat to accounting implicit in the propositions of Hawkins and of the others referred to above. If it ever became accepted that accounting might be used to achieve other than purely measurement ends, faith in it would be destroyed [16] just as faith in

---

[13] The letter dated October 6, 1977, addressed to the FASB chairman-designate by Senator William Proxmire (D-Wisconsin) and four Wisconsin congressmen and reported in the FASB *Status Report* no. 55, "Persons Opposing the FASB Exposure Draft on Oil and Gas Accounting Apparently Seek Support in Congress for Retention of Alternatives," October 14, 1977, is a case in point.

[14] There is nothing farfetched about this. In *The Final Days* (New York: Avon Books, 1977, p.177), Bob Woodward and Carl Bernstein state that "late in 1971, Nixon had summoned the White House personnel chief, Fred Malek, to his office to discuss a 'Jewish cabal' in the Bureau of Labor Statistics. The 'cabal,' Nixon said, was tilting economic figures to make his administration look bad." Another example came to my notice when I was in Singapore in 1976. There the administration was accused of keeping the price index down by changing the grade of rice included in the collection of food items going into the index.

[15] In my Price Waterhouse lecture at Stanford University in 1972 entitled "Financial Accounting Standards: Regulation or Self-Regulation?"

[16] Support for this view is to be found in Arthur R. Wyatt's article, "The Economic Impact of Financial Accounting Standards," *Arthur Andersen Chronicle*, September 1977, p.49. Somewhat ironically in the circumstances, the same view has been espoused more recently by the chairman of the SEC. In his Statement of August 29 on accounting practices for oil and gas producers, setting aside FASB Statement no. 19, Harold M. Williams said: "If it becomes accepted or expected that accounting principles are determined or modified in order to secure purposes other than economic measurement—even such virtuous purposes as energy production—we assume a grave risk that confidence in the credibility of our financial information system will be undermined."

The Journal of Accountancy, November 1978

speedometers would be destroyed once it was realized that they were subject to falsification for the purpose of influencing driving habits.

Hawkins's view that "because the [FASB] has the power to influence economic behavior, it has an obligation to support the government's economic plans" is, I believe, not only destructive of accounting but it is also infeasible. Governments have a habit of changing their plans from year to year, and even from month to month. Are accounting standards to be changed with every change in the political climate? One has only to recall President Nixon's turnabout from a "no wage and price controls" stance to an espousal of rigorous controls in 1971-72—or President Ford's switch from proposals for tax increases to "whip inflation now" to an acceptance of tax cuts to stimulate employment in 1974—to see how futile it is to talk about supporting the government's economic plans or how impossible it would be for a standards board to keep up with the government.

The Importance of Neutrality

Simply because information has an effect on human behavior does not mean that it should not seek to be neutral as between different desired modes of behavior. Unless it is as neutral as the accountant can make it, it is difficult to see how it can be relied on to guide behavior. As Chambers observes, "If the form of accounting is permitted to change with changes in policy, any attempt to scrutinize and to evaluate specific policies will be thwarted."[17]

Neutrality in accounting implies representational accuracy. Curiously, it has been little discussed, though other terms related to it have received more attention. The American Accounting Association's 1977 committee on concepts and standards for external financial reports gets near the heart of the matter when it says: "Users of financial information prefer that it have a high degree of reliability. Reliability is that quality which permits users of data to depend upon it with confidence as representative of what it purports to represent. But reliable information is not necessarily useful. It could, for example, be reliable but unrelated to the use at hand. Several relatively general terms are often used as synonyms for, or to cover parts of, the concept of reliability. Thus, verifiability, objectivity, lack of bias, neutrality, and accuracy all are related to reliability. Like relevance, reliability (above some minimal level) is a necessary but not a sufficient condition for usefulness of data."[18]

If the preceding sentence is true, these two qualities (relevance and reliability) together go far toward ensuring usefulness. Relevance comprehends subsidiary characteristics of information one might list such as timeliness. And the essential element in the reliability of information (at least for our present purpose) is that it shall as accurately as possible represent what it purports to represent.[19] This implies neutrality.

Neutrality, in the sense in which the term is used here, does not imply that no one gets hurt. It is true, as the AAA 1977 committee on the social consequences of accounting information says, "Every policy choice represents a trade-off among differing individual preferences, and possibly among alternative consequences, regardless of whether the policy-makers see it that way or not. In this sense, accounting policy choices can never be neutral. There is someone who is granted his preference, and someone who is not."[20] The same thing could be said of the draft, when draft numbers were drawn by lot. Some people were chosen to serve while others escaped. It was still, by and large, neutral in the sense that all males of draft age were equally likely to be selected.

Accounting as Financial Cartography

Information cannot be neutral—it cannot therefore be reliable—if it is selected or presented for the purpose of producing some chosen effect on human behavior. It is this quality of neutrality which makes a map reliable; and the essential nature of accounting, I believe, is cartographic. Accounting is financial mapmaking. The better the map, the more completely it represents the complex phenomena that are being mapped. We do

[17] Raymond J. Chambers, *Accounting, Evaluation and Economic Behavior* (Englewood Cliffs, N.J.: Prentice-Hall, Inc., 1966), p.326.

[18] Committee on concepts and standards for external financial reports, *Statement on Accounting Theory and Theory Acceptance* (Sarasota, Fla.: American Accounting Association, 1977), p.16.
[19] This is close to Yuji Ijiri's statement that "in general, a system is said to be reliable if it works the way it is supposed to" (*The Foundations of Accounting Measurement: A Mathematical, Economic, and Behavioral Inquiry* [Englewood Cliffs, N.J.: Prentice-Hall, Inc., 1967], p.137). But his more formal definition of reliability is couched more in terms of the predictive value of information, an aspect of the matter with which I am not here concerned.
[20] Committee on the social consequences of accounting information, *Report of the Committee on the Social Consequences of Accounting Information* (Sarasota, Fla.: AAA, 1978), p.24.

not judge a map by the behavioral effects it produces. The distribution of natural wealth or rainfall shown on a map may lead to population shifts or changes in industrial location, which the government may like or dislike. That should be no concern of the cartographer. We judge his map by how well it represents the facts. People can then react to it as they will.

Cartographers represent different facts in different ways and match the scale of their maps to their purpose. Every map represents a selection of a small portion of available data, for no map could show physical, political, demographic, climatological, geological, vegetational and numerous other kinds of data and still be intelligible. The need to be selective in the data that one represents does not normally rob the map of its neutrality, although it could.

As with the geographic features that cartographers map, different financial facts need to be represented in different ways, and different facts are needed for different purposes. It is perfectly proper for measurements to be selected with particular political ends in mind or to be adapted to a political end if it is made clear to users of the measurement what is being done. For example, the government is entitled, for taxation purposes, to define taxable income in whatever way suits it. It would be quite another matter for it to tell accountants that they were to use this definition for all purposes to which an income number might be put.

Some Contrary Views

There have recently been some expressions of a different view of accounting from mine that deserve comment here. Sometimes the difference in the weight to be given to economic impact in standard setting is merely one of emphasis. Sometimes it is more fundamental in nature. Sometimes neutrality is dismissed on other grounds.

Probably no one argues that those who formulate accounting standards should do so with total unconcern for their economic consequences. Indeed, without some concern for such consequences, the selection of problem areas that call for standards could not be made. It was the economic consequences of not having a standard to deal with some particular problem which presumably directed attention in that direction in the first place. To require the FASB to report on the probable economic impact of a proposed standard when an exposure draft is issued[21]—if it can be done, for the impact will often not be clear or unambiguous—is not at all objectionable, so long as the standard is designed to bring about a better representation of the facts of a situation, with whatever behavioral results flow from that, and not to promote some preselected economic objective or mode of behavior.

Some of those who would play down the value of neutrality in accounting standards do so because, they argue, the financial phenomena which accountants must report are not independent of the reporting methods selected. This view is expressed by the AAA 1977 committee on the social consequences of accounting information in the following passage from its report: "The view that measurement merely involves representing or describing stocks and flows is a static view. It assumes that the stocks and flows are history, fixed forever, no matter how you measure them. But what about tomorrow's stocks and flows? They are governed by the business decisions of enterprises—decisions which might change depending upon how you choose to measure the stocks and flows. The traditional framework fails to take this interdependence of measurement and decisional behavior into consideration."[22]

It is true that, where human beings are the subjects of measurement, behavior and measurements are not independent of each other. But this does not make neutrality a less desirable quality of measurement in such cases. If one substitutes speedometers for accounting and driving behavior for stocks and flows in the AAA committee's statement above, one can see that as an argument against neutrality it is quite unconvincing. There is nothing static about the relationship between the speed of a vehicle and the reading on the speedometer, and there is unquestionably feedback. The behavior of the driver is reflected on the dial, and what is on the dial affects the behavior of the driver. Speedometers still should register speed accurately and neutrally. The decision about how to react to the reading must be left to the driver.

A different criterion for the selection of approved accounting methods is put forward by William Beaver and Roland Dukes in a discussion of interperiod tax allocation: "The method which produces earnings numbers

---

[21] As recommended by Prem Prakash and Alfred Rappaport in "The Feedback Effects of Accounting," *Business Week*, January 12, 1976, p.12.
[22] Social consequences committee, p.23.

having the highest association with security prices is the most consistent with the information that results in an efficient determination of security prices. Subject to [certain] qualifications . . . , it is the method that ought to be reported."[23] And, having found that "deferral earnings are most consistent with the information set used in setting security prices," they conclude that "if one accepts market efficiency, the results suggest that the [Accounting Principles Board] made the 'correct' policy decision . . . in the sense that it requires a method which is most consistent with the information impounded in an efficient determination of security prices."[24]

Beaver and Dukes themselves point out that any inferences to be drawn from their evidence are "conditional upon the prediction models used to test the accounting measures. . . . Any findings are the joint result of prediction models and accounting methods, and only appropriately specified joint statements are warranted."[25] In other words, the identification of the accounting method found to generate earnings numbers or cash flow numbers most closely associated with security prices depends on the way that "unexpected returns" are defined. The results of this analysis do not point unambiguously, therefore, toward a particular accounting method.

This could explain why, left to themselves, companies do not all choose the same accounting methods. They do not all use the same prediction models, and therefore the accounting method that has the most information content for one company is not the one with the most for another company. One moral that might be drawn from this is that we do not need accounting standards at all but, rather, that in an efficient market laissez-faire should prevail. A different conclusion about the Beaver and Dukes study is reached by Gonedes and Dopuch when they say that "under the contemporary institutional setting, capital market efficiency—taken by itself—does not imply that the prices of firms' ownership shares can be used in assessing the desirability of alternative information-production decisions."[26] In any case, whichever

way the efficient market points us, it does not point us toward politically motivated accounting standards.

Limitations of the Analogy With Cartography

There is a danger, with any analogy, of pushing it too far, and the analogy between accounting and cartography is no exception. Most maps represent external phenomena that have an independent existence of their own. The accountant is on safe ground only when he is doing the same thing—representing external phenomena such as cash flows, contractual rights, market values, etc. Of course, cartographers have sometimes amused themselves by drawing maps of fictitious countries, like Erewhon or Atlantis, an activity which, too, has had its accounting counterparts.

Whatever limitations representational accuracy may have in pointing us toward right accounting answers, it will at least sometimes enable us to detect a wrong answer. For instance, FASB Statement no. 2, which requires all R&D expenditures to be expensed as incurred, is bad cartography because to represent the value of the continuing benefits of past research expenditures as zero will usually not be in accord with the facts of the situation, however expedient the treatment may be. Off-balance-sheet financing requires that certain unattractive features of the landscape be left off the map, so that again the map is defective. The criterion by which rules are to be judged is not the effect which they may or may not have on business behavior. It is the accuracy with which they reflect the facts of the situation.

Conclusion

It is not at all palatable for accountants to be confronted by a choice between appearing to be indifferent to national objectives or endangering the integrity of their measurement techniques. But if the long-run well-being of our discipline is what matters, the right choice should be easy to make. It is our job —as accountants—to make the best maps we can. It is for others, or for accountants acting in some other capacity, to use those maps to steer the economy in the right direction. If the distinction between these two tasks is lost sight of, we shall greatly diminish our capacity to serve society, and in the long run everybody loses. ■

[23] William H. Beaver and Roland E. Dukes, "Interperiod Tax Allocation, Earnings Expectations, and the Behavior of Security Prices," *Accounting Review*, April 1972, p.321. They add, in a footnote, that "the criterion suggested above provides a simplified method for preference ordering of alternative measurement methods."
[24] Ibid., p.331.
[25] Ibid., p.332.
[26] Gonedes and Dopuch, p.92.

UNIFORMITY IN ACCOUNTING: A HISTORICAL PERSPECTIVE

An illustrative overview of the evolution of uniformity—from generations ago to the Metcalf and Moss reports.

by Barbara D. Merino and Teddy L. Coe

History can be viewed as an extension of experience fostering greater sophistication and judgment in addressing contemporary issues. Accountants sometimes fail to examine issues in historical perspective, thereby ignoring valuable insights that might enable the profession to respond more forcefully to contemporary demands. Consider the concept of uniformity in accounting, which has been the subject of debate for many generations. Historians who have examined the concept of uniformity in relation to political theory have concluded that the "horrible logic of any policy of uniformity starts with the fear of heterodoxy, becomes regimentation of opinion, hardens into poisonous orthodoxy, and ends in pathological terror of contradiction" (Schafer, 1969, p.11). Accountants, likewise, have rejected uniformity as a panacea for the development of accounting theory. Since the staff reports of the late Senator Lee Metcalf (D-Mont.) and Congressman John E. Moss (D-Calif.) have

once again advocated uniformity (although in different forms), it seems beneficial to highlight the historical evidence with respect to this issue.

This article will discuss briefly the various definitions of uniformity, trace the evolution of the concept of uniformity as (seemingly) advocated by Metcalf and Moss and assess the historical validity of accountants' rejection of the concept. The examples given here should be considered illustrative, since it would require a voluminous literature to tell the complete story of the history of uniformity.

The Current Climate Toward Uniformity

Accountants today rightfully feel besieged. Congressional committees, the Securities and Exchange Commission,* the courts and the financial community have strongly criticized the accounting profession. Such criticisms include lack of uniform financial accounting standards, alleged dominance of the eight largest international CPA firms and the American Institute of CPAs, the lack of auditor independence and the imprecision of the fairness standard. Many critics have resorted to a simplistic solution by advocating uniform accounting principles as the answer to the profession's problems.

The term "uniformity" as applied to accounting has never been satisfactorily defined. However, the following classifications provide a framework of ways in which the word has been used:

☐ Strong form—no variance in practice allowed; principles and rules are prescribed to indicate a single accounting rule for each type of recognizable accounting event (including rules governing event recognition).

☐ Moderate–strong form—general uniformity in the application of accounting principles with specific rules of implementation; some variance allowed where it is impractical to gain uniformity.

BARBARA D. MERINO, Ph.D., is assistant professor at New York University. An associate member of the Kentucky Society of CPAs, she is also a member of the Academy of Accounting Historians and the American Accounting Association. Dr. Merino is the author of several articles that have appeared in professional publications. **TEDDY L. COE**, CPA, Ph.D., is associate professor at New York University. A member of the American Accounting Association and the National Association of Accountants, Dr. Coe has had a number of articles published in professional publications.

The Journal of Accountancy, August 1978

* Ed. note: For an article on historical impressions of the SEC and its chief accountants, see Gary John Previts, this issue's Statement in Quotes department, pages 83–91.

☐ Moderate–weak form—general uniformity in the application of accounting principles with a choice of principles resting on the particular industrial and firm economic and technological conditions.

☐ Weak form—general uniformity to be achieved by limiting the number of accounting choices available, but the choice of a particular accounting principle is left to management.

Metcalf and Moss appear to call for different types of uniformity. Metcalf's staff report advocates the strong form of uniformity: "A comprehensive set of Federal accounting objectives should encompass such goals as uniformity, consistency, clarity, accuracy, simplicity, meaningful presentation, and fairness in application. . . . Congress should establish specific policies abolishing such 'creative accounting' techniques as percentage of completion income recognition, inflation accounting, 'normalized' accounting, and other potentially misleading accounting methods. . . . The Federal Government should directly establish financial accounting standards for publicly-owned corporations" (U.S. Congress, Senate 1976, p.21).

The Moss report appears to recommend the moderate–strong form of uniformity: ". . . to the maximum extent practicable, the SEC should prescribe by rule a framework of uniform accounting principles. In instances where uniformity is not practicable, the SEC should require the independent auditor to attest that the accounting principles selected by management represent financial data most fairly" (U.S. Congress, House 1976, pp.51–52).

The committees appear to assume that uniformity will result in more accurate financial reports. This attempt to gain greater uniformity in accounting is not the first; indeed, interest in the topic predates this century, even though it did not receive widespread attention until the twentieth century. An examination of the historical evidence suggests that the committees' assumption that uniformity would result in better financial reporting may not be warranted.

Uniformity, of course, is not the only issue that has been the subject of recurring debate. Some historians find it ironic that the accounting profession is criticized for the dominance of large firms. A major concern of congressional leaders at the turn of the century was that small accounting firms could not maintain their independence in the face of the enormous powers of investment bankers like J. P. Morgan. The merger movement

among accounting firms that began in the first decade of this century was viewed as salutary. Indeed, it was suggested that accountants could not achieve professional status unless the individual firms were large enough to be independent of clients and provide a countervailing power to protect the public interests when auditing corporations like Standard Oil.[1]

Historical Background— Initial Attempts at Uniformity

The Interstate Commerce Law passed by Congress in 1887 marked an early attempt to regulate industry in the United States. Although the Interstate Commerce Commission was given broad regulatory powers, it is generally agreed that regulation had been ineffective before the turn of the century (U.S. Industrial Commission, 1902, p.353). But the establishment of the ICC secured the idea

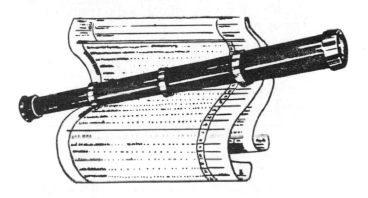

that government had the right to regulate certain industries.

The Hepburn Act (1906) significantly increased the broad powers of the ICC, including authority over accounting systems of regulated industries. The federal agency established "uniform systems of accounting" making it "unlawful for . . . carriers to keep any other accounts, records or memoranda than those prescribed or approved by the Commission" (JofA, Nov. 06, p.36).

Accountants responded positively to the ICC requirements that all railroads make annual financial reports public and available to the regulatory agency. The proposal of uniform accounts did not incur the wrath of accountants, simply because they did not be-

---

[1] Editorial, JofA, Nov.27, pp.366-367, which states that, of 15,000 surveyed companies, only 892 issued audited financial reports. Of the 892 audits, 579 companies were audited by 10 different accounting firms while 199 other accounting firms audited the remaining 313 companies.

lieve that the ICC intended to advocate the strong form of uniformity. In response to a somewhat hysterical comment in *Railway Age*, the editor of the *Journal of Accountacy* admitted that uniformity could lead to some undesirable results if one assumed that the ICC would insist on "an inflexible form of accounts." Certainly, he conceded, if "all corporate accounts are to be prescribed by government officials and no others can be kept," then, accounting progress would be checked. But the editorial noted that "all government officials are not so bureaucratically stupid as the pro-railroad people are inclined to make out." Henry C. Adams, the chief statistician of the ICC, was highly respected, and most accountants believed he could be trusted to avoid the pitfalls of "rule-book" uniformity (JofA, Nov.06, pp.36–37).

The American Association of Public Accountants (AAPA, now the AICPA) committee on interstate commerce offered to help the ICC in any way it could and relations between the two, at least initially, were harmonious (JofA, Nov.06, p.77). The criticism of uniform systems came not from American accountants but from their British brethren. An editorial in the *Accountant* (July 20, 1907) condemned the law since it might be designed to reduce rates by requiring railroads to report only minimum operating costs. "The 'reform' is curiously interesting," suggested the editor, "inasmuch as it affords us the rather pathetic spectacle of the United States striving to go back to the low level of British railroad statistics and Great Britain struggling to attain the fullness of perfection exhibited by the now discarded American method."

But the actions of the ICC seemed to suggest that such fears were unwarranted. The ICC's initial concern was not with a rule-book approach but with such broader issues as whether depreciation was a cost of doing business. Accountants supported the commission's assertion that depreciation was an operating expense and were pleased that the ICC did not attempt to prescribe a specific method of depreciation. Strangely, management, which would benefit since rates would be increased because of lower reported income, became indignant. The explanation was simply that the panic of 1907 had reduced profits to a low level and most firms did not want to be compelled to report additional expenses.[2] CPAs did not oppose ICC regulation because it failed to mandate independent audits as subsequently charged; opposition came when the ICC, in an apparent effort to reduce rates to a bare minimum, began to require that all depreciation be calculated on a straight-line basis. This interpretation of uniformity met with strong criticism, for accountants contended that railroads were being systematically destroyed by the shortsighted policy of regulators. With the low return on investment afforded by the ICC policy, it had become difficult to attract new capital or to maintain existing capital. The accountants' view that profits had been grossly overstated because of inadequate provisions for operating expenses appears to have been justified in the light of the subsequent monumental failure of railroads. The attempts of the ICC to dictate a rule-book approach caused accountants to rebel.

The accountants' response to the ICC reflects a pattern of criticism to such proposals that has been followed by subsequent generations. They said that uncertainty and different environmental conditions made it unfair to treat all business concerns alike and that only incorrect and misleading information results from such treatment.

Ironically, it was the public accounting profession itself that made politicians aware of the benefits of a uniform classification of accounts. At the turn of the century, reformers had demanded greater accountability on the part of public officials. Several CPAs had received national recognition for their work in this area, and the financial press lauded their efforts. By 1901, the *Chronicle* (New York, New York) observed that the "one great advantage in having a uniform or standard system of accounts is that by means of the same it became possible to compare one place with the corresponding results for another" and thus determine the efficiency of political leaders. The AAPA, in response to a Conference on Uniform Municipal Accounting called by the U.S. Census Bureau (1904), had appointed a committee "to consider the practical application of true accounting principles in connection with standard schedules for uniform reports on municipal industries and

---

[2] For the railroad's view, see M. P. Blauvelt, "Railroad Accounting Under Government Supervision," JofA, June08, pp.81-92; for an accountant's rebuttal, see J.F. Calvert, "Depreciation in Railway Accounting," JofA, Aug.08, pp.229–233; for the ICC's view, see Henry C. Adams, "Railway Accounting in Its Relation to the Twentieth Section of the Act to Regulate Commerce," JofA, Oct.08, pp.381–393.

public service corporations." Harvey Chase, chairman of the committee, conducted a highly successful campaign to convince municipalities to adopt the association's uniform system (AAPA, *Report of the Committee on Standard Schedules for Uniform Reports on Municipal Industries and Public Service Corporations, 1906*). CPAs worked closely with the National Municipal League and by 1910 could report that uniform legislation was being adopted in many states (JofA, Apr. 10, p.453). Naturally politicians asked why such a simple solution could not be extended to the private sector.

Uniform Cost Systems

Edward N. Hurley, chairman of the Federal Trade Commission in 1916, noted that regulated companies were using uniform charts of accounts and that the Harvard Business School had been experimenting with a uniform system of cost accounting for shoe retailers. He asked if such systems would not be advantageous to businessmen. He argued that "intelligent cost accounting lies at the base of efficient management. . . . Men go into business to make money." In 1916, his major concern was that goods were not being properly priced because costs were not known. He said that "90% of all manufacturers of the United States are pricing their goods arbitrarily" and, therefore, engaging in destructive "cutthroat competition" (Hurley, 1916, pp.3-14).

Accountants could find no fault with these arguments for they had been trying to convince businessmen of the need for proper cost systems for several generations. But they were uncertain of Hurley's motives, for the FTC was established as a reform agency to administer most of the antitrust legislation and prevent price discrimination and unfair competition.[3] There was some fear that Hurley was attempting to create another ICC, which had resulted not only in temporary displacement of auditors in the railroad in-

---

[3] The wariness of the association's leadership is clearly shown in the minutes of that group. In 1916, Robert Montgomery characterized Hurley as an "unknown quantity" (minutes, 1916, 110ff.) but by 1917 he was lamenting "the loss of our boy in Washington" (minutes, 1917, 30ff.). The view that Hurley was "pro business" and in favor of "private control" is supported in the historical literature. See Gabriel Kolko, *The Triumph of Conservatism; A Reinterpretation of American History, 1900–1916* (New York: The Free Press of Glenco, 1963). Even revisionist historians who disagree with Kolko's general thesis that the majority of the FTC commissioners were pro-business concede that Hurley's primary concern was to ensure a "fair return" to business.

dustry but in the development of rule-book accounting, and accountants were naturally wary. Hurley, however, asked the AAPA to review the uniform systems developed by the FTC, and relations were cordial. The benefits of such cost systems to businessmen were soon obvious.

Uniform Financial Accounting

While accountants could accept with equanimity uniform municipal and cost accounting systems—for they were essentially classificatory and involved no profit calculations—they were caught unaware when Hurley blithely suggested that uniform systems be extended to financial accounting. He proposed that (1) a standard financial statement form for all credit purposes be developed; (2) a set of rules and regulations for the valuation of all assets and the ascertainment of liabilities be developed; and (3) all statements accepted by bankers be verified by an

> "Accountants were not surprised or unprepared when, in the thirties, political leaders began to advocate the strong form of uniformity."

accountant registered with the Federal Reserve Board or with the federal reserve banks (1916, p.175).

The national organization was disconcerted by Hurley's suggestion of federal registration; however, the AAPA attempted to meet Hurley's other demands, and later those of Frank Delano, of the Federal Reserve Board, by at least appearing to acquiesce in their call for a "scientific methodology," for the development of an accounting rule book. *Uniform Accounting* (later reissued under the more appropriate title *Approved Methods for Preparation of Balance Sheet Audits*) neither advocated uniformity nor dealt with accounting principles. *Uniform Accounting* was simply an adaptation of an internal control memorandum prepared by J. Scobie for Price Waterhouse (Demond, 1951, p.140f.).

The demand for uniform financial accounting was a simplistic extension of the concept of uniform cost systems, which was not warranted. Uniform cost systems were designed on an industry-by-industry basis, giving recognition to the different technological and economic environments of various industries; the cost systems for each industry were sufficiently flexible to allow for differences among companies. Indeed, these systems were designed more as uniform charts of accounts rather than as comprehensive accounting systems. In the uniform cost systems, little or no attention was given to such questions as valuation or income–expense recognition. While the cost systems appeared to use the historical cost assumption, the methods of computing depreciation and the valuation of inventories were not specified. Such cost systems were not designed to obtain complete uniformity. However, when demands for uniform financial accounting arose, they appeared to be calls for a strong or moderate–strong form of uniformity.

Uniform Accounting left room for considerable variability in the application of accounting methods, and many matters were simply left to professional judgment. The book's name, however, suggested that there was a uniform accounting methodology accepted by most practitioners. That, of course, was not true. A 1929 editorial in the *Journal of Accountancy* accurately assessed the impact of this document, stating that "prominent members of business at that time were led to extremes by their desire for reform and there was suggestion of a uniform system of accounting and auditing for all sorts of conditions of business." The editorial went on to say that "this excess of zeal [for uniformity] retarded progress" (1929, p.357).

The SEC—Reviewing the Debate Over Uniformity

Accountants were not surprised or unprepared when, in the thirties, political leaders began to advocate the strong form of uniformity. This time they did not avoid the issue but firmly rejected the idea of absolute uniformity. There is overwhelming evidence that if the profession was wary of federal regulation, it had reason to be. The intent of Congress was not clear and, historically, that body had sought unsophisticated remedies for financial reporting problems.

As early as 1906, accountants had noticed the tendency of government officials to resolve all evils by legislative fiat. "For a long time," wrote Joseph Sterrett, "the lazy man's shortcut [has been] pass a law, create a department or bureau. . . ." He added that this has two results: it provides a "modest income" for some employees, but, more important, it lulls the financial community into a "fancied security very far removed from reality" (Sterrett, 1906, p.21). Certainly, the immediate reaction of one legislator to the

crash of 1929 indicates that not all political leaders understood the economic system. A U.S. senator is purported to have wired the following message to the New York Stock Exchange: "Today's activity in your Exchange demonstrates absolute necessity for immediate adoption of a rule limiting amount of loss on any stock during a single session. The country is not prepared to withstand the effect of repetition of what happened today. Unless a rule is adopted and published establishing a reasonable amount of depreciation in any one session, campaign for reform will immediately take shape with possible result either closing Exchange entirely or placing the same under government supervision" (*Chronicle,* July 22, 1933, p.581).

One hopes this was an atypical reaction, but it does seem clear that accountants were genuinely concerned that legislation would be enacted which implied that financial reports were merely summations of facts. Accountants claimed that this would be unrealistic and misleading because of the uncertainty of the business environment. This was not a remote threat given the extravagant claims that had been, were and are still made about the "reliability" and "truth" that could be presumed in audited financial statements.

The profession had been genuinely shocked, if not horrified, by Ripley's assertion in the twenties that the "balance sheet is an instantaneous photograph of the condition of a company" (May 1933, p.8). Accountants had warned that such claims were absurd. Robert Montgomery wrote that "our most precious asset is our independence in thought and action. Our method of expressing the use of our asset is by means of opinion and judgment" (JofA, Oct. 27, p.253). The Institute showed the direction the profession would take in response to governmental demands for certitude in financial reports when it titled an original draft of its correspondence with the New York Stock Exchange "Value and Limitations of Corporate Accounts and General Principles for Preparation of Reports to Stockholders."[4]

---

[4] This pamphlet was introduced into evidence at the securities hearings by the New York Stock Exchange and was issued by the American Institute of Accountants under the more familiar title *Audits of Corporate Accounts,* Correspondence Between the Committee on Cooperation With Stock Exchanges and the Committee on Stock List of the New York Stock Exchange (New York, AIA, 1934).

While the document established six broad general principles, it stressed the need for professional judgment and the fact that the balance sheet was "merely a reflection of opinion subject to, possibly wide, margins of error" (AIA, 1934, pp.3–4). This emphasis on the limitations of financial reports could be viewed as an adverse reaction to increased responsibility being placed on the profession, but it is probably more accurate to interpret this trend as an effort by accountants to warn investors that financial reports could never attain photographic accuracy.

Initially, it did appear that the desire for certainty, a characteristic of the depression mentality, would lead Congress to demand absolute uniformity. The SEC had the right to dictate accounting principles and several of its leaders had suggested that uniformity should be its goal. George O. May was successful in convincing Judge James M. Landis of the SEC, who had originally favored uniformity, that such a goal was unobtainable (Wiesen, 1978). May agreed that uniformity in classification (such as in treatment of operating expenses of routine transactions) was beneficial, but he warned that income determination involved uncertainty and risk, which, despite wishful thinking, could not be eliminated by legislation or regulation (1937, p.346). The SEC's emphasis on consistency and disclosure rather than on uniformity was considered salutary by the accounting profession.

In 1939, Charles Couchman reviewed the various attempts to establish uniform accounting principles, noting that the ICC, the Federal Power Commission and public service corporations in many states had "experimented with uniform systems." He predicted that "in the ensuing years there may be such growth of bureaucratic control over all forms of industry that accounting will be shackled by it in a manner as to allow us no freedom of discretion or judgment." But, he concluded, if attained, uniformity would not endure since truth must prevail and truth "can't be bound by a rule or a law." Government bureaus, he said, "usually function to protect one class or user group [and] are not fair to all." More important, Couchman believed that politicians would eventually realize that uniformity was an unattainable goal. Writing that CPAs "lacked adequate training, knowl-

edge or prophetic endowment to forsee the future and overcome uncertainty," he added that "administrators are also lacking in this respect" (1939, p.3).

Conclusion

While accounting principles have continued to be storm centers of controversy, the profession had established its position with respect to this issue by the late thirties: Namely, that uniformity, when used in the context of absolute rules, was not only impracticable but dangerous. The American Accounting Association's "Tentative Statement of Accounting Principles Affecting Corporate Reports" summarized the position the profession had taken: "Business enterprises are so different in nature that principles applied to any single corporation must make allowance for its individual characteristics and for the character of the industry as well. In fact, it may be said that any complete statement of

> "An evaluation of previous attempts at uniformity had probably had a significant impact on the rejection of uniformity as a basis for establishing accounting principles."

fundamental principles must include suitable explanations, extensions and qualifications" (1936, p.188).

One finds unusual unanimity on this point within the profession and regulatory bodies. The AIA committee on accounting procedure's stated objective was to limit needless variations by recommending "one or more alternative procedures as being definitely superior in its opinion to other procedures which have received a measure of support . . ." (AIA minutes, 1939, p.5ff.). This objective was certainly consistent with the goals of the SEC as expressed by William Werntz, who wrote that the "soundness or correctness of an accounting practice is determinable only by the facts of a particular situation, circumstances alter cases," and, therefore, he thought that consistency, comparability and disclosure should be focal points for financial reporting (Werntz, 1939, p.17ff.).

An evaluation of previous attempts at uniformity had probably had a significant impact on the rejection of uniformity as a basis for establishing accounting principles. Indeed, the attempts of the ICC to use a rulebook approach to regulate railroads had ended in dismal failure, while the national bank examiners using a similar approach had afforded little protection against the flagrant abuses of the twenties. Thus, the historical evidence with respect to uniformity suggested that even when a regulatory agency, seeking to protect the interests of one specific group, had mandated uniform systems, changes in environmental and political objectives had often necessitated a departure from the rule-book approach or resulted in unfortunate consequences.

The issue became not uniformity but the extent of the profession's responsibility to select appropriate alternatives. Academicians thought that "it should be possible to agree on a foundation which will tend to eliminate random variations in accounting procedures resulting not from the peculiarities of individual enterprises but rather from varying ideas of financiers and corporate executives as to what will be expedient, plausible or persuasive to investors" (AAA, 1936, p.188).

A key but unresolved issue has been whether the accounting profession has the authority commensurate with its responsibility. Much of the subsequent criticism of the AIA committee on accounting procedure and the Accounting Principles Board stemmed from the charge that auditors failed to exercise professional judgment in application of principles once they became "generally accepted."

Contemporary Criticism

If one examines contemporary criticism of the state of accounting principles, there is little to suggest that uniformity should be resurrected as an appropriate response to alleged abuses. The SEC's criticism of the profession has been directed not at the lack of uniformity but, rather, at auditors for placing too much reliance on GAAP. Auditors, it has been alleged, have not assessed risk and uncertainty in various transactions, thereby permitting alternative methods to be used simply because they were in accord with GAAP, even though they were inappropriate and resulted in misleading investors (Accounting Series Release no. 173). Even the vocal academic critic Abraham J. Briloff states that he is "willing to take the framework of GAAP with its alternatives." But an "accountant [should] use those rules or applicable principles that he believes best reflect the situation as he sees it" (*Barron's*,

April 26, 1976, p.18). An example of failure to assess alternative procedures with respect to risk and uncertainty can be seen in the continuing debate over the question of percentage-of-completion accounting.

Revenue realization is one area where advocates of strong uniformity would reduce the number of reporting alternatives. Percentage-of-completion revenue realization has come under severe criticism, with some suggesting that it be outlawed. This technique results in recognizing revenue as the contracted work is performed if there is reasonable assurance that the specified cash payments will be received. The alternate method —completed contract—recognizes revenue only when the contract is fully performed and when there is reasonable assurance that the specified cash payments will be received. The completed contract method is clearly appropriate when there is any considerable uncertainty; it is, however, clearly inappropriate when there is reasonable assurance that the cash will be collected. If revenue realization is made more uniform by outlawing the percentage-of-completion method, the economic performance of some firms will be obscured; circumstances differ, and to ignore these differences in financial reporting results in loss of information, inaccurate information and statements that serve no useful economic purpose.

The basic question that seems to remain unresolved is how the accounting profession with limited power can fulfill its responsibility to exercise professional judgment. The suggestion that uniformity can be substituted for judgment, which seems to be implicit in the Metcalf and Moss reports, is not a realistic remedy. If someone must assess risk and uncertainty to determine the applicability of any given principle, then "rules" simply will not suffice. It is also clear that once a rule is established, with rare exceptions, the administrative process does not facilitate expeditious responses to the dynamic, changing business environment. Uniformity, in its strong form, implies a certainty that does not exist. Accountants have not reacted negatively to such suggestions out of perversity or fear but from a deep-seated conviction that such schemes are not feasible. Despite consistent efforts by the profession to disclaim any suggestion that they are reporting "facts," one consistently finds statements to the contrary made by regulators and politicians. The ultimate goal, everyone seems to agree, is "truth," "fairness," "justice" or perhaps, more simply, that financial statements not be misleading. But these concepts are essentially ethical—and not absolute—terms requiring that someone make a determination of what is fair.

An overriding concern to the Metcalf and Moss committees, as it is to the Financial Accounting Standards Board and to the accounting profession in general, is how to obtain better financial information for economic decisions. Unfortunately, the Metcalf and Moss reports focused on the unworkable but historically popular solution—uniformity. It seems unfortunate for several reasons. First, it ignores the lessons of history, which show that successful attempts to gain absolute uniformity occurred only when the resulting uniformity allowed for similar events to be similarly reported and different events to be reported differently. The success of the uniform cost systems is partially attributed to such recognition. Second, the imposition of strong uniformity as in the regulated industries has not resulted in better protection of or in better information for all user groups. Uniformity in financial accounts for the regulated industries was devised to foster some public policy rather than to reflect a firm's financial condition.

The Trueblood report correctly defined the crucial issues of uniformity to be the elimination of *needless* variations by making like things look alike, and unlike things look different (AICPA, 1973, p.59). When uniformity has been proposed, the accounting profession has, in our view, rightly rejected attempts that did not allow for the recognition of the uncertainty inherent in the business world.

Apparently, the search for uniformity by the outside world—outside of the profession, that is—has turned up a will-o'-the-wisp, and it is unlikely that anything more concrete will be found. But history has taught us that the search will undoubtedly be begun again by legislators or others seeking perfection. History, as we know, is condemned to repetition, and it is perhaps with this understanding that the profession can better understand the cyclical nature of demands made on it in the name of the public. ∎

References

American Accounting Association (1936) "A Tentative Statement of Accounting Principles Affecting Corporate Reports." *Accounting Review* (March), pp. 187-91.

American Institute of Accountants (1934) *Audits of Corporate Accounts.* New York: AIA.

American Institute of Accountants (1939) Committee on accounting procedure correspondence file regarding Accounting Research Bulletin no. 1. New York: AICPA.

American Institute of Certified Public Accountants (1959) "Organizational Operation of Accounting Research Program and Related Activities." (October) manuscript file. New York: AICPA.

American Institute of Certified Public Accountants (1973) *Objectives of Financial Statements.* New York: AICPA.

Briloff, A. (1976) "No Last Trumpet." "Corporate Pay-Offs." "Accountable Accountants." *Barron's* (April 12, 19, 26).

Couchman, Charles (1939) "The Haunted Balance Sheet." 19 pages, mimeographed, AICPA library, New York.

Demond, C. W. (1951) *Price Waterhouse in America.* New York: Comet Press.

Hurley, Edward N. (1916) *Awakening of American Business.* New York: Doubleday, Page & Co.

May, George O. (1937) "Improvement in Financial Accounts." *Journal of Accountancy* (May), pp. 333-69.

May, George O. (1933) "Transcript of a Speech Before the Illinois State Society." (December 6) AICPA library, New York.

Montgomery, Robert H. (1927) "Accountants' Limitations." *Journal of Accountancy* (October), pp. 245-66.

Schafer, Robert Jones, ed. (1969) *A Guide to Historical Method.* Homewood, Ill.: Dorsey Press.

Sterrett, Joseph E. (1906) "Profession of Accountancy." *Annals of the American Academy of Political and Social Science* (July), pp. 16-27.

"Uniform Accounting" (1917) Washington, D.C.: Federal Reserve Board.

U.S. Congress, House (1902) *Final Report of the Industrial Commission.* H. Doc. 380, 57th Cong., 2nd sess.

U. S. Congress, House (1976) *Federal Regulation and Regulatory Reform.* Report by the Subcommittee on Oversight and Investigations of the Committee on Interstate and Foreign Commerce. 94th Cong., 2nd sess., October.

U. S. Senate (1976) *The Accounting Establishment.* A staff study prepared by the Subcommittee on Reports, Accounting and Management of the Committee on Government Operations, 94th Cong., 2nd sess., December.

Werntz, William (1939) "What Does the Securities and Exchange Commission Expect of Independent Auditors?" AIA, *Papers on Auditing Procedure and Other Accounting Subjects,* pp. 17-26.

Wiesen, Jeremy (1978) *The Securities Acts and Independent Auditors: What Did Congress Intend?* Commission on Auditors' Responsibilities Research Study no. 2. New York: AICPA.

LIFO ... OR FIFO?

Careful consideration should be given before choosing either inventory method. An arbitrary decision could result in, among other things, lost tax benefits.

DALE MORSE
Assistant Professor of Accounting
Cornell University

The recent inflationary period has caused business executives to reexamine methods of adapting to a world of changing prices. One approach is to use alternative methods for costing inventory: the "last-in-first-out" (LIFO) method or the "first-in-first-out" (FIFO) method. During periods of rising inventory costs, LIFO creates lower income numbers than FIFO and thus lowers income taxes. This accounting option, however, has surprisingly not been universally adopted by the business community. A survey in *Accounting Trends and Techniques*, 1979, showed that only 57 percent of the major corporations use any form of LIFO, and only 2 percent use LIFO exclusively. In addition, there have been several cases of companies changing from FIFO to LIFO in an inflationary period.

Are business executives acting irrationally? Not necessarily. There are some valid economic reasons for using either method. But before investigating the economic effects of inventory costing methods, the following example should be reviewed. It demonstrates the impact of each method on the balance sheet and income statement. There are many variations of these methods, but the relative effect on the financial statements is approximately the same.

Suppose a company that produces boxes incorporates at the beginning of 1979. Throughout 1979, 55 boxes are produced at the following costs:

3/1/79
    10 boxes @ $1.00 per box
6/1/79
    15 boxes @ $1.25 per box
9/1/79
    10 boxes @ $1.50 per box
12/1/79
    20 boxes @ $2.00 per box

The number of boxes sold during the year was 30. Therefore, the final inventory at year-end (12/31/79) was 25. The problem is how to allocate the production costs of the year to the final inventory and the boxes that were sold.

If FIFO is used, the first 30 boxes produced are treated as the boxes that were sold. Therefore, the cost of boxes sold would be calculated by adding the production costs of the first 30 boxes:

10 boxes
    @ $1.00/box = $10.00
15 boxes
    @ $1.25/box = $18.75
5 boxes
    @ $1.50/box = $7.50
Cost of boxes sold= $36.25

The remaining production costs [(5 × $1.50) + (20 × $2.00)], or $47.50, are allocated to ending inventory.

With LIFO, the last 30 boxes produced are treated as the boxes that were sold. Production costs would be:

20 boxes
    @ $2.00/box = $40.00
10 boxes
    @ $1.50/box = $15.00
Cost of boxes sold= $55.00

The remaining production costs [(10 × $1.00) + (15 × $1.25)], or $28.75, are allocated to ending inventory.

The previous examples can also be used to compare how the various methods allocate costs during periods of inflationary inventory costs. With the cost of producing inventory increasing, FIFO allocates a greater proportion of costs to the final inventory balance, while LIFO allocates more of the costs to cost of goods sold. Therefore, using the LIFO method would cause the net income and the corresponding income tax to be lower. The FIFO method, on the other hand, would cause a higher final inventory cost on the balance

"Reprinted from *Financial Executive*, February 1980, with permission of the publisher."

sheet. If the inventory costs were decreasing over time, the LIFO and FIFO methods would cause opposite effects, and FIFO would yield a lower income number, with corresponding tax savings.

The distinctions occur because of different allocations of costs over time. The total income over all the years that a corporation exists would be the same for each method. If the tax rate didn't change, the total tax liability over all the years would also be the same for each inventory method. The difference between FIFO and LIFO during periods of inflationary inventory costs would be higher income, with FIFO during the early years offset by lower income in the last or later years. Therefore, use of LIFO for tax purposes would yield lower taxes in the early years. The benefits of LIFO over FIFO may be interpreted as an interest-free loan from the government. No business would ever want to pass up such an opportunity. Why, then, would FIFO be used by anyone during periods of price inflation?

ACCOUNTING THEORY

Before further examining the economic impact of the inventory costing decisions, a brief comment on accounting theory may be helpful. Changes from LIFO to FIFO or vice versa are usually accompanied by a statement explaining why one method more adequately reflects the true income. This implies that there is a true income and that the purpose of accounting is to approximate that income. Neither statement

is correct. Income is often defined as the change in value of a business over a period of time. Without a market-determined price for the business, an individual may perceive different changes in value. Therefore, there is not necessarily a universally accepted measure of true income. The FASB has further stated in its conceptual framework that the purpose of accounting is not to measure value. Thus, the choice of an inventory costing method is purely arbitrary from an accounting theory point of view.

WHY CHOOSE FIFO

Given that there is no theoretical accounting reason for using FIFO or LIFO, managers would be expected to turn to LIFO

> **"The benefits of LIFO over FIFO may be interpreted as an interest-free loan from the government."**

during periods of inflation to obtain the tax benefits. Indeed, **Figure I,** p. 16, shows that through the years there have been more changes to LIFO during periods of inflation. This was especially noticeable in the late 1940s and mid-1970s. Yet the transition to LIFO has not been complete. Why is there a reluctance to convert to LIFO?

Inflation is not necessarily uniform over all goods. During periods of inflation, some goods

may even decrease in price. One example of this is the electronics industry. **Figure II,** p. 16, provides a comparison of the wholesale prices of various goods over time. Television prices have decreased over time. Therefore, if only tax effects are considered, then producers of televisions would be less likely to use LIFO than those companies working with petroleum and steel. A recent survey by *Accounting Trends and Techniques* revealed that 36 percent of those companies producing electrical equipment used LIFO, while 89 percent of the steel companies and 92 percent of the petroleum companies used LIFO. Therefore, an important criterion in choosing an inventory costing method is the expected price change of the specific inventory item, not general price level changes.

There are uncertainties about factors other than future inventory cost changes. If the future tax rate is expected to increase, then there may be reasons not to postpone the recognition of income. With increasing inventory costs, FIFO would recognize income earlier at a lower tax rate and may be preferable.

Future inventory levels may also be uncertain. If ending inventories tend to fluctuate, there may be years with near-zero inventory. This reduces the potential tax savings of using LIFO with increasing inventory costs. Following a zero final inventory level, a company would have to begin a new LIFO base, after recognizing a large profit from using the previous LIFO base.

Of course, the magnitude of the tax benefits depends on the

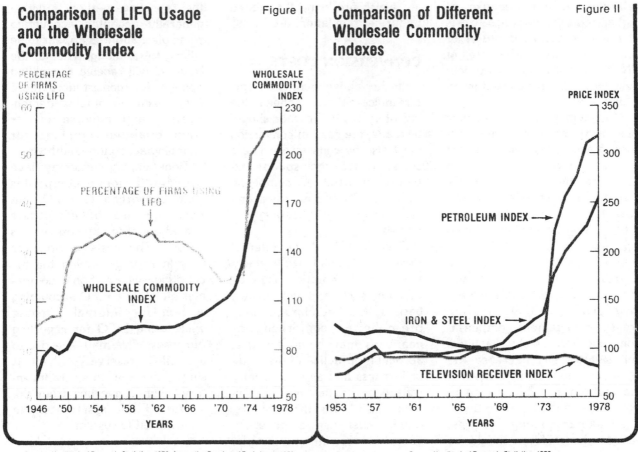

Comparison of LIFO Usage and the Wholesale Commodity Index

Figure I

PERCENTAGE OF FIRMS USING LIFO

WHOLESALE COMMODITY INDEX

PERCENTAGE OF FIRMS USING LIFO

WHOLESALE COMMODITY INDEX

1946 '50 '54 '58 '62 '66 '70 '74 1978

YEARS

Comparison of Different Wholesale Commodity Indexes

Figure II

PRICE INDEX

PETROLEUM INDEX →

IRON & STEEL INDEX →

TELEVISION RECEIVER INDEX →

1953 '57 '61 '65 '69 '73 1978

YEARS

Sources: Handbook of Economic Statistics, 1979; Accounting Trends and Techniques, 1979

Source: Handbook of Economic Statistics, 1979

level of final inventory. The greater the inventory, the more likely a company would use LIFO with rising inventory costs. If a company normally has a very low inventory level, the company may be indifferent about which inventory costing method it uses.

The Internal Revenue Service allows for the write-down of inventory to the lower of cost or market if FIFO is used. If the market price of inventory is less than the cost, then the company can immediately recognize the difference as a loss. This would provide immediate tax savings. Under LIFO, the lower of cost or market rule is not allowed. Given that costs and market prices are generally increasing, the likelihood of the market price dipping below the LIFO base cost is low and should not be an important factor.

FINANCIAL REPORTING EFFECTS

Until now, the tax implications of the LIFO/FIFO choice have been discussed. The IRS has ruled, however, that if LIFO is used for tax purposes, it must also be used for financial reporting purposes. LIFO may then become a two-edged sword. During rising inventory costs, LIFO lowers income for tax savings, but the lower income may not be appealing to the shareholders.

Recent research on securities markets addresses this problem. The efficient market hypothesis suggests that the market price would not decrease just because a new accounting method lowered the reported income number. This hypothesis has been backed by considerable research. Therefore, an inventory

accounting choice should not be made on the basis that the market can be "fooled" by choosing an accounting method that increases the reported income.

There is the possibility, however, that corporate contracts may be based on reported accounting numbers. Two such contracts that are very common are debt covenants and management compensation. Debt covenants are made to protect bondholders from corporate decisions that would benefit shareholders while decreasing the value of the debt. These covenants may include restrictions on the debt/equity ratio or dividends paid out of earnings. Reported accounting numbers are used to verify compliance with the debt covenants. During periods of rising inventory costs, the use of FIFO would make compliance relatively easier because of higher reported earnings. Costs of rewriting bond indentures or refinancing make the use of FIFO economically practical even when there is a greater tax liability.

Management compensation is seldom referred to when discussing accounting changes. Yet bonuses are often tied to reported income. A simple method of increasing reported income and bonuses is to use FIFO during periods of increasing inventory costs. This is, of course, a situation where the interests of management and the interests of shareholders may diverge. FIFO may increase management compensation, but greater tax liabilities and salaries will decrease the value of outstanding shares in the corporation. Because management and the board of directors make accounting decisions, outside shareholders should be aware of the potential effects of these decisions.

Recently, reported accounting numbers (especially profit figures) have been used by politicians and social activists to attack "big business." Profits have even been declared "obscene." With this anti-big business atmosphere (and increased regulation), corporations now have incentives to report the lowest profits possible because large profits will only arouse public outcry and further regulation. These potential political costs suggest that corporations should consider LIFO over FIFO when inventory costs are increasing. This would reduce reported earnings. As mentioned previously, a high percentage of petroleum companies, which are being threatened by further regulation, use LIFO.

CONVERSION COSTS

If the above-mentioned factors indicate that a change in the inventory costing method should be made, the costs of conversion must also be considered. These costs include the special expenses incurred by complying with the IRS and auditors, and also include bookkeeping expenses.

Section 471 of the Internal Revenue Code of 1954 states that "... inventories shall be taken by such taxpayer on such basis as the Secretary ... may prescribe as conforming as nearly as may be to the best accounting practice in the trade or business and as most clearly reflecting the income." Essentially this means that the taxpayer must use a generally accepted accounting principle, which includes both LIFO and FIFO. The IRS places greater weight on consistency. A change now may preclude a change later. Exactly how strict the IRS has been is unclear. Some corporations have changed as much as three times since 1956. No advance permission is required to change to LIFO. The business need only fill out an additional form with the tax return. On the other hand, a change from LIFO to FIFO will often cause the business to incur a lump-sum tax liability. Through agreements with the IRS, payment of these excess taxes may be spread over several years.

Auditors must also accept an accounting change for financial reporting purposes. As long as the reporting method is within generally accepted accounting principles, auditors appear to be willing to go along. Though the business will receive a qualified opinion for consistency, there have been no studies demonstrating any adverse effects from qualified opinions for changing accounting methods.

Bookkeeping costs may have prevented some companies from converting to LIFO, but now the use of computers should equalize any costs of this nature. The costs would arise only in reprogramming the accounting system. Some companies maintain a FIFO accounting system for internal purpose while using LIFO for reporting purposes. This may give rise to a "LIFO reserve," which is simply the adjustment to inventory when converting from the internal FIFO system to the external LIFO system.

CONCLUSIONS

The choice of an inventory costing method is not as direct and obvious as it may appear. The tax effects depend on the size of the inventory, the changing costs of inventory, fluctuations in inventory, and potential changes in future tax rates. There are also other factors that may influence the choice of an inventory costing method. There may be contracts tied to reported income numbers that are influenced by the inventory costing method. Political costs and conversion costs must also be considered when making the choice between LIFO and FIFO. Each of these factors must be carefully weighed to make an optimal decision. □

Federal Taxation

by Joseph M. Flynn, CPA

Joseph M. Flynn, CPA, is a partner in the firm of Arthur Young & Company, Boston, Massachusetts.

New Inventory Rules

In the March 2, 1980 issue of the Internal Revenue Bulletin, the Internal Revenue Service published Revenue Procedure 80-5 and Revenue Ruling 80-60. These two documents discussed the Internal Revenue Service's position with respect to a recent Supreme Court decision, the *Thor Power Tool Company* case *(Thor Power Tool Company* v. *Commissioner* 43 U.S. 522 (1979)). That case dealt with a company which had excess inventory which was written down to a nominal value. This writedown was different from the normal lower-of-cost-or-market writedown and was, in effect, a writedown to net realizable value which in most cases was determined to be scrap value. The taxpayer in the *Thor Power* case did not dispose of any of these inventory items, but kept them in inventory and from time to time sold them at original prices. The belief was that it was necessary for the company to keep these items on hand to provide full service for all of its customers. However, in order to present its financial statements fairly, it was believed that these inventories should be kept at scrap value. The Commissioner challenged the writedown and stated that that writedown had not taken place in accordance with requirements of Regulation 1.471-2 which requires such writedowns to be supported by bona fide attempts to offer the goods for sale within 30 days of the balance sheet date at the written down price.

The Supreme Court held that even though the practice followed by the taxpayer constituted good account-ing, it nonetheless failed to meet the specific requirement of the regulation, and the taxpayer was denied the deduction for the writedown to net realizable value. The Revenue Service has announced in Revenue Procedure 80-5 that any taxpayer which has a writedown of excess inventories which has not met the requirements of Section 1.471-2 of the Regulations must restore that writedown to income for the first tax year ending after December 25, 1979. This restoration is mandatory and will take place in the normal ten-year fashion with, however, several exceptions. If the *Thor Power Tool* method has been used for less than ten years, then the restoration to income will take place over the same number of years. If the writedown is entirely attributable to the prior taxable year, then the entire amount must be restored to income in the year of change. Where two-thirds or more of the adjustment is attributable to the first, second, or third immediately preceding tax period, the highest percentage attributable to such first, second or third prior taxable year will be taken into account ratably over a three-year period beginning with the year of change. Any remaining balance will be taken into account ratably over an additional period of time not to exceed ten years. If any of the writedown is attributable to a period prior to 1954, that portion of the writedown will escape taxation, but only if the taxpayer elects to restore the entire remainder of the balance of the writedown in one taxable year. Even if the taxpayer is able to restore the writedown evenly over a ten-year period, this restoration will be accelerated if the value of the year-end inventory for any year subsequent to the year of change drops below two-thirds of the beginning inventory value for the year of change, if the taxpayer ceases to engage in business before the expiration of the "spread period", if the taxpayer is a partnership and either goes out of business or incorporates in a tax-free incorporation, or if a sole proprietor decides to incorporate in a tax-free incorporation.

If a taxpayer is using the ten-year spread and decides to adopt the LIFO method of valuing inventories, then the entire remainder of the restoration must be taken into account as an item of ordinary income in the year in which the LIFO method of inventory valuation takes place. This mandatory change in accounting method is effected by filing two copies of Form 3115. One copy is filed with the taxpayer's timely filed original return for the year of change and the second copy is sent directly to the National Office of the Internal Revenue Service. Detailed examples are provided in Revenue Procedure 80-5.

Revenue Ruling 80-60 contains the following paragraph: "Taxpayers have an obligation to file returns prepared in accordance with appropriate laws and regulations; income tax return preparers are subject to similar obligation in preparing returns. Therefore, if a taxpayer files a federal income tax return not using the 'prescribed method' of inventory valuation, the taxpayer will have filed a return not in accordance with the law."

The meaning of that quotation should be clearly understood by tax return preparers. The Service is saying that returns which have arbitrary writedowns (as distinguished from appropriate writedowns for obsolescence or for cost or market whichever is lower) have been improperly prepared. Consequently, the preparers of such returns may be subjected to penalties and the taxpayer itself may be penalized for disregard of the regulations.

More on Tax Return Preparers' Penalties

In Revenue Ruling 80-28 (IRB 1980-4, 14) the Internal Revenue Service discussed three situations.

In the first one a tax return preparer failed to report on an individual income tax return a minimum tax liability of $300 resulting from a capital gain deduction shown on the taxpayer's return. The preparer believed that the taxpayer might have had some basis in the assets sold which would eliminate any minimum tax due. However, the preparer was unable to confirm a basis in the assets before filing the return. The Service held that the preparer was negligent and penalized him $100.

In another situation discussed in this ruling, the facts were the same as in the prior example; however, the reason the minimum tax was not paid was that the tax return preparer inadvertently failed to include it in the tax liability. The Service held that inadvertent oversight is not sufficient to establish that the omission was not negligent. Consequently, the preparer was penalized $100.

In the final situation in the Ruling, the facts were the same as in the prior examples except that the tax return preparer was not aware of the fact that the minimum tax applied. In this situation also, the preparer was held to be subject to the negligence penalty of $100. The Service held that a tax return preparer should be familiar with all of the information contained in the instructions for an individual income tax return. ☐

FINANCIAL REPORTING— FACT OR FICTION?

The AICPA president calls for a reappraisal of the approach to financial reporting.

by Wallace E. Olson

In the wake of the bewildering array of initiatives directed at financial reporting in Washington, in the courts and within the profession, it is not surprising that our profession wonders what can reasonably be expected of financial reporting and whether we are trying to achieve far more than is reasonable.

Obviously, various groups have a stake in financial reporting, and their expectations differ. These expectations, in fact, are so diverse that I believe financial reporting should not attempt to satisfy them all. Financial analysts, investors and creditor grantors, for example, are interested principally in determining whether an investment is, or will be, both safe and profitable. It should be noted that financial statements are only one of many kinds of information needed or desired to meet this objective.

Principally the Securities and Exchange Commission would like to assure through regulation that the securities markets function both fairly and free of fraud. The federal agency's first objective is to make sure that investors are not cheated through fraud or manipulation. Over the years, however, the commission has tended to take on the responsibility of seeing that investors make sound investments.

I submit that there is a real difference in emphasis between protecting investors from fraud and helping them make wise decisions. This extension of the commission's role is at the root of the ever-expanding volume of disclosure requirements we are experiencing today.

Congress has a variety of objectives that depend on or use financial reporting to a significant degree. Financial statements are an important factor in the business regulatory processes of Congress. We are rapidly becoming a planned society, and financial reports are essential to economic and social planning policies established by Congress. Any changes in financial reporting, such as current value accounting, can have a serious effect on income tax revenues, which are the lifeblood of governmental projects legislated by Congress.

Independent auditors are mainly concerned about being able to satisfy themselves as to the reliability of financial reporting. Their concern centers on auditability. Hence, they tend to resist any movement toward data reporting that focuses on projections of the future and therefore does not lend itself to objective verification.

Academics are generally more interested in a search for "truth" in financial reporting. This search for truth takes the form of a yearning for a set of basic principles—a conceptual framework—from which answers to all accounting measurement and disclosure questions will flow. Generally, academics seem to have as an objective the bringing together of economic concepts and financial reporting.

Finally, there are the issuers of financial reports. They normally prefer to keep the costs of external reporting to a minimum by keeping the volume of information as low as possible.

Admittedly, enlightened issuers are interested in giving a fair picture of their companies, but this is motivated principally by a desire to present their companies in a favorable light to maintain a good market for their stock.

WALLACE E. OLSON, *CPA, is president of the American Institute of Certified Public Accountants. Formerly executive partner of Alexander Grant & Company in Chicago, Mr. Olson has been chief staff officer of the Institute since August 1972. The present article is an adaptation of a speech given before a group of Michigan and Indiana CPAs, in South Bend on March 17, 1977.*

The Journal of Accountancy, July 1977

Issuers are torn by conflicting desires, however, because they prefer not to disclose information that might do harm to their competitive positions. On balance, issuers can be counted on to resist extensions of or additions to the financial reporting process.

Given the diversity of objectives and expectations, is it any wonder that the setting of standards for financial reporting has become a subject which gives rise to strong emotions and is subject to intense pressures from many directions?

Clearly, each group answers the question of "financial reporting—fact or fiction?" from the perspective of its own needs and expectations. What may be "fact" for one group is "fiction" for another. This is not to assert, however, that there is no commonality. I am merely making the point that financial reporting is faced with the almost impossible task of trying to satisfy needs that are to a considerable degree diametrically opposed.

Traditionally, we have tried to meet these needs with a single set of general purpose financial reports. This has been the only practical approach. But because we have been trying increasingly to meet the needs of all comers, we are reaching the point where the message is getting lost because of the sheer volume and complexity of information we are trying to communicate. Most people recognize this overload problem but don't know how to solve it.

Are we doomed to go on forever expanding the quantity of information in financial reporting? Or is there a solution?

This brings me back to my main question: Are we trying to achieve far more than can be reasonably expected of financial reporting?

Myths About Financial Reporting

In attempting to answer this question, I have identified what I consider to be three persistent myths about financial reporting that add to our confusion about the objectives of such reporting.

The first myth is that financial reports play a dominant role in making decisions about investments. While it is true that financial data is a factor, I believe that the importance of its role in making investment decisions has been greatly oversold. If the efficient market theory is partially valid—as many people think it is—then financial reports serve principally to confirm after the investment has been made whether it was a wise or unwise choice. These reports are apparently not as much help as might be thought in serving as the principal basis for making the investment decision in the first place. And those who would attempt to determine how investment decisions are made may well end up concluding that the answer is as diverse as the number of decision makers.

We simply cannot reduce the making of sound investment decisions to a neat formula. Because this is not possible, we should recognize that financial reports have limited usefulness in making investment decisions. They serve to confirm or refute our prior predictions of future events. In this sense they become one factor among many other types of information which we take into account in our forecasts.

This limitation has great significance with respect to our aspirations for financial statements. We are no longer obliged to strive

"…the most we can hope to achieve is a basic package of financial information that will have general utility for all groups but will probably not fully meet the needs of any one group."

toward reflecting economic "truth." Rather, consistency of measurement, comparability and disclosure of information about potential changes in circumstances become of primary importance. Put more simply, the method of measurement becomes less important than the need to be consistent and to disclose facts relevant to potential changes in circumstances.

The second myth is the belief that most of the difficulties with respect to financial reporting stem from our failure to establish a basic set of principles or a conceptual framework of accounting. This notion that there are certain basic truths which await our discovery overlooks the fact that financial accounting standards are simply conventions derived from experience and through general acceptance.

The yearning for a conceptual framework that would yield a set of accounting principles that are completely consistent internally is understandable. It would give us the comfort of feeling we had discovered "truth" and had developed a surefire defense against challenges to the validity of particular accounting principles. We might then be provided with ready answers to all of our future accounting problems.

To believe such goals can be achieved is to ignore the existence of the multiple groups described earlier, each with conflicting objectives and expectations in its use of accounting data. It is the tension between the motivations of these groups that makes the establishment of accounting standards essentially a process of weighing diverse objectives with the goal of finding a balance. Success in setting standards depends not so much on the discovery of an internally consistent framework as on the art of seeking a middle ground between conflicting interests. The phrase "generally accepted" correctly recognizes that the validity of accounting standards depends on a broad base of acceptance rather than on objective proof.

Stated another way, accounting standards are established through a consensus in a highly charged environment of strong advocacy by disagreeing parties. The Financial Accounting Standards Board, the SEC and Congress have all participated in that process and in all probability will continue to do so. Under these circumstances, it is folly to assume that some scheme of basic principles or definitions of terms or priority of emphasis between the balance sheet and statement of earnings will eliminate the differences of opinion over accounting standards or lead to widespread agreement that financial reporting is all fact and no fiction.

It may well be that some benefit can be derived from defining more precisely our terms or our objectives. But we should not waste our energies searching for a "holy grail" which will only be trampled underfoot on the legislative battleground.

The third myth, which is almost the same as the second, is the belief that we can develop a scheme of financial reporting that will meet, at least to a reasonable degree, the objectives and expectations of all the groups described earlier. We ought to recognize that the many conflicts in interests will continue to hinder progress toward this goal.

We shall always face tradeoffs between costs and benefits. Thus, adoption of multiple rather than general purpose financial reports is unlikely to be an acceptable solution.

We shall always be torn between the need for objective auditability and a desire to move closer to economic reality through the use of soft data.

There will always be differences in the types of data that are best suited for regulatory purposes as contrasted with economic planning or the making of investment decisions.

We cannot escape the fact that the need for comparable data is not compatible with the need for data that is more precisely tailored to a particular set of circumstances.

Given these many conflicting objectives, the most we can hope to achieve is a basic package of financial information that will have general utility for all groups but will probably not fully meet the needs of any one group. If we accept this fact, it can have a significant bearing on our approach to financial reporting. We can abandon what seems to be our current goal of trying to satisfy fully everyone's needs. We can concentrate on developing a sound basic package that will yield a high degree of comparability. We can accept the fact that financial reports do not necessarily reflect economic reality. We can adopt an approach to disclosure on an exception basis rather than the current all-inclusive basis.

My point is simply this. We are trying to achieve more than can reasonably be accomplished with financial reporting. We need to stop clinging to the myths described here and adopt more modest goals for financial reporting. If we do this in a realistic fashion, we will greatly reduce our frustration and stop the erosion of credibility which is certain to continue if we go on striving to attain goals and objectives for financial reporting that are unrealistic.

A Suggested Approach

If we are to adopt more modest goals, what approach should we pursue? Our principal

objective should be to report important factual information on a uniform basis to permit a maximum degree of comparability. Our main concern should be to thwart manipulation within financial reports. Thus, prevention of fraud and the needs of regulation should serve as our guide in designing the form and content of financial reports and in establishing accounting standards.

We should abandon the notion of trying to help investors and credit grantors make good decisions, except to the extent that prevention of fraud helps them avoid being misled. It is impossible to design a reporting and disclosure system that can anticipate all the vagaries of the decision making process, and we should not try.

We should design a basic package of information that includes data about generally recognized indicators of operating success or failure. This basic package should be carefully defined so as to set practical limits on the amount of disclosure.

Based on such a basic package of information, issuers of financial reports should be charged with disclosing additional material facts on an exception basis. What constitutes a material fact would depend on the individual circumstances but would usually be information about developments that might have a substantially abnormal effect or influence on earnings.

We should also change the format of financial reports to group all information by the functional areas of a business to make it more understandable. At present, information about similar subjects is scattered throughout annual reports in the president's letter, in management's analysis of operations, in the financial statements and in footnotes. We should consider grouping all information in sections by subject, which might be classified by functions within a business such as sales and marketing, manufacturing, labor relations and personnel, etc. If this were done, the current financial statement format might be retained but in greatly condensed form as a link to past practices.

If the foregoing approach were adopted, the following changes in emphasis would occur:

□ The burden of disclosing material facts on an exception basis would be placed on issuers and no longer would be a mechanistic responsibility for complying with detailed rules. Thus, the continuing increase in the volume of all-inclusive disclosure requirements would be halted.

□ Users would be charged with the task of using the information for decision making in whatever way that satisfied them.

□ Auditors would be required to verify on a test basis the reliability of the basic information and to search for additional material facts that should be disclosed to prevent investors from being misled.

□ By not trying to help investors and credit grantors to make "good" decisions, we need have less concern about reflecting economic values. Rather, our emphasis could be placed on uniformity to gain a maximum degree of comparability. As a result, we could be less concerned about searching for "truth" in accounting standards and be more successful at eliminating alternative accounting methods.

Summary

To summarize, I believe that over the years the SEC, the academics, the issuers and the auditors have succumbed to the siren song of the users. That song has been that the main objective of financial statements is to help users make "good" decisions—to reduce the risks in investment decisions.

I submit that financial statements cannot meet such an ambitious objective. They can help reduce the risk of users' being misled by fraud or manipulation and they can confirm whether prior investment decisions proved to be wise or unwise. But designing a financial report that would substantially reduce the incidence of "bad" decisions is an impossible task and ignores the tremendous complexity of the decision making process and the vagaries of the future.

If we adopt more modest objectives for financial reporting, our focus can be sharper and we can be more effective. We can adopt uniform measurement as our guide in setting accounting standards and can gain greater comparability, which is a strong antidote to manipulation. As a goal, reliability can be placed ahead of economic reality.

The question would become not "financial reporting—fact or fiction?" but "financial reporting—reliable or unreliable?" ■

The Penn Central: A Predictable Situation

by Paul E. Dascher

The failure of the Penn Central Transportation Company shook the financial world. The accounting profession has been criticized for its role in this failure: the adequacy of reporting standards and the accuracy of the figures reported in the financial statements have been questioned in the public and financial press.[1]

Certainly, the failure of a corporation the size of the Penn Central (approximately $7 billion in assets reported in 1969) raises many complex issues. Much of the criticism to date has focused on individual instances of deviation from "generally accepted accounting principles." Considering that many different accounting techniques were applied to a great amount of data to generate the financial reports, however, some deviations were both possible and probable.

The purpose of this paper, however, is neither to evaluate nor defend the specific applications of accounting principles for the Penn Central. Rather, the emphasis is on the final result of such activity —the published financial reports. This article suggests that if existing techniques for detecting financial weakness had been applied to the published financial data for Penn Central they would have predicted failure.

Previous Studies of Financial Failure

Several empirical studies have been conducted in an attempt to identify conditions which can forecast the failure of an enterprise. Notable relationships between predicted failures and characteristics of selected financial ratios were found in four of these efforts.[2] These approaches, which defined failure as the inability to meet maturing financial obligations, may contribute to the present study.

In 1932, FitzPatrick, using a paired sample technique, found differences in the ratios of failed and nonfailed firms for at least three years prior to failure. The net worth to debt and the net profit to net worth ratios proved to be the most useful predictors.[3] In 1935, Winakor and Smith observed a significant worsening of average ratio values prior to business failure.[4] A similar relationship

---

1. Footnotes appear at end of article.

PAUL E. DASCHER *is Assistant Professor of Accounting at Virginia Polytechnic Institute and State University.*

between ratio trends and continuity was identified in 1942 by Merwin for up to six years before failure.[5] Two recent reports by Beaver deserve special attention because of the results and the methodology employed.

The Beaver Studies

In 1966, Beaver reported on the results of a study designed to evaluate the ability of financial ratios to predict business failure.[6] He employed a paired sample design to distinguish between 79 firms that failed and 79 firms that didn't. Pairings were made on the basis of industry classification and asset size.

Beaver made ratio calculations using annual data for each of the five years prior to the failure of the failed firm in each pair. The differences (as evidenced by the ratio values) were noted for each sample pair and used as a basis for prediction. Although his results were significant, specific ratios differed in their predictive ability. Beaver concluded:

> The ability to predict failure is strongest in the cash-flow to total-debt ratio. . . .
> Clearly all ratios do not predict equally well. The net-income to total-assets ratio predicts second best, which is to be expected, since its correlation with the best ratio is higher than the correlation of any other ratio with the best ratio. The total-debt to total-assets ratio predicted next best, with the three liquid-asset ratios performing least well.[7]

In 1968, Beaver reported on an extension of his 1966 study.[8] The objective was to compare the actual predictive ability of financial ratios with expectations found in the literature. In general, these expectations were identified by Beaver as suggesting that, ". . . the liquid asset ratios will predict failure better than the nonliquid asset ratios one and two years before failure, whereas the nonliquid asset ratios will predict better four and five years before failure."[9]

Again, he studied a sample of 79 failed and 79 nonfailed firms, making ratio calculations on financial information taken from *Moody's Industrial Manuals,* and using a simple classification test as an index of predictive ability. The status of a firm (either failed or nonfailed) was predicted by comparing its ratios with a ranked list of the entire sample. A cutoff point was established and firms ranking above or below this point were classified as nonfailed or failed respectively.

The expectations found in the literature were *not* confirmed by the results of the study.

No single liquid asset ratio predicts as well as any of the nonliquid asset ratios (cash flow to total debt, net income to total assets and total debt to total assets).

Surprisingly, the superior predictive power exists not only in the long term but also in the years shortly before failure.[10]

Thus, using 38 different industries, Beaver's study demonstrated the general usefulness of nonliquid asset ratios in predicting impending financial failure.

The apparent success of this approach to prediction appears to be related to two basic characteristics of financial ratios. First, ratios rely on the financial statements in total, rather than on individual transactions; the impact of a given event is lessened. Second, the nonliquid asset ratios are not easily subject to "window dressing," and as Beaver notes, "Because failure is so costly to all involved, the permanent rather than the short-term factors largely determine whether or not a firm will declare bankruptcy. . . ."[11]

The Current Study

The current study uses Beaver's technique to predict the failure of the Penn Central Transportation Company. Because of the nature of the current study, however, certain changes in the sampling and evaluation procedures were necessary: Since the Penn Central merger was not fully consummated until early in 1968, prior years' data were not considered in the analysis (the merged company was considered to be different from the sum of its component parts). The collection of data was limited to 1968 and 1969 and the basis for prediction was, necessarily, short-run. As a standard for evaluation, a sample of comparable companies was selected, using size and operational similarity as the criteria. The Penn Central was ranked first (by operating revenues) in Fortune magazine's 1970 listing of transportation companies. The next ten railroads on the list were initially included in the sample. Because one of these companies, the Burlington Northern, was formed through a merger in 1970, comparable data for the previous years was absent, forcing its removal.[12] Data were collected for all of the remaining companies, including the Penn Central, from Moody's Transportation Manual, and four-

teen financial ratios were computed for each company for the years 1968 and 1969.

Prediction requires a technique or rule for associating historical observations with future expectations. The Beaver results suggest that when the values of relevant ratios are below established levels the company is headed for trouble. The more significant the difference, the greater the potential for failure. In the current study, average values of the nine other railroads served as a norm.

An Overview

The first step in the analysis compares the Penn Central's performance to that of the sample railroads. Table I presents the results of a ranking based on the ratio values for the years 1968 and 1969.

Table I. Penn Central Financial Ratio Ranks in Relation to the Industry Sample

	Penn Central Rank* 1968	1969
Nonliquid Asset Ratios		
Cash flow to total debt	10	10
Net income to total assets	10	10
Total debt to total assets	7	9
Liquid Asset Ratios		
Current assets to total assets	8	7
Quick assets to total assets	8	7
Net working capital to total assets	10	9
Cash to total assets	9	9
Current assets to current debt	10	9
Quick assets to current debt	10	9
Cash to current debt	10	10
Current assets to sales	7	5
Quick assets to sales	7	6
Net working capital to sales	10	9
Cash to sales	9	9

*Where 1 is most favorable and 10 is least favorable.

The performance of the Penn Central is consistently low compared to other railroads included in the sample. Its ratio performance overall did improve in 1969 as evidenced by a decrease in the mean ratio rank (for all fourteen items) from 8.92 to 8.43. However, the most important indicators, the nonliquid asset ratios, moved away from this general trend and deteriorated from an average rank of 9.00 to 9.67. In terms of both rank and trend, the Penn Central's performance was certainly ominous.

Unfortunately this approach, which is similar to Beaver's, has limited value for two reasons: First, performance *trends* were established for only one company, making interfirm trend comparisons difficult, and second, the Beaver approach does not provide any basis for a statement concerning the importance of the observed differences. In many industries all of the companies are soundly financed, so that a small deviation might be sufficient to cause one company to fall at the bottom of the list.

A Statistical Approach

To help solve these problems, the sample ratios were averaged in order to form a general performance standard. Table II presents comparisons between the Penn Central and the industry average for each of the fourteen ratios. The performance of the Penn Central was consistently below the industry average for all ratios in both 1968 and 1969.

To provide a measure of the importance of these results, appropriate statistical tests were made. A null (or test) hypothesis of equal performance by all railroads was specified. In those cases where the differences were found to be statistically significant the corresponding level of significance was indicated in the table. This level reflects the probability that the observed difference could have been generated by a railroad in the sample; the smaller the level, the greater the assurance that significant differences do in fact exist between the Penn Central and the industry sample. For example, from Table II we note that in 1969 Penn Central's cash flow amounted to one per cent of its total debt, while the industry sample has a cash flow equal to 14 per cent of its total debt. At the indicated level of significance (0.001) there is only one chance in a thousand that the Penn Central's ratio is *not* drawn from a different universe than the railroads in the industry sample.

Consider the three nonliquid asset ratios listed at the top of Table II: In 1968 Penn Central's nonliquid asset ratios were sufficiently below the industry sample to be classified as statistically significant. The ratios for 1969 were even worse.

The Spearman rank correlation coefficient, a distribution free (nonparametric) statistic, was used to determine the validity of the ratio performance trends, based on ratio performances of the sample of railroad companies and the Penn Central over the two-year period. The results are presented in Table III.

The correlation coefficient measures the association of two factors. A value of one (either plus or minus) represents perfect correlation, while zero indicates a complete lack of correlation. As Table

Table II. Penn Central and the Industry Sample Compared

	1968			1969		
	Penn Central	Industry Average	Level of Significance*	Penn Central	Industry Average	Level of Significance*
Nonliquid Asset Ratios						
Cash flow to total debt	.0295	.1442	.01	.0104	.1403	.001
Net income to total assets	− .0060	.0315	.001	− .0144	.0333	.001
Total debt to total assets	.5036	.4340	ns	.5533	.4441	.05
Liquid Asset Ratios						
Current assets to total assets	.0833	.0964	.05	.1017	.1021	ns
Quick assets to total assets	.0657	.0831	.02	.0826	.0886	ns
Net working capital to total assets	− .0301	.0079	.01	− .0238	.0009	.01
Cash to total assets	.0100	.0388	.01	.0151	.0401	.01
Current assets to current debt	.7343	1.1215	.01	.8105	1.0115	.01
Quick assets to current debt	.5789	.9671	.01	.6584	.8791	.01
Cash to current debt	.0880	.4520	.01	.1208	.3954	.01
Current assets to sales	.2479	.3299	ns	.2892	.3440	ns
Quick assets to sales	.1954	.2818	ns	.2350	.2965	ns
Net working capital to sales	− .0897	.0228	.01	− .0676	− .0113	ns
Cash to sales	.0297	.1320	.01	.0431	.1132	.05

*Only levels of significance of .05 or below are shown. The notation "ns" indicates that the difference was not significant at the .05 level. A two-tailed t-test was used.

III indicates, the coefficients were all closer to one than to zero, with 0.75 being the lowest. The right-hand column of Table III indicates that these correlation coefficients were all statistically significant, confirming the results of the analytical tests presented in Table III.

Table III. Ratio Correlation Between 1968 and 1969 for the Industry Sample and the Penn Central

	Correlation Coefficient	Level of Significance
Nonliquid Asset Ratios		
Cash flow to total debt	.9636	.01
Net income to total assets	.9030	.01
Total debt to total assets	.9636	.01
Liquid Asset Ratios		
Current assets to total assets	.6091	.05
Quick assets to total assets	.6000	.05
Net working capital to total assets	.7455	.05
Cash to total assets	.8303	.01
Current assets to current debt	.7455	.05
Quick assets to current debt	.8061	.01
Cash to current debt	.9030	.01
Current assets to sales	.8424	.01
Quick assets to sales	.8545	.01
Net working capital to sales	.8303	.01
Cash to sales	.8182	.01

Summary and Conclusions

The current study is based on a technique developed by Beaver for analyzing financial statements to identify potential corporate failures. The current author introduced certain analytical modifications, and applied the technique to financial data of the Penn Central Transportation Company.

Based on hindsight application to the Penn Central, the prediction value of this technique seems to be quite high. The failure of the Penn Central Transportation Company, although unexpected at the time, was not improbable. ◆

FOOTNOTES

1. For example, see: Rush Loving, Jr., "The Penn Central," *Fortune* (August, 1970) and Abraham J. Briloff, "Six Flags at Half Mast," *Barron's* (January 11, 1971).
2. A citation to the use of the current ratio appeared in the literature in 1908. See, William M. Rosendale, "Credit Department Methods," *Bankers Magazine* (1908), pp. 183-84.
3. Paul J. FitzPatrick, "A Comparison of the Ratios of Successful Industrial Enterprises With Those of Failed Companies," *Certified Public Accountant* (October, November and December, 1932), pp. 598-605, 656-62 and 727-31.
4. Arthur Winakor & Raymond F. Smith, *Changes in Financial Structure of Unsuccessful Industrial Companies* (Urbana: University of Illinois Press, 1935).
5. Charles L. Merwin, *Financing Small Corporations in Five Manufacturing Industries, 1926-36* (New York: National Bureau of Economic Research, 1942).
6. William H. Beaver, "Financial Ratios as Predictors of Failure," *Empirical Research in Accounting: Selected Studies, 1966*, Supplement to Vol. 4 of the *Journal of Accounting Research*, pp. 71-111.
7. *Ibid.*, pp. 85-86.
8. William H. Beaver, "Alternative Accounting Measures as Predictors of Failure," *The Accounting Review* (January, 1968), pp. 113-22.
9. *Ibid.*, pp. 114-15.
10. *Ibid.*, p. 117.
11. *Ibid.*
12. The nine remaining railroads included: Southern Pacific, Norfolk and Western Railway, Chesapeake and Ohio Railway, Santa Fe Industries, Union Pacific, Southern Railway, Seaboard Coast Line Industries, Missouri Pacific System and Louisville and Nashville Railroad.

CONTROVERSIES ON THE CONSTRUCTION
OF FINANCIAL STATEMENTS

Patrick S. Kemp*

AT THE present time, both accountants and users of accounting data are quite properly concerned with the usefulness or lack of usefulness of financial statements for various purposes.[1] Some gross misconceptions have arisen in the myriad of discussions surrounding this problem, leading to disagreements both within the accounting profession and between accountants and other interested groups. Some of these disagreements might well be resolved if the misconceptions and misunderstandings could be swept away and clear thinking and communication substituted in their place. The purpose of this article is to examine carefully some of the areas of disagreement and to suggest means of resolving them.

Financial Statements for Whom? One of the primary areas of controversy revolves around a misunderstanding as to who should be expected to use financial statements or, stated differently, to whom the statements should be directed. Many people, both accountants and others, seem to be concerned with the notion that financial statements frequently are not clear and comprehensible to the "man on the street" or the uninformed layman. Many suggestions for simplification and even modification of the conventional statements have come about due to this concern for the uninformed reader of these statements. For example, the current attention to "cash flow" analysis[2] seems to be directed toward protecting the financial statements reader who is not properly equipped to understand, interpret, and use accounting data presented on the widely accepted accrual basis of accounting.

A serious question arises as to whether this concern for the unqualified user of financial statements is warranted. Does the average "man on the street" expect to be able to read, comprehend, and make decisions based upon legal documents without competent assistance? He does not, if he is at all a wise person. Rather, he seeks the advice and assistance of an attorney, as well he should. Neither is the lawyer particularly concerned with simplifying legal materials so that the uninformed layman can understand and use them without professional assistance. The same analogy can be applied to the physician, the engineer, or a member of any other recognized profession. In all these cases, the professional people involved and, it would appear, the laymen as well recognize the need for expert assistance in interpreting matters related to those professions. Why then should the professional accountant be concerned with making his reports—the financial statements—comprehensible to the uninformed layman? The layman should be made to recognize here, as in other professional areas, that professional assistance is necessary for intelligent interpretation of reports.

On the other hand, accountants certainly should strive to improve the usefulness of their statements to informed, qualified users. Such techniques as the use

_____

* Patrick S. Kemp is Associate Professor and Chairman of the Department of Accounting in the University of Richmond, Richmond, Virginia. He has contributed previously to THE ACCOUNTING REVIEW and to the *NAA Bulletin.*

[1] See, for example, "What's Wrong with Financial Reporting?" (A Symposium), *The Journal of Accountancy,* August 1961, pp. 28–33.

[2] See Perry Mason, "*Cash Flow*" *Analysis and the Funds Statement* (*Accounting Research Studies No. 2*), A.I.C.P.A., 1961.

Construction of Financial Statements

of charts and graphs to supplement conventional statements, the use of comparative statements, and the constant search for more meaningful accounting terminology serve as examples of this type of worthwhile endeavor. Equally clearly, the accounting profession has a concurrent duty to educate the public in the proper use of financial statements. This educational responsibility involves both explaining the basic tenets upon which financial statements are based in order to help more laymen become qualified users of those statements and indoctrinating the public in the wisdom of seeking competent, professional advice and assistance when needed.

Uniformity vs. Flexibility in Accounting. Even if accountants agree that financial statements should not be designed for the uninformed user, there still remains the problem of making the statements as useful and meaningful as possible to the informed, qualified reader. With this problem in mind, much has been written lately concerning the controversy over whether accounting should be "uniform" or "flexible."[3] Advocates of each position seem to be a bit confused as to just what the other side is proposing. The biggest area of misunderstanding seems to lie in determining just what portions of accounting theory and practice should be uniform and which should be flexible. It would be difficult to find an intelligent, thinking, professional accountant who would advocate that all accounting be reduced to a set of hard and fast rules—a "cookbook" which any person of reasonable intelligence could follow —for this would reduce accountants to the status of mere clerks. On the other hand, it would be equally difficult to find an intelligent, thinking, professional accountant who would support the idea of allowing each accountant to simply select any methodology which happens to suit his fancy. Obviously, a middle ground must be found.

Two significant reasons exist for the concern over uniformity and flexibility. The first involves the reliance which the public can place in the opinions on financial statements issued by Certified Public Accountants. Both accountants and laymen ask the question: "How can accountants state that financial statements are presented 'in accordance with generally accepted accounting principles' when they cannot agree among themselves as to these principles?" Second, many people, particularly financial analysts, are concerned with the lack of comparability of financial statements of companies employing different accounting methods. Both of these ideas apparently have played a large part in stirring the desire for "uniformity" in accounting. Each has some validity, but each also can be answered satisfactorily if clear thinking is applied to the problem.

Principles vs. Methods and Procedures. A major part of the problem revolves around defining the basic postulates and principles upon which accounting theory and practice are founded. This search for definition has occupied the attention of accountants and professional accounting societies for many years. The American Institute of Certified Public Accountants, through its research staff and the Accounting Principles Board, is presently attempting to accomplish this considerable task. Four publications, including two of fundamental importance, *The Basic Postulates of Accounting*, by Maurice Moonitz, and *A Tentative Set of*

---

[3] As examples, see the following:

Maurice Peloubet, "Is Further Uniformity Desirable or Possible?," *The Journal of Accountancy*, April 1961, pp. 35–41.

Leonard Spacek, "Are Accounting Principles Generally Accepted?", *The Journal of Accountancy*, April 1961, pp. 41–46.

Charles J. Gaa, "Uniformity in Accounting Principles," *The Journal of Accountancy*, April 1961, pp. 47–51.

Carman G. Blough, "Principles and Procedures," *The Journal of Accountancy*, April 1961, pp. 51–53.

"Uniformity and Flexibility" (Editorial), *The Journal of Accountancy*, April 1961, pp. 33–34.

Albert J. Bows, "The Urgent Need for Accounting Reforms," *N.A.A. Bulletin*, September 1960, pp. 43–52.

The Accounting Review, January, 1963

Broad Accounting Principles for Business Enterprises, by Robert T. Sprouse and Maurice Moonitz, have already resulted from the new research program of the Institute, and more are imminent. The Accounting Principles Board emphasizes the tentative nature of these publications. In connection with the *Principles* study it said: "The Board believes, however, that while these studies are a valuable contribution to accounting thinking, they are too radically different from present generally accepted accounting principles for acceptance at this time."[4]

As far as *present* generally accepted accounting principles are concerned, I submit that the extent of agreement is far greater than is supposed in some critical quarters. Such familiar accounting concepts as the going concern, objectivity, consistency, full disclosure, cost as the primary measure of value, the matching of costs and revenues, realization, etc., do, in fact, form a basis for accounting theory and practice. On the other hand, these concepts have been called variously postulates, principles, conventions, doctrines, standards, etc. Although unanimous agreement probably will never come about, the areas of disagreement today appear to be more in the realm of semantics than concept. Regardless of what we call the accounting concepts on this high plane of accounting theory, substantial general acceptance is not only possible but existent.

As we move away from the area of basic accounting principles to accounting procedures, the means of implementing the principles, we encounter perhaps the major area of controversy. The proponents of "uniformity" deplore the variety of "acceptable" procedures and methods available to accountants in several areas—for example, the several inventory valuation procedures (LIFO, FIFO, moving average, etc.) and the many depreciation methods

(straight-line, sum-of-the-years'-digits, declining balance, units-of-production, etc.). They speak of these various procedures, however, as *alternatives*, implying that any one is equally acceptable to any other in a given situation. They then express concern that financial statements purporting to reflect similar, or even identical facts of operations may yield quite different results. This concern is unwarranted if it is recognized that the various procedures and methods available to implement the accounting principles are not alternatives at all, but merely constitute varying methodology which is necessary to reflect varying sets of facts. Although, to be sure, these procedures are not always treated in this manner in practice, this fact is not a legitimate indictment of accounting theory, but of accounting practice and of some practicing accountants.

Illustrative Case. An example may serve to illustrate the above comments. Let us hypothesize two companies, which buy on the same day identical assets, paying the same price for those assets. Assume further that the assets are to be put to exactly the same use by the same companies and that all circumstances surrounding their use are identical. There is little question in the minds of most accountants that these assets represent unexpired costs to the two companies and, as such, should be recorded as assets at their acquisition price. This conclusion is based on an idea commonly termed "the cost principle." Nor is there any doubt that the costs of these two assets should be allocated to the accounting periods constituting the useful lives of the assets. This is the principle of matching costs and revenues. The question is: "By what means shall the costs be allocated?"

Many depreciation methods are avail-

---

[4] "Accounting Principles Board Comments on 'Broad Principles'," *The Journal of Accountancy*, May 1962, p. 10.

Construction of Financial Statements

able, but these are not *alternative* methods, as the proponents of "uniformity" seem to believe. That is to say, one of the above companies could not *correctly* use straight-line depreciation and the other *correctly* use the declining balance method. Since we *hypothecated* identical assets which would be put to identical uses under identical circumstances, only one depreciation method can possibly be correct. The correct method is that one which most nearly accurately describes the using up of the service potential embodied in each asset. Both of the indicated methods may be incorrect, but both certainly cannot be correct. If one is the correct method, then the other is by definition incorrect. The idea that the two methods represent equally acceptable alternatives is ridiculous.

The same reasoning applies to inventory valuation and to any other area in which varying accounting procedures or methods are available. The various methods do not represent equally acceptable alternatives; only one is acceptable for a given set of circumstances. The fact that some businessmen may view them as alternatives and, even worse, that some C.P.A.s may render unqualified opinions when any "recognized" method is used, under the assumption that they are alternatives, is not a valid criticism of accounting theory, but of the people involved. The answer does not lie in a uniform set of accounting procedures, but in a realization by practicing accountants that they are charged with a responsibility to see that the *proper* method is selected.

The Purpose of Financial Statements. A high degree of general acceptance, and hence "uniformity" in regard to accounting postulates and principles seems clearly desirable. As mentioned above, our profession renders opinions on financial statements every day using the phrase "generally accepted accounting principles."

Without rather widespread agreement in the area of accounting principles, the integrity of financial statements seems indeed jeopardized. But all too frequently, one overriding principle of accounting appears to be ignored—that the goal of financial statements is to reflect as nearly accurately as possible the financial facts of business operation.

Most accountants recognize the significance of the doctrines of full disclosure and objectivity (although Maurice Moonitz refers to these as postulates). The doctrine of full disclosure tells us that financial statements should not fail to disclose any information the absence of which would render the statements misleading. The related doctrine of objectivity points out that the information appearing in these statements should be based on objective, verifiable evidence. If we view these doctrines together, we can arrive at the corollary statement that financial statements should reflect, as nearly accurately as possible, the financial facts concerning a business entity. To be sure, accountants need a generally accepted or "uniform" set of broad principles and postulates to guide them in the recording, assembling, and classification of financial data. Equally surely, however, these financial data vary from one company to another and even within a given company. Thus, the procedures and methods by which the accounting principles are implemented should not be uniform—indeed, they cannot be. The duty of the public accountant, as the guardian of the public interest, must always be to insure that accounting methods and procedures are not chosen at the whim of management, but that the best available method is selected to present a given set of facts. The goal must always be to seek the truth, or in less poetic language, to attempt to reflect in the financial statements the financial facts of a business enterprise as nearly accurately as possible.

The Accounting Review, January, 1963

The Guardian Status of Accountants. This "guardian status" of the accountant requires some further discussion. All too frequently in recent times, the C.P.A. has begun to think of himself as the counsel and advocate of his client.[5] The role of counsel is quite appropriate in management services engagements; the role of advocate is appropriate in income tax work. But the foundation of public accounting continues to be the audit function and the resulting expression of formal opinions on clients' financial statements. In this capacity, the C.P.A. is neither counsel nor advocate. In fact, his responsibility in expressing his opinion is not to guard the interest of his client, but to assure the unbiased presentation of financial facts to the interested public. Thus, there is no place here for selection of a particular accounting method because it is expedient, because it is advantageous for income tax purposes, or because it presents the kind of picture which management would like to present. Only that method which most nearly accurately presents the facts is appropriate.

At this point, it may be fruitful to examine the standard short form report used by most C.P.A.s, in order to determine just what the C.P.A. is saying when he renders a formal opinion. The opinion paragraph of the short form report reads as follows:

> In our opinion, the accompanying balance sheet and statement(s) of income and surplus present fairly the financial position of the X Company at December 31, 19—, and the results of its operations for the year then ended, in conformity with generally accepted accounting principles applied on a basis consistent with that of the preceding year.[6]

The wording of this paragraph furnishes a useful insight into the C.P.A.'s responsibility in expressing such an opinion. It furnishes a clear case for strong, individual action on the part of the C.P.A. as opposed to mere reliance on a set of rules promulgated by the A.I.C.P.A. or by any other body. Notice first the opening phrase, "In our opinion." This is an *opinion* expressed by the C.P.A. or firm of C.P.A.s. Notice also that the phrase "present fairly" precedes the notation of "conformity with generally accepted accounting principles." The C.P.A. is expressing an opinion *primarily* on the fairness with which the statements present the financial position and the results of operations, and only secondarily on the conformity with generally accepted accounting principles.

It is certainly possible to have conformity with generally accepted accounting principles without fairness in presentation. For example, the straight-line method of depreciation conforms with generally accepted accounting principles, the primary principle involved being the matching of costs and revenues. But if the predictable expiration of service value of the asset in question is related to, let us say, the number of miles it is driven rather than a number of time periods, then straight-line depreciation must result in an *unfair* presentation simply because it does not present the facts insofar as they can be determined. Thus, in this situation, the C.P.A. must reject straight-line depreciation as an acceptable method. There is no such thing as a "generally accepted accounting *method*"; accounting methods can be acceptable only if they both fit the facts and implement generally accepted accounting principles.

For far too long, many C.P.A.s have hidden behind the shield of "generally accepted accounting principles" in dealing with their clients. If the C.P.A. is to render an *opinion*, then logically he must make up his own mind, not depend on a set of

---

[5] The term "client" is used here in reference to the management of a client company, although technically the C.P.A.'s client may be either the stockholders or the board of directors of that company.

[6] *Codification of Statements on Auditing Procedure,* A.I.C.P.A., 1951, p. 16.

Construction of Financial Statements

"*rules*" to do it for him. A defensive position soon becomes untenable, and the C.P.A. finds himself following the wishes of his client rather than his own professional judgment. A typical comment of a C.P.A. (off the record, of course) sounds something like this: "My client wishes to use LIFO. Now, I don't think that the method yields reasonable results in his case, but how can I tell him that he can't use it when it *is* an acceptable method?" The answer to this question is simple—there is no such thing as an acceptable accounting method *per se;* it must fit the particular situation before it is acceptable in that situation. If the LIFO method does not result in a fair presentation on the balance sheet and income statement in the above case, then the C.P.A. cannot honestly render a report which states, "In my opinion, the accompanying balance sheet and statements of income and surplus present fairly the financial position . . . and results of operations . . . " After all, the C.P.A. is a professional person rendering a professional opinion. If the statements covered by that opinion are to be relied upon, it must be just that—a professional opinion—unaffected by the natural biases of client management.

Comparability of Financial Statements. The answer to the comparability problem lies in the resolution of a simple misconception. The idea that financial statements of two companies should be comparable is based upon the assumption that the companies themselves are comparable, which might or might not be true. It is perfectly reasonable to expect that the statements of both companies be based on the same generally accepted accounting principles, but unreasonable to expect that the same accounting methods be employed by both. To illustrate, the users of financial statements have every right to expect that the statements of Company A and Company B use cost as the measure of asset valua-

tion. On the other hand, there is no reason at all to expect that the same method be used to record the expiration of asset costs unless, in fact, the assets in question expire in exactly the same manner.

This notion of operational incomparability is often overlooked, however, and the statements of two companies are adjusted by the user in order to *make* them comparable. This approach can only distort at least one of the company's statements. For example, suppose that Company X uses the LIFO method of inventory valuation and Company Y uses the FIFO method. Accepting the premise that there is only one correct method for a given set of facts, assume further that each of these companies is using the best available method to reflect the facts of its operations. Then suppose that the statements of Company X are adjusted to a FIFO basis in order to make them comparable with the statements of Company Y. The two sets of statements would be comparable (at least mechanically comparable), but the comparison would be fallacious because the revised statements for Company X would simply be wrong.

Attempts to force comparability where none in fact exists can result only in distortion. The users of financial statements must be made to recognize that those statements can be expected to be comparable only if the companies represented thereby are comparable. If the companies are not comparable, or even if parts of their operations are not comparable, then no amount of manipulation can change those facts. Forced comparability where no real comparability is present is necessarily misleading.

Summary and Conclusions. The confusion regarding the usefulness or lack of usefulness of present day financial statements may be resolved through answering three important questions. First, for whom are financial statements intended? Second,

The Accounting Review, January, 1963

should accounting principles be "uniform" or "flexible"? Third, can the reader of financial statements logically expect to find a high degree of comparability among the statements of different companies? The following paragraphs summarize the answers to these questions provided in the body of this article.

For whom are financial statements intended? The idea that financial statements should be comprehensible to the uninformed layman, "the man on the street," is unwarranted. Financial statements are, after all, technical reports rendered by members of the accounting profession. There is no more reason to expect that the uninformed layman should be able to understand these reports without competent professional assistance than that he should be able to comprehend technical reports prepared by members of any other profession. Financial statements, then, should be directed toward the informed, competent reader. Further, the profession should be concerned with educating the public to the proper use of financial statements, including knowing when to seek professional assistance.

Should accounting principles be "uniform" or "flexible"? The answer to this question lies in a clear distinction between accounting principles on the one hand and accounting procedures and methods on the other. The principles are broad guides to action, on which there is, in fact, substantially general agreement among accountants. The procedures and methods are means of implementing the principles. No general agreement exists here because none is possible. A variety of procedures and methods is needed to reflect a variety of circumstances. Various depreciation methods, for example, have been developed to fit a variety of sets of conditions. Any one of these will implement applicable accounting principles *provided* that it fits the facts of the particular case. There is no such thing as an acceptable accounting procedure or method *per se;* a particular method or procedure is acceptable only if it "presents fairly" the financial facts of the company concerned. Thus, it seems clear that a high degree of general agreement (or "uniformity") in accounting principles is desirable, whereas "flexibility," or a variety of methodology is necessary in the area of procedures and methods.

Can the reader of financial statements logically expect to find a high degree of comparability among the statements of different companies? The financial statements of two or more companies can be expected to be comparable only if the companies themselves are comparable. Based on the ideas presented above, one should not expect to find all companies using the same depreciation method, the same inventory method, the same treatment of deferred compensation, etc. unless the facts in these companies are the same. When incomparable situations are encountered, the reader must accept that incomparability; attempts to force comparability through adjustments result only in distortion.

Above the answers to all three of these questions looms the responsibility of the public accountants to guard the interest of the public through assuring that financial statements "present fairly the financial position . . . and the results of operations . . . " of their client companies.

———◆———

How useful are annual reports to investors?

*The following article by
Kenneth S. Most, CPA, professor
of accounting, and Lucia S. Chang,
associate professor of accounting,
at Florida International University, presents the results of
the "Florida survey." This survey,
which was begun in 1976, is
the first part of a research
project that is aimed to produce
evidence on an important
topic—the use and usefulness
of financial statements in annual
reports. We think the findings
are noteworthy and will be of
interest to all practitioners.
Readers who are interested in
the complete study and its findings
should write to Professor Most
at the university, Tamiami
Campus, Miami, Florida 33199.*

Certified public accountants who
produce and report on the financial
statements that form part of corporate annual reports do not usually
acknowledge doubts about the
value of the statements. Nevertheless, the use and usefulness of the
annual report as a whole and of
the financial statements have been
questioned critically.[1]

This article reports the findings
of the Florida survey—the first
part of a major research project
designed to produce objective evidence on the use and usefulness
of annual financial statements.[2]

The Florida survey: methodology

The first stage of this research
project was the mailing of questionnaires to three user groups: individual investors, institutional investors and financial analysts. This
stage is called the Florida survey
because the individual investors
were selected randomly from the
mailing list of the Florida office of
a national stockbrokerage firm.
The institutional investors and financial analysts were selected
randomly from various national
directories.

After pretesting, 2,034 questionnaires were sent out: 1,034 to individual investors and 500 each to
institutional investors and financial
analysts. This mailing was done in
March 1976. One month later a
second questionnaire was mailed
to those who had not yet replied.

The questionnaires were identical except that certain questions
were adapted to the circumstances
of each of the three groups. Part I
of the questionnaire asked for respondents' investment objectives
and their views on the relative importance and usefulness of different sources of information available for making decisions about
buying, holding or selling common
stocks. It also included questions
about the need for additional types
of investment information. Part II
asked respondents to disclose their
personal characteristics such as
age, education and investment experience.

The response rate was 21.5%
for individual investors, 34.5% for
institutional investors and 33.3%
for financial analysts. The overall
response rate was 27.7%.

The project had the benefit of
advice and criticism by a professional statistician at all stages, and
the tabulation and analysis were
carried out with a computer, by a
student in mathematics.[3]

The Florida survey: findings

☐ *Investment objectives.* For individual and institutional investors,
the first question in part I asked
those surveyed to rate various investment objectives in order of importance. Long-term capital gains
was the objective rated most important by both groups. Almost

[1] For the annual report, see Reynolds
Girdler, "18,000,000 Books Nobody
Reads," *Saturday Review*, April 13,
1963, p.71. For financial statements,
see Wallace E. Olson, "Financial Reporting—Fact or Fiction?" JofA, July
77, pp.68–71.
[2] The authors gratefully acknowledge
financial support received from the
Florida International University Foundation for this project.

[3] The authors gratefully acknowledge
the invaluable criticisms and suggestions of Dr. Carlos W. Brain, assistant
professor of mathematics at Florida
International University, and the assistance of Eduardo Caso, FIU student.

equally important, however, was the objective of a combination of dividend income and capital gains. Dividend income alone was considered much less important and short-term capital gains, unimportant. Some respondents mentioned safety of capital. Investors with portfolios under $10,000 in amount rated the objective of short-term capital gains higher than did investors with large portfolios. Individual investors were compared with institutional investors and no statistically significant differences were found.

□ *Information sources.* The three user groups were then asked: "When making decisions about buying, holding or selling common stocks, what are your important sources of information?"

Individual investors rated corporate annual reports most important (46.8%); newspapers and magazines came second (38%); and stockbrokers' advice and advisory services ranked third and fourth (33.3% and 32.1%, respectively).

Institutional investors rated corporate annual reports most important (47.8%); advisory services came second (39.9%); newspapers and magazines were third (25.5%). This group rated all other sources lower than did individual investors.

Financial analysts rated annual reports as even more important than did the other two groups (82.6%). This group was also asked about interim reports, communications with management, prospectuses and corporate press releases, and, as expected, it rated

them as relatively important: prospectuses (78.6%); communications with management (75.8%); interim reports (61.1%). By contrast, corporate press releases were rated less important (27.3%), suggesting that analysts rate information originating from accountants as more important than information originating from public relations specialists.

□ *Financial statements.* All three user groups were asked to rate the importance of selected parts of the annual report. The question included the financial statement items as well as nonfinancial information. It was clear from the responses that the most important parts of the annual report, for all three groups, were the financial statements and related information. The least important part of the annual report was the pictorial material.

All three groups rated as very important the income statement, the summary of operations for the last 5 or 10 years and the statement of changes in financial position. Institutional investors and financial analysts also rated as very important the balance sheet, the statement of accounting policies and other footnotes. Individual investors rated these three items as important and the footnotes as slightly important. No other part of the annual report was rated as very important by individual and institutional investors, and only the 10-K report was also rated as very important by financial analysts.

Conclusions

The responses to the Florida survey reveal that all user groups surveyed view annual financial statements as an important source of information for their investment decisions. Institutional investors (who are responsible for very large investment decisions) and financial analysts (who may be assumed to advise major individual and institutional investors) place even greater importance on financial statements as a source of information than do individual investors. The survey's finding that the importance of financial statements increases with the size of investment portfolio and with education and training in accounting and business administration provides

evidence of the usefulness of financial statements.

Additional indirect evidence of their usefulness is provided by respondents' ratings of the relative importance of different parts of the annual reports. If the value of a stock is largely a function of its earning power, and the prospect of dividend flows can be predicted in part from past flows of funds, then the most useful financial statements to the investor would be the income statement and the statement of changes in financial position. Respondents rated as most important the income statement, the summary of operations for the last 5 or 10 years and the statement of changes in financial position.

It is also interesting to note from the results of this survey that there is much more heterogeneity in the individual investor group than in the institutional investor and financial analyst groups. The findings suggest that individual investors should not be regarded as a single user group, and that the needs of financial analysts should not be allowed to dictate the quantity and quality of investment information provided for individual investors.

Above all, the findings suggest that the individual investor group is a sophisticated one. The questionnaire gave the opportunity to the group to note if it found the annual report's accounting information to be incomprehensible. It did not do so, and this fact, together with the large percentage who viewed financial statement information as very important, refutes the contention that the average investor should be excluded from the target user group and attention directed solely to the needs of professional analysts.

Finally, the findings of the Florida survey provide empirical evidence of the weakness of the efficient markets hypothesis. The findings suggest that rather than the extensive testing of this hypothesis, which characterizes much contemporary research, researchers should attempt to learn the ways accounting information is used by investors as a much needed basis for evaluating changes in accounting disclosure requirements.

SECTION IV

Valuation in Accounting

Questions of valuation provide for a basic articulation between the balance sheet and income statement or the resource base and earning ability of the firm. Informed individuals recognize that alternatives exist in this important area ranging from the traditional historical cost model through price level accounting to replacement cost accounting.

In recent years, increased professional attention has been devoted to questions of valuation. While the student attempts to grasp the mechanics of a method, he or she must also be prepared to accept the inevitability of change and to recognize bases of thought relative to other proposals. This section is divided into four parts which focus on the three major alternatives and present readings of a general nature relative to the entire valuation question.

Most principles of accounting courses deal exclusively with the historical cost approach to valuation. This is logical for several reasons. First, historical cost has been and remains the foremost means of external reporting. Secondly, an understanding of the application of historical cost provides a solid overview of the workings of the accounting process and permits students to delve into the inherent mechanics.

However, the economy in various parts of the world and in the United States has in recent years moved through periods of drastic change. These changes have impacted on the meaning and content of financial statements. Consequently, alternative valuation bases have been suggested and sometimes implemented.

An appreciation of the content, ramifications and implications of these changes lends important insights into the future of the profession. Recent authoritative pronouncements have mandated consideration of these alternatives for many companies and industries. While not moving into specific details of the complexity of implementation, the readings in this section do address valid considerations important for an understanding and appreciation of valuation alternatives in accounting. A questioning mind in the principles of accounting course can provide an openness to grasp more advanced material. Valuation alternatives, when explored from various perspectives, enhance this ability.

Opinion No. 29: A New Valuation Method

Not only is it inconsistent, but the new method produces values that are not relevant to the economic substance of the exchange being recorded.

By Eugene A. Imhoff, Jr. and Paul A. Janell

One analysis of APB Opinion No. 29 concluded that the opinion expanded the use of "fair value accounting, thereby giving accounting a more logical foundation." [1] This evaluation, upon closer inspection, seems to be both incomplete and inaccurate. Our examination of APB No. 29 will show that not only is it an extension of *fair value* accounting, but it also is inconsistent with any other accounting valuation method currently employed.

APB No. 29, "Accounting for Nonmonetary Transactions," deals with exchanges and non-reciprocal transfers which involve *principally* nonmonetary items. The basic principle of accounting for nonmonetary exchanges is to record the exchange at the fair value of the asset(s) given or received, whichever is the most objectively determinable. [2] The major provisions of Opinion No. 29 are twofold: 1. to clarify the treatment of a nonreciprocal transfer ("a transfer of assets for which no assets are received or relinquished in exchange" [3]); and 2. to elaborate on the accounting procedures that should be employed for those exchange situations which involve little or no cash or other monetary consideration.

Background of Exchange Accounting

In order to evaluate the changes resulting from Opinion No. 29, we will review the recording of exchange situations prior to the issuance of the Opinion. In Table 1, a situation is described in which an existing asset is exchanged for a new asset. Three values are given for the old asset: the net book value ($2,600); the trade-in value allowed by the seller ($3,200); and the fair value of the old asset ($2,900). As shown in Table 1, prior to Opinion No. 29, there were three alternative methods that could be employed to account for the exchange. Each of these methods, along with their theoretical justification, is briefly explained below.

According to tax law, the gain on the exchange is nontaxable and thus no gain or loss can be recognized in recording this exchange. The elimination of the old asset from the books and the outflow of cash are two elements of the entry which are common to each alternative treatment. The recorded amount for the new asset should be adjusted to reflect the economic substance of the transaction. Since no gain or loss is recognized under the tax method, the new asset is recorded at an amount equal to the sum of the net book value of the old asset plus the cash outflow ($4,400). While this method does not accurately account for the value of the acquired asset in an economic sense, it is consistent with the intent of the tax laws, since the general theory of taxation is to tax gains only when there is a cash inflow. As a result, while the tax method may not yield a meaningful economic value for the new asset, it is appropriate for income tax purposes.

The list method is based on the assumption that the list price of the new asset is equal to its fair value. As a result, the new asset is recorded at $5,000, its list price. The elimination of the old asset from the books along with the cash outflow is recorded as before, and the gain recognized is $600. This gain reflects the difference between the list price ($5,000) and the sum of the net book value plus the cash outflow ($4,400). The list method accurately records the exchange at fair value only when the list (asking) price is a close approximation of the market value of the asset being acquired. In many cases, such as with vehicles and machinery, the list price is not an accurate reflection of market value.

The fair value method is based on the premise that asset(s) acquired should be recorded at the fair value of the asset(s) given up or received, whichever is the most readily determinable. To determine market value, it is often necessary to get an outside appraisal of the fair value of either the old asset or the new asset. A fair value of the new asset would be the cash price acceptable to the seller *without* the exchange of the old asset.[4] A fair value of the old asset would be the value offered by other vendors dealing in such assets. Either of these values should help us to arrive at approximately the same new asset value in a rational marketplace. In fact, the cash or market value of the old asset plus the cash given should equal the cash price of the new asset on a straight purchase.

In the example above, the fair value of the new asset ($4,700) is the economic value given up in exchange ($1,800 cash plus an old asset worth $2,900). This implies that a $300 discount from the list price should reasonably be expected in a straight cash acquisition. In order to explain the apparent inconsistency with the list method, the $300 discount was added to the fair value of the old asset to arrive at its inflated $3,200 trade-in value. It should also be noted that when the list price is the fair value, the list method and fair value method will yield the same result.

Fair Value Most Logical

The fair value method is clearly the most logical of the three, and is in keeping with the basic accounting principle of *fair value of exchange* cited earlier. The only potential drawback of this method is the possible absence of an objective fair market value for the old asset (or cash value of the asset being acquired). However, if management is rational in its decision making, it would not acquire an asset unless the present value of the future benefits exceeded the economic value given in exchange. In other words, management must have at least estimated the market value of the old asset, either implicitly or by using other markets. Therefore, it should be possible in most cases for management to arrive at a reasonable approximation of the market value of the exchanged asset,

and for an independent third party to test the reasonableness of such a valuation.

Nonreciprocal Transfers and Fair Market Values

The alternatives illustrated in Table 1 do not cover the problem of nonreciprocal transfers. It was required that such transfers be recorded at the donor's book value when received from nonowners prior to Opinion No. 29. As a result of

Table 1
ALTERNATIVE JOURNAL ENTRIES

	Tax method		List method		Fair value method
Old asset—acc. depr.	1600		1600		1600
New asset	4400		5000		4700
Old asset		4200		4200		4200
Cash		1800		1800		1800
Gain on exchange		–0–		600		300
Old asset cost						$4,200
Old asset accumulated depreciation						—1,600
Old asset—net book value						$2,600
Old asset—trade-in value per dealer						$3,200
Old asset—fair market value						$2,900
New asset—list price						$5,000
Cash given						$1,800

Opinion No. 29, however, such donations must now be recorded at fair market value by both the donor and donee, with any resulting gain or loss recognized on the books of the donating firm. Nonreciprocal transfers with owners follow the same guidelines, except when the transfer is a "form of reorganization or liquidation or in a plan that is in substance the recission of a prior business combination. . . ."[5] In such cases, the transfer is recorded at the book value of the transferred asset. The changes in nonreciprocal transfers provide a welcomed expansion of the use of fair market values in recording certain one-way transfers.

The most significant change created by Opinion No. 29 alters the acceptability of the alternatives described in Table 1 under certain conditions. In those cases where the exchange involves similar nonmonetary assets, or when the exchange involves dissimilar nonmonetary assets which culminate an earnings process, the fair value concept demonstrated in Table 1 now is the only acceptable method. However, when the exchange involves *principally* nonmonetary assets that are similar and do not culminate an earnings process, then the new method developed in Opinion No. 29 should be used.

Table 2 presents the same facts as before but now considers the firm acquiring the new asset (Firm A) and the firm selling it (Firm B).

Journal Entries to Record the Exchange

The assumption that the asset being acquired is "new" is dropped, making it simply an exchange of one asset plus $1,800 *boot* for another asset. The entry recorded for Firm A is exactly the same entry required for tax purposes and illustrated in Table 1. For Firm A, the two alternatives, the list method and the fair value method, are no longer acceptable in this particular situation according to Opinion No. 29. This is true even though the fair value of the asset is both available and necessary to record the exchange on the books of Firm B! Even though the fair value is known for both assets, the new accounting treatment for this situation requires the recording of both assets at something other than their fair value. It may be observed in the formula for computing the recognized gain for Firm B in Table 2 that the fair market value of the asset being received is a necessary input. In the absence of this value, the fair market value of the asset given in the exchange is to be substituted for the cash plus the fair value of the asset received. For the above case, the latter alternative would have resulted in the same $306 gain for Firm B.

The situation differs considerably, however, when a loss on the exchange results. Consider Table 3, where all facts remain the same except the market value of Firm A's asset is assumed to be $1,600 and the value of Firm B's asset is not clearly determinable. In this case, both Firm A and Firm B recognize the loss just as it would be recognized under the fair value method in Table 1. For Firm A, the asset received in the exchange is recorded at the fair value of the asset given up ($1,600) plus the cash given ($1,800). For Firm B, the asset received is recorded at its known fair value. In short, for loss situations the principle of fair value is applied, but for gains a new valuation method must be used. It seems as if Opinion No. 29 has developed a new valuation principle: "lower-of-modified-fair-value-or-fair-value" for certain qualifying exchange situations.

The major point is that the only possible problem with applying the fair value method illustrated in Table 1 was in obtaining the market value of the asset given or received in the exchange. This problem is recognized and discussed in the Opinion and is considered a major reason for the change in accounting treatment. In applying the major provisions of Opinion No. 29, as illustrated in Tables 2 and 3, the fair market value must be known. Yet for situations involving similar nonmonetary assets which do not culminate an earnings process the fair value is ignored. This is clearly inconsistent with the fair value principle expounded in the literature and in pronouncements, such as FASB Statement No. 12, "Accounting for Certain Marketable Securities."

Opinion No. 29 Qualifications

If the conditions for determining the applicability of Opinion No. 29 are carefully examined, it may be shown that they introduce more subjectivity than objectivity. First, the new method applies only to those exchanges that consist *principally* of nonmonetary assets. However, the term principally is not defined and could easily be interpreted to mean anything that is more than 50% of the total value involved in the exchange.

Table 2
ACQUIRING AND SELLING THE ASSET

	Firm A (purchaser)	Firm B (seller)
Cost of machine	$4200	unknown
Accumulated depreciation	1600	unknown
Book value	$2600	$3900
Fair value	$2900	$4700
Cash paid	1800	—
Cash received	—	1800

Journal Entries to Record the Exchange

Firm A

Old asset—acc. depr.	1600	
Firm B asset	4400	
Old asset		4200
Cash		1800

Firm B

Cash	1800	
Firm A asset	2406*	
Old asset (net)		3900
Gain on exchange of an asset		306**

*Forced—see below

$$**\text{Recognized gain} = \text{Cash received} - \left(\substack{\text{Book Value} \\ \text{of Firm A's} \\ \text{asset}} \times \frac{\text{Cash}}{\text{Cash} + \text{fair value} \\ \text{of asset received}} \right)$$

$$= \$1800 - \left(\$3900 \times \frac{\$1800}{\$1800 + 2900} \right)$$
$$= \$1800 - (\$3900 \times .3829787)$$
$$= \$1800 - \$1494$$
$$= \$306$$

Table 3
MARKET VALUE NOT DETERMINABLE

	Firm A (purchaser)	Firm B (seller)
Cost of machine	$4200	—
Accumulated depreciation	1600	—
Book value	$2600	$3900
Market value	1600	Not determinable
Cash paid	1800	—
Cash received	—	$1800

Second, the new method applies to assets that are similar in nature. Consider three vehicles: a station wagon, a two-ton pickup truck, and a six-ton diesel truck. Which of these vehicles are similar, if any? The similarity attribute may not be as definitive a guideline as necessary to determine when Opinion No. 29 should be applied.

Finally, the qualification that the transaction does not culminate an earnings process is required for application of Opinion No. 29. This requirement, under a very narrow interpretation, would only be met in the case of the liquidation of the entity involved. Alternatively, under a broad interpretation, every asset which leaves the firm culminates its earning process. In Table 2, if Firm B is considered to be a new equipment dealer, has the sale of the equipment to Firm A for cash plus used equipment culminated the earnings process? The answer to this is contingent upon one's interpretation and definition of the earning process being considered.

In short, it appears as though the criteria for applying Opinion No. 29 do not significantly contribute to the uniformity of its application to similar situations. In fact, Opinion No. 29 can be viewed as expanding the alternatives in Table 1 to include a new method which is substantively inconsistent with the principle of fair value based accounting. This new method prohibits the use of market values to record certain exchanges unless the use of market value results in a loss. As a result, not only is it internally inconsistent, but it also fails to promote uniformity and consistency of accounting practice within and among firms, thus, in effect, increasing the number of generally accepted accounting alternatives available for similar events. Further, this new method produces values that are not relevant to the economic substance of the exchange being recorded, thereby reducing the general utility of accounting information. Aside from conservatism, there is not a single theoretical justification for such an innovation in GAAP.

Sound Accounting Theory?

In the case of nonreciprocal transfers, Opinion No. 29 has broadened the use of fair value as a basis of accounting, and provides a meaningful addition to the consistency and theoretical basis for generally accepted accounting principles and procedures. At the same time, the development of a new valuation basis for recording exchanges of similar assets that are principally nonmonetary in nature and do not culminate an earnings process seems to take a step in the other direction. The new "lower-of-modified-fair-value-or-fair-value" method, while innovative, lacks the support of sound accounting theory and is not consistent with most generally accepted accounting principles. As a result, it falls short of achieving its objective of improving accounting practices on a basis that is consistent with prior generally accepted accounting principles and procedures.   □

Is APB No. 29 a new valuation basis that takes a step in another direction?

1 S.J. Lambert and J.C. Lambert, "Concepts and Applications in APB Opinion No. 29," *The Journal of Accountancy*, March 1977.
2 APB Statement No. 4, "Basic Concepts and Accounting Principles Underlying Financial Statement of Business Enterprises," AICPA, New York, N.Y., 1970.
3 APB Opinion No. 29, "Accounting for Nonmonetary Transactions" AICPA, New York, N.Y., 1973.
4 *Ibid*, para. 25.
5 *Ibid*, para. 23.

WHAT IS VALUE?

Any asset can have a number of values which vary according to the business transaction or purpose to which they are applied and the circumstances involved.

BY JOHN HEATH, JR.
Director of Business Development
Marshall and Stevens, Incorporated

What is value? Can you answer this question? Before you try, what about other commonplace words used in and by the business community? Such words as appraisal, valuation, opinion, worth, cost, merger, acquisition, pooling, purchase, reproduction, replacement, depreciation, deterioration, tangible, intangible, fair market value, actual cash value?

These words are similar, but for some who use them they might as well be in different languages because they mean different things to different people. Unfortunately, they are often misunderstood and misused.

It is not surprising that businessmen are somewhat confused when even Webster's Dictionary is not very clear or precise on valuation terms. It defines "worth" as "monetary value, and equivalent of specific amount," and then defines "value" as "monetary worth, marketable price,—see worth."

DEFINITIONS

To prevent further confusion, let's then attempt to define various terms used in appraising values and discuss each in light of current business practices. The 10 most common terms are the following: reproduction cost, re-placement value, depreciated reproduction cost, actual cash value, original cost, book value, tax basis, liquidation, fair market value, and subjective value—value to an appreciative owner.

Reproduction cost is the amount it would cost to reproduce a particular property, based upon an analysis of current market prices of materials, labor, contractor's overhead, profit, and fees. It presumes replacing the property in question in new condition of exactly like kind and as a complete unit at one time.

Replacement value is the cost to replace the property in question with a modern unit in new condition and of equivalent capacity. Replacement cost takes into consideration modern materials and design concepts. In most instances, the replacement cost may be quite different, either higher or lower, than the cost of reproduction described above.

Depreciated reproduction cost is reproduction cost, as defined previously, less an allowance for accrued depreciation as evidenced by observed physical deterioration and condition, age, utility, remaining serviceable life, with consideration given to functional and economic obsolescence. Also normally considered is the assumption that the facilities will be continued in use at the present location and for the purposes designed.

Actual cash value is a term used in insurance policies, but, to our knowledge, not defined by insurance companies. In many states, this term has taken on a meaning the same as depreciated reproduction cost as defined above. Other states permit the "board evidence rule," wherein market factors can be considered.

Original cost is the initial capitalized cost of the item in the hands of the present owner, for accounting and tax purposes. It generally includes the purchase price of an item, but it may or may not include such items as sale tax, freight, cartage, and installation labor.

Book value, sometimes called

"It is one thing to express an opinion as to the fair market value of a property at a given time, but it is entirely another problem to express an opinion of the fair market value of a business entity."

net book value or unrecovered cost, is the capitalized cost for the item in question, less depreciation taken for accounting purposes, which is based on the adopted corporate method for computing depreciation over the useful life of the asset.

Tax basis is the capitalized cost less depreciation taken for federal income tax purposes wherein depreciation is computed in a prescribed manner over the allowed or allowable life for tax purposes. It may or may not be the same as the book basis.

It is important to realize that the accountant's concept of depreciation — determined by a fixed method over a given life period—is entirely different from the appraiser's connotation of the same word. The latter considers loss in value based on facts and circumstances embracing wear and tear, age, utility, and functional and economic obsolescence.

Liquidation is the amount in dollars the property in question is likely to bring under forced sale conditions within a specific amount of time. Very often liquidation is associated with an auction.

Subjective value is sometimes defined as the "value to an appreciative owner." It is the amount the object is worth to its owner, generally for emotional reasons, regardless of its worth or value to another. An example of something that has subjective value might be an old picture of one's ancestors, a serviceman's flag from World War I and II, a ticket stub to a national convention, or some other memorabilia.

Fair market value is the price at which property would change hands between a willing buyer and a willing seller, each having reasonable knowledge of all pertinent facts and neither being under compulsion to buy or sell. Fair market value is without a

doubt the best-defined valuation term. As a result of many court cases, attorneys, appraisers, and others involved in valuation work generally agree on the aforementioned definition.

In actual practice, however, there is more to determining fair market value of certain assets than considering the willing buyer, willing seller concept. One must properly consider such matters as the terms, conditions, and limiting factors, such as to whom, for what, and when the property is sold. When these factors receive proper consideration, they may change the answer radically from the willing buyer, willing seller concept.

It is one thing to express an opinion as to the fair market value of a property at a given time, but it is entirely another problem to express an opinion of the fair market value of a business entity. In the latter situation, the proper determination of fair market value embraces the deliberate consideration of past earning performances, future earnings potential, economic climate of the industry, and in any particular business, a study of the health, ability, vitality, and the age of the personalities involved.

Since appraising is not an exact science, most valuation processes contain an element of opinion. The expression of an opinion of the fair market value of a business or a group of assets is subject to considerable subjective thought and deliberation, and consequently the determination of fair market value can generate wide divergence of opinion among appraisers. Furthermore, the answer to a fair market value study can be somewhat theoretical or even fictitious. Seldom do the circumstances surrounding determination of fair market value include a complete willing buyer and a

complete willing seller, each having reasonable knowledge of all pertinent facts and equal negotiating ability.

Let's consider just one example to illustrate the point. Recently an aerospace company wished to acquire the government equipment located at its plant. The government was willing to sell the equipment—at fair market value. Here we had a willing buyer and a willing seller. But— what was fair market value? The original cost to the government of some 1600 pieces of equipment of all kinds installed in the contractor's plant between 1950 and 1969 amounted to $22 million. Assuming maximum utility by the aerospace company and earnings to justify a proper return on the investment and other relevant factors, the appraiser felt that the equipment assembled in place for continued use had a value to the company of $15 million. However, if the company had told the government to remove the equipment, and the government had to sell the equipment in an orderly manner on the open market, it would bring only about $4.5 million.

Both sale of the equipment to the aerospace company and sale of the equipment on the open market contained the factors of a willing buyer and a willing seller; the terms and conditions radically changed the selling price, hence the value.

One further comment: fair market value should not be confused with purchase price. Sometimes it is synonymous, but fair market value is the theoretical answer, and purchase price is the amount at which a transaction actually takes place and depends on the ability of the negotiators involved and the relative value of the assets in question to one or the other of the parties involved in the transaction.

COMPARISON OF VALUES

Now that we have defined terms prevalent in valuation

work, we must strongly emphasize that there is no set relationship between any of the foregoing terms used in valuation work. Here are a few examples.

First, let's take the case of an old castle being used as a machine shop. The insurable value, based on the reproduction cost less depreciation, with today's labor, would be an astronomical figure. However, if the castle was to be sold, its fair market value would probably be considerably less. Who could afford to maintain and operate a castle today and to what business purpose could it be put because of its obsolete design?

As a second example, let's consider the buildings erected by a fast-food carry-out business which operates nationally on a franchise basis. Each building in the chain is virtually the same, whether built five years ago or yesterday. As such, the reproduction cost is nearly the same at any time for any building. However, the fair market value of a particular building may be higher or lower than the reproduction cost, depending on whether the franchise is attached to it. In other words, a building with a franchise is a special-purpose structure and is worth considerably more than the same building without the franchise.

It is hoped that these examples illustrate and emphasize the fact that there is no set relationship between these terms used in valuation work. There is no formula to convert one term to another.

DIFFERENT VALUES

Let's take one last example which will show how a given item or an entire industrial complex can be worth various amounts under different circumstances. As an example, a machine was purchased new in 1960 and given a 16-year useful life. Today it has the following "values":

Reproduction cost, because of inflation factors, would be $45,-150.

Replacement value, because of modern technology, would be $58,815.

Depreciated reproduction cost, considering normal maintenance, etc., $33,862.

Actual cash value, excluding the foundation since it would be excluded for insurance purposes, might be $33,300.

Original cost, including freight, cartage, and installation, was $33,825.

Book value, for accounting purposes, using straight-line depreciation, would be $12,684.

Tax basis, using an accelerated method of depreciation, would be $5,223.

Liquidation value, if disassembled and placed on the loading dock for sale to a used machinery dealer, might be $24,000.

Fair market value, considering continued use in place as part of a going concern involved in a merger or acquisition, $28,000.

Subjective value, or value to its appreciative owner, might vary from zero if the company has had trouble with the machine—up to $50,000 or even $100,000 if by chance the owner placed sentimental value on it.

How much is something worth? Many answers may be proper. It depends upon the usage and conditions.

SUMMARY

The question of "value," whether applied to land, building, equipment, capital stock, patents, goodwill, or other assets, has become increasingly complex. "True value" and "absolute value" are misnomers; any given asset can have a number of values which vary according to the business transaction or purpose to which they are applied and the circumstances involved.

And often a given word or term can be defined in different ways. We have seen that the accountant's concept of "depreciation" is entirely different from the appraiser's connotation of the same word. It is important, therefore, that the parties in any business transaction involving valuation terminology take the time and effort to assure themselves that they are "on the same wave lengths" that they understand each other and speak the same language.

Some concepts or terms used in valuation work have resulted from court decisions, while others are the result of established practice. Some terms are well defined; others are not. "Fair market value" is undoubtedly the best-defined valuation term. "Actual cash value," the famous three-word phrase of fire insurance policies, has never been defined by insurance companies, although they continue to write policies using the term which contractually bind both the carrier and the insured.

Nevertheless, an understanding of valuation terms and concepts and knowledge of the proper valuation term (or terms) used in various types of business transactions is essential for the parties involved in the transaction. Thus, the question "what is worth?" or "what is value?" can be answered without confusion and a possible resulting breakdown of negotiations. ▪

John Heath, Jr. is director of business development for Marshall and Stevens Incorporated, international firm of appraisers and valuation consultants. He has more than 13 years' experience in the appraisal profession as district representative, district manager, regional sales manager, and director of market planning. He is a graduate in civil engineering from the California Institute of Technology and the executive program of the UCLA graduate school of business administration. Mr. Heath is the author of articles in several professional publications and is a regular speaker for American Management Association seminars on mergers and acquisitions.

A Proposal for Accounting Under Inflationary Conditions

This proposal by Ernst & Ernst recommends a relatively simple change in *both corporate reporting and federal income taxation* — in order to offset the undesirable effects of inflation on capital formation, on investor information and thus on the economy.

The recommendations in this article are taken from a 1976 position paper of the firm. The original publication includes additional discussions of (1) the advantages of retaining the historical cost basis and (2) the problems with current value accounting.

Inflation is a disruptive and burdensome force in any economy. It falls on individuals as well as companies. Its effects are anything but equitable, punishing those with fixed incomes and large investments in depreciable assets, and often rewarding debtors at the expense of creditors. Its impact has been described as similar in effect to regressive taxation.

For both financial statement preparers and users, inflation magnifies the problems of effective financial reporting. In addition, we must not neglect the fact that inflation imposes an additional financial burden on industry through effective tax rates higher than those legislated. We believe that these are two facets of the same problem and should be resolved together. Halfway measures that appear to solve the financial reporting problem without meeting the tax impact of inflation on a business enterprise are inadequate. None of the many proposals on "accounting for inflation" which we have reviewed meets both aspects of the inflation issue satisfactorily.

In a number of other countries, sustained inflation has reached levels that far exceed anything ever experienced in the United States. Faced with conditions that we believe would be near disastrous to business activity as conducted here, authorities in those countries have imposed or proposed major accounting changes. Nothing has yet occurred in the United States that would justify similar action in this country.

We counsel against precipitate major changes in financial reporting. Hasty action either to meet an assumed emergency or to keep up with others, whose problems are much different than ours, is unlikely to provide satisfactory long run results. We need a carefully considered method that fits the needs of our economy; not one borrowed from a different set of economic circumstances.

Practical Usage of Financial Statements

In seeking an acceptable solution to the problem of accounting and inflation, we felt it important to note that the income statement is understood by most people to be the principal measure of a company's past success and future prospects. The balance sheet is important and useful in presenting certain aspects of liquidity but as a measure of success is generally of less importance to users than the income statement.

As a result, we felt that our search for an acceptable method of responding to inflationary influences on accounting should be guided by the following:

• The proposed response should not be so complex as to negate any reasonable chance of acceptance by diverse groups of financial statement users such as institutional investors, small shareholders, creditors and the management and employees of the enterprise.

• Net income should continue to receive the highest priority and should be adjusted to recognize the most material effects of inflation on a company's costs (cost of sales and depreciation).

• Proposed changes in income determination are unlikely to be accepted by taxing authorities unless the changes are administratively feasible.

• Balance sheet valuation can reasonably continue to be based substantially on historical cost which effectively presents current assets and liabilities as elements of a conservatively portrayed financial position.

Our approach has been a practical one. Given that one of our objectives was to identify an economic as well as an accounting solution to the effects of inflation, we recognize that the difficulty of mobilizing necessary support for change in our nation's income tax laws might well be directly propor-

"Reprinted from *The CPA Journal*, August 1977, with permission of the authors."

tionate to the complexity of a proposed solution. We feel that what follows is, for all users of financial statements, an equitable, understandable and readily implementable solution to the problem.

Advantages of LIFO Under Inflationary Conditions

We have long recommended LIFO accounting for inventories as a partial solution to the problem of inflation. LIFO has a twofold effect. By bringing the most recent costs incurred into cost of goods sold, to be matched with current revenue dollars, a more understandable net income figure results than would otherwise be obtained during a period of inflation. In addition, because LIFO is accepted for tax purposes, it has positive financial benefits to the companies which adopt it. The immediate cash flow advantages of LIFO through reduced income taxes help a company bear the financial burden of inflation.

Needed: a LIFO-Type Result for Depreciation Accounting

During periods of inflation, depreciation on a historical cost basis understates, in terms of current dollars, the cost of replacing depreciable property consumed through operations.[1] To compensate for this, and to prevent capital erosion, proposals have been made to "restate" assets and depreciation on a replacement cost or some other basis.

None of the present proposals, in our judgment, has a realistic expectation of the dual benefits of LIFO adoption—both income statement and positive cash flow effects. Proposed accounting adjustments for depreciation tend to reduce reported income, thereby decreasing the company's relative ability to obtain capital and credit, without any compensating improvement in cash flow. Rather than helping affected companies bear the burden of inflation, such restatement levies an additional burden. Something more than this is needed.

[1] Hereafter in this article, "depreciation" should be read to include depreciation, depletion and amortization of long-lived, tangible assets.

Briefly stated, we urge acceptance of increased depreciation for both income tax and financial reporting purposes so that affected companies retain more cash to permit acquisition of replacement assets at higher prices.

We believe that the most common understanding of corporate net income would describe it as the increase in net assets which a company has obtained through operations and which it can distribute to its shareholders without reducing the company's ability to continue as a going concern at approximately the same scale of activity. During an inflationary period, historical cost depreciation does not measure asset use in current cost terms so historical cost net income overstates the amount that could be distributed to shareholders if the company is to replace its assets at current prices. Yet the reduction in net income that would result from charging depreciation on a current cost basis would also make it more difficult for a company to raise funds in the capital market.

The solution to this problem is to charge depreciation on a current cost basis for both book and tax purposes. In this way, a net income amount more closely approximating the common concept of net income is obtained and, at the same time, the increased depreciation results in reduced income taxes and a cash flow advantage to assist in replacing tangible capital assets at increasing costs.

Is this equitable and socially desirable? We think it is. Upward restatement of depreciation and downward restatement of net income with no cash flow accompaniment penalizes a company and discourages capital formation at a time when it is sorely needed. Positive cash flow through reduced federal income taxes for those companies whose income is affected by inflation will assist them to retain their viability in the capital market. It also results in an effective rate of taxation closer to the statutory rate.

Is it administratively feasible? We think it is. Alternative proposals, such as complete current value models, are so new, so indefinite, so subject to varying interpretation in specific situations, and so lacking in standards for implementation

that they would present intolerable problems of administration if applied for income tax purposes. Accordingly, their adoption for that purpose is highly improbable in time to help counter present inflation. But the restatement of depreciation alone, using approved indices, would be sufficiently objective to cause no significant problems of Treasury Department interpretation and administration.

Essentials of Proposed Depreciation Accounting

We think our depreciation proposal, when combined with LIFO, provides both a better measure of corporate net income under inflationary conditions and more equitable income taxation. It is also practical and feasible. The close tie-in of financial reporting and income tax results is important. Neither is adequate without the other.

We propose that the Treasury Department and Internal Revenue Service accept restated depreciation for tax purposes. If they find it necessary, the depreciation deduction could be related to capital asset acquisitions on some appropriate basis. Insofar as accounting technique is concerned, the procedure is uncomplicated and readily understood. It provides that:

1. The property and associated accrued depreciation accounts would be maintained on a historical cost basis with no necessary change in method of computation or estimate of life.

2. Depreciation charged against income for both book and tax purposes would be computed on historical cost restated to current dollars by application of selected indices acceptable to the Treasury Department.

3. Accrued depreciation in excess of historical cost depreciation would be credited to a special account in the shareholders' equity section of the balance sheet which would accumulate during inflation and decrease during deflation.

4. As long as reinvestment occurs, there would be no attempt to recapture the restated depreciation for either book or tax purposes. Gain or loss on retirement or sale of a capital asset would be calcu-

A PROPOSAL FOR ACCOUNTING UNDER INFLATIONARY CONDITIONS / ≡cpa JOURNAL

lated on the basis of historical cost amounts.

5. The amount and method of determining restated depreciation would be disclosed by footnote.

Note the rather unusual combination of effects if this depreciation methodology is accepted for both book and tax purposes. Assuming that a company already uses LIFO for inventory purposes, the following would result:

• Net income would be reduced by the amount of the increased depreciation less the resulting tax saving.

• Although net income is reduced, equity would be enlarged because the credit for the increased depreciation, not reduced for any tax effect, would be carried directly to a special equity account.

• Net cash flow would be increased by the amount of the tax saving resulting from acceptance of the increased depreciation for tax purposes.

The simplified illustration shown in Table 1 presents the essentials of current cost depreciation. Assume a company with the following balance sheet on December 31, 1976. Its accounts are kept in accordance with generally accepted accounting principles.

The company's income statement for 1976 includes the data as shown in Table 2.

To apply current cost depreciation in this situation, assume that the properties and equipment are being depreciated over ten years, and that the cost indices appropriate to those assets have gone up an average of 40 percent since the assets were acquired. The current cost of the assets, therefore, is $700,000, and depreciation at a 10 percent rate for the current year is $70,000. An income statement for 1976 using current cost deprecia-

TABLE 2

Revenues	$1,000,000
Other costs	850,000
Depreciation	50,000
	900,000
	100,000
Federal income tax	50,000
Net income	$ 50,000

tion would appear as shown in Table 3.

This company's year-end balance sheet for 1976 under current cost depreciation would appear as shown in Table 4.

Use of Indices

Our recommendation for the establishment of authorized indices contemplates procedures which are substantially identical to those which are now used by many retail companies. For LIFO inventories determined using the retail pricing method, the Treasury Department has published regulations which provide that indices prepared by the United States Bureau of Labor Statistics are acceptable. We envision development of authorized indices for adjustment of depreciation expense following the precedent which has already been established in gaining acceptance for LIFO inventories. Not only have these procedures proven acceptable to both government and industry, but many of the implementation details, which are often quite troublesome in adapting to change, have already been carefully established.

Why This Proposal?

A number of proposals for accounting for inflation have been put forward, some of them in consider-

TABLE 3

Revenues	$1,000,000
Other costs	850,000
Depreciation	70,000
	920,000
	80,000
Federal income tax	40,000
Net income	$ 40,000

able detail. Why then recommend still another? Each proposal we have seen does well at serving the desires of one or more of the several interests in financial reporting but gives little consideration to the concerns of other interests. We offer a proposal that favors no one group yet effectively serves the interests of all.

For readers of financial statements, it provides a restated net income that largely avoids inventory profits and deducts depreciation in terms of current dollars.

For companies and their investors, it provides cash flow benefits to ease the difficulties of capital formation.

For the Treasury Department, it is not only administratively practical but taxes income at real rates much closer to statutory rates and provides an opportunity to tie the tax benefits to maintenance or expansion of productive capacity, thereby creating jobs and related economic benefits.

For all concerned, it provides a readily understood procedure, one that is objectively verifiable and that causes minimum interference with present generally accepted accounting principles and practices.

We propose it as a sensible, sound, equitable and feasible solution to the problem of accounting for inflation.

The Case for Historical Cost

We are firmly in favor of retaining historical cost as the basis for corporate financial reporting. As the succeeding section will show, we have examined the major alternatives to historical cost and find them greatly lacking in objectivity and usefulness. But this does not mean that we fail to recognize the limitations of historical cost. We have examined historical cost with

TABLE 1

Other assets	$400,000	Other liabilities	$285,000
		Taxes payable	15,000
Properties and equipment	500,000		
Less depreciation	200,000	Shareholders' equity:	
	300,000	Capital stock	200,000
		Retained earnings	200,000
			400,000
	$700,000		$700,000

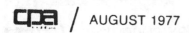 / AUGUST 1977

TABLE 4

Other assets	$400,000	Other liabilities	$285,000
		Taxes payable	5,000
Properties and equipment	500,000		
Less depreciation on a		Shareholders' equity:	
historical cost basis	200,000	Capital stock	200,000
	300,000	Retained earnings	190,000
		Accumulated current	
		cost depreciation	20,000
			410,000
	$700,000		$700,000

equal thoroughness and are familiar with the arguments of its critics. They fail to persuade us.

The Purpose of Accounting

The thought that comes through to us after reading what has been argued by the critics of historical cost accounting is that they apparently misunderstand its purpose. They criticize historical cost on the grounds of its alleged failure to do a number of things that it was never designed to do.

Conventional accounting was never intended to provide shareholders with a precise measure of the value of their shares. That is a function of the stock market.

Conventional accounting does not purport to show economic values, either of a company or of its individual assets. Indeed, economic concepts of value vary so much that to attempt to state "economic value" will almost certainly mislead someone whose interpretation of the term differs from that of the one making the statement.

Conventional accounting does not purport to report the economic income of a company. Economic income is essentially a personal income concept that can be adapted to business corporations only after severe modification of the basic concept.

What conventional accounting was intended to do—and what it still does well—is to provide a reliable record on an objective basis of the actual transactions and events to which the reporting company was a party during the period of the report.

Accounting does so under the theory that a reliable record of the immediate past, together with trends over a period of years, pro-

vides information useful for predicting future transactions and events. Although this is a less dramatic role than some of its critics would attribute to accounting, its usefulness is clear. Accounting has no need to make exaggerated claims about that information because a great variety of interests in business have found such objective reports of actual transactions to be of great usefulness, if not indispensable, in the performance of their functions. A danger is that, in trying to make accounting something different, the practical usefulness of a reliable record of actual events will be lost.

Balancing Objectivity and Relevance

Once one departs from a factual report of past events, reliability decreases even if relevance to the needs of some specific interest may increase. If accounting were to be completely objective, it might restrict its reporting to purchases, sales and cash transactions, and be much less useful. On the other hand, if it had no concern with objectivity, it could engage in forecasts and all forms of "what if" accounting. Generally accepted accrual accounting principles represent what management, accountants and the various users of accounting information have agreed is a reasonable balance between objectivity and relevance.

Over the years of its development, accounting has seen a continuing effort to balance objectivity and relevance. Early theorists, eager to inject some discipline into financial reporting practices which they felt were almost completely dominated by the immediate wishes of corporate management, urged the acceptance of historical cost established in arm's-length transac-

tions to which the reporting company was a party as a means of curbing the reporting of assets and income having little real substance.

To support this concept, they proposed that accounting be viewed as a process of cost allocation rather than one of asset valuation. The history of accounting over the last several decades is largely a record of attempts to improve accounting as a process of cost allocation.

At the same time that strenuous efforts were made to improve cost allocation practices, critics of historical cost as a basis for accounting were calling for the introduction of "current value" which they contended came closer than historical cost to approaching "economic reality" in an economy with a continuing inflationary tendency. Cited as examples of the irrelevance of historical cost were substantial changes in the values of certain securities and land.

Practical Modifications of Historical Cost

While the theorists argued with one another at length, corporate management and accounting practitioners adopted a far more pragmatic attitude. Accepting historical cost as the appropriate basis for the preparation of financial statements did not prevent them from modifying historical cost in those circumstances where they felt its strict application was not the most useful practice. Very early, provision was made for the anticipated uncollectibility of accounts receivable on an experience basis. Inventories were priced at the lower of cost or market as a practical way of measuring loss of utility and salability. Anticipated permanent declines below cost in the values of investments were recorded as write-downs. At the same time, experience convinced these practical businessmen that unless alleged increased values of assets were corroborated by the judgment of another entity expressed in an arm's-length purchase transaction, those values might prove to be illusory and the familiar realization test of a completed transaction was adopted.

Consequently, traditional or conventional accounting practice

A PROPOSAL FOR ACCOUNTING UNDER INFLATIONARY CONDITIONS /

continued to be based on historical cost, but it gradually adopted a number of modifications which were inconsistent with the strictest interpretation of the historical cost concept. This encouraged the critics of accounting, some of whom saw every such adaptation as evidence that historical cost was inappropriate, to argue for a valuation or economic approach which they believe would provide a logical and internally consistent theory on which to report the results of operations and financial condition of business corporations.

We have examined both sides of this controversy with care. We recognize that conventional accounting has both conceptual and implementation problems. Our examination of current value concepts leads us to the conclusion that these present even greater conceptual and implementation problems. Furthermore, traditional accounting is in place and working. The possibility of trying to make a major shift in our basis of accounting presents untold problems. Contracts and agreements of all kinds, business practices and legal requirements and precedents are all based on conventional accounting practice. We have been accounting on a cost basis for the corporate entities which constitute the most important components of this nation's economy for a long time. Those who manage these entities, those who share in the proceeds of their activities, those who invest in them or advance credit to them, members of regulatory bodies—indeed, everyone concerned with corporate business relies on present accounting practice in one way or another. Traditional accounting is an important part of our economic culture.

Traditional Accounting and Managerial Decision Making

Our attachment to traditional accounting is both theoretical and practical. We accept the role for accounting on which historical cost is based, yet we accept the desirability of periodic modification and adaptation to meet the needs of changing circumstances.

Consider some of the advantages of present accounting. It provides a readily understood income concept that fits the corporate executive's decision processes in the great majority of business situations. The accounting calculation of income is a reflection of the way corporate executives think about their work and about meeting the needs and desires of their customers. It provides some major information on which they make operating decisions. For most companies, buying and selling, rather than mere holding, are essential parts of business activity. The pursuit of profit requires that a company add sufficient utility of time, place or form to the materials, product or services it buys so they can be sold above cost. The most common, the best understood, the simplest, the most versatile concept of profit is the excess of selling price over cost.

A decision to continue or to discontinue a product, a division, a department or a plant hinges to a considerable extent upon whether continuation of the operation is expected to show a favorable spread between projected revenue and cost. This concept of profit can be applied to a few or to many transactions, to a simple or a complex operation, to the results of the activities of the entire business or to any part of it, to past activities or future expectations.

The matching principle grows directly out of this concept of profit. Costs and revenues are matched on a basis of their relationship to one another so that management and others can judge whether those costs should continue to be incurred. Have they been successful in producing adequate revenue or have they not? Any shift to an asset valuation basis for income determination will depart directly from the kinds of decisions that must be made to operate most business enterprises.

Traditional accounting provides an appropriate and recognized basis for evaluating operating results. Present historical cost financial statements report those transactions which have actually taken place, not those which might have taken place under some other assumed conditions. The income statement brings together a record of management's efforts in the form of costs incurred with management's accomplishments in the form of revenues. And both of these are measured in terms of actual transactions entered into by the company, not in terms of subjective estimates of asset values. We can think of no more rational or equitable basis for evaluating performance, whether for the total company or for any one of its parts.

"Holding," an activity emphasized in some analyses of business income, and much emphasized by current value advocates, is no more than an incidental aspect of most corporations' productive operations. Where it is of sufficient independent importance to warrant attention, that attention can be given by supplementary disclosure without revolutionizing all financial reporting.

Thus traditional accounting holds firmly to objectively determined facts—actual transaction data, the most reliable information available. Plans, intentions and expectations may be disclosed in the annual report if desired, but one of the great advantages of generally accepted accounting principles is that such interpretive material is clearly distinguished from factual transaction data. A clear separation between completed and possible events is maintained.

Finally, traditional accounting is the result of decades of effort to strengthen and improve financial reporting practice. From the time companies first began to report their results of operations to outsiders, professional accountants, both in industry and in public accounting, have worked together to develop standards adequate to distinguish acceptable from unacceptable financial reporting. The AICPA Committee on Accounting Procedure, the Accounting Principles Board, the Financial Accounting Standards Board, the Financial Executives Institute, the American Accounting Association, the National Association of Accountants, the stock exchanges, the Securities and Exchange Commission and other regulatory agencies—all aided by scores of committees and great individual efforts—have improved corporate financial reporting by narrowing the range of acceptable practice and by requiring essential disclosures.

The Role of Accounting Theory

We wholeheartedly support the idea that accounting must have a conceptual base. No art applied by so many people under such varying circumstances and relied on for such important decisions as accounting can serve satisfactorily without some core of established concepts and principles.

But it is not always clear just what those concepts should be. The current controversy between those who support traditional accounting and those who favor current value as the basis for financial reporting illustrates the difficulty of deciding how accounting and financial reporting can best serve all those who use the financial information it produces. Under such conditions, we rely on a cost/benefit test: In the specific circumstances, what works best for the majority of those concerned? What are the costs of change? Who will bear them? What are the established—not merely claimed—benefits? Unless persuasive evidence exists that the total economic benefit exceeds the total cost, change is unwise.

In applying that approach, we would deny our professional responsibility if we are so bound by any theory that we permit it to override our professional judgment. As yet, we have not met any general accounting theory which we believe satisfies all needs and all occasions so well that it can be applied without thoughtful consideration of its appropriateness in the specific circumstances. We feel obliged to recommend departures from prevailing theory when our best judgment tells us this is necessary to meet the needs of the situation. Such departures are and should be relatively rare; otherwise the value of a conceptual basis is negated.

Our reasons for this judgmental attitude toward accounting grow out of our perception of business as a dynamic process presenting an endless number and variety of actions and effects. Accounting must have flexibility to meet the innovations and adaptations of

business activity. It should respond to business activity, not dominate or restrict it. Accounting is an appropriate tool for use by those charged with responsibility to direct, control or regulate business, but accounting itself is not intended to be such a regulator. In our view, accounting should seek to report facts fairly and objectively, uncolored by the accountant's subjective approval or disapproval of the actions reported.

The difficulty of doing this is apparent. If only those facts that are completely and objectively measurable were accounted for, accounting would be much less useful. Accounting would also be much less useful if it lost its emphasis on objectivity. One of the responsibilities of accountants and accounting—and a factor in the usefulness of both—is a continuing effort to obtain the best mixture of faithfulness to basic concepts and adaptability to new circumstances, an emphasis on traditional objectivity balanced by a recognition of changing needs.

Problems with Current Value Accounting

Two general types of current value proposals have been made: (1) internally consistent theoretical models which give little attention to the problems of application in a wide variety of companies and situations; and (2) somewhat more realistic models directed almost completely to the details of implementation with little concern for theoretical consistency as long as the specific valuation techniques employed fit within the general category of current value.

Although we expect that the more realistic models will be proposed for actual implementation purposes, we feel obligated to consider the theoretical models also because our criticisms run to the basic concepts as well as to the very serious problems of implementation.

Conceptual Difficulties with Current Value Accounting

Theoretical models fall into three types on the basis of the way they value a company's assets: (1) the present value of discounted fu-

ture cash flows, (2) current realizable value and (3) replacement costs.

Change in Present Value of Future Cash Flow

Most current value proposals are urged as a reasonable approximation of an economic income concept based on the present value of future cash flows which is often cited as the basic economic concept of value. The theory is that if the amount and timing of the future cash flows from a given asset—whether that asset be a security, a machine or a company—were known, these could be discounted to the present at an appropriate rate of interest and the result would be the value of that asset in the most realistic economic terms.

There is an interesting result in this approach. If a company could be recorded at the present value of its future receipts, the company's net income in any period would then become nothing more than a rate of interest applied to its value. The most revealing information about the differences among companies would be found, not in such a statement of income for each company, but in the calculation of the future cash flows necessary to determine present values. All the differences between companies would be worked out in determining the future cash flows from their anticipated activities. Once the future cash flows were determined and a rate of interest selected, income determination would consist of applying the interest rate to accumulate the present values back up to the amounts of the cash flows.

This approach works ideally with a federal government bond which comes as close to certainty of cash flows as we have in our uncertain world. It would also work for some rental properties under lease for the duration of their lives. But it is quite another matter to apply it to a variety of assets, such as the components of a production line, which must be associated with one another in order to produce an income stream. And, of course, a company is far more difficult to value based on the present value of future cash flows because it in-

A PROPOSAL FOR ACCOUNTING UNDER INFLATIONARY CONDITIONS /

cludes a variety of assets, not all of which are a matter of record.

For example, how does one determine anticipated cash flows from such intangibles as created goodwill, from a successful marketing program, from a research and development department? Included in the idea of income as the change in the present value of future cash flows is the frequently overlooked idea that if we can approximate the present value of each of a company's individual assets, these can be added to reveal the current value of the company. We have difficulty in accepting the idea, even on a conceptual basis, that all the assets which contribute to a company's cash flows can be identified and valued on any basis that provides dependable information.

Most people concede that, with rare exceptions, the implementation difficultues in applying discounted cash flow concepts of value and net income to the operating assets of many companies on a realistic basis are overwhelming. For the assets of most companies, future productivity is so uncertain that we just do not know and cannot estimate with any degree of objectivity what future cash flows will be. Neither can we find sufficiently reliable evidence of the appropriate interest rate at which they should be discounted. Hence, change in the present value of future cash flows is held by some to constitute an ideal which cannot be attained in practice but should at least be sought.

We do not argue with the idea of present value of future cash flows as a useful economic concept of value. We do disagree strongly with the contention that such a concept has any valid application to the financial statements of a modern corporation. An income concept that presumes (a) to identify as assets all the factors that contribute to a company's future cash flows, (b) to measure the specific cash flows resulting from such factors, (c) to effectively equalize such flows with a discount rate, and (d) then to total the results to obtain the value of the company and to determine its income is so far removed from real world uses and problems of corporate income data as to have little, if any, perceivable relevance to corporate financial reporting.

Current Realizable Value

Another group of theorists argues that the major economic decision facing management is whether to continue in its present line of activity or to convert the capital under its control to some other course of action. For example, if the rate of return on government bonds is greater than the return from making steel, the company's assets used for making steel should be disposed of and the amount realized should be invested in government bonds or whatever other available activity promises the highest rate of return commensurate with the risk the company is willing to accept.

But to make such a decision, the argument runs, management must know what the current realizable value of its assets actually is. It does no good to sell the steel mill and find the amount realized is so small that less will be earned on the government bonds that would have been earned if the company still made steel. Therefore, at the end of each period, the current realizable value of the company's assets should be determined. Under this theory, the change in the current realizable value of the company's assets from the beginning of the period to its end, taking into account additional investments and withdrawals, represents its income.

The implementation problems in ascertaining current realizable values are similar to those faced in attempting to discover future cash flows. As a matter of fact, in concept they are much the same. If markets were "perfect," every asset could always be priced at the present value of its future cash flows. In this uncertain world with limited and imperfect markets, a variety of questions arise. What is the current realizable value for a steel mill? Do we plan on selling the assets on a piece-by-piece basis or seek bids on the plant as a whole? Does one assume forced sale liquidation or disposition on a going concern basis? What value is to be used if no sales of plants of this kind or size have taken place recently?

We have great difficulty in finding any usefulness in such information even if it could be obtained. Certainly management must be alert

to the possibility that other opportunities exist for employment of its capital. But going out of business is not a decision that needs to be made at every balance sheet date, nor should possible liquidation dominate financial reporting when the normal expectation is that the company will continue.

Replacement Cost

Replacement cost, a term that seems to mean many things to many people, is often advocated as the closest practical approximation of discounted future cash flows. Conceptually, except for market imperfections, replacement cost, current realizable values and the present values of future cash flows should be the same. The assumption is that the market is willing to pay for any asset no more than the present value of what the asset will produce in the future in the way of cash flows. Thus, the present replacement cost of any asset is the market's estimate of the future cash flows of such an asset discounted at what the market considers to be a reasonable rate of interest.

We have already noted what we consider to be the fundamental flaw in that approach to asset valuation and income determination. Equally serious implementation issues require resolution.

The difficulty with replacement cost arises when we consider the nature and circumstances of the asset to be replaced. A simple staple like a ten-pound bag of sugar will likely be replaced by a ten-pound bag of sugar so similar that telling them apart might be nearly impossible. But replacing a complex piece of production machinery presents another problem entirely. If it were to be replaced at all, it might be by a greatly improved machine designed to perform the same function, or by a substantially different machine designed to use new technology for attaining the same results, or by equipment that produces a different product to perform the same function as the old product. A conceptual question concerns the extent to which replacement cost of property and equipment should recognize technological change.

In general, the following versions of replacement cost are all possibilities:

• *Reproduction cost of existing assets.* The cost to replace existing assets without considering technological improvement. Reproduction cost is frequently approximated through price-level adjustment of historical cost amounts using specific price indexes.

• *Replacement cost of existing assets.* The cost to replace a single asset or groupings of congruous assets with other assets of equivalent productive capability. Replacement cost is equivalent to reproduction cost only in those relatively rare instances when there has been no technological change.

• *Replacement cost of existing capacity.* The cost to replace productive capacity without regard to existing assets or their physical distribution. This approach represents a forecast of how the company might proceed if it were to establish a competing business with identical productive capacity. For this purpose, technological change, economies of scale and other anticipated savings are all considered. Variations in the way these influence replacement cost seem unavoidable.

In addition to the possibility of confusing these, some pose significant implementation shortcomings. The lack of an adequate and accepted technology to develop replacement cost data, absence of a reasonably identifiable set of standards to reduce subjectivity to a satisfactory minimum, and a widespread failure to understand either the purpose or limitations of replacement cost data represent important deficiencies. We believe that adoption of replacement cost for financial statement purposes would introduce problems of measurement and interpretation that would far exceed those now faced in conventional financial reporting.

The SEC has introduced yet another application of replacement cost, one that tends to emphasize implementation over theory.

SEC Requirement for Supplementary Replacement Cost Data

A modification of replacement cost accounting was adopted by the Securities and Exchange Commission on March 23, 1976, in its Accounting Series Release No. 190.[2] The new SEC rule calls for the disclosure on a supplementary basis, by certain large companies, of the following items of information:

• The current replacement cost of inventories at each fiscal year-end for which a balance sheet is required.

• For the two most recent fiscal years, the approximate amount which cost of sales would have been if it had been calculated by estimating the current replacement cost of goods and services sold at the times when the sales were made.

• The estimated current cost of replacing (new) the productive capacity together with the current depreciated replacement cost of the productive capacity on hand at the end of each fiscal year for which a balance sheet is required.

• For the two most recent fiscal years, the approximate amount of depreciation, depletion and amortization which would have been recorded if it were estimated on the basis of average current replacement cost of productive capacity.

The requirement differs from the typical proposal for replacement cost accounting in both purpose and detail. It does not call for determination of a net income amount based on replacement cost, although an invitation to make such a calculation seems implicit in provision of the replacement cost data. The SEC release states that the information is offered as supplementary data intended to provide information to investors which will assist them in obtaining an understanding of the current costs of operating the business which cannot be obtained from historical financial statements taken alone. A secondary purpose is stated to be to provide information which will enable investors to determine the current cost of inventories and productive capacity as a measure of the current economic investment in these assets existing at the balance

sheet date.

A distinguishing feature of the SEC's replacement cost rule appears in its definition of replacement cost as the current cost to obtain an asset of equivalent productive capability in accordance with management's normal or most likely replacement policy. Thus if a given item of equipment which cost $1,000 and is still profitable could be replaced either by a similar piece of equipment at a current cost of $1,200 or by a technologically improved machine at $1,500, the replacement cost to be used would depend on management's policy. It if is assumed that management's policy would be to acquire the technologically improved machine at time of replacement, the replacement cost of the machine would be reported at $1,500 under the SEC rule.

In this illustration, SEC replacement cost results in an asset valuation greater than that which could result under other definitions of replacement cost. The difference exists because the SEC calls for replacement cost to be determined using management's normal approach to replacement.

SEC replacement cost and "ordinary" replacement cost will approximate one another when any technological advance is reflected in the asset cost. If that technological advance appears instead in the use of less material because spoilage is reduced, or in lower labor costs or in energy consumption, replacement cost under the two approaches may be significantly different.

Companies are currently seeking to apply the SEC replacement cost concepts. We expect that most companies will be able to do so, although at some cost and management effort. But to what end? Will the resulting information have any practical use? Nothing in the SEC release answers the kinds of conceptual and implementation objections we have to replacement cost accounting but we strive to keep an open mind until the considerable experience to be acquired during the next year or two will provide a better basis for evaluating the usefulness of the required information and the implementability of the rule as it stands.

---

[2] Ernst & Ernst Financial Reporting Developments, *SEC Requires Replacement Cost Disclosures for Large Companies,* April 1976, Retrieval No. 38450.

Implementation Problems in Current Value Accounting

As mentioned previously, models advanced by practitioners tend to adopt current value as a general goal of financial reporting, a goal to be reached in specific circumstances by whatever valuation technique seems both available and appropriate. For example, current market quotations would be used for marketable securities; inventories would be valued at the lesser or current replacement cost or current realizable value; income producing property at exit or discounted value; plant and equipment at replacement cost or exit value with replacement cost selected from (1) reproduction cost, (2) the replacement cost of existing assets, (3) the lower of replacement cost or reproduction cost, or (4) the lower of replacement or reproduction cost provided the resulting amount does not exceed the present value of future cash flows.

Although general agreement might be reached among current value advocates on the appropriate valuation procedure for many assets and liabilities, a number of items present special problems. Included among these are intangible assets such as goodwill, patents and copyrights; land in use under productive facilities; natural resources such as oil reserves; and even long-term receivables and payables when interest rates are changing.

Consider the determination of financial statement amounts for long-term receivables and payables. Some current value proponents would have companies revalue all such long-term items at every balance sheet date. Fluctuations in interest rates would then influence reported income. To the extent that a company has entered into a long-term financing transaction at a current market rate, we feel that rate should govern the accounting for the receivable or payable until settled or until another transaction is consummated.

Neither the lender nor the borrower can control prevailing interest rates, and it is economically impracticable to refinance obligations or dispose of assets at every rate change. Of course interest rates influence the profits of companies engaged in financial activities but we believe financial statement readers are interested in the results of actual transactions, not in every change that would have influenced other transactions if they had been entered into.

Net Income in Current Value Models

In reporting net income, current value models exhibit differences similar to those found in their valuation methods. Most models try to subdivide the present net income figure into a variety of components including, for example, operating income, realized value changes and unrealized value changes. Some would include a provision for capital maintenance based on the decline in the general purchasing power of the dollar. Others would adjust reported income for general purchasing power gains or losses on net monetary items.

Segregation of holding gains (generally defined as the increase in value of an asset during the time it is held by a company) is a relatively common characteristic of current value reporting proposals. This is apparently done on the theory that such gains are so different from operating income that they should not be combined with it. In some cases, the contention seems to be that they are not actually enterprise income at all. The purpose in separating them from other income items is so that financial statement readers will identify holding gains as something they cannot count on to be repeated in future years.

As a practical matter, holding and operations are often inseparable. Manufacturing and sales operations cannot be conducted without holding inventories and other assets for a period of time, and to report these activities as if they were separable can be misleading. In other cases, holding gains are the result of wise management planning and purchasing and are as much a result of management action as are operating gains. We concur that extraordinary market changes may result in holding gains that are not indicative of a company's ability to sustain reported earning power but we feel that such changes can be disclosed without major modifications to the conventional income concept.

Because we believe the present concept of corporate net income has demonstrated great usefulness, we are opposed to the idea that what is now reported as net income should be subdivided into a number of separate elements with new designations and descriptions. The present concept of net income is so much a part of the way investors, management, credit grantors, labor, regulatory authorities and others think about business success and failure that proposals to change it in major ways impress us as unreasonable. Such a proposal would place a significant burden on financial statement readers who would then be left to their own devices to formulate and apply some concept of enterprise net income. The failure to identify and determine net income is not likely to be received by financial statement users as progress.

Loss of Discipline Under Current Value Proposals

It seems curious that some of those who now complain that present financial reporting already includes far too wide a range of acceptable practices should advocate abandonment of historical cost. One can only conjecture about the total range of asset valuation practices that would be proposed as acceptable if current value amounts were injected into financial statements. Certainly the discipline now incorporated in conventional accounting, the hard-earned results of decades of work by many individuals and organizations, is likely to be sacrificed if a new basis of accounting is adopted, and the long, tedious and painful process of developing authoritative standards will have to commence anew.

Financial Statements Adjusted for Changes in General Purchasing Power

An entirely different method of adjusting accounting data for the impact of inflation was proposed by

CPa / AUGUST 1977

the Financial Accounting Standards Board in an exposure draft entitled "Financial Reporting in Units of General Purchasing Power." Ernst & Ernst opposed the issuance of that proposal as a financial accounting standard.[3]

Our primary opposition focused on the recommendation that the purchasing power gain or loss from holding net monetary items be included in net income although it is an item that will never constitute realized net income in the sense that most readers of financial statements understand that term. It represents a "gain" that will never be received by the reporting company in cash and as such cannot be reinvested or distributed to shareholders. We commented further:

On this point, GPP net income for conservatively capitalized companies will compare unfavorably to that of highly leveraged companies, because the latter will include larger purchasing power gains as part of their net income. Users may not understand that income in leveraged companies is influenced by the amount of debt and could errroneously conclude that prospects for leveraged companies are unrealistically better than future cash flows will ever justify. The opposite conclusion may be reached for conservatively capitalized companies. Should this occur, reported net income would be misleading as a measure of past success and future prospects.

We also objected to the proposal on the grounds of its general lack of understandability, the questionable usefulness of price-level adjustments for economic predictive purposes involving specific

[3] Ernst & Ernst Financial Reporting Development, *Price Level Accounting*, August 1975, Retrieval No. 38350.

companies based on a single general index, the cost of not only implementing the proposal but of educating financial statement users to an understanding of its meanings and limitations, and the widespread lack of enthusiasm for a procedure which has been available for years.

We did take that occasion to advocate the reporting on a supplementary basis of depreciation expense adjusted for price-level changes, a position included in the recommendations of this article.

In June 1976, the FASB announced that it had decided to defer further consideration of a statement on financial reporting in units of general purchasing power.

Conclusions about Current Value Accounting

Our approach to resolving accounting issues is essentially an application of a cost/benefit test. What are the net advantages or disadvantages of historical cost? What are the net advantages or disadvantages of current value? How do they compare? Such an evaluation, of course, should be made keeping in mind the varying interests in and uses of accounting data. We recognize that others may place different evaluations on some of these factors but, given our experience and practical orientation, we find the decision an easy one.

In favor of historical cost we find its demonstrated usefulness over time and under a variety of circumstances. It has wide acceptance and understanding, and is supported by a body of well established standards and practices. Literally innumerable decisions are made every day on the basis of conventional accounting data and those who make them are not the ones calling for a change to current value. On the negative side we recognize its limitations during times of inflation or deflation and the desirability of supplementing it with specific value information under some conditions. Both of these de-

ficiencies can be remedied, the first by the proposals in this article, the other by supplementary disclosures.

We also support continuing efforts to narrow the range of acceptable practices insofar as this is possible without unduly restricting application of the judgment necessary to recognize the influence of circumstances and conditions on transactions.

Current value advocates claim great usefulness for financial statements prepared on that basis but such claims are as yet completely unsupported by any significant amount of experience. They also claim conceptual conformity with economic concepts, but this claim is subject to challenge. On the negative side are anticipated but as yet unknown problems of implementation. We consider these of great importance. There is also an absence of experience, of acceptance and of discipline in the form of established standards or accepted practices. An additional negative is the cost of change if current value is substituted for historical cost, a change that can result in great confusion and distress to those who fail to understand the results.

Given such a summary, we can come to no other conclusion than that the clear balance of usefulness at this time remains with the modest departure from historical cost we have recommended. If we put ourselves in the position of corporate managers, investors, analysts, regulators, taxing authorities, creditors or whatever interest you choose, and consider whether we would prefer to have traditional financial statements, modified as proposed in this article, or some version of current value with all the disadvantages we envisage in the implementation of that method of accounting, we find historical cost to be the better choice by far. On any cost/benefit test we can apply, society would be ill served by the adoption of current value accounting as the basis for corporate financial reporting. Ω

Accountants, Accountancy and the Future

by R. F. J. DEWHURST, MA, FCA
Senior Lecturer in Finance, University of Warwick

In an earlier article (*The Accountant*, October 12th, 1978), the author tried to point out that historical accounting was not necessarily right simply because it had existed for several hundred years. He also argued that qualified accountants with their long training in accounting methods based on historical input figures would inevitably find it hard to consider with favour any other approach.

In order to present the argument for a different (replacement account) approach a very simple example was used in my original article. To concentrate on the main issue — that historical accounting was not necessarily right — this example did not differentiate between two possible alternative replacements (if the word be allowed); namely physical capital maintenance and real capital maintenance.

This example was taken one stage further — and better — by Professor French, Mr Waldron *et al*. In a letter published in *The Accountant* of November 2nd, 1978, Professor French used this example:

'I buy a ton of sugar for £100 at the beginning of a year in which the general index of prices moves from 100 to 200 and sell it at the end of that year for £400 when its replacement cost to me is £350.'

He then differentiated between three possible definitions of profit, [see examples opposite] and went on to say 'Because profit is a creature of definition we cannot say that one of these approaches is right and the others wrong. We must choose between them by some pragmatic test, such as their *usefulness*' (my italics).

Professor French is, of course, quite correct in saying that profit (like so many basic terms in accountancy such as cost) has no absolutely 'right' definition; we must choose. But which is the most useful choice? Which has really had the most use?

	£	£
Historical		
Sales	400	
Less Purchases	100	
	——	300
Replacement or physical capital maintenance		
Sales	400	
Less Replacement cost	350	
	——	50
Real capital maintenance		
Sales	400	
Less Opening wealth re expressed in end year £s	200	
	——	200

Physical maintenance

My article deliberately started with the origin of trading. Before money was invented, a man would deal with physical items. If he dealt with sugar and had one bag both at the start and at the end of the year, he would say he had made no profit; his trade was sugar, and it is with his trade that he would be concerned. Hence his simple basic idea of profit would be rooted in the physical maintenance concept — though he might not be all that aware of it in those terms.

With the increasing complexity of trading, as time went on,

THE ACCOUNTANT, March 15th, 1979

"This article, by R.F.J. Dewhurst, MA, FCA, of the University of Warwick, first appeared in *The Accountant* of March 15th, 1979."

our trader would perhaps extend the range of his products. He might deal in white and brown sugar, even conceivably branch into other items totally unconnected with his original trade. How could he work out the profit that his business made in such trying circumstances?

Fortunately, money was invented with its dual role of storing wealth and, more importantly, making possible comparisons between the value of different commodities. It would then be possible to express the value of (say) one bag of white and one bag of brown sugar in common (money) terms, and hence arrive at the joint profit on the trading of the two different types expressed in one unit. But does this mean that he has to turn away from the commonsense concept on which he originally based his trading; ie, physical maintenance or replacement accounting? It is true that, with the advent of money, he has the facility to use another measure, ie, money's wealth, or real capital maintenance. But primarily he is not dealing with money; he is dealing in sugar, and it is by his ability to trade in that commodity that he should still be judged.

Money indeed is a useful unit for measuring. It is entirely necessary in a business organisation where trading is in a range of products. Indeed there is no other practical way of arriving at total profit without using money. But because we need to use money does not mean that we have to believe that it acquires a mystical significance in its own right. The sugar man trades in sugar, not in money; he should be judged by how well he does at this trade. That is what a trading and profit and loss account says, and that is what it should mean.

It is interesting to note that in Holland (the birthplace of replacement accounting) even those businesses which prefer to present their published accounts in historical terms often keep their asset records in replacement cost form. They argue – as do we – that this form is the most useful.

I have put Professor French's example to a large number of first-year students (most of whom were having their first exposure to accounting matters), with no intentional prior recommendation. Their view of the 'right' figure for profit is shown in the following table:

	Approx number of students
Historical figure of 300	40
Replacement figure of 50	35
Real capital maintenance figure of 200 ..	30

So there was no clear consensus of opinion. Some, too, it should be added, were undecided or would not commit themselves.

Other views

In *The Accountant* of January 11th, 1979, Dr Boersema took a whole article to comment on the first simple example given in my October article. He said 'Justification of the use of replacement costing solely by an appeal to common sense fails to recognise, opposing viewpoints expressed through the relevant literature'.

He went on to list 13 reasons for advocating purchasing power of capital, some 14 reasons for arguing that the replacement cost alternatives (which do not – as Dr Boersema suggests – include the temporarily necessary, but unhappy, compromise of Hyde) 'are still subject to some very significant problems' and some 13 advantages for another possible way of arriving at profits not yet mentioned: namely, net realisable value.

Not too much time need be spent on this last alternative;

both on a conceptual basis and, perhaps more obviously, on a pragmatic level, it is unsatisfactory. How can one even think of attributing, every year, values to all the assets of a business this way? Clearly it would be, in practice, prohibitively difficult.

But the main fault is the conceptual error; the basis is wrong, since there is no intention of realising the assets. The business is going on; there is no thought of selling it; all we are trying to do is to assess how well it has done over that highly arbitrary period of one year – the time the Earth takes to go round the Sun.

What is profit?

If Professor French is right – and it seems clear that he is – and profit is a creature of definition, this does not mean that we cannot arrive at some sensible way of looking at it.

An analogy may help. What we think of as 'Mount Everest' varies with our viewpoint. Even such an apparently certain thing as its height varies with the viewer. The first men who saw it must have thought it immensely tall; to a jet pilot it is still high, but less awesome; to an astronaut it must be almost insignificant. We all have our perceptions of Mount Everest, much as we all have our views of profit. Indeed, for both, there is no clearly agreed reality.

Mount Everest physically changes a little all the time. Even where it starts, its base as it were, is uncertain. The only way to agree on Mount Everest is to define its physical limits and the viewpoint of the observer. That way we shall be able to arrive at an agreed perceived view of Everest. And this is useful not only in its own right, but is particularly helpful in that it makes possible valid comparisons with other mountains.

It is the same with profit. We must have an agreed viewpoint, preferably rooted in something firm and understandable such as physical maintenance. This is the way it was long before money problems complicated the issue and made other ways possible, and apparently attractive.

The future

The United Kingdom was the first major industrial country to try and turn away from historical (and the associated CPP) accounting to a form of physical replacement accounting. The attempted transition can now be seen as having been far too radical and too swift. It brought, understandably, a sharp reaction from the profession. This reaction itself was too strong. It attempted to put right the grave error in the speed and positiveness of the initial implementation of Sandilands. It, too, overcompensated.

There are very clear signs of a further swing of the pendulum back to replacement accounting. At the time of writing it seems certain that the next step (after the unhappy Hyde compromise) will be a current cost accounting supplement to historical accounting. This supplement will probably follow along much the same lines as Sandilands (except that gains or losses on holding monetary liabilities or assets will be included). In brief, this means historical plus a Sandilands supplement.

If the argument used in this article for replacement accounting is right; if the analysis of recent changes showing a long-term trend away from historical towards replacement accounting is correct, too, then there is no doubt what the future will be for published accounting statements. Not historical plus a Sandilands supplement. No: the two sets of accounts will be changed about. Historical accounts will be relegated to their rightful place – that of a supplement to Sandilands.

Laurence A. Friedman, CPA, Ph.D.

What *Is* Current Value?

The author describes in simple terms the various
inflation accounting proposals and questions whether
the SEC's so-called replacement cost information is
meaningful. Alternatives are considered to be
developed from the supply of data presently available
to companies.

THE initial reaction to the SEC's requirement that
large firms disclose supplemental replacement cost
information has, for the most part, been negative. The
requirements that firms disclose the replacement costs
of inventory, property, plant and equipment as well as
the replacement cost depreciation expense and replacement cost of goods sold is criticized as being
costly with no appreciable benefits. For example, General Motors Company characterized the requirements
as " . . . of no value because of the subjectivity necessarily involved in making these estimates and because
the concept is based on an unrealistic premise, i.e.,
the total replacement of all productive capacity at one
time."[1]

On the other hand, most accountants agree that
some measures should be taken to inform users of the
effect on financial statements of the inflationary tendency of the economy. Many critics of ASR 190 seem
to agree that some measure of the effect of changing
prices should be disclosed but that the SEC's version
of replacement cost accounting is not appropriate.[2]

Among other things, they criticize the use of replacement costs as defined by the SEC as not representing current values. Approximately 50 percent of the
10–K reports the author examined contained criticisms,
such as:

> . . . replacement cost data . . . are not representa-
> tive of the current value of existing inventory and
> productive capacity.[3]

[1] The General Motors Company, annual report, 1976.
[2] Bastable, C. W., "Is SEC Replacement Cost Data Worth the
Effort," *Journal of Accountancy*, October 1977, pp. 74–76.
[3] The Dow Chemical Company, 10–K report, 1976.

*Laurence A. Friedman, CPA, Ph.D., is an Associate Professor
of Accounting at the University of Colorado, Boulder. He is a
member of the American Accounting Association, the AICPA,
and the Colorado Society of CPAs and has authored numerous articles in academic and professional accounting journals.*

> . . . it cannot be assumed that the reported re-
> placement cost bears any relationship to the actual
> current value of existing property, plant and equip-
> ment . . .[4]

> . . . replacement cost should not be interpreted as
> the current value of existing productive capacity.[5]

Most of the reports give no explanation of what is
meant by "current value." But if progress is to be
made toward reaching a consensus regarding reporting
in periods of changing prices, interested parties must
be specific in their suggested solution. Users, preparers and auditors must all make known their needs for
current value information and the practical difficulties
of meeting those needs. The purpose of this article is
to summarize various valuation approaches that could
all be called "current value." Perhaps this will enable
accountants to understand some of the different methods of current value accounting and will encourage
them to come forward with specific suggestions, which
they feel can be implemented at reasonable cost, for
improving reporting in periods of changing prices.

The Current Price Debate

Sterling set up a framework to describe the various
valuation approaches. Basically, he suggests that two
types of prices exist: input and output. Also, one can
examine three different states of time: the past, present
and future. Each intersection of time and price provides a possible method of valuation. "Thus, there are
four major valuation methods that have been proposed:
1. Historical cost (HC);
2. Replacement cost (RC);
3. Exit value (EV); and
4. Discounted cash flows (DCF)."[6]
His classification is reproduced in Table 1.[7]

[4] Wheeling-Pittsburgh Steel Corporation, 10–K report, 1976.
[5] Handy and Harman, 10–K report, 1976.
[6] Sterling, Robert R. "Decision Oriented Financial Accounting,"
Accounting and Business Research, Summer 1972, p. 202.
[7] Ibid.

TABLE 1			
Price	Past	Present	Future
Input	HC	RC	DCF
Output	Irrelevant	EV	DCF

He does not include general price level adjustments because they could be added to any of the above, resulting in four more alternatives. He suggests that one should adjust for changes in the general price level but that selection of the valuation method is a separate problem which must be solved first. The author agrees with this suggestion, but a discussion of general price level adjusted historical costs is appropriate since that is the subject of APB Statement No. 3 and a withdrawn FASB exposure draft.[8]

Before reviewing the various valuation alternatives, however, an attempt is made to discover which of the various valuation alternatives seem to be implied by the use of the term "current value." One report states "Replacement costs . . . should not be interpreted to be current value or the price for which the assets could be sold."[9] Unfortunately, that statement could mean either that current values are current selling prices or that current values are something different from current selling prices. Another report includes that statement that " . . . replacement cost amounts should not be interpreted to represent amounts at which the assets could be sold or any other measure of current value."[10] This implies that current selling prices are a measure of "current value," but that others exist also.

Thus, while the term "current value" may mean selling prices, it may not; it may refer to a variety of valuation approaches. Even if we could define "current value" it is not clear from the statements quoted above (or from any other remarks in the replacement cost footnotes of the companies already cited) that use of some form of "current value" is in fact an appropriate method of accounting in periods of changing prices. Therefore rather than continue to try to determine what is meant by current value, I will briefly summarize the major valuation alternatives which have been suggested, all of which could be considered methods of current valuation.

Replacement Cost

A reasonable starting point for this discussion is with replacement cost accounting since this is the cur-

'. . . while the term current value may mean selling prices, it may not; it may refer to a variety of valuation approaches.'

rent value method mandated by the SEC. The replacement cost of an asset must be considered to be a current value since it is a measure of what current buyers would have to pay for a similar asset.

The SEC is in the process of developing detailed rules and regulations specifying how replacement costs are to be determined. This process is likely to take years. In the meantime, the basic guideline provided requires the preparer of supplemental replacement cost information to determine how much it would cost to replace existing productive facilities and inventories *in the manner in which they would actually be replaced.*

This guideline reflects the SEC's definition of replacement cost and is one of the most serious flaws in the disclosure requirement. The flaw results from the fact that, as most companies replace their productive facilities, they become either increasingly capital intensive or technologically sophisticated. Much of the reason for incurring higher capital outlays is to reduce labor costs and to create tax shelters. But the SEC will not allow a company to reduce the depreciation expense which is based on the replacement cost of the capital intensive productive capacity by an amount equal to the anticipated labor and tax savings. Thus, the information could be misinterpreted.

As an example, consider the United States steel industry. As the industry currently exists, much of its productive capacity is still from an era of reasonably inexpensive labor and is highly labor intensive. As labor costs have increased, the new steel plants which have been built have been more automated, more expensive and less dependent on labor. Evidence exists to indicate that this trend will not change. Therefore, if steel companies calculate replacement costs based on the newer technologically advanced productive capacity, the price will be much higher than the older labor intensive plants. But these additional expenditures probably are economically sound given the size of the anticipated labor savings. The SEC version of replacement cost accounting recognizes the escalating capital costs, but does not require the quantification of the labor savings. Thus, the charges that the SEC's replacement cost numbers are misleading.

The flaw in the SEC's approach is one of implementation, rather than of conceptual weakness. It could be remedied in several ways. One of the most obvious, but least satisfactory from the companies'

[8] Accounting Principles Board, *Statement No. 3, Financial Statements Restated for General Price-Level Changes*, AICPA, June 1969; and Financial Accounting Standards Board, *Exposure Draft: Financial Reporting in Units of General Purchasing Power*, 12-31-1974.
[9] International Business Machines Corporation, 10-K report, 1976.
[10] Kraft, Inc., 10-K report, 1976.

CPA JOURNAL   NOVEMBER 1978

viewpoint, would be to encourage disclosure of anticipated savings due to replacement of existing productive equipment with technologically superior equipment. But many companies may balk at this type of disclosure because it may be considered proprietary. Also, disclosure of anticipated labor savings would be an extension into forecasting, whereas conceptually replacement cost accounting is concerned with reporting past and present phenomena.

Perhaps a different definition of replacement cost is more appropriate. The SEC's definition of replacement cost is their own and it does not correspond to that in any of the major works dealing with replacement cost accounting. Another definition of replacement cost is the current cost to acquire productive capacity *which would provide the current level of economic services.* In other words instead of using replacement costs for the existing facilities, the measure would be the cost of providing similar economic services.

Continuing the steel industry example, the replacement cost under the alternative definition of replace-

> 'From a theoretical point of view, use of exit values is significantly different from use of replacement costs.'

ment cost would be the cost to build a new plant which utilizes approximately the same technology then in existence. This definition is advantageous because the calculation is based on what the company actually has rather than on some nonexistent future plant which the company may or may not build. Thus, the replacement cost figures would be more relevant to the then present activities of the company.

Another advantage of the alternative definition is that the replacement cost figures are based on a plan of the size of that being used. The SEC's definition of replacement cost may result in numbers which reflect much higher levels of productive capacity because newer technology may only be economically feasible at higher output levels.

To summarize, use of replacement cost data might be much less subject to criticism and more valuable as a source of information if a more reasonable definition were adopted. Thus, a more viable method of accounting in periods of changing prices would retain the use of replacement costs, but modify the operational definition so that more reasonable, reliable and meaningful information would be obtained.

Exit Values

Another measure which may be used to represent "current value" is exit value. Exit value is the amount which may be obtained in the current market by selling an asset. From a theoretical point of view, use of exit values is significantly different from use of replacement costs. From a practical viewpoint, however, most differences may be so small that they are immaterial.[11]

Exit values may be easier to determine because one does not have to be concerned with valuing assets which are no longer produced. We are no longer concerned with buying replacements, but rather with selling those assets we have. Thus, a manager does not have to try to determine what it would cost to buy an asset which cannot be bought. Use of exit values would have several other advantages. One of the major advantages is that it would avoid cost allocation. Depreciation expense is simply the decline in selling price of an asset during a period. Thus, no life estimates are necessary.

Another advantage of an exit value approach is that it is probably the most easily understood of the current value alternatives. The exit value is simply what a company could expect to receive for its assets if it were to sell them in small groups rather than use them or sell the firm as a whole. This is a concept which laymen should be able to easily comprehend. But, valuation problems will still exist for unique assets which are infrequently traded. Estimates will still be necessary to determine what assets could be sold for. A more serious problem relates to defining the hypothetical sale. Would one assume that assets have to be sold immediately (a distress sale) or could the company assume some reasonable time period in order to dispose of its assets in favorable markets? In addition, would the hypothetical costs of selling the assets be deducted from the selling prices?

Exit values have several other disadvantages. One is that an exit value system does not lend itself to traditional income statement presentation. Income, in an exit value system, is simply the difference between the valuation of the net assets at the end of the period and net assets at the beginning of the period, after adjustment for any capital transactions. Thus, revenues and expenses are not an integral part of the system. Furthermore, income, as measured in an exit value system, is time related rather than based on events.

---

[11] Assets which are traded in good markets, such as commodities, are likely to have buying and selling prices which move together. Because of this the income measures based on these prices should also be very similar. Assets which are not actively traded, such as specialized ones, are likely to have a more significant difference in price. Thus, the income measurement for these items will be more divergent. An interesting project would be to try to determine the relative percentage of the assets of a company which are actively traded.

Thus, measurements of revenues and expenses are not facilitated by the system. While income statements have been designed, no general agreement has been reached as to which is most appropriate. Of course, given that the SEC has required disclosure of only supplemental information, this may not be a serious problem.

Another disadvantage of exit value measurements is conceptual: assets are held to be used rather than resold. Thus, the prices reported in an exit value system are based on assumptions which may be contrary to intent. As is the case with replacement cost, exit values may be considered hypothetical. Nevertheless, the exit value approach may be a useful method of accounting in periods of changing prices.

Discounted Cash Flows

Discounted cash flow valuation is widely discussed by economists and accounting theorists as the theoretically correct way to value assets and measure income. Accountants, however, usually ignore discounted cash flow valuation because of the practical difficulties inherent in implementing such a system. Projecting future cash flows and determining the appropriate discount rate is considered by many to be a completely subjective exercise, not sufficiently objective to be useful for external reporting purposes.

Staubus has suggested that discounted cash flows is the most relevant valuation method. He also recognizes the difficulty of determining discounted cash flows and indicates that they can be approximated by using current market prices.[12] He suggests that net realizable values (current selling prices less costs of selling) be used in valuing inventory, because inventory is held for sale and net realizable value should be a good surrogate for present value of the future proceeds.

On the other hand, Staubus suggests replacement costs be used for assets held for use. He argues that if the company did not have these assets they would have to buy them in the future. These future purchases would require outflows which can be approximated by current replacement costs. The replacement cost provides an indication of what it will cost to use these assets in the future.

Staubus' suggestion makes use of both current market values. Therefore, while the system may be conceptually different from either of the valuation approaches discussed earlier, the practical advantages and disadvantages are the same as for the others.

[12] Staubus, George "The Relevance of Discounted Cash Flow Valuation," *Asset Valuation*, Robert R. Sterling, editor, University of Kansas Press, 1971, pp. 42–69.

> **'Accountants . . . usually ignore discounted cash flow valuation because of the practical difficulties inherent in implementing such a system.'**

General Price Level Adjusted Historical Costs

As mentioned earlier in this paper, the author concurs with Sterling's and others' suggestion that general price level adjustments be added to any valuation system which is used. Some accountants have suggested that adding general price level adjustments to historical cost amounts would provide sufficient information about changing prices and alleviate any need for current values.

Such an approach has the advantages of being easier to implement than the others and of being objective in the sense that the necessary data are readily available. Implementation is easier because little is added to the historical cost records which are already kept. The historical cost records are adjusted by means of a general price level index. The only extra information needed is the index and the acquisition date of the assets. Since general price level indexes are government developed, they are objective and readily available. The adjustments are relatively simple and could even be programmed on a computer. Thus, the prime advantages of this system are ease of implementation and no loss of objectivity.

Among the disadvantages of the system is that it does not really report the effect of changing prices. Implicit in the system is the assumption that all company assets are affected by inflation in the same manner as are average goods and services in the economy. In other words, each asset's value is determined by adjusting its cost for the price change of the goods and services used in the index construction. Yet it is well known that an index is nothing more than a composite average. It is unlikely that the price of any one asset will change exactly by the same amount as the average of the general index goods and services. In a period of rising prices in general, some asset prices may fall, some may rise more slowly than average, some faster than average, but few will be exactly average. Therefore, while general price level adjustments may be useful as a general indicator of the effects of inflation, they cannot provide information about the effects on any specific company.

Another disadvantage of general price level adjustments relates to the determination of monetary gains

CPA NOVEMBER 1978

> 'General price level is neither what it would cost to buy the item nor what the item could be sold for.'

and losses. One of the criticisms leveled at the FASB's general price level exposure draft was that highly leveraged companies would recognize large monetary gains and would look better than companies that do not use such large amounts of debt financing. Furthermore, Kaplan has demonstrated that it is conceptually incorrect to determine monetary gains by applying general price level adjustments to historical amounts of debt. He shows that the correct gain is determined only when current prices are used to value debt.[13] Using historical amounts borrowed to calculate monetary gains is the reason that highly leveraged companies seem to benefit so substantially from general price level adjustments. If current market prices for the debt instrument were used, the magnitude of purchasing power gains from holding debt would probably be much smaller.

The last disadvantage to be discussed is that general price level adjustments are not likely to be easily understood. It is easy to say that these are nothing more than scale adjustments similar to changing feet to yards. But most scale adjustments take place at an instant in time, whereas general price level adjustments are intertemporal. For example, if we measure a board

---

[13] Kaplan, Robert "Purchasing Power Gains on Debt: The Effect of Expected and Unexpected Inflation," *Accounting Review*, April 1977.

to be six feet long we also know it is two yards long. But if we measured a board as six feet last year, we cannot say it is two yards now unless we know that nothing has happened in the meantime. Yet with general price level adjustments we try to make scale conversions across time while knowing things have changed.

Therefore, if one were to ask the meaning of a general price level adjusted cost the answer would be difficult to understand. It is neither what it would cost to buy the item nor what the item could be sold for. It is the cost of the item when originally purchased expressed in current sized dollars. Since this adjusted price may not actually exist in the world, interpretation is likely to be difficult.

Summary

In this paper we indicated some of the major valuation techniques which could be considered to provide measures of current value. These techniques include replacement cost accounting, exit value accounting, discounted cash flow accounting and general price level adjusted historical cost. Each of the alternatives uses a price in the valuation process. The difference hinges on the market and time from which the price is taken. One common feature is that all of the methods could be general price level adjusted.

The author hopes that his discussion will enable accountants to be more specific in their thinking on how to account in periods of changing prices. Perhaps one of the systems discussed, or some combination of them is the answer. It is likely that, if the issues are more completely understood and if suggestions become more concrete accountants will find an acceptable method of accounting in periods of changing prices. Ω

The Numbers Game

Waist Deep In Big Muddy

IT'S A FUNNY THING about accounting; the deeper you get, the more confusing it gets. The harder you try for the precise truth, the more it eludes you. Indeed, as Pontius Pilate asked: "What *is* truth?"

Take inflation accounting. The accounting profession has been concerned with reflecting the effects of inflation for many years. In 1974 when inflation was rampant, the Financial Accounting Standards Board, under pressure to act quickly, plucked a previously worked-out approach off the shelf and offered it as its proposed way to account for inflation. It met with tremendous opposition and it may never go into effect.

Because it did not agree with the FASB proposal, the Securities & Exchange Commission came up with its own proposal. It calls for disclosure in the footnotes of four pieces of information: 1) current replacement cost of inventories, 2) the effect on cost of sales if goods and services had been booked at current replacement cost, 3) the replacement cost of depreciable, depletable and amortizable assets and 4) the effect on depreciation charges if depreciation had been calculated on replacement rather than historical cost.

Replacement cost is today's cost. Historical cost is yesterday's cost—cost at time of purchase. Simple example: You bought a car five years ago for $3,000 and depreciated it over the five years. The price of the car is now $5,000. The $3,000 you set aside for depreciation of the original car is not enough to buy a new car. That, in a nutshell, is what is wrong with standard accounting in an inflationary period.

Inflation makes profits look better than they really are. It creates inventory profits that are not really profits. It causes depreciation to be understated (in the simple case above the understatement was $2,000).

According to the Treasury Department, nonfinancial corporations reported aftertax profits of $53.7 billion in 1973. In 1974 reported earnings were up about 14%—to $61 billion. But then the figures were adjusted for inflation—allowing for higher replacement costs and taking out inventory profits. The difference was dramatic and frightening. Instead of being up 14%, corporate profits were *down* a resounding 44%!

Obviously it is of importance to provide investors with more information on how inflation affects companies. But does the SEC proposal do the job? It doesn't seem so.

The primary benefit of the SEC proposal would be to show empirically the dangerous degree of underdepreciation in American business today. U.S. Steel's comptroller, Bracy D. Smith, says that for U.S. Steel the true depreciation (to *replace* fixed assets) should be two to three times what it is. Doubling depreciation would add about $300 million to Big Steel's costs, which would come out of aftertax profits and would have lowered reported 1975 earnings per share from $10.33 to under $5.

Okay. The SEC proposal would make depreciation and cost of goods more realistic. But it does not deal at all with a host of other issues, many of which would have a beneficial effect on earnings. For example, it requires no procedures for revaluing monetary items like debt or nonmonetary items like investments. Under the SEC's proposed disclosures, banks would show little impact from inflation. Most of their assets are in loans and equity investments, neither of which would be revalued. Yet banks have not been immune to inflation.

Borrowers Are Winners

"In inflationary times, companies that borrowed money have achieved an economic gain, because you pay back in cheaper dollars," says Gary Depolo of Transamerica Corp. "If you ignore that, you're not reflecting business strategies. Many business consultants advise that in inflationary times the winners are those who borrow heavily." The logic of this is obvious: Money due in 1978 will be more burdensome than debt due in 2000. The one will be paid back in dollars worth maybe 90 cents in current terms; the latter in dollars worth maybe 40 cents. So, while inflation increases replacement costs, it probably decreases debt burden.

The SEC's chief accountant, John C. Burton, concedes the partial nature of the disclosure called for, but adds: "We don't have in mind a final end. We have in mind a beginning."

The particular danger of such a piecemeal approach, however, is that investors may get a distorted view of what "real earnings" are; they would see only one side of the picture.

The lack of specific guidelines in the SEC proposal is a still more serious problem, and one that troubles many companies. Each company would have to make its own assumptions and estimates on replacement cost. This adds an element of subjectivity to accounting that is pure poison to accountants. Take the replacement cost of a plant. The SEC proposal would work like this: Say a plant was built seven years ago at a cost of $10 million. It has a life of 25 years and is currently 40% depreciated. The replacement cost is determined to be $15 million. The company would depreciate 40% of the replacement cost immediately and the balance—$9 million—on a straight-line basis over the remaining 18 years of the life of the asset.

Doesn't sound too difficult. But how was the replacement cost determined? Was it the cost of building a new plant exactly like the old one? Or does it incorporate any technological changes that have occurred? It is up to the companies to decide. A technologically updated plant might cost more to build, but it might also reduce operating and production costs, neither of which would be required to be reflected under the SEC's proposal. Or take a New York City office building that cost $8 million to build. It might cost $10 million to replace, but could only be sold for $6 million. 'What value should be booked? The SEC has not said.

In short, there seems to be considerable question as to how useful the SEC's proposal will really be. "This thing is going to cost a lot of money, but it has not been demonstrated that there will be a benefit," says A.L. Monroe, controller of Exxon.

How much *would* it cost to comply with the SEC proposal? Estimates vary considerably. AT&T, which favors the change, thinks it could be done for the whole Bell System for under $1 million. On the other hand United Telecommunications, the nation's third-largest telephone company, but with only 3% of AT&T's assets, complains that it would cost a minimum of $3 million and probably far more.

There is some sentiment within the accounting profession that the proper agency to deal with inflation accounting is not the SEC but the accountants' own Financial Accounting Standards Board. The FASB has a project under way dealing with the whole issue of current value accounting (of which replacement cost is only one part), but it is unlikely that there will be a final rule until some time in 1977.

There is considerable criticism of the FASB's failure to act more quickly, but Vice Chairman Robert Sprouse defends the FASB's deliberate approach: "The SEC proposal provides few guidelines on how replacement-cost data is to be determined. It is really a very fuzzy sort of thing. I am also concerned about the partial nature of the disclosure. We're not in a position to do that. Our pronouncements become part of Generally Accepted Accounting Principles."

Slow But Steady

In other words, the FASB must come up with rules for a fully articulated set of financial statements. It cannot duck the issue of monetary items simply because it is a difficult issue. It cannot be vague on what it wants and how data is to be developed. It must be precise because, unlike the SEC's proposal, disclosure under its rules would have to be audited. Such precision takes time.

Some companies, General Electric and J.C. Penney among them, would prefer a period of experimentation before *requiring* disclosure. At least one accounting firm agrees. In January Touche Ross & Co. began a nationwide effort to get companies to experiment with all aspects of current-value accounting, and has suggested procedures to provide a fully articulated set of financial statements. "We feel that there are tremendous distortions in current financial statements," says TR partner Tom Porter. "Historical-cost figures may be objective and easy to get, but in an inflationary period, they are no longer relevant."

What seems clear is that requiring the disclosure of piecemeal data is both misleading and expensive. For the SEC to *require* partial disclosure now seems an unnecessary burden to place on companies, especially when they might have to change their systems again to comply with a future FASB ruling. A hastily devised and partial stopgap measure like the SEC proposal merely adds one more expensive regulation to an already over-bureaucratized business environment.

Don't get us wrong. We're not against letting investors know the facts, but we *are* against rushing into anything this important on an incomplete basis. Sure, inflation hurts most businesses, but it also helps them in some ways. A system that deals only with the hurt and not with the benefit may be worse than no system at all. ∎

Replacement Cost Accounting: Another Answer*

In this article the author analyzes the effects of historical cost, general purchasing power and replacement cost accounting by creating financial statements for a simple business entity.

John M. Lacey, CPA, received his MBA and BS degrees from the University of Southern California. This article was written while he was research assistant to the National Accounting and Auditing Partner of Laventhol & Horwath, Los Angeles. He is currently pursuing a Ph.D. degree in Accounting at the Graduate School of Business, Stanford University.†

While the dollar's purchasing power has been eroding through inflation, accountants have continued to report financial information in terms of historical cost. Recently, however, in the face of an increasing rate of inflation, the Financial Accounting Standards Board (FASB) and the Securities and Exchange Commission (SEC) have proposed standards to disclose the effects of inflation upon financial statements.

The topic of inflation is not new to the accounting profession. Since 1947 authoritative pronouncements have included references to its impact.[1] More recently, Accounting Principles Board (APB) Statement No. 3 recommended, but did not require, that companies issue general price-level financial statements as supplementary information. On December 31, 1974 the FASB issued an exposure draft[2] of a proposed standard which would, if it becomes effective, *require* disclosure of general purchasing power (general price-level) information in financial statements prepared in conformity with generally accepted accounting principles.

The inclusion of general pur-

chasing power information in the category of required financial disclosure represents a major change in financial reporting that will affect all users of financial statements. Currently, several companies are preparing general purchasing power statements on a trial basis. The results of these trials, along with the comments received by the FASB before the close of the comment period on September 30, 1975, will likely influence the FASB's final position. If the FASB statement is adopted as proposed, it will be effective for fiscal years commencing on or after January 1, 1976.

The SEC favors limited replacement cost disclosures as a method of showing the effects of inflation. The Commission has proposed that footnote disclosure be made of the cost to replace inventory and productive assets, and that cost of sales and depreciation, depletion or amortization be calculated using replacement costs. The proposal does not call for additional financial statements or changes in the presentation of net income.

The results of reporting on a basis of Historical Cost, General Purchasing Power and Replacement Cost in a period of rising prices are compared here in simple examples.

How Does Inflation Affect the Financial Statements?

Consider Corner Candy Store which buys and sells only candy bars and has only assets of cash, accounts receivable, inventory and a cash box. (The historical basis income statement and balance sheet of Corner Candy Store for Years 1, 2 and 3 are shown in Exhibit 1.) The

---

* *Editor's Note.* See this issue's Auditing and Reporting department for an article by Professor Donald F. Arnold on other aspects of this subject.

† The author wishes to express his gratitude to Robert Richter, partner, Laventhol & Horwath, Philadelphia, for his helpful comments and counsel.

[1] See Accounting Research Bulletin No. 43, Chapter 9A "Depreciation and High Costs" (originally issued as ARB 33 in 1947). See also Accounting Research Study No. 6, "Reporting the Financial Effects of Price-Level Changes."

[2] "Financial Reporting in Units of General Purchasing Power," FASB, December 31, 1974. Copies of this exposure draft and the discussion memorandum entitled "Reporting the Effects of General Price-Level Changes in Financial Statements" are available from the Financial Accounting Standards Board.

cpa / MARCH 1976

EXHIBIT 1
Corner Candy Store
Income Statements (Historical Cost)
Year Ended 12/31/Year 1, 2 and 3

	December 31, Year 1	December 31, Year 2	December 31, Year 3
Sales	$20.00	$30.00	$30.00
Cost of goods sold	10.00	10.00	20.00
Gross profit	10.00	20.00	10.00
Depreciation	5.00	5.00	5.00
Net income before tax	5.00	15.00	5.00
Income tax expense	2.50	7.50	2.50
Net income	$2.50	$7.50	$2.50

Corner Candy Store
Balance Sheets (Historical Cost)

	January 1, Year 1	December 31, Year 1	December 31, Year 2	December 31, Year 3
Cash	$0.00	$2.50	$5.00	$12.50
Accounts receivable	0.00	5.00	5.00	5.00
Inventory (200 candy bars)	10.00	10.00	20.00	20.00
Equipment (cash box)	15.00	15.00	15.00	15.00
Less: Accumulated depreciation	0.00	5.00	10.00	15.00
Net	15.00	10.00	5.00	0.00
Total assets	$25.00	$27.50	$35.00	$37.50
Liabilities	$5.00	$5.00	$5.00	$5.00
Owners equity	20.00	22.50	30.00	32.50
Total liabilities and owners' equity	$25.00	$27.50	$35.00	$37.50

candy store keeps 200 candy bars in inventory and sells exactly that many bars each year. When the store opened, 200 candy bars were purchased for 5¢ each in anticipation of selling the bars for 10¢ each. During Year 1 the 200 bars were sold for 10¢ each ($20). After deducting the $10 cost of the candy bars sold, $5 of depreciation (which results from depreciating the cash box over a three-year life) and income tax expense of $2.50 (at an assumed 50 percent rate), net income for Year 1 is $2.50. During Year 1 the stock was replenished at a cost of $10.

On January 1, Year 2, a wholesale price increase of 5¢ was announced by candy bar manufacturers, raising the cost to 10¢ each and the retail price of all bars was increased by 5¢ to make the new selling price 15¢ per bar. During Year 2 the candy store sold for 15¢ the candy bars which it had purchased for 5¢, so an extra profit of 5¢ each, or $10, was earned on the bars purchased during Year 1 and sold during Year 2. Sales increased to $30 in Year 2 while the cost of the bars sold was $10. After deducting depreciation, the cost of the

bars and taxes, the net income was $7.50 for Year 2. During Year 2 the inventory was replenished with candy bars which cost 10¢ each, or $20 in total.

In Year 3 the candy store sold for 15¢ each the candy bars bought for 10¢ each in Year 2, returning to the normal 5¢ gain on the sale of each candy bar. Sales for the year totaled $30 while the cost of the candy bars sold increased to $20. After deducting depreciation and taxes, the net income for Year 3 was $2.50, the same as the amount earned in Year 1.

How much better off is the Corner Candy Store after three years of profitable operations? The inventory account has doubled, but the number of candy bars which it owns remains the same. The store has $12.50 in cash and $5 in accounts receivable that it did not have on January 1 of Year 1, but how about that fully-depreciated cash box? Its three-year life has expired and if the store is to remain in business it needs to be replaced. A cash box cost $15 at the beginning of Year 1, but with inflation it will cost $20 to replace at the end of Year 3. Where will the $20 come

from? There is $12.50 in cash in the business and, even if the $5 of accounts receivable could be collected immediately, that still means that the owner will need to invest an additional $2.50 to buy the new cash box.

Did Corner Candy Store really earn a profit during the three-year period if the owner must invest an additional $2.50 just to maintain the original asset base of 200 candy bars and a cash box?

How Would the Operations Be Reported Using General Purchasing Power Accounting?

General Purchasing Power (GPP) accounting adjusts the historical cost financial statements to reflect changes in the general purchasing power of the dollar. A general purchasing power index (the Gross National Product Implicit Price Deflator) is used to make the adjustments.

In GPP accounting a distinction is made between monetary and nonmonetary assets and liabilities. Monetary assets are cash and claims to specific amounts of cash which do not change regardless of the change in the price level, such as notes and accounts receivables. Monetary liabilities are debts to be repaid in a specified amount regardless of the change in the specific price level, such as accounts payable and notes payable.

How are the holders of monetary assets and liabilities affected by inflation? Consider the example of a child who is saving allowance money to buy candy bars. If the price of candy bars is 10¢ and the child has saved $3, the child's purchasing power is 30 candy bars. When the price of candy bars increases to 15¢, the purchasing power of the child's $3 falls to 20 candy bars. It is clear that a price rise in the intended purchase causes a loss in purchasing power to the holder of cash. Similarly, the purchasing power loss realized by a holder of receivables can be demonstrated by a situation in which the child loans $3 to a friend when the price of candy bars was 10¢ and is repaid when the price has risen to 15¢. The child loaned purchasing power of 30 candy bars and is repaid the power to purchase only 20.

REPLACEMENT COST ACCOUNTING: ANOTHER ANSWER / THE CPA

The friend enjoys the benefit which accrues to debtors in a time of inflation, by borrowing purchasing power of 30 candy bars and repaying purchasing power of 20.

Rather than considering the changes in specific prices, GPP accounting measures changes in the general purchasing power. The FASB has proposed that the Gross National Product Implicit Price Deflator (GNPIPD) is to be used to measure the change in general purchasing power of the dollar.

Holders of nonmonetary assets and liabilities (all assets and liabilities other than monetary) are not necessarily affected by a change in the purchasing power of the dollar, since the value of those assets may fluctuate along with the change in general purchasing power.

In GPP financial statements, monetary assets are not restated since they already reflect current purchasing power. Nonmonetary assets and liabilities are reported at historical cost adjusted by the change in the GNPIPD. For example, an asset purchased for $10 when the GNPIPD was 100 would be reported at purchasing power of $12 in a period when the GNPIPD had risen to 120 (120/100 × $10.00 = $12.00). In this manner all amounts are presented in current purchasing power. Gains and losses are measured for changes in the purchasing power of monetary assets and liabilities.

Consider again the Corner Candy Store example presented previously. Assume for purposes of this example that the GNPIPD is:

Beginning of Year 1	100
End of Year 1	110
End of Year 2	120
End of Year 3	130

Assume also that the change in the GNPIPD is uniform throughout the year (for example, the average GNPIPD for Year 1 would be equal to 105), and that sales occur uniformly throughout the year. Using these GNPIPD numbers and the Historical Cost financial statements in Exhibit 1, GPP financial statements can be created.

The first step in creating GPP financial statements is to restate the income statement items to a GPP basis. Since sales are made uni-formly throughout the year, the ratio of the end-of-the-year GNPIPD and the average GNPIPD is applied to the sales to compute the amount of sales in terms of purchasing power at the end of the year. For Corner Candy Store for Year 1, the computation is as follows: Sales = (110/105 = 1.0476) × $20.00 = $20.96. This is the amount used for sales in the Year 1 GPP income statement (see Exhibit 2).

The next computation is cost of goods sold. Although only one number is listed on the income statement, three calculations are required. First, beginning inventory must be restated from beginning of the year dollars to end-of-the-year dollars using the ratio 110/100 = 1.10, then purchases and ending inventory are restated with the same factor used above for sales.

Beginning Inventory	10.00 × 1.1.0	=	$11.00
Purchases	10.00 × 1.0476	=	10.48
Goods Available for Sale			21.48
Less: Ending Inventory	10.00 × 1.0476	=	10.48
Cost of Goods Sold			$11.00

Depreciation expense is calculated by computing the ratio of the current GNPIPD to the GNPIPD at the time of purchase of the depreciable asset and multiplying the result times the historical depreciation. The depreciation for Year 1 is: Depreciation expense = (110/100 = 1.10) × $5.00 = $5.50.

EXHIBIT 2
Corner Candy Store
Income Statements (General Purchasing Power) for Years Ended

Year 1
(End of Year 1 dollars)

	December 31, Year 1
Sales	$20.96
Cost of goods sold	11.00
Gross profit	9.96
Depreciation	5.50
Income before GPP gain or loss	4.46
GPP gain	.14
Income after GPP gain	4.60
Income tax expense	2.62
	$1.98

Year 2
(End of Year 2 dollars)

	December 31, Year 1	December 31, Year 2
Sales	$22.87	$31.31
Cost of goods sold	12.00	11.43
Gross profit	10.87	19.88
Depreciation	6.00	6.00
Income before GPP gain or loss	4.87	13.88
GPP gain or (loss)	.15	(.34)
Income after GPP gain or loss	5.02	13.54
Income tax expense	2.86	7.83
Net income	$2.16	$5.71

Year 3
(End of Year 3 dollars)

	December 31, Year 1	December 31, Year 2	December 31, Year 3
Sales	$24.77	$33.91	$31.20
Cost of goods sold	13.00	12.38	22.60
Gross profit	11.77	21.53	8.60
Depreciation	6.50	6.50	6.50
Income before GPP gain or loss	5.27	15.03	2.10
GPP gain or (loss)	.16	(.37)	(.72)
Income after GPP gain or loss	5.43	14.66	1.38
Income tax expense	3.10	8.48	2.60
Net income	$2.33	$6.18	$(1.22)

Computation of the GPP gain or loss is somewhat more complex. As discussed previously, with inflation, holders of monetary assets lose purchasing power while debtors gain. The computation of this gain or loss is shown in Exhibit 3.[3]

The last item on the income statement is income tax expense. Since income tax expense accrues uniformly throughout the year, the computation is: Income tax expense = (110/105 = 1.0476) × $2.50 = $2.62.

The result of these restatements is to report a GPP net income of $1.98 as compared to the $2.50 net income in the historical income statement for Year 1.

Similar adjustments are made to the historical balance sheet to create a GPP balance sheet. Monetary items on the balance sheet are not adjusted because the monetary items are already stated in terms of end-of-the-year purchasing power. The amounts reported for cash, accounts receivable and liabilities for Corner Candy Store are the same for the GPP and historical financial statements.

Because inventory is acquired throughout the year, its cost is adjusted by the ratio of the end of the year GNPIPD and the average GNPIPD: Inventory = 110/105 = 1.0476 × $10.00 = $10.48.

Equipment and accumulated depreciation are adjusted using the ratio of current GNPIPD and the GNPIPD at the time of purchase of equipment: Equipment = 110/100 × $15.00 = $16.50; Accumulated depreciation = 110/100 × $5.00 = $5.50.

Restating owners' equity requires a separate computation for invested capital and earnings. For Corner Candy Store, the investment portion is restated by applying the end-of-the-year GNPIPD: Owners' investment = (110/100 = 1.10) × $20.00 = $22.00.

Since the net income amount is already stated in end-of-Year 1 dollars on the GPP income statement, that amount can be transferred directly to the GPP balance sheet. This results in total GPP owners' equity of $23.98 at the end of Year

[3] See Meigs, Mosich, Johnson and Keller, *Intermediate Accounting*, New York: McGraw-Hill, 1973, for a good explanation of computing GPP gain or loss.

EXHIBIT 2—*Continued*
Balance Sheet (General Purchasing Power)

Year 1
(End of Year 1 dollars)

	December 31, Year 1
Cash	$2.50
Accounts receivable	5.00
Inventory	10.48
Equipment	16.50
Less: Accumulated depreciation	5.50
Net	11.00
Total assets	$28.98
Liabilities	$5.00
Owners' equity:	
Original investment	22.00
Net income	1.98
Total owners' equity	23.98
Total liabilities and owners' equity	$28.98

Year 2
(End of Year 2 dollars)

	December 31, Year 1	December 31, Year 2
Cash	$2.73	$5.00
Accounts receivable	5.46	5.00
Inventory	11.43	20.87
Equipment	18.00	18.00
Less: Accumulated depreciation	6.00	12.00
Net	12.00	6.00
Total assets	$31.62	$36.87
Liabilities	$5.46	$5.00
Owners' equity:		
Original investment	24.00	24.00
Net income, year 1	2.16	2.16
year 2		5.71
Total owners' equity	26.16	31.87
Total liabilities and owners' equity	$31.62	$36.87

Year 3
(End of Year 3 dollars)

	December 31, Year 1	December 31, Year 2	December 31, Year 3
Cash	$2.96	$5.42	$12.50
Accounts receivable	5.91	5.42	5.00
Inventory	12.38	22.60	20.80
Equipment	19.50	19.50	19.50
Less: Accumulated depreciation	6.50	13.00	19.50
Net	13.00	6.50	0.008
Total assets	$34.25	$39.94	$38.30
Liabilities	$5.91	$5.42	$5.00
Owners' equity:			
Original investment	26.00	26.00	26.00
Net income, Year 1	2.34	2.34	2.34
Year 2		6.18	6.18
Year 3			(1.22)
Total owners' equity	28.34	34.52	33.30
Total liabilities and owners' equity	$34.25	$39.94	$38.30

1 as compared to owners' equity on historical financial statements of $22.50.

Similar adjustments have been made to the historical financial statements for Year 2 and Year 3 to create GPP financial statements for those years.

REPLACEMENT COST ACCOUNTING: ANOTHER ANSWER /

EXHIBIT 3
Computation of GPP Gain or Loss

	Year 1			Year 2			Year 3		
	Histori-cal	Conver-sion Factor	Restated to 12/31/ Yr. 1 Dollars	Histori-cal	Conver-sion Factor	Restated to 12/31/ Yr. 2 Dollars	Histori-cal	Conver-sion Factor	Restated to 12/31/ Yr. 3 Dollars
Monetary assets and liabilities at beginning of period:									
Monetary assets	-0-			7.50			10.00		
Less: Monetary liabilities	(5.00)			5.00			5.00		
Net monetary assets	(5.00)	× 1.1000	(5.50)	2.50	× 1.0910	2.73	5.00	1.0830	5.42
Sources of monetary assets:									
Sales	20.00	× 1.0476	20.96	30.00	× 1.0435	31.31	30.00	1.0400	31.20
	15.00		15.46	32.50		34.04	35.00		36.62
Uses:									
Purchase	10.00	× 1.0476	10.48	20.00	× 1.0435	20.87	20.00	× 1.0400	20.80
Income tax	2.50	× 1.0476	2.62	7.50	× 1.0435	7.83	2.50	× 1.0400	2.60
Total uses	12.50		13.10	27.50		28.70	22.50		23.40
Net monetary items at end of year	2.50			5.00			12.50		
Restated net monetary items	2.36		←2.36	5.34		←5.34	13.22		←13.22
GPP gain or (loss)	.14			(.34)			(.72)		

For comparative GPP financial statements, previous years must be restated to purchasing power at the date of the latest balance sheet presented. Therefore, all items on the GPP income statement and balance sheet for Year 1 have been adjusted when presented as a comparative statement in Year 2 or Year 3, and Year 2 financial statements have been adjusted when presented as a comparative statement in Year 3. The restatement factors were computed as follows: Year 1 presented in Year 2, 120/110 = 1.091; Year 1 presented in Year 3, 130/110 = 1.182; Year 2 presented in Year 3, 130/120 = 1.083.

Net income reported in GPP amounts would be lower than historical cost net income as follows:

		GPP	
	Historical	As re-ported for each year	In Year 3 pur-chasing power
Year 1	$2.50	$1.98	$2.33
Year 2	7.50	5.71	6.18
Year 3	2.50	(1.22)	(1.22)

Is There Another Method of Accounting for the Effects of Inflation?

GPP accounting shows the effect on the business enterprise of the change in the general purchas-ing power of the dollar. GPP finan-cial statements do *not*, however, show the effect of changes in re-placement cost of the specific goods and services bought and sold by a company, nor do they show the effect of changes in the replacement cost of the assets held by the company.

The effects of changes in the replacement cost may be shown in Replacement Cost (RC) financial statements.[4] The following addi-tional information about the change in replacement cost of the cash box is required to apply this method to the Corner Candy Store example:

Date	Replacement Cost
Beginning of Year 1	$15.00
End of Year 1	16.00
End of Year 2	18.00
End of Year 3	20.00

Replacement Cost financial statements for Corner Candy Store are shown in Exhibit 4 The differ-ences between Replacement Cost financial statements and Historical Cost financial statements lie primar ily in the change in replacement cost of inventory and depreciable

---

[4] Replacement Cost accounting is fre-quently called Fair Value accounting. The term *replacement cost* is used to differentiate this method from others which are also re-ferred to under the more general term *fair value*. The specific method illustrated in this article is proposed by the author.

assets The Year 1 Replacement Cost income statement for Corner Candy Store shows depreciation at $5.33 instead of $5 as on the histori-cal income statement. The Replace-ment Cost depreciation is based upon the replacement cost of the cash box at the end of Year 1: ($16.00/3 = $5.33). The additional depreciation of 33¢ reduces Year 1 net income from $2.50 on a Histori-cal Cost basis to $2.17 on a Re-placement Cost basis.

The Replacement Cost balance sheet shows the equipment account and accumulated depreciation ac-counts at replacement cost. The Re-placement Cost retained earnings balance is lower because the Re-placement Cost net income is lower.

A special account has been es-tablished entitled "unrealized asset increase due to replacement cost valuation." In the example, the $1 balance in this account at the end of Year 1 is due to the increase in the replacement cost of the cash box from $15 to $16. This increase in asset amount is credited directly to this account, *not* to income. This account helps to identify the capital which will be required to finance the increased replacement cost of the company's asset base.

The $4.17 loss reported in the Replacement Cost income state-ment for Year 2 is a dramatically different result from the net income of $7.50 reported in the historical statement for the same period. The

THE CPA JOURNAL / MARCH 1976

EXHIBIT 4
Corner Candy Store

Income Statements (Replacement Cost)
For Years Ended

	December 31, Year 1	December 31, Year 2	December 31, Year 3
Sales	$20.00	$30.00	$30.00
Cost of goods sold	10.00	20.00	20.00
Gross profit	10.00	10.00	10.00
Depreciation	5.33	6.00	6.67
Operating income	4.67	4.00	3.33
Adjustment of prior years depreciation caused by increase in replacement cost of depreciable assets	0.00	(.67)	(1.33)
Income before tax		3.33	2.00
Income tax expense	2.50	7.50	2.50
Net income (loss)	$2.17	$(4.17)	$(.50)

Balance Sheets (Replacement Cost)

	December 31, Year 1	December 31, Year 2	December 31, Year 3
Cash	$2.50	$5.00	$12.50
Accounts receivable	5.00	5.00	5.00
Inventory	10.00	20.00	20.00
Equipment	16.00	18.00	20.00
Less Accumulated depreciation	5.33	12.00	20.00
Net	10.67	6.00	0.00
Total assets	$28.17	$36.00	$37.50
Liabilities:	5.00	5.00	5.00
Owners' equity:			
Original investment	20.00	20.00	20.00
Net income (loss) Year 1	2.17	2.17	2.17
Year 2		(4.17)	(4.17)
Year 3			(.50)
Total owner's equity	22.17	18.00	17.50
Unrealized appreciation due to replacement cost valuation	1.00	13.00	15.00
Total liabilities, owners' equity and increased replacement costs	$28.17	$36.00	$37.50

difference is caused by reporting a greater amount for cost of goods sold and depreciation. Cost of goods sold is reported at $20 instead of the $10 historical amount because the current replacement cost of candy bars during the year was 10¢ each, or a total of $20 for the 200 candy bars sold. The Replacement Cost depreciation expense for the current year, $6, is based upon the current replacement cost ($18.00/3 yrs. = $6.00). The separate line item in the Replacement Cost income statement is titled "adjustment of prior years depreciation caused by increased replacement cost of depreciable assets" results from the effect of the increased replacement cost on the

adequacy of the balance of the accumulated depreciation account. Based upon the new replacement cost of $18 and the life of the asset which has expired, the accumulated depreciation balance should be $6 (1/3 × $18.00 = $6.00). The "adjustment of prior years" Replacement Cost income statement amount is computed by subtracting the balance of the accumulated depreciation account as reported in the previous year's Replacement Cost balance sheet ($5.33) from the balance that should be reported based upon the current replacement cost of assets ($6). The Replacement Cost income statement amount is, therefore, 67¢ ($6.00 − $5.33 = 67¢).

The cause of this 67¢ charge is the increase in the replacement cost of the asset which took place in Year 2, so the 67¢ should be charged against income in Year 2. The 67¢ charge does not, however, have the characteristics of depreciation expense. Depreciation expense is a systematic allocation of cost (or in this case replacement cost) of the asset to periods during which the life of the asset expires. The 67¢ amount results from the effects of current replacement cost changes on the adequacy of depreciation charged in *previous* years and is unrelated to the asset life expiration of the current year. It is, therefore, included in the income statement as a separate charge.

The Replacement Cost income statement for Year 3 shows a loss of 50¢ compared to the historical net income of $2.50. The difference results from additional depreciation based upon the increased replacement cost of the asset and the adjustment of prior years' depreciation.

Examining the trend of earnings, it is obvious that the critical problem occurred in Year 2. In that year the sale of old cost inventory at the new, higher price caused a taxable profit. This "profit," which was required to replace old inventories with new, higher cost inventory, was reduced by 50 percent because of income taxes. (Similarly, the income required to replace the depreciable assets at the new, higher replacement cost was reduced by taxes in all three years.)

Comparison of the Effect of Each Method

The net income of the Corner Candy Store as reported under the three methods is shown below:

	Historical	GPP	RC
Year 1	$2.50	$2.33	$2.17
Year 2	7.50	6.18	(4.17)
Year 3	2.50	(1.22)	(.50)
Total	$12.50	$7.29	$(2.50)

Which method best exhibits the economic progress of Corner Candy Store? The historical statements report what appears to be economic progress when inflation has caused the store owner's economic position to regress.

The GPP information shows profits in the first two years and a loss in the third. This method, like Historical Cost, appears to indicate overall economic progress, but with a negative trend in earnings.

Replacement Cost accounting, on the other hand, shows a profit only in the first year, followed by losses which result in a reduction in owners' equity of $2.50 during the three-year period. This reduction of $2.50 in owners' equity coincides with the earlier calculation of the additional investment which the owner will be required to make. The earnings reflect the initial economic progress and the subsequent economic regress caused by rising prices.

Conclusion

The example presented shows that inflation can have a significant impact upon financial statements. A comparison of financial statements prepared on Historical Cost, General Purchasing Power and Replacement Cost basis for a simple entity indicates that, for the example presented, replacement cost accounting appears to best report the economic progress of the business. It is recognized that this simplified example does not deal with the many difficult problems of meas-

urement and evaluation which are inherent in replacement accounting. Nevertheless, it illustrates the differences in the basic concepts of income determination.

Both GPP accounting and Replacement Cost accounting have been proposed as solutions to the general problem of financial reporting in times of inflation. Since it appears from the example that Replacement Cost accounting may be the better answer to this general problem in some circumstances, it seems important that the FASB give this method serious study before adopting the proposed statement entitled "Financial Reporting in Units of General Purchasing Power." Ω

Frank T. Weston, CPA

Accounting for Inflation

This article analyzes various proposals for dealing with the impact of inflation on financial reporting and expresses some conclusions about possible future developments in this area.

Frank T. Weston, CPA, is a partner of Arthur Young & Company. He is a graduate of Dartmouth College and Columbia Graduate School of Business. He served seven years on the Accounting Principles Board and was a member of the AICPA study group on objectives of accounting. Recently, he has been visiting professor at the Graduate School of Business at Harvard University.

The impact of inflation on a family's lifestyle is well-known to every housewife in this country. In the business, professional, academic, and governmental communities few other subjects have received more attention during the past year. As the period for exposure of the accounting standard proposed by the Financial Accounting Standards Board draws to a close, interest will heighten.

The Problem

In any discussion of inflation accounting it is important to understand the nature of the problem. Much of the opposition to proposed methods of dealing with inflation in accounting appears to result from a lack of understanding of various facets of this particular problem and of related problems.

First for a definition: *Inflation* is generally considered to represent the decline in the purchasing power of money (in this case, the dollar); the diminution in its command over goods and services over time.

Financial accounting measurements and financial statements are expressed in dollars. There is an implicit assumption in these processes that the value of the measuring unit, the dollar, is stable over time. Otherwise, accounting for long-lived assets and comparing of results for different time periods would be nonsensical.

Given these conditions, it is not difficult to understand the problems for financial accounting and reporting caused by inflation. In periods of inflation the important assumption as to the stability of the measuring unit is not valid. Accordingly, financial accounting data stated in historical dollars do not adequately reflect revenues and expenses and resources and obligations during or after periods of inflation. (A similar effect is also caused by deflation, but this article will focus on inflation.) Important financial ratios based on such financial statements are affected, as are conclusions concerning trends.

In short, the inherent usefulness of financial statements is seriously impaired by the impact of inflation, unless corrective reporting measures are taken.

The Consequences

Consider the consequences of inflation. Management decisions on the pricing of products or services, new or expanded investments in operating property or income producing ventures, labor remuneration, dividend policies, and a host of others, are affected because the data on which management relies do not adequately measure what they purport to measure. Operating results measured by combining dollars of widely different purchasing power—say, 1945 dollars and 1975 dollars—are materially misstated and probably misleading.

Investor decisions regarding debt and equity securities are affected. Debt investors may be misled by the apparent high rate of interest being offered, without realizing that when the debt is repaid they will receive dollars of much less purchasing power than those they loaned. Furthermore, the operating results and other data such as "times interest earned" may be misleading unless adjusted for the impact of inflation. Equity investors will likewise be misled as they view such ratios as return on investment and dividend payout and such trend data as increases in earnings per share, revenues, and net income.

On a broader scale, government decisions are also affected. The manner in which the income tax burden is shared among corporations and individuals is modified invisibly during periods of inflation. Regulatory agencies involved in the setting of rates for utility-type monopolies may be misled by unadjusted data. The consequences are widespread and serious.

On a still broader scale, the effectiveness of the allocation of capital resources among industries and companies may be affected. This is particularly unsatisfactory from a socioeconomic point of view because one of the main functions of the financial accounting and reporting process is to furnish reliable and useful information to investors and others for the purpose of achieving an efficient allocation of capital resources.

The Proposed Solutions

Preliminary Considerations. A number of solutions have been proposed for accounting in an inflationary era. Before discussing the proposed solutions, it is important not only to understand the problem but also to distinguish it from other problems that may appear similar. First, we must keep in mind the definition of inflation previously given. It is a historical phenomenon. Second, we must realize that prices of individual items may rise or fall due to conditions other than inflation, such as supply and demand, and that the rates of these changes will often differ from the rate of inflation. Further, we must realize that investors are interested in future earnings and that financial data which are basically historical in nature may not be useful in forecasting results of future operations. Earnings forecasts must consider the rates of future inflation as well as the rates at which the prices of specific items will rise or fall in relation to other items.

Two other thoughts are appropriate here. First, there is a danger in attempting to adopt measures to solve all the above problems at once. They have different causes and are different in nature. Second, there are limitations on the nature and extent of the changes which can be made in the financial accounting and reporting process in a short time. Major changes should be made one at a time. Determining the priority of such changes is an important exercise.

Heeding this cautionary advice, let us examine some of the solutions which currently find some favor in the financial community.

Price-Level-Adjusted Financial Statements

This proposed solution to the reporting problems caused by inflation has been on the scene for a number of years. It is currently under intensive study in this country, as well as in Canada and the United Kingdom. The exposure draft, "Financial Reporting in Units of General Purchasing Power," issued for comment by the Financial Accounting Standards Board in December 1974 is based largely on the statement of the Accounting Principles Board "Financial Statements Restated for General Price-Level Changes," issued in recommendation form (i.e., not as a required standard) by the APB in June 1969. A great deal of experimentation is currently being conducted to apply the provisions of the exposure draft and to assess the usefulness of the resulting data. This is obviously a major educational and technical effort.

The method consists of two interacting techniques whose purpose is to express financial statements at a date and for periods ended that date in dollars of current purchasing power. One technique relates to the restatement at year-end of "nonmonetary items" to reflect the amount of purchasing power expended in their acquisition. This is an upward restatement during (and after) periods of inflation. These assets, such as property, plant, and equipment, are still stated at cost, but in cost stated in dollars of the reduced purchasing power at the closing balance sheet date. "Monetary items" (e.g., cash, accounts receivable, accounts payable, long-term debt), whose claim is in dollars of current purchasing power, need not be restated at the balance sheet date.

The second technique is to restate or "roll forward" the balance sheet at the beginning of the year (which has been previously adjusted as explained) into dollars of purchasing power at the end of the current year. This is a mechanical process, based on the ratio of the price indices at the beginning and the end of the year.

The result is a set of comparative financial statements

expressed entirely in dollars of common purchasing power. As a result of the restatement of the monetary items at the beginning of the year into dollars of year-end purchasing power, a new item is introduced into the income statement, "general price-level gain or loss." This is the increase or decrease in purchasing power, expressed in year-end dollars, resulting from holding monetary items during a period of inflation (or deflation).

There are problem areas in the above process, some of which are treatment of deferred income taxes, treatment of preferred stock, particularly those issues with redemption requirements, and treatment of resources, obligations, and operations overseas. Experience during the testing period should suggest appropriate solutions for each of these problem areas.

Will the resulting data be useful? It seems obvious that price-level-adjusted financial data will be more useful to certain parties than will unadjusted data. Management should benefit by obtaining results expressed in a stable measuring unit. Trends and comparisons with prior periods will be more informative, being more soundly based. Conclusions drawn from such data will be based on a proper recording of the underlying transactions, not on measurements with a flexible unit, the effects of which are not disclosed. Management will have a precise measure of the impact of inflation on its operations.

Other users of the data will also benefit. Investors will be in a much better position to compare results of industries and of companies within industries when their results are measured in constant dollars. The "real" ratios and other relationships can be assessed. Also, investors can consider the effectiveness of various managements in countering the effects of inflation, to the extent deemed feasible in view of operating and other restraints. With this type of information available on a wide scale, government can begin to assess the impacts of inflation and can consider whether present taxing allocations and other regulatory positions are logical and equitable. The broad process of allocating resources to competing investments should be improved when financial statements reflect the results of operations in a common counter, and the effects of inflation are clearly segregated and displayed.

We must, of course, realize what price-level-adjusted statements do *not* do. They do not introduce current value information into the financial accounting and reporting process. They do not insure that management will be able to counteract the effects of inflation, since other factors may have a greater bearing on the decisions that must be made to keep the business operating. They also do not necessarily match current replacement costs with sales during the period, nor do they purport to forecast the rate of future inflation, replacement costs, or gross margins. They do, however, eliminate the effects of inflation on the measurement process and thus furnish valuable information to investors, management, and government.

LIFO Method of Inventory Accounting

This method of inventory accounting is sometimes proposed as a partial solution to the problems of inflation reporting. Under this method income is charged with the costs of products most recently purchased or produced, regardless of the physical flow. The amounts shown in the balance sheets thus represent costs incurred at lower cost levels (in times of inflation).

Are financial statements which reflect inventories in the balance sheet at costs incurred many years previously and cost of products sold at the latest incurred costs useful? The understatement of the balance sheet amount for inventories certainly makes for a misleading presentation of "financial position" under any justifiable criterion. Whether the income statement offers compensating advantages is an open question. From a management point of view, since the usual way of applying the method is to compute inventories on a first-in, first-out or average

method and then to convert to the LIFO method, the amount of the difference in method can be identified and evaluated. Whether this information is useful is another matter. Presumably, every management closely monitors current cost data in setting prices and is aware of the necessity of maintaining a sufficient margin to insure replacement of quantities sold. The LIFO method does not, of course, segregate the effects of inflation, and therefore management must wrestle with the question of how much of the LIFO adjustment is a matter of inflation (or loss of purchasing power of the measuring unit) and how much is due to price changes peculiar to the products being purchased. This is a disadvantage of LIFO.

Use of the LIFO method might be considered indirectly helpful to investors in that it reduces income taxes and increases cash flow as compared with other inventory methods. However, a number of very complex problems are involved in the use of the method. This is particularly true for interim periods when prices, price levels, and quantities fluctuate. All things considered, its main advantage is the reduction in income taxes.

NIFO Method of Inventory Accounting

The NIFO, next-in, first-out, method of inventory accounting is also sometimes proposed as a partial solution to the problems of accounting for inflation. Under this method income is charged with the costs of currently replacing the products sold. The method may be applied in two ways—through supplemental disclosure or through formal reflection in the financial statements.

The Disclosure Method. The disclosure method has received quite a bit of attention in recent months, first as a means of reporting so-called "inventory profits," and later in more formal proposals, in each case by the Securities and Exchange Commission. In Accounting Series Release No. 151, issued on January 3, 1974, the Commission urged companies to make disclosure of inventory profits, which it defined

as the result of holding inventories during a period of rising inventory costs, to be measured by the difference between the historical cost of an item and its replacement cost at the time it is sold. The release points out the obvious—that such profits are "not normally repeatable in the absence of continued price-level increase." The release states: "The Commission therefore believes that it would be in the best interest of both statement preparers and users to disclose the extent to which reported earnings are comprised of potentially unrepeatable and usually unsegregated 'inventory profits'." The Commission also recognizes that such a disclosure might be misleading: "If a company is able to raise selling prices immediately upon realizing cost increases (or in anticipation of cost increases), its net income in dollar terms benefits from inflation." Therefore, the release urges companies to discuss the relationship of costs and prices experienced in the current year in connection with disclosing inventory profits.

The Financial Statement Method. The other approach under NIFO is to introduce replacement cost data for all resources and obligations into the financial statements. Thus, the balance sheet would reflect amounts for inventories computed on a replacement cost basis, as well as for other assets, such as property, plant, and equipment. Changes in the replacement costs of such items would be shown as an element of income or changes in stockholders' equity, depending on the approach taken. Cost of products sold could be based on replacement cost, with the excess over historical cost shown separately, or on historical costs. Replacement cost is a partial step toward introducing current values for all items in the financial statements, discussed below.

Limitations of NIFO Method. In spite of the views of the Commission outlined above, neither replacement inventory cost disclosures nor full replacement cost accounting for all items will segregate or identify the effects of inflation. The results under these methods will do so only in the unlikely event that the rate of inflation coincides (exactly) with the rate of price increase for the products and services purchased by the company. To claim that disclosure of "inventory profits" will show the effects of inflation indicates a misunderstanding of some of the fundamentals of the accounting process or of the proper definition of inflation. Use of replacement accounting during a period of inflation for this purpose is misleading. The result combines the effects of inflation—changes in the purchasing power of the dollar—with the effects of unrelated price changes in specific items. Thus, the results are a complex mixture of data which the reader may well find hard to understand.

As the release correctly points out, however, the important fact for the investor is to understand how much of the increase in earnings is due to inflation—which price-level-adjusted statements would reveal—and how much is due to inventory turnover and cost and pricing mechanics. Segregating these elements would, hopefully, help the investor to forecast the changes which might occur in the future in these two quite different elements. Consideration of recent experiences in industries such as oil and gas, sugar, and real estate will quickly indicate the difference between inflation and the movement of prices of specific items. It would appear that replacement cost accounting is being asked to solve too many problems at once—and ends up solving no one problem adequately.

Current Value Accounting

This method of accounting reflects all resources and obligations of the company in its balance sheets at current values. The opening balance sheet is not restated (rolled forward) as in price-level-adjusted statements, since the objective is to depart from historical cost and reflect current values at each reporting date. Current value accounting gives effect to all of the factors affecting the value of a particular asset (e.g., supply and demand, geographical location, forces of nature, changes in the environment). Changes in such values are usually segregated in the income statement between

those which are "realized" and those which are "unrealized." (Some accountants would carry the unrealized changes in value directly to the balance sheet and consider them as outside the definition of income.)

Will statements prepared on this basis be useful? It is indeed unfortunate that to date more time and effort has been spent on arguments about which of several valuation methods should be used and about the proper display of value changes in the income statement than in attempting to determine just how useful the resulting data would be. There seems little doubt that, in many cases, the introduction of current value data would be useful to investors and to management. A lengthy period of education would, no doubt, be required before full-fledged statements would be understood by most users. However, it seems clear to the writer that, because of the obvious relevance of the information, it is only a matter of time before current value data is introduced into financial statements, followed by complete statements within, say, five to eight years.

It is also clear that current value statements do not measure or segregate the effects of inflation. In fact, as is true for replacement cost data, they "bury" its effects in what are improperly described as "value changes." If current value statements are to be useful, it would appear that the impact of inflation must be segregated in order to make them of maximum usefulness—as is true of historical-cost-based statements. With the impact of inflation segregated, value changes could be identified and evaluated on a consistent and useful basis.

The Future

Of the various proposals offered to deal with the impact of inflation on financial accounting and reporting, it should be evident that the only proposal which adequately deals with inflation per se is the use of price-level-adjusted statements. The other proposals should be evaluated based on what they in fact purport to do. None of them

adequately identifies or segregates or eliminates the impact of changes in the measuring unit—the dollar—on financial statements. If this conclusion were accepted, then much of the present confusion regarding various proposals would be eliminated. Each proposal could be evaluated based on its own particular claims, not on claims that it solves all types of problems for which it was not designed.

There are limitations on the nature and extent of changes that can be made in the financial accounting and reporting process within a reasonable time. For this reason, the most important problem should be faced first. This would be to deal with inflation, and to adopt the requirement that price-level-adjusted data be furnished in the near future, as is proposed by the Financial Accounting Standards Board. This is a technique for which procedures exist. It can be applied consistently in an objective manner by various types of companies, and its purpose and results can be understood by users of financial statements with a minimum of education and explanation. Other proposals, such as the introduction of current value information, should wait their turn, after price-level-adjusted statements have been in use for a few years. The interim period can be used in experimentation and education—of which a great deal will be needed. Those who favor the immediate introduction of current value accounting should concede that the timely (later) introduction of that useful data will, in the long run, be more helpful to users than will the rapid introduction of such current value data, particularly if the effects of inflation are not segregated from "real" changes in value. Disregarding the necessity for this segregation would indeed be a disservice to users of financial statements.

In my view, based on results obtained in other countries and on the results of testing in this country, the Financial Accounting Standards Board will conclude that the evidence clearly supports the proposals of its exposure draft and it will therefore require that supplemental price-level-adjusted data be included in financial statements for fiscal years beginning on and after January 1, 1976. While a reduction in the rate of inflation in this country might be considered a reason for not moving ahead with this standard, the *cumulative*

impact of inflation on historical-cost financial statements resulting from inflation such as we have experienced in recent years should be sufficient to warrant issuance of

the standard. Requiring such supplemental data will represent a very useful improvement in the financial accounting and reporting process.Ω

The Numbers Game

Oops! We Overlooked That

WHAT worries us about the accountants is the profession's occasional tendency to make things worse in a sincere but confused effort to make them better. The latest case in point is the Financial Accounting Standards Board's exposure draft on inflation accounting, which is now being circulated through the profession and through industry generally.

The proposal is, in essence, to apply a single general-purchasing-power adjustment to all figures of all companies—and report the figures so adjusted as a supplement to their regular financial statements. Unfortunately, the FASB exposure draft also has a grave flaw—one that FASB members themselves admit they completely overlooked.

What is behind the proposal, of course, is the havoc that inflation has played with figures based on historical cost: Assets depreciated or depleted on the basis of their historical cost cannot be replaced by the total of the amounts thus reserved. What the FASB proposed is to adjust such historically based figures by a general, nationwide index of inflation—the gross national product deflator, for example.

This is a crude adjustment at best, since inflation rates vary from industry to industry and from one geographical area to the next. Thus, while the adjusted figures may come closer to current realities, it is almost coincidental whether they reflect accurately the fair market value of an item or its cost of replacement.

You would expect that any kind of inflation adjustment would tend to reduce reported earnings because it would increase depreciation charges every year in line with the inflation rate. A company with $10 million in depreciation, given a 10% inflation rate, would have to reserve $11 million the next year even if it didn't buy a single new machine. So, pretax earnings "drop" by $1 million.

But that is only half the story. You have to consider the effect of inflation on liabilities as well as on assets. Inflation reduces *liabilities* in terms of real dollars; when you pay off the debt, you do so in cheaper dollars. Under this new kind of accounting, a company loses earnings from higher depreciation but gains earnings from the reduction of the debt. The exposure draft provides that this gain on

"... a company could show huge earnings gains all the way to bankruptcy."

debt be credited directly to earnings.

Please follow us in some simple arithmetic. A company borrows $100 at the start of 1974 and buys a machine with it. By the beginning of 1975, after a year of 12% inflation, the company is permitted to take a $12 credit because the debt has decreased by that amount in constant dollars. But now let's look at the machine. It gets written up to $112—although the extra $12 isn't flowed through to income—with the result that depreciation charges go up. Let's take 10% straight-line depreciation. Under present rules the depreciation is $10; under the new rules it is $11.20—10% of $112.

The bottom line now looks like this: Credit to earnings: $12. Debit to earnings from higher depreciation: $1.20. Net gain: $10.80. Terrific!

But wait a minute. We're sorry to say that there's yet another complication. Any business has receivables: cash due it. Obviously, these receivables are depreciating in value during a period of inflation. Like debt, these are "monetary" items. So, while the company gets a *credit* for the reduction in the burden of its debt, it

gets *debited* for the reduction of its receivables.

This is rough on a company with high receivables and little debt. Such a company gets hit by inflation accounting on *both* sides of the balance sheet. Take Eastman Kodak, which last year had about $1.6 billion in receivables and cash items and $1.2 billion in debt. On 12% inflation, Kodak would gain a credit of about $144 million on its debt, but would "lose" $192 million on its receivables. Moreover, its depreciation charges would rise by more than $25 million. Overall, Kodak's earnings would have been lowered by $73 million. This, of course, oversimplifies the situation, but makes the point that a conservatively financed company would be penalized under the proposed rules.

Restated this way, most companies earnings *do* come out lower than those they reported. In a recent book, *Accounting—The Language of Business*, Professor Sidney Davidson of the University of Chicago Business School and three colleagues applied the FASB guidelines to the 1974 results of 65 industrial companies. The 30 Dow Jones industrial companies

The Numbers Game

showed a median reduction in earnings to 88% of reported earnings. For the other 35 companies, the median was 94%. Some companies were tremendously impacted. Chrysler, for example, would have shown triple the loss it reported. General Motors would have shown a loss, and United Technologies' restated earnings would have been only 25% of those actually reported in 1974.

Still others would have been little affected, and some would have benefited. Procter & Gamble's restated earnings would have been 98% of the $317 million it did report. Alcoa, more highly leveraged, would have shown 27% greater earnings by restatement.

Are utility earnings so much better than anyone except possibly Ralph Nader suspected? Rather the opposite, in fact. If one eliminated monetary item adjustments (*see column two of the table*), all the companies showed sharp earnings *declines*. Consumers Power, a Michigan utility generally considered in trouble, showed restated earnings only 37% of those reported. But include monetary items, and Consumers Power would show restated earnings more than triple and per-share earnings six times those that were reported.

Consumers Power shows this precisely *because* it is in such woeful shape. As a highly leveraged utility

fect of sharply *decreasing* earnings—not increasing them as would the FASB approach. Indiana Telephone, for example, has restated earnings of $1.93, vs. $3.96 on a historical cost basis—an approach that its auditors, Arthur Andersen & Co., say in their letter of certification *more fairly* represents the true financial condition of the company.

What worries the utilities is that rate-making commissions might treat the higher restated earnings as true current earnings—something that FASB Vice Chairman Robert Sprouse expressed a fervent hope would not occur. But rate commissions are more noted for their grasp of political expediency than their grasp of accounting intricacy.

The heart of the utility objection is the FASB's different treatment of monetary items, like debt and receivables, and nonmonetary items, like plant and equipment. They would prefer both items to be treated the same way in regulated industries, where the allowed return is based on recovery of historical cost. Sprouse concedes this problem, although it never came up in the FASB committee's initial discussions.

What kind of inflation accounting will be used by U.S. business is not merely a question of adjusting the disagreement between the utilities and the FASB. The Securities & Exchange Commission is likely to enter the fray with its own preferred method, replacement-cost accounting, which restates fixed assets and inventory on the balance sheet and cost of sales and depreciation in the income statement in terms of replacement cost. It also raises the confusing prospect that financial statements could show *three* sets of numbers: the traditional, the FASB's and the SEC's, although the latter two sets of figures would be supplementary to the first.

Replacement-cost accounting is admittedly more complex than the FASB method, which John C. Burton, the SEC's chief accountant, argues is confusing and does not reflect financial reality. But one can agree with Burton's reservations without accepting the SEC's alternative.

It's too bad that life isn't simple, but since it is so complicated, the accountants and the regulatory authorities should work together rather than at cross purposes so that they don't end up confusing investors instead of better informing them. ■

Electric Utilities Earnings, FASB Style

| | | —Adjusted Income— | | | |
| | Reported 1974 income (millions) | Before gain on monetary items (millions) | Including gain on monetary items (millions) | Common Share Earnings Reported | Common Share Earnings Adjusted |
Utility					
American Elec. Power	$176	$117	$488	$2.06	$7.21
Cleveland Elec. Illum.	61	45	127	3.68	9.60
Commonwealth Edison	180	108	395	2.88	8.21
Consolidated Edison	209	148	499	2.68	8.79
Consumers Power	61	23	202	1.34	8.31
Detroit Edison	89	55	255	1.46	6.00
Houston Lighting & Power	69	54	149	2.92	6.98
Niagara Mohawk Power	96	65	216	1.70	4.86
Pacific Gas & Elec.	261	179	515	3.27	8.24
Philadelphia Elec.	129	94	294	1.81	5.94
Public Service Elec. & Gas	154	106	351	2.35	7.03
Southern Calif. Edison	218	169	409	4.10	9.76

Source: Financial Analysts Journal, September/October, 1975.

That set Davidson to thinking. He decided to look at some highly leveraged industries. In an article to appear in the September-October issue of *The Financial Analysts Journal,* he and Roman Weil of Georgia Tech report on the consequences of applying the FASB guidelines to the utilities.

The results, if the pun is permissible, are electrifying. Utility earnings would have increased in every case, usually by more than double. The impact on earnings per share was even more dramatic. As shown in the table above, median earnings per share of electric utilities would triple.

its "earnings" from discounted debt are huge, but without any more cash flow—it is all a paper profit. "It sounds as though a company could show huge earnings gains all the way to bankruptcy," snaps Controller Ralph Heumann of Chicago's Commonwealth Edison, echoing the fears of many other utilities.

It's not that the utilities are constitutionally opposed to inflation adjustments. Some, like Indiana Telephone and Toledo Edison, already publish inflation-adjusted figures. But both *defer* the benefit of inflation on long-term debt, and that has the ef-

accounting for inflation: the controversy

by Lawrence Revsine and Jerry J. Weygandt

As all Americans know these days, inflation is a fact of life. For the entire second half of 1973, consumer prices rose at a 9.4 percent yearly rate, although the price for all commodities other than food rose only 5.6 percent.[1] Although many countries are experiencing a much higher inflation rate than the United States (e.g., Great Britain, Japan), it is clear that the United States' rate of inflation is serious, that this induces systematic

wealth redistribution and that a number of social problems are being encountered in such a cycle.

Most accountants have always recognized the necessity for the formulation of a set of objectives to help in the solution of many accounting controversies. Various practicing and academic individuals have argued ad infinitum about the proper way to account for such diverse issues as the investment credit, business combinations, inventory valuation and the necessity for price level adjustments. In some cases, it is possible that all viewpoints involved in a discussion were correct, given their stated or implied objectives. Unfortunately, too often the objectives are not stated accurately, if they are stated at all, and, as a consequence, arguments and misunderstandings continue.

We would like to address ourselves to one of the objectives recommended by the Study Group on the Objectives of Financial Statements and in-

Lawrence Revsine, *CPA, Ph.D., is visiting professor of accounting and information systems at the University of Wisconsin, Madison (on leave from Northwestern University). A member of the AICPA and AAA, he has served as a consultant to the AICPA's Accounting Objectives Study Group and is chairman of the AAA Committee on Concepts and Standards—External Financial Reports. Professor Revsine is a frequent contributor to academic journals and is the author of* Replacement Cost Accounting *(Prentice-Hall, Inc., 1973).*
Jerry J. Weygandt, *CPA, Ph.D., is associate professor of accounting and information systems at the University of Wisconsin. He is a member of the AICPA, the AAA and the Accounting Research Association. He is the author of numerous articles in professional journals including the* Journal of Accountancy *and is coauthor of* Intermediate Accounting *(John Wiley, 1974).*

The Journal of Accountancy, October 1974

[1] Paul McCracken, "1974's Basic Problem—Inflation," *The Wall Street Journal*, February 21, 1974, p. 12.

Using general price level indexes to adjust individual firms' financial statements may give rise to misleading inferences.

dicate how this objective might help in solving the complex issue of accounting for price level adjustments. As indicated by the Study Group, one objective of external financial reporting is to "provide information useful to investors and creditors for predicting, comparing and evaluating potential cash flows to them in terms of amount, timing and related uncertainty."[2]

The Study Group noted that both creditors and investors were interested in information related to actual and prospective dividend and interest payments (cash flow). Barring complications, it was suggested that security prices rise and fall with changes in investors' expectations about the enterprise's ability to pay future dividends and interest. It appears, then, that the problem of accounting for price level adjustments might be examined in the following manner: Given the objective to predict, compare and evaluate cash flows, what type of adjustment for inflation should be made?

To answer this question, given the stated objective, one must be able to differentiate between a general and a specific price level adjustment and understand the normative model developed as a basis for predicting cash flows.

General price level adjustments

A general price index (purchasing power index) is a weighted average relationship between money and a given set of goods and services. A problem exists in determining what items to include in the index, the price of the items included and the relative economic importance of the items and in allowing for changes in the methods of production and consumer attitudes and in the technological improvements in goods and services.[3]

In Accounting Principles Board Statement No. 3, the APB concluded that "general price level information is not required at this time for fair

---

[2] *Objectives of Financial Statements* (New York: American Institute of Certified Public Accountants, October 1973), p. 20.

[3] For a discussion of some problems inherent in the construction of general purchasing power indexes, see Denis S. Karnosky, "A Primer on the Consumer Price Index," *Federal Reserve Bank of St. Louis Review* (July 1974), pp. 2-7.

presentation of financial position and results of operations in conformity with generally accepted accounting principles in the United States."[4] The APB recommended the preparation and publication of financial statements restated for general price level changes as supplemental to the basic historical dollar financial statements, prohibiting presentation of the adjusted statements as the only or basic financial statements.

As part of its guide for preparing general price level adjusted financial statements, the APB urged that

1 The same accounting principles used in preparing historical dollar financial statements should be used.

2 An index of the general price level, not an index of the price of a specific type of goods or services, should be used (GNP Implicit Price Deflator recommended).

3 General price level financial statements should be presented in terms of the general purchasing power of the dollar at the latest balance sheet date.[5]

It should be noted that in spite of the APB recommendation, general price level adjustments have not been adopted.

Both the Financial Accounting Standards Board and the Securities and Exchange Commission are examining the issue of accounting for price level adjustments. The FASB recently issued a discussion memorandum on the subject in an attempt to seek views on reporting the effects of general price level changes in financial statements.[6] The SEC in Accounting Series Release No. 151 recommends that where significant differences exist between historical and replacement cost of goods sold, additional disclosure is needed to inform the investing public that the reported profits may be inflated because older costs are matched against current revenue figures.[7] It is interesting to note that whereas the FASB is addressing itself to general price level adjustments, the SEC is concerned with specific price changes.

Specific price level adjustments

The use of replacement cost (current costs) has long been discussed by accountants but has only recently received serious attention as an external reporting method. The replacement cost concept is differentiated from the general price level (purchasing power) concept in that replacement cost is concerned with the price pattern of specific items, whereas a purchasing power concept is concerned with the overall change in the price of all goods and services (the value of the dollar). Replacement cost introduces the use of current market prices or appraisals or highly specific indexes to account for each asset or set of homogeneous assets in the financial statements.

To illustrate the replacement cost approach, assume that a retailer has two units of inventory on hand at the beginning of year 1 with an original cost (and current replacement cost) of $80. One unit of inventory is sold at the end of year 1 for $150, at which time its current replacement cost is $100. If for simplicity we assume that this is the only item sold during the period, then income statements prepared under both historical and replacement cost concepts for year 1 would appear

---

The income determination method that best reflects the maintenance of the actual physical operating level of the firm is preferred.

---

as shown in Exhibit 1, page 75. In the traditional income statement, accounting income is determined to be $70, which is subject to claims for dividend distribution and income taxes. In the replacement cost income statement, current operating profit is computed by subtracting expenses measured on a replacement cost basis. This figure indicates what portion of gross inflows can be distributed, given prevailing factor prices, without contracting the firm's future operating level. Thus, current operating profit is regarded as a primary measure of the current (and potential future) profitability of existing operations. By contrast, holding gains are nonoperating in origin and may or may not recur in future periods. In a period of rising prices current operating profit ($50 in this case) is normally less than accounting income, and total replacement cost income (i.e., current operating profit plus holding gains) is normally greater than accounting income.

Normative model—maintenance of physical operating level

We now consider what method of inflation accounting best provides information to predict, compare and evaluate cash flows.

It is generally agreed that in the long run, the value of a firm's ownership shares is determined

---

[4] APB Statement No. 3, "Financial Statements Restated for General Price-Level Changes" (New York: AICPA, 1969), p. 12.
[5] Ibid., pp. 13-14.
[6] Financial Accounting Standards Board, "Discussion Memorandum Reporting the Effects of General Price-Level Changes in Financial Statements," February 15, 1974.
[7] Securities and Exchange Commission, Accounting Series Release No. 151, January 3, 1974.

Exhibit 1

Historical cost income statement	
Revenues	$150
Cost of goods sold	80
Accounting income	$ 70

Ending inventory: 1 unit @ $80

Replacement cost income statement	
Revenues	$150
Replacement cost of goods sold	100
Current operating profit	50
Holding gain ($100-80) x 2	40
Total replacement cost income	$ 90

Ending inventory: 1 unit @ $100

by the level of its cash operating flows.[8] Observation of management behavior indicates that managers are vitally concerned about the level of their firm's share prices. While they will obviously do better if they can, at a minimum management can be assumed to be constantly striving to maintain existing share prices. If in the long run share prices are determined by levels of operating flows, then in order to maintain existing share prices management must simultaneously maintain operating flows at their current level.

The operating flows generated by a firm are a function of two variables: the physical level of its operations and the prevailing prices for its inputs and outputs. Price levels are dictated by existing competitive conditions and are thus largely beyond the control of the firm. Accordingly, management's primary controllable variable in attempting to maintain operating flow levels is to maintain the prevailing physical level of operations on the assumption that the margin between input and output prices will remain constant.

Following this logic, if we adopt the recommendation of the Accounting Objectives Study Group with regard to the primacy of cash flow predictions, we have a criterion for evaluating alternative inflation accounting methods. Specifically, whichever inflation accounting method generates an income figure that best reflects the maintenance of the physical operating level of the firm ought to be preferred. That is, insofar as an income concept reflects the maximum dividend that can be paid without impairing physical operating level, investors have some means for estimating the maximum potential future dividends

emanating from the security. Thus, our criterion for evaluating alternative inflation accounting options is clear: the income determination method that best reflects the maintenance of the actual physical operating level of the firm is preferred.

Illustration

It seems clear that, in terms of current price levels, existing profits are overstated and reported income does not reflect maintenance of physical operating level. It has recently been estimated that profits for nonfinancial corporations would drop by $24 billion, or roughly one-fourth of total profits, if inflationary profits were excluded. Of that $24 billion overstatement of profits, inventory profits amounted to around $17 billion and most of the rest was attributed to underdepreciation of plant and equipment.[9] Companies are beginning to recognize that, to combat this inflationary cycle, Lifo inventory valuation, for example, should be employed. Recently CPC International reported that, after shifting to Lifo, it cut 1973 net income by about $8.6 million, or $.36 per share. As the president noted, "By charging current earnings with current costs, the results are realistically stated, and future earnings won't be penalized by these inflated costs."[10] It should also be noted that the Machinery and Allied Products Research Division finds that "the accelerated methods utilized for depreciating plant assets have underdepreciated existing capital assets by as much as $7 billion."[11]

Thus there appears to be wide agreement that "real" profits are currently being overstated. But

[8] This cash flow orientation is generally accepted in both the traditional individual security literature (e.g., Alexander A. Robichek and Stewart C. Myers, *Optimal Financing Decisions* (Englewood Cliffs, N.J.: Prentice-Hall, Inc., 1965)), and in the share pricing model that underlies the two-parameter portfolio theory model (e.g., Eugene F. Fama and Merton Miller, *The Theory of Finance* (New York: Holt, Rinehart and Winston, 1972), pp. 295-304).

[9] Henry C. Wallich and Mable I. Wallich, "Profits Aren't as Good as They Look," *Fortune* (March 1974) p. 127.
[10] "The World at Work," *Barron's* (February 25, 1974) p. 21. It should be noted, however, that the proportion of Lifo users at present is smaller than in the 1960s. *Accounting Trends and Techniques* (New York: AICPA, 1973), p. 99. Corporations are apparently reluctant to switch to Lifo because of the depressing effect on earnings and in some cases because complications in computing such a figure exist.
[11] Wallich and Wallich, p. 129.

since there are two divergent approaches for reflecting price changes—general and specific price adjustments—the crucial question is this: Which of the two inflation accounting alternatives generates an income figure that reflects the amount of resource inflows that could conceivably be distributed as a dividend without impairing the physical operating level of the firm? The income figure that best reflects maintenance of physical operating level is deemed superior, because it reflects the maximum amount of potential dividend flows that the investor might expect to receive and thus facilitates predictions of future cash flows emanating from the security.

We now address this issue of alternative inflation accounting methods within the context of a descriptive case.

For discussion purposes, assume the existence of two firms in a single industry (e.g., cement) in widely dispersed locations. Both firms began operations at the start of the current year and are identical in all respects except that the markets in which each purchases its inputs differ considerably. Firm A's purchasing power is constantly deteriorating. All of the inputs it uses in operations have risen considerably in price. A labor shortage in its area has driven wage rates upward and similar increases are continuing. Land is expensive and constantly increasing in price. Gravel, sand and other cement ingredients must be bid away from other firms in various industries, all of which are prospering in Firm A's location. As a consequence, the prices of materials have risen and continue to rise at a rapid rate. In summary, all costs incurred by Firm A are much higher today than they were a year ago.

By contrast, Firm B is in a depressed area. Textile mills, the primary industry in its area, have

> ... uniform reliance on general price indexes as an inflation adjustment mechanism can lead to adjustments that do not conform to the specific purchasing power change experienced by individual firms.

been closing and unemployment is high. As a result, wage rates paid by Firm B have not risen. Indeed, as openings arise, currently unemployed workers are hired at wage rates below those of departed workers. Land is cheap and, in some cases, has actually fallen in price. As firms have exited

from the area, the demand for raw materials has fallen sharply. In an effort to increase demand and reduce overstocks, suppliers of gravel, sand and other cement ingredients have drastically lowered prices over the year. In summary, all costs incurred by Firm B are much lower today than they were a year ago.

With regard to output, assume that volume and selling price are similar for Firms A and B. Further assume that the general level of prices in the U.S. (as reflected by the GNP Implicit Price Deflator) has increased over the year.

Advocates of general purchasing power adjustments would suggest that the financial statements of Firms A and B should be adjusted by a general purchasing power index—e.g., the GNP deflator. Were this procedure adopted, the net effect would be to lower adjusted profits for both firms below reported historical cost profits.

However, Firm B has not suffered a decline in its real purchasing power. On the contrary, despite general inflation throughout the U.S., the price of the specific goods and services it uses in production has fallen; it has experienced an increase in its real purchasing power. Were we to adjust the historical cost numbers of Firm B by a general purchasing power index, the direction of the adjustment would be opposite to the specific price changes that the firm actually experienced. As a consequence, the resultant income measure would understate the amount of inflows which could be distributed as a dividend by Firm B while maintaining physical operating level intact. All other factors being equal, this would tend to worsen investor estimates of Firm B's dividend-paying ability.

Our point is not to argue that the above case is empirically dominant. It clearly is not. Rather, it represents an extreme case that illustrates our point: Given the investor information needs for predicting cash flows, it is the purchasing power of the individual firm that is important, since it is individual purchasing power that will determine the amount of current flows which can be distributed as a dividend without reducing physical operating levels. Insofar as individual-firm and economy-wide purchasing powers diverge (in either direction), it is inappropriate to use general purchasing power changes to adjust individual firms' statements.

Our example is intended to illustrate the anomalous results that arise when a general index is used despite the existence of nonparallel movements in general vs. specific price levels. While our illustration is hypothetical, a check of available statistics indicates that the general price level and the specific price level have indeed diverged significantly in certain economic sectors. For example, the GNP deflator in 1955 was 77.5 and in 1971 was 120.7. Specific price changes for certain wholesale price

I...ex categories, however, were significantly different, as shown by the following statistics: the index for household appliances was 112.9 in 1955 and 107.2 in 1971; manmade fiber textile products was 123.5 in 1955 and 100.8 in 1971; paint materials was 104.4 in 1955 and 102.4 in 1971; plastic resins and materials was 126.5 in 1955 and 88.9 in 1971; plywood was 120.4 in 1955 and 114.7 in 1971; and home electronics equipment was 120.0 in 1955 and 93.8 in 1971.[12] (The base for all of these indexes is 1967 = 100.0.)

This indicates that nonparallel price movements do indeed occur in realistic economic settings. As a consequence, uniform reliance on general price indexes as an inflation adjustment mechanism can lead to adjustments that do not conform to the specific purchasing power change experienced by individual firms. Indeed, in some instances the adjustment can be in the opposite direction from the actual purchasing power change for an individual entity. Given the possibility of nonparallel price movements, and given the objective of cash flow prediction, it would appear that the specific price change approach would provide users with more reliable information.[13]

Objections to the specific price adjustment approach

We are cognizant that objections will be made to our recommendations for a variety of reasons. We would like to address ourselves to several issues that arise when specific price adjustments are discussed and to provide some new perspectives on these issues.

Adaptability of the firm. The index selected to reflect price changes and thus to compute depreciation implicitly incorporates specific assumptions regarding the firm's reinvestment policy as assets physically deteriorate. For example, when highly specific indexes are used to reflect changes in the price of the firm's existing assets, the implicit assumption is that the firm will replace existing assets with essentially similar assets. To illustrate this more concretely, assume that there are no income taxes and a firm regularly pays out 100 percent of its reported income as a dividend. In this circumstance, the amount of computed depreciation expense represents that portion of revenue inflow that must be shielded from dividends in order to maintain capital (however defined).[14] When depreciation is measured using *specific* price indexes, the dividend shield is computed by reference to the price changes that have affected the specific assets currently used. This assumes that the firm will reinvest the shielded funds in equivalent assets whose movements are reflected by the specific index used to compute depreciation.

By contrast, when a *general* price index (e.g., GNP deflator) is used to compute depreciation, the implicit reinvestment assumption is different. Here depreciation does not reflect price changes for the specific assets used by the firm. Instead, the price movements that determine depreciation charges (and thus the dividend shield) reflect a weighted average of changes in the prices of all goods and services. This use of a general index implies that the funds shielded from dividends are potentially available for reinvestment in any type of assets the firm deems appropriate.

Since each index approach assumes a different reinvestment policy, the issue of specific vs. general adjustments must also address the issue of which reinvestment assumption is more appropriate. It is conceivable that for a highly diversified conglomerate enterprise, the reinvestment assumption implicit in the GNP deflator approach may be approximately correct; that is, the depreciation shield may indeed be reinvested in a group of assets whose price changes tend to approach the weighted average of all price changes in the economy. But for this reinvestment assumption to be even approximately correct, the conglomerate enterprise must be quite large and its existing and contemplated lines of activity must be diverse.

For all other types of firms, the reinvestment assumption implicit in the specific index approach would appear to be superior. That is, if the firm is in a single line of activity, the reasonable assumption is that the firm will not soon become sufficiently diversified to validate the reinvestment assumption implicit in the general index approach. Such firms may (and probably will) diversify in the future, but only into a few areas and only over a lengthy period. Since the diversification transi-

---

[12] *Handbook of Labor Statistics*, Bulletin 1790, U.S. Department of Labor.

[13] Insofar as general price levels tend to move in tandem with an entity's own unique purchasing power, general price level adjustments would also provide useful information. The reason is not because general price level adjustments are relevant per se, but rather because the general price level adjustments would tend to give the same results as do the "theoretically correct" specific adjustments. Indeed, one might argue that the entire justification for reflecting general price changes is that general and specific price levels will usually be covariant.

[14] When the prices of long-lived assets are continuously changing over time, replacement cost income must take cognizance of such price changes if the resultant income number is intended to help preserve physical operating level. The issue arises because the replacement cost of a long-lived asset on the books reflects the current value of the asset in its present (used) condition. If replacement prices have continuously been increasing, then past replacement cost depreciation has not shielded sufficient inflows from possible dividend distribution to allow eventual replacement of the asset with a new asset at its current higher price. If income is to reflect maintenance of physical operating level, the current replacement cost depreciation charge must consist of two components: (1) the prorata share of current-year depreciation based on existing price levels and (2) adjustment to compensate for past underdepreciation because of rising price levels.

tion—if it takes place at all—will be slow, and since we cannot know in advance which new area (or areas) the firm will choose, the best reinvestment assumption is likely reflected by reference to the assets currently in use. Insofar as firms tend to diversify into areas related to their current activity in order to capitalize on existing expertise, this observation is reinforced.

Inflation-adjusted income — firm vs. investor. Some have justified the use of a general index for inflation adjustments by reference to the diversity of the corporate ownership group. The rationale is that since ownership of large corporate enterprises is geographically dispersed and represents a disparate group with dissimilar expenditure patterns, a general index seems appropriate for computing the income accruing to "typical" corporate owners. The problem with this argument is that it confuses two distinct notions: (1) the impact of price changes on the real income of the enterprise and hence on its dividend-paying ability and (2) the impact of price changes on the real value of the dividend to the recipient once its amount is determined. For simplicity we will refer to these concepts as inflation-adjusted income to the firm and inflation-adjusted income to the investor, respectively.

If a firm is concerned with maintaining its physical operating level intact, inflation-adjusted income to the firm would consist of the amount of current operating flows that can be distributed as a dividend without contracting physical operating level. For this computation, it is the specific purchasing power of the individual firm that is important; that is, the maximum dividend that a firm could pay without reducing physical operating level must be computed by reference to the price changes that have affected the specific resources used or contemplated for use by the specific firm for which the statements are prepared.

By contrast, inflation-adjusted income to the investor is computed without reference to changes in the individual firm's purchasing power. For example, if one wished to compute the inflation-adjusted dividend yield to an individual investor, it is the investor's purchasing power that is relevant to this calculation; that is, a price index relevant to the individual consumption preferences of the investor would be used to adjust initial investment to present dollars and to compute the inflation-adjusted return.

Thus, the process of computing inflation-adjusted income should ideally encompass two sets of inflation index calculations. The determination of income to the firm would employ price indexes that reflect changes in the unique purchasing power of the firm. The firm would use this income calculation to determine the amount of inflows that could conceivably be distributed as a dividend without contracting the physical operating level of the firm. Once this amount is computed, the firm will determine its cash needs for expansion and other purposes and distribute some portion of its inflation-adjusted income as a dividend. After the dividend is received by the investor, it is no longer necessary to consider the firm's purchasing power. Now it is the purchasing power of the investor that determines the amount of real income received. Were these two separate purchasing power calculations merged by the use of some general index to determine firm income, the danger is that the resultant inflation-adjusted income number will not reflect the real price changes experienced by the firm. As a consequence, the physical operating level of the firm could conceivably be diminished.

Conclusion

Accounting for the inflation in the United States must be considered a top priority of the accounting profession. As indicated in the discussion memorandum of the FASB, the problem is acute and answers must be forthcoming shortly. Already, comments are appearing in the press that are critical of the accounting profession's failure to move in this area. As one recent commentator noted, "The consequences are already serious, and the profession should give this problem intellectual leadership or court a serious backlash not so far down the way."[15]

In its discussion memorandum, the FASB suggests that general vs. specific inflation adjustments represent two separate issues that can be addressed individually.[16] However, we have contended that, if one adopts the Study Group's objective of cash flow predictions, the use of general price level indexes to adjust individual firms' financial statements can give rise to misleading inferences. As a consequence, we have argued for the use of the specific price change approach as a means of adjusting for the impact of inflation. ■

15 McCracken, *Wall Street Journal,* p. 12.
16 FASB Discussion Memorandum, p. 6.

Harper A. Roehm, CPA, DBA, and Joseph F. Castellano, Ph.D

Inflation Accounting: A Compromise

This article presents an alternative to proposals for replacement cost and/or purchasing power adjustments. The authors believe this proposed solution gives a net income that can be distributed without jeopardizing the company's ability to maintain its asset base in an inflationary environment.

MANY financial analysts and journalists have been unable to resist the temptation to adjust individual company financial statements for the replacement cost information presented in accordance with ASR 190. Despite the warnings of the SEC, accountants, and chief financial officers, these adjustments are likely to continue. Several authorities would argue that the information provides an incomplete analysis. The data fails to measure (1) holding gains and losses from changes in replacement cost, (2) price level losses from holding monetary assets, and (3) price level gains from holding monetary liabilities. The purpose of this article is to examine how financial information regarding inflation may be further enhanced by not only requiring the adjustments prescribed by ASR 190 but also requiring the disclosure of purchasing power gains and losses from holding monetary assets and liabilities. In effect, we are proposing an accounting model which could be characterized as General Price Level (GPL) Adjusted Replacement Cost. A model presented by Robert Sterling[1] and later modified by Raymond Chambers[2] is the basis for our model.

In deciding which attributes financial statements should measure, Sterling states that the attribute must be interpretable and relevant.[3] He goes on to say that for financial statements to be both interpretable and relevant, they must measure a firm's command over goods (COG) at a point in time and the change in command over goods between two points in time. Sterling demonstrates that command over goods can be measured through "price level adjusted current value" financial statements and that this model meets the tests of interpretability and relevance.[4] He adjusts financial statements for general price level changes and replacement cost using cash and securities as his only assets. Many accountants believe that one or the other adjustment is required but not both.

For example, assume a business was started on January 1 with a contribution of $2,000 and immediately purchased securities for $1,200. Its balance sheet would appear as in 1.

EXHIBIT 1

Firm
Balance Sheet
Jan. 1, Yr 1

Cash	$ 800
Marketable Securities	1,200
Total Assets	$2,000
Invested Capital	$2,000
Retained Earnings	-0-
Total Owner's Equity	$2,000

Assume further that between January 1 and December 31 of Year 1 the gross national product price deflator index changed from 1.0 to 1.5 and that the market price of the securities purchased was 2,000 at December 31, Year 1. Also, there were no other transactions during the year. Using "price level adjusted

Harper A. Roehm, CPA, DBA, is a Professor of Accountancy at Wright State University. He is a member of the AAA and is also author of a number of articles in professional journals. Joseph F. Castellano, Ph.D., is an Associate Professor and Chairman of the Accountancy Department at Wright State University. He is a member of the AAA and the NAA and has authored articles for many professional journals.

[1] Robert R. Sterling, "Relevant Financial Reporting in An Age of Price Changes," *The Journal of Accountancy*, February 1975, pp. 42-51.
[2] R. J. Chambers, "NOD, COG, an PuPu: See How Inflation Teases," *The Journal of Accountancy*, September 1975, pp. 56-62.
[3] See Sterling, pp. 44-45.
[4] See Sterling, p. 50.

INFLATION ACCOUNTING: A COMPROMISE

EXHIBIT 2

Firm Balance Sheet January 1, Year 1		Firm Balance Sheet December 31, Year 1	
Cash (1.5 × 800)	$1,200	Cash	$ 800
Marketable Securities		Marketable Securities	2,000
(1.5 × 1,200)	$1,800		
Total Assets	$3,000	Total Assets	$2,800
Invested Capital		Invested Capital	$3,000
(1.5 × 2,000)	$3,000		
Retained Earnings	-0-	Retained Earnings	(200)
Total Owners Equity	$3,000	Total Owners' Equity	$2,800

Firm Income Statement For Year 1	
Revenue	-0-
Cost of Sales	-0-
Gain from holding security (2,000 - 1,800)	200
Loss from holding cash (1,200 - 800)	(400)
Net Loss	$(200)

current value" as a basis, Sterling would present financial statements by December 31, as shown in Exhibit 2.

The January 1 balance sheet is converted to December 31 dollars by using the gross national product price deflator of 1.5. The December 31 balance sheet indicates the actual cash on hand and the market price of the securities. (Note that this is a replacement cost adjustment using "exit value," a *different definition*

from what the SEC is using.) When these two amounts are added they represent the current dollars available and the firm's command over goods. In the equity section, the invested capital is also adjusted by 1.5. The retained earnings of ($200) is explained by the income statement which reflects the causes of the firm's changes of command over goods from $3,000 to $2,800. The $200 gain from holding the securities is

EXHIBIT 3

Financial Presentation December 31

Balance Sheet January 1		Balance Sheet December 31	
Cash	$ 800	Cash	$ 800
Marketable Securities	1,200	Marketable Securities	2,000
Total Assets	$22,000	Total Assets	$2,800
Invested Capital	$2,000	Invested Capital	$3,000
Retained Earnings	-0-	Retained Earnings	(200)
Total Owners' Equity	$2,000	Total Owners' Equity	$2,800

Income Statement For Year 1	
Increment from trade	-0-
Price variation adjustment (Marketable securities change of 1,200 to 2,000)	$ 800
Capital Maintenance Adjustment (1.5 × 2,000) = $3,000 - 2,000 = 1,000)	(1,000)
Net Loss	($ 200)

THE CPA JOURNAL   SEPTEMBER 1978

only that gain which is in excess of price level adjustments of 1.5. This holding gain is more than offset by the $400 purchasing power loss from holding cash.

Chambers agreed with Sterling's $200 net loss in the income statement but objected to the December 31 presentation of the January 1 balance sheet.[5] He recommended the approach and presentation at December 31 as shown in Exhibit 3.

Chambers also disagreed with the format of Sterling's income statement which "nets off" the effects of inflation on a specific asset. His income statement would show a holding gain on marketable securities and a capital maintenance adjustment.

The January 1 balance sheet is not restated in December 31 year end dollars. The income statement shows the entire holding gain on marketable securities $800 (a replacement cost or exit value at December 31 of securities would be $2,000) and a capital maintenance adjustment which restates the purchasing power of the net assets. Chambers refers to his model as COCOA (continuously contemporary accounting).[6]

An Expanded Analysis

While our method is similar to Sterling's and Chamber's (a technique utilizing both a general price level and current value approach) substantial differences exist.

---
[5] See Chambers, p. 58.
[6] See Chambers, p. 59.

Neither the Sterling or Chambers models considered the inflationary impact on holding monetary liabilities. They also did not consider inventory and fixed assets in their example. More importantly our model introduces a concept which discloses replacement cost gains and losses in the balance sheet, and purchasing power gains and losses on net monetary items in the income statement. The net result of this treatment is that the income figure represents (excluding legal restrictions) income available for distributions as dividends while allowing a firm to maintain its capital base.

In an attempt to expand on their analysis and to illustrate why ASR 190 does not go far enough in its requirements, we have developed an example which contrasts the balance sheets, income statements, and selected ratios for a fictitious company (Inflato Corporation). The example illustrates the results that would be reported under three different accounting models: (1) historical cost, (2) replacement cost, and (3) general price level adjusted replacement cost.

Recognizing that there are a variety of replacement cost techniques, we have chosen ASR 190 and its limited requirements as the basis for our replacement cost adjustments. We recognize that the SEC does not require or recommend a calculation of net income using the adjustments it prescribes. However, such figures are being reported. Consequently, our replacement cost adjustments are for inventory, fixed asset, and depreciation and show how they would be accounted for and disclosed in the financial statements if such

---

EXHIBIT 4

Inflato Balance Sheet December 31, 1977			Inflato Income Statement For Year Ended Dec. 31, 1977	
Assets				
Cash		$ 1,000	Net Sales	$40,000
Accounts Receivable		2,000	Cost of Sales-other than Depreciation	(25,000)
Inventory		2,000		
Current Assets		$ 5,000	Cost of Sales-Depr.	(5,000)
			Gross Profit	$10,000
Fixed Assets	$25,000			
Less Acc. Depr.	5,000	20,000	Operating expenses	6,000
		$25,000	Net income before taxes	4,000
			Taxes @ 40% rate	1,600
	Liabilities & Equity		Net income after taxes	$ 2,400
Accounts Payable		$ 2,500		
Bonds Payable		12,700		
Invested Capital		7,400		
Retained Earnings		2,400		
Total Liabilities & Stock Equity		$25,000		

THE CPA JOURNAL   SEPTEMBER 1978

statements were required. Our GPL adjusted replacement cost model starts with the results obtained under the SEC version of replacement cost adjustments but expands the adjustment process to include monetary assets and liabilities. Our purpose in illustrating these comparisons is to show the limitations and misleading inferences that might be drawn from utilizing financial data that has been adjusted solely on a replacement cost basis.

Assume that the Balance Sheet and Income Statement for the Inflato Company at the end of December 31, 1977 is as described in Exhibit 4.

The following assumptions are pertinent to the analysis:

1. Inflato is a manufacturing firm and all fixed assets are engaged in manufacturing.

2. The accounts payable are a current liability and bonds payable are long term.

3. The price levels both general and specific have been stable through December 31, 1977. Price Index = 1.0.

4. The inflation effects for 1978 are as follows:
A. The average general price level index during 1978 was 1.2.
B. The average specific index for fixed assets was 1.3.
C. Since inventory turns over very rapidly historical cost ending inventory approximates replacement cost and no adjustment was necessary. Beginning Inventory in 1978 was adjusted by 10 percent for the average specific change in the inventory index.

5. A $1,500 dividend is declared and paid at the end of 1978.

Comparative balance sheets and income statements for 1978 based on historical cost, replacement cost and general price level adjusted replacement cost are given in Table 1.

Net income after taxes is different in each case. The $1,400 difference between historical and replacement cost is a result of the increase in depreciation ($1,200) and beginning inventory ($200) which were necessary to place cost of sales on a replacement cost basis.[7] In the case of GPL adjusted replacement cost the difference in net income (as compared to historical cost) is partially offset by the purchasing power gain from holding net monetary liabilities. Note that the COP after taxes is the same in the replacement cost and GPL adjusted replacement cost method since the $1,400 increase in cost of sales as explained above is common to both methods. However, the purchasing power gain has offset $1,180 of that increase.[8]

One final comment about our replacement cost income statement format is in order. Some authors contend that $1,400 increase in cost of sales under the replacement cost method should be added back to COP after taxes in the replacement cost income statement as a realized holding gain. The Stockholders'

---

[7] Historical cost depreciation = $4,000. Multiplying this times the specific index for fixed assets 1.3 gives depreciation on a replacement cost basis 4,000 × 1.3 = $5,200. $5,200−4,000 = $1,200 increase due to replacement cost. The same procedure is followed for Beginning Inventory using the specific index for inventory 1.1. Historical cost of Beginning Inventory $2,000 × 1.1 = 2,200−2,000 = $200 increase in Beginning Inventory on a replacement cost basis.

[8] The net monetary liabilities at the end of 1978 are $5,900 (ML = 9,600−3,700 MA = $5,900 NML). Since the GPL increased 20% (1.0 to 1.2) and the company was in a NML position, a $1,180 purchasing power gain has occurred (5,900 × 20% = $1,180) since the firm will be repaying debt with dollars of less purchasing power.

TABLE 1
Inflato
Comparative Income Statements For Year Ended Dec. 31, 1978

	Historical Cost		Replacement Cost		GPL Adjusted Replacement Cost	
Net Sales		$50,000		$50,000		$50,000
Cost of Sales						
Other than Depr.	$31,000		$31,200		$31,200	
Depr.	4,000	35,000	5,200	36,400	5,200	36,400
Gross Profit		$15,000		$13,600		$13,600
Operating Expenses		6,000		6,000		6,000
Current Operating Profit (COP)						
Before Taxes		9,000		7,600		7,600
Taxes @ 40% Rate		3,600		3,600		3,600
Current Operating Profit						
After Taxes		5,400		4,000		4,000
Purchasing Power Gain		-0-		-0-		1,180
Net Income After Taxes		$ 5,400		$ 4,000		$ 5,180

TABLE 1 (Continued)
Inflato
Comparative Balance Sheets December 31, 1978

		Historical Assets		Replacement Costs Assets		GPL Adjusted Replacement Cost Assets
Cash		$ 1,300		$ 1,300		$1,300
Accounts Receivable		2,400		2,400		2,400
Inventory		3,600		3,600		3,600
		7,300		7,300		7,300
Fixed Assets	$25,000		$32,500		32,500	
Less Acc. Dep.	9,000	16,000	11,700	20,800	11,700	20,800
Total Assets		$23,300		$28,100		$28,100
		Liabilities & Stock Equity		Liabilities & Stock Equity		Liabilities & Stock Equity
Accounts Payable		$ 2,800		$ 2,800		$ 2,800
Bonds Payable		6,800		6,800		6,800
Invested Capital		7,400		7,400		8,880
Retained Earnings		6,300		4,900		6,080
Inflation Adjustment		-0-		6,200		3,540
Total Liabilities & Stock Equity		$23,300		$28,100		$28,100

Equity section of the balance sheet would then show only unrealized holding gains. Of course COP after taxes would still differ by the amount of the holding gains. Our presentation is consistent with those authors who chose not to disclose these holding gains in the income statement. We believe that final "net income" should reflect as much as possible the full inflationary impact during the period and the amount available for dividend distributions. A more comprehensive discussion of these issues is beyond the scope of this article. Our presentation (in the GPL adjusted replacement cost income statement) of the purchasing power gain from net monetary liabilities is consistent with the position taken by the Accounting Principles Board in Statement No. 3. However, it should be noted that the APB was not recommending a change in the historical cost model only that supplemental statements might be useful.

Several changes should be noted in the balance sheets. Under both replacement and GPL adjusted replacement cost, net fixed assets are increased. However, this increase is reflected differently in the stockholders' equity section of the balance sheet. The inflation adjustment balance represents additional capital that must be maintained as a result of inflation. Under the historical cost model no such provision is made and the danger of distributing dividends from the capital base is present.

Under GPL adjusted replacement cost, the amount needed to maintain the capital base is reduced since the firm generated purchasing power gains from holding net monetary liabilities. In addition, the invested capital account was adjusted by the GPL index. Under our GPL adjusted replacement cost model the purchasing power gain was taken into income and would be available for dividend distributions. Appendix A contains a simplified example demonstrating how a firm with a purchasing power gain on net monetary liabilities could distribute these gains as a dividend and yet have sufficient cash flow available to replace its non-monetary assets. The underlying assumptions are: (1) product sales price is increased at least at the same rate as GPL inflation, and (2) the firm desired to maintain its present debt/equity ratio.

Comparative Ratios

Selected ratios for the Inflato Company for 1978 under each model are given in Table 2.

The limitations of historical cost based accounting data in financial statement analysis are clearly evident when compared to inflation adjusted data. This is especially true in the rates of return and earnings per share measures. However, the replacement cost model is also an extreme alternative and represents "inflationary adjustment over-kill." Hence, the

	Historical Cost	Replace-ment Cost	GPL Ad-justed Replace-ment Cost
TABLE 2			
Return on Sales	11%	8%	10%
Return on Assets	23%	14%	18%
Return on Stock-holders' Equity [1]	39%	22%	28%
Earnings Per Share [2]	$1.08	.80	$1.03
Price Earnings Ratio [3]	9.2	12.5	9.7
Payout Ratio (Dividends/NI) [4]	28%	38%	29%
Tax as a % of COP [5]	40%	47%	47%

[1] Stockholders' Equity = Invested Capital, Retained Earnings and Inflation Adjustment.
[2] Assume 5,000 shares of stock outstanding.
[3] Market Price of stock = $10.
[4] Dividends paid = $1,500.
[5] Taxes paid = $3,600.

usefulness of the accounting data developed in this model must come into serious question. Inflationary erosions occur in monetary as well as nonmonetary items. To ignore either in proposing alternatives to historical cost based data is not only incorrect but seriously misleading to those who will rely on an analysis of the data. General price level adjusted replacement cost corrects for the inadequacies of historical cost and avoids the incomplete adjustments that result from a pure replacement cost accounting model. A finanaical analyst comparing Inflato Company's results for 1978 on a historical and replacement cost basis would, we believe, assess the inflationary impact as more severe than is warranted. To properly appraise management's ability to conduct operations in an inflationary environment, attention must be given to the firm's ability to manage all its resources, monetary as well as nonmonetary. In our example, inflation has taken its toll, but not to the degree reflected by a replacement cost model that would only adjust inventory and fixed assets.

A close examination of the ratios finds the results for GPL adjusted replacement cost falling between historical cost and replacement cost (except for taxes as a percent of COP). Some might be quick to argue that this is a "masking" of inflations impact. For Inflato Company, the moderating effect of using GPL adjusted replacement cost resulted because the firm was in a net monetary liability position. If the firm had been in a net monetary asset position a purchasing power loss would have been recognized and net income under

GPL adjusted replacement cost would have been less than income under replacement cost. If a firm's ability to manage its resources in an inflationary environment is to be measured, the effect on all resources must be considered.

Summary and Conclusion

The pressure on the accounting profession to deal effectively with the question of inflation and its impact on financial statements is not likely to lessen. We appear to be at the crossroads on this issue. The profession can adopt a "hands off" position and continue to take its direction from the SEC which obviously favors replacement cost disclosures as an answer to the problem. The FASB could renew its call for GPL adjustments and hope that at a minimum the SEC would permit an additional set of disclosures for GPL adjustments apart from its ASR 190 requirements. To date the SEC has shown little enthusiasm for the comprehensive GPL adjustments proposed by the APB in Statement No. 3 and endorsed by the FASB in a prior exposure draft.

We believe the present impasse is an outgrowth of the view that tends to view GPL and replacement cost adjustments as mutually exclusive choices. As a result, the SEC has taken the initiative in this vital area of financial reporting. This is unfortunate for several reasons. First, replacement cost adjustments as prescribed by ASR 190 are not a solution to the inflation accounting problem. The SEC, FASB, accounting profession, and industry are well aware of this, and so the many warnings against an indiscriminate use of the data. Unfortunately the warnings are being ignored by many analysts and journalists and perhaps by a growing number of investors. Consequently, the sooner we can provide a better method of adjusting for inflations' effect the better since the analysts' appetite for inflation adjusted data seems to be increasing. Perhaps they subscribe to the theory that it is better to be vaguely right than precisely wrong. Secondly, at present the FASB has lost the initiative to the SEC in this vital area of financial reporting. True, the FASB is attempting to clarify the question of the objectives of financial statements and ultimately will have to address inflation in that context, but a speedy resolution of the objectives question is not likely. As a result the SEC is likely to gain an even greater foothold in this area and moving them to a new position once the objectives issue is settled is likely to be a difficult task.

We believe the alternative that we have proposed offers the best chance for the profession to regain the initiative in this area. The SEC would be able to retain its replacement cost preference for the items specified in ASR 190 and the FASB's preference for GPL adjustments for monetary items would be preserved.

Obviously what we are calling for represents a compromise for both groups. Both types of adjustments would be disclosed in supplemental financial statements (GPL adjusted replacement cost statements). We believe the timing is excellent for such a compromise since the SEC is actively studying the experiences to date of applying ASR 190. The fact that an improper use of replacement cost data is occurring might also improve the chances for compromise.

A cessation of the debate on the merits of the many inflation models that have been proposed in the literature is long overdue. The SEC has taken the initiative and appears very serious in its approach to the problem. We can continue to discuss the "theoretically" best method of inflation accounting and what attributes we should be measuring. If we do the SEC, under pressure itself, will continue to move forcefully in this area. Such a situation is likely to affect not only the inflation question but the very essence of the objectives question as well. Unknowingly we may be abdicating our role in this vital area. Ω

APPENDIX A

Assume:
1. One asset (a machine) which costs $10,000, has a life of one year and produces 10,000 units.
2. Sales price of $1.20 per unit.
3. An average inflation of 5%.
4. The price of the unit will increase an average of 5%.
5. The replacement cost of machine will increase by 5%.
6. Company A finances machine with $4,000 at 10% debt and $6,000 equity.
7. Company B finances machine with $10,000 equity.

Company A
Balance Sheet
January 1, 1978

Asset		Liabilities & Equity	
Machine	$10,000	Note	$4,000
		Equity	6,000
Total	$10,000		$10,000

Company B
Balance Sheet
January 1, 1978

Asset		Equity	
Machine	$10,000		
		Equity	$10,000
	$10,000		$10,000

Assume further that the only cost is depreciation.

Company A
Income Statement

Sales (1.20 X5%) X 10,000	$12,600
Depreciation (10,000 + 500)	10,500
Operating Income	2,100
Interest (10% X 4,000)	400
	1,700
Purchasing Power Gain (5% X 4,000 Debt)	200
Income Available for Distribution to Owners	$ 1,900

Company B
Income Statement

Sales	$12,600
Depreciation	10,500
Operating Income	2,100
Income Available for Distribution to Owners	$ 2,100

Owners Return on Investment (NIAT Owners Equity)

$$\frac{1,900}{6,000} = 31\%$$

$$\frac{2,100}{10,000} = 21\%$$

APPENDIX A (Continued)

Company A Balance Sheet December 31, 1978		Company B Balance Sheet December 31, 1978	
Cash (12,600-400-1,900)	$10,300	Cash	$10,500
Machine	10,500		
Acc/Depr.	(10,500)		
Asset	10,300		10,500
Note	4,000		
Inflation Adjustment (500 on Asset -200 Purchasing Power Gain)	300	Inflation Adjustment	500
		Equity	10,000
Equity	6,000		
Total	$10,000	Total	$10,500

Both companies can replace the asset without raising additional equity (see note 1).

Company A (assuming the same debt to equity ratio):

	Dr.	Cr.
Note Payable	4,000	
Cash		4,000
(Cash account equals 10,300−4,000 = 6,300)		
Machine	10,500	
Cash (60% X 10,500)		6,300
Notes Payable (40% X 10,500)		4,200 (see note 2)
(Cash account 6,300−6,300 = 0)		
Company B		
Machine	10,500	
Cash		10,500

NOTE 1:
In attempting to make the basic point illustrated in the example, i.e., that the purchasing power gain is available for dividend distribution, we have ignored the effects of inflation on holding cash. We could have addressed this problem by assuming that all cash flow was invested in marketable securities (a nonmonetary asset) and then converted back to cash at year end for balance sheet purposes. In any case, the basic difference between the two companies is the same.

NOTE 2:
The $4,200 is the equivalent of the $4,000 debt as of January 1, 1978.

relevant financial reporting in an age of price changes

by Robert R. Sterling

This article has the modest goal of clarifying the concept of price level adjustments. Since price level adjustments have been debated for a great many years, it may seem that the concept has previously been made quite clear. Perhaps so, but my reading of the recent literature, especially the testimony presented to the Financial Accounting Standards Board, persuades me that concept clarification is needed rather desperately. To put it negatively, I fear that if we take action on price levels

—establish a standard—prior to further clarification of the concept, we may make things worse instead of better.

A highly simplified case will be considered in this article. The advantages of simplified cases are that they are easily understood by both the reader and the author and they are more easily solved. If we cannot solve the simplified cases, then we can be fairly certain that we also cannot solve the complex cases. Thus, if a particular approach fails to provide a solution for simplified cases, then we can avoid wasting effort by trying that approach on complex cases. The main disadvantage of simplified cases is that even if we can solve them, there is no guarantee that the obtained solution can be extended to realistic cases. But the problem with realistic cases is that they are too complex to be easily understood or solved. I chose the simplified case in this article in the

Robert R. Sterling, *Ph.D., is currently Jesse H. Jones Distinguished Professor at Rice University's Department of Economics and Accounting in Houston. Among the numerous academic honors he has received is the AICPA accounting literature award for his article "Accounting Research, Education and Practice," which appeared in the September 1973* Journal of Accountancy. *He has been involved in much committee work for the American Accounting Association and has been a prolific contributor of books, articles and papers to the field of accounting. This article has been adapted from a speech given on Accounting Day at the University of California at Berkeley, May 30, 1974.*

The Journal of Accountancy, February 1975

Author's Note: I am grateful for the support of Arthur Young & Company in the preparation of this article. The conclusions, however, are mine and do not necessarily reflect the views of Arthur Young & Company.

Only price level adjusted current value financial statements fully meet the primary objectives of accounting—relevance and interpretability.

hope that the concept, once clarified, can be extended to more complex cases.[1]

The necessity of choosing attributes and the criteria for choosing

A measurement requires that one consciously decide which attribute is to be measured. Consider a physical object. It is impossible to measure that object; instead, one must decide which attribute (e.g., length, weight, hardness, color, density, carbon half-life, etc.) of that object is to be measured. The same is true for accounting measurements: we must decide which attribute is to be measured.[2]

The decision as to which attribute ought to be measured cannot be made on the basis of one's being "wrong" and the other's being "right." In regard to measuring a physical object, for example, one cannot say that it is wrong to measure the attribute of, say, length and right to measure the attribute of, say, weight. For some purposes,

---

[1] The choice of a simplified case reflects my general feeling that we accountants often err by immediately tackling the complex cases. I think that one of the reasons we can't get more solutions (or more agreement) is that we try to run before learning to crawl. Compare the procedure in the sciences where they first study highly simple cases. As Nelson Goodman (*Fact, Fiction, and Forecast* (New York: Bobbs-Merrill, 1965), p. xii) puts it:

". . . science has to isolate a few simple aspects of the world. . . . This, admittedly, is over-simplification. But conscious and cautious over-simplification, far from being an intellectual sin, is a prerequisite for investigation. We can hardly study at once all the ways in which everything is related to everything else."

By contrast, in accounting we seem to think that simplification is an intellectual sin. I think we would make more progress more rapidly if we took the roundabout route of examining simple cases before going on to the complex cases.

---

[2] Unfortunately, a single accounting term is often used to describe different attributes. It is clear, for example, that the income figure derived by using Fifo is different from the one derived by using Lifo, yet we refer to both as "income." Similarly, "price-level adjusted income" and "unadjusted income" are measures of different attributes despite the fact that both are called "income." The point is that it does not help to simply state that the attribute sought is "income" because that single term is used to refer to different attributes. Precise distinction of these attributes requires the use of different names —jargon—in this article.

length is the relevant attribute and, for other purposes, weight is relevant. The same is true in accounting. We cannot say that unadjusted figures are wrong and adjusted figures are right. Instead, we must provide interpretations of the attributes that are being measured and then decide which one we ought to measure. The decision as to which attribute we ought to measure must be based on the relevance of the attributes, not on one's being wrong and the other's being right.

> Consideration of what we ought to measure requires that we focus on the appropriate criterion—relevance.

The interpretation of an attribute is related, but not identical, to its relevance. A thorough discussion of interpretation and relevance requires distinctions that cannot be drawn here. The reader interested in pursuing these notions should see May Brodbeck, especially the discussion of the significance of concepts,[3] or Carl G. Hempel, especially the discussion of the theoretical import of concepts.[4] For the purpose of this article, the following brief discussion will suffice.

Interpretation

When an attribute involves an arithmetical calculation, the "empirical interpretation" of that attribute requires that it be placed in an "if . . . then . . ." statement. For example, the attribute "area" is defined as the product of the length and width of a plane, i.e., $A = LW$. To repeat the definition of that attribute is not an empirical interpretation. Instead, an empirical interpretation would require a statement such as "if this space were to be covered with tiles of this size, then it would require x tiles." This "if . . . then . . ." statement provides the listener with an understanding of the meaning of "area" as well as demonstrating one of the uses of the concept.

A counter example will show that the repetition of the definition does not aid in understanding the meaning of an attribute. I hereby define the attribute "ster" as the quotient of the length and width of a plane, i.e., $S = L/W$. If you were to ask me the meaning of that attribute, you would be justly disappointed if I simply repeated that it is the quotient of the length and width of a plane. Since "ster" cannot be inserted in an "if . . . then

. . ." statement, it is not empirically interpretable and, therefore, it should be regarded with suspicion. We don't have any idea of the meaning or use of "ster" because we haven't been able to interpret it. We should be highly suspicious of attributes if we don't understand their meaning or use. We therefore arrive at Criterion 1: *Attributes must be interpretable.*

Relevance

Everyone agrees that accounting information should be useful. As with other abstractions (e.g., truth, justice, fairness), however, we run into difficulty when we try to apply the concept. In an attempt to be more precise, to make the concept more concrete, in previous works I have replaced the term "usefulness" with the term "relevance."[5] I define relevance as follows:

"If a decision model specifies an attribute as an input or as a calculation, then that attribute is relevant to that decision model."

The negation, of course, is that if the attribute is not specified by the model, then that attribute is not relevant to that model.

Consider, for example, the decision about which object one should select as a life raft. One needs to know which, if any, of the available objects will float on water. The decision model specifies two attributes (weight and volume) as inputs and one attribute (density, the quotient of weight and volume) as a calculation. Then it specifies that one compare the density of the object to the density of water. Indeed, the interpretation of the calculated attribute of density is "if object x is less dense than fluid y, then x will float on y." Thus, three attributes—weight, volume and density—are relevant to the model. All other attributes are irrelevant.[6]

---

[3] May Brodbeck, ed., *Readings in the Philosophy of the Social Sciences* (New York: Macmillan, 1968), pp. 6-9.

[4] Carl G. Hempel, *Fundamentals of Concept Formation in Empirical Science* (Chicago: University of Chicago Press, 1952), p. 46.

[5] For example, see Robert R. Sterling, "Decision Oriented Financial Accounting," *Accounting and Business Research*, Summer 1973.

[6] Note the distinction between relevant to the decision *model* and relevant to the decision *maker*. Some decision makers may think that, say, area (instead of volume) is relevant to the decision. Others may think that color is relevant. Still others may think that a third attribute is relevant. Given a large number of decision makers, it would be impossible to supply measures of all of the attributes that all of them think are relevant. Moreover, all attributes other than weight, volume and density are of no help to the decision maker, despite the beliefs to the contrary.

The analogy fits accounting. We service a large number of decision makers (e.g., investors and potential investors), many of whom have demonstrably erroneous ideas about which attributes are relevant to their decisions. For example, despite the fact that the efficient market research has demonstrated that "technical analysis" (price charting) is of no use in trading the market, many investors and financial analysts still use it. Others use other attributes. It is impossible for us to supply measures of *all* the attributes that *all* investors think are relevant. Worse, such attributes are of no help in making the decision despite the fact that decision makers use them and think that they are relevant. Hence, we must define relevance in relation to decision models, not decision makers.

As the example makes clear, relevance is concerned with what ought to be measured. If someone were to measure the area of the object, it would not be wrong—it would simply be irrelevant to the decision. The area attribute meets the interpretability criterion, but it does not meet the relevance criterion. Applying this to accounting means that the selection of the attributes that we ought to measure and report requires that we examine the decision models and determine which attributes are specified by those models. Therefore we arrive at Criterion 2: *Attributes must be relevant.*

Complete exchange case

Description of the case

Consider the highly simplified problem of accounting for a trader on the New York Stock Exchange. The only activities of this simplified firm are the purchase and sale of securities in a near perfect market. To further simplify, assume that there are zero transaction (e.g., commission) costs and that all exchanges are for cash. There are no liabilities, which means that the total assets figure is equal to that of total owner's equity. In addition, assume that at the time of statement preparation all of the inventory has been sold so that the only asset on hand is cash.[7] Hence, there is only one asset—cash—to account for.

To simplify even further, assume that the only good that the trader consumes is bread, so that the Consumer Price Index is just the ratio of the prices of bread at two dates. Thus, there are only two real (nonmonetary) goods in this economy: securities (measured in shares) are the only producers' goods, and bread (measured in loaves) is the only consumers' good.

The facts of the case are that at January 1 the firm had $1,000 in cash. At the same date it purchased 100 shares for $10 per share. At February 1 the price has increased to $15 per share, and the entire inventory is sold. During the same period the price of bread increased from $.50 to $.60 per loaf, resulting in a Consumer Price Index of 1.2 (= $.60/$.50).

Measuring NOD

Exhibit 1, this page, shows the standard (unadjusted) financials for this firm. The interpretation is straightforward. The attribute being measured

---

[7] This is what I mean by a "complete exchange." See Robert R. Sterling, *Theory of the Measurement of Enterprise Income* (Lawrence: University Press of Kansas, 1970), pp. 27-28, for further discussion. For a discussion of the related notion of "complete cycles," see *Objectives of Financial Statements*, a report of the Accounting Objectives Study Group, Robert M. Trueblood, chairman (New York: AICPA, 1973).

Exhibit 1

Measuring number of dollars

Complete exchange case

| | Comparative balance sheets | |
	January 1	February 1
Cash	$1,000	$1,500
Invested capital	$1,000	$1,000
Retained earnings	-0-	500
Total owner's equity	$1,000	$1,500

	Income statement Month of January
Revenues	$1,500
Cost of securities sold	1,000
Net income	$ 500

---

is number of dollars (NOD). The balance sheets report the stocks of NOD at two dates, and the income statement reports the increment in NOD during the period.

Many people assert that unadjusted financials, such as those in Exhibit 1, are "wrong." Accompanying this assertion are a variety of comments about "changing purchasing power," "changing value of the dollar," etc. Although many different terms are used to make the criticism, they all refer to the ability of dollars to command goods and services. It is true that the financials in Exhibit 1 do not measure command over goods (COG). However, it is equally true that those financials accurately measure NOD. Thus, the criticism cannot possibly be that the financials are "wrong," because they are quite correct. I believe that the critics intend to say that the financials do not measure the relevant attribute—the COG attribute.

I don't mean to quibble over words. However, I do want to be clear as to the source of the difficulty. If the objective is to measure NOD, then auditors must certify the financials in Exhibit 1. However, if we decide that the objective is to measure COG, then it is easy to demonstrate that those financials do not meet that objective. This is an important distinction. It shifts the basis of the argument from wrong vs. right to what we ought to measure and report. Consideration of what we ought to measure requires that we focus on the appropriate criterion—relevance.

It is axiomatic that money per se is not desirable. Rather, it is the ability of money to command real goods that is desired. Witness Confederate money. Measuring the stocks of or incre-

Exhibit 2

Measuring command over goods in price level adjusted dollars

Complete exchange case

	Comparative balance sheets	
	Jan. 1	Feb. 1
Cash (January 1=$1,000 x 1.2)	1,200	$1,500
Invested capital ($1,000 x 1.2)	$1,200	$1,200
Retained earnings	-0-	300
Total owner's equity	$1,200	$1,500

	Income statement Month of January
Revenues	$1,500
Cost of securities sold ($1,000 x 1.2)	1,200
Net income	$ 300

---

ments in Confederate money is irrelevant—no one is interested in the results of such measurements—precisely because that money has no ability to command goods. As the extreme case of Confederate money makes clear, measurements of NOD are not specified by decision models; hence, NOD is irrelevant. Instead, decision models specify the measurement of COG; thus, Proposition 1: *COG is the relevant attribute.*

Measuring COG

As the name makes clear, the command over goods (COG) attribute is a measure of the number of goods that could be commanded in the market. Since the goods that could be commanded are physical objects, COG is a physical measure. The measurement is accomplished by multiplying the monetary units by a price index. The purpose of such price level adjustments is to permit the adjusted monetary units to be interpreted as physical units. Economics and statistics textbooks state this point explicitly. Wallace C. Peterson, for example, writes, "If we adjust by the above price index, the result will be a measure of *physical output*. . . ."[8] To put it another way, if price level adjustments are done properly, then the resulting figures can be interpreted as a measure of physical units.

Recall that there is only one consumer good in this simple case and therefore the Consumer Price

[8] Wallace C. Peterson, *Income, Employment, and Economic Growth* (New York: W. W. Norton & Co., 1962), p. 68.

Index is the ratio of the prices of that good at the two dates. The price of bread was $.50 and $.60 at January 1 and February 1, respectively. Hence, the Consumer Price Index is 1.2 (= $.60/$.50). In order to convert the NOD attribute in Exhibit 1 to the COG attribute, we need only multiply each of the January 1 figures by 1.2. The result is shown in Exhibit 2, this page.

The point to be stressed is not the procedure, however, but rather the ability to interpret those figures. We can divide all of the figures in Exhibit 2 by the $.60 per loaf price of bread at February 1 and obtain the following interpretation:

☐ If all of the assets of the firm had been used to purchase bread at January 1, then 2,000 loaves (= $1,200/$.60) could have been purchased.

☐ If all of the assets of the firm had been used to purchase bread at February 1, then 2,500 loaves (=$1,500/$.60) could have been purchased.

☐ Hence, the increment (income) in COG is 500 loaves (= $300/$.60).

The figures can be interpreted; therefore, they meet the interpretability criterion. Indeed, in this simple case we could prepare financials in physical units as shown in Exhibit 3, this page. One can check the accuracy of these financials by using the unadjusted January 1 figures and dividing by the price per loaf at January 1. For example, the unadjusted cash on hand at January 1 was $1,000 and the price per loaf was $.50. Therefore, the firm could have commanded 2,000 loaves (= $1,000/$.50) at January 1. In addition, note that all of the ratios of the figures in Exhibit 3 are the same as those in Exhibit 2. For example, Exhibit 2 shows a $300 net income on sales of $1,500, a return on sales of 20 percent. Exhibit 3

Exhibit 3

Measuring command over goods in physical units

Complete exchange case

	Comparative balance sheets	
	January 1	February 1
Cash	2,000 loaves	2,500 loaves
Invested capital	2,000 loaves	2,000 loaves
Retained income	0 loaves	500 loaves
Total owner's equity	2,000 loaves	2,500 loaves

	Income statement Month of January
Revenues	2,500 loaves
Cost of securities sold	2,000 loaves
Net income	500 loaves

shows a 500 loaf net income on sales of 2,500 loaves, a return of 20 percent.

Market basket interpretation. Interpretation of price level adjusted figures is usually more difficult because the price index is made up of a collection ("market basket") of goods. However, the concept is identical to the one-good index used in this

> . . . price level adjusted historical costs do not fully meet the criteria. The cash figures are interpretable and are measures of the relevant COG attribute. However, the securities and total asset figures are not interpretable (by me), are not specified by any decision model that I know of and are not measures of COG.

simple case. To illustrate, consider a two-good, equally weighted index composed of bread and milk.

Assume prices of $.50 per loaf and $1 per gallon at January 1 and $.60 per loaf and $1.20 per gallon at Febuary 1. Thus, the index is the same: ($.60 + $1.20)/($.50 + $1) = 1.2.

The January 1 cash figure of $1,000 would be adjusted to the same $1,200 (= $1,000 x 1.2). The interpretation, however, requires the use of both goods with equal budget allocations. One-half of the adjusted $1,200 divided by $.60 per loaf and by $1.20 per gallon yields 1,000 loaves (= $600/$.60) and 500 gallons (= $600/$1.20). Thus the interpretation is:

☐ If all of the assets of the firm had been used to purchase bread and milk with equal budget allocations at January 1, then the firm would have been able to buy 1,000 loaves of bread and 500 gallons of milk.

With a two-good index the preparation of financials in physical units would be cumbersome. The addition of more goods to the index would make it even more cumbersome. However, the concept is the same. The price level adjustment converts a monetary measure into a physical measure. It allows one to interpret the figures as the number of physical units that could have been bought.

Incomplete exchange case

Description of case

The difference between the "incomplete exchange" and the "complete exchange" cases is that, in the former, some noncash assets are held; hence, some

securities have been bought but, since they have not yet been sold, the exchange (or cycle from cash to cash) is said to be "incomplete." Assume that on January 1 the firm purchased 70 shares at $10 per share, leaving a cash balance of $300. No other transactions occur. The price of the securities has increased, as before, to $15 per share. Also, as before, the price of bread has increased from $.50 to $.60, resulting in a Consumer Price Index of 1.2.

Although this case is highly simplified, its consideration is complicated because there are four different proposed methods of accounting for it:
1 Historical cost.
2 Price level adjusted historical cost.
3 Current value.
4 Price level adjusted current value.

Historical cost. The familiar historical cost financials are presented in Exhibit 4, this page. Despite the increase in the prices of both bread and securities, the February 1 figures are exactly the same as those at January 1. It seems to me that these financials do not meet the criteria.

First, I am unable to interpret the figures. I don't know how to place them in an "if . . . then . . ." statement. Thus, I don't think they meet the interpretability criterion. However, my inability to interpret them may be due to a deficiency in my thinking rather than a deficiency in the figures. Therefore, instead of concluding that they are not interpretable, I will challenge the readers to provide an interpretation.

Second, I have not been able to find decision models that specify the figures. Thus, I don't think they meet the relevance (or usefulness) criterion.

Exhibit 4

Unadjusted historical cost

Incomplete exchange case

| | Comparative balance sheets | |
	January 1	February 1
Cash	$300	$300
Securities	700	700
Total assets	$1,000	$1,000
Invested capital	$1,000	$1,000
Retained earnings	-0-	-0-
Total owner's equity	$1,000	$1,000

	Income statement Month of January
Revenues	$ -0-
Cost of securities sold	-0-
Net income	$ -0-

Exhibit 5

Price level adjusted historical cost

Incomplete exchange case

	Comparative balance sheets	
	Jan. 1	Feb. 1
Cash (January 1 = $300 x 1.2)	$360	$300
Securities ($700 x 1.2)	840	840
Total assets	$1,200	$1,140
Invested capital ($1,000 x 1.2)	$1,200	$1,200
Retained earnings (deficit)	-0-	(60)
Total owner's equity	$1,200	$1,140

	Income statement Month of January
Revenues	$ -0-
Cost of securities sold	-0-
	-0-
Loss in COG from holding cash ($360-$300)	60
Net income (loss)	$(60)

Again, however, since I may have overlooked the decision models that specify these figures, I will challenge the readers to demonstrate their relevance rather than concluding that they are irrelevant.

Third, the figures clearly do not measure the COG attribute. There is no way to interpret them —prepare financials in physical units such as Exhibit 3—as measures of the ability to command goods.

Price level adjusted historical cost. A number of people have suggested—e.g., see Accounting Research Study No. 6[9]—that historical cost financials be adjusted by the following procedure:

1 Multiply the January 1 cash balance by the price index and take the difference between the adjusted January 1 balance and the unadjusted February 1 balance as a loss.

2 Multiply the January 1 securities cost by the price index and carry that adjusted figure forward to the February 1 balance sheet.

Financials adjusted by this procedure are shown in Exhibit 5, this page. The cash figures can be interpreted as follows:

☐ If the firm had used its cash at January 1 to purchase bread, then it could have purchased 600

loaves. (Adjusted cash of $360 divided by February 1 price per loaf of $.60 equals 600 loaves. Alternatively, the unadjusted cash of $300 divided by the January 1 price per loaf of $.50 equals 600 loaves.)

☐ If the firm had used its cash at February 1 to purchase bread, then it could have purchased 500 loaves (= $300/$.60).

☐ Hence, the loss from holding cash is $60 (= $360 − 300), which is equivalent to 100 loaves (= $60/$.60 and = 600 − 500).

Thus, the cash figures are (1) interpretable and (2) measurements of the relevant COG attribute. This is a major improvement over the unadjusted historical cost financials.

The problem lies with the figure for securities at February 1. First, I cannot find a true interpretation of the figure. I am not able to place it in an "if . . . then . . ." statement. Perhaps the figure is interpretable. Perhaps it is just that I don't know how to do it. For that reason, I will again challenge the readers to provide an interpretation rather than concluding that it is not interpretable.

Although I am not certain of the proper interpretation, I am certain that the figure cannot be interpreted as either NOD or COG:[10]

☐ If the securities were sold (or replaced) at February 1, then the NOD received (or required) would *not* be $840.

Thus, NOD cannot be the proper interpretation.

☐ If the securities were sold at February 1 and the cash proceeds used to purchase bread, then

---

[9] Accounting Research Study No. 6 *Reporting the Financial Effects of Price Level Changes* (New York: AICPA, 1963), p. 11.

---

[10] It is possible to interpret the figures as a measure of both NOD and COG by making the contrary to fact assumption of proportional price changes.
☐ If the securities were sold (or replaced) at February 1 and *if price changes were proportional,* then the NOD received (or required) would be $840, which is equivalent to COG of 1,400 loaves (= $840/$.60).
The statement is false. Price changes were not proportional in the case under consideration. More importantly, they are not proportional in the real world. In fact, many changes are in opposite directions. For example, last year refined petroleum products went up 79.5 percent while animal feeds went down 26.5 percent, both of which are components of the Wholesale Price Index which went up 16.4 percent. Clearly then, we cannot assume proportional price changes any more than we can assume a stable measuring unit.
When writing *Enterprise Income* (p. 347), it occurred to me that since price level adjusted historical costs were interpretable if all price changes were proportional, perhaps the proponents had implicitly assumed proportional price changes. I rejected the idea, however, because the assumption was contrary to fact. That the proponents were implicitly assuming proportional price changes now seems more plausible because several authors mention what would be the case if it were true. For example, in "Problems of Implementing the Trueblood Objectives Report," *Empirical Research in Accounting: Selected Studies* (Chicago: Institute of Professional Accounting, 1974), Richard M. Cyert and Yuji Ijiri correctly claim that "[price level adjusted historical costs] are exactly the same as current values if all prices move up or down in the same proportion." The problem is that price changes have not been proportional in the past and they are not likely to be proportional in the future.

the number of loaves that could be purchased (i.e., the COG) is *not* 1,400 (= $840/$.60).

Thus, COG cannot be the proper interpretation. This makes it difficult to interpret the total assets figure. As demonstrated earlier, the cash figures can be interpreted as COG and it seems clear that the intent of ARS No. 6, among others, is to measure COG. So, the cash figure is a COG measure, and the securities figure is not a COG measure. Since the total assets figure is the sum of a measure of COG and a measure of not-COG, what is its interpretation? For the reasons given above, I again challenge the readers to provide an interpretation.

Second, I do not know of any decision model that specifies the securities or the total assets figure; therefore, I will tentatively (until the readers demonstrate otherwise) conclude that these figures are irrelevant. I can firmly conclude that they are irrelevant in regard to Proposition 1 since they do not measure COG.

In summary, price level adjusted historical costs do not fully meet the criteria. The cash figures are interpretable and are measures of the relevant COG attribute. However, the securities and total asset figures are not interpretable (by me), are not specified by any decision model that I know of and are not measures of COG.

> We should not be arguing that one set of figures is right and another is wrong; instead we should be arguing about which attribute we ought to measure and report. Selection of the attribute that ought to be measured requires precise criteria, rigorously applied.

Current value. The current value financials are shown in Exhibit 6, this page. Recall that 70 shares were purchased at January 1 for $10 per share. Hence, the current value of securities at January 1 was $700 as shown. At February 1 the price has increased to $15 per share for 70 shares or $1,050 current value.

The figures can be interpreted as measures of NOD:

☐ If the securities were sold at February 1, then $1,050 would be received.

The total assets figure can be interpreted similarly:

☐ If all of the assets of the firm were converted into cash at February 1, then the firm would hold $1,350.

Exhibit 6

Current value

Incomplete exchange case

	Comparative balance sheets January 1	February 1
Cash	$300	$300
Securities	700	1,050
Total assets	$1,000	$1,350
Invested capital	$1,000	$1,000
Retained earnings	-0-	350
Total owner's equity	$1,000	$1,350

	Income statement Month of January
Revenues	$ -0-
Cost of securities sold	-0-
	-0-
Gain on price increase of securities	350
Net income	$350

That is, there is no difficulty in adding the $300 on hand to the number of dollars that could be acquired if the securities were sold. The sum is a straightforward interpretation of the number of dollars that would be held if the securities were sold.[11] The income statement shows the increment in NOD due to the $5 per share price increase for 70 shares. If desired, this increment could be labeled "unrealized" since the securities haven't been sold.

The figures for individual and total assets can also be interpreted as measures of COG. For example:

☐ If the firm had used all of its assets at February 1 to purchase bread, then it could have purchased 2,250 loaves (= $1,350/$.60).

This is a major improvement over the price level adjusted historical cost financials.

The problem lies with the income figure. The $350 NOD increment (net income) does not reflect the increment in COG. COG at January 1 was 2,000 loaves (= $1,000/$.50) and, at Febru-

[11] Technically, there is a difference between this figure and the NOD figure in the complete exchange case. Perhaps they should be distinguished by calling the above figure COD (command over dollars) instead of NOD. However, since the difference is slight and since I have already tried the readers' patience by introducing new jargon, I didn't make the distinction. Interested readers should consult Raymond J. Chambers (*Accounting, Evaluation, and Economic Behavior* (Englewood Cliffs, N.J.: Prentice-Hall, 1966)) for a description of current cash equivalents (CCE) which is, as I read it, identical to COD. Chambers also provides for a price level adjustment of CCE.

Exhibit 7

Price level adjusted current value (measuring command over goods in price level adjusted dollars)

Incomplete exchange case

	Comparative balance sheets	
	Jan. 1	Feb. 1
Cash (January 1 = $300 x 1.2)	$360	$300
Securities (January 1 = $700 x 1.2)	840	1050
Total assets	$1,200	$1,350
Invested capital		
($1,000 x 1.2)	$1,200	$1,200
Retained earnings	-0-	150
Total owner's equity	$1,200	$1,350

	Income statement Month of January
Revenues	$ -0-
Cost of securities sold	-0-
	-0-
Gain from holding securities ($1,050-$840)	210
Loss from holding cash ($360-$300)	(60)
Net income	$150

Exhibit 8

Interpretation of price level adjusted values (measuring command over goods in physical units)

Incomplete exchange case

	Comparative balance sheets	
	January 1	February 1
Cash	600 loaves	500 loaves
Securities	1,400	1,750
Total assets	2,000 loaves	2,250 loaves
Invested capital	2,000 loaves	2,000 loaves
Retained earnings	-0-	250
Total owner's equity	2,000 loaves	2,250 loaves

	Income statement Month of January
Revenues	-0- loaves
Cost	-0-
	-0-
Gain from holding securities	350
Loss from holding cash	(100)
Net income	$250 loaves

ary 1, it was 2,250 loaves (= $1,350/$.60), an increment of 250 loaves. Division of the $350 NOD increment by the January 1 price per loaf of $.50 yields 700 loaves. Division by the February 1 price per loaf of $.60 yields 583⅓ loaves. Since neither division yields the actual 250 loaf increment, the current value income statement does not measure the COG increment.

In summary, current values do not fully meet the criteria. All of the figures are interpretable as measures of NOD, but only the assets figures are interpretable as measures of COG. The income figure can only be interpreted as NOD. Since COG is the relevant attribute, current value income does not meet the relevance criterion.

Price level adjusted current values. In order to "price level adjust" the current value financials in Exhibit 6, we need only multiply each of the January 1 figures by the Consumer Price Index of 1.2[12] The adjusted financials are shown in Exhibit 7, this page.

All of the individual figures as well as the sums and differences in Exhibit 7 can be interpreted:

☐ If all of the assets of the firm had been used to purchase bread at January 1, then 2,000 loaves (=$1,200/$.60) could have been purchased.

☐ If all of the assets of the firm had been used to purchase bread at February 1, then 2,250 loaves (=$1,350/$.60) could have been purchased.

☐ Hence, the increment (income) in COG is 250 loaves (= $150/$.60), which is the net of a gain of 350 loaves (= $210/$.60) from holding securities and a loss of 100 loaves (= $60/$.60) from holding cash.

The complete interpretation is given in Exhibit 8, this page. As before, note that the ratios of all the figures in Exhibit 8 are the same as those in Exhibit 7. For example, the increase in total assets is 12.5 percent in both exhibits.

The figures can be interpreted. Moreover, they are interpreted as measures of the relevant COG attribute. Therefore, price level adjusted current values meet both criteria.

Summary and conclusion

The modest objective of this article was to clarify the concept of price level adjustments. The first clarification was concerned with what we ought to be arguing about. We should not be arguing that one set of figures is right and another is wrong; instead we should be arguing about which attribute we ought to measure and report. Selection of the attribute that ought to be measured requires

---

[12] This is "inflating" the past financials. It is possible to "deflate" the current financials without destroying the interpretability. The reasons for preferring to adjust the past financials is given in Sterling, *Enterprise Income,* p. 339. For the same reasons, I prefer the "roll-forward" procedure.

precise criteria, rigorously applied. I agree fully with the Trueblood Committee that the primary objective (or criterion) of accounting is usefulness. The substitution of "interpretability" and "relevance" for "usefulness" was an attempt to make that criterion more precise and more concrete, not a disagreement.

The criterion of interpretability is that a given attribute be capable of being placed in a true "if . . . then . . ." statement. The failure of an attribute to meet that criterion should cause us to be skeptical of that attribute. The criterion of relevance is that an attribute be specified by a decision model. This must be what is meant by "usefulness," since if an attribute is not specified by any decision model, then I can't imagine how it could be useful.

These criteria were utilized in the examination of the simple problem of accounting for a trader on the New York Stock Exchange under the two cases of a complete and an incomplete exchange. The examination of the first case—complete exchange—revealed that although the NOD attribute is interpretable, it is irrelevant. COG is the relevant attribute. The conclusion that COG is the relevant attribute permitted a more precise application of the relevance criterion in examining the incomplete exchange case, i.e., determination of whether or not the attribute could be interpreted as COG.

When accounting for an incomplete exchange, there are four competing methods. Each of these methods was subjected to the criteria. Some methods partially meet the criteria but only one method —price level adjusted current values—fully meet them. The results are summarized in Exhibit 9, this page. Since the cells that contain "no" may be due to a deficiency in my examination rather than a deficiency in the figures, the readers were challenged to demonstrate their interpretability and relevance. Until such a demonstration is provided, I will maintain that only price level adjusted current value financials fully meet both criteria.

It follows that the appropriate procedure is to

Exhibit 9

Method \ Criteria	Interpretable	Relevant
Historical cost	No	No
Price level adjusted historical cost	No	No
Current value	Yes	No
Price level adjusted current value	Yes	Yes

(1) adjust the present statement to current values and (2) adjust the previous statement by a price index. It is important to recognize that *both* adjustments are necessary and that neither is a substitute for the other. Confusion on this point is widespread. For example, a business executive recently announced that his firm had converted to current value accounting when, in fact, the firm had done nothing but make price level adjustments to historical costs. In addition, several CPAs seem to be saying that current value accounting is a substitute for price level adjustments. Also, although I am not entirely clear on the Securities and Exchange Commission's position on this issue, it seems that it is leaning toward current replacement costs as a substitute for price level adjustments. Finally, the phrasing of the FASB's questions seemed to indicate that it thought of current values and price level adjustments as competing methods, only *one* of which should be selected.

I hope that the consideration of this simple case demonstrates that both are required. ∎

Robert T. Sprouse, Ph.D.

Understanding Inflation Accounting*

This article offers a good understanding of the several proposals and requirements advanced by various authorities in the United States and abroad to reflect the effects of inflation in financial reporting.

Robert T. Sprouse, Ph.D., is Vice Chairman of the FASB. He was Professor of Accounting at the Stanford University Graduate School of Business for eight years, after having taught at the University of California and Harvard Business Schools. He has coauthored numerous technical papers and research studies and has been published frequently in professional journals. Consultant and board member of many corporations, Dr. Sprouse was president of the American Accounting Association.

* Extracted from a presentation given in Puerto Rico to the National Retail Merchants Association, Financial Executives Division.

It is important, in talking about reporting the effects of inflation in financial statements, to agree on a common meaning of the term "inflation." According to *Webster's New Collegiate Dictionary*, the phenomenon of inflation is characterized by a substantial and continuing rise in the general price level. Stated another way, inflation is characterized by a decrease in the *general* purchasing power of the monetary unit. Due to a variety of economic factors, the prices of specific types of goods and services acquired by a business enterprise may change more or less than the *general* inflationary trend or even change in the opposite direction. For example, pocket calculators are getting better and better, yet in spite of inflation they are also getting cheaper and cheaper. It is important, therefore, that inflation not be confused with changes in the price of a specific item.

Some Effects of Inflation

One striking illustration of the effect of changes in purchasing power is the experience of many with Series E savings bonds. A private inducted into the Army in 1942 signed up for a payroll deduction to buy Series E savings bonds. Each payday $6.25 was deducted from his $50 per month pay and at the end of one year he was the proud and prosperous possessor of a $100 bond that had cost a total of $75. Held to maturity at the end of ten years, the effective rate of interest was about 2.9 percent compounded semiannually. At their maturity, he found it was necessary to report to the IRS $25 income on each $100 bond. That is, based on the unadjusted historical cost of $75, he had income of $25 during the ten-year period; he had more dollars at the end of the ten-year period that he had at the beginning. According to the Consumer Price Index, however, anyone who invested $75 in such bonds during 1942 would have to receive about $122 in 1952 merely to recover the amount of purchasing power origi-

nally invested. Based on the historical cost adjusted for changes in the general price level (as measured by the CPI), there was a loss of 22, 1952 dollars during the ten-year period; the holder actually had $22 less purchasing power at the end of the ten-year period than he had at the beginning. To make a bad matter worse, he was required to pay federal income taxes on the $25 income. Assuming an income tax rate of about 20 percent, he was required to pay five 1952 dollars in federal income taxes. The $5 tax brought the total loss of purchasing power to 27, 1952 dollars.

Note that the recognition of "current values" would not have alleviated this distorted measure of "income" in any way whatsoever. The current values were readily and objectively determinable; indeed, a schedule of "current values" was printed right on the savings bond itself. After the first couple of years a new and higher current value was attained each six months. As a matter of fact, in this case, selling price and replacement cost and the present value of future cash flows were identical; presumably, all "current values" advocates would be satisfied, regardless of the variation they prefer.

A business holding monetary assets during a period of inflation has the same kind of purchasing power loss, but because it usually is also holding monetary liabilities, such as accounts payable and long-term debt, it also has a purchasing power gain. That is, less purchasing power will be required to settle those obligations than was obtained at the time the obligations were originally incurred. Those who have mortgages on their homes are probably familiar with this latter phenomenon. The current value of a home is probably keeping pace with inflation but the amount of the mortgage is fixed; as a result there is a gain in wealth.

Some have suggested that a general purchasing power gain on long-term debt be offset against

THE **CPa** JOURNAL / JANUARY 1977

interest expense in order to reflect the "real" interest cost of such debt. Perhaps it is not as important *where* the gain is reported as it is whether the gain *is* reported.

Some have argued that the measure of the change in the general purchasing power of net monetary items (monetary assets less monetary liabilities) would be crude because of the problems of general price index construction. This may be true, but general price indexes have become widely understood— particularly the Consumer Price Index and the Gross National Product Implicit Price Deflator.

Others argue that an index at the gross national product level does not purport to measure changes in the overall prices paid by any specific enterprise or consumer. This is also true, but there is increasing use of such indexes. For example, an article appeared in the *New York Times* recently, entitled, "Have Athletes' Salaries Hit Ceiling?" It reported that the top sports star in 1975 earned $500,000 compared to $60,000 earned by the top sports star in 1925. That sounds like quite an increase but the article pointed out that in 1975, taking inflation and higher tax rates into account, it would take an income of $500,000 to produce the same amount of purchasing power as represented by an income of $60,000 in 1925. Thus, while the top star in 1975 received eight times as many dollar bills as the top star of 1925, their disposable incomes would purchase the same amount of goods.

Proposals for Change

If we were asked what accounting model is used today for financial reporting, most of us would probably quickly respond, "the historical cost model." For example, we are particularly aware that inventories and property and equipment are recorded at the cost incurred at the time they were acquired. However, while it may be true that our present system is dominated by historical cost measurement, it is important to recognize that the present system is not a pure historical cost system. As an example, we presently record receivables at their net realizable value—not their historical cost. Also, we presently use the equity method to record investments in common stock of unconsolidated subsidiaries and certain other investees, not the cost method. There are many other examples of items that are not presented at their historical cost in today's financial statements. When there is good reason to depart from historical cost, we have done so.

The increased rate of inflation in recent years has led many people to question the usefulness of the so-called conventional "historical cost" model. But while many agree that a change in our present accounting model is necessary, few agree on the kind of change that is appropriate. Three kinds of proposals have surfaced.

General Purchasing Power Accounting

Some of those who favor a change advocate only that conventional financial statements be restated in terms of units of general purchasing power. It is important to emphasize that such restatement alone would adhere to historical cost as the primary basis of valuation; the restatement would merely convert historical cost now measured in terms of numbers of dollars to historical cost measured in terms of units of general purchasing power. This point is emphasized because considerable confusion continues to exist about the purpose and result of restating conventional financial statements in terms of units of GPP. General purchasing power restatements of historical costs are not intended to measure any form of "current value." It would be sheer coincidence if the historical cost of an asset restated for changes in the general purchasing power of the dollar resulted in a measurement which was equivalent, in any sense, to the asset's "current value."

The FASB issued an exposure draft in December 1974 that, if adopted, would require financial statements to include certain supplemental information restated in terms of units of general purchasing power. At that time, inflation was at its double-digit peak. Over

470 letters of comment were received in response to that exposure draft and valuable input from 84 companies that applied the exposure draft to their 1972, 1973 and 1974 financial statements was also received. There is no question about being able to make general purchasing power restatements in a practical and objective way; the restatement process is completely mechanical. The question is primarily one of meaning and usefulness.

Similar proposals have been put forth by authoritative groups in other countries. Perhaps the most interesting developments abroad are in the United Kingdom. In the U.K., the Accounting Standards Steering Committee issued an exposure draft in January 1973 recommending supplementary disclosure of financial statements restated to reflect changes in the general price level. In May 1974, they issued a "provisional standard" adopting the proposals in the earlier exposure draft and a large number of companies in the U.K. have published general purchasing power information. Presumably, the U.K. standard would have been mandatory rather than provisional if the British Parliament had not interceded by establishing a committee called the "Sandilands Committee of Inquiry" to study the potential economic impact of such a requirement. The Report of the Sandilands Committee was issued in September 1975, and recommended that beginning after December 24, 1977, companies should prepare their basic—not supplemental—financial statements on the basis of what is called "current cost accounting." Furthermore, the Report recommended that no general purchasing power restatement be made.

The Australian Accounting Standards Committee issued an exposure draft entitled "A Method of Accounting for Changes in the Purchasing Power of Money" in December 1974. While that proposal was still being exposed, the Committee issued another exposure draft entitled "A Method of Current Value Accounting" for the public to consider at the same time as the general purchasing power proposal. The two proposals were similar to the FASB exposure draft on general purchasing power accounting and the SEC proposal for disclosures of current replacement cost information that were outstanding concurrently.

An exposure draft on reporting in units of general purchasing power has also been issued in Canada; and recently, the International Accounting Standards Committee issued an exposure draft entitled "Accounting Treatment of Changing Prices," which states:

> Enterprises should present in their financial statements information that represents a systematic response to specific price changes or to changes in the general level of prices, or to both.

Current Value Accounting

Some in the U.S. who believe that a change in our present accounting model is necessary, advocate changing from historical cost to some type of "current value" accounting. In FASB jargon, that alternative calls for a change in the attribute being measured, in contrast to a change in the unit of measurement. That is, instead of using historical cost as the attribute to be measured, some form of "current value" would be measured.

It should be noted that "current value" has been used as a general term embracing any valuation other than historical cost. A list of some of the attributes of assets that might be encompassed by this general term "current value" appears in Exhibit A. Replacement cost accounting is in the forefront now because of the SEC's recent issuance of Accounting Series Release 190. Replacement cost accounting reflects the amount that would have to be paid if the same asset were acquired currently. But, what exactly is meant by the "same asset?" To some, it would mean replacement of an asset with an identical asset; to others—for example, in SEC ASR 190—it means replacement of the productive capacity represented by an asset.

The Sandilands Report calls for "value to the business" which it defines as "the loss the company would suffer if it were deprived of the asset." The Report states that in the majority of cases this value will be the cost to replace the asset in kind. However, the Report states that:

> in certain circumstances the "value to the business" of an asset will be less than its replacement cost—that is, where its net realizable value and its "economic value" are lower than replacement cost.

Economic value is determined by the use to which an asset is to be put and the expected cash flows from that use.

Current exit value is another type of valuation which falls under the broad term "current value." Current exit value refers to the amount of cash that could be obtained currently by selling an asset in orderly liquidation—that is, its market value. This valuation system has been supported strongly by a well-known Australian, Ray Chambers, who describes it as "current cash equivalents" and argues that it is the only consistently relevant measurement of an asset.

With all the different methods of determining "current value" one is never certain what someone is advocating when they are said to favor "current value accounting." The only thing one can be certain of is that they favor a departure from historical costs.

General Purchasing Power and Current Value

A third group advocates a change that would include both general purchasing power restatement and current value accounting. They suggest that both a common measuring unit and a change in the attribute being measured are neces- sary in order to supply users of financial statements with useful information that is comparable from period to period in times of inflation. General purchasing power accounting and current value accounting are sometimes characterized as alternatives, but they are not alternatives; they deal with entirely different problems. General purchasing power accounting is concerned solely with the measuring unit. That is, should financial statements be stated in units of money that vary in economic significance or be stated in terms of units of general purchasing power or both? On the other hand, the change to current value is concerned with the attribute being measured. That is, should financial statements report historical costs or report some form of "current value?"

Illustration of Different Theories

A simple illustration may help clarify this important distinction. Assume a company purchased an investment in marketable securities on January 1, 19X1 for $100,000. During that year the market value increased $20,000 to $120,000. However, during the same year the general-price-level index increased 12 percent.

Exhibit B shows four possible sets of information derived from varying: (1) the unit of measure, and (2) the attribute being measured. If historical cost is the attribute being measured and units of money are the measuring units, we would report marketable securities on December 31, 19X1 at $100,000 and no gain or loss for 19X1. If historical cost is the attribute being measured and units of general pur-

---

EXHIBIT A

"Current Value"

A. *Current Cost*
   1. Replacement in kind.
   2. Replacement of productive capacity.
B. *Value to the Business (Sandilands' Report)*
   1. Replacement in kind.
   2. Net realizable value (expected exit value).
   3. Economic value (present value of expected cash flows).
C. *Current Exit Value (Current Market Value)*

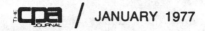 / JANUARY 1977

Exhibit B

Marketable Securities

Facts

January 1, 19X1	Cost	$100,000
December 31, 19X1	Market Value	$120,000

General Price Level Increased 12% During 19X1

Balance Sheet

	Historical Cost		"Current Value"	
	Money	GPP	Money	GPP
Marketable Securities	$100,000	$112,000	$120,000	$120,000
Capital Stock	$100,000	$112,000	$100,000	$112,000
Retained Earnings	–	–	20,000	8,000
	$100,000	$112,000	$120,000	$120,000

Income Statement

December 31, 19X1	Market Value	$120,000	$120,000
	Cost	100,000	112,000
Holding Gain		$ 20,000	$ 8,000

chasing power are the measuring units, we would report that marketable securities cost the equivalent of 112,000 year-end dollars but no gain or loss for the period would be recognized. If "current value" is the attribute being measured and units of money are the measuring units, we would report marketable securities at $120,000 and a $20,000 holding gain for the period. If current value is the attribute being measured and units of general purchasing power are the units of measure,

we would report marketable securities at 120,000 year-end dollars and a holding gain of 8,000 year-end dollars. I leave it to you to select the most meaningful answer.

The important point is that, because general purchasing power accounting is concerned with the measuring unit and current value accounting is concerned with the attribute being measured, the merits of each can and should be evaluated independently. They cannot rightfully be viewed as alterna-

tives. General purchasing power restatement is just as applicable to current value statements as it is to historical cost statements.

Conclusion

The FASB, with the help of 84 corporations, conducted extensive field tests in connection with the exposure draft on "Financial Reporting in Units of General Purchasing Power." Those field tests were costly and time-consuming for both the FASB and the participating companies. It should be emphasized that while this field test procedure has been costly and time-consuming, the Board believes it is necessary to follow such deliberate procedures in connection with projects with such broad ramifications. The Board would propose to follow similar deliberate procedures in its consideration of the current value question.

The FASB is not competing with the SEC. It will not now rush to issue a statement on "current value" accounting because of the SEC's release. It will follow the deliberate procedures which we feel are so important. Much work remains to be done in considering the concepts and implementation issues related to "current value" accounting; and the Board will look to those who work with financial information on a day to day basis for help in resolving these issues.Ω

The Financial Accounting Standards Board's (FASB) new Statement No. 33, "Financial Reporting and Changing Prices," which requires the nation's largest public companies to report the effects of inflation on their financial statements, is controversial and extremely complex. It is the most significant pronouncement issued by the FASB to date. Understanding the new rule's concepts will require a major educational effort.

FASB Chairman Donald J. Kirk describes the Statement as meeting "an urgent need for information about the effects of changing prices." He cites the following as consequences that would result if this supplemental information is not provided:

■ Investors' and creditors' understanding of a company's performance and their ability to assess future cash flows may be severely limited, and

■ Government officials may lack information on the implications of their decisions on economic policy.

SCOPE AND EFFECTIVE DATE

The disclosures are effective for fiscal years ending after December 24, 1979, but, as explained later, companies may postpone disclosure of the 1979 current cost information until their 1980 annual reports. Only public companies having either $1 billion of assets or $125 million of inventories and gross properties at the beginning of the year are required to present the supplemental information.

A SUMMARY OF THE FASB'S INFLATION ACCOUNTING RULES

Statement No. 33 is considered to be one of the most important steps taken by the FASB so far. This article offers an overview of its effects.

DENNIS R. BERESFORD
Partner

NORMAN N. STRAUSS
Partner

JOHN R. KLEIN
Supervisor
Ernst & Whinney

FINANCIAL EXECUTIVE January 1980

All enterprises, however, are encouraged to make these disclosures. Many banks, insurance companies, and other large financial institutions which did not have to report under the Securities and Exchange Commission's (SEC) replacement cost rule are covered by the FASB standard.

While the FASB has decided to stay with historical cost in the primary financial statements, Statement No. 33 specifies the minimum changing prices disclosures that are to be presented as supplementary information in annual reports. The delibera-

tions on the changing prices standard generated a great deal of controversy among preparers, auditors, and users of financial statements over how the FASB should proceed on its inflation accounting experiment. Realizing that a consensus could not be reached on how to report the effects of inflation on business enterprises, the FASB concluded that companies should report under two fundamentally different measurement approaches—historical-cost/constant-dollar accounting, which deals with general inflation (i.e., changes in the purchasing

power of the dollar), and current-cost accounting, which addresses specific price changes.

ILLUSTRATIVE DISCLOSURES

Figures I (below) and **II** (p. 14), illustrate disclosures of the current year information contained in Statement No. 33. These disclosures must be included in a company's annual shareholders report and Form 10-K. The information can be presented either outside the financial statements or in an unaudited footnote. The follow-

---

FIGURE I
Statement of Income from Continuing Operations
Adjusted for Changing Prices For the Year Ended December 31, 1980
(In 000s of Dollars)

	As Reported in the Primary Statements	Adjusted for General Inflation	Adjusted for Changes in Specific Prices (Current Costs)
Net sales and other operating revenues	$253,000	$253,000	$253,000
Cost of goods sold	197,000	204,384	205,408
Depreciation and amortization expense	10,000	14,130	19,500
Other operating expense	20,835	20,835	20,835
Interest expense	7,165	7,165	7,165
Provision for income taxes	9,000	9,000	9,000
	244,000	255,514	261,908
Income (loss) from continuing operations	$ 9,000	$ (2,514)	$ (8,908)
Gain from decline in purchasing power of net amounts owed		$ 7,729	$ 7,729
Increase in specific prices (current cost) of inventories and property, plant, and equipment held during the year*			$ 24,608
Effect of increase in general price level			18,959
Excess of increase in specific prices over increase in the general price level			$ 5,649

*At December 31, 1980, current cost of inventory was $65,700 and current cost of property, plant, and equipment, net of accumulated depreciation, was $85,100.

ing examples cover 1980 reporting, when data reflecting both measurement methods are required to be presented.

Figure I shows income becoming a loss after inflation adjustment (an extreme example). The actual effect of applying the Statement's requirements will vary from company to company, depending on such factors as whether LIFO is used in the basic financial statements

(rather than FIFO as in this illustration), the age and relative amount of properties, and the changes in specific prices of the company's assets.

In the previous example, the income statement information is presented under the different measurement bases. Alternatively, a "reconciliation format" can be used, as indicated in **Figure II,** below, which shows the adjustments to historical

income from continuing operations to arrive at the inflation-adjusted amounts.

HISTORICAL-COST/CONSTANT-DOLLAR BASIS

Constant-dollar accounting is a method of reporting financial statement items in dollars having a fixed purchasing power. It attempts to portray how general inflation has affected the exchange value of the dollar. The concept has been around for over 40 years under different names—"price-level accounting" in Accounting Principles Board Statement No. 3 (1969), and "general purchasing power accounting" in a 1974 FASB proposal.

A comprehensive application of historical-cost/constant-dollar accounting to each financial statement item is not required by Statement No. 33. Instead, the FASB decided to focus on the items most often affected by inflation—inventories, property, plant, equipment, and monetary assets and liabilities. Therefore, the Statement requires disclosure for the current year of only:

■ Historical income from continuing operations adjusted for average current year constant-dollar measurements of cost of goods sold and depreciation, depletion, and amortization. (To simplify the disclosures, other revenues and expenses are not adjusted because the FASB believes many already reflect average current-year dollars. Similarly, because cost of goods sold for companies using the LIFO inventory method would

---

FIGURE II
Statement of Income from Continuing Operations Adjusted for Changing Prices For the Year Ended December 31, 1980
(In 000s of Average 1980 Dollars)

Income from continuing operations, as reported in the income statement		$ 9,000
Adjustments to restate costs for the effect of general inflation		
Cost of goods sold	(7,384)	
Depreciation and amortization expense	(4,130)	(11,514)
Loss from continuing operations adjusted for general inflation		(2,514)
Adjustments to reflect difference between general inflation and changes in specific prices (current costs)		
Cost of goods sold	(1,024)	
Depreciation and amortization expense	(5,370)	(6,394)
Loss from continuing operations adjusted for changes in specific prices		$ (8,908)
Gain from decline in purchasing power of net amounts owed		$ 7,729
Increase in specific prices (current cost) of inventories and property, plant, and equipment held during the year*		$ 24,608
Effect of increase in general price level		18,959
Excess of increase in specific prices over increase in the general price level		$ 5,649

*At December 31, 1980, current cost of inventory was $65,700 and current cost of property, plant, and equipment, net of accumulated depreciation, was $85,100.

---

already reflect current-year dollars—assuming no liquidation of prior years' layers has occurred—a constant-dollar adjustment for cost of goods sold would be unnecessary when a company uses LIFO), and

■ Purchasing power gain or loss on net monetary items. (This constant-dollar disclosure attempts to show the gain or loss in purchasing power that results from holding monetary assets and liabilities during periods of inflation.)

The FASB does not require items such as investments in affiliates, intangible assets, and deferred charges and credits to be restated. But, companies wishing to present comprehensive supplementary financial statements on a constant-dollar basis may do so.

The Consumer Price Index for All Urban Consumers has been chosen to measure general inflation, principally because it is available on a monthly basis.

CURRENT-COST BASIS

This is a method of measuring assets and related expenses at current cost at the balance sheet date or at the date of sale or use. It focuses on the specific price changes for individual assets, rather than price changes caused by general inflation. Current-cost measurements are usually made for the assets presently owned and used by a company, and not for assets that might replace existing assets, like SEC replacement-cost accounting (which has recently been dropped).

As under the historical-cost/constant-dollar basis, the FASB directs current-cost accounting at inventories, property, plant, and equipment. Companies will be required to disclose for the current year:

■ Historical income from continuing operations adjusted for current-cost measurements of cost of goods sold and depreciation expense,

■ Increases or decreases in current-cost amounts of inventories, property, plant, and equipment, net of the effects of general inflation, and

■ Current cost of inventories and net current cost of property, plant, and equipment as of the latest balance sheet date.

The FASB's current-cost basis includes certain elements of current-cost/constant-dollar accounting. For example, the inflation component of the increase or decrease in current costs is a constant-dollar concept, which enables a comparison of how the specific price changes of a company's resources fared against general inflation. Also, companies wishing to present comprehensive supplementary financial statements on a current-cost/constant-dollar basis may do so.

The Statement allows companies a considerable amount of flexibility in selecting methods of determining current cost, ranging from indexing historical costs with specific price indexes to direct pricing techniques (e.g., invoices and unit pricing). Despite this flexibility, and the fact that most affected companies have been presenting replacement-cost information, the FASB realizes that some companies may encounter problems in developing the current cost disclosures for inclusion in 1979 annual reports. Therefore, companies are not required to make initial disclosure of the current cost information for 1979 until their 1980 annual reports.

IMPLEMENTING CURRENT COST

Because of the affected companies' experience under the SEC's Accounting Series Release No. 190, it is expected that many companies will be able to use much of their replacement-cost data when determining current cost. For example:

■ Inventories—replacement-cost measurements can generally be used to determine the current cost of inventories and the cost of goods sold. Also, as a practical matter, the Statement acknowledges that cost of goods sold determined by the LIFO inventory method (assuming no layer liquidations) will provide an acceptable approximation of cost of goods sold at current cost, and

■ Properties — companies whose replacement-cost approach yielded a reproduction cost (or replacement cost in kind)—either by indexing historical costs or more direct methods—may use this data to determine current cost. Where replacement with technologically superior or substantially different assets was assumed, adjustments can be made to replacement-cost data to arrive at current cost. In some instances, however, the determinations necessary to make the needed adjustments to replacement-cost data, such as the effect of potential operating cost savings, may be so subjective that management may decide to develop a different approach to compute current cost.

Indexing historical cost is a very cost-effective and objective method of determining current cost. Further, indexing is tailored to the FASB's dual measurement approach in that the same historical-cost data can be

the historical-cost/constant-dollar basis and the current-cost basis (merely, net assets reported in the financial statements adjusted for the revised amounts of inventories and properties),

■ Per-share amounts of income from continuing operations under the historical-cost/constant-dollar basis and the current-cost basis,

■ Net sales and other operating revenues,

■ Cash dividends per share,

forward to current-year dollars) each year. Companies that use base-year dollars avoid the annual restatement problem but will show different amounts of income from continuing operations in the five-year summary and in the current-year disclosures (which must be in current dollars), perhaps a more confusing result.

Figure III, p. 17, shows a FASB example of a five-year summary that would appear in a company's 1980 annual report.

SEC DROPS REPLACEMENT-COST RULE

The SEC's ASR No. 271 deletes the replacement-cost requirement for fiscal years ending on or after December 25, 1980; the date on which the FASB's current-cost disclosures become mandatory. Until that time, the SEC provides an automatic waiver from reporting replacement-cost information to companies that present current-cost disclosures in their annual reports, and to others that would otherwise be required to report replacement cost for the first time. On the other hand, companies taking advantage of the FASB's one year postponement of current-cost disclosures must show replacement-cost data in their 1979 Form 10-K.

Future SEC actions are expected, including

■ a safe harbor provision for the FASB inflation accounting disclosures, and

■ an amendment to Regulation S-K that will require inflation accounting disclosures in financial reports filed with the Com-

> **"Only public companies having either $1 billion of assets or $125 million of inventories and gross properties at the beginning of the year are required to present the supplemental information. All enterprises, however, are encouraged to make these disclosures."**

used to compute constant-dollar data and current-cost data by the application of general and specific indexes.

FIVE-YEAR SUMMARY

Companies are also required to present a five-year summary of selected financial data to aid users in assessing trends. In addition to the required current year historical-cost/constant-dollar and current-cost information discussed above, this summary must include the following (all expressed in constant dollars):

■ Net assets at year-end under

■ Market price per share at year-end, and

■ Average consumer price index.

Only the sales, dividends, market price, and consumer price index disclosures are required to be reported for years before 1979.

Although all the information in the five-year summary must be presented in constant dollars, companies will have a choice between using current-year dollars or base-period dollars (currently 1967). If companies present the information in current-year dollars, the prior year information must be restated (rolled

FIGURE III
Five-Year Comparison of Selected Supplementary Financial Data Adjusted for Effects of Changing Prices
(In 000s of Average 1980 Dollars)

	Years Ended December 31,				
	1976	1977	1978	1979	1980
Net sales and other operating revenues	$265,000	$235,000	$240,000	$237,063	$253,000
Historical cost information adjusted for general inflation					
Income (loss) from continuing operations				(2,761)	(2,514)
Income (loss) from continuing operations per common share				(1.91)	(1.68)
Net assets at year-end				55,518	57,733
Current cost information					
Income (loss) from continuing operations				(4,125)	(8,908)
Income (loss) from continuing operations per common share				(2.75)	(5.94)
Excess of increase in specific prices over increase in the general price level				2,292	5,649
Net assets at year-end				79,996	81,466
Gain from decline in purchasing power of net amounts owed				7,027	7,729
Cash dividends declared per common share	2.59	2.43	2.26	2.16	2.00
Market price per common share at year-end	$ 32	$ 31	$ 43	$ 39	$ 35
Average consumer price index	170.5	181.5	195.4	205.0	220.9

mission (e.g., registration statements).

FOREIGN OPERATIONS

Despite the size tests explained earlier, a publicly held non-U.S. company would be subject to Statement No. 33 requirements only when its primary financial statements are prepared in U.S. and in accordance with U.S. generally accepted accounting principles (GAAP).

The Statement also gives guidance on applying the dual-measurement approach to foreign operations that are included in consolidated financial statements:

■ Constant-dollar accounting—inventories, properties and related expenses measured in a foreign currency should first be translated to U.S. dollars in accordance with Statement No. 8 and then restated to constant dollars, using the U.S. Consumer Price Index,

■ Current-cost measurements—if current cost of inventories and properties is measured in a foreign currency, it should be translated to U.S. dollars at the rate in effect at the balance sheet date. But, to ease compliance, many U.S. parent companies will be expected to make current-cost determinations for their foreign subsidiaries. For example, these companies may translate properties first into U.S. dollars at historical rates, and then apply appropriate indexes similar to constant-dollar accounting.

SPECIALIZED INDUSTRIES

Early in 1979, the FASB appointed task groups to study

implementation and measurement problems in six specialized industries–banking and thrift institutions, insurance, forest products, oil and gas, mining, and real estate. These task groups issued preliminary reports, conducted public hearings, and published interim reports containing their recommendations to the FASB.

The task groups generally reported that no distinctive problems would be encountered in implementing the proposed historical-cost/constant-dollar disclosures. But a wide range of views was expressed on the current-cost disclosures and on the need to disclose values in lieu of, or in addition to,

dollar requirements. And banks and insurance companies also must make current-cost disclosures when the effect of current-cost depreciation is material (see next section), and

■ For the purposes of applying the $125 million size test, inventories, property, plant, and equipment would include the unprocessed natural resources and income-producing real estate.

The FASB will consider current-cost measurement problems for these assets and address them in a forthcoming Exposure Draft, with a final Statement expected in 1980. In the

how to determine current cost for assets assigned to contracts in process. The FASB decided that items (such as materials) assigned to partly completed contracts should be measured at current cost at the date of use on or on commitment to the contracts. Changes in current cost of such assets will not be recognized after they have been committed to a contract. But these contracts in process, in many cases, will be monetary assets, as they are effectively receivables, and therefore should be considered when computing the purchasing power gain or loss.

FINANCIAL INSTITUTIONS

Financial institutions, such as banks and insurance companies, are not given any special guidance in the Statement. At a minimum, the purchasing power gain or loss on net monetary items would be presented and some financial institutions will have to report constant-dollar data (and possibly current-cost data as well) for their properties because the effect on depreciation expense will be material to income from continuing operations. These entities generally have not had experience in applying inflation accounting, since they were not subject to the SEC's replacement-cost rules. If they have not previously aged their properties, first-year implementation efforts could be significant.

MAJOR CHANGES FROM THE EXPOSURE DRAFT

The most significant change from the Exposure Draft (issued

". . . the FASB realizes that some companies may encounter problems in developing the current-cost disclosures for inclusion in 1979 annual reports. Therefore, companies are not required to make initial disclosure of . . . [such] information for 1979 until their 1980 annual reports."

current-cost disclosures. The FASB considered the views of the task groups when finalizing Statement No. 33 and decided that:

■ All six specialized industries will be required to report historical-cost/constant-dollar data,

■ The only assets that will be allowed special treatment for current cost disclosures for 1979 are unprocessed natural resources (mineral resource assets: oil, gas, mining, and forest products) and income-producing real estate. Such assets, however, are still subject to constant-

meantime, if a company with natural resources or real estate operations decides to provide current-cost information in its 1979 annual report, it may measure those assets and related expenses "at their historical-cost/constant-dollar amounts or by reference to an appropriate index of specific price changes." Therefore, the assets cannot be excluded from current-cost data presented in 1979.

While a task group was not established for long-term contractors (e.g., the aerospace and construction industries), the Statement provides guidance on

December 28, 1978) is the required dual-measurement approach (the proposal strongly suggested that commercial and industrial companies follow the current-cost basis). But, other major changes were made concerning some controversial aspects of the Exposure Draft:

■ Historical income tax expense will not be allocated between income from continuing operations and realized "holding gains." This is a significant improvement over the allocation method originally proposed. Now current-cost income will reflect a high effective tax rate, and this should enhance the possibility for tax reform. (Also, despite many comments received to the contrary, the FASB still maintains that pro forma income taxes should not be provided on unrealized current cost adjustments.),

■ The preferential ordering of the various methods of computing current cost was removed. Therefore, companies can use specific indexing without any implication that such an approach is of lesser quality than the other methods of determining current cost,

■ "Lower recoverable amounts" (net realizable value or value in use) need only be measured for inventory and properties in those unusual circumstances where they are materially and permanently lower than historical-cost/constant-dollar and current-cost measurements,

■ "Holding gains or losses" are

now more neutrally described as "increases or decreases in current cost," as the FASB has not yet decided whether these items actually qualify as gains or losses,

■ Foreign exchange gains and losses will not be segregated and disclosed apart from income from continuing operations,

■ The unit of measure for the current year constant-dollar measurements is average-for-the-year dollars rather than end-of-year-dollars. But, companies presenting comprehensive supplementary financial statements on the historical-cost/constant-dollar basis or the current-cost/constant-dollar basis may use either unit of measure, and

■ The option under the proposed current-cost basis of presenting the five-year summary in either nominal (unadjusted) dollars or constant dollars was removed. All information in the five-year summary must be stated in constant dollars.

AUDITOR INVOLVEMENT

Although the inflation accounting disclosures are supplemental in nature, they still constitute GAAP, which must be followed by affected companies. Therefore, some degree of auditor involvement is necessary. The current plan, based on an American Institute of Certified Public Accountants' (AICPA) Auditing Standards Board draft, is that the data would be unaudited, but that auditors would review the reasonableness of the

disclosures, just as replacement-cost disclosures were reviewed.

Regarding auditors' reporting responsibilities for this data and any other supplemental information that may be required under GAAP (e.g., oil and gas reserve quantities), a recently proposed Statement on Auditing Standards would require auditors to explicitly report (via negative assurance) on the data only when it is presented outside the financial statements, and not when it is included in an unaudited footnote.

FUTURE OF THE EXPERIMENT

Realizing that understanding the mass of new disclosures will entail a substantial learning process, the FASB believes that clear narrative explanations and presentations are essential. Therefore, it has organized an advisory task force of senior corporate executives to develop illustrative disclosures on ways to present and explain the inflation accounting disclosures. The task force plans to publish sample disclosures in December.

In addition, FASB intends to assess the usefulness of the experimental changing prices disclosures required by Statement No. 33. This ongoing assessment process is expected to provide a basis for decisions on whether the dual approach should continue, and on whether other requirements should be changed. The FASB has also announced plans to "undertake a comprehensive review of this Statement no later than five years after its publication." □

SECTION V

Rule-Making Bodies

Like many major professions, accounting has a proud history of internal reliance. For many years, the profession itself assumed sole and total responsibility for the development of its procedures and practices. Recent years have seen other organizations enter into the area of rule-making for the accounting profession. Yet, it should be realized that accounting remains essentially independent of external forces and continues to assume the major responsibility for developments effecting the practice of the profession.

This section is divided into six parts which present articles relating to major organizations effecting the development of accounting rules. These range from the Financial Accounting Standards Board and the American Institute of Certified Public Accountants, which are professional in nature and represent the commitment of the accounting profession to its own development, through four levels of governmental agency involvement in accounting practice. An appreciation of the scope and activity of these groups can be useful in gauging an accurate assessment of the status of accounting.

Within the accounting profession, rules, so to speak, do not lay down a set of absolute procedures but rather specify guidelines and goals for the accountant. Much of the actual detail inherent in the accounting process comes from the judgment base and decision-making ability of the accounting practitioner. While several rule-making bodies exist, their output does not match the magnitude of situations and transactions faced by the accountant in contemporary business practice. Consequently, a significant part of the accounting process relies on the individual practitioner and its ultimate success is a function of the ability of the individual. The activities of various rule-making bodies provide insights into the details specified by these organizations, but more importantly, suggest avenues of individual opportunity. It is indeed interesting to contrast the specifics mandated for accounting versus specifics mandated for other professions of which students have knowledge.

CURRENT EFFORTS TO DEVELOP
A CONCEPTUAL FRAMEWORK
FOR FINANCIAL ACCOUNTING AND REPORTING*

by

William G. Shenkir

*This paper was submitted to The Academy of Accounting Historians for in-
clusion in its Working Paper Series prior to the release of FASB Discussion
Memorandum, "Conceptual Framework for Financial Accounting and Reporting:
Elements of Financial Statements and Their Measurement" and "Tentative
Conclusions on Objectives of Financial Statements of Business Enterprises,"
(December 2, 1976).

Working Paper No. 30
February, 1977

"'Current Efforts to Develop Conceptual Framework for
Financial Accounting and Reporting' by William G. Shenkir,
*The Academy of Accounting Historians Working Papers
21-40*, Vol. 2, Edward N. Coffman, ed. The Academy of Ac-
counting Historians, Georgia State University, Atlanta,
Georgia, 1979, pp. 166-183."

CURRENT EFFORTS TO DEVELOP
A CONCEPTUAL FRAMEWORK
FOR FINANCIAL ACCOUNTING AND REPORTING*

by

William G. Shenkir
Visiting Professor of Accounting
Graduate School of Business Administration
New York University

*An earlier version of this paper was presented at a Symposium sponsored by the Arthur Andersen Faculty Fellow, Pennsylvania State University, Pittsburgh, Pennsylvania, April 29-30, 1976. At that time, the author was a Project Director on the technical staff of the Financial Accounting Standards Board and was assigned to the conceptual framework project. The views expressed in this paper are those of the author and do not necessarily reflect the views of the author's former employer, the Financial Accounting Standards Board.

Current Efforts to Develop
A Conceptual Framework
For Financial Accounting and Reporting

One of the more important tasks undertaken to date by the Financial
Accounting Standards Board (occasionally referred to in this paper as the
FASB or the Board) is its project on a "Conceptual Framework for Financial
Accounting and Reporting: Objectives, Qualitative Characteristics, and
Information." That project is being approached in a series of coordinated
steps. By approaching the project in a well-coordinated step-by-step
process, the FASB hopes to succeed where previous authoritative accounting
bodies have not.* The purpose of this paper is to review the FASB's work
to date on this project and to discuss two basic considerations in establishing a conceptual framework for financial accounting and reporting.

First Phase of Project

When the FASB selected its initial technical agenda in April 1973,
one of the seven projects chosen from a list of more than thirty possibilities suggested by the Financial Accounting Standards Advisory Council
and others was the topic of "Broad Qualitative Standards for Financial
Reporting."[1] The original intent of the FASB was "to develop qualitative
standards to provide guidance in determining the substance of a transaction
or event, regardless of its form, and a qualitative basis for fair presentation in financial reports."[2] It was expected that the Report of the Study
Group on the Objectives of Financial Statements,[3] (occasionally referred to
in this paper as the Objective Study or the Trueblood Study) when completed,
would be of assistance in the project.

After working on the Broad Qualitative Standards project and meeting
with some members of the Trueblood Committee, the FASB concluded that the
scope of the Broad Qualitative Standards project should be broadened to
encompass the entire conceptual framework of financial accounting and
reporting, including objectives, qualitative characteristics, and the information needs of users of accounting information. Accordingly, the name
of the project was changed. A ten-member task force composed of individuals
from industry, public accounting, the financial community, and academe was
selected for the project in December 1973.[4]

The task force held its first meeting in early 1974. The initial step
in this ongoing project recognized the primacy of the objectives of financial
statements in the adoption of financial accounting standards. Accordingly,
the FASB issued, with the advice and counsel of the task force, a Discussion
Memorandum on the subject of objectives of financial statements and qualitative

---

*The work of the two predecessors of the FASB--the Committee on Accounting
 Procedure and the Accounting Principles Board--to develop a conceptual
 framework for financial accounting and reporting is reviewed in Appendix A.

characteristics of financial reporting. That Discussion Memorandum, published in June 1974, relied almost exclusively on the Objectives Study.[5]

The Discussion Memorandum raised four general questions about the objectives and qualitative characteristics of the Trueblood Report for public consideration and comment, and it raised specific questions on each of the twelve objectives in the Report. In addition, a hierarchical arrangement of the various elements of a conceptual framework system was discussed in an Appendix to the Memorandum.[6] That hierarchy, presented in Figure 1, attempts to portray the way in which the many facets of financial accounting and reporting might fit together to form a cohesive and operable whole. The hierarchy is tentative and may be modified as the project continues.

According to Figure 1, objectives provide a basis for the development of the remainder of the elements. The hierarchy provides for more than one basic objective should that be considered appropriate; it also allows for those objectives which might be considered subsidiary in that they are supportive of the basic objective(s). At the next level in the hierarchy are the qualititive characteristics which are the attributes of accounting information that tend to enhance its usefulness. The Objectives Study sets forth the following seven "qualitative characteristics of accounting:" (1) relevance and materiality, (2) form and substance, (3) reliability, (4) freedom from bias, (5) comparability, (6) consistency, and (7) understandability. The "information needed" section involves identification of the broad categories of financial information needed by users. As an example, the Objectives Study mentions specific types of financial statements and some of the information that should be contained in those statements to meet the information needs of users. The statements mentioned in the Trueblood Report were a statement of financial position, a statement of periodic earnings, a statement of financial activities, and financial forecasts.

At the next level in the hierarchy are the fundamentals of accounting and reporting such as definitions of assets, liabilities, capital, earnings, revenue and expense. Each of the fundamentals is critical in fulfilling the objectives and is also important in resolving most of the specific accounting issues that confront the FASB. Included in this level are issues concerning valuation bases in accounting. The Trueblood Report did not really deal with the contents of this box. More will be said about its contents at a later point in the paper.

Below the fundamentals box are two boxes labeled accounting and reporting standards and interpretations of standards. The Statements and Interpretations of Statements issued to date by the Board are examples of the contents of those two boxes. The final element is labeled accounting practices which are the means to achieve the objectives and include the decisions made by managements and auditors in applying the contents of all the other boxes to specific situations. In essence, financial statements are reflections of those applications.

FIGURE 1

HIERARCHY OF ELEMENTS IN A
CONCEPTUAL FRAMEWORK FOR
FINANCIAL ACCOUNTING AND REPORTING

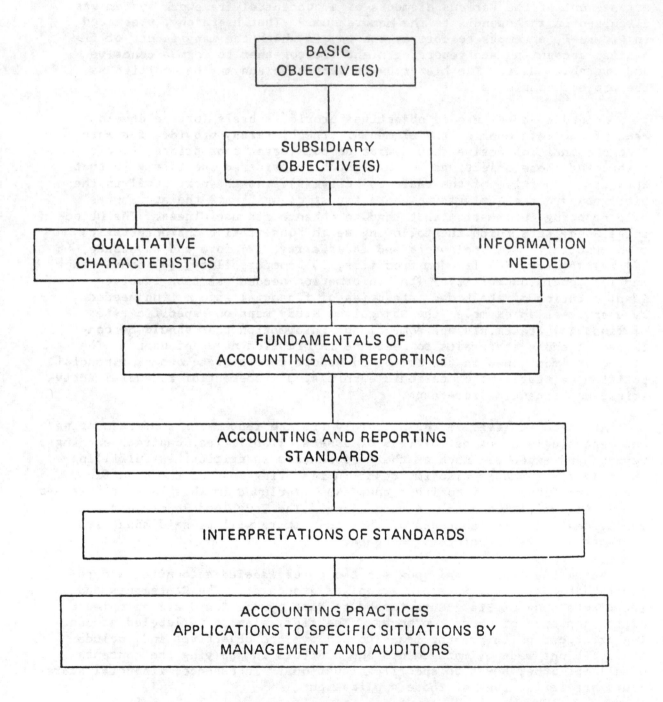

Source: "Conceptual Framework for Accounting and Reporting: Consideration of the Report of the Study Group on the Objectives of Financial Statements," FASB Discussion Memorandum (Stamford: FASB, 1974), p. 15

Summary of First Phase

The first phase of the conceptual framework project dealt primarily with the contents of the top four boxes of the hierarchy since that is the predominant thrust of the Objectives Study. The FASB received ninety-five position papers containing a wide spectrum of responses to the Memorandum on the Objectives Study. The papers included 58 from industry, 17 from public accounting, 15 from academe, 3 from government and 2 from the securities industry. Since the papers included responses from several professional organizations, the representation was even broader than the number of position papers might indicate. A public hearing on the objectives of financial statements was held in New York City on September 23-24, 1974. That hearing provided an opportunity for 20 interested parties to present their views orally and enabled the Board members to question them.

In thinking about the Objectives Study and responses to the Memorandum, two observations may be appropriate. First, as Cyert and Ijiri stated in a paper presented shortly after publication of the Objectives Study:

Financial statements are not just statements reporting on the financial activities and status of a corporation. They are a product of mutual interactions of three parties: corporations, users of financial statements, and the accounting profession.[7]

Disagreement on the objectives of financial statements may exist between the three parties (inter-party) as well as within a single constituency (intra-party). If complete agreement existed within each party and between the three parties there would have been little need for a Study Group on Objectives.

A second pertinent observation is one that was made by Justin Davidson in discussing the Cyert and Ijiri paper. He stated that the Objectives Study is "primarily a value statement. It sets forth the judgment of a group of able, intelligent, and ethical people about how to trade-off the conflicting interest, costs, and benefits of various groups who are affected by the supply of financial information within our society."[8] He also noted that "a major and immediate problem of implementing the Report will be in obtaining agreement with its general value judgments."[9] An analysis of all responses to the Discussion Memorandum indicates that there is a diversity of opinion concerning the twelve objectives in the Trueblood Report:

-25% of the respondents recommended immediate adoption;
-17% favored further study;
- 7% urged deferral of the project;
-30% of the responses were either unclear, or did not address the questions in the Discussion Memorandum; and,
-21% recommended that the objectives be rejected.

It is not possible to discuss all the concerns raised by respondents about each of the specific objectives. However, several of those concerns pertaining to Objectives One through Six have been selected and are covered briefly. In general, the responses to the Memorandum indicate that the level

of support for the specific objectives contained in the Trueblood Report
begins to taper off after Objective Six in favor of further study or
deferral/rejection of the objectives. This is not to say, however, that
all of the notions contained in Objectives One through Six received the
same level of support because there were numerous comments on the meaning
and implication of those objectives.

The Trueblood Report identifies the basic objective of financial statements as providing "information useful for making economic decisions." One
might ask: Could there really be disagreement with a statement such as this?
APB Statement No. 4, which was published in 1970, was the first document
issued by the AICPA to recognize this decision-usefulness objective.[10] Even
so, there continues to be some opposition to embracing it as the basic objective. Some of those who disagreed with this tenet generally took the position
that the basic function of financial statements was to report on management's
stewardship of the enterprise's assets--and that the information needs of
readers was of secondary importance. Another concern expressed about this
objective was its focus on economic decisions. Some were of the opinion that
the term encompassed a far broader range of decisions than those accountants
had in mind when they constructed financial statements. For example, it was
thought that the term encompasses "macro-economic decisions, pricing decisions,
federal revenue-raising decisions, and decisions concerning levels of wages
desired by a labor union." Not surprisingly, the user group responding to the
Memorandum agreed with the Trueblood Report's basic objective. Disagreement
was expressed in responses from some corporations as well as in several of
those received from accounting firms.

Objective Two in the Trueblood Report identifies the primary user group
as those "who have limited authority, ability, or resources to obtain information and who rely on financial statements as their principal source of information about an enterprise's economic activities." Several respondents
commenting on that objective offered another basis for specifying the primary
user of financial statements such as current and/or potential shareholders
(creditors were also mentioned by some respondents), reasonably well informed
or reasonably prudent investors, and sophisticated investors or analysts. Other
respondents stated that it is not necessary to specify a primary user. There
was a clear indication that respondents did not favor the preparation of more
than one set of financial statements differing in degree of summarization,
selectivity of data presented, classification of data, or in other ways. For
example, there was definite opposition to the preparation of a set of financial
statements for the credit grantor or financial analyst, and another set for the
holder of securities who may be relatively unschooled in financial affairs.

Objectives Three and Four were considered together in the Discussion
Memorandum. The Study Group's phrase, "predicting, comparing, and evaluating,"
appears in both objectives. Objective Three is concerned with cash flow to
the investor or creditor, and Objective Four is concerned with earning power
which the Trueblood Report notes in the long run is equivalent to "cash generating ability" of the enterprise. The Study Group asserts that cash generation and earnings approximate each other over long periods. From their
reading of those two objectives, some respondents to the Discussion Memorandum
apparently concluded that the Trueblood Committee was calling for a cash basis
of accounting rather than accrual accounting. In a few instances, those expressing that concern supported it by quoting the objective dealing with financial forecasts (Objective Ten). There was some uncertainty expressed about

the implications of the emphasis on cash for asset valuation and revenue recognition. Closely related to this overall concern over the Trueblood Report's emphasis on cash was the question of who is responsible for the "predicting" that is mentioned in both objectives. It was suggested by several respondents that prediction is the responsibility of users of financial statements, not preparers.

Objective Five calls for information "useful in judging management's ability to utilize enterprise resources effectively in achieving the primary enterprise goal." Some respondents interpreted this objective as the traditional stewardship reporting function and found it acceptable. Others, however, thought that financial statements could not be designed in such a way to meet this objective. Another concern expressed about this objective was directed at the validity of the assumption that the primary enterprise goal was to maximize cash to owners.

Objective Six recommends that factual information should be distinguished from interpretation. There were some respondents who questioned whether this objective could be implemented. A view expressed by some that seemed to make the objective implementable for them was that it called for disclosure of significant assumptions and principles (i.e., explanatory material) on which the financial statements were based.

Second Phase of Project

The second phase of this project has been underway since the initial public hearing was held in September 1974. All the input recieved in response to that hearing has been summarized and reviewed for the Board's use in its deliberations on objectives. In addition, interviews have been conducted with all task force members to seek their advice on the direction and scope of the second phase of the project. The entire task force has met on three occasions to discuss the next phase of the project. The FASB staff has developed the necessary background material to support and supplement the Board's tentative conclusions on objectives and to help provide a basis for the other considerations in the second Memorandum. Research has been underway to determine the issues related to the fundamental elements of financial statements and on the various alternative valuation bases. At this time, it is anticipated that the second Discussion Memorandum will begin with the Board's tentative conclusions on the objectives of financial statements based on the "Report of the Study Group on the Objectives of Financial Statements," the previous FASB Discussion Memorandum, and the letters of comment and the public hearing on that Discussion Memorandum. In addition, the Memorandum will comprise three parts.

Part I will include background material that supports and supplements the tentative conclusions and that provides a basis for Parts II and III.

Part II will probably revolve around the fundamental elements of financial statements (assets, liabilities, capital, earnings, revenues and expenses). Issues will be raised with respect to those elements. This part will also include a discussion of the balance sheet approach (earnings are derived from changes in economic resources and obligations) and the income statement approach (earnings are independently defined and assets and liabilities are dependent, at least in part, on that definition). A decision regarding those two approaches seems critical in establishing a conceptual framework for financial accounting and reporting. Both approaches are discussed in the next section of this paper.

Part III will probably raise issues related to the measurement of the elements of financial accounting. The focus is on five attributes of assets and liabilities that might be measured. Those are:

(1) historical entry value (historical cost)
(2) current entry value (current replacement cost)
(3) current exit value in orderly liquidation (current market value)
(4) expected exit value in due course of business (net realizable value)
(5) present value of future cash flows

Each attribute is considered as a possible basis of valuation for five major categories of assets and three classes of liabilities.

Two Basic Issues in Establishing a Conceptual Framework

Two issues emerge in thinking about a conceptual framework for financial accounting and reporting that seem basic. Each is briefly discussed below.

The first basic issue can be stated as follows: What perspective should a conceptual framework have? Two possibilities are: (1) an internal perspective; and (2) an external perspective.

In essence, perspective is concerned with the emphasis, if any, that is to be given in the establishment of a conceptual framework to users of financial statements and their information needs. One possibility is to focus on the accounting process in developing a framework rather than upon users and their needs. That approach may be viewed as an internal one. Accounting is defined, and the statement of financial position and earnings statements are assumed to be useful. A set of fundamental accounting concepts is then developed. An example of that approach is found in Accounting Research Study No. 1 by Maurice Moonitz.[11]

In contrast, the Trueblood Committee's approach was that a framework should be derived from a study of users and their information needs. The Study Group's approach can be viewed as an external one in which the initial focus is on processes external to accounting. The Trueblood Report stated that "the basic objective of financial statements is to provide information useful for making economic decisions." The Report identified the users of financial statements and made certain assumptions about their information needs. The Study Group emphasized the need to supply users with information to enable them to predict, compare, and evaluate potential cash flows to the enterprise and, in turn, potential cash flows to them.

In summary, the Study Group emphasized initially processes external to accounting and from those it derived the accounting (i.e., financial statements and fundamentals) needed to meet the needs of external processes.

A second basic issue to be addressed in establishing a conceptual framework is: Should the determination of financial position--that is the measurement of assets and liabilities--determine income? That can be called a balance sheet or asset and liability approach. Or should the measurement of income--that is, the process of matching costs and revenues--determine the balances that are necessarily carried forward in the balance sheet? That can be called an income statement or revenue and expense approach. It is extremely important to recognize that the issue is not whether the balance sheet or income statement is the more important statement. Rather, the issue is whether the process of income determination should be based on a systematic matching of costs and revenues or on a measurement of the change in net assets. According to the income statement approach, matching costs and revenues is the center of attention in accounting, and the identification of assets and liabilities is partly dependent on the matching process. Under the balance sheet approach, the focus is on the measurement of assets and liabilities and precise definitions of those terms is essential in a conceptual framework.[12]

Several implications of the balance sheet and income statement approaches can be noted. The wording and emphasis in defining fundamentals of accounting may vary depending on whether a balance sheet or income statement approach is pursued. For example, a definition of revenue under an income statement approach might be:

> Revenue results from the sale of goods and the rendering of services and is measured by the charge made to customers, clients, or tenants for goods and services furnished to them. [Accounting Terminology Bulletin No. 2, "Proceeds, Revenue, Income, Profit, and Earnings" (New York: AICPA, 1955), p. 34.]

In contrast, a definition of revenue under the balance sheet approach might be:

> Revenue is the increase in the net assets of an enterprise as a result of the production or delivery of goods and the rendering of services. [Robert T. Sprouse and Maurice Moonitz, Accounting Research Study No. 3, "A Tentative Set of Broad Accounting Principles for Business Enterprises" (New York: AICPA, 1962), p. 9.]

The difference in the two definitions is in the thrust.

The orientation or point of view taken in resolving specific accounting issues might also vary depending on the approach adopted. For example, under a balance sheet approach, questions such as the following are important:

Is the item (under discussion) an asset?
Is an asset impaired?
Is a liability incurred?

Under an income statement approach, questions such as the following are important:

Is revenue realized?
Is the cost appropriately related to revenue of the period? (Or when does a cost become an expense?)

Another difference of the two approaches concerns the attitude of each towards income smoothing. The income statement approach, with emphasis on matching costs and revenues, seems to lend itself more readily to spreading or deferral methods of accounting which may be achieved and rationalized more easily under the guise that they achieve proper matching. On the other hand, the balance sheet approach, with its focus on the measurement of assets and liabilities, makes it more difficult to adopt spreading or deferral methods of accounting. An example of a recent accounting problem in which the two approaches were implicit is that of the treatment of an exchange gain or loss once determined through foreign currency translation. A number of suggested approaches called for deferral of exchange losses and were generally supported on the basis that they would not distort income; it did not matter if the amount to be deferred failed to meet a reasonable test for an asset. In contrast, it was difficult to support deferral of an exchange loss under a balance sheet approach since such an item does not meet reasonable tests for recognition as an asset.

The balance sheet and income statement approaches seem to be essentially neutral on the issue of valuation or selection of the measurement basis in accounting. That is, neither approach has an edge on reporting current value information. It can be argued that the income statement approach leads to selection of the most "relevant" value. For example, the LIFO method of inventory valuation is justified on the basis that it provides a better matching of costs with revenue. On the other hand, some balance sheet advocates argue that the balance sheet approach is a more appropriate framework from which to support the reporting of current value information because its focus is on the measurement of assets and liabilities. It is difficult to maintain that the goal of reporting current value information is inherent in either approach while the other is essentially wedded to historical cost.

Concluding Remarks

The FASB has been approaching the conceptual framework project as an ongoing one consisting of a number of coordinated steps with each step planned to progress from the preceeding one. That approach on such a project seems appropriate since obtaining agreement on a comprehensive framework in one sweeping effort is probably an unrealistic goal. The second Discussion Memorandum should make a significant contribution to the development of an accepted conceptual framework.

Appendix A

Efforts by the Committee on Accounting Procedure and the
Accounting Principles Board to Develop a Conceptual Framework
for Financial Accounting and Reporting

The two predecessors of the FASB--The Committee on Accounting Procedure (CAP) and the Accounting Principles Board (APB)--attempted to develop
a conceptual framework for financial accounting and reporting. The CAP's
endeavor was referred to as a "comprehensive statement of accounting principles"; initially the APB had two projects--"basic postulates" and "broad
principles." This appendix reviews the efforts taken by the CAP and APB
to develop a conceptual framework for financial accounting and reporting.[13]

Efforts by the Committee on Accounting Procedure (1938-1959)

During its 21-year history, the CAP on various occasions considered
the desirability of preparing a "comprehensive statement of accounting
principles that would be virtually all-inclusive."[14] The CAP first considered the matter at its initial meeting[15] but "very quickly rejected
the idea."[16] The reason given in its final report, issued in 1959, for
that early decision was:

> It would doubtless have taken a very long period before any
> such statement could have been agreed upon. In the meantime,
> the committee would have been performing little or no service
> in the direction of reducing current controversies over account-
> ing procedures. Furthermore, it seemed doubtful whether it
> would be feasible to prepare a statement of accounting principles
> that would be sufficiently comprehensive to afford a practical
> guide to settling any very large number of accounting problems.
> Accordingly, the committee decided to deal with specific areas
> of difference.[17]

Carman Blough provided additional insight concerning the reasoning
underlying the Committee's decision:

> At first it was thought that a comprehensive statement of
> accounting principles should be developed which would serve
> as a guide to the solution of the practical problems of day
> to day practice. It was recognized that for such a state-
> ment to be of much help to the practitioner it would have
> to be much more comprehensive and in far greater detail
> than the "Tentative Statement" of the American Accounting
> Association issued two years previously. [1936 AAA State-
> ment]

After extended discussion it was agreed that the preparation
of such a statement might take as long as five years. In
view of the need to begin to reduce the areas of differences
in accounting procedures before the SEC lost patience and
began to make its rules on such matters, it was concluded
that the committee could not possibly wait for the development of such a broad statement of principles.[18, 19]

The CAP considered the question of a comprehensive statement of accounting principles again in 1940 and decided "that it might be constructive to
review the postulates implied in much accounting literature, often without
direct expression."[20] Accordingly, subcommittees of the CAP were appointed
to consider the monographs--A Statement of Accounting Principles, by
Sanders, Hatfield, and Moore, and An Introduction to Corporate Accounting
Standards, by Paton and Littleton. Although the subcommittee reports were
published in The Journal of Accountancy in 1941,[21] apparently the CAP
never acted on the reports. The country's involvement in World War II was
probably a reason for this inaction since "the committee on accounting procedure was forced to devote itself almost exclusively to questions involving
war transactions."[22] The research department of the American Institute of
Accountants published a brief statement entitled "Corporate Accounting Principles" in 1945,[23] which was based on the Accounting Research Bulletins
issued to that date, the 1936 AAA Statement, and the SEC's Accounting Series
Releases.

According to Carman Blough, the CAP "never gave up the idea that it
would be desirable to develop a comprehensive statement of accounting principles," and the Committee undertook another effort in 1949 by appointing
a subcommittee to work on a statement. Although the subcommittee did considerable work, the results were "highly unsatisfactory."[24] The effort was
abandoned in favor of a revision and restatement of previous Bulletins,
which was published in 1953 as Accounting Research Bulletin No. 43.

The CAP did not produce a comprehensive statement of accounting principles during its 21-year life. A review of the historical record reveals
that the CAP's general approach to a conceptual framework for financial
accounting and reporting would have probably been to develop in one sweeping
effort a "comprehensive statement of accounting principles." As already
noted, the CAP initially decided against proceeding with the project because
of concern that it would take too much time and doubt that it could be
accomplished. The CAP had to move before the SEC "lost patience." To have
taken the time to develop a comprehensive statement of accounting principles
"may have deferred or even made less attainable the degree of professional
acceptance actually secured for the independent accountant by the Institute."[25]
Later consideration of the problem by the CAP did not result in the desired
statement; it led instead to special reports and a codification of existing
pronouncements.

Efforts by the Accounting Principles Board (1959-1973)

The APB responded to its charter rules[26] and decided at its first meeting on September 11, 1959, that "work on basic postulates and principles should begin as promptly as possible."[27] The two projects were assigned to competent accounting scholars. Apparently, the Board believed that the basic postulates of accounting (assumed to be few in number) could be identified through high quality research and that further research would lead to "a fairly broad set of co-ordinated accounting principles." Indeed, a common thread running throughout the 1957 speech by Alvin Jennings[28] (which led to the establishment of the Special Committee on Research Programs), the report of the Special Committee, and the charter rules of the APB is the "emphasis upon research."

Two years after the APB's initial meeting, Accounting Research Study No. 1, "The Basic Postulates of Accounting," by Maurice Moonitz, was published. Moonitz selected a "problem-oriented" approach in which the focus was upon "the problems that accountants deal with." The "pragmatic" approach was rejected because its emphasis on usefulness required answers to questions such as "useful to whom? and for what purpose?"[29]

Moonitz later said that Accounting Research Study No. 1 "did not evoke much reaction from the APB or the profession generally at the time of its publication" as both were waiting for the research study on principles.[30] Since there was little precedent in accounting for a study like that on postulates, many readers were probably unable to understand its implications.[31] Only one member of the project advisory committee, Leonard Spacek, published comments in the study. (Several notes by individual committee members were contained in the body of the text.) Mr. Spacek disagreed with the basic approach in Accounting Research Study No. 1 and indicated that "the essential prerequisite of the establishment of a sound framework of accounting theory must be a clear determination of the purposes and objectives of accounting."[32] A summary by the AICPA's Research Division of fifty-two comment letters received on the study stated that "many persons" agreed with Spacek's position.[33] In an article considering both the postulates and broad principles studies, Vatter stated that the "central idea in any methodology is one of . . . objectives," and "postulates are not objectives."[34] He also noted:

> Before we specify the problems with which accounting must deal, we must first establish a set of purposes or aims to be served, what should be measured, recorded, and reported? To whom and under what circumstances are reports to be directed? How should the data to be reported be structured with respect to the persons who will read the reports and the uses they try to serve?[35]

A careful reading of Accounting Research Study No. 1 indicates that some objectives may be implied, for example, in the discussion on "quantification" and "rational decisions."[36] However, objectives are not highlighted and unequivocally stated in the study.

According to Zeff, the thrust of the foundation presented in the postulates study was lost by its immediate translation into principles. Publication of Accounting Research Study No. 3, "A Tentative Set of Broad Accounting Principles for Business Enterprises," by Robert T. Sprouse and Maurice Moonitz, in April 1962 diverted attention "to the policy implications of the foundation."[37]   Sprouse and Moonitz were guided in their work by a requirement of "compatibility" with the "basic postulates." The "tentative" set of principles called for reporting inventories and plant and equipment at current values and receivables and payables at present (discounted) value. The study's focus on the measurement of assets and liabilities shattered tradition and differed from the cost and revenue allocation model that the APB had inherited from the CAP.

The principles study caused considerable controversy among the project advisory committee. Only one of the nine comments from that group, which were published in the study, was favorable. Each copy of Accounting Research Study No. 3 that was distributed publicly was accompanied by a statement from the APB stating that Accounting Research Study Nos. 1 and 3 were "too radically different from present generally accepted accounting principles for acceptance at this time."[38]   Although the contributions of the two studies to accounting thought have since been recognized and several recommendations contained therein were eventually adopted by the APB,[39] the results of developing in a two-stepped effort postulates and broad principles did not meet with approval from the APB.

The next effort to establish a conceptual framework occurred in 1965 with the publication of Accounting Research Study No. 7, "Inventory of Generally Accepted Accounting Principles for Business Enterprises," by Paul Grady. The APB approved the undertaking of this study in June 1963. Unlike Accounting Research Study No. 3, which had been concerned with "what ought to be" (a normative approach), Accounting Research Study No. 7 was concerned with "what is" (i.e., a description or codification of existing practices). It has been stated that since Grady had been associated with the Committee on Auditing Procedure that produced the set of generally accepted auditing standards, he "had every reason to expect that Accounting Research Study No. 7 would satisfy the profession's need for a code from which it could progress.[40]   The APB, however, did not take formal action on Accounting Research Study No. 7; this study served as one of the sources used by the APB in its next effort to develop a conceptual framework.

The time was 1965 and, after working six years, the APB had not been successful in adopting a conceptual framework. Concern over the lack of success was apparent. The first recommendation in the final report of the AICPA's Special Committee on Opinions of the Accounting Principles Board (Seidman Committee) indicated in part:

At the earliest possible time, the Board should:

(a) Set forth its views as to the purposes and limitations of published financial statements and of the independent auditor's attest function.

    (b) Enumerate and describe the basic concepts to which
        accounting principles should be oriented.
    (c) State the accounting principles to which practices
        and procedures should conform.[41]

The Special Committee actually reiterated a directive contained
initially in the APB's charter. The Special Committee believed that
Accounting Research Study No. 7 contained "most of the raw material"
needed to fashion the type of document or documents implied in its
recommendation.[42]

In response to the Seidman Committee's Report, the chairman of the
APB appointed a subcommittee, which met for the first time in May 1965
and worked diligently until publication in October 1970 of APB Statement
No. 4, "Basic Concepts and Accounting Principles Underlying Financial
Statements of Business Enterprises." At the beginning of the project,
the plan was to develop a series of pronouncements on fundamentals of
financial reporting to serve as a foundation for more specific Opinions
on the application of accounting procedures. According to Clifford
Heimbucher, then chairman of the APB, the first three of the series were
to cover: (1) the nature and objectives of financial statements, (2)
basic concepts underlying financial statement preparation, and (3) broad
accounting principles.[43] The documents were expected to be published as
"brochures or booklets" with "the full status of Opinions of the Board"
but clearly distinguishing "between those portions constituting Opinions,
departure from which will in the future call for disclosure, and those
portions representing merely explanatory or background material."[44]

Two points about Statement No. 4 are pertinent: First, it was issued
as a Statement which did not have the authority of APB Opinions although
earlier drafts of the document carried the label of "Opinion."[45] Second,
Statement No. 4 was an attempt to develop in one sweeping effort a conceptual framework for financial accounting and reporting.

Statement No. 4 contains two sections that are succintly summarized
as follows:

The first discusses the environment in which accounting
exists, the present objectives of financial accounting and
financial statements, and the basic features and elements
of financial accounting. The second describes present
generally accepted accounting principles.[46]

Some parts of Statement No. 4 are similar to Accounting Research Study
No. 7--descriptive not prescriptive. However, unlike Accounting Research
Study No. 1 on postulates, Statement No. 4 does contain a specific section
devoted to the objectives of financial accounting and financial statements.
A noticeable shift in emphasis is found in the "new" definition of accounting.[47] The emphasis is no longer on "internal" accounting processes (recording,
classifying, and summarizing) but on the processes "external" to accounting
(economic decision-making). However, the shift is merely one of interpreting

accepted accounting practices from a "more user-oriented viewpoint" rather than any shift in the fundamentals of accounting.[48]

Evaluations of Statement No. 4 have been mixed. The author of Accounting Research Study No. 1, Moonitz, observed that it "does not satisfy the need for a comprehensive authoritative definition of generally accepted accounting principles," nor does it satisfy "the directive from the April 1965 meeting of the AICPA Council with respect to matters other than the codification of accounting principles."[49] The author of Accounting Research Study No. 7, Grady, also stated that Statement No. 4 does not fulfill the task assigned in the APB Charter and in the Special Committee's final report.[50] On a more positive note, Staubus concluded that Statement No. 4 is "a big step forward" and that the section on objectives of financial accounting and financial statements is "progressive" and the Statement's "strongest feature."[51] Ijiri stated that the APB "should be congratulated for its courage and effort in tackling this difficult task and in publishing the results," although an important missing factor was the "Board's authentication" of Statement No. 4.[52]

A final effort by the APB in the area of a conceptual framework came in 1968 when a subcommittee was appointed to work on a statement of objectives of financial statements.[53] Some staff work and Board discussion occurred. However, after the President of the AICPA appointed the Study Group on Objectives of Financial Statements (Trueblood Committee) in April 1971, the APB subcommittee did not actively pursue its task.

FOOTNOTES

[1]Financial Accounting Standards Board, Status Report, No. 1, June 18, 1973, p. 1.

[2]Financial Accounting Standards Board, Status Report, No. 8, December 27, 1973, pp. 1-2.

[3]American Institute of Certified Public Accountants, Accounting Objectives Study Group, Objectives of Financial Statements (New York: AICPA, October, 1973).

[4]Financial Accounting Standards Board, Status Report, December 27, 1973, pp. 1-2.

[5]"Conceptual Framework for Accounting and Reporting: Consideration of the Report of the Study Group on the Objectives of Financial Statements," FASB Discussion Memorandum (Stamford: FASB, 1974).

[6]Ibid., pp. 13-17.

[7]Richard M. Cyert and Yuji Ijiri, "Problems of Implementing the Trueblood Report," Studies on Financial Accounting Objectives: 1974, Supplement to Volume 12 of the Journal of Accounting Research, p. 29.

[8]H. Justin Davidson, "Discussion of Problems of Implementing the Trueblood Objectives Report," Studies on Financial Accounting Objectives: 1974, Supplement to Volume 12 of the Journal of Accounting Research, p. 44.

[9]Ibid.

[10]Statement of the Accounting Principles Board No. 4, "Basic Concepts and Accounting Principles Underlying Financial Statements of Business Enterprises" (New York: AICPA, 1970).

[11]Maurice Moonitz, Accounting Research Study No. 1, "The Basic Postulates of Accounting" (New York: AICPA, 1961).

[12]For a discussion of some aspects of the two approaches see: Robert T. Sprouse, "The Balance Sheet--Embodiment of the Most Fundamental Elements of Accounting Theory," Williard E. Stone (editor), Foundations of Accounting Theory (Gainesville, Fla.: University of Florida Press, 1971), pp. 90-104.

[13]The author acknowledges that the preparation of this appendix was greatly facilitated by the following studies: John L. Carey, The Rise of the Accounting Profession, Volume II (New York: AICPA, 1970); Maurice Moonitz, Studies in Accounting Research No. 8, "Obtaining Agreement on Standards in the Accounting Profession," (Sarasota: AAA, 1974); and Stephen Zeff, Forging Accounting Principles in Five Countries: A History and an Analysis of Trends (Campaign: Stepes Publishing Company, 1972).

[14]"History of the Accounting Procedure Committee--from the Final Report," The Journal of Accountancy, November, 1959, pp. 70-71.

[15]Carman G. Blough, "Development of Accounting Principles in the United States," Berkeley Symposium on the Foundations of Financial Accounting (Berkeley: Schools of Business Administration, University of California, 1967), p. 7.

[16]"History of the Accounting Procedure Committee--from the Final Report," op. cit., p. 70.

[17]Ibid.

[18]Blough, "Development of Accounting Principles in the United States," op. cit., pp. 7-8.

[19]Although the 1936 AAA Statement was not considered by the CAP to be of sufficient detail, it probably had some impact by serving as a broad outline for a conceptual framework for financial accounting and reporting. Regarding the 1936 AAA Statement, John Carey has observed: "The issuance of this statement irritated many practitioners of accounting. It appeared to be a step toward establishment of a uniform code of accounting principles-- a concept formally rejected by the Institute, which was co-operating with the SEC in the 'common-law' approach of settling each case on its merits in view of the surrounding circumstances." (Carey, The Rise of the Accounting Profession, Volume II, op. cit., p. 9.)

[20]Midyear Report of the Committee on Accounting Procedure, 1940 Yearbook of the American Institute of (Certified Public) Accountants, p. 161.

[21]"Reports on 'An Introduction To Corporate Accounting Standards' and 'A Statement of Accounting Principles,'" The Journal of Accountancy, January, 1941, pp. 48-62.

[22]Carey, The Rise of the Accounting Profession, Volume II, op. cit., pp. 16 and 49.

[23]"Corporate Accounting Principles," The Journal of Accountancy, October, 1945, pp. 259-266.

[24]Blough, "Development of Accounting Principles in the United States," op. cit., p. 11; and "History of the Accounting Procedure Committee--from the Final Report," op. cit., p. 71.

[25]A. C. Littleton and V. K. Zimmerman, Accounting Theory: Continuity and Change (Englewood Cliffs: Prentice-Hall, 1962), p. 143.

[26]"Report to Council of the Special Committee on Research Program," The Journal of Accountancy, December, 1958, p. 63. Also, see: Organization and Operation of the Accounting Research Program and Related Activities (New York: AICPA, October, 1959), p. 6.

[27]APB Minutes of Meeting--September 11, 1959, (Unpublished) p. 5.

[28]Alvin R. Jennings, "Present Day Challenges in Financial Reporting," The Journal of Accountancy, January, 1958, pp. 28-34.

[29]Maurice Moonitz, Accounting Research Study No. 1, "The Basic Postulates of Accounting" (New York: AICPA, 1961), pp. 4-5.

[30]Moonitz, "Obtaining Agreement on Standards in the Accounting Profession," op. cit., p. 18.

[31]Zeff, Forging Accounting Principles in Five Countries: A History and An Analysis of Trends, op. cit., p. 174.

[32]"Comments of Leonard Spacek," in Moonitz, "The Basic Postulates of Accounting," op. cit., pp. 56-57.

[33]"Comments on 'The Basic Postulates of Accounting,'" The Journal of Accountancy, January, 1963, pp. 45-46.

[34] William J. Vatter, "Postulates and Principles," Journal of Accounting Research, Autumn, 1963, pp. 182-183. For other sources emphasizing the need to determine objectives see: Carl Thomas Devine, "Research Methodology and Accounting Theory Formation," The Accounting Review, July, 1960, pp. 387-399; and Alfred Rappaport, "Establishing Objectives for Published Corporate Accounting Reports," The Accounting Review, October, 1964, pp. 951-962.

[35]Vatter, "Postulates and Principles," op. cit., p. 183. On the relationship of postulates and objectives, Hendriksen has stated: "In the field of accounting, the objectives can be considered part of the postulates in the formal structure or they can be viewed as a set of propositions above or at the same level as the postulates. But it cannot be denied that some agreement on objectives is necessary to determine what postulates are relevant to accounting." [Eldon S. Hendriksen, Accounting Theory, Revised Edition (Homewood: Richard D. Irwin, Inc., 1970), p. 102].

[36]Moonitz, "The Basic Postulates of Accounting," op. cit., pp. 21-22, 26-28.

[37]Stephen A. Zeff, "Discussion," Berkeley Symposium on the Foundations of Financial Accounting, op. cit., pp. 24-25.

[38]Statement by the Accounting Principles Board, April 13, 1962. For a discussion of the APB debate on Research Study No. 3 see: Moonitz, "Obtaining Agreement on Standards in the Accounting Profession," op. cit., pp. 18-19.

[39]George A. Gustafson, "Status of Accounting Research Study Nos. 1 and 3," The Journal of Accountancy, March, 1970, pp. 56-60.

[40]Moonitz, "Obtaining Agreement on Standards in the Accounting Profession," op. cit., p. 21.

[41]Report of Special Committee on Opinions of the Accounting Principles Board (New York: AICPA, 1965), p. 12.

[42]Ibid., p. 13.

[43]Clifford V. Heimbucher, "Improving Financial Accounting and Reporting," The Fourth Annual Hayden, Stone Accounting Forum, November 18, 1965, p. 15.

[44]Ibid.

[45]Maurice Moonitz, "The Accounting Principles Board Revisited," The New York Certified Public Accountant, May, 1971, p. 342.

[46]"APB Approves Fundamentals Statement," The CPA, November, 1970, p. 1.

[47]The "new" definition of accounting is: "Accounting is a service activity. Its function is to provide quantitative information, primarily financial in nature, about economic entities that is intended to be useful in making economic decisions--in making reasoned choices among alternative courses of action." [Statement of the Accounting Principles Board No. 4, "Basic Concepts and Accounting Principles Underlying Financial Statements of Business Enterprises," (New York: AICPA, 1970), par. 40.] The old definition formulated in 1941 stated: "Accounting is the art of recording, classifying, and summarizing in a significant manner and in terms of money, transactions and events which are, in part at least, of a financial character, and interpreting the results thereof." [Accounting Research Bulletin No. 9, "Report of Committee on Terminology" (New York: AICPA, 1941), p. 67.]

[48]Yuji Ijiri, "Critique of the APB Fundamentals Statement," The Journal of Accountancy, November, 1971, p. 45.

[49]Moonitz, "Obtaining Agreement on Accounting Standards," op. cit., p. 22.

[50]Paul F. Grady, "Development of Accounting Principles--A Review of the Past Fifty Years," The Florida Certified Public Accountant, January, 1972, pp. 20-21.

[51]George J. Staubus, "An Analysis of APB Statement No. 4," The Journal of Accountancy, February, 1972, pp. 36-43.

[52]Ijiri, "Critique of the APB Fundamentals Statement," op. cit., p. 50.

[53]Zeff, Forging Accounting Principles in Five Countries, op. cit., p. 198.

Keith G. Stanga, CPA, Ph.D. and Jan R. Williams, CPA, Ph.D.

The FASB's Objectives of Financial Reporting

The FASB has taken the first step toward a long-awaited
goal—publication of a conceptual framework. The
authors describe the important features of this release
and the context of the Board's action.

THE FASB recently issued Statement of Financial Accounting Concepts No. 1, *Objectives of Financial Reporting by Business Enterprises.*[1] This Statement establishes the objectives of general purpose external financial reporting by business enterprises. It may be viewed both as the ending and the beginning of lengthy processes. On the one hand, the document represents the tentative completion of long debate and discussion concerning the objectives of financial statements. On the other, the document represents the first in a series of pronouncements designed to ultimately constitute the long-sought conceptual framework for financial reporting.

The purpose of this article is to review the content of SFAC #1, hoping to capture the predominant theme of the pronouncement and encourage the reader to study the pronouncement in its entirety. Additional considerations are to place the pronouncement in perspective and to make some interpretative and evaluative comments.

The Objective-Setting Process

The desire to identify specific objectives of financial reporting is inherent in the process of establishing standards of financial reporting. This is particularly true where a selection must be made between alternative accounting principles. The need for objectives to assist in this selection process is obvious.

Previous attempts to codify the conceptual basis for financial statements have relied on implicit objectives

even though these objectives were not identified as such.[2] Perhaps the first detailed listing of objectives of financial statements appeared in APB Statement #4, *Basic Concepts and Accounting Principles Underlying Financial Statements of Business Enterprises,* published in 1970. This study relied heavily on the description of then current financial reporting, and the stated objectives consist primarily of verbal descriptions of the financial statements.

In the 1970s, interest in the establishment of stated objectives intensified with the following major steps being taken:

• Issuance of the Report of the Study Group on the Objectives of Financial Statements, by the AICPA in 1973 (The Trueblood Report).

• Issuance of the Discussion Memorandum on the Conceptual Framework for Accounting and Reporting: Consideration of the Report of the Study Group on the Objectives of Financial Statements, by the FASB in 1974.

• Issuance of the FASB's Tentative Conclusions on Objectives of Financial Statements of Business Enterprises in 1976.

• Issuance of the Exposure Draft of SFAC #1, Objectives of Financial Reporting and Elements of Financial Statements of Business Enterprises, by the FASB in 1977.

The most recent step is the issuance of the pronouncement which is the major concern of this article.

Statements of Financial Accounting Concepts

SFAC #1 is the first in a series of new pronouncements which are intended to represent a step-by-step construction of the conceptual framework of financial reporting. This first Statement deals with the objectives of financial reporting. Future Statements are expected to cover the elements of financial statements and their recognition, measurement and display; capital maintenance; unit of measure; criteria for distinguishing information to

---

[1] Statement of Financial Accounting Concepts No. 1, "Objectives of Financial Reporting by Business Enterprises," FASB, November 1978.

Keith G. Stanga, CPA, Ph.D. is associate professor of accounting at the University of Tennessee, Knoxville. His articles have been published in The CPA Journal, Management Accounting, The Journal of Accountancy, Financial Management, Accounting and Business Research, CA Magazine *and other journals. Jan R. Williams, CPA, Ph.D. is professor of accounting at the same university. His articles have been published in several professional journals, including* The CPA Journal, The Accounting Review, The Journal of Accountancy, Management Accounting, CA Magazine *and others.*

---

[2] See, for example, Moonitz, Maurice *Accounting Research Study No. 1,* "The Basic Postulates of Accounting," AICPA, 1961; and Sprouse, Robert T. and Moonitz, Maurice *Accounting Research Study No. 3,* "A Tentative Set of Broad Accounting Principles for Business Enterprises," AICPA, 1962.

be included in financial statements from that which should be provided by other means of financial reporting; and criteria for evaluating and selecting accounting information.

Donald J. Kirk, the Chairman of the FASB, describes SFAC #1 as "the cornerstone, the first in a series of FASB Statements that will, in effect, comprise a 'constitution' for financial accounting and reporting."[3]

Harold M. Williams, Chairman of the SEC, has emphasized the importance of the project as follows:

> The conceptual framework project exemplifies the kind of important and fundamental undertaking which the profession can perform best, and is one of the foremost existing opportunities . . . for accountants to demonstrate to Congress and to the profession's critics its effectiveness and resolve in confronting the important issues facing it . . . The project must be an exercise in leadership—an effort to create a set of principles which can serve as a goal—a visionary guide—for the profession to work toward as it develops and refines disclosure techniques during the coming decade.[4]

A clear distinction is made between this series of Statements and FASB Statements of Financial Accounting Standards and FASB Interpretations. The purpose of FASB Statements of Financial Accounting Concepts is to set forth fundamentals on which financial accounting and reporting standards will be based. The concepts Statements are not intended to invoke the application of Rule 203 of the Rules of Conduct of the Code of Professional Ethics of the AICPA, as is the case with Statements of Standards and Interpretations. In due course, the concepts Statements will serve as the basis for a re-evaluation of existing Statements of Standards and Interpretations and the issuance of new ones. It is reasonable to expect that the new series of pronouncements will have a significant impact on the form and content of financial statements in the future.

Context for Objectives

Prior to the declaration of specific objectives, the FASB discussed a number of points which help to provide a context for the objectives. These points should be viewed as parameters established by the FASB. In some cases they represent characteristics of the environment in which financial reporting resides; in other cases they represent conscious choices made by the FASB. The more important of these considerations are discussed in the following paragraphs.

The FASB chose to state objectives in terms of the broad context of financial reporting rather than limiting them to financial statements specifically. Financial reporting is a broad term which encompasses financial statements as well as many other disclosure media such as

corporate annual reports and separate booklets describing a firm's social impact. Boundaries of distinction between financial reporting and financial statements will be more clearly drawn in other parts of the conceptual framework project or in Statements of Financial Accounting Standards.

The objectives set forth stem largely from the needs of those who use financial information but who lack the authority to require the information they want from a given firm. The informational needs of these users depend significantly on the nature of economic activities and the decisions with which the users are involved. Thus, the objectives stated are affected by the economic, legal, political and social environment of the United States. The numerous complexities and unique features of the economic system have an influence on the stated objectives. In this context, the function of financial reporting is to provide information that is useful to those who make economic decisions about business enterprises.

There are certain characteristics and limitations of financial reporting which have an influence on the stated objectives. These include the following:

• Information provided is to a significant extent based on approximate measures of the financial effects of past transactions and events.

• Information cannot be provided or used without incurring a cost.

• Information provided is generally quantified and expressed in units of money, usually based on exchange prices.

• Information provided pertains to individual business enterprises rather than to industries or the economy as a whole.

• Information provided often results from approximate rather than exact measures, and involves numerous estimates, judgments and allocations.

• Information provided is combined with information from other sources, such as information about general economic conditions, political events, etc.

Numerous groups have potential interest in information provided by financial reporting. Some have direct economic interests in the reporting enterprise (e.g., investors, lenders, suppliers); others have derived or indirect interests (e.g., financial analysts, regulatory authorities, labor unions). The stated objectives are presented in terms of the perceived needs of external users of financial information as opposed to internal users. These external users are generally interested in a firm's ability to generate favorable cash flows because their decisions relate to amounts, timing and uncertainty concerning expected cash flows.

Finally, the stated objectives are those of general purpose financial reporting which is directed toward the common interests of various potential users of financial information. The primary focus is on information for investment and credit decisions, largely for pragmatic reasons. These reasons include the desire to make the objectives fairly concrete as opposed to vague, the fact that investment and credit decisions have enormous signifi-

[3] FASB Status Report No. 77, December 6, 1978, p. 1.
[4] Ibid.

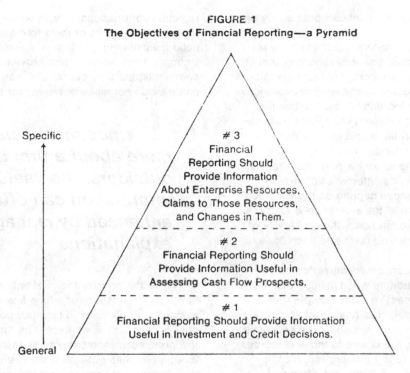

FIGURE 1
The Objectives of Financial Reporting—a Pyramid

Specific

General

\# 3
Financial
Reporting Should
Provide Information
About Enterprise Resources,
Claims to Those Resources,
and Changes in Them.

\# 2
Financial Reporting Should
Provide Information Useful in
Assessing Cash Flow Prospects.

\# 1
Financial Reporting Should Provide Information
Useful in Investment and Credit Decisions.

cance for the allocation of resources in the economy, and perhaps most importantly, the fact that the financial information needed by investors and creditors will also likely be useful to other external users.

Objectives of Financial Reporting

SFAC #1 specifies three major objectives which the authors feel may be conveniently visualized as a pyramid (see Figure 1). At the base or foundation of the pyramid is the broadest, most general objective. Resting on this foundation, the remaining two objectives are progressively more narrow or specific in scope.

> ' . . . the scope of financial reporting will not be confined to one, or even a few, major user groups.'

Objective number 1 states that "financial reporting should provide information that is useful to present and potential investors and creditors and other users in making rational investment, credit and similar decisions. The information should be comprehensible to those who have a reasonable understanding of business and economic activities and are willing to study the information with reasonable diligence." Thus, financial reporting is to be built on the foundation of usefulness.

The Board's response to the traditional questions of Useful to whom? And for what purpose?'' was quite

broad. As a result, the scope of financial reporting will not be confined to one, or even a few, major user groups. Instead, financial reporting will attempt to simultaneously serve many diverse parties. However, these parties are expected to have a reasonable understanding of business affairs. In addition, users must be willing to spend reasonable amounts of time and effort to analyze accounting information. Certainly, accountants should strive to produce reports that are understandable. However, naive users of accounting information should consider taking steps to enhance their understanding of business matters. Alternatively, they should rely on the services of professional advisors.

> ' . . . users must be willing to spend reasonable amounts of time and effort to analyze accounting information.'

The second objective is that "financial reporting should provide information to help present and potential investors and creditors and other users in assessing the amounts, timing and uncertainty of prospective cash receipts from dividends or interest and the proceeds from the sale, redemption, or maturity of securities or loans.''

Rational investment, credit and similar decisions are made after careful consideration of factors such as expected cost, risk and return. Thus, an investor or creditor who commits cash to a business would like to know if, when, and how much cash will be returned. Information that helps to resolve these uncertainties would surely be regarded as useful.

"Since investors' and creditors' cash flows are related to enterprise cash flows, financial reporting should provide information to help investors, creditors and others assess the amounts, timing and uncertainty of prospective net cash inflows to the related enterprise." Notice that this objective differentiates between cash flows to investors and creditors and cash flows to a given enterprise to which they have committed funds. Naturally, a given investor or creditor wants to know his personal chances of receiving cash via dividends, interest or otherwise. However, his personal chances depend on the expected cash flows to the enterprise. If the enterprise is successful in generating favorable cash flows, the probability of investors and creditors receiving favorable cash flows is enhanced.

The third objective is concerned with information helpful to investors and creditors when making their assessments regarding prospective cash receipts from a business enterprise. This objective holds that "financial reporting should provide information about the economic resources of an enterprise, the claims to those resources (obligations of the enterprise to transfer resources to other entities and owners' equity), and the effects of transactions, events, and circumstances that change its resources and claims to those resources."

Some of the most significant transactions and events that change a firm's resources and the claims to those resources are used to measure financial performance. Investors and creditors may use past measures of financial performance in making their predictions concerning expected future performance. The Statement asserts that "the primary focus of financial reporting is information about an enterprise's performance provided by measures of earnings and its components." Thus, investors and creditors may use past measures of earnings to help predict future earnings, and indirectly, to help predict their chances of receiving cash from a given enterprise.

> *' . . . accountants provide useful historical measurements, but they cannot accurately predict the future and they do not make decisions for information users.'*

The Board feels that the application of accrual accounting results in performance measures that are superior to those under cash basis accounting. However, the Statement emphasizes that "accrual accounting provides measures of earnings rather than evaluations of management's performance, estimates of 'earning power', predictions of earnings, assessments of risk, or confirmations or

rejections of predictions or assessments. Investors, creditors and other users of the information do their own evaluating, estimating, predicting, assessing, confirming or rejecting." Thus, accountants provide useful historical measurements, but they cannot accurately predict the future and they do not make decisions for information users.

> *' . . . since management knows more about a firm than outsiders, the usefulness of information can often be enhanced by management's explanations . . . '*

While the primary focus of financial reporting is on earnings, information regarding financial position as well as significant changes in financial position (besides earnings) is important when assessing an enterprise's cash flow prospects. Moreover, since management knows more about a firm than outsiders, the usefulness of information can often be enhanced by management's explanation of the financial impact of certain transactions, events and circumstances.

Concluding Comments

The need for an authoritative conceptual framework for financial accounting and reporting has existed for many years. Certainly, the objectives specified in SFAC #1 are an important part of this framework. In a sense, the FASB has achieved a delicate balance in its initial pronouncement on concepts. On the one hand, the objectives appear specific enough to provide a clear sense of direction for external financial reporting. On the other hand, the objectives are broad enough to support many alternative accounting theory structures. For example, a theory structure emphasizing current value accounting could conceivably (though not necessarily) result from SFAC #1.

The FASB has suggested that it may be the major user of its new series of Statements of Financial Accounting Concepts. However, it seems that everyone concerned with corporate financial reporting will benefit from a greater understanding of the nature, purpose and limitations of external accounting information. For instance, independent CPAs as well as corporate accountants will have a logical framework within which to explain GAAP to company managers, stockholders and others.

SEC Chairman Williams has said that the conceptual framework project must be an exercise in leadership. Like democratic leaders, the FASB has sought and evaluated the views of the financial community throughout its process of formulating objectives. Now it appears that these objectives deserve the support of the Board's constituency. Ω

STATEMENTS IN QUOTES

The SEC and its chief accountants: historical impressions

In this fascinating and enlightening study adapted from a paper presented at the Haskins History Seminar of the New York University Ross Institute for Accounting Research, Gary John Previts, *professor of accounting at the University of Alabama, traces the history of the office of chief accountant of the SEC from Carman Blough to John Burton. We learn the backgrounds and accomplishments of each chief accountant, as well as being treated to Previts' observations and insights toward each administration.**

A perspective

The stability and progress of business and government in a society as complex as ours are unlikely to persist without strong capital markets, and it seems equally unlikely that confidence in capital markets can persist without confidence in the people who operate them and in the Securities and Exchange Commission and other governmental agencies that supervise them. The role of adequate information in the process of trading securities and valuing securities is interlaced and imbedded in this overall social order. Revelations in the past decade of excesses, frauds and abuses in the institutions of government, business and the professions have brought the existing capital market structure and its ability to command the public trust into question. The ability of the public accounting pro-

* Ed. note: For another article dealing with the historical perspective of an important accounting topic, uniformity, see Barbara D. Merino and Teddy L. Coe's piece in this issue, pages 62-69.

fession to command the respect and confidence of the individuals and institutions of the capital markets would appear to be central to the issue of reexamining the balance and worthiness of our economic, political and social order.

The market crash of 1929 and the trauma of the early 1930s, capped by the collapse of the Kreuger and Toll Empire, heightened the legislative ardor to investigate the operations of the securities markets. Also, Ferdinand Pecora had begun a series of investigations under the U.S. Senate Committee on Banking and Currency relative to investment bankers and the banking system. A Senate committee subsequently engaged in extensive inquiries about the Kreuger and Toll collapse even though the principle accounts of Kreuger and Toll had been audited by Swedish accountants (a U.S. subsidiary had been audited by Price Waterhouse & Co. and another American accounting firm was also indirectly involved). The financial press highlighted this episode and generated substantial pressures on the accounting profession, referring to inadequate auditing and accounting safeguards. In the capital markets, confidence had reached an all-time low. The newly elected President Franklin D. Roosevelt, as a part of his New Deal platform, promised reform of the capital markets. Among his confidential advisers was a young Columbia University law professor, Adolph A. Berle. Berle had been influenced by the writings of Professor William Z. Ripley, the author of a series of articles that first appeared in the *Atlantic Monthly* in the 1920s and were later published in the book, *Main Street and Wall Street.*

In 1932, Berle and Gardiner Means, an economist also on Columbia's faculty, published *The Modern Corporation and Private Property.* This work identified and analyzed the phenomena of the modern corporation and the separation of ownership and management relative to securities and property control. John L. Carey and other writers assert that Berle's influence in the Roosevelt administration (as Berle was a member of the young intellectual "brain trust") led to the structuring of securities legislation to address the basic bifurcation of management control and ownership.

The keywords in this new legislation were "full and fair disclosure." James M. Landis, who served as a commissioner during the early years of the SEC, commented with regard to the legislative history of the 1933 Securities Act that among the multiple considerations in the minds of those who drafted the legislation, it was clear that the government did not seek to pass upon the investment quality of any security. Landis further stated that the theory of the English Companies Acts was fundamental in guiding the deliberations of that small group who were charged with constructing the provisions and exemptions under this initial "registration" act.

Edward N. Gadsby, then chairman of the SEC, wrote in the *George Washington Law Review* in 1959, "It is doubtful that history affords an example of more timely and necessary legislation than the federal securities acts." In his view, the federal securities acts responded to the need to restore confidence in order to maintain an important source of investment identified as "people's capitalism" (a view that, during the 1920s, public subscription of corporate securities had followed upon the favorable experience of individual investors in the liberty bonds program of World War I). After the casino-like atmosphere of the 1920 stock market, with speculation and market manipulation, the basis for public confidence in the investment process had been eroded if not all but destroyed.

The 1933 securities law first required registration of new offerings of securities upon the public exchanges. The registration of such securities required the certification by an *independent* public or certified accountant. This requirement had not initially been in the drafts of legislation, but had come about through the testimony of Arthur H. Carter, then managing partner of Haskins & Sells and, at that time, president of the New York State Society of CPAs. Carter's testimony before the Senate Banking Committee is acknowledged to have influenced Congress to include this requirement for certification of financial statements. The 1934 legislation, which established the SEC and other requirements for periodic reporting to that commission, contained no certification requirement. However, the broad powers granted to the commission under the law were later specified by the commission to require such certification of the 1934 act periodic reports filed. With the passage of the 1934 law, all the filings for public disclosures under registrant companies under the 1933 act were transferred from the Federal Trade Commission to the SEC. These laws had given the commission power to prescribe the accounting disclosure policies (sec. 19—1933 act; sec. 13—1934 act) to be followed in filings and had also placed responsibility and liability on accountants who undertook to practice and present statements to the commission.

The chief accountants

Carman G. Blough (December 1935–May 1938). Blough had come to the SEC after several years of professional experience and teaching accounting at several universities. While working at the commission, he accepted the newly created position of chief accountant in December 1935. The task before Blough was to establish a basis of policy to provide formal interpretation of the law the commission was to enforce with regard to the practice of accountants. While Blough was not encumbered by precedent, he was not afforded any of the guidance that is normally provided by such precedent. The literature of the profession of this period, as characterized by the editorial by Eric Kohler in the *Accounting Review,*

refers to the fact that the profession was "nervous" as to the outcome of its role in its new relationship with the SEC. The stipulation of independence, while not new, had never before been clearly defined as a legal or operational term. Furthermore, the authority of the commission extended not only to filings with it but, under the proxy rules, the potential for the commission's authority to extend to periodic and annual reports, normally provided by management to shareholders, also existed (but it was not exercised in these early years). The profession was to find that the decision of the commission (in Accounting Series Release no. 4, April 25, 1938) to permit financial statements to be filed with the commission in accordance with accounting principles—a decision which had substantial authoritative support—was the start of a new generation of accounting thought and practice. The term "substantial authoritative support" was the key concept in this generation. Earlier, Blough had remarked: "There is, of course, a dividing line between acceptable and unacceptable accounting practices; that line is a hairline, the location of which is a matter for the individual judgment of the accountant."

Only ASRs nos. 1 through 8 are attributed directly to Blough, as he resigned from office in 1938; but the role of the chief accountant for several years had been set in the precedent of his path-breaking judgments, precedents such as in ASR no. 4[1] and the notion of substantial authoritative support. As John Carey has observed,[2] Blough was "not only a competent accountant, but was temperamentally ideally qualified for the job. A minister's son, he was attracted by public service. He was vigorous, industrious, and self-confident, but open-minded and judicious—not doctrinaire. When convinced he was right, he stood his ground, but he could disagree without being disagreeable. His candor, complete honesty, and good nature inspired confidence. He was not without a gift of diplomacy. He got along well with people. He had a sense of humor. He could relax convivially. He had no pretentions."

[1] Accounting Series Release no. 4, April 25, 1938. 11 F.R. 10913.

The Securities and Exchange Commission today issued the following statement of its administrative policy with respect to financial statements:

"In cases where financial statements filed with this Commission pursuant to its rules and regulations under the Securities Act of 1933 or the Securities Exchange Act of 1934 are prepared in accordance with accounting principles for which there is no substantial authoritative support, such financial statements will be presumed to be misleading or inaccurate despite disclosures contained in the certificate of the accountant or in footnotes to the statements provided the matters involved are material. In cases where there is a difference of opinion between the Commission and the registrant as to the proper principles of accounting to be followed, disclosure will be accepted in lieu of correction of the financial statements themselves only if the points involved are such that there is substantial authoritative support for the practices followed by the registrant and the position of the Commission has not previously been expressed in rules, regulations, or other official releases of the Commission, including the published opinions of its chief accountant."

[2] Carey, J. L., "The CPA's Professional Heritage—Part IV," The Academy of Accounting Historians—Working Paper Series, December 1977.

William W. Werntz (May 1938–April 1947). Historically, we must acknowledge the significant influence of Blough in guiding the commission's ruling on ASR no. 4 with regard to accounting principles. Similarly, we find under the chief accountantship of Werntz an important precedent as to the establishment of auditing standards under the direction of the profession in the wake of the *McKesson-Robbins* case.

In December 1938, McKesson-Robbins, a large, widely known company principally engaged in drugs and chemicals, was suspended from trading in the New York Stock Exchange in light of a suit and other revelations with regard to the financial representations of the corporation. Assets approximating $19 million (total consolidated assets $87 million) were subsequently found to have been fictitious. For the prior year ended December 31, 1937, the financial statements had been certified by Price Waterhouse & Co. Other investigations revealed that the president of the corporation was in reality an individual who had previously been convicted of several commercial frauds and that other principal officials in McKesson had been acting under assumed names. All this added up to a juicy bit of scandal.

The SEC commenced hearings on the McKesson-Robbins frauds in 1939, shortly after the revelations had been made. In the meanwhile, the CPA profession began to act independently, establishing a special committee to deal with auditing procedures. At issue was whether the generally accepted auditing procedures for the examination of assets and the presentation of financial statements were adequate to discover such frauds and to protect the investing public. The outcome, in part because of the expeditious action of the profession, was the issuance of the first auditing standard, Statement on Auditing Procedure no. 1, *Extensions of Auditing Procedure.* The gist of this pronouncement was to require that the observation of inventories and confirmation of receivables be required where reasonable and practicable to do so. When the SEC concluded its hearings in April 1939, it began to deliberate the appropriate course of action with regard to the professional competence of independent accountants as a result of the deficiencies determined. By this time, however, the procedures that had now been set forth under SAP no. 1 had been approved by the council of the American Institute of CPAs. ASR no. 19, issued in December 1940, revealed the findings and conclusions of the SEC with regard to McKesson-Robbins. While noting that the auditors had failed to employ the degree of vigilance and inquisitiveness necessary in a professional undertaking, the commission also acknowledged that the profession had acted promptly to address the overall procedural deficiencies through the issuance of SAP no. 1. In this way, the commission recognized auditors' efforts to establish their authority over their own rules of work. While some may contend that this issue was never in question since the language of the law does not clearly authorize the commission or its principals to mandate auditing procedures, others have held that had the profession not acted promptly and appropriately, action or legislation to empower the SEC to do so might have been forthcoming.

Also in 1939, a significant precedent emerged in the *Interstate Hosiery Mills* case. While this case did not primarily involve an issue of the responsibility for financial information, the judgment indicated that the management of a company subject to SEC jurisdiction had the responsibility for the financial information filed with the commission. The findings in this case tended to establish and reinforce a prevalent belief that management had primary responsibility for the selection and application of accounting principles and that the auditors' duties extended to the satisfaction of their own judgment as to the propriety of such principles under the norm of substantial authoritative support.

In February 1940, the commission established a revision of previous filing rules relative to the acts that it had now taken the responsibility for enforcing. This revision had been directed by Werntz since he had come to the commission as a member of the forms division under Harold Neff. Werntz had compiled the rules for what had originally been identified as Regulation Z, later retitled Regulation S-X, issued in 1940. Regulation S-X specified the form and content of financial information and statements to be filed with the commission. It was also during Werntz's term as chief accountant, in 1941, that Regulation S-X was revised to require that the certificate of the independent accountant refer to conformity with generally accepted auditing standards.

During his term as chief accountant, Werntz also tackled the difficult issue of independence, which had been rather unclearly dealt with on a preliminary basis in ASR no. 2, wherein a net worth measure of conflict of interest had been established. In ASR no. 25, using the issue of independence as the basis of decision, Werntz ruled that the agreements between registrants and accountants to hold the accountant harmless from all losses and liabilities arising out of his certification (i.e., to indemnify the accountant) would seriously impair the independence of the accountant, such that the chief accountant would not recognize the independence of the public accountant in certifying financial statements to be registered with the commission. Werntz sought to further operationalize the concept of independence by citing specific cases relative to the matter of independence in ASR no. 47, issued in January 1944. The principles of compiling and considering these cases had been set forth a few months earlier in ASR no. 44 wherein the commission had stated that an accountant would not be considered independent with respect to a registrant in whom he had a substantial interest, direct or indirect, or with whom he was, during the period of report, connected as a promoter or underwriter, voting trustee, director, officer or employee.

The notion of independence had by now become one of considerable importance to both the public accounting profession, the registrant and the SEC. It continues today to be a critical matter in the nature of the professional service offered by the accountant who certifies the statements of the publicly held corporation filing with the commission.

As if addressing the issues of authority over auditing rules, the matter of management responsibility for the selection of accounting principles and the issuance of Regulation S-X were not enough, it was Werntz who instituted proceedings under rule II (e) of the rules of practice of the commission (wherein the disciplined practitioners were found to be deficient in independence and competence with regard to their practice before the commission). All of this activity, of course, was taking place during the very difficult and demanding years of World War II.

After resigning from the commission in May 1947, Werntz turned to public practice as a member of the firm Touche, Niven, Bailey & Smart. Among his early responsibilities at that firm were duties relative to the Seaboard Commercial Corporation. The annual report of that corporation for the fiscal year ended December 31, 1947, became the basis for an accounting series release issued nearly a decade later (ASR no. 78, March 25, 1957). In instituting proceedings under rule II (e), the commission asserted that the financial statements of Seaboard at December 31, 1947,

were materially misleading, in that inadequate reserves had been reflected for accounts known to be doubtful of collection and that current assets were overstated as a result. Because of the newly formed status of the firm, and because of the involvement of Werntz on that assignment, the determination of the commission as to the degree of responsibility held by Werntz was unclear. Nevertheless, the firm and Werntz were sanctioned and denied the privilege of practicing before the SEC for 15 days.

In studying the history of the commission, there is irony in this situation, in that someone who formally was in charge of the accounting policy of a regulatory agency could subsequently be considered to have practiced improperly before it immediately after departing from the commission.

In his writings, Werntz not only evidences his scholarship, but his understanding of the relationship between law and accounting. Among the cogent quotes is the following,[3] made with regard to accounting as a control device:

"It was impossible that this development of accounting as a control device originating in the business world would go unnoticed by legislative bodies and judicial and administrative officials. It was inevitable, in the search for an effective means of obtaining data as a social and economic phenomena, [that] early resorts should be had to accounting data. Thenceforth, it was but a short and logical step to reliance on the accounting process, first, as a means of regularly observing the activities of economic units, and then as a means of prescribing and proscribing courses of action. It is most interesting to note, in passing, that the effective use of accounting as a control over government itself has lagged far behind the use of accounting by government as a means of policing and controlling those whom it governs. Only recently have some of the most obvious improvements of business

[3] Werntz, W. L., "The Influence of Administrative Agencies on Accounting," Handbook of Modern Accounting Theory, 1955, pp. 99-118 (Morton Backer, ed.).

accounting been enlisted in an effort to control governmental activities."

Werntz observed that administrative agencies had been a significant influence on the development of accounting in the last half century predating 1950 and that overall they enforced and enlarged a greater amount of detail data collecting and probably contributed by the improvement of accounting methods that might have otherwise not have been developed. On balance, he concluded, it seems probable that accounting thought and practice progressed further and faster under the stimulus of such agencies than it would otherwise have done.

Werntz's writings suggest not only the awareness as to the potency of accounting as a control device, but also of the potential for legislative and governmental agencies to use accounting information primarily for social control and economic planning.

Earle C. King (April 1947–November 1956). King had come to the commission's registration division in 1934 and was assigned to Blough when the chief accountant's office was created. In April 1947, he succeeded William Werntz and continued in that position until November 1956, when he resigned. King is perhaps the least well known of the chief accountants of the SEC. This lack of recognition deserves to be addressed. An editorial in the June 1947 *Journal of Accountancy,* pertaining to the years preceding King's chief accountantship, suggests that "a happy state of affairs" had existed relative to the tenure of Werntz and Blough. And it seemed, since fewer than two dozen accounting series releases were issued under King, that this condition continued. (One might saucily observe that such a modest number of ASRs would not even have been a fair night's work for "Sandy" Burton in his heyday during the mid-1970s.)

The lack of productivity, however, does not necessarily indicate a lack of activity on the part of the commission in matters relating to financial reporting and disclosure. King's philosophy was not to use the commission filings as a proving ground for innovations in reporting techniques. One might observe that the existing rules for reporting and measurement were deemed to be suitable and in the eyes of the chief accountant innovation or "proving" of new disclosure techniques should take place in the periodic reports (management's reports to shareholders), rather than in the statutory disclosures to the commission. King, much like his predecessors, was attuned to the "disclosure qua remedy" theme that had been sounded by Professor Ripley 25 years earlier. An important accomplishment of the King term as chief accountant includes the major revision of Regulation S-X set forth in ASR no. 70. This comprehensive amendment of Regulation S-X included eliminating old, awkward and unsuitable terminology, such as reserves and surpluses, as had been recommended and encouraged for at least the preceding decade. The release was finally issued in December 1950, undertaken amidst an environment of the rapidly changing expectations and multiple economic uncertainties of the post-World War II period.

Confrontation on income disclosure

Battlelines became drawn on the issuance of Accounting Research Bulletin no. 32, under the authority of the Committee on Accounting Procedure (CAP) of the Institute. The committee had issued the bulletin, which endorsed the current operating concept of net income. The commission had previously expressed a preference for an all-inclusive concept of income and, in keeping with this, King requested that in conjunction with the published announcement of ARB no. 32, his letter to the committee be published in the *Journal of Accountancy*. It was so published in the January 1948 issue. The letter, dated December 11, 1947, contained the following statement: "The Commission has authorized the staff to take exception to financial statements which appear to be misleading, even though they reflect the application of Accounting Research Bulletin no. 32."

The CAP attempted compromise by issuing ARB no. 35 but

the clash continued and subsequently was to be accented by other conflicts, although as we have observed, King had otherwise limited the number of ASRs as to technical matters.

The accounting academic community also exercised its view with regard to the controversy between the SEC and the CAP on the matter of accounting for net income. In one of its moments of academic decisiveness (during the term of Professor Perry Mason's presidency), the American Accounting Association passed a resolution at its annual meeting "condemning" the SEC for deciding accounting principles. It is not known what the effect of this resolution was on the commission, but it is important to learn that academics can muster the resolve to take a position.

The feud between the Institute and the SEC did resolve some differences between the two groups. The commission withdrew the term "principles" in its revised text of Regulation S-X and left it as a "disclosure" requirements document. This was undertaken with the understanding that the Institute would get to work to create the proper accounting principles.

It is probably important to note from the point of view of hindsight that income statement disclosure as it now is established

takes the form of a "modified, all-inclusive" arrangement. While the term "modified" suggests compromise, the form indicates that an all-inclusive vs. a current operating approach has been followed, and would seem to indicate that the commission influenced the profession as to the approach.

Lest the reference to the "happy state of affairs" above and the lack of a deluge of accounting series releases be taken to indicate that King had become "soft on the accounting profession," it should be noted that during his term as chief accountant, the first rule II(e) proceedings against one of the eight largest international CPA firms were instituted (ASR no. 73) in the matter of Haskins & Sells and Andrew Stewart and their client Thomascolor. The results of the hearings resulted in the suspension of practice for both Haskins & Sells and Andrew Stewart for 10 days. While this suspension seems to be a minor penalty, it should be remembered that when a firm itself is denied practice before the commission for a period of time, innocent clients of the firm are inconvenienced and punished. Therefore, the commission does not take lightly the imposition of such a suspension. And since suspensions of this nature tended to inconvenience clients, they served as an economic sanction for firms, in that clients who were prohibited from entering the public capital markets during this period, because they lacked CPA representation, might choose to be represented by other independent accountants.

Andrew Barr (November 1956– January 1972). Barr had been recruited to the SEC by Carman Blough in 1938. When Earle King resigned his position, Barr, who had been the assistant chief accountant, was selected as King's successor. His tenure was to last until January 1972, and the number of ASRs issued during his term as chief accountant would number nearly 60. Because of his extensive experience at the commission, Andy Barr quickly stepped in and accepted the responsibility for continuation of the policies that had been established by his predecessors. He was equally familiar with the personalities and predilections of each, having served with them over a period of almost 20 years.

Barr's views on independence provided the basis for the actions that led to the current Institute rule of professional conduct with regard to that subject. Furthermore, his innovative techniques for disclosing nonconsolidated significant subsidiaries (as in the *Atlantic Research Corporation* case of 1964) provided a precedent for adequate disclosure within the maze of conflicting alternatives for consolidated reports during the merger period of the 1960s. Barr also dealt with the issue of the commission position on the investment credit in the early 1960s. He was also involved in the deliberations relative to the 1964 amendments to the exchange act, which extended the authority of the commission and its accounting rules to the wide body of "over-the-counter securities" for companies with $1 million of assets and (now) 500 shareholders. The significant extension of the 1964 amendments to include such companies was in part a response to concerns that many insurance and bank corporations whose securities had not been traded on public exchanges were employing woefully inadequate accounting and disclosure practices. The annual reports to the Congress by the SEC for 1964 describes the intent in the 1964 legislation. Transportation companies such as railroads were now included as a result of the 1964 amendments, that is to say, they were subject to file with the SEC for the first time but were permitted to use statements prepared for the Interstate Commerce Commission, and because the ICC had prescribed the disclosure requirements, the reports were not required to be certified by public

accountants. However, following the Penn-Central disaster in the late 1960s, the commission now requires that information follow the rules established for other commercial companies. As a result of the 1964 amendments, banks that were under the control of federal bank regulatory agencies would not be required to file under the regulations of the commission, but any banks not subject to federal bank regulatory agencies would be so required under the 1964 amendments. Reporting by insurance companies, while extremely complicated by the fact of state regulations, was expanded to include insurance companies that were involved in interstate commerce and that met the size test of $1 million of assets and 500 security holders.

Barr's term might be characterized as one of dedication to the processes that were initiated by his predecessors. ASR no. 4 remained at the heart of the administration of the securities acts relative to accounting principles. But the difficulty of abiding by the partnership as established on those terms (substantial authoritative support) was becoming all too apparent as evidenced in the matter of ASR no. 96 on investment credit, issued January 10, 1963. Prior to this ASR, the Accounting Principles Board (APB), the newly formed senior technical committee of the Institute which was vested with the authority to establish accounting principles for practitioners, had directed to treat the investment credit on the deferred basis. The commission had to decide to accept this treatment in filings or to accept either the deferred or the flow-through treatment. As the day of final deliberation was reached, it was noted that in the area of public utilities, where the treatment of investment credit was a most critical factor, the major corporations were about equally split with regard to the treatment between deferral and flow-through. The commission had no basis in practice for preferring one treatment over the other. Further, the APB was not sufficiently constituted by all major firms to insure that its promulgations would be followed. Necessary professional sanctions did not exist

as a means to discipline those who might choose to disagree with an APB pronouncement. Thus, perhaps with some reluctance, the commission directed that either approach would be acceptable.

In the history of the accounting profession's attempts at self-regulation in the development of accounting principles, this episode is often regarded as a critical one, in that the SEC, through lack of cooperative support, is considered to have "broken the back" of this attempt by the CPA profession at self-determination.

When viewed from the position of the chief accountant, the lack of clear support in law or theory for one approach over the other, it is understandable that the commission chose to permit either technique. This episode was also a bellwether of the fact that industry had come of age in recognizing the importance of alternative treatments of accounting principles with regard to potential economic consequences. Without precedent and without research to determine the potential outcomes of investment credit legislation, the commission had little choice but to allow either treatment.

Despite the profession's setback on the issue of authority related to the determinations of APBs nos. 2 and 4, the SEC worked cooperatively with the APB affording the profession the opportunity to deal with such issues as leases, pensions and earnings-per-share disclosures.

Critics of the commission have claimed that this period of SEC policy was clearly one of abandoning the duties and responsibilities of the commission by permitting the APB to establish, or attempt to establish, accounting principles. But from the commission's point of view, it would appear that the willingness to accept the profession's leadership was consistent with the policy set in ASR no. 4, as well as with a belief that management had a right to express its point of view in the periodic reports. Without Barr's patience and the cooperation of the commission, it seems likely that the trial and error procedures which the APB underwent in the process of perfecting a private sector standard-setting approach might never have taken place, particularly if the commission had acted vigorously during this period.

But we can reserve speculation on such a matter and point to the fact that as the chief accountantship of Andrew Barr came to a close, it had become apparent that a new view was necessary if the partnership between the commission and profession was going to address effectively the changing technological and investment forces which were impacting the capital market structure of the country.

John C. "Sandy" Burton (June 1972–September 1976). Burton came from the Graduate School of Business at Columbia University to the office of chief accountant at the age of 39. His prior experience as an academic, including host coordinator of the Seaview Symposia (which dealt with important disclosure and ethical considerations in the capital markets of the 1960s and 1970s), familiarized him with the concerns of the many parties who had a vested interest in the disclosure system as it existed under the securities laws. One might appropriately term these the years of "the sound and the fury," but that might be unfair and a poor attempt to add humor to a very important period in the history of our profession.

With the economy of the early 1970s struggling to maintain the confidence of the American people, and the political environment not being necessarily conducive to extensive capital market adventure, Burton's record, one of clear activism, displays an impressive accomplishment. To begin with, in the areas of lease disclosure and of treasury shares, we find attempts to halt questionable accounting practices, and in later pronouncements we find disclosure innovation and disciplinary actions that suggest some degree of intestinal fortitude.

From the end of 1945 when the Institute numbered a mere 9,000 members, to the mid-1970s when its membership numbered over 130,000, it became clear that the public accounting profession had lost the ability to give itself clear direction.

Resource managers in the capital markets, who had grown to depend on the representations of the independent accountant, were getting misty information signals. Double-digit inflation was also eroding the meaningfulness of financial disclosures. Periodic management reports to shareholders submitted in support of proxy solicitations were still prepared under generally accepted accounting principles as determined by "substantial authoritative support" which afforded no clear basis of authority. Watergate, Equity Funding, Lockheed payments and other political and economic matters had laid low the confidence of the general investing public. Burton dealt courageously and creatively with the many issues he encountered. First, he indicated support for the attempt of the accounting profession to establish its own independent rule-making agency (ASR no. 150). Indeed ASR no. 150 was the cornerstone of a new era of disclosure policy, just as ASR no. 4 had been the cornerstone of the previous one. ASR 150 recognized the Financial Accounting Standards Board as the agency whose pronouncements were considered to have substantial authoritative support.[4]

When considered along with ASR no. 159 and the related amendments to the proxy rules (which accomplished what had

[4] Accounting Series Release no. 150, issued December 20, 1973, says, in part:

"The [SEC] intends to continue its policy of looking to the private sector for leadership in establishing and improving accounting principles and standards through the FASB with the expectation that the body's conclusions will promote the interests of investors.

"In Accounting Series Release No. 4 (1938) the Commission stated its policy that financial statements prepared in accordance with accounting practices for which there was no substantial authoritative support were presumed to be misleading and that footnote or other disclosure would not avoid this presumption. It also stated that, where there was a difference of opinion between the Commission and a registrant as to the proper accounting to be followed in a particular case, disclosure would be accepted in lieu of correction of the financial statements themselves only if substantial authoritative support existed for the accounting practices followed by the registrant and the position of the Commission had not been expressed in rules, regulations, or other official releases. For purposes of this policy, principles, standards, and practices promulgated by the FASB in its Statements and Interpretations will be considered by the Commission as having substantial authoritative support, and those contrary to such FASB promulgations will be considered to have no such support.

"Accounting Research Bulletins of the Committee on Accounting Procedure of the American Institute of Certified Public Accountants and effective opinions of the Accounting Principles Board of the Institute should be considered as continuing in force with the same degree of authority except to the extent altered, amended, supplemented, revoked, or superseded by one or more Statements of Financial Accounting Standards issued by the FASB.

"It should be noted that Rule 203 of the Rules of Conduct of the Code of Ethics of the AICPA provides that it is necessary to depart from accounting principles promulgated by the body designated by the Council of the AICPA if, due to unusual circumstances, failure to do so would result in misleading financial statements. In such a case, the use of other principles may be accepted or required by the Commission."

long been recognized as feasible under the acts, namely that the commission had the authority to dictate not only the contents of the reports filed with it but also the contents of any reports submitted in solicitation of proxies), ASR no. 150 stands as the policy hallmark for this new generation of chief accountants. ASR no. 159 was the start of the end of the "dual stream" of financial reporting (the 10-K and the corporate annual report). Notwithstanding Burton's commitment to "differential disclosure," what has now evolved is the policy tool to afford the commission the control over both 10-K and periodic report contents. Even more, when viewed as the constructs of a new disclosure policy, ASR nos. 150 and 159 amalgamate the authority of the private sector and the public sector over both the filings with the commission and management disclosures in the annual report to shareholders.

Burton's exhortations via ASRs and his innovative Staff Accounting Bulletins (SABs) were not limited to the matter of the authority of the commission in relationship to the accounting principles. Indeed, in the area of auditing policy an important issue with regard to interim reports involving "the auditor of record" became a matter of confrontation. In an attempt to add credibility to the limited review of interim financial statements as required under ASR no. 177, Burton sought the assistance of the Auditing Standards Executive Committee (AudSEC) to develop guidelines for such reviews. The controversy surrounding Statement on Auditing Standards (SAS) no. 10 included some important last minute changes in posture by AudSEC such that an "acceptable" audit "disclosure" was finally achieved.

Burton initiated several important precedent-setting sanctions against national public accounting

firms, one of the most important of which was the sanction of Peat, Marwick, Mitchell & Co., as detailed in ASR no. 173. Such creative sanctioning introduced the concept of a firm peer review. It is important to recognize that the process of disciplining a firm, at that time, was unavailable to the Institute through its rules of professional conduct, which were capable of individual sanction only. The notion of peer review established a basis for evaluating the competence of the firm as well as the policies of that firm to include its internal quality controls.

If the sanctions imposed and the pressures relative to SAS no. 10 were not sufficient to draw the fire of the accounting profession on the new chief accountant, his actions with regard to the independent accountant's responsibility for newly adopted principles set forth in the interpretation of ASR no. 177 clearly afforded a choice target. Whether such a preferability judgment need be made by the independent accountant may one day need to be decided by the courts.

Burton's innovations did not stop with ASR no. 177. In fact, they did not reach a zenith until ASR no. 190, requiring the unaudited disclosure of replacement costs by certain large registrants. ASR no. 190, and its accompanying safe-harbor provision, ASR no. 203, were attempts by Burton to address the issue of inflation accounting. Taken in perspective, ASR nos. 190 and 203 represent a logical extension of the hallmark of the term of this "first" chief

accountant in this "new" generation. ASR no. 190 is consistent with a structure of unaudited interim information data, other socially relevant data and the proposal for forecast information within a new trend of soft data. This "soft data" accountability distinguishes this new generation of chief accountants from the preceding one, which was identified with historical cost and financial data disclosure.

If all these changes are taken in light of the "scienter" limitations established by the Supreme Court ruling on the 1934 act liability provisions (the *Hochfelder* decision), perhaps the accounting profession can find some solace when considering the Burton years. One might note that this is what would be expected from the son of a former managing partner in a national public accounting firm. My view is less cynical: Burton had guts and gusto and displayed them both.

ACCORD and Coming Attractions. When Sandy Burton resigned his position and took on the task of Deputy Mayor of Finance for the City of New York, the job of chief accountant fell vacant and has remained so. Some have suggested that the new chairman of the commission, Harold M. Williams, is in effect serving in the chief accountant capacity, as well as fulfilling the duties of the chairmanship. In one respect, with the able talent of A. Clarence Sampson, acting chief accountant, there may be little concern for the ability of the commission to continue to implement the innovative policies that were introduced by Burton.

New issues have also evolved and new pronouncements (some of which were to some extent initiated under Burton's tenure as chief accountant) have come to fruition, including segment reporting, another proposal for forecast disclosure and the potential for involvement by public accountants in the process of disclosing questionable or illegal payments by registrants. All this has occurred under the close political scrutiny of congressional committees (and others charged with a sense of public-spirited curiosity and wrath) relative to the problems of disclosure and the capital markets.

The deliberations of the Advisory Committee on Corporate Disclosure (ACCORD), as contained in its report of November 1977, provides added insight to the role which the SEC may play in this new era. While the commission's position toward the recommendations of the advisory committee falls short of a blanket endorsement of the recommendations, its response (as contained in Release 34-14471) endorses the recommendations made by the committee and, in many respects, action that has already been taken by the SEC tends to strengthen the prospects for accomplishing a major number of important recommendations in ACCORD, including additional soft information disclosures, such as earnings projections and other future-oriented information, and the study of differences in the cost-benefit relationship of various disclosure rules of the commission with regard to large and small registrant companies.

The commission also has embarked recently on investigations relative to corporations' policies for payments of perquisites to management. The chairman of the commission has gone on record as encouraging limited participation by active members of management on the board of directors of registrants.

Further, an amendment to the 1934 securities act created by the passage of the Foreign Corrupt Practices Act of 1977 will likely increase the involvement of the commission and the office of the chief accountant in matters of internal control policies and as to disclosure of the adequacy of such systems.

A final observation with regard to recent developments includes noticing comments by the newest SEC commissioner, Roberta Karmel, as to the interest of the commission in matters of "competition." In a speech before the U.S. Air Force Academy on alternatives to government regulations, she said

"Government regulations are necessarily a reactive force which

seems to have limited ability for creating initiatives in the economics sphere. One of my concerns about overregulation is that it is a drag on private sector development and innovation. There are at least two alternatives to greater government regulation which play an important role in the SEC's administration of federal securities law, namely *disclosure and competition* (emphasis added). Disclosure enables investors to exercise their judgment through their voting rights as to whether or not directors and officers have acted in a company's best interest. Disclosure may lead to public debate on the morality of public conduct." Later she said, "I believe that a competitive environment is generally more conducive to responsible business behavior than an environment characterized by regulatory controls."

Does this statement suggest that the SEC will become active in judging disclosure in light of competition? Is such a role consistent with its legislative authority and conducive to the free enterprise notion of market derived competition? Only time will tell the significance of these statements.

As to the period that began with the term of Carman Blough and ended with the term of Andrew Barr, we can note (1) the establishment of the notion of professional independence as contained in the rules of professional conduct and (2) the development of the concept of substantial authoritative support which is linked to the second generation through ASR no. 150. We also find established a customary view of the role of recognizing management's responsibility for the determination of appropriate accounting principles and policies and we see the evolution of the "strong, silent type of cooperation" between the chief accountant and the accounting profession. Overall, this initial generation is characterized by concern with disclosure of historical cost-based financial data.

It is probably appropriate to characterize this initial era as one of mixed "public interest" and "capture." The critical accounting series releases number at least a

half dozen, including ASRs nos. 4, 19, 62, 78, 90 and 96.

By the end of the first generation of chief accountants, the capital markets in the American economy, not to mention the American public accounting profession, had matured and evolved into a different interdependent state, one that was characterized by the high technology of computers and mass communication facilities. The new and yet to be fully characterized second generation of chief accountants, as established by the policies of John C. Burton, is one of "soft data" and social "accountability." Much remains to be decided about where this disclosure philosophy will lead. Does the prospect for social and political control as noted in Werntz's writings in the 1950s exist and is there a chance that it will be enhanced under this type of approach? Only time will tell. What is clear about the new generation is that it has afforded the accounting profession both the opportunity, through creative new disclosure programs (including quarterly and replacement cost disclosures) and through programs which provide for firm discipline (namely, peer review) to reestablish a positive and respected public image among consumers of accounting information within the capital markets.

In conclusion, two observations are required. First, the office of the chief accountant has become an institution, not only in the United States but in the western world. Second, accountancy as an economic institution is in a phase of evolution such that it must now be examined from the point of view of political science, as well as from that of an art of recording and reporting financial based transactional data. ∎

Examination vs. Inspection of Taxpayer's Returns: The Internal Revenue Service Criteria for Examination of a Taxpayer's Subsequent and Prior Year Returns.

by Max J. Singer, Chief, Examination Division

Max J. Singer, a career employee of the Internal Revenue Service, has been Chief of the Examination Division in the Boston district since 1972. He is a Certified Public Accountant who has been with the Federal Agency since 1950 when he became a Revenue Agent.

The administration and enforcement of Federal Internal Revenue taxes are required by law to be performed by or under the supervision of the Secretary of the Treasury.[1] In the Department of the Treasury the official immediately in charge of the Internal Revenue Service is the Commissioner of the Internal Revenue. Under the existing organizational structure the Commissioner is assisted in the administration of the Internal Revenue laws by Assistant Commissioners, Regional Commissioners and District Directors.

The mission of the Service is to encourage and achieve the highest possible degree of voluntary compliance with the tax laws and regulations and to maintain the highest degree of public confidence in the integrity and efficiency of the Service. The primary function of the Internal Revenue Service is the determination, assessment and collection of taxes.

In conjunction with the determination of taxes the Commissioner has delegated to the Chief of Examination Division in each District Office responsibility for the examination of all classes of returns.[2] The usual reason for selecting a tax return for examination is to verify the correctness of income, exemptions or deductions that have been reported on the return. However, some returns are selected as part of a random sample for research studies.

Where it appears that the explanation and questioning can be handled by correspondence or office interview the "Office Audit" branch handles the case. Where it is necessary to audit or check the books and records, the examinations are conducted through the "Field Audit" branch by Revenue Agents. The scope of the audit examination varies according to different problems presented on the return.

In recent years some confusion has developed among both practitioners and taxpayers alike as to the Service's distinction between an examination of a taxpayer's return vs. a mere inspection of the return by a member of the Examination Division staff.

By definition, an examination is . . . "the act of examining or the state of being examined," whereas an inspection is . . . "the act of inspecting."[3] Specific provisions and guidelines are contained within the Internal Revenue Manual as to what constitutes an inspection of a taxpayer's return. An inspection is essentially equivalent to the classification of a return to determine if an examination is necessary. This means that no record should be examined and no questions asked the taxpayer concerning the copy inspected.[4] Simply stated, once an examiner, be it an Office Auditor or a Revenue Agent, makes a single inquiry of a single item appearing on the return, then an examination has been initiated. This requires a report of examination by the examiner for the tax year questioned.

As noted in the preceding, the Manual provisions are quite specific as to the distinction between an examination vs. inspection of a taxpayer's return. Examiners are constantly reminded of this Manual section to achieve uniformity in the inspection procedures to avoid taxpayer and practitioner confusion in this matter. Where an examiner requests either from a taxpayer or a practitioner a retained copy of the subsequent and/or prior year return he/she will immediately advise the party that the request is to determine if an examination of these returns is necessary.

As a general rule when examiners make field examinations of assigned returns, the taxpayer's retained copy for the subsequent year should be inspected. The prior year return will be inspected only if the examiner determines that issues on the assigned return warrant inspection.[5] In office interview examinations of business returns not

EXAMINATION VS. INSPECTION . . .

requiring precontact analysis and of nonbusiness returns, the initial contact letter should not include an automatic request that the taxpayer bring in a retained copy of the subsequent and/or prior year return to the interview. However, in office interview examinations of business returns requiring precontact analysis when the examiner determines that issues on the return warrant inspection of a subsequent and/or prior year return, the initial contact with the taxpayer should include a request that the taxpayer bring in a retained copy of the subsequent and/or prior return.[6]

In correspondence examinations contact with the taxpayer should not include a request for an inspection of a subsequent and/or prior year return.[7]

Regarding this question, Internal Revenue Manual section 4228.(1) states in part, . . . "When adjustments respecting income or deductions are made by examiners and such adjustments affect returns filed for years other than the year under examination, the examiner will ensure that appropriate adjustments are made in the prior and subsequent years which are open under the statute of limitations. This action will be taken whether the adjustment results in a deficiency or an overassessment."

In summary: If it is determined the examination of the subsequent and/or prior year return is warranted, they will be examined concurrently with the assigned return under examination. The taxpayer in turn will be informed as soon as the examiner decides to extend his/her examination to include the subsequent and/or prior year return(s).

Footnotes

1. IRC Sec. 7801(A)
2. I.T. Regs. Sec. 601.105
3. The American Heritage Dictionary of the English Language
4. Internal Revenue Manual 4217:(1)
5. Internal Revenue Manual 4217:(1)
6. Internal Revenue Manual 4217:(3)
7. Internal Revenue Manual 4217:(4)

Lane K. Anderson, Ph.D., CPA

An Update of the CASB

Here is a refresher on the important work of the
CASB. It reviews pronouncements and other activities
of the Board in the two years since this subject was
last presented in the *CPA Journal*.

MOST CPAs have only fleeting acquaintance with the Cost Accounting Standards Board (CASB), its purpose, and its accomplishments. This is surprising, considering the number of companies directly influenced by its promulgations. The constituency of the CASB, as designated by Congress, consists of contractors awarded negotiated defense contracts in excess of $100,000. There are more than 4,000 prime defense contractors, representing more than 25,000 profit centers performing defense contracts, and thousands of subcontractors. They represent all sizes of business and all industries. About $26 billion in defense contracts are subject to CASB promulgations annually. In addition, the General Services Administration has amended the federal procurement regulations to apply CASB promulgations to practically all nondefense government contracts in excess of $100,000. The number of companies and the multitude of products involved means that the standards issued by the CASB widely affect the business community.

Fuller, in the January 1976 issue of *The CPA Journal*,[1] covered the historical background and operations of the CASB, and summarized Cost Accounting Standards 401 through 409. Since that time, the CASB has promulgated an additional seven cost accounting standards and two interpretations of earlier standards. This article summarizes these additional promulgations and describes other important work of the CASB.

Reasons for Involvement in CASB Matters

To start with, a question—why should a CPA be concerned about the potential impact of CASB on his clients and his practice. There are at least five reasons:

1. A client's failure to comply with CASB promulgations can result in an adverse adjustment of costs and profits related to government contracts.

2. Promulgations can significantly affect a client's cash flow and the inventory values attached to government contracts in process.

3. The cost/benefit equation may require clients to adopt cost accounting standards for any commercial work. For example, the establishment of longer service lives for depreciable assets may make it impractical to keep separate depreciation records for government and commercial costing due to the distribution of depreciation through service centers and overhead pools.

4. The CASB is an authoritative organization created by law and its promulgations represent a body of knowledge concerning cost accounting, if only for government work. This body of knowledge may serve at least as an informal guide in dealing with cost accounting practices for nongovernment contracts.

5. CPAs, when using generally accepted auditing standards, will be concerned with evaluating whether a company's current and proposed cost accounting practices comply with the promulgations. This work is usually an integral part of the audit.

A significant reason over the longer term for being acquainted with the work of the CASB is the potential impact it may have in shaping the accounting profession. *The Accounting Establishment*, a staff study prepared by the Senate Subcommittee on Reports, Accounting and Management of which Senator Lee Metcalf was Chairman, made several recommendations[2] affecting the accounting profession. Recommendation five states: "The Federal Government should directly establish financial accounting standards for publicly-owned corporations." In discussing ways this recommendation could be implemented, the report said that one alternative would be ". . .a Federal Board similar in operation to the CASB. . ." Earlier, in recommendation two, the report concluded that the "Cost Accounting Standards Board had benefited from its specific statutory mandate to achieve 'uniformity and consistency' in cost accounting standards. . ." Congress, if it determines that the federal government should establish fi-

Lane K. Anderson, Ph.D., CPA, associate professor of accounting at Texas Tech University, was, until recently, an assistant director on the staff of the CASB. He is a member of the AAA, AICPA and NAA. Dr. Anderson is the author of several articles on management/cost accounting and financial information systems.

[1] "Impact of CASB Standards," K. John Fuller, The *CPA Journal*, January 1976, p. 19.
[2] U.S. Congress, Senate, Committee on Government Operations, *The Accounting Establishment*, by the Subcommittee on Reports, Accounting and Management; Committee Print, Staff Paper (Washington, D.C.: Government Printing Office, 1976), pp. 20–24.

FEBRUARY 1979

nancial accounting standards, could either expand the role of the CASB or use it as a model for a separate Board.

> **'The constituency of the CASB, as designated by Congress, consists of contractors awarded negotiated defense contracts in excess of $100,000. There are more than 4,000 prime defense contracts, and thousands of subcontractors. They represent all sizes of business and industries.'**

Summary of Cost Accounting Standards 410-416

CAS No. 410, Allocation of Business Unit General and Administrative Expenses to Final Cost Objectives; Effective Date: October 1, 1976. The purpose of this standard is to provide criteria for the allocation of business unit general and administrative (G&A) expenses to final cost objectives based on their beneficial or causal relationships. These expenses represent the costs of the management and administration of the business unit as a whole. The base for allocating the G&A expense pool to final cost objectives is a cost input base representing the total activity of the business unit for the period. The cost input base may be (1) total cost input, (2) value-added cost input, or (3) single element cost input. This standard also provides criteria for the allocation of home office expenses received by a segment to the cost objectives of that segment.

CAS No. 411, Accounting for the Acquisition Cost of Material; Effective Date: January 1, 1976. Most material used on government contracts subject to these standards is purchased specifically for and charged directly to the appropriate contract. This standard permits direct charging of such costs provided the specific contract was specified at the time of purchase or production of the units.

Some materials, of course, are drawn from existing inventories. Such material may be priced into contracts using one of the following costing methods consistently applied:
1. The first-in, first-out (FIFO) method;
2. The moving average cost method;
3. The weighted average cost method;
4. The standard cost method;

5. The last-in, first-out (LIFO) method.

Contractors are required to have and consistently apply written statements of accounting policies and practices for accumulating material costs and allocating them to cost objectives. The cost of materials which are used solely in performing indirect functions or which are not a significant element of production cost may be charged to an indirect cost pool and allocated as part of the pool.

CAS No. 412, Composition and Measurement of Pension Cost; Effective Date: January 1, 1976. This standard provides guidance for determining and measuring the components of pension costs. Its provisions fall within the requirements of the Employee Retirement Income Security Act of 1974 (ERISA).

In the case of defined-benefit pension plans, the amount of pension cost is determined by an actuarial cost method which measures separately the normal cost of the period, a part of any unfunded actuarial liability, an interest equivalent on the unamortized portion of any unfunded actuarial liability, and an adjustment for any actuarial gains and losses. Each actuarial assumption used to measure pension cost must be separately identified and must represent the contractor's best estimates of anticipated experience under the plan.

For defined-contribution pension plans, the pension cost is the net contribution required to be made during the period.

The pension cost assignable to a period is allocable to cost objectives of the period only to the extent that liquidation of the liability for such cost can be compelled or liquidation is actually effected in that period.

CAS No. 413, Adjustment and Allocation of Pension Cost; Effective Date: March 10, 1978. This standard provides guidance for adjusting pension cost by measuring actuarial gains and losses and assigning such gains and losses to cost accounting periods.

> **'A significant reason over the longer term for being acquainted with the work of the CASB is the potential impact it may have in shaping the accounting profession.'**

Actuarial gains and losses are calculated annually and assigned to the accounting period for which the actuarial valuation is made and subsequent periods. The number of subsequent periods involved is determined by the actuarial cost method used: (1) where an immediate gain actuarial cost method is used, amortize the gains and losses over a 15-year period; or (2) where a spread-gain actuarial cost method is used, include the gains and losses in current and future normal cost and spread over the remaining average working lives of the work force.

'This standard takes a giant step forward in accounting theory by recognizing imputed interest as a cost.'

The actuarial value of the assets of a pension fund, used for measuring actuarial gains and losses, may be determined by any recognized asset valuation method which provides equivalent recognition of appreciation and depreciation in the value of pension fund assets. However, the total asset value must fall within a corridor from 80 to 120 percent of market value of the assets, determined as of the valuation date.

Contractors must allocate pension cost to each segment having participants in a pension plan. The standard provides criteria for such allocation.

CAS No. 414, Cost of Money as an Element of the Cost of Facilities Capital; Effective Date: October 1, 1976. This standard takes a giant step forward in accounting theory by recognizing imputed interest as a cost. The purpose of this standard is to establish criteria for the measurement and allocation of the cost (imputed interest) of capital committed to existing facilities of a contractor. The cost of money rate for any cost accounting period is the arithmetic mean of the interest rates specified by the Secretary of the Treasury pursuant to Public Law 92-41 (85 Stat 97). Provisions in the standard explain the proper criteria for allocating the imputed interest to the final cost objectives.

CAS No. 415, Accounting for the Cost of Deferred Compensation; Effective Date: July 10, 1977. This standard provides criteria for the measurement of deferred compensation and the assignment of such cost to cost accounting periods.

The cost of deferred compensation is assigned to the cost accounting period in which the contractor incurs an obligation to compensate the employee. An obligation is incurred when the following conditions are met:

• There is a requirement to make the future payment(s) which the contractor cannot unilaterally avoid.

• The award is to be satisfied by a future payment of money, other assets or shares of stock of the contractor.

• The amount of the future payment can be measured with reasonable accuracy.

• The recipient of the award is known.

• If the terms of the award require that certain

events must occur before an employee is entitled to receive the benefits, there is a reasonable probability that such events will occur.

For stock options, there must be a reasonable probability that the options ultimately will be exercised.

For awards which require that the employee perform future service to receive the benefits, the obligation is deemed to have been incurred as the future service is performed for that part of the award attributable to such future service. In the event no obligation is incurred prior to payment, the cost of deferred compensation is the amount paid and is assigned to the cost accounting period in which the payment is made.

The measurement of the amount of deferred compensation is the present value of the future benefits to be paid by the contractor. If the award provides that the amount to be paid includes the principal of the award plus interest, such interest is included in the computation of the amount of the future benefit. If no interest is included in the award, the amount of future benefit is the amount of the award.

Each award is considered separately for purposes of measurement and assignment of its costs to accounting periods. However, if the deferred compensation for the employees covered by a plan can be measured with reasonable accuracy on a group basis, separate computations for each employee are not required.

CAS No. 416, Accounting for Insurance Costs; Effective Date: July 10, 1979. This standard provides criteria for measuring insurance costs, assigning them to cost accounting periods, and allocating them to cost objectives.

A company may cover its exposure to risk of loss either by purchased insurance, by a trusteed fund, or by a self-insurance program. Under any of these alternatives, the amount of insurance cost assigned to a cost accounting period is the projected average loss for the period plus insurance administration expenses of the period. The projected average loss is represented by the premium for purchased insurance plans and by payments to the fund for trusteed plans. The standard contains the criteria for determining the projected average loss for self-insurance programs.

Summary of Interpretations

Interpretation No. 1 to CAS No. 402; Effective Date: July 1, 1972. This interpretation requires that a contractor support the percentage factors used in estimating the direct material costs to cover expected material losses such as those occurring when items are scrapped, fail to meet specifications, are lost, are consumed in the manufacturing process, or are destroyed in testing and qualification processes. The factors may be supported with accounting, statistical, or other relevant data from past experience, or by a program to

FEBRUARY 1979

accumulate actual costs for comparison with such percentage estimates.

Interpretation No. 1 to CAS No. 402; Effective Date: July 1, 1972. This interpretation specifies that costs incurred in preparing, submitting and supporting proposals pursuant to a specific requirement of an existing contract are incurred in different circumstances from those under which costs are incurred in preparing proposals which do not result from such specific requirements. The difference is based on the theory that costs of preparing proposals specifically required by the provisions of an existing contract relate only to that contract while other proposal costs relate to all work of the contractor.

Important Proposed Standards

The CASB has devoted major effort to research on problems related to the allocation of indirect costs. This effort has resulted in five separate, closely-related proposed standards, which were published for public comment on March 16, 1978. They are:

Distinguishing between direct and indirect costs. This proposal covers the accounting concepts and principles governing consistent classification of costs as direct or indirect, and the criteria for making distinctions.

> **'. . .many participating contractors agreed that one benefit of the Disclosure Statement was information gained about cost accounting practices actually in use. Contractors completing the Disclosure Statement for the first time have remarked how little they really knew about their accounting systems.'**

Allocation of service center costs. This proposal provides a hierarchy of measures for the allocation of service center costs to other cost objectives. In descending order of preferability the allocation measures are: (1) a resource consumption measure, (2) an output measure, and (3) a surrogate that represents the resources used. The proposal also provides guidelines for allocating service center costs among service centers.

Allocation of material-related overhead costs. Material-related overhead costs are the costs incurred for the activities associated with acquiring, handling and controlling materials. The proposed standard gives criteria for the creation of cost pools and selection of allocations bases pertaining to material-related overhead costs.

Allocation of manufacturing, engineering and comparable overhead. This proposal provides criteria for accumulating manufacturing, engineering and comparable overhead costs and for selecting bases for allocating the costs thus accumulated to final cost objectives.

Allocation of indirect costs. This proposed standard governs the accumulation of costs in indirect cost pools and the selection of allocation measures for those items of costs not specifically covered by another standard. The proposal gives guidance in determining the homogeneity of an indirect cost pool, and establishes a hierarchy of allocation measures.

Projects in Progress

There are a number of research projects which may later result in standards. Because these projects may be expanded, divided or deleted, there is little purpose in listing them. The Board's annual report, *Progress Report to the Congress*, gives the current topics, their scope and current status.

Disclosure Statement

The law creating the CASB contained a provision that contractors receiving negotiated defense contracts must disclose, in writing, their cost accounting practices. The Board has prepared a Disclosure Statement to be used in complying with the law. CASB regulations require a separate Disclosure Statement from each of the contractor's profit centers, divisions or similar organizational units whose costs are included in the total price of any contract exceeding $100,000. A Disclosure Statement is also required for each corporate or group office whose costs are allocated to one or more corporate segments performing contracts subject to the standards. These requirements apply to prime contractors as well as subcontractors.

The principle purpose of the Disclosure Statement is to provide the government personnel with a tool to help them understand the cost accounting practices contractors plan to follow and to help assure consistency in estimating and accounting for the cost of government contracts. The Disclosure Statement is a 35-page document plus continuation sheets provided for explanatory purposes and instructions. It is subdivided as follows:

· Part I—General Information;
· Part II—Direct Costs (Material, Labor, other);
· Part III—Direct v. Indirect;
· Part IV—Indirect Costs;
· Part V—Depreciation and Capitalization Practices;

• Part VI—Other Costs and Credits (Vacation, Holiday, Sick Pay, Incidental Receipts, etc.);

• Part VII—Deferred Compensation and Insurance Costs;

• Part VIII—Corporate or Group Expenses.

Under CASB regulations a completed Disclosure Statement will not be made public in any case where the contractor indicates that it contains privileged and confidential information. The CASB does believe that aggregate information not identified to particular contractors should be made available. In its annual report, *Progress Report to the Congress*, the CASB presents aggregated responses in statistical form.

The practical effect of the Disclosure Statement requirement is the development and maintenance of accounting manuals. As an interesting sidelight, the Board held an evaluation conference in June 1975; many participating contractors agreed that one benefit of the Disclosure Statement was information gained about cost accounting practices actually in use. Contractors completing the Disclosure Statement for the first time have remarked how little they really knew about their accounting systems.

Conclusion

Promulgations of the CASB[3] have influenced accounting policies and practices of companies performing on defense contracts. CPAs need to be aware of the CASB and its promulgations if they are to assess its influence on their client's accounting systems, inventory valuation and cash flow. This also presents opportunities for increased client services. Besides reviewing or designing cost accounting systems for compliance with these standards, CPAs can provide counsel and assistance on CASB matters, and interface with government auditors and contracting officers. Ω

---

[3] A publication, "Standards, Rules and Regulations of the Cost Accounting Standards Board-Basic Manual and Supplement," is available from the Government Printing Office. The "CCH Cost Accounting Standards Guide" summarizes the history and background preceding the establishment of the Cost Accounting Standards Board by Public Law 91-379, and contains the Disclosure Statement, the Contract Clause, promulgated Standards and Interpretations and a section called "New Developments."

Comparing Cost Accounting Standards with Existing Accounting Standards

Although the variety of cost accounting standards is large, it is nowhere near as large as for existing accounting standards, which cover the entire scope of accounting.

By Fathi A. Mansour and James H. Sellers

The Cost Accounting Standards Board, created by Public Law 91-379, has been in operation since 1970 and has issued a series of cost accounting standards which affect companies dealing with the federal government. The purpose of this article is to examine Cost Accounting Standards 401 through 415 and their relationship to existing accounting standards. If consistency is truly the goal of accounting standards, then the standards promulgated by the CASB should be compatible with the standards used by firms for external reporting.

The Development of the CASB

The Department of Defense grants negotiated contracts based on cost to the contractor of the work performed. Until 1970, determination of cost was based on the cost principles outlined in the Armed Services Procurement Regulation (ASPR). Many of these principles refer to GAAP and IRS regulations as guidelines. The availability of acceptable alternative accounting principles, however, led to disagreements between contractors and the defense department regarding the proper method of cost determination.

In 1968, the comptroller general undertook a study to determine the feasibility of establishing cost accounting standards for defense contracts. The accounting profession, professional organizations, and government agencies indicated that such principles were feasible. Defense contractors, however, did not perceive cost accounting standards to be either feasible or desirable.

As a result of the feasibility study Congress enacted Public Law 91-379, which established the Cost Accounting Standards Board with the following charge:

> "The Board shall from time to time promulgate cost-accounting standards designed to achieve uniformity and consistency in the cost-accounting principles followed by defense contractors and subcontractors under Federal contracts." [1]

Cost Accounting Standards

Since its inception, the CASB has issued statements on a variety of subjects. Cost accounting standards tend to be detailed instructions for the treatment of particular items of cost as opposed to most existing accounting standards which, although dictating a particular treatment of an item, generally tend to be less detailed. Although the variety of cost accounting standards is large, it

Fathi A. Mansour is Assistant Professor of Accounting at the University of Wyoming. He is a CPA and holds a B. Com. degree from the University of Alexandria, Egypt, an M.S. degree from the University of Minnesota, and a Ph.D. degree from the University of Mississippi.

This article was submitted through the Northeast Mississippi Chapter.

is nowhere near as large as for existing accounting standards, which cover the entire scope of accounting. Exhibit 1 describes the cost accounting standards as well as the related accounting standards in use. A discussion of the similarities and differences in the two sets of standards follow.

CAS 401

Cost Accounting Standard 401 relates to consistency in estimating, accumulating and reporting costs and is related to APB Opinions Nos. 20 and 22. Standard 401 states that:

> "a. A contractor's practices used in estimating costs in pricing a proposal shall be consistent with his cost accounting practices used in accumulating and reporting costs.
>
> "b. A contractor's cost accounting practices used in accumulating and reporting actual costs for a contract shall be consistent with his practices used in estimating costs in pricing the related proposal." [2]

Consistency as developed in APB Opinion No. 20, is described as follows:

> "In the preparation of financial statement there is the presumption that an accounting principle once adopted should not be changed for events and transactions of a similar type." [3]

APB Opinion No. 22 states:

> "A description of all significant accounting policies of the reporting entity should be included as an integral part of the financial statements." [4]

The two standards aim to satisfy the same purpose; that is, consistency in the application of accounting principles and procedures should be maintained by the business entity. Each standard has a slightly different emphasis. It could be argued, however, that the existing accounting standard could be easily extended to include the objective of the cost accounting standard. Implementation of the existing accounting standard implies or presumes consistency in the application of methods and procedures of estimating costs, for example, estimating the cost of work in process.

CAS 402

Cost Accounting Standard 402, relating to the allocation of costs incurred for the same purpose,

James H. Sellers is Associate Professor of Accountancy at the University of Mississippi. He is a CPA and holds a B.B.A. degree from the University of Texas at Austin, an M.B.A. degree from the University of Houston and a Ph.D. degree from the University of Arkansas. Dr. Sellers is a member of the Northeast Mississippi Chapter.

Exhibit 1

COST ACCOUNTING STANDARDS COMPARED WITH EXISTING ACCOUNTING STANDARDS

	Cost Accounting Standards	Existing Accounting Standards	Comment
401	Consistency in estimating accumulating and reporting costs	APB Opinions Nos. 20 and 22	
402	Consistency in allocating costs incurred for the same purpose	APB Opinions Nos. 20 and 22	
403	Allocation of home office expense to segments	No Standard	
404	Capitalization of tangible assets	No Standard	Financial accounting practice and theory is in complete agreement with Standard.
405	Accounting for unallowable costs	No Standard	This Standard is related specifically to government contracts.
406	Cost accounting period	No Standard	This Standard adopts the fiscal Accounting period.
407	Use of standard costs for direct material and direct labor	ARB No. 43	
408	Accounting for costs of compensated personal absence	No Standard	This Standard is compatible with financial accounting practice and theory.
409	Depreciation of tangible capital assets	Accounting Terminology Bulletin	
410	Allocation of business unit G&A expenses to final cost objective	No Standard	There is conflict between this Standard and financial accounting practice.
411	Accounting for acquisition costs of material	ARB No. 43, Ch. 4	
412	Composition and measurement of pension cost	APB Opinion No. 8	
414	Cost of money as an element of the cost of facilities capital	No Standard	APB Statement No. 3 recommends supporting statements for adjusted data.
415	Accounting for the cost of deferred compensation	APB Opinions Nos. 12 and 25	

Note: Standard No. 413 was not issued.

is also related to APB Opinion Nos. 20 and 22. This Standard states:

"All costs incurred for the same purpose, in like circumstances, are either direct costs only or indirect costs only with respect to final cost objectives. No final cost objective shall have allocated to it as an indirect cost any cost, if other costs incurred for the same purpose, in like circumstances, have been included as a direct cost of that or any other final cost objective. Further no final cost objective shall have allocated to it as a direct cost any cost, if other costs incurred for the same purpose, in like circumstances, have been included in any indirect cost pool to be allocated to that or any other final cost objective." [5]

Two major points are included in this Standard. The first is the consistency concept discussed above. The cost and existing accounting standards are in agreement regarding this concept. The second is the allocation of incurred costs to cost objectives. There is no equivalent existing accounting standard even though the concept is important in such financial accounting problems as inventory valuation.

The consistency principle can be satisfied by uniform application of accounting principles from period to period. However, such mechanical application does not ensure that the essence of the principle is maintained. For example, an inventory valuation method such as FIFO could be applied consistently from period to period, and the amount of direct materials cost charged to the final cost objective could vary even if treatment of other procurement costs changed.

CAS 403

This standard is related to the allocation of home office expenses to segments of the business and is not directly related to any existing accounting standard.

"Home office expenses shall be allocated on the basis of the beneficial or causal relationship between supporting and receiving activities. Such expenses shall be allocated directly to segments to the maximum extent practical." [6]

No existing accounting standard is equivalent to the above cost accounting standard. There is no specified way to deal with the allocation of common costs between products or departments. However, if corporations are required to report results by segments, such vital questions as allocation of common costs should be addressed by the accounting profession.

CAS 404

Cost Accounting Standard 404 presents a rather detailed treatise on the capitalization of tangible assets. This Standard reads, in part:

"a. The acquisition cost of tangible capital assets shall be capitalized. Capitalization shall be based upon a written policy that is reasonable and consistently applied.
"b. The contractor's policy shall designate economic and physical characteristics for capitalization of tangible assets . . .
"d. Costs incurred subsequent to the acquisition of a tangible capital asset which result in extending the life or increasing the productivity of that asset (e.g., betterment and improvement) and which meet the contractor's established criteria for capitalization shall be capitalized with appropriate accounting for replaced asset accountability units. However, costs incurred for repairs and maintenance to a tangible capital asset which either restore the asset to, or maintain it at, its normal or expected service life or production shall be treated as costs of the current period." [7]

No specific accounting standard is equivalent to the above cost accounting standard. Nevertheless, all authoritative sources in financial accounting treat the capitalization of fixed assets subject in the manner described in CAS 404.[8] Therefore, cost and existing accounting standards and procedures are in complete agreement regarding the treatment of capital and revenue expenses. The only difference is that the cost accounting standard is more detailed and provides specific rules and procedures to be followed.

CAS 405

Standard 405 relates to costs which are incurred but are not allowable for government contracting purposes. The Standard merely prohibits the inclusion of specified costs in determining the allowable costs for government contracts. Because this Standard relates specifically to government contracts, there is no equivalent standard in financial accounting.

CAS 406

The cost accounting period is the subject of Standard 406 which states:

"A contractor shall use his fiscal year as his cost accounting period, except . . ." [9]

It requires that the financial accounting period be used as the cost accounting period unless special circumstances require another treatment. Complete agreement between financial and cost accounting exists in this area.

"The consistency principle can be satisfied by uniform application . . ."

"Accrual accounting requires the recognition of costs incurred..."

Those responsible for financial accounting have not paid much attention to the potential and the problems of standard costs as a basis of an accounting system. It has been assumed that standard costs constitute a cost accounting problem and of little consequence to financial accounting. Such is not the case. Problems concerning the nature of standards used and disposition of variances must be dealt with by financial accounting.

CAS 407

Cost Accounting Standard 407 addresses this problem.

"Standard costs may be used for estimating, accumulating and reporting costs of direct material and direct labor only when all of the following criteria are met:

a. Standard costs are entered into the books of account;

b. Standard costs and related variances are appropriately accounted for at the level of the production unit; and

c. Practices with respect to the setting and revising of standards, use of standard costs, and disposition variances are stated in writing and are consistently followed." [10]

Financial accounting has dealt with standard costs in relation to inventory valuation. *Accounting Research Bulletin No. 43* states:

"Standard costs are acceptable if adjusted at reasonable intervals to reflect current conditions so that at the balance-sheet date standard costs reasonably approximate costs computed under one of the recognized bases. In such cases descriptive language should be used which will express this relationship, as, for instance, 'approximate costs determined on the first-in first-out basis,' or, if it is desired to mention standard costs, 'at standard costs, approximating average costs.' " [11]

The cost and existing accounting standards regarding the use of standard costs for materials are similar and compatible. The cost accounting standard requirement that standard costs be used in the books of account is of particular significance.

CAS 408

Standard 408 is another specialized standard regarding the accounting for personal absence from work by employees. This Standard states:

"a. The costs of compensated personal absence shall be assigned to the cost accounting period of periods in which the entitlement was earned.

"b. The costs of compensated personal absence for an entire cost accounting period shall be allocated prorata on an annual basis among the final cost objectives of that period." [12]

The essence of part a. of the above Standard is applicable in financial accounting in determining periodic income through the matching process. Accrual accounting requires the recognition of costs incurred in producing the revenue realized during the period. Therefore, such items as deferred vacation costs, allowance for ordinary maintenance, and warranty costs should be charged to the period in which they were incurred. Part b. of the Standard is considered to be outside the interest of financial accounting. Standard No. 408 is, therefore, compatible with existing accounting standards. Here again, however, this Cost Accounting Standard provides operational rules to be used in its application, a situation which is lacking in financial accounting.

CAS 409

Standard 409 addresses the question of depreciation. This Standard reads, in part:

"a. The depreciable cost of a tangible capital asset (or group of assets) shall be assigned to cost accounting periods in accordance with the following criteria:

1. The depreciable cost of a tangible capital asset shall be its capitalized cost less its estimated residual value.

2. The estimated service life of a tangible capital asset (or group of assets) shall be used to determine the cost accounting periods to which the depreciable cost will be assigned ...

"b. The annual depreciation cost of a tangible capital asset (or group of assets) shall be allocated to cost objectives for which it provides service in accordance with the following criteria." [13]

Accounting Terminology Bulletin defined depreciation as:

"... a system of accounting which aims to distribute the cost or other basic value of tangible capital assets, less salvage (if any), over the estimated useful life of the unit (which may be a group of assets) in a systematic and rational manner. It is a process of allocation, not of valuation." [14]

The cost and existing accounting standards regarding depreciation are almost identical with the cost accounting standard giving more detail.

CAS 410

Standard 410 relates to the allocation of general and administrative expenses to final cost objectives. This Standard reads, in part:

"a. Business unit G & A expenses shall be grouped in a separate indirect cost pool which shall be allocated only to final cost objectives.

"b. The G & A expense pool of a business unit for a cost accounting period shall be allocated to final cost objectives of that cost accounting period by means of a cost input base representing the total activity of the business unit ... The cost input base selected shall be the one which best represents the total activity of a typical cost accounting period." [15]

General and administrative expenses are generally considered to be period costs; that is, noninventoriable costs. Therefore, there is a conflict between existing and cost accounting standards regarding such costs. For example, the CASB requires contractors to follow Standard 410 in determining cost, but it permits them to follow existing standards for financial reporting.

CAS 411

The CASB has adopted the existing accounting methods of inventory valuation. These are addressed in Standard 411 which states:

"a. The contractor shall have, and consistently apply, written statements of accounting policies and practices for accumulating the costs of material and for allocating costs of material to cost objectives.

"b. The cost of units of a category of material may be allocated directly to a cost objective provided the cost objective was specifically identified at the time of purchase or production of the units." [16]

The Standard also specifies that one of the following inventory costing methods be used when issuing material:

1. The first-in-first-out method
2. The moving average cost method
3. The weighted average cost method
4. The standard cost method
5. The last-in, first-out method.

It is therefore in complete agreement with generally accepted accounting principles regarding accounting for materials and inventory valuation.

CAS 412

Standard 412 deals with pension costs and is similar to the financial accounting treatment of pension costs.

"For defined-benefit pension plans, the amount of pension cost of a cost accounting period shall be determined by use of an actuarial cost method which measures separately each of the components of pension cost ...

"The amount of pension cost computed for a cost accounting period is assignable only to that period. Except for pay-as-you-go plans, the cost assignable to a period is allocable to cost objectives of that period to the extent that liquidation of the liability for such cost can be compelled if liquidation is actually effected in that period." [17]

This Standard is compatible with APB Opinion No. 8. In any case, the two standards are detailed and comprehensive. CAS 412 adds a provision allocating the pension cost to cost objectives.

CAS 413, 414

The accounting profession has long been aware of the problem of inflation and its effects on the reliability of historical financial statements. However, it was unable to deal directly with the problem. Twice the accounting profession recommended, but did not require, disclosure of the effects of inflation on the financial statements. ARB No. 43, issued in 1953, in discussing the effect of inflation on depreciation, stated that the committee on accounting procedure "gives its full support to the use of supplementary financial schedules, explanations or footnotes by which management may explain the need for retention of earnings." On the other hand, APB statement No. 3, issued in 1969, stated that: "General price-level information may be presented in addition to the basic historical-dollar financial statements, but general price-level financial statements should not be presented as the basic statements." It is interesting to note that the CASB did not attack the problem directly; instead it used a surrogate, the cost of money, to deal with the problem of inflation.

The CASB considered the promulgation of two new Standards: Standard 413—Adjustment of Historical Depreciation Cost for Inflation and Standard 414. The Board concluded that since the available research shows a strong correlation between interest rates and the rate of change of the price level, the interest rate used in measuring the cost of capital would include some allowance for inflation. The Board reasoned that issuing these two Standards would result in overlapping coverage; therefore, it withdrew the proposed Standard 413 and issued Standard 414, which reads, in part:

"a. A contractor's facilities capital shall be measured and allocated in accordance with

"The accounting profession has long been aware of the problem of inflation and its effects ..."

". . . cost standards are detailed . . . accounting standards are general . . ."

the criteria set forth in this standard. The allocated amount shall be used as a base to which a cost of money rate is applied.

"b. The cost of money rate shall be based on interest rates determined by the Secretary of the Treasury . . ." [18]

No existing accounting standard is equivalent to Standard 414.

CAS 415

Deferred compensation is similar in many respects to pension costs. It is discussed in Standard 415.

"The cost of deferred compensation shall be assigned to the cost accounting period in which the contractor incurs an obligation to compensate the employee. In the event no obligation is incurred prior to payment, the cost of deferred compensation shall be the amount paid and shall be assigned to cost accounting period in which the payment is made."

"The measurement of the amount of the cost deferred compensation shall be the present value of the future benefits to be paid by the contractor." [19]

This Standard is compatible with APB Opinion No. 12—Deferred Compensation Contracts and APB Opinion No. 25—Accounting for Stock Issued to Employees.

Summary and Conclusion

The cost accounting standards promulgated thus far by the CASB can be classified into these groups: (1) Standards 401, 402, 404, 406, 408, 411, 412, and 415, which are basically similar to existing accounting standards; (2) Standards 403 and 410, which could be in conflict with generally accepted accounting principles; and (3) Standards 405 and 414, which have no equivalent existing accounting standards. Most of these standards are, however, compatible with GAAP.   □

[1] U.S. Congress, *An Act to Amend the Defense Production Act of 1950,* Public Law 91-379, 91st Congress, 1970.
[2] *Federal Register,* February 29, 1972, p. 4172.
[3] APB Opinion No. 20, Paras. 15 and 17, AICPA, New York, N.Y., July 1971.
[4] APB Opinion No. 22, Paragraph 8, AICPA, New York, N.Y., April 1972.
[5] *Federal Register,* February 29, 1972, p. 4173.
[6] *Federal Register,* December 14, 1972, p. 22683.
[7] *Federal Register,* February 27, 1973, p. 5321.
[8] See, for example, Paul Grady, *Inventory of Generally Accepted Accounting Principles for Business Enterprises,* ARS No. 7, AICPA, New York, N.Y., 1965, p. 156.
[9] *Federal Register,* November 7, 1973, p. 30732.
[10] *Federal Register,* April 1, 1974, p. 11871.
[11] *Accounting Research Bulletin* No. 43, AICPA, New York, N.Y., 1961.
[12] *Federal Register,* September 19, 1974, p. 33684.
[13] *Federal Register,* January 29, 1975, p. 4264.
[14] *Accounting Research and Terminology Bulletins,* p. 25.
[15] *Federal Register,* April 16, 1976, p. 16135.
[16] *Federal Register,* May 5, 1975, p. 19428.
[17] *Federal Register,* September 24, 1975, p. 43873.
[18] *Federal Register,* June 2, 1976, p. 22244.
[19] *Federal Register,* July 30, 1976, p. 31797.

**AICPA board issues statement
on ads, solicitation, encroachment**

The American Institute of CPAs board of directors has issued a statement related to the membership votes on advertising, solicitation and encroachment. The statement follows:

"By mail ballots in 1978 and 1979, the membership of the Institute has decided to remove the rule against encroachment and to permit any advertising or solicitation that is not false, misleading or deceptive. These most recent changes in the Rules of Conduct permit AICPA members to inform the public of the availability of professional accounting services and the terms on which those services may be obtained by those having need of them. The Board of Directors supported these changes, which are designed to provide the public the opportunity to make informed and unpressured choices among those offering to fill its needs for accounting services.

"The Board is confident that AICPA members will exercise sound professional judgment and show due regard for the public they serve by refraining from the kinds of solicitation, including advertising, that would tend to mislead or otherwise result in substandard or unnecessary work.

"It is clearly understood that Institute members are engaged in competition on a professional level. It is in the interests of clients and the public that Institute members compete first and foremost in the quality of the services they render. Any solicitation or advertising ought to be aimed at promoting better understanding of services offered. Promotional activities should not diminish the quality of the services or in any way detract from the reliability of those services or the reliance the public is entitled to place on them.

"The Institute believes that the recent changes in its Rules of Conduct regarding solicitation, advertising and encroachment should not result in the misuse or abuse of those practices. In the final analysis, every profession does and must rely upon the discretion, integrity and professionalism of its members to act in a manner consistent with the best interests of the public."

The Journal of Accountancy, September 1979

Professional

AICPA asks governmental units to participate in experiment to improve accounting methods

The American Institute of CPAs will soon ask hundreds of state and local governments throughout the nation to cooperate in an experiment designed to provide insight into the merits of the experimental principles that are considerably different from those now used by governmental units to account for public funds.

A set of experimental accounting principles, developed by the Institute state and local government accounting committee, is being sent to members of such groups as the Municipal Finance Officers Association and the Association of Government Accountants.

Participants will be asked to prepare, for study by the committee, general purpose financial statements using full accrual basis accounting and consolidation of all funds under control of the governmental unit.

"We want to accumulate some experience with methods that represent significant changes in governmental accounting," said Paul Rosenfield, director of the AICPA accounting standards division. "For now, we are not recommending that participants issue these statements publicly," he said. "Instead, we would like an opportunity to evaluate their usefulness and to learn whether the changes cause unforeseen problems."

Participants will be asked to submit their statements by April 30, 1980. Results of the test program will be published as an aid to municipal governmental units and to organizations responsible for developing uniform accounting and reporting practices for state and local governments.

The Journal of Accountancy, October 1979

The Foreign Corrupt Practices Act of 1977 (the Act), aimed at ending foreign bribery by U.S. companies, has charged corporate directors and officers with increased legal responsibilities. They are subject to a maximum five-year jail term and a $10,000 fine if convicted of violating the law. Similarly, corporations are subject to penalties of up to $1 million. It is not clear whether, or under what circumstances, foreign subsidiaries of U.S. corporations are covered by the law. If it is determined, however, that the law does apply to foreign subsidiar-

FCPA'S IMPACT ON DIRECTORS

Directors and officers can receive stiff penalties for violating the Foreign Corrupt Practices Act. Here's how they can comply with the law.

DANIEL S. VAN RIPER
Partner
Peat, Marwick, Mitchell & Co.

ies, U.S. directors and officers could be prosecuted and convicted if they know about or authorized payments by a foreign subsidiary.

The antibribery law is an outgrowth of the revelations by over 300 U.S. corporations in recent years of "questionable" payments to further business interests in foreign countries. The Securities and Exchange Commission took the lead in pressing for "voluntary" disclosures by public corporations. In addition, the Internal Revenue Service received domestic and foreign payments data in response to about 2,000 questionnaires sent to large corporations. To date, attention has focused on significant payment disclosures made by large, publicly held corporations, and perhaps there has been a feeling by officials of medium-sized and small-size companies with foreign operations or business, that somehow the public concern over foreign questionable payments is not directed to them.

The law, however, with its stiff criminal and civil liability provisions, should put to rest any such notions. It applies to all U.S. companies, small as well as large, privately owned as well as publicly owned. While many large publicly owned companies have taken formal actions intended to eliminate illegal activities by establishing corporate codes of conduct and other specific policies on foreign business activities, small or privately owned corporations probably are not as well prepared. Few private corporations have an audit committee of the board of directors. Frequently, boards of privately owned corporations only include inside officer/stockholder directors. If there are outside directors, they may not be fully aware of their responsibilities, and may be unduly influenced by the actions and opinions of inside directors. Now, however, directors of public and private corporations must insist on remaining fully informed of corporate business practices and must actively acquire more detailed knowledge of corporate financial affairs by meetings with financial and operations executives and outside auditors.

"A violation occurs when [officers, directors, employees, agents or stockholders] . . . provide something of value to a foreign official, foreign political party, or any candidate for foreign political office, to assist in obtaining, retaining, or directing business to any person."

GLOBAL COMPLIANCE

Aside from the U.S. anti-bribery law, measures have been taken on an international level to deter corrupt corporate practices. The U.S. Department of State has entered into bilateral agreements with several countries, which provide for the exchange of information on illegal corporate practices. In July 1975, the Permanent Council of the Organization of American States adopted a resolution " . . . to condemn in the most emphatic terms any act of bribery, illegal payment, or offer of payment by any transnational enterprise; any demand for or acceptance of improper payments by any public or private person . . . ." In July 1976, and as revised in June 1979, a Declaration on International Investment and Multinational Enterprises was adopted by the Council of Ministers of the Organization for Economic Cooperation and Development. Voluntary guidelines aimed at eliminating corrupt corporate practices are included in the Declaration. Late in 1977, a report entitled "Extortion and Bribery in Business Transactions" was adopted by the Council of the International Chamber of Commerce. This report, which includes "rules of conduct" to combat extortion and bribery, has been circulated to the government and business communities of the member nations of the ICC.

During the past two years, the U.S. has actively considered the problem of illicit payments. Further, the United Nations Commission on Transnational Corporations is considering this matter and may release a corporate code of conduct or a guideline. With the Act now signed into law, new initiatives may be forthcoming from the U.S. Department of State.

PROVISIONS

Some of the Act's provisions should be reviewed. It has three major subsections:

■ Accounting Standards,

■ Foreign Corrupt Practices by Issuers (i.e., registrants), and

■ Foreign Corrupt Practices by Domestic Concerns.

The term "domestic concern" means any individual who is a citizen, national, or resident of the U.S.; or any corporation, partnership, association, joint stock company, business trust, unincorporated organization, or sole proprietorship, which has its principal place of business in the U.S., is organized under the laws of a state of the U.S., or is a territory, possession, or commonwealth of the U.S. The Act grants power to the U.S. attorney general to seek injunctive relief or a temporary restraining order to prohibit apparent violations of the Act.

The Accounting Standards Subsection is applicable to every issuer having a class of securities registered pursuant to Section 12 of the Securities Exchange Act of 1934, and every issuer that is required to file reports pursuant to Section 15(d) of The Securities Exchange Act of 1934. The Accounting Standards provisions do not apply to other domestic concerns.

The Standards section requires every issuer to "(A) . . . keep books . . . which in reasonable detail, accurately and fairly reflect the transactions and dispositions of the assets of the issuer; and (B) devise and maintain a system of internal accounting controls sufficient to provide reasonable assurances that—

(i) transactions are executed in accordance with management's general or specific authorization;

(ii) transactions are recorded as necessary (I) to permit preparation of financial statements in conformity with generally accepted accounting principles or any other criteria applicable to such statements, and (II) to maintain accountability for assets;

(iii) access to assets is permitted only in accordance with management's general or specific authorization; and

(iv) the recorded accountability for assets is compared with the existing assets at reasonable intervals and appropriate action is taken with respect to any differences."

At first glance, these Standards provisions may not appear awesome. Upon reflection, however, it probably will be necessary for issuers to formally review and test their system of internal accounting controls, and to devise a procedure for monitoring changes in the system. The Securities and Exchange Commission has under consideration the requirement that registered companies include a management statement on internal accounting control in their annual reports. Increased emphasis will most likely be directed, as a result of these developments, to the general controls of the enterprise that support an environment conducive to establishing a strong system of internal control. But, because of their very nature, these controls are frequently not documented. It would appear desirable for issuers to review and document their general controls. To test the depth of the controls in force, issuers might consider the following questions:

■ Is the organization structure documented and communicated sufficiently among employees?

■ Are procedures and policies sufficiently defined to identify authority and responsibility for decision-making?

■ What is the degree of objectivity, independence, and com-petence of any internal audit activity?

■ How well is the accounting function administered? Are there sufficient records (such as budgets and non-financial reports on operations) to facilitate analytical review and comparison of accounting reports to minimize the potential for errors?

■ What is the possibility of management override of the administrative and accounting control systems?

■ What measures are employed to safeguard physical assets, critical documents, data files, and other records? How security-conscious is the organization?

The Standards provisions should also influence management's concern for the Statement on Auditing Standards No. 20, "Required Communication of Material Weaknesses in Internal Auditing Control," which requires communication—preferably in writing—to senior management and the board of directors or its audit committee of material weaknesses in internal accounting control that come to the auditor's attention during an examination of financial statements made in accordance with generally accepted auditing standards and that had not been corrected before the time they came to the auditor's attention. The assessment of the materiality of a weakness in internal accounting control requires considerable judgment by the auditor. Concerning the concept of what constitutes such a weak-

ness, Statement No. 20 quotes a portion of a section of Statement on Auditing Standards No. 1:

". . . a condition in which the auditor believes the prescribed procedures or the degree of compliance with them does not provide reasonable assurance that errors or irregularities in amounts that would be material in the financial statements being audited would be prevented or detected within a timely period by employees in the normal course of performing their assigned functions."

Nevertheless, there are many auditors who believe that neither this definition nor existing authoritative auditing literature provides sufficient guidance for the auditor to measure objectively and uniformly the materiality of weaknesses in systems of internal accounting control. In fact, a special advisory committee of the American Institute of Certified Public Accountants, principally comprising financial and internal audit executives, recently issued a report on internal accounting control, which includes guidance on procedures and techniques to use in evaluating internal accounting control.

Statement No. 20 also permits the auditor, if requested, to issue a letter to the board confirming the absence of material weaknesses in internal accounting control, if no such weaknesses were discovered by the auditor. Regarding the Accounting Standards provisions of the Act, it would seem desirable for issuer boards of directors to request such a letter from the auditor to further document that the issuer complies with the provision to devise and maintain a system of internal accounting control. Of course, any such letter issued by an auditor at the request of the board of directors should not be construed as an affirmation that the company is in full compliance with any applicable laws pertaining to internal control.

The Accounting Standards provisions of the Act are applicable to issuers only. But issuers and domestic concerns and their officers, directors, employees, agents, or stockholders acting on behalf of the enterprise are prohibited from engaging in foreign corrupt practices. A violation occurs when such individuals provide something of value to a foreign official, foreign political party or any candidate for foreign political office, to assist in obtaining, retaining, or directing business to any person. "Foreign official" means any officer or employee of a foreign government or any department, agency, or instrumentality, or any person acting in an official capacity for or on behalf of such government or department, agency, or instrumentality. This does not include any employee whose duties are essentially ministerial or clerical.

The definitions of business purpose and "foreign official" are important, as the law apparently is intended to exclude commercial bribery as well as facilitating or "grease" payments to minor officials to expedite such matters as customs clearances. It should also be noted that the use of a conduit to transfer any consideration to

a foreign official, political party or candidate would also be a prohibited transaction, assuming it was known or there was reason to know of the ultimate recipient.

A PLAN OF ACTION

Compliance with the U.S. antibribery law begins in a corporate environment that exhibits integrity of management in its day-to-day business dealings. Because of the importance of this law, the board of directors should assume ultimate responsibility for compliance and frame the environment through a corporate code of conduct. Now, one might say that a code of conduct is not really necessary, as there is little to be gained by establishing a corporate code that says, in effect, "thou shalt not break the law." But, a carefully prepared corporate code adopted by the directors will create a corporate environment that encourages integrity of management and compliance with the law.

Develop a Code of Conduct

The board should monitor the operation of the code by designating a committee of the board, such as the audit committee or a new committee. In adopting a code, the board of directors should be concerned about

■ Establishing clearly understood policies that define the corporation's business ethics and conduct,

■ Implementing a strong system of internal control that requires integrity of financial statements

through accurate and timely recording of transactions and events,

■ Hiring and promoting only individuals of high character and performance with a sense of responsibility for the total enterprise,

■ Engaging vendors and seeking customers that appear to meet the same high standards of business ethics of the corporation, and

■ Promoting employees' attitudes, whereby they sense an obligation to report corporate policy exceptions or perceived irregularities.

Check Up On Foreign Operations

The board of directors should remain informed of the manner of conduct and business plans of the corporation's foreign operations. Some may interpret the law as excluding foreign subsidiaries and therefore the board may remain uninformed about them, but this may not be a good long-range approach. Whether or not this law applies to foreign subsidiaries, it would be advisable to consider inviting chief executives of the more significant foreign subsidiaries to board meetings to establish open and direct communication on the subsidiary's operations and business plans. The parent company's chief executive or general counsel should implement controls to monitor pending and threatened litigation and unasserted claims affecting both U.S. and foreign operations, and should make the board of directors aware of such matters. Clear communication channels to the parent company should be established with foreign law firms serving foreign subsidiaries and their local executives.

The board should adopt a policy that requires corporate officers, division heads, and foreign subsidiary chief executives to report periodically to the chief executive on compliance with the Act: Executives reporting to the chief executive should document the procedures used regarding their subordinates, and the chief executive should submit a summary of such reports to the board.

Confer with Outside Auditors

The board or a designated committee of the board should meet with the corporation's outside auditors to review their procedures regarding illegal or possibly illegal corporate acts. Statement on Auditing Standards No. 17, entitled "Illegal Acts by Clients," provides guidance to the auditor when he discovers such acts or believes such acts may have occurred. This Statement does not require an auditor to search for such acts, and an examination made according to generally accepted accounting practices (GAAP) can not be expected to provide assurance that illegal acts will be detected. It does require, however, that material and immaterial illegal or questionably illegal corporate acts that come to the auditor's attention be communicated to the client's management at a high enough level of authority so that appropriate

action can be taken and sufficient information can be obtained.

The outside audit firm for the company's worldwide corporate organization can greatly assist the board of directors in monitoring compliance with the Act. As auditing standards vary considerably worldwide, it is important that examinations of foreign subsidiary financial statements be conducted according to U.S. GAAP, thereby providing a uniform approach to the audit of the total enterprise. This examination should be planned and directed from one office. Specific audit instructions should be sent by the head engagement partner to participating offices of the audit firm, which will focus on specific matters applicable to the total enterprise audit. The instruction letter would provide guidance and direction on such matters as the preparation of financial statements, reporting weaknesses in the system of internal control, compliance with U.S. auditing standards, and specific procedure requests of the board of directors.

Encourage Internal Compliance

Internal audit departments are becoming more independent and objective of management in discharging their responsibilities. More and more, internal audit departments are reporting directly to the board of directors or have a dual reporting line within the enterprise. The demonstrated interest by boards in the current and planned examinations of the internal audit

department has contributed to this increased objectivity. A competent and dedicated internal audit department can be valuable to assure adherence to a corporate code of conduct. As internal auditors visit corporate locations throughout the world, they can demonstrate a clear concern for compliance. They can design inquiries and tests that may identify exceptions to the code or an environment that is not conducive to compliance. As an arm of the board, their professionalism and example should stimulate the success of a functioning code of conduct.

Headquarters executives should also play an important role. They, too, can demonstrate concern for conformance with the corporate code during visits to foreign subsidiary locations. Finally, compliance with the code and any other related policies could sometimes be included on the agenda of important corporate or divisional meetings and seminars.

CONCLUSION

Some have said that the survival of our free business enterprise system is dependent upon business leaders adopting socially acceptable values which will permeate the corporation. Under the U.S. antibribery law, directors and officers are responsible, and should therefore assume leadership for framing a corporate environment that encourages the good conduct and integrity of the business; because ultimately, individuals run the business and commit the illegal acts—not the impersonal corporation. □

SECTION VI

Contemporary Topics in Accounting

The world changes, and as it does, so changes the informational demands of users of accounting statements. Also, changes in the business environment can present new issues to be dealt with by the profession. Obviously, as most dynamic fields of study and practice, accounting confronts its scholars with a broad and continually expanding range of contemporary topics.

To understand the present and capture the future, one can benefit from viewing the responses of accounting practitioners, academicians and observors to contemporary issues, as they arise. Obviously, much debate and discussion will be necessary before a final resolution to these problems is reached, but the process underlying such a resolution is fundamental and continual.

This section is divided into four parts which address current issues in the field of accounting. The articles encompass divergent views from alternative sources. Each sheds a different type of perspective on an issue.

Contemporary topics in accounting emerge from a variety of business needs. Some result from unique situations not previously encountered in the practice of the profession. Others represent continuations of items of question which have historically been faced by accounting practitioners. The opportunity to read views in these areas gives insight not only into current topics but also affords the reader a broadened scope of the range and magnitude of contemporary topics.

Evaluating Leases with LP

Management accountants can furnish better information for capital expenditure decisions if they use such techniques as linear programming and sensitivity analysis.

By Jane O. Burns and Kathleen Bindon

Jane O. Burns is an assistant professor of accounting at Indiana University. A CPA, she has a Ph.D. degree from the Pennsylvania State University. She is a member of the Indianapolis Chapter through which this article was submitted.

Kathleen Bindon, a doctoral candidate at the Pennsylvania State University, is an instructor at the University of Alabama. She is a member of the Central Pennsylvania Chapter.

The authors gratefully acknowledge the assistance provided by Kimberlee T. Young.

Leasing is not a new concept. It has been associated with the use of land since ancient times. In recent years, however, emphasis has shifted to personal property with virtually everything available for leasing. Concurrently, the increase in dollar volume of leased property has been phenomenal, reaching the $100 billion level in 1976, according to one banker.[1]

Because capital expenditure commitments are often sizable not only in initial cost outlays and time involved but also because these decisions establish the overall direction a firm takes, management needs to use the best methods available for analyzing capital expenditure decisions. The evaluation process is further complicated when critical variables consist of both quantitative and qualitative information. In addition, quantitative data may seem to defy logical analysis because it is reported in nonadditive dimensions such as dollars, square feet, personnel, and production units. Fortunately, mathematical concepts—such as linear and integer programming models—have been devised that are capable of comparing and evaluating capital expenditure decisions. These two models, capable of processing a variety of information, select the optimum solution from among proposed alternative strategies. The optimum solution can then be subjected to sensitivity analysis. Using this technique, management can examine the sensitivity of the optimum solution to changes in variables. In this article, we compare three hypothetical equipment leases using linear programming and sensitivity analysis techniques.

Linear programming (LP) is a mathematical computer-assisted technique used to organize, summarize, and analyze various quantifiable data to facilitate the solution of complex matters. A business problem that benefits from LP must have a quantifiable goal (objective function) and relevant alternatives (variables) each of which is subject to certain limitations (constraints). For example, the objective function for a capital asset acquisition problem may be to maximize profits. The different machines and financing terms available to the company comprise the variables. Constraints on variables may relate to limitations of available space for housing the equipment, available manpower qualified to operate the equipment, output volume the equipment can produce each period, and annual costs a company is willing to incur. Linear programming does not provide the absolute solution to a problem since only quantifiable information can be included in the LP model. It does, however, provide an efficient method for processing all quantifiable (both monetary and nonmonetary) data. As a result, it is applicable to many business decisions that are dependent on accouting data. While LP has been applied to a wide variety of business and government problems, accountants' use of the concept has been limited.

B & B Company Leases

To illustrate the use of LP, let's examine three operating leases of the B & B Manufacturing Co., a fictional company. B & B is a medium-sized firm engaged in the manufacture of automobile parts and accessories. Its management is offered a three-

0025-1690/80/6108-2422/$01.00/0

year contract to supply directional compasses to an automobile manufacturer. The compasses will be a part of a special optional equipment package installed at the auto factory. The contract requires that B & B supply the auto company with as many compasses as possible up to a maximum of 500,000 each year at $7 per compass. The officers of B & B believe the market for directional compasses will grow but expect some improvements in manufacturing equipment to take place over the next few years. Because directional compasses are a small part of their present business, new manufacturing equipment must be acquired to fill the contract. A number of factors including a shortage of available cash, expected technological changes in manufacturing equipment, and the uncertainty of compass sales after three years leads management to prefer leasing over purchasing the necessary equipement. Investigation reveals that three different machines are available. Before making a leasing decision, management would like to know which one or ones are most economical within established company constraints. See Table 1 for a summary of leasing agreements.

Table 1
TERMS OF LEASE AGREEMENTS

	Reliable X	Flexible Y	Futura Z
Annual production capacity	50,000 units	45,000 units	35,000 units
Lease period	10 years	5 years	4 years
Annual lease cost	$50,000	$60,000	$70,000
First renewal period		5 years	3 years
Annual lease cost		$40,000	$60,000
Second renewal period			3 years
Annual lease cost			$50,000
Annual maintenance cost	$2,000	$3,000	Included in annual lease
Labor requirements	4 people	3 people	1 person

Table 2
SCHEDULE OF CONTRIBUTION MARGINS

	Reliable X	Flexible Y	Futura X
Annual units of production	50,000	45,000	35,000
Sales ($7 per unit)	$350,000	$315,000	$245,000
Variable lease costs:			
Materials ($3.50 per unit)	$175,000	$157,500	$122,500
Direct labor ($15,000 per person)	60,000	45,000	15,000
Maintenance costs	2,000	3,000	-0-
Indirect labor (14% of direct labor)	8,400	6,300	2,100
Employee benefits (20% of total labor)	13,700	10,300	3,400
Heat, light, power	2,000	2,000	2,000
Total variable costs	$261,000	$224,100	$145,000
Sales less total variable costs	$ 88,900	$ 90,900	$100,000
Present value of sales less total variable costs (10 years at 10% cost of capital)	$546,300	$558,500	$614,600
Present value of lease payments (10 years at 10% cost of capital)	307,200	321,600	387,600
Present value of contribution margin	$239,100	$236,900	$227,000

All three lease agreements include a guarantee of replacement at renogotiated lease rentals if the machine becomes technologically obsolete. The lessor pays all insurance and property taxes. The lessee pays all operating expenses except maintenance costs. Production capacity of each machine is based on an eight-hour day and a 50-week year. A schedule of estimates for each machine, prepared by B & B's accounting department, is shown in Table 2.

All amounts included in Table 2 are rounded to the nearest $100 to simplify math, and more importantly, to avoid attributing more accuracy to the figures than they perhaps deserve. These are estimates and this is an important point to convey to the decision maker.

This analysis compares leases for ten years. It also would be useful to compare leases for three years. The procedure is the same except the cost of cancelling lease agreements at the end of three years must be included for each of the machines.

A 10% discount rate was chosen. It is not within the scope of this article to discuss the applicability of a borrowing rate or an internal rate of return in this case. All costs are assumed to occur at the beginning of each year. A more detailed study would require the use of monthly and daily discount tables.

Information gathered by the accounting department indicates that quantifiable constraints are:

1. Approximately $600,000 will be available for annual lease rental.
2. Approximately 30 workers (considering turnover) trained to operate the machines can be hired.
3. Available plant capacity is 2,000 square feet, requirements for machines X, Y, and Z are 175, 210, and 250 square feet, respectively.
4. Working capital needs can be met by advances from the automobile company and by favorable credit treatment from suppliers.[2]

From the foregoing infomation, a linear programming model is created. See Table 3. The LP formulation allows the following advantages:

1. Leases with different rental payments, different labor and space requirements, and different outputs can be compared.
2. All relevant quantifiable data that are available can be incorporated into the model, not just monetary data.
3. Various quantifiable constraints are analyzed by the LP model to provide the maximum contribution margin without violating any constraint.
4. Information for sensitivity analysis is provided. Thus, before a decision is made, the most critical or sensitive variables can be identified and

the degree of acceptable error computed.

5. Considerable quantitative information is summarized for examination in conjunction with qualitative information and sensitivity analysis.

An important advantage of LP is that the individual using the tool need not know how to solve the LP formulation mathematically. Although LP solutions can be derived by hand, the volume of computations is prohibitive except for very small problems. Because a number of computerized LP programs are available to companies with computer capability, accouting efforts can be concentrated on gathering information about the objective function, variables, and constraints and on constructing the model. As in any decision situation, better inputs generally result in a more reliable solution.

Although LP is an invaluable tool, it has one important disadvantage when analyzing leases. The optimal solution contains fractions. According to the computer printout summarized in Table 4, the best strategy for B & B is to lease 6.6667 Reliable X machines and 3.3333 Futura Z machines. Since it is not possible to lease a portion of an asset, the optimal LP solution is unacceptable to the company. This is not necessarily an insurmountable problem. First, the LP optimal solution should be truncated. A decision to lease six Reliable X and three Futura Z machines is tentatively accepted as an optimal solution. (See Table 5.) Next, the contribution margin (objective function) for the tentative optimal solution is calculated and compared with the LP solution. If the decrease in the contribution margin is not material, the truncated LP optimal solution may be accepted on the basis that the cost of further testing probably will exceed its benefits.

Since B & B's problem is small and the contribution margin decreases by 10% (from $2,350,667 to $2,115,600), further testing is desirable. The tentative LP solution should be examined to determine if the constraints allow an additional machine—either X, Y, or Z—to be leased. Table 5 indicates that leasing an additional Reliable X violates the labor requirement, and leasing either another Futura Z or a Flexible Y exceeds available plant capacity. Based on these constraints, the optimal LP solution for B & B is to lease six Reliable X and three Futura Z machines.

Although the LP printout contains fractions, it is possible to use computer programs that provide optimal solutions in whole numbers. Integer or discrete programming is simply LP without fractions in the solution. However, integer programming requires considerably more reiterations than required by LP and, therefore, is more time-consuming and costly. In addition, integer LP computer programs are not as widely available as are LP programs. For these reasons, historically, the

Table 3
LINEAR PROGRAMMING MODEL

	Reliable X	Flexible Y	Futura Z	Limits
Maximize:				
contribution margin	239,100X +	236,900Y +	227,000Z	
Subject to constraints:				
Production capacity	50,000X +	45,000Y +	35,000Z =	500,000
Annual lease cost	50,000X +	60,000Y +	70,000Z =	600,000
Annual maint. cost	2,000X +	3,000Y +	=	30.000
Labor requirements	4X +	3Y +	Z =	30
Plant capacity	175X +	210Y +	250Z =	2,000

Table 4
LINEAR PROGRAMMING OPTIMAL SOLUTION

	Reliable X	Flexible Y	Futura Z	Total
Lease	6.667	-0-	3.3333	10
Contribution margin (present value, 10 years at 10%)	$1,594,000		$756,667	$2,350,667
	Units available (constraints)	Units consumed (solution)	Units remaining (slack)	
Production capacity	500,000 units	450,000 units	50,000 units	
Annual lease cost	$600,000	$566,667	$33,333	
Annual maintenance cost	$30,000	$13,333	$16,667	
Labor requirements	30 people	30 people	-0-	
Plant capacity	2,000 sq. ft.	2,000 sq. ft.	-0-	

noninteger LP solution has been truncated and tested as shown in Table 5. However, since the field of integer programming did not develop until the late 1950s, its efficiency and resulting usage is expected to increase with improving computer technology. Whenever possible, integer programming should be used in capital expenditure analysis. The most important reason is that integer programming provides more relevant information for sensitivity analysis.

The Optimal Solution and Sensitivity Analysis

After obtaining the optimal solution to the LP problem it is natural for decision makers to have some doubts. When they established the goals and constraints, estimates were made. What if some of these estimates were too low or too high? Or maybe management would be willing to relax some of the constraints in exchange for more profit. The LP model is capable of incorporating each of these adjustments and solving the problem anew. However, such changes may be infinite and solving the problem again and again becomes computationally inefficient, even with a computer.

Decisions to acquire capital assets generally have long-range impacts. Such acquisitions usually result in large, relatively permanent commitments that influence the firm's operations and, thus, flexibility and earning power for several years. The fact that these decisions affect the future increases the difficulty of analysis. Although some elements may be ascertained with relative

Table 5
MACHINES TO BE LEASED

| | Optimal solution | Alternate solutions | | | |
		One	Two	Three	Four
Reliable X	6.667	6	7	6	6
Flexible Y	0	0	0	0	1
Futura Z	3.3333	3	3	4	3
Contribution margin[1]	$2,350,667	$2,115,600	$2,354,700	$2,342,600	$2,352,500

CONSTRAINTS

| | Units available | Optimal solution | Units consumed | | | |
| | | | Alternate solutions | | | |
			One	Two	Three	Four
Production capacity (in units)	500,000	500,000	405,000	455,000	440,000	450,000
Annual lease cost (in dollars)	600,000	566,667	510,000	560,000	580,000	570,000
Annual maint. cost (in dollars)	30,000	13,333	12,000	14,000	12,000	15,000
Labor requirements (in no. of persons)	30	30	27	31[2]	28	30
Plant capacity (in square feet)	2,000	2,000	1,800	1,975	2,050[2]	2,010[2]

[1]Present value, 10 years at 10%.
[2]Exceeds the units available and is not an acceptable solution unless the constraint is relaxed.

This is a minor problem when on-line, real-time interactive computer models are available. If batch processing is used, the time delay may be significant.

Sensitivity analysis also indicates which variables and which constraints are most critical to the final solution. This requires examination of estimates used to develop the contribution margins (Table 3) and LP model (Table 4). Those elements which are most critical to the decision-making process are reviewed. Management should reconsider the tightness of the constraints whose limits are reached, and therefore prevent an additional machine from being leased. In doing so, it may appear necessary to re-examine some of the critical estimates. Because management has limited time and resources that it can devote to information gathering, sensitivity analysis aids in deciding which estimates require refinement. Without the direction afforded by the analysis, it would be difficult, if not impossible, to determine which variables are sensitive, that is, which ones can affect the optimal solution with a small change in value. Not only is the LP model valuable to the accountant as a means for preparing and presenting data for capital expenditure decisions, the sensitivity analysis related to it can assist in allocating time to any data refinement deemed necessary.

The Contribution Margin

For B & B, the contribution margin related to the labor constraint is $239,100. This is how much the value of the objective function would increase if one additional machine operator were available. B & B estimates that it is able to hire only 30 trained workers to operate the machines. Theoretically, B & B should be willing to pay up to the contribution margin of $239,100 for the 31st machine operator. In reality, B & B should do everything possible to recruit the additional worker as long as the cost does not exceed $239,100.

Adding one more person has an additional advantage. Due to the original labor constraint of 30 people, B & B is able to lease only six Reliable X and three Futura Z machines. If the labor constraint is increased to 31, B & B would be able to lease a seventh Reliable X. This decision would require 1,975 square feet of floor space, which is less than the space available to B & B for the machines.

In addition to data about constraints, the LP computer program provides information referred to as shadow prices. For B & B, the shadow price reveals how much Flexible Y's profit contribution margin must increase for it to become an attractive alternative. Certainly, any decrease will make Y a less viable alternative since it is rejected at its present level. According to the LP printout, Y's contribution margin must be at least $243,175 for it to be a profitable alternative. At exactly this

certainty, measurement of most variables involves considerable risk. Generally, variables can be satisfactorily measured by estimating expected results, by establishing averages or ranges, or by adopting a method of sensitivity analysis. Hertz suggests a common approach to risk and uncertainty is to list assumptions made about the variables, establish a point estimate based on the best available information, and then adjust the firm's acceptable minimum performance level to reflect the perceived degree of risk and uncertainty.[3] In another work, Hertz writes, "... to understand uncertainty and risk is to understand the key business problem—and the key to business opportunity."[4]

Sensitivity analysis is extremely useful under conditions of risk and uncertainty. However,

> ... sensitivity analysis cannot totally eliminate mistakes in decisions making, nor can it eliminate entirely the risk that future events may render even the best decision a poor one. Yet this kind of analysis can show where the greatest risks may lie, and perhaps, how to avoid them.[5]

Sensitivity analysis focuses on estimation errors by indicating the degree of error that can exist before decisions change. It also indicates how close the alternatives not selected are to being included in the final decision, i.e., what their lowest attractive profit contribution margin would be for the company. Decision changes are significant when a new optimal solution requires that different alternatives be chosen. If a change is indicated, a new optimal solution must be calculated and new information for sensitivity analysis generated.

level, an alternate optimal solution exists. Anything above $243,175 makes leasing arrangements including Y more profitable than the present optimal solution. In terms of Y's contribution margin, an increase of $6,275, ($243,175 less $236,900), is not particularly large. That much of an increase in profit could be caused by Flexible Y producing an additional 144 units per year.

Alternatively, profits can be increased if plant capacity is expanded to allow B & B to acquire a Flexible Y machine or a fourth Futura Z machine. The company's contribution margin will be increased by $236,900 if the Flexible Y machine is leased and by $227,000 if an additional Futura Z is leased. The Flexible Y machine requires plant capacity to be increased by ten square feet, while the Futura Z machine requires an additional 50 square feet.

B & B should concentrate of three possible adjustments and their consequences:

1. The addition of one worker, allowing a seventh Reliable X to be leased, increases profits by $239,100.
2. The addition of ten square feet of plant capacity, allowing a Flexible Y to be leased, increases profit by $236,900, less the cost of increasing plant capacity be ten square feet.
3. The addition of 50 square feet of plant capacity, allowing a fourth Futura Z to be leased, increases profits by $227,000 less the cost of increasing plant capacity by 50 square feet.

Based on the LP model and sensitivity analysis, B & B's alternatives are:

1. If neither labor nor plant capacity can be increased, lease six Reliable X and three Futura Z machines.
2. If labor can be increased but plant capacity cannot, lease seven Reliable X and three Futura Z machines.
3. If labor cannot be increased but plant capacity can be increased by ten square feet but less than 50 square feet, lease six Reliable X, one Flexible Y, and three Futura Z machines. This alternative is acceptable, however, only if the contribution margin exceeds the net present value of the cost of additional plant capacity.
4. If labor cannot be increased but plant capacity can be increased by 50 square feet, management must decide if it is better to lease a Flexible Y or a fourth Futura Z machine. This alternative is acceptable, however, only if the contribution margin exceeds the net present value of the cost of additional plant capacity. While the contribution margin of the Flexible

Y machine exceeds that of the Futura Z by approximately 4.4%, other factors may negate this advantage.
5. If both labor and plant capacity can be increased to add any one of the three machines, management must weigh the advantages and disadvantages of the alternatives.

Focusing on the Greatest Risk

Sensitivity analysis, by itself, does not provide management with an optimal decision. Nor does it eliminate estimation errors. It does allow adjustments for errors in the original objective function and constraints without the necessity of re-solving the entire problem. Its major contribution is that it provides information concerning the effect changes in the original assumptions have on the current solution. It allows management to focus attention on elements having the greatest risk. Sensitivity analysis reveals the extent to which assumptions may change before a different optimal solution occurs. Thus, management receives information not only concerning the best choice from among the variables but also the range of error allowed in the data before the optimal solution is changed. If small adjustments in the variables or constraints have significant effects, more investigation is necessary. If large adjustments are required to change the optimal solution, the factors are relatively insensitive and management should have considerable confidence in the LP solution.

Linear programming and sensitivity analysis have considerable application in accounting for multiple lease comparisons as well as for other capital budgeting situations. Such analysis offers the accountant a valuable tool when trying to estimate future events in that it indicates critical areas where the greatest efforts should be concentrated when refining data. This is extremely important because it can provide the accounting profession with a viable means of assisting management in decision making. It also allows the accounting process to become more than an information gathering and presenting function, i.e., one that can help in making decisions that have a significant impact on a company's future. By applying quantitative business analysis techniques, management accountants can expand their area of usefulness. □

Because LP programs are available, accounting efforts can be concentrated on gathering data—not working out the math.

[1] "Leasing Offers Many Advantages," *Credit and Financial Management*, 176, January 1977.
[2] This assumes away the problem incurred when considering the cost of working capital in an analysis of this type. If the problem is viewed from a total system approach rather than an incremental approach, the analysis should include opportunity costs. That is, the firm presumably has the opportunity of using its working capital and its plant capacity to pursue alternative actions.
[3] David B. Hertz, "Investment Policies that Pay Off," *Harvard Business Review*, January-February 1968.
[4] Hertz, "Risk Analysis in Capital Investment," in *Contemporary Issues in Cost Accounting*, edited by Hector R. Anton and Peter A. Firmin, Houghton Mifflin Co., Boston, Mass., 1966.
[5] Nabil Hassan, R. Penny Marquette, and Joseph M McKeon, Jr., "Sensitivity Analysis: An Accounting Tool for Decision-Making," MANAGEMENT ACCOUNTING, April 1978.

PLANT CLOSINGS: THE PENSION COST CONTROVERSY

Despite the lack of specificity in accounting literature, an examination of basic reporting principles can eliminate confusion and achieve reporting comparability.

LAWRENCE C. BEST
Professional Accounting Fellow
Securities and Exchange Commission*
PAUL A. GEWIRTZ
Consultant
Towers, Perrin, Forster & Crosby

*The Securities and Exchange Commission, as a matter of policy, disclaims responsibility for any private publication or statement by any of its employees. The views expressed herein are those of the author and do not necessarily reflect the views of the Commission or of the author's colleagues on the staff of the Commission.

Goliath Industries' David Plant operated in the red for many years. Unable to turn the plant around and no longer willing to sustain the continuing losses, Goliath management decided to discontinue the David Plant operations and redeploy its assets to areas with greater profit potential. In its financial statements, Goliath Industries reported a loss of $30 million in connection with the shutdown, but predicted an upswing in profits due to the David Plant closing.

After three years Goliath Industries' profits were still depressed. Management stated that one factor contributing to the low level of reported profits was the continuing write-off of $18 million in unfunded pension liabilities from the David Plant. An outside director is now questioning management's policy of charging current operations with costs related to a plant abandoned three years earlier.

THE CONTROVERSY

Although the above example is a hypothetical case, the situation is not unusual. There is enough controversy surrounding accounting for pension costs related to a plant closing, and enough of a dollar swing inherent in the different accounting treatments, that the issue should be of concern to financial executives.

In recent years many companies have embarked upon significant asset redeployment programs. In many of these situations, marginal or unprofitable operations have been discontinued and significant employee groups terminated, but the question of the appropriate accounting for pension costs related to the terminated employee group has continually surfaced. Unfortunately, the response heard far too often is that accounting literature in this area is unclear and several alternatives exist.

Some companies choose to view pension costs exclusively on a company-wide basis, emphasizing their long-term nature. Such companies conclude that a shutdown does not trigger any acceleration of the accrual of pension costs. Other companies contend that a shutdown does accelerate the accrual of pension costs, but only to the extent that special benefits are called for under collectively-bargained plans. They maintain that any unfunded vested liability that existed before the shutdown should not be included. Instead, they continue to amortize the unfunded vested liability over the same number of years originally established before the closing. Still others believe that all previously unrecorded costs associated with the shutdown should be immediately recognized. In the charge to operations they include the pre-closing unfunded vested liability, as well as any additional liability arising from the shutdown.

Not surprisingly, these different views result in significantly different charges. As a consequence, financial reporting falls short of achieving comparability in reporting, one of its most basic objectives.

We believe that generally accepted accounting principles for discontinued operations do not provide a supermarket of alternatives. Although the principles set forth in the accounting literature may not be crystal

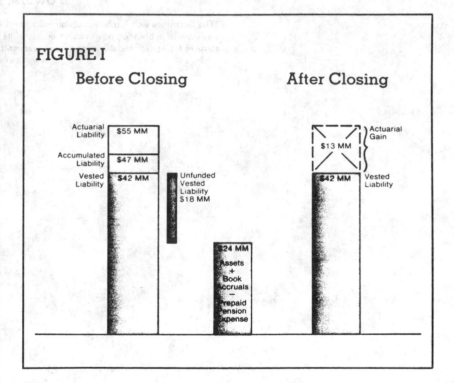

FIGURE I
Before Closing   After Closing

clear, the present accounting framework provides more guidance than it is credited with. We suggest that many of the so-called alternatives in practice today are inappropriate, as the illustrations show.

A SIMPLE SCENARIO

Figure I depicts the David Plant pension liabilities before

and after closing. The middle bar represents the level of assets plus book accruals minus prepaid pension expense at that time, a total of $24 million. The two outer bars show the levels of pension commitments before and after closing.

The liability for vested benefits before the closing was $42 million; the liability for all accumulated benefits was $47 million. The actuarial liability, a partial allocation of total prospective pension costs under a selected actuarial cost method, was $55 million. After the closing, the only remaining commit-

ment was the $42 million liability for vested benefits.

No change in commitments was triggered by the plant closing. There could have been a change if management had chosen to vest the $5 million of non-vested accumulated benefits, or if there had been negotiated shutdown benefits designed to take effect upon closing.

There was, however, an actuarial gain under the plan. The actuarial liability of $55 million that existed before the closing decreased to the $42 million liability for vested benefits after the closing. As defined by actuaries, any unanticipated decrease in actuarial liability arising from experience is an actuarial gain. In this simple illustration, the actuarial gain amounted to $55 million minus $42 million, or $13 million. Faced with similar facts, companies have struggled with the question of what to record as a charge to operations.

THE ACCOUNTING LITERATURE

In part, the controversy over appropriate accounting practice can be traced to confusion over the delicate interplay between two accounting standards. Also at fault are the subtle differences in terminology between the accounting and the actuarial professions. But to a great extent the controversy can be tied to an unfortunate lack of specificity in accounting literature, which some see as justification for flexibility in practice. The two accounting opinions that play a major role in this area are Opinion 30, *Reporting the Results of Operations,* and Opinion 8, *Accounting for the Cost of Pension Plans.*

Opinion 30 gives guidance in accounting for a discontinued operation. Although this Opinion speaks directly to the disposal of a "segment of a business," the guidance and measurement principles are applicable to discontinued operations that may not meet the definition of a segment of a business. This could include the shutdown of an entire plant or even a partial plant closing.

Under Opinion 30, when a company decides to close a plant or other operation, an assessment process is begun and the consequences of the decision are measured in terms of a gain or loss. This gain or loss is computed by converting to a liquidation basis of accounting, thus offsetting the estimated realizable value of all assets against all identifiable obligations.

Opinion 8 appears to contribute to this gain or loss determination by stating that any actuarial gain or loss resulting from plant closings ". . . should be treated as an adjustment of the net gain or loss . . . " This seems to imply some additional provision for the actuarial gain or loss beyond what is already measured by Opinion 30.

Further, Opinion 30 emphasizes the need to include in the gain or loss determination "costs and expenses directly associated with the disposal," including items such as "severance pay, additional pension costs and employee relocation expenses. . ." This emphasis on "additional pension costs" is the cause of much of the controversy and confusion.

Except for the phrase "additional pension costs," Opinion 30 does not specifically mention the other components of pension costs that should be considered such as the pre-closing unfunded vested liability or any actuarial gain or loss generated by the closing. As a consequence, these items often are not properly considered in the gain or loss determination.

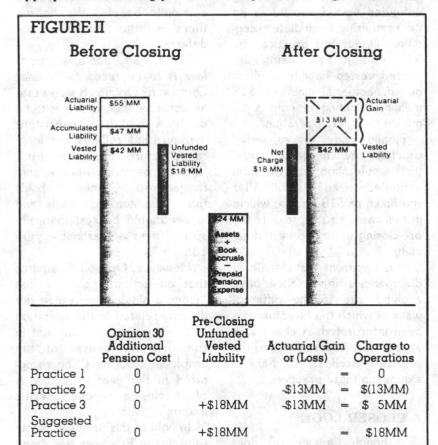

FIGURE II

Before Closing   After Closing

Actuarial Liability $55 MM
Accumulated Liability $47 MM
Vested Liability $42 MM

Unfunded Vested Liability $18 MM

24 MM Assets + Book Accruals − Prepaid Pension Expense

Net Charge $18 MM

Actuarial Gain $13 MM

$42 MM Vested Liability

	Opinion 30 Additional Pension Cost	Pre-Closing Unfunded Vested Liability	Actuarial Gain or (Loss)		Charge to Operations
Practice 1	0			=	0
Practice 2	0		-$13MM	=	$(13MM)
Practice 3	0	+$18MM	-$13MM	=	$ 5MM
Suggested Practice	0	+$18MM		=	$18MM

This situation is fairly common in non-bargained plans. There are no special shutdown benefits. However, the pre-closing vested liability is unfunded by $18 million. The suggested charge to operations is $18 million.

INTERPRETING
THE LITERATURE

Although undefined in Opinion 30, the term "additional pension costs" has generally been interpreted by companies to mean an increase in the vested benefit liability that occurs at the closing, usually resulting from either the special negotiated shutdown benefits or the existence of plan assets that exceed the vested liability before closing. In the latter case, the IRS requires that non-vested accumulated benefits be vested to the extent of excess assets.

In practice, most companies are able to identify these additional pension costs related to a plant closing. It is what many companies do not include—such as the pre-closing unfunded vested liability—or do include—such as the actuarial gain or loss—that seems to contribute most to the inconsistencies in practice.

We suggest that all unrecorded pension obligations associated with the plant closing be included in the overall gain or loss determination. We believe the requirement in Opinion 30 to determine the gain or loss includes the pre-closing unfunded vested liability as well as any additional pension cost. We also believe that further inclusion in the computations of any actuarial gain or loss envisioned by Opinion 8 will result in double counting.

Our views, however, have not always been followed in practice. **Figure II**, which is the same situation as in Figure I but with actual and suggested practices inserted, illustrates the variations we have found.

Faced with this scenario, some companies (using Practice No. 1) interpret Opinion 30 as requiring no provision for pen-

sion costs in determining the gain or loss at shutdown because there are no "additional pension costs" in the first place, and because these companies interpret the literature as not requiring immediate recognition of the pre-closing unfunded vested liability of $18 million.

Other companies (using Practice No. 2) also agree that no additional pension costs are generated under Opinion 30, but separately consider the provisions of Opinion 8. They believe the $13 million actuarial gain should be a credit to current operations in determining the gain or loss on shutdown.

In yet another variation, some companies (using Practice No. 3), in addition to the actuarial gain, consider the pre-closing unfunded vested liability as an item requiring immediate recognition. Under this practice, the $18 million pre-closing unfunded vested liability is offset by an actuarial gain of $13 million, resulting in only a $5 million charge to operations.

Finally, under the suggested practice, the charge to operations would simply be the total unfunded vested obligation after shutdown of $18 million, which, in this case, also represents the pre-closing unfunded vested liability.

It is apparent that significant divergencies in practice have evolved due to the different ways in which the literature has been interpreted. A closer look at some key issues as well as the literature itself should help in examining these practices.

A CLOSER LOOK

Although Opinion 30 does not specifically address the question of whether the pre-closing unfunded vested liability should be recognized earlier

than originally planned, we believe the answer is implicit in the Opinion. Because Opinion 30 calls for a final liquidation accounting for the operation being closed, an accountant should refer to the pervasive measurement principles in the literature for recognizing costs and expenses. These principles include a convention of immediately recognizing costs that provide no discernible future economic benefit and cannot be associated with earnings in any future period.

In a shutdown, the pre-closing unfunded vested liability should be viewed as an obligation still to be recorded in winding up the plant's affairs. This obligation represents unrecorded costs that have no discernible future economic benefit. We believe there is little justification for deferral.

What, if any, actuarial gain or loss is to be recognized under Opinion 8? Opinion 8 states that an actuarial gain or loss is to be dealt with "in a consistent manner that reflects the long-range nature of pension cost." Because pension costs are long-range costs, Opinion 8 holds that most actuarial gains and losses should be systematically spread over a reasonable period.

However, Opinion 8 requires that an actuarial gain or loss "from a single occurrence not directly related to the operation of the pension plan and not in the ordinary course of the employer's business" be recognized in the year it occurs. A plant closing is one specific example given.

In light of this provision, some think (as in Practices No. 2 and No. 3) that any actuarial gain arising from a plant closing should be recognized immediately as a credit to any gain or loss from discontinuance. We believe this is a misunderstanding of the accounting implications of Opinion 8.

Accountants sometimes go astray by assuming that the actuarial gain supplied by the actuary is the same actuarial gain referred to in Opinion 8. This is not so. For accounting purposes, the immediately recognizable actuarial gain envi-

funded after the closing. Further, this actuarial gain is already reflected in the overfunded position of the vested liability. Separate inclusion in the gain or loss determination would therefore be double counting.

On the other hand, a plant closing could give rise to an actuarial loss, for example, when substantial shutdown ben-

Opinion 30. Here separate inclusion of the actuarial loss in the gain or loss determination would also be double counting.

MORE EXAMPLES

Figure III represents a non-bargained plan with no special shutdown benefits involved. However, assets plus book accruals minus prepaid pension expense exceed the pre-closing vested liability by $10 million. In this case, the IRS requires that any assets above the vested liability be used to cover the non-vested accumulated liability. Of the $10 million in excess assets, $5 million must therefore be used to vest the non-vested accumulated liability. Hence, the additional $5 million in vested liability is categorized as "additional pension costs" even though it is covered by existing assets.

Note that $5 million of the $8 million actuarial gain can be considered an Opinion 8 actuarial gain because $5 million is the amount of prior accruals now unnecessary. But separately including the $5 million gain in the computations would be double counting. It is already implicit in the overfunded position for the vested benefit liability.

The suggested accounting practice in **Figure III** adds the $10 million pre-closing overfunded vested liability (as a credit) to the $5 million additional pension costs and arrives at a $5 million credit to operations. The other three practices develop answers varying from a $13 million credit to a $5 million charge.

Figure IV shows a plant closing that triggers special shutdown benefits, a common situation in bargained plans in major industries. The shutdown benefits increase the vested liability

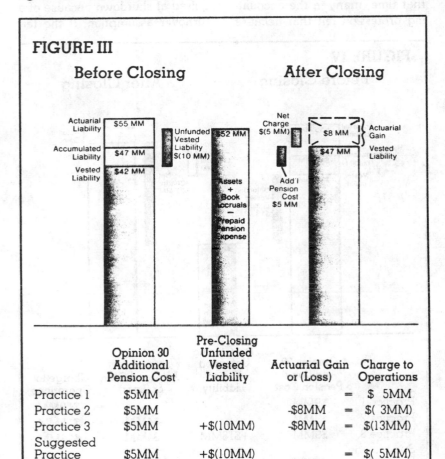

FIGURE III

	Opinion 30 Additional Pension Cost	Pre-Closing Unfunded Vested Liability	Actuarial Gain or (Loss)		Charge to Operations
Practice 1	$5MM			=	$ 5MM
Practice 2	$5MM		-$8MM	=	$(3MM)
Practice 3	$5MM	+$(10MM)	-$8MM	=	$(13MM)
Suggested Practice	$5MM	+$(10MM)		=	$(5MM)

Although there are no bargained shutdown benefits here, this plan's vested liability increases $5 million anyway. The IRS requires at shutdown that any assets above the vested liability be used to cover any non-vested accumulated liability. But because the pre-closing vested liability is overfunded by $10 million, the suggested accounting is a $5 million credit to operations.

sioned by Opinion 8 can exist only to the extent that previous pension accruals become unnecessary in retrospect. This can occur only in a plan that is over-

efits are triggered by the closing. The accountant would have recorded the cost of these shutdown benefits in computing the additional pension costs under by $9 million, while the pre-closing vested liability is unfunded by $18 million. The suggested charge to operations is $27 million, compared to $5 million, the lowest charge observed in practice.

Figure V is similar to **Figure IV** except that assets plus book accruals minus prepaid pension expense exceed the pre-closing vested liability by $3 million. Practices Nos. 1 through 3 would produce a charge as low as $2 million or as high as $9 million. The suggested practice adds the $3 million pre-closing overfunded vested liability (as a credit) to the $9 million additional pension costs to arrive at a charge to operations of $6 million.

Finally, **Figure VI** depicts a plant closing where the $18 million in special shutdown benefits is large enough to increase the vested liability by $5 million beyond the pre-closing actuarial liability, creating a $5 million actuarial loss. Although this is an Opinion 8 actuarial loss, separately including it in the computations would be double counting. It is already implicit within the "additional pension costs" recognized under Opinion 30.

The most direct method of calculating the suggested charge in each of these cases is simply to subtract the assets plus book accruals minus prepaid pension expense from the final vested liability after shutdown.

THE PAST SERVICE COST AND TURNOVER ARGUMENTS

In discussions with various practitioners, we occasionally encountered views that were based almost entirely on Opinion 8. For example, some practitioners argue that no special accounting is required at plant

shutdown by drawing an analogy to past service costs under Opinion 8. Just as these costs can be deferred to future years, so too, they claim, can the unfunded vested liability at shutdown.

Those familiar with the development of Opinion 8, however, will recall that the most controversial issue concerned accounting for past service costs. At that time, many in the accounting profession felt that because

past service costs are associated with active employees who will continue to produce income for the company, the recognition of these past service costs should be spread over their remaining future service lives. We share

this view, although Opinion 8 did not specifically identify the theoretical basis for spreading past service costs. We also believe that immediate recognition of the remaining unfunded vested liability following a plant closing is appropriate because there are no remaining future service lives.

Still other practitioners argue that no special accounting is required at shutdown because of a turnover assumption. If the terminated employees participated in a company-wide pension plan, these practitioners maintain, nothing further is called for, especially if total employee turnover was within the normal assumption for the year.

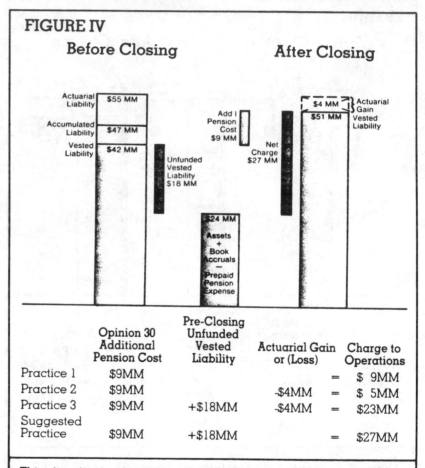

FIGURE IV

	Opinion 30 Additional Pension Cost	Pre-Closing Unfunded Vested Liability	Actuarial Gain or (Loss)		Charge to Operations
Practice 1	$9MM			=	$ 9MM
Practice 2	$9MM		-$4MM	=	$ 5MM
Practice 3	$9MM	+$18MM	-$4MM	=	$23MM
Suggested Practice	$9MM	+$18MM		=	$27MM

This situation is quite common in major industry bargained plans. Special shutdown benefits in this plan increase the vested liability by $9 million, while the pre-closing vested liability is unfunded by $18 million. The suggested charge to operations is $27 million.

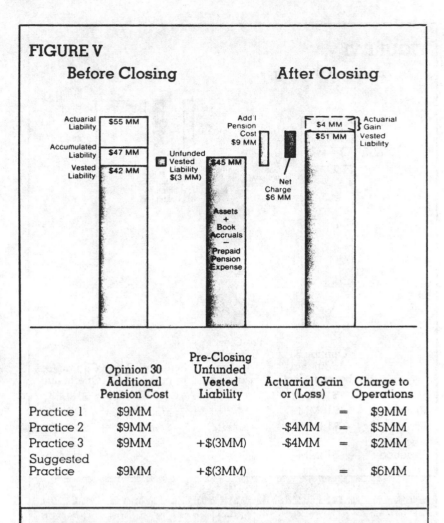

FIGURE V

| | Before Closing | After Closing |

Actuarial Liability $55 MM
Accumulated Liability $47 MM
Vested Liability $42 MM

Unfunded Vested Liability $(3 MM)

$45 MM

Assets + Book Accruals − Prepaid Pension Expense

Add'l Pension Cost $9 MM

Net Charge $6 MM

$4 MM
$51 MM

Actuarial Gain
Vested Liability

	Opinion 30 Additional Pension Cost	Pre-Closing Unfunded Vested Liability	Actuarial Gain or (Loss)		Charge to Operations
Practice 1	$9MM			=	$9MM
Practice 2	$9MM		-$4MM	=	$5MM
Practice 3	$9MM	+$(3MM)	-$4MM	=	$2MM
Suggested Practice	$9MM	+$(3MM)		=	$6MM

This situation is occasionally seen as a variation of Figure IV. The only difference in this plan is that assets plus book accruals minus prepaid pension expense exceed the pre-closing vested liability by $3 million. The suggested charge is $9 million + ($3 million), or $6 million.

"... generally accepted accounting principles for discontinued operations do not provide a supermarket of alternatives."

However, these practitioners are overlooking the difference in accounting treatment that Opinion 8 requires for normal employee turnover and for turnover arising from a plant closing. Basically, Opinion 8 distinguishes the two events by their origins. Normal employee turnover is a regular occurrence. A plant closing, on the other hand, is a reduction in work force that is not considered to be a regular occurrence under Opinion 8 and any resulting actuarial gain or loss therefore requires immediate recognition.

REMAINING ISSUES

In this article we have attempted to identify only the most fundamental issues involved with the pension cost controversy. Additional issues need to be dealt with. One gray area involves the unfunded vested liability relating to employees who retired or were terminated long before the plant closing. Although there may be merit in including this liability in the total charge in order to further unencumber future income streams from prior pension obligations, the issue warrants further study.

Another issue is the choice of appropriate actuarial assumptions for calculating the final unfunded vested liability and the approach to be taken if future experience requires a "change in estimate."

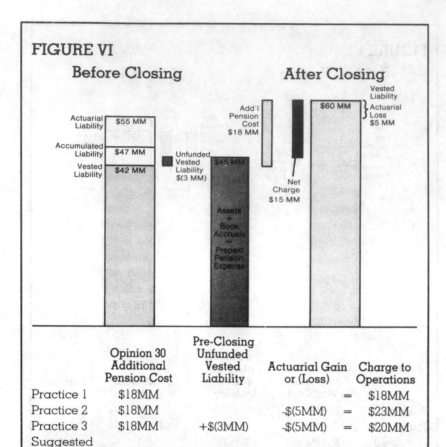

FIGURE VI

Before Closing

Actuarial Liability $55 MM

Accumulated Liability $47 MM

Vested Liability $42 MM

Unfunded Vested Liability $(3 MM)

$45 MM

Assets + Book Accruals − Prepaid Pension Expense

After Closing

Add'l Pension Cost $18 MM

Net Charge $15 MM

$60 MM

Vested Liability

Actuarial Loss $5 MM

	Opinion 30 Additional Pension Cost	Pre-Closing Unfunded Vested Liability	Actuarial Gain or (Loss)		Charge to Operations
Practice 1	$18MM			=	$18MM
Practice 2	$18MM		-$(5MM)	=	$23MM
Practice 3	$18MM	+$(3MM)	-$(5MM)	=	$20MM
Suggested Practice	$18MM	+$(3MM)		=	$15MM

Unlike Figure V, $18 million of special shutdown benefits in this plan are large enough to increase the vested liability $5 million beyond the pre-closing actuarial liability, creating a $5 million actuarial loss. Although this is an Opinion 8 actuarial loss, adding it in would be double counting. The suggested charge is $18 million + ($3 million), or $15 million. This can also be derived as the final unrecorded obligation, which is $60 million − $45 million, or $15 million.

> "Much of the pension cost controversy arises from subtleties in terminology and lack of specificity in Opinions 30 and 8."

Finally, unfunded welfare benefit liabilities are, in some cases, just as significant as unfunded pension liabilities. Many companies have accepted the obligation to continue death and medical benefits after shutdown, at least for retirees. Because accounting for these welfare benefits is often on a *pay-as-you-go* basis, many companies will discover significant unfunded welfare benefit liabilities at shutdown. We think these liabilities should be handled in the same manner as unfunded pension liabilities.

CONCLUSION

Much of the pension cost controversy arises from subtleties in terminology and lack of specificity in Opinions 30 and 8. But basic financial reporting principles should be followed despite any shortcomings in language. We believe these principles require that whatever was not expensed before the closing should be expensed at the closing, so as not to burden future income streams.

Perhaps practitioners have instinctively followed this rule on more occasions than not. However, we think it is advisable to eliminate the potential for confusion when Opinions 30 and 8 are redrafted or reinterpreted. Otherwise, it seems inevitable that instances will occur where the wrong numbers will be supplied to the right questions. □

Pension Plans: What Companies Do— and Do Not—Disclose

One cent of every dollar of revenue for the surveyed companies is transferred to an employee pension fund.

By James W. Deitrick and C. Wayne Alderman

James W. Deitrick is assistant professor of accounting, Graduate School of Business, The University of Texas at Austin. He has a doctorate in business administration from The University of Tennessee—Knoxville. This article was submitted through Austin Area Chapter.

Since the Employee Retirement Income Security Act (ERISA) was signed into law in 1974, interest in pension accounting and reporting has snowballed. Investors, creditors, employees, federal agencies, and company management especially are interested in the abilities of companies to satisfy their annual pension obligations. Legitimate concerns have been expressed about the effects of pension costs on future cash flows and reported income. To make reasonable projections about these factors, complete pension information is usually beneficial; however, financial analysts, accountants, and others[1] have been critical of corporate pension disclosures. Much of this criticism cannot be dismissed as unwarranted. As a result, the Financial Accounting Standards Board (FASB) currently has pension accounting and reporting requirements under study for possible revision.

Recent articles in MANAGEMENT ACCOUNTING[2] have continued to bring pension accounting and reporting to the attention of those who prepare corporate financial statements and their related footnotes. Yet, little empirical information has been included in these articles. To fill this void, we designed a survey with the objective of reviewing pension disclosures in both annual reports and 10-Ks. From the results, we obtained some key measures of the impact of pension plans.

The survey's results indicated that although pension plans represent a significant burden for many companies, essential pension information is not always disclosed in either the annual report or the 10-K. Moreover, important information is often reported in the 10-K but does not appear in the annual report to shareholders—a reporting phenomenon known as differential disclosure.

The Study's Design

Sixty companies were randomly selected from *Fortune's* 1978 listing of the 500 largest U.S. industrial corporations. Because of incomplete or unavailable data, eight firms were subsequently deleted. A distribution of the rankings of the 52 companies comprising the final sample is presented in Table 1. The results of an examination of these companies' pension disclosures in both annual reports and 10-Ks for fiscal years ending between July 1, 1977 and June 30, 1978, are presented below.

Currently, Accounting Principles Board (APB) Opinion No. 8, "Accounting for the Cost of Pension Plans" and Financial Accounting Standards Board Interpretation No. 3, "Accounting for the Cost of Pension Plans Subject to the Employee Retirement Security Act of 1977: An Interpretation of APB Opinion No. 8," govern the account-

0025-1690/80/6110-2835/$01.00/0

ing for and reporting of defined-benefit pension programs. Briefly, APB Opinion No. 8 requires disclosure of:

1. A statement that a plan exists and identification of employees covered.
2. A statement of the company's accounting and funding policies.
3. The annual pension cost for the period.
4. The excess of any actuarially computed value of vested benefits over pension fund assets and balance sheet accruals, less any pension prepayments or deferred charges; and
5. Any changes or events regarding the pension program that would materially affect comparability for all periods presented.

These disclosures normally appear in a company's annual report. Moreover, the Securities & Exchange Commission, in addition to the above, requires disclosure in the 10-K of any unfunded pension liabilities as of the most recent valuation date. A detailed profile of the reported pension information and key financial ratios for the sample companies is presented in Table 2.

Table 1
DISTRIBUTION OF SAMPLE RANKINGS

Fortune 500 ranking	Number of firms
1 - 10	1
11 - 100	6
101 - 200	11
201 - 300	12
301 - 400	16
401 - 500	6
Total	52

Generally, the required pension disclosures can be found in a company's annual report and 10-K; however, it is not uncommon for the information to be scattered throughout these statements. Pension information for many firms is distributed among management's analysis of operations, the body of the financial statements, regular footnotes, and supplementary footnotes (usually in the 10-K). Further, there is little or no cross-referencing of pension data. As a result, if a financial-statement user is not specifically aware of the required disclosures, there is a strong likelihood that some valuable pension information will be overlooked. Indeed, the organization of pension data for many firms is inefficient, inconvenient, and confusing.

To compound the difficulty of learning about a firm's pension costs by examining its annual report, many enterprises provide little, if any, information beyond what is actually mandatory. For example, 11 of the 52 (21.2%) sampled companies did not report the number of years used for funding or amortization purposes. In some cases of those supplying the data, the disclosure appeared

in the 10-K but not in the annual report. Seldom does a company state its actuarial cost method or actuarial assumptions. There are at least five different cost methods acceptable under ERISA and they can produce widely different results. Major actuarial assumptions include the level of future wage increases, the rate of return on pension fund investments, employee turnover, and mortality. According to financial analysts,[3] these are significant pieces of information that, if disclosed, would better enable users to develop a reasonable understanding of a firm's pension costs and to assess the impact of a pension plan on future operations.

DIFFERENTIAL DISCLOSURE.   For many companies, there is a dramatic difference between the quality of pension disclosures in the annual report and the 10-K. As previously mentioned, some firms present their amortization or funding periods in the 10-K but not in the annual report. Twenty companies did not disclose the amount of unfunded pension liabilities in the notes to their annual reports; however, this information was reported by 18 of the 20 in the 10-K. Differentially-disclosed information causes stockholders and other users of annual reports to incur additional costs of time and money if they want more complete pension information. Since the information is already prepared for the 10-K, there would be little or no extra cost to have it also printed in the annual report. Although management's pension disclosures in the annual report conform with generally accepted accounting principles (APBO No. 8), the spirit of full and fair disclosure appears to be sometimes lacking.

PENSION EXPENSE.   Annual pension expense is a function of each company's actuarial cost method and unique set of actuarial assumptions. Because of available alternatives and inadequate disclosures, it is difficult to make comparisons across companies. Nevertheless, it is apparent from Table 2 that pension expense represents a major burden on corporate profits and cash flows. In most cases, annual pension expense is funded as accrued. This amounts to a total of $1,001,235,000 for the 52 sampled firms for an average of $19,254,519 per firm. Pension expense averaged 32% of bottom line net income and 1.3% of revenues. In effect, one cent of every dollar of revenue for the sampled companies is transferred to an employee pension fund. Table 3 presents the five largest ratios of pension expense to income (largest is 2.4 to 1) and to revenues (largest is .035 to 1).

EXCESS OF VESTED BENEFITS OVER PENSION FUND ASSETS.   Essentially, reported vested benefits are the present value of pension payments due employees if they should leave the company today. For most plans, vesting does not take place immediately upon employment but occurs only after an employee has been with a company for a

C. Wayne Alderman is an assistant professor of accounting at Auburn University. He has a doctorate in business administration from The University of Tennessee—Knoxville.

Table 2
PROFILE OF SAMPLE COMPANIES AND THEIR PENSION COSTS (IN MILLIONS)

Fortune 500 ranking	Company	Annual pension expense	Excess of vested benefits over fund assets	Unfunded pension liability
200	ABBOTT LABS	$ 14.668	$ 0	$ 65.000
284	AKZONA INC	8.587	18.400	47.000
152	AMERICAN BROADCASTING	5.160	4.307	22.294
65	AMERICAN CAN	86.400	126.000	351.000
371	AMSTED INDUSTRIES	16.430	49.000	92.100
136	ANHEUSER BUSCH	21.447	60.000	10.845
299	AVNET INC	2.804	.785	2.175
396	BELL + HOWELL	1.293	0	2.360
283	BLACK + DECKER	9.433	3.100	15.000
49	BOEING CO	90.600	60.600	191.500
464	BRIGGS + STRATTON	11.220	0	14.838
113	BRISTOL MYERS	18.800	.500	3.600
497	BUTLER MANUFACTURING	4.299	2.444	14.080
105	CARNATION	11.200	0	0
334	CESSNA AIRCRAFT	8.800	12.800	36.000
377	CONAGRA INC	1.920	1.150	6.950
453	CONGOLEUM	3.924	29.200	35.000
296	CUMMINS ENGINE	13.300	18.000	106.000
360	DAYCO	3.333	2.847	18.808
81	DRESSER INDUSTRIES	33.000	22.000	166.000
46	FIRESTONE TIRE	72.000	128.400	413.100
366	FLEETWOOD ENTERPRISES	4.436	0	0
351	FLINTKOTE	5.372	11.800	23.200
368	GANNETT INC	8.120	0	10.000
59	GULF + WESTERN	49.100	145.000	330.000
8	GULF OIL	110.000	40.000	466.000
148	HERCULES	48.600	36.000	216.315
184	HEWLETT PACKARD	37.500	0	69.000
425	HUGHES TOOL CO	4.149	0	8.100
341	INDIAN HEAD	.190	0	.299
256	JOSEPH SCHLITZ BREWERIES	11.254	ND	ND
266	MCA INC	12.100	ND	0
426	MEMOREX	1.500	0	4.800
118	NABISCO INC	32.134	60.000	103.000
356	NEWMONT MINING	12.248	32.045	63.605
230	POLAROID CORP	16.584	0	0
305	POTLATCH	10.588	21.039	48.178
162	QUAKER OATS	12.900	0	45.000
55	RALSTON PURINA	15.200	0	34.700
295	REXNORD INC	15.066	31.154	61.933
203	ROHM + HASS CO	24.708	34.200	ND
471	ROPER CORP	3.171	7.518	13.519
373	SAXON INDUSTRIES	1.095	1.600	8.300
234	SUNBEAM CORP	10.950	0	38.500
352	SYBRON	12.655	6.900	46.000
198	TIME INC	8.100	ND	4.700
248	TIMKEN CO	33.860	109.540	273.400
399	TRANE CO	5.450	8.065	24.942
391	TWENTIETH CENTURY FOX	2.700	6.738	7.251
217	UPJOHN CO	17.308	ND	69.000
435	WASHINGTON POST	6.879	ND	5.655
182	WHITE CONSOLIDATED	28.700	137.000	252.400
Total		$1,001.235	$1,228.132	$3,847.447

Average ignoring nondisclosures
Average ignoring nondisclosures and values of zero

ND = Not disclosed   * = Cannot be determined

Amortization or funding period	Pension expense		Executive vested benefits			Unfunded liabilities		
	Income	Sales	Total assets	Net worth	Income	Total assets	Net worth	Income
40 yrs	.124	.012	0	0	0	.052	.098	.552
ND	1.141	.011	.027	.061	2.446	.070	.157	6.248
30	.047	.003	.004	.009	.039	.023	.044	.203
30	.796	.025	.068	.135	1.160	.161	.375	3.232
30	.462	.030	.161	.215	1.376	.303	.404	2.587
ND	.233	.012	.043	.088	.653	.008	.016	.118
ND	.070	.004	.002	.003	.020	.006	.009	.054
10-30	.110	.003	0	0	0	.006	.013	.200
30	.183	.012	.004	.006	.060	.021	.037	.290
25	.502	.022	.025	.049	.336	.078	.156	1.062
30	.299	.025	0	0	0	.061	.084	.396
30	.108	.009	.000	.001	.003	.002	.004	.021
20	.231	.012	.012	.021	.131	.072	.119	.757
ND	.103	.005	0	0	0	0	0	0
30	.238	.014	.031	.061	.347	.086	.170	.975
30	.127	.004	.006	.014	.076	.037	.085	.459
15-40	.159	.010	.110	.191	1.180	.131	.229	1.415
30-40	.198	.011	.022	.047	.269	.128	.278	1.582
40	.245	.006	.009	.031	.209	.058	.203	1.381
10-30	.178	.013	.010	.020	.119	.076	.154	.897
25	.653	.016	.038	.079	1.165	.122	.255	3.749
ND	.250	.007	0	0	0	0	0	0
ND	.258	.009	.025	.049	.567	.050	.096	1.115
40	.117	.015	0	0	0	.019	.026	.144
25-40	.327	.013	.035	.118	.965	.081	.273	2.235
15	.146	.006	.003	.005	.053	.033	.064	.620
30	.839	.029	.024	.048	.621	.146	.286	3.734
30	.309	.027	0	0	0	.060	.084	.568
30	.096	.009	0	0	0	.017	.025	.187
ND	.123	.007	0	0	0	.001	.015	.193
ND	.569	.012	.015	.031	.562	*	*	*
ND	.127	.014	.013	.021	.117	0	0	0
30	.027	.003	0	0	0	.015	.042	.085
40	.412	.015	.056	.123	.769	.097	.212	1.320
40	2.401	.020	.027	.051	6.282	.054	.102	12.469
10	.180	.016	0	0	0	0	0	0
30	.171	.015	.031	.055	.340	.072	.126	.779
20	.175	.008	.0	0	0	.045	.091	.611
30	.107	.004	0	0	0	.020	.040	.243
40	.342	.020	.062	.110	.706	.123	.219	1.404
ND	.542	.022	.033	.065	.750	*	*	*
40	.403	.013	.041	.088	.955	.073	.158	1.717
40	.155	.002	.004	.014	.226	.022	.074	1.171
30	.245	.009	0	0	0	.051	.113	.863
40	.463	.022	.016	.030	.253	.105	.200	1.684
10	.089	.006	.011	.020	.123	.004	.009	.052
ND	.455	.035	.141	.189	1.472	.351	.472	3.673
30	.218	.011	.022	.037	.323	.068	.116	.998
25	.053	.005	.016	.039	.133	.017	.042	.143
40	.189	.015	.011	.020	.121	.066	.126	.754
20	.194	.016	.040	.079	.313	.020	.040	.159
15-40	.533	.020	.147	.395	2.546	.270	.727	4.691
	.322	.013	.026	.050	.534	.068	.133	1.356
	.322	.013	.028	.055	.579	.074	.145	1.474

predetermined period of time. An excess of vested benefits over pension fund assets indicates that the pension fund is presently incapable of satisfying these promised payments. Normally, this difference will be made up by future funding and expected appreciation in the value of pension fund investments.

To help protect employees' guaranteed benefits, ERISA created the Pension Benefit Guarantee Corporation (PBGC). The PBGC, a federal agency, can attach a tax lien on corporate assets up to 30% of net worth if a plan is terminated and pension fund assets are not sufficient to cover the guaranteed benefits. The attachment has the status of a federal tax lien and ranks ahead of unsecured creditors. Thus, bankers, suppliers, and other corporate creditors are interested in the relationship between excess vested benefits and a company's net worth.

For the sampled companies, the total excess of vested benefits over pension fund assets was $1,228,132,000. Significantly, this amount must be charged to operations and be funded in future years. Fourteen of the 52 companies (26.9%) are fully funded and five firms (9.6%) did not mention the relationship between vested benefits and pension fund assets in either the annual report or

10-K. Therefore, the total of $1.2 billion is produced by just 33 firms (63.5%) for an average of $37,216,121 per company.

The average ratio of reported excess vested benefits to total company assets is 2.8%. In regard to net worth, the average ratio is 5.5% (just one firm was above the PBGC's critical 30% level). The average ratio based on net income is 57.9%. Significantly, this particular ratio for eight firms (15.4%) was 100% or more. Table 4 presents the five largest measures for each ratio.

UNFUNDED PENSION LIABILITIES. This variable represents the actuarially computed value of vested and unvested pension obligations (normally, unfunded past or prior service costs) that are not covered by pension fund assets. The magnitude of unfunded pension liabilities is a significant item because, usually, it will be charged against future operations and become funded. However, as pointed out earlier, this variable is not required to be reported by APB Opinion No. 8 but is required by the SEC. Interestingly, 18 firms (34.6%) did not report their unfunded pension liabilities in their annual reports but did disclose them in the 10-Ks. In all, for the 18 firms, potential charges to future periods amounting to $1.5 billion were omitted from their annual reports.

> *Unfunded liabilities constitute a potential future drain on cash flows and severely reduce reported income.*

Table 3
FIVE LARGEST PENSION EXPENSE RATIOS

Ranking	Income	Ranking	Sales
356	2.401	248	.035
284	1.141	371	.030
148	.839	148	.029
65	.796	184	.027
46	.653	65	.025
		464	.025

Table 4
FIVE LARGEST RATIOS INVOLVING EXCESS VESTED BENEFITS

Ranking	Total assets	Ranking	Net worth	Ranking	Income
371	.161	182	.395	365	6.282
182	.147	371	.215	182	2.546
248	.147	453	191	284	2.446
453	.110	248	.189	248	1.472
295	.062	65	.135	371	1.376

TABLE 5
FIVE LARGEST RATIOS INVOLVING UNFUNDED LIABILITIES

Ranking	Total assets	Ranking	Net worth	Ranking	Income
248	.351	182	.727	356	12.469
371	.303	248	.472	284	6.248
182	.270	371	.404	182	4.691
65	.161	65	.375	46	3.749
148	.146	148	.286	148	3.734

According to data obtained from both annual reports and 10-Ks, total unfunded pension liabilities were $3,847,447,000 for 46 (88.5%) of the sampled companies. This is an average of $83,640,152 per company. Four companies (7.7%) specifically noted that they had no unfunded pension liabilities, and there were no disclosures for two companies (3.8%).

As might be expected, unfunded liabilities are considerably greater than the excess of vested benefits over pension fund assets. In fact, for this sample of firms, they are over three times as large. Consequently, the differences between unfunded liabilities and total assets, net worth, and net income become even more pronounced. The average ratios for unfunded liabilities and these three variables are .068, .133, and 1.356, respectively. Table 5 reports these five largest ratios.

Unfunded liabilities constitute a potential future drain on cash flows and may severely reduce reported income. The sizes of the various ratios involving this variable indicate why analysts and creditors are especially concerned about companies' abilities to absorb this obligation. Unfunded liabilities are greater than 10% of total assets for ten of the 52 companies (19.2%). They exceed 10% of net worth for 24 firms (46.2%) and the ratios for 42 companies (80.8%) are above 10% of net income. Moreover, 19 firms (36.5%) have ratios of unfunded liabilities to net income that exceed 1.000. Because of the magnitude and importance of this variable, it becomes understandable why some companies elect not to report unfunded pension liabilities directly to their stockholders. But if the economy suffers a prolonged downturn, many of these companies will have trouble obtaining the resources to meet their obligations for unfunded vested and, perhaps, unvested pension benefits. This could come as a shock to stockholders because some of these obligations are not now disclosed to them in the annual report.

More Efficient Disclosure Needed

This study of the pension cost disclosures of 52 companies appearing in the 1978 *Fortune* 500 indicates that the vast majority of firms adhere to the reporting standards of the FASB and SEC. However, the reported information is often divided among several locations throughout a financial statement. This fragmentation is not in the best interest of financial statement users. More efficient disclosure of all pension cost information, e.g., in one clearly identified section, would assist all user groups. Further, the level of differential disclosure between the annual report and 10-K creates unnecessary costs for users who must obtain and evaluate both documents. The significance of most pension plans is such that the additional information reported to the SEC, e.g., unfunded pension liabilities, should also be reported to stockholders

and creditors by means of the annual report.

Tables 3 through 5 present numerical measures of reported pension costs and its potential burden on future periods. Pension plans are indeed a substantial cost for most companies, but the nature of the off-balance sheet disclosures makes it difficult for analysts and others to evaluate these obligations. If an objective of financial statements is to assist users in appraising and predicting enterprise cash flows and earning power, then a strong argument can be made for disclosure of a company's actuarial cost method, material actuarial assumptions, and its funding and amortization periods. Only with this type of information can users reasonably assess reported pension costs and project the effects of future inflation, an expected recession, or possible changes in retirement benefits and actuarial assumptions on a firm's cash flows and net income. For example, the significance of actuarial assumptions on annual pension expense becomes evident when it is realized that a 1% increase in the interest rate assumption can reduce pension expense by 20 to 25% or a 1% reduction in the wage assumption can lower the annual pension contribution by about 13%.[4]

The findings of this study bring into focus two other financial reporting issues that are of particular concern to corporate accountants. First, the SEC is currently campaigning to make annual reports as informative as the 10-K. This could lead to increased regulation regarding the form and content of annual reports. The SEC's involvement could lead to the complete replacement of the annual report with the 10-K. It is not clear that this action would be in the best interests of the company or its stockholders. On the other hand, the evidence of frequent differential pension disclosures illustrates that management does not always report important but potentially negative information to its stockholders.

Second, the FASB recently has proposed two new pension reporting guidelines. One would establish additional financial accounting and reporting standards for all defined-benefit pension plans. The other proposal would require greater pension disclosure by employers in their annual reports. The new disclosures would include identification of the significant assumptions and methods used in determining actuarial costs, the present value of accumulated benefits as well as any vested benefits, and a description of the accounting policies. Corporate accountants and their auditors will follow both proposals with interest. □

The different cost methods acceptable under ERISA can produce widely different results.

[1] For example, see Patrick J. Regan, "Potential Corporate Liabilities Under ERISA," *Financial Analysts Journal,* March-April 1976; Joe J. Cramer, Jr. and Charles A. Neyhart, "Accounting for Pensions: A Contemporary Perspective," *The CPA Journal,* June 1976; and A. F. Ehrbar, "Those Pension Plans Are Even Weaker Than You Think," *Fortune,* Nov. 1977.
[2] In particular, see Jack Smith, "Needed: Improved Pension Accounting and Reporting," MANAGEMENT ACCOUNTING, May 1978, and Frank G. Burianek, "An Actuary's View on Pension Plan Accounting and Reporting," MANAGEMENT ACCOUNTING, January 1979.
[3] See Patrick J. Regan, "Interpreting the Pension Data in 1977 Annual Reports," *Financial Analysts Journal,* March-April 1978.
[4] Ehrbar, p. 106.

ATTITUDES OF FINANCIAL EXECUTIVES TOWARD FOREIGN EXCHANGE ISSUES

Results of a survey indicate that financial executives are taking new directions in foreign exchange management. Is there a move away from hedging and trading in exchange markets toward risk management through sales and investment diversification?

IKE MATHUR
Department of Finance
Southern Illinois University

A multinational firm in its day-to-day business operations can realize gains and losses due strictly to the changes in the values of its foreign currency denominated assets. Exporting, importing, and investing in subsidiaries abroad create foreign exchange risk for the firm. Recent years have seen large changes in the relative value of currencies. These changes in currency values have made the management of foreign exchange risks one of the most difficult and persistent tasks for financial executives of multinational firms.

Many studies have provided guidelines for foreign exchange management, and a few have reported on actual foreign exchange risk management practices. But, there has been a noticeable lack of detailed studies on the attitudes of financial executives toward foreign exchange issues. This report hopes to fill that gap.

HISTORICAL PERSPECTIVE AND RISKS DEFINED

The importance of comparative currency values and their impact on world trade made obvious the need for some mechanism to regulate or oversee currency values. The 1944 Bretton Woods Agreement was designed to bring order to the foreign exchange market. Under the Bretton Woods Agreement, central banks of the various countries were expected to intervene in the exchange markets to correct supposedly temporary imbalances in exchange rates. If demand and supply situations indicated permanent imbalance, then exchange rates were to be adjusted. In recent years rapid changes in exchange rates led to the abandonment of the Agreement in 1973. Since then the exchange rates for currencies have been constantly changing.

Currency exchange rates fluctuate daily on the basis of demand and supply. Multinational firms face risks generally not encountered by uninational firms. These risks are sovereign risk, transaction risk, and translation risk.

Sovereign risk is associated with conducting business abroad under the rules and regulations of a foreign government. Multinational firms at times have had their assets in certain countries nationalized or confiscated. Still other multinational firms frequently have found it difficult to convert their holdings in foreign currencies into American dollars.

Transaction risk occurs when a domestic firm imports or exports goods from or to a foreign country. The invoice may be denominated in a foreign currency and since time may lapse between the date of the transaction agreement and the date when payment is made, there is a risk that the exchange rate will change.

Translation risk is also called accounting risk. It is derived from attempts to value foreign subsidiary firms in terms of the balance sheet currency of the parent/domestic company. At any point in time, the accounting value of a multinational firm is defined as the total value of both the parent firm and its subsidiaries. Since exchange rates change, multinational firms incur accounting risk due to the necessity of recording the effects of changes in currency valuations for balance sheet and income statement items.

Financial Accounting Standards Board's Statement No. 8, *Accounting for the Translation of Foreign Currency Transactions and Foreign Currency Financial Statements,* mandated the procedure that U.S. firms

"Reprinted from *Financial Executive*, **October 1980** with permission of the publisher."

would have to use in translating foreign-currency denominated financial statements of their subsidiaries. FASB No. 8 has become quite controversial because of its impact on the reported earnings of U.S multinationals. The next section of this paper presents the survey results related to the attitudes of financial executives of U.S. multinationals toward foreign exchange risk and FASB No. 8.

RESEARCH METHODOLOGY

This study was designed to look at the attitudes of financial executives toward a variety of foreign exchange issues and to examine the risk management practices of U.S. multinationals. Only the attitudinal portion of the study is reported here. Questionnaires were mailed to the vice presidents of finance of 300 companies. The 300 companies were selected from the *Fortune 500* list. These firms were also cross-listed in the Dun and Bradstreet's *Directory of International Companies.* The respondents were asked to complete a 45 item questionnaire, and were assured of the anonymity of their responses.

Among those surveyed, 55 useful responses were received. Total assets for the 55 firms varied from $70 million to $22.1 billion. The average total assets for the responding firms was $3.04 billion. Total annual sales for these firms had a range of $182 million to $42.8 billion, with an average of $5.4 billion; 40 companies in the sample had sales in excess of $1 billion.

One of the 55 responding firms manufactured/sold in 168 countries. On the other end of the spectrum, one dealt only with two countries. The average firm in the sample was manufac-

turing/selling in 43 countries; 50 firms were conducting business in ten or more countries. All of the firms analyzed derived at least 10 percent of their sales overseas. While one firm was deriving 86 percent of its sales from abroad, the average figure for foreign sales was 31 percent of total sales.

ORGANIZATIONAL POLICIES

To gain better understanding of the attitudes of financial executives toward foreign exchange issues, firms were asked to respond to a variety of questions related to corporate policies for their foreign exchange transactions.

Some 67.3 percent of the firms responding had written policies governing foreign exchange transactions. **The existence of a written foreign exchange policy was positively related to the relative size of foreign sales and to total assets.** This indicates that the more a firm relies on foreign sales, the more it emphasizes foreign exchange policy. Larger firms also appear to opt more often for formalizing foreign exchange policy.

The survey also revealed that 89 percent of the firms considered capital structure in establishing foreign exchange policy. Only six of the 55 firms did not. Approximately 63.6 percent of the firms explicitly considered dividends on common stock when foreign exchange decisions are made. Of the 55 firms, 49 (or 89 percent) consider cash liquidity in their foreign exchange policy.

Respondents were asked to characterize their foreign exchange risk management policy: 25:5 percent answered that minimizing foreign exchange

transaction losses was the basic corporate policy; five, or 9.1 percent, indicated minimizing these translation losses; and 32 (58.2 percent) indicated minimizing both. Of the 55 firms, 39 (70.9 percent) executed a majority of their foreign exchange transactions at corporate headquarters. Firms with centralized decision-making evidenced greater use of hedging for covering exposure to foreign exchange losses.

In the sections that follow, the attitudes of financial executives toward importance of foreign exchange factors, translation and transaction exposure, and efficiency in these markets are examined.

RANKING OF FACTORS

Foreign exchange risk management requires consideration of a variety of factors. First, exchange rates for currencies change, thereby creating transaction risk. Devaluations and revaluations directly affect the dollar value of assets held abroad and of assets denominated in the affected currencies. (FASB No. 8 establishes the guidelines for translating foreign currency denominated financial statements, and is generally accredited with magnifying translation exposure for U.S. firms.) And, political stability is another important factor in foreign exchange risk management. Political upheavals create the risk of nationalization or confiscation of assets.

Foreign exchange managers for the 55 multinationals in the study were asked to rank, in order of decreasing importance, factors they felt were significant in foreign exchange risk management. The most important factor was floating exchange rates—28 of the 55 managers rated it most important. The average rating for this factor was 1.78. As indicated previously, respondents were also requested to answer questions related to a variety of foreign exchange risk management practices. Correlation analysis indicated that those managers who attached greater importance to floating exchange rates were also the ones who were placing major emphasis on forecasting foreign exchange rates. Finally, these same managers were basing their forecasts on a cash flow rather than accounting basis.

The second most important factor in foreign exchange management was devaluations and revaluations. Devaluations/revaluations directly affect the balance sheets and income statements when foreign currency denominated items are converted into dollar entries. **Managers who attached greater importance to devaluations/revaluations were also prone to increased utilization of foreign exchange adjustment clauses in their contracts.**

FASB No. 8 was considered to be the third most important factor—25 of the 55 respondents felt that it was the least important factor in foreign exchange management. Given the tremendous displeasure that managers have expressed about FASB No. 8, it was surprising to note that relatively few managers attach any significance to FASB No. 8. In general, those managers who felt that FASB No. 8 was relatively more important also believed that FASB No. 8 provided the investing public with additional needed information.

The least important factor in foreign exchange management

was political upheavals. Only six of 55 respondents felt that it was the most important factor. Its average ranking was 3.02. Responses to other parts of the questionnaire indicated that only two firms out of the 55 had experienced confiscation or nationalization of assets in the past year. Given that, on the average, each of the 55 respondents was operating in 44 different countries, the incidence of confiscation/nationalization is remarkably low. This fact may explain the relatively low importance attached to political instability.

ATTITUDES TOWARD FASB NO. 8

Basically, FASB No. 8 requires that all "non-monetary" items on the balance sheet, such as inventories, plant, and equipment, be expressed in dollar terms. For a firm with non-monetary assets or liabilities abroad, the values of these foreign currency denominated assets or liabilities are to be translated at "historical" exchange rates. Historical rates are the ones that prevailed on the day the non-monetary items were acquired. "Monetary" items, such as accounts receivable, current liabilities, and long-term debt, are to be translated at current exchange rates. Any translation gains or losses, even if they occur only on paper, have to be reported on the current income statement. **In general, the accounting practices mandated by FASB No. 8 have tended to increase the volatility of reported earnings of U.S multinational firms.**

The financial executives of the 55 firms were asked to indicate whether they felt that FASB No. 8 had a negative

impact on the price of the common stock of their firms: Seven of 55, or 12.7 percent of the executives, felt that FASB No. 8 had impacted negatively on the price of their common stock. Considering the adverse publicity that FASB No. 8 has received, it was surprising to note the small percentage who felt that FASB No. 8 had been detrimental to the performance of common stock. It may be that the executives felt that investors in general recognize the vagaries of FASB No. 8 and properly recognize its effects in pricing common stock.

Executives were asked to indicate the effects of FASB No. 8 on reported earnings. Almost 51 percent stated that without FASB No. 8 reported earnings would have been higher, while 43.6 percent indicated that earnings would have remained the same. These responses provide a clear indication of the impact of FASB No. 8 on reported earnings. The majority of firms would have been able to report higher earnings without FASB No. 8. This factor may be a partial explanation for the unpopularity of FASB No. 8.

Respondents were asked to indicate whether they felt that FASB No. 8 provided the investing public with additional needed information. Only 10 of 55 executives responded positively. The vast majority of the executives were of the opinion that FASB No. 8 did not provide the investing public with any useful information. In general, those executives who felt that FASB No. 8 provided useful information were also the ones who felt that benefits of hedging were greater than the costs of hedging. Additionally, these same executives also felt that eliminating accounting exposure to foreign exchange risk was more important than eliminating transaction exposure. If, in fact, FASB No. 8 provides useful information to investors, then it is logical to engage in hedging activities for managing accounting exposure resulting from FASB No. 8.

TRANSACTION EXPOSURE

Firms are exposed to both translation and transaction exposure in conducting business overseas. FASB No. 8 requires that all gains or losses resulting from translation and transaction exposure are to be reported in the current period. Prior to FASB No. 8, multinational firms had great latitude in how they reported gains and losses from their foreign exchange operations. The use of reserves was an acceptable practice among most multinational corporations.

FASB No. 8, of course, does not allow for gains or losses to be applied to reserve accounts. The 55 executives were asked to indicate how translation gains and losses should be recognized—10 of the 55 indicated that gains and losses should be recognized every reporting period, without using reserves.

This response is consistent with the reporting requirements of FASB No. 8; 24 of the 55 executives (43.6 percent) favored reporting gains and losses every period, using reserves. **This approach is the one that firms could employ prior to FASB No. 8.** The remaining executives felt that translation gains or losses should be recognized only when they actually occur. The last approach is most consistent with the monetary/non-monetary method for realizing translation gains and losses. Responses to recognition of translation gains

and losses indicate the general dissatisfaction of executives with the reporting requirements of FASB No. 8.

Executives were also asked to indicate whether eliminating accounting exposure to foreign exchange risk was more important than eliminating transaction exposure, with seven of the 55 executives responding positively to this question. The responses indicated that the vast majority of executives place much more emphasis on foreign exchange risk arising from business transactions than risk arising from translation exposure, which generally results in paper gains and losses.

Positive responses to this question were positively related to the relative importance of FASB No. 8. Those executives who attached greater significance to eliminating accounting exposure were also the ones who generally felt that FASB No. 8 was relatively more important. These executives also felt that losses due to currency fluctuations could be eliminated through the use of trading rules. These same executives also represented firms which were relatively more active in hedging their foreign exchange transactions in forward markets. The results appear to indicate that the small number of firms that place greater emphasis on reported earnings engage in a variety of foreign exchange transactions, which are mainly motivated by a desire to counteract the impact of FASB No. 8 requirements.

PERCEPTIONS OF EFFICIENCY

A growing body of evidence appears to indicate that stock markets, as well as foreign exchange markets, are rela-

tively efficient. Efficiency in stock markets implies that security prices are based on an assimilation of all relevant information and that no abnormal returns can be derived by further information processing. In efficient markets, stock prices fluctuate randomly around a trend and adjust instantaneously to new information. **The concept of efficiency in foreign exchange markets implies that present information regarding currency devaluations and revaluations, foreign trade balances, political instability and so on are fully reflected in the prevailing spot and future exchange rates.** In efficient foreign exchange markets, there are basically little, if any, benefits to be derived from trying either to anticipate changes in exchange rates or engaging in external hedging activities.

The 55 respondents were asked a variety of questions related to their perceptions of efficiency in foreign exchange markets. As a reference point, the 55 executives were asked to indicate whether U.S. stock market prices fluctuate around a trend in a random fashion: 39 of 55 executives (70.9 percent) responded positively to this question. In general, a large percentage of high-level financial executives believe in the efficiency of U.S. stock markets.

Of the 55 respondents, 25 (45.5 percent) indicated that they believed foreign exchange rate fluctuations were random. Responses to this question are in sharp contrast to the one dealing with efficiency in U.S. stock markets, where a much larger percentage of respondents expressed a belief in the efficiency of the markets. The responses to these two questions correlated at a very low level, indicating that executives perceive the exchange rates adjustment process to be quite different from the adjustment process for stock prices.

Those who generally do not put faith in the efficiency of markets tend to feel that trading rules can be effectively utilized to "beat the market." The respondents were asked to indicate if they felt that losses due to currency fluctuations can be eliminated through using trading rules in the future markets. Agreeing with the statement were 11 of the 55 respondents; 80 percent indicated that the utilization of trading rules would not help them in beating the exchange markets. Positive responses to this question were negatively related to percent of sales derived from abroad. In general, executives of firms with relatively smaller levels of foreign sales were more apt to feel that currency exchange losses could be eliminated through trading.

By and large, proponents of efficient exchange markets argue that since exchange rates fully reflect all present knowledge, hedging is not essential to managing foreign exchange risk. Respondents were asked to indicate whether they agreed with the statement that benefits of hedging are greater than costs of hedging and 19, or 34.5 percent, agreed with this statement, thus indicating their doubts about efficiency in exchange markets.

CONCLUSIONS

The survey provided interesting and enlightening results. As expected, the most important issue facing multinational financial executives is floating exchange rates. Surprisingly, FASB No. 8 was relegated to a

". . . hedging is not essential to managing foreign exchange risk."

relatively lower level of importance. The continued hue and cry over FASB No. 8 has forced the Financial Accounting Standards Board to propose changes in corporate accounting for exchange gains and losses. It may be that the proposed changes will accomplish only the obvious, generating a new set of criticisms.

With the world political order in what some charitably claim is a state of orderly chaos, financial executives do not appear to be very perturbed with the notion of political upheavals disrupting the activities of their firms. Political upheavals were considered to be least important in managing overseas business. The low incidence of confiscation and nationalization indicates that business firms, in general, are adept at evaluating and coping with global political realities.

FASB No. 8 does not allow for gains or losses resulting from currency valuations to be applied to reserve accounts. Critics of FASB No. 8 feel that procedures specified by this standard increase the volatility of reported earnings. Yet the survey results indicated that the earnings of almost one-half of the responding firms were not affected by the reporting requirements of FASB No. 8. The results indicate that firms, in general, can learn to live with various reporting standards.

The study indicated that almost 70 percent of the respondents would prefer reporting translation gains and losses by

using reserve accounts. It appears that the FASB may be able to accommodate the wishes of this large majority. The salient features of the changes to FASB No. 8 tentatively approved in March 1980 by the FASB are as follows:

■ Translation gains and losses would be shown as a separate component of stockholders' equity.

■ All foreign currency denominated assets and liabilities would be translated at current exchange rates.

The first change is equivalent to using reserve accounts and would tend to dampen volatility in earnings induced by translation gains and losses. The second change would help remove the distortions caused in gross margins, which are caused by translating inventories at historical exchange rates.

Financial executives of multinationals also feel that U.S. stock markets are more efficient than foreign exchange markets. One could argue that such was the case prior to the demise of the Bretton Woods Agreement in 1973. Under the Bretton Woods Agreement, central bankers could step in to try to bring into balance their relative exchange values. The artificial demand and supply situation resulting from central bank interventions allowed foreign exchange traders to consistently beat the market.

Evidence now indicates that the value of trying to outguess the foreign exchange markets is zero. It may be that U.S. multinationals are slowly moving away from hedging and trading in exchange markets toward risk management through sales and investment diversification. □

The Future of Forecasting

Advice to management: if you publish a forecast of your earnings,
also include a time-series extrapolation of historical earnings figures
for comparison.

By Wm. Brent Carper, M. Frank Barton, Jr.
and Haroldene F. Wunder

In 1975, the Securities and Exchange Commission
attempted to set up an elaborate system of voluntary disclosure for companies choosing to make
projections public. A majority of respondents opposed the proposals so the Commission withdrew
them.

Last November, the Commission issued a statement again encouraging disclosure of projections,
and also authorized the publication of guides for
preparation and filing of registration statements.
At the same time, the agency proposed for comment a safe-harbor rule for projection disclosure.

Published forecasts continue to be a controversial subject in the accounting field. Another look
could help us discern the possible future of forecasting.

Several studies which offer support for the hypothesis that managements' forecasts will not be
used in their present manner of presentation by
either investors or financial analysts. We urge that
management, in order to lend credibility to its
earnings forecasts, present with the published
forecasts supplementary projections derived from
a time-series extrapolation of historical earnings
figures.

Although the SEC and accounting bodies have
recognized the value of publishing projections,
forecasts can be misleading. The average investor

may misinterpret the significance of a published
forecast. In a study conducted by Asebrook and
Carmichael, members of three respondent groups
(Institute of Chartered Financial Analysts, Financial Executives Institute, and American Institute
of CPAs) indicated they feel the average investor
would misunderstand or misinterpret forecasted
statements published by management.[1] (See Table
1.) To interpret forecast data intelligently the
reader must understand the assumptions that are
inherent in the forecast.

Possibility of Managed Earnings

Another concern is that published forecasts
may lead to managed earnings on the part of companies issuing such forecasts. In situations where
forecasts turn out to be conservative, companies
might hold down profits in an effort to meet the
forecast. Profits could be depressed in the year of
the conservative forecast, thus building up a cushion of profits for subsequent years. Managed earnings could lead to the sacrifice of long-run goals in
order to attain short-run objectives and forecasted
earnings to the potential detriment of the stability
and soundness of the corporation.

At this point, one should ask: Will investors and
financial analysts *use* forecasts published by management? One cannot accurately predict, or forecast, if you will, the future action of investors and
financial analysts, but the following three cases
are presented as evidence that, in the past, neither

Wm. B. Carper, CPA, is
associate professor of
accounting, Memphis
State University. He
holds a Ph.D. in
business administration
from the University of
Alabama.

M. Frank Barton, Jr.,
CPA, is assistant
professor of
accounting, Memphis
State University. He
has a Ph.D. in business
administration from the
University of
Mississippi.

Haroldene F. Wunder is assistant professor of accounting, University of Pennsylvania. She has a Ph.D. in business administration from the University of South Carolina.

investors nor financial analysts have indicated they actually will use published forecast figures.

Case No. 1—The Fuqua Forecast

Fuqua Industries, Inc., is a diversified Atlanta-based corporation. In 1972, Fuqua issued a *preliminary* 1972 annual report which contained unaudited figures for 1972 and a *forecast* of its 1973 earnings. Fuqua was the first company to issue such a report.

Project earnings were broken down by product line. Fuqua's reason for this breakdown was:

"We thought our stock was undervalued, and we believed that if analysts could see where our earnings came from, they would also see that our stock is undervalued . . . We are a highly leveraged company, so we broke out our interest expense. This is a figure many analysts following Fuqua like to see."[2]

It is interesting to note the reaction of the investment community to Fuqua's forecast. Fuqua distributed 12,000 copies of the 1972 preliminary annual report containing the forecasts of operations and earnings per share for 1973 to analysts with requests for feedback. Only approximately 50 replies were received. In 1973, the response was again slight; the 1974 Fuqua annual report did *not* contain forecasts.

Case No. 2—Information Needs of Security Analysts

Because few attempts have been made in the past to determine the information needs of external financial statement users, Chandra undertook a study to directly ascertain the information requirements of professional security analysts. A questionnaire was distributed to 400 chartered financial analysts, randomly selected from the membership directory of the Institute of Chartered Financial Analysts. The questionnaire contained 58 items, only two of which concern us: earnings per share and budgetary predictions and forecasts. The respondents were asked to rate each information item on a five-point scale: Five points—very important; four points—important; three points—neither important nor unimportant; two points—unimportant; and one point—very unimportant.

One hundred eighty complete, useable replies were received. (It is significant that the majority of the respondents had more than ten years' experience as financial analysts.) Arithmetic means were calculated for each item, and each item was categorized as: (1) item of high value; (2) item of moderate value: (3) item of low value: (4) item of neutral value; and (5) unimportant item.

The study revealed that, on the basis of responses received, security analysts are very interested in *actual* earnings per share, but only moderately interested in the disclosure of projections and forecasts.[3]

Several explanations can be offered for investors' and analysts' apparent lack of strong interest in forecasts. Investors may not understand what the projected figures represent and may consequently ignore them. Investors and analysts may be skeptical of managements' representation of future earnings. Security analysts may hesitate to use forecast figures because of the lack of audit and reporting standards pertaining to forecasts. Security analysts often use the expected rate of return on incremental capital in analyzing two companies, rather than their respective predicted earnings per share, and finally, security analysts may prefer to develop their own forecasts, based on past earnings data and current economic conditions.

Case 3—CFAs on the Need for Forecasted Financial Data

A study conducted by two of the authors was designed to analyze the opinions of chartered financial analysts concerning earnings forecasts with a view toward determining the direction in which the accounting profession should move in improving its communication with equity investors.[4]

This survey contained six items relating to forecasting: two multiple choice questions; two viewpoint assessments written as equal-appearing-internal scales; one completion question; and one open-ended question for additional comments.

There are almost 3500 chartered financial ana-

Table 1
ATTITUDES ON FORECASTING

Respondent groups	% who feel misinterpretation:	
	Would take place	Would not take place
ICFA	47	31
FEI	57	21
AICPA	48	36

lysts listed in the *Directory of Members* of the Institute of Chartered Financial Analysts. Of that total, 1,065 are employed in brokerage and investment banking houses and, therefore, are in a direct advisory capacity to the investing public. Our initial sample consisted of 50% of this latter group selected systematically (every other directory entry). Of the 533 questionnaires mailed out, 190 replies were received, a response rate of 36%. This was considered to be an adequate response rate for our purpose.

We found that CFAs are not very interested in

the inclusion of earnings forecasts in financial reports. Table 2 contains a summary of their opinions. One hundred eighty-five CFAs responded to this survey item. Of that number, 53 agreed that earnings forecasts should be included. Forty-eight respondents were indifferent, 59 disagreed, and 25 strongly disagreed with the inclusion of earnings forecasts. The measures of central tendency bear out this lack of interest in forecasts in financial reports. The *highest* measure was a median of *zero*.

CFAs are of the opinion that earnings forecasts

Table 2
IT IS IMPORTANT THAT EARNINGS FORECASTS BE INCLUDED IN INTERIM AND ANNUAL REPORTS?

+2	+1	0	−1	−2
13	40	48	59	25

+2 — Strongly agree   Respondents = 185
+1 — Agree   Mean = −.23
  0 — Indifferent   Median = 0
−1 — Disagree   Mode = −1
−2 — Strongly disagree

if presented at all should be in the president's letter section of the financial report. In Table 3, dealing with the location of earnings forecasts, 147 of the 179 respondents (82.1%) indicated that preference.

There is no doubt in the minds of CFAs as to

Table 3
WHERE SHOULD THE EARNINGS FORECAST IN THE FINANCIAL STATEMENT BE LOCATED?

	Number	%
On the face	7	3.9
In a footnote	7	3.9
In the president's letter	147	82.1
Other	18	10.1
Total	179	100.0

whom should prepare earnings forecasts if they are to be included in financial statements. Of the 165 CFAs responding to this item as shown in Table 4, 147 (89.1%) indicated that earnings forecasts should be prepared by company management. There was a difference of opinion as to the need for independent auditors to evaluate and comment on the credibility of the methods used in preparing earnings forecasts. Eighty-five CFAs (51.5%) felt that such evaluation and comment was unnecessary while 62 CFAs (37.6%) indicated a preference for such evaluation and comment.

The CFAs apparently are not completely satis-

Table 4
WHO SHOULD PREPARE THE EARNINGS FORECAST?

	Number	%
Company management	85	51.5
Company management (credibility of method used evaluated and commented on by independent auditors)	62	37.6
Independent auditors	3	1.8
Other	15	9.1
Total	165	100.0

fied with their present sources of information concerning the future earning power of companies. CFAs were asked, in one survey item, "How would you expect a systematic method of earnings forecasting included in financial reports to compare with their present sources of information?" Their replies are presented in Table 5. Seventy-two respondents indicated that they preferred their present sources, and 49 indicated that such information would be useful. Fifty-six were indifferent to the concept. Again, the highest mathematical rating for this topic was a median of indifference. Apparently CFAs put more stock in their existing evaluation techniques than they do the earnings forecasts of managements—but not a whole lot more.

Finally, CFAs were asked to rank their present sources of information concerning earnings forecasts (Table 6). Participants ranked their sources of information from one (most preferred) to five (least preferred). It is apparent that the CFAs trust first, their own contacts in industry, then their own research, and only to a much lesser extent, industry statistics and the work of other analysts. This pattern seems to fit that established by prior data illustrated in the other tables. We conclude CFAs are not very interested in the inclusion of earnings forecasts in financial reports. But there is a clear mandate that if earnings forecasts

Published forecasts may lead to managed earnings.

Table 5
HOW WOULD A SYSTEMATIC METHOD OF EARNINGS FORECASTING INCLUDED IN INTERIM AND ANNUAL REPORTS COMPARE WITH YOUR PRESENT SOURCES OF INFORMATION?

+2	+1	0	−1	−2
7	42	56	61	11

+2 — Most useful   Respondents = 177
+1 — More useful   Mean = −.152
00 — Equally useful   Median = 0
−1 — Inferior   Mode = −1
−2 — Highly inferior

are included in interim reports, they should be included in the president's letter.

CFAs strongly agree that earnings forecasts, if prepared, should be made by management. It is less clear, however, as to whether such earnings forecasts should be evaluated and commented on by the independent auditors.

CFAs are not completely satisfied with their present sources of information concerning future earning power of companies. However, they appear to believe that a systematic method of earnings forecasting in financial reports would not be an improvement over their present sources of information.

Finally, CFAs believe that their bread and butter depends upon their ability to gather financial data from company contacts, own research, industry statistics, other analysts and other sources. They believe that there is no magic formula that

Will a time-series model yield an accurate prediction of future earnings?

technique. It is relevant to stress that subjectivity can only be reduced, not eliminated, because any forecasting technique which uses historical accounting data as input is inherently subjective because of the existence of alternatives for the treatment of depreciation, inventory costing, leases, and other variables.

Also, in situations where there is no significant statistical difference between management's forecast and the time-series forecast, more credence can be placed in management's projections. When there is a significant discrepancy between management's figures and the time-series projections, management will be placed in a position of having to offer substantiation for its forecast, i.e., changes in the economic environment in which it operates, the introduction of a new product, or the availability of new technology.

In addition, the time-series technique will offer

Table 6
WHAT ARE YOUR PRESENT SOURCES OF EARNINGS FORECASTING DATA?

	Rank	1	2	3	4	5
Company contacts		56	28	24	8	9
Own research		55	15	5	1	
Industry statistics		19	14	14	7	3
Other analysts		12	17	2	8	11
Historical financial data		8	12	8	5	4
Economic forecasts		7	7	10	3	
Competition		1	7	2	6	1
Computer simulation						2
Field trips			1			
Government agencies				2		
Industry & trade sources		1	7	17	3	5
Public relations of a promotional nature						1
Retired directors						1
Rumor						2
Wall Street sources		1	4	9	3	4

can be used in forecasting earnings. They believe that there are many imponderables that experience and judgment can process that escape the statistical analysis of those not a part of the financial analysts' profession.

This most recent study tends to further underscore what earlier studies have suggested. A systematic method of earnings forecasting by management and somehow attested to by the CPA *will not* improve significantly the validity and reliability of the CFA's investment decision.

A Look at the Future

We support the suggestion that companies issuing forecasts of operations and earnings should supplement their own management-derived forecasts with forecasts developed from a time-series extrapolation of past earnings data. What are the advantages of such dual presentation?

The subjectivity of managements' earnings forecasts would be tempered by an objective statistical

additional information for decision making. As Chandra suggests, security analysts currently often rely on forecasts developed from past earnings data.[5]

Most important, the time-series forecast would serve to limit the public accountant's legal liability if he is required, at some point in the future, to attest to the fairness of management's published forecasts.

Accuracy of Time-Series Forecasts

A relevant question at this point is: Will a time-series model yield an accurate prediction of future earnings? Lorek, McDonald and Patz undertook an empirical investigation in an attempt to test the hypothesis "that forecasts by informed management should be superior to models relying solely upon past earnings performance."[6]

The authors used the Box-Jenkins Methodology,[7] with a sample composed of 40 management forecasts obtained from the *Wall Street Journal*.

The four years from 1966 to 1970 were studied in order to have a period characterized by changing economic conditions. The original population of 201 management forecasts was dichotomized into relatively accurate (prediction error less than or equal to 10%) and relatively inaccurate (prediction error in excess of 10%). Random samples were taken from each of the two groups until four forecasts were taken from each group for each of the five years under consideration, yielding a final sample size of 40 management forecasts.

Quarterly earnings of the companies represented by the management forecasts described above provided the data bases for application of the Box-Jenkins model. The quarterly earnings data ended with the quarter prior to the year of the forecast. The result of the Box-Jenkins methodology was "40 firm-specific time series models," which were used to predict the annual earnings of the firm.[8]

The resulting model-predicted earnings were then compared with the management forecasts to determine which generated the smaller relative prediction error, computed as:

$$\frac{\text{Actual earnings—Predicted earnings}}{\text{Predicted earnings}}$$

Rather than describe the results of the study in detail, the study being available to the interested reader, only the conclusions relevant to this discussion are presented. In cases where management forecasts were reasonably accurate (relative prediction error $\leq 10\%$), their accuracy did not exceed that of the model generated forecasts. In instances where management forecasts were associated with a relative prediction error in excess of 10%, the Box-Jenkins forecasts were significantly more accurate.

Accordingly, the hypothesis that forecasts by informed management are far more accurate than those generated by time-series models which rely *solely* on past earnings performance was rejected, based on the data used in this application of the Box-Jenkins methodology.

In an attempt to determine the usefulness of management's earnings forecasts (in their current form of presentation) as they relate to the financial statement user's decision-making processes, this discussion has offered support for the contention that reliable management forecasts are potentially beneficial. In practice, many observers doubt their usefulness.

The Lorek, McDonald and Patz study showed that the model-derived forecasts were at least as accurate as management's forecasts for the companies and time period under consideration. A dual presentation would tend to decrease the subjectivity of management's own forecasts. The appropriate statistical method to be used in the time-series extrapolation of past earnings is a matter which requires further empirical investigation.

One concluding comment: The plain fact is security analysts and specifically CFAs do not place much stock in forecasted financial data in its current form. Hence, it seems clear that a new approach to forecasted financial data is needed. Application of some time-series model may just be the way to go. □

> CFAs do not place much stock in forecasted financial data.

[1] Richard J. Asebrook and D. R. Carmichael, "Reporting on Forecasts: A Survey of Attitudes," *Journal of Accountancy*, August 1973.
[2] John K. Shank and John B. Calfee, "Case of the Fuqua Forecast," *Harvard Business Review*, November-December, 1973.
[3] Gyan Chandra, "Information Needs of Security Analysts," *Journal of Accountancy*, December 1975.
[4] M. Frank Barton, Wm. Brent Carper, and Thomas S. O'Connor, "CFAs Speak Out on the Information Content of Interim Financial Statements," *The Ohio CPA*, Winter Quarter 1979.
[5] Chandra, *Op. Cit.*
[6] Kenneth S. Lorek, Charles L. McDonald, and Dennis H. Patz, "A Comparative Examination of Management Forecasts and Box-Jenkins Forecasts of Earnings," *The Accounting Review*, April 1976.
[7] See G.E.P. Box and G. M. Jenkins, *Time Series Analysis: Forecasting and Control*, Holden-Day Inc., San Francisco, Calif., 1970, for additional information on the methodology.
[8] Lorek, McDonald, and Patz, *Op. Cit.*

A Closer Look at Management Forecasts

Is there a sound basis for judging the forecasting ability of corporations?

By Eugene A. Imhoff, Jr.

Eugene A. Imhoff, Jr. is associate professor of accounting at the University of Michigan—Ann Arbor. He holds a Ph.D. degree from Michigan State University and is a member of the Ann Arbor Chapter, through which this article was submitted.

The SEC has taken positive steps to encourage the reporting of financial forecasts by publicly-traded companies. While they are not a requirement at this time, forecasts disclosing key assumptions and comparing actual results to previous forecasts are encouraged. It is clear that the Commission's position is to attempt to encourage management to provide forecasts to the public on a timely and uniform basis, allowing all interested parties equal access to such forward looking data. While not requiring forecasts, the SEC probably will use any forthcoming experience with financial forecasts as a basis for reviewing the effectiveness of its current policy.

Because of the controversy that resulted from the SEC guidelines, the Commission established a safe harbor for financial forecasts. The rules limit a company's liability in case a forecast made in good faith and prepared on a reasonable basis is not achieved. The final SEC rules also state that the burden of proof for misleading forecasts is on the plaintiff rather than the defendant. The safe harbor also covers forecasts concerning capital expenditures and financing, dividends, capital structure, and statements of managements plans and objectives for future operations and economic performance. These items, in addition to revenues,

income, and earnings per share, were granted safe harbor from the liability provisions of the federal securities laws for both the issuer and the third party reviewer. While the statement of any key underlying assumptions is encouraged, the statement of assumptions are not necessary to be granted safe harbor.

Perhaps the most demanding aspect of the final SEC rules is that which requires management to revise its forecasts to reflect new material facts, both favorable and unfavorable, which might cause the prior forecast to be misleading to users who might have relied on prior foward-looking data. Overall, the disclosure and safe harbor rules are as liberal as any which have been considered by the SEC. The current position seems to reflect the SEC's desire to encourage registrants to include forecasts as much as possible, short of requiring registrants to forecast.

In 1979 the AICPA developed a proposed guide, titled "Review of a Financial Forecast." The forecast must be prepared in accordance with the guide for a report on the forecast to be issued by a CPA. The guide includes most of the content of Management Advisory Services Guideline Series No. 3 regarding the preparation of a financial forecast and Statement of Position (SOP) No. 75-4 regarding the presentation and disclosure of financial forecasts. In addition, the guide discusses how

0025-1690/80/6111-2978/$01.00/0

to review the financial forecasts of management and the report forms to be issued in various circumstances. One of the major inconsistencies between the AICPA and the SEC concerned the amount of information included in the projection. The SEC, in setting its safe harbor rules, seemed reluctant to expand the data covered by the safe harbor as mentioned earlier.

On the other hand, the AICPA encouraged full financial statement forecasts, including balance sheet, income statement, and changes in financial position statement, and would consider anything less than the seven items in SOP 75-4 as inadequate disclosure which the CPA could not issue a report on. The seven items include such things as gross profit, provision for income taxes, disposal of a segment and extraordinary or unusual items, both primary and fully diluted earnings per share, and any significant anticipated changes in financial position which are not mentioned by the SEC's safe harbor rules. This seems to suggest that compliance with the AICPA exposes management to liability concerning data not covered by the safe harbor provisions.

It would be ideal if complete financial forecasts of management were available to evaluate in the context of existing SEC and proposed AICPA guidelines. Unfortunately, very little forecast data is available for public inspection. The one element which has been forecasted by companies with some frequency has been earnings per share. Let's look at some of the forecast experience as covered in several recent studies with a view of evaluating the implications of this issue in the future.

Management Forecast Accuracy

In order for forecasts to be useful to users they must reduce uncertainty about future earnings. More *accurate* management forecasts are, therefore, considered to be more useful to external financial statement users than less accurate forecasts. When the SEC first became involved in management forecasts, it considered the size of the forecast error as a key element of the forecast disclosure policy proposal. The early guidelines for forecasting (Release No. 5581) suggested that a $\pm$ 10% error in the forecast would be reasonable, with errors greater than 10% being considered material deviations from planned results. These error measures are relative measures. For purposes of this article, forecast error will be defined as:

$$\frac{\text{Actual Earnings} - \text{Expected Earnings}}{\text{Expected Earnings}}$$

unless otherwise stated. This permits all positive errors to be defined as underestimated earnings, and negative errors as overestimated earnings.

A number of research studies have examined actual management earnings forecasts (one element of forecast data) to determine their accuracy. Most forecast studies have been based on management earnings per share forecasts voluntarily published in *The Wall Street Journal,* where management will sometimes provide an annual earnings forecast in conjunction with a first quarter earnings report or dividend announcement.

Two such studies by Imhoff and McDonald measured the accuracy of management forecasts.[1] Both of these studies evaluated only point estimate forecasts, for example, $3.25 per share, which were taken from *The Wall Street Journal.* Open-ended estimates, such as "at least $3.00 per share," and range estimates such as "between $3.00 and $3.75 per share" were not used in these two studies. While some controversy exists as to the value of point estimates versus range estimates,[2] the measurement of forecast errors for point estimates can be made without assuming anything about the probability distribution around the estimate. On the other hand, for range estimates, in order to measure the forecast error it is necessary to assume that the earnings estimates within the stated range are distributed symmetrically, and that the midpoint is the expected overall value. There is no way to test the assumption that estimates within the range of, say, $3.00 to $3.75 are symmetrically distributed. As a result, measurement of forecast errors using range estimates are not capable of measuring the unexpected element of earnings. While some studies have used range estimates and some authors have argued that they contain more information, their use in measuring forecast error is questionable.

The management forecasts for both studies were taken from the January 1 to April 30 issues of *The Wall Street Journal* for the years 1966-1970 (McDonald) and 1971-1974 (Imhoff). The total of 318 forecasts, excluding several outliers with very large errors, are summarized in Table 1[3].

Two points should be made concerning this evidence on management forecast accuracy. First, most of the annual average forecast errors across all firms are less than $\pm$ 10%, with some tendency toward overestimated earnings. These data seem to suggest that the 10% guidelines originally proposed by the SEC might be a realistic hurdle. However, it should also be pointed out that these annual average forecast errors are biased downward when computed by using the *sign* (+ or −) of the forecast error. A +25% error and a −25% error result in a zero average error. The bias of this procedure becomes clearer when you compute the average *absolute* error for comparison. In the above case, a +25% and a −25% error would yield an average *absolute* error of 25%. While the average absolute errors were not provided by the first study, the Imhoff study reported

Forecast pressures could cause some companies to manipulate earnings, thereby distorting earnings in the short-run.

both error measures for a subset of 95 firms as shown in Table 2[4].

In the case of absolute errors, the 10% limit seems more unreasonable. Based on the Table 2 data, companies issuing forecasts are in error by more than 10% on the average. In evaluating an individual forecast, it seems clear that the sign of the error might be important, with overestimates suggesting bad news and underestimates suggesting good news since the time the forecast was issued. However, in aggregating forecasts it is not clear that one measure is superior to the other, only that they are different.

Table 1
MANAGEMENT FORECAST ERRORS

Year of forecast	Number of forecasts	Average forecast error	Std. deviation of errors
1966	43	.7%	14.00%
1967	30	-9.4%	18.50%
1968	40	-8.8%	19.30%
1969	42	-10.2%	14.60%
1970	34	-14.8%	41.50%
McDonald subtotal	189	-10.2%	22.2 %
1971	28	-5.04%	16.96%
1972	28	+1.63%	30.37%
1973	38	+2.25%	20.30%
1974	35	-3.66%	31.73%
Imhoff subtotal	129	-1.07%	25.53%

There is a key point which needs to be made at this stage. The evidence on average forecast errors would seem to be useful to policy makers in addressing the question: "Can management forecast accurately?" However, the analysis in Table 2 demonstrated that the way in which guidelines are stated may have a significant impact on the number of firms which can meet a forecast error standard.

A second point to be made regarding forecast accuracy is that, even with real error measures (+ and −) as the basis for a guideline, the average values are still misleading. For example, an average overall forecast error of −1% combined with a standard deviation of 25% (as is the case for 1971-1974) could result in the majority of firms exceeding a ± 10% error limit. Figure 1 shows the distribution of errors based on the data above assuming the errors approximate a normal distribution. The data from the study by Imhoff did approximate a normal distribution, with skewness and kurtosis being very small. The kurtosis from the distribution of forecast errors suggests a flatter, lower peaked distribution, with more observations than normal in the tails of the distribution. Less than 40% of the forecasts fall within ± 10%. As a result, more than one half of the companies which have voluntarily issued earnings projections would have exceeded the ± 10% limit previously suggested as being reasonable by the

SEC. It would seem, based on the existing evidence from firms which have voluntarily issued earnings forecasts, that management forecasts are frequently in error by 10% or more, and that a 10% materiality criterion might be unreasonable. However, there is no way of knowing whether earnings errors are representative of other forecast errors.

The new SEC rules are intended to encourage companies to forecast financial information. It will be interesting to see if the number of firms forecasting or the amount of financial data being forecasted actually increase from past levels of disclosure. It should be noted that the group of companies which have willingly provided forecasts of certain data in the past might not be representative of all companies in terms of their ability to forecast or the usefulness of the forecasted information. Also, the group of firms which forecast as a result of the recent SEC rule changes will not necessarily be representative of all companies. If the SEC is planning to use its experience with voluntary forecasts produced under its current policy as a basis for evaluating a mandatory forecast policy, it should do so with caution. It might be argued that companies which have and will provide forecast information on a voluntary basis might be companies whose managers are more confident of their ability to forecast than their counterparts in nonforecasting companies.

Controversial Issues and Analysis

It is difficult to consider one isolated attribute of forecasting, such as errors, as a basis for evaluating their usefulness to owners and investors. It is entirely possible that an eight-month forecast within 10% of actual annual earnings for Company X would be useful to one investor but not another because of their different materiality functions. Also, a 10% forecast error for a firm in the steel industry may be much more tolerable than a 10% forecast error for a firm in the cosmetics industry because of the inherently different risk levels associated with those industries. Further, for those investors and creditors with a preference for risk aversion, a 10% underestimated earnings forecast may be more tolerable than, say, a 5% overestimated earnings figure. And finally, it is most likely that an annual earnings forecast within 10% of actual, issued 10 months in advance of year-end would be more useful than the same forecast issued eight months in advance of year-end.

The forecasts themselves and the various aspects of their formulation and issuance are complex enough to present a number of potential problems which have not yet been completely resolved. Additional aspects which affect the utility of earnings forecasts to users of financial information need to be considered by the SEC in order to effectively evaluate existing forecast policy and future policy developments. At least three additional points concerning the evaluation of current forecast policy and future proposals should be considered: earnings pressure, independent review of earnings forecasts, and representativeness problem.

EARNINGS PRESSURE

The evidence concerning forecast accuracy discussed above suggests that many companies would feel some pressure in achieving an earnings figure within a 10% range of their forecast. In theory, the conventional accrual accounting model of earnings should tell users something about a company's long-run future cash generating ability as well as its past performance, which should, in turn, help creditors and investors in evaluating the firm as an investment. To the extent that required forecasts may put pressure on management to meet a target earnings figure by way of artificial (noneconomic-based) accounting earnings adjustments, the forecast requirement could reduce the relationship between accounting earnings and future cash flows, thereby reducing the utility of the forecasts. An example of such a noneconomic based accounting change would be a change from accelerated to straight-line depreciation.

Alternatively, to the extent that management might make real economic adjustments in the company (for example, cut back on research or maintenance projects) to meet its current earnings target, the long-range cash generating ability of the company could be adversely affected. If the existing forecast disclosure policy results in pressure to achieve targeted earnings numbers, it is likely to have a negative effect on the usefulness of accounting earnings in the valuation of the company. This, in turn, would undermine the utility of the earnings forecasts themselves because it would reduce the ability of the forecast of earnings *and* actual earnings to predict the long-run cash generating ability of the firm. In short, the manipulation of earnings, through either economic or noneconomic-based actions by management, for the purpose of meeting an earnings forecast will tend to distort earnings in the short-run and will tend to reduce the ability of earnings to predict the long-run cash-generating ability of the firm. While forecasts are not required at this time, it is expected, according to current policy, that once a company starts to forecast it will continue to do so in future years unless some reasonable basis for discontinuing the practice of providing forecast data is given.

Another type of earnings pressure which could result from current forecast policy might be pressure from competing companies which have voluntarily provided forecasts. The accuracy of forecasts from an organization's competitors might

place undue emphasis on forecast activity and the resulting forecast accuracy, bringing about the same sort of undesirable earnings adjustments mentioned above. This could be a problem even within a group of companies in the same industry, which might have major financial differences that would reduce their ability to forecast with comparable accuracy. This systematic market riskiness of companies has been found to be substantially dif-

Table 2
REAL AND ABSOLUTE FORECAST ERRORS

Year	Number of firms	Average real forecast error	Average absolute forecast error
1971	21	−6.49%	12.54%
1972	20	+3.07%	16.36%
1973	27	+5.91%	12.61%
1974	27	+.94%	22.15%
Totals	95	+1.16	16.10%

ferent within given and well-defined industries. Even an industry like public utilities, which many view as a homogeneous group of companies, has been found to be made up of companies with substantially different levels of risk, return, leverage, and so on.

For example, debt to equity ratios and capital (versus labor) intensity may vary substantially among firms in the same industry. Higher ratios of debt to equity should result in more volatile

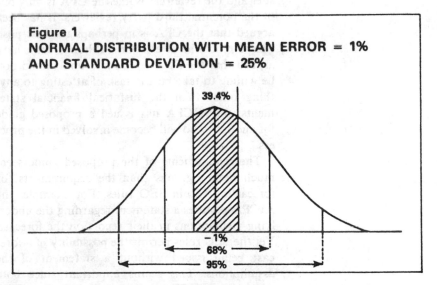

Figure 1
NORMAL DISTRIBUTION WITH MEAN ERROR = 1% AND STANDARD DEVIATION = 25%

earnings per share figures than low debt to equity ratios. This would make forecasting more difficult for firms with high debt to equity ratios because of the greater sensitivity of their earnings to fluctuations in revenues. The same line of reasoning will show that capital-intensive companies, with a higher percentage of fixed charges, should find forecasting more difficult than their less mechanized (more labor intensive) competition, all else being equal.

While companies in a given industry might feel

pressure to match the forecast activity and accuracy of their competitors, it is entirely possible that the real economic differences among companies within an industry would make comparable accuracy difficult to achieve. Such a reaction could, again, result in pressure to adjust earnings figures in order to achieve short-range earnings targets, resulting in potential dysfunctional long-range effects on earnings.

To the extent that current forecast policy creates pressure on management to achieve target earnings figures, the relationship between accounting earnings, cash flow, and the valuation of the company might be impaired. Such an outcome, in turn, would reduce the utility of the forecast itself.

The SEC should be urged to proceed with caution when reviewing its forecast policy.

INDEPENDENT REVIEW OF EARNING FORECASTS

The current SEC policy does not require a third party review of management's forecast data but does encourage such a review. Some of the comments received by the SEC suggested that two problems could result from such a review. First, a review by a third party might imply greater credibility to the forecast information than outsider users should reasonably expect. Also, it was pointed out that shopping for favorable reviews would be possible under the suggested guidelines. The SEC has not really addressed these concerns by issuance of a safe harbor which includes both the issuer and the reviewer. While the CPA is only one of the potential third party reviewers, it has been argued that the CPA is in perhaps the best position to render an attestation. Although some have argued that the CPA would not, and should not, be willing to take on the task of attesting to anything other than the historical financial statements, the AICPA has issued a proposed guide for auditors who will become involved in the process.

The requirements of the proposed guide seem much more rigorous than the requirements for forecasting within SEC rules. For example, the AICPA requires a statement regarding the underlying assumptions in their report on the forecast. Yet the SEC rules permit the possibility of a forecast being issued without a statement of the assumptions. This seems important since both managers and CPAs agree that the value of the forecast data usually turns on the accuracy or reasonableness of the underlying assumptions. At the same time, it would seem to be extremely difficult for either management or the third party reviewer to assess the accuracy of these assumptions. There are two key problems with this process which should be addressed. First, everyone to date seems to use the actual outcome of the projected data as the benchmark for evaluating the reasonableness of the forecast data and the underlying assump-

tions. However, it may not be accurate to call such differences errors. In theory, a forecast error would be the difference between the stated earnings forecast and the true or correct forecast that should have been issued based on all of the information available at the date of the forecast. It is only reasonable to assume that new information regarding things related to earnings occurring after the date of the forecast would have the potential to revise the forecast. Therefore, in order to use the actual year-end earnings figure as a basis for evaluating forecasts, it would seem necessary to determine how the new information surfacing between the date of forecast and year-end should have affected the forecast. This would be as difficult as determining what the true forecast should have been at the date of the stated forecast. Yet this is essentially what would be required if management were asked to identify, and auditors to verify, incorrect forecast assumptions in order to explain material forecast errors.

A second point is that, given the original forecast assumptions and the benefit of hindsight, the differences in assumed and actual events can be identified. However, the differences are not self-explanatory, nor are they independent events that affect one element of the forecast alone. For example, if the forecast assumes inflation will be 8% and that GNP will rise 12%, and when inflation actually is found to be 10% and GNP increased 11%, what is the impact of these differences on any given forecast? If no other assumptions were incorrect, does that necessarily mean that these two items automatically account for all the differences between forecast and actual? What if items, such as stockouts or machine breakdowns, not explicitly considered in the forecast assumptions had a material impact on the results? Can the auditor identify and review all possible variables both specified in the forecast assumptions and unspecified that might account for forecast errors?

To explain meaningfully the exact cause of differences can be a complex undertaking. It is not clear how such a complex task can be made by an independent third party reviewer who typically has less information and knowledge of the business than the issuer of the forecast. Existing micro-cconomic thought is not capable of explaining the impact of changes in the economy on the company in a static environment. In the dynamic environment of the company, it is doubtful that the auditor or other third party reviewer will be able to attest objectively to management's explanations of why material forecast errors occurred.

REPRESENTATIVENESS PROBLEM

From the available evidence concerning voluntarily-issued management earnings forecasts, the following two conclusions may be drawn: (1) management forecast errors tend to average somewhere below ± 10%, but with well over half of the forecast errors in excess of ± 10%; (2) management forecasts are not significantly better than analysts' forecasts. It is entirely possible, however, that the evidence from those companies which have voluntarily provided forecasts is not a sound basis for evaluating management earnings forecasts. The forecast companies which voluntarily issued earnings projections may not be representative of non-forecast companies. If the non-forecast companies are somehow different, then the evidence that is available regarding forecast accuracy along with the new evidence that becomes available under recent policy changes will probably not be useful for evaluating either current policy or proposed future policy, especially proposals to mandate forecasting.

There are many reasons why one might suspect forecast companies to be different from their non-forecast counterparts. The fact that a company makes an overt statement regarding expected earnings is evidence that it wants that information to be used somehow by investors, which could easily suggest the issuance of knowingly biased forecasts. For example if a utility were about to apply to some regulatory body for permission to increase its rates, it might want to project a bleak earnings outlook. In the study by Imhoff, this seemed to be the case. Only forecasts issued by utilities called for a decline in earnings. Alternatively, if a company wanted to fend off an expected takeover bid, or if it wanted to make a public offering of a new issue, it might want to be overly positive in its earnings forecast in hopes of increasing the market price of its securities. There could be any number of reasons why a firm might want to issue biased projections on a one time basis in hopes of achieving some short-term reactions from users.

The possibility that these forecast companies may not have been forecasting in earnest places voluntarily-issued forecast evidence in a questionable position. One might ask how the previously cited result, showing management and analysts to be near equals at predicting, could have occurred if the management forecast errors were somehow planned. One simple explanation could be that the two forecasts for any given company were not made independently. In other words, management may have influenced, or been influenced by, analysts in the process of issuing a forecast. This suggests the possibility that both analyst and management forecasts for forecast companies might be of limited utility as a basis for formulating a forecast policy.

A recent study by Imhoff attempted to determine the relationship between representative forecast companies and their non-forecast counterparts. The study compared certain key attributes of forecast companies with non-forecast companies, and reported several significant differences between the two groups. Specifically, the research reported that forecast companies had more stable accounting earnings over time, and more volatile market prices for their stock. These results suggest that forecast companies might be able to forecast accounting earnings more accurately than non-forecast companies, assuming both groups are forecasting in earnest, but that the market will not necessarily view forecast companies as being less risky because of their more stable earnings numbers.

The available evidence suggests that forecast companies are not representative of non-forecast companies in a number of important respects, and should probably not be used as a basis for evaluating current or proposed forecast policy. Based on the above interpretation, it might be expected that non-forecast companies would produce larger forecast errors than those observed in the forecast companies. However, without actually observing forecast errors on non-forecast companies, by definition an impossibility, there is no way to know what the actual outcome would be. A SEC proposal does call for mandatory forecasts for electric and gas utility companies.[3] However this group of companies is also not representative because they tend to be more stable, predictable, and highly regulated entities. As a result, the SEC's experience with these companies also will tend to be biased and not useful to the policy evaluation and formulation process.

Forecast Policy—Where Will It Go from Here

Management forecasts have been a topic of interest to investors, analysts, and auditors for some time. Current developments by both the SEC and AICPA should provide an important new phase to the forecasting area. It will be interesting to observe how effective the recent developments are at stimulating voluntary forecast activity and what impact these results will have on policy evaluation and formulation.

Several important issues remain somewhat controversial at this stage of forecast policy development. For one, the pressure to achieve target earnings figures could seriously undermine the relationship between accounting earnings, past performance of the company, cash flows and the valuation of the company. Secondly, it may be very difficult for the accounting profession and others involved in third party review to develop procedures which will enable an auditor to evaluate objectively the assumptions of management in developing the forecast, and the probable impact of deviations from those assumptions. Finally, the little evidence which is available on management forecast accuracy at this time is probably not a sound

Most of the annual average forecast errors across all the firms are less than ± 10%.

SECTION VII

Accounting Information
for Management

External users are just one source for the product of the accounting process. An equally important set of users is management of the firm. These individuals, charged with daily operating responsibility for the organization, can benefit from varying types of information included in the accounting system.

Over the years, accountants have responded to management needs in a variety of ways. The profession of managerial accounting has developed in direct response to this situation. However, it is difficult to isolate a top manager from the full flow of information within the firm. Consequently, accountants can view the propriety and opportunity of developing specific reports for management.

Included in such considerations is a full range of issues ranging from the management reporting and budgetary process through considerations of the behavioral aspects of accounting and internal control issues. The opportunity for the accountant to broaden his or her scope and view the totality of the management process is clearly present when one deals in the area of accounting information for management.

This section is divided into six parts which range from the basic to the behavioral, from internal planning to internal control, and from direct costing to managerial responsibility. Many issues are not new; the perspectives are and the challenges confront the future.

Often, traditional textbooks give the impression that managerial needs are specified to the accountant and the practitioner need only respond to these requests. However, this is not the case. The accountant must understand that as an information specialist, numerous opportunities are available for an initiative to be taken in response to available information and situations. Many of the readings in this section present suggestions from accountants and others involved with the profession about internal reporting.

Internal or managerial reporting is a significant need and also gives the accountant the most direct form of feedback as to the success of his or her endeavors. Managerial practice faces a full range of informational needs and normally has ready access to the accounting staff. These needs and this access present a challenge to and opportunity for the profession.

Managerial Accounting: A Frame of Reference

By WILLIS J. DOMBROVSKE

IN OUR INCREASINGLY complex and competitive business environment, management has an ever mounting need for pertinent information. As our business environment has grown, the rising manager has found it increasingly difficult to accumulate the necessary personal experience so needed to manage effectively. No longer can he expect to gather all of his own first-hand knowledge of situations within his firm or even to rely upon his intuition to evaluate the complex factors which affect the great majority of our business decisions.

First hand inspection of the organization is most desirable for every level of management and imperative for the operating executive. Every manager should strive to accomplish as much of it as is humanly possible. It is as Ford Bell expressed in his excellent series of memos to a rising executive, "feeling the pulse of the organization."[1] The manager's first-hand observations coupled with the factual and analytical data provided by others, serve him as a dual resource in his planning and decision making function.

[1] Ford Bell, *You're in Charge,* Doubleday & Company, Inc., New York, 1964, p. 4.

Modern management is placing more and more reliance on information which is developed by others, both within and without the company. To be useful to the manager, this data must be assembled quickly and transmitted to him by means of a highly efficient information system.

This information flow is imperative for the successful manager in the performance of the basic tasks in the management cycle:

1. The establishment of his firm's objectives.
2. Formulation of plans to reach the desired objectives.
3. The implementation of these plans.
4. The appraisal of the performance of the organization in carrying out these plans.
5. The feeding back of revised (corrective) action and additional plans.

The information needed to accomplish this method of managing has its own requirements. First, it must contain the "right" data—necessary for effective performance of each function of the management process at all of its various levels. Second, it must be completely accurate and pertinent to the action at hand. Third, the data must be presented in a form that is clearly understandable to the

WILLIS J. DOMBROVSKE, Minneapolis *Chapter 1960,* *is Treasurer and Controller of Transistor Electronics Corporation, Minneapolis, Minn. He was formerly Accounting Supervisor of Armco Steel Corporation. Mr. Dombrovske holds a B.A. degree from St. John's University, Collegville, Minn., and an M.B.A. degree from the University of Minnesota. He was awarded two NAA Certificates of Merit, one in 1963-64 and the other, for this article, in the 1964-65 Chapter Competition year.*

person responsible for acting on it. Fourth, the information must be provided to the persons whose actions can be improved by it. Fifth, it must be received in time to influence the action which it is supposed to assist.

These considerations that lead to what Lawrence Appley describes as the "Management Factor."[2] This factor is the "something" a manager does to produce results different from those to be expected if events are left to follow their own course.

When a manager "does something about it" a planned change is in the offing. Nor does the manager stop here. Projecting past results into the future does not in itself ensure their attainment. The manager, referred to here as the managerial accountant, must possess a sensitivity to his own power to influence people and events. He must follow a process such as the following:

1. Identity of the *need* for change.
2. Develop an idea, and alternatives, that will *fill the need.*
3. *Transmit* the need and idea to the minds of others.
4. Determine the best *program* to activate the idea.
5. *Test* the economics of his program.
6. Aid in the *selection* of the individual or group qualified to carry out this idea.
7. *Follow* the program to conclusion with instruction and corrective action.
8. *Report* on the results.

The connotation for the accountant becomes increasingly apparent. The accountant today bears the tremendous responsibility of gathering data, placing them in meaningful format, interpreting them and quickly transmitting the information to the appropriate management level.

Basic Objectives of the Accounting System

In the consideration of his changing role in the management function of a company the accountant will do well to seriously concern himself with the basic objectives of his accounting system. The classification which follows will serve to focus one's attention on the various objectives of the accounting system. It will likewise aid in distinguishing among decisions as to what plans the business should adopt, the measurement of detailed performance against these plans, and the overall financial results of the performance.[3]

Custodial accounting—the financial accounting for the assets entrusted to the company. The basic concern here is with the preparation of the reports for groups or individuals outside of the management group: stockholders, creditors, the regulatory commissions, or the government.

Performance accounting — the quantitative matching of performance against some plan by organizational responsibility. It includes all those accounting procedures and reports which exist in order to evaluate organizational performance. Likewise, it includes the functions referred to as responsibility accounting, i.e. the collection of costs by organizational responsibility. It also deals, however, with quantitative data other than costs. It may include such items as product line revenue, physical workload statistics, and internal net income reports. It implies the use of standards and budgets. The distinguishing characteristic here is the measurement of *actual* performance against *planned* performance by responsibility.

2 Lawrence P. Appley, *The Management Evolution*, American Management Association, New York, 1963, p. 36.

3 Robert Beyer, *Profitability Accounting for Planning and Control*, The Ronald Press Company, New York, 1963, p. 17.

AUGUST 1965

Decision accounting—the quantitative evaluation of alternative courses of action. This includes all the disciplined techniques for providing quantitative information in the form which can best assist a *specific* management decision at the time when the decision must be made. This area includes such things as profit planning, product pricing, make-or-buy decisions, inventory policies and the choice of alternative production methods. This is the area of accounting on which business has historically depended for special analyses and memorandum reports.

We shall refer to performance and decision accounting under the classification of *managerial accounting* and to custodial accounting as *financial accounting*. These classifications are not unrelated. The accounting structure which is established to carry out the custodial objectives will handle most of the data used in the decision-making process as well as measuring performance. The raw data on operations (cost and revenue) is recast to evaluate performance. Variance from objectives or budgets is one such example. This data is in turn rearranged to provide for decisional accounting requirements. An analysis of product profitability would involve this type of special data arrangement.

The development of accounting structures toward this objective of providing a firm's management with the highest order of quantitative information is a further advancement in the art of accounting. The accountant who can anticipate the reporting and interpreting structure tailored to his firm's need becomes a functioning participant in management rather than a producer of statistics. Further, he takes the valuable data of custodial accounting a step beyond the formal financial accounting area into the future. This step moves him from recording to forecasting. Within the realm of financial accounting the future cannot be quantified. On the positive side of this comment is the fact that the value of financial reporting is increased to those parties outside of the firm. Moreover, the precision with which financial accounting is executed provides management with the sound basis that it must have for progress.

The Necessity for Managerial Accounting

Managerial accounting is the expansion of the accounting structure to meet the needs of management at all levels. As one progresses through these levels of management, the use of data goes further and further into the future. Consider, for example, the needs of a departmental manager, a division manager, a general manager, the president and the board of directors. The objectives may move from the short term of one week for the department manager to the long term of a five-year projection for the directors.

The managerial accountant must develop the ability to design his accounting structure so that it will produce tailored information for these levels of managerial need. The structure must provide for data that will become the basis for decision making at each level. As the level of managerial responsibility rises, economics enters with increasing impact on the data presented by the managerial accountant; this is an important consideration for him to recognize and respect. He is now well beyond the facts of purely financial accounting and into the area of projection. This is the area where the corporate manager finds himself and one in which he needs the soundest counseling he can obtain. The management accountant, with his access to the final resting place of the firm's operations expressed in monetary terms, is the logical choice to provide this counseling.

He must have at his disposal an accounting structure which is capable of providing data to meet these needs. The structure, if it is to assist, must be conceived with its function clearly defined by the managerial accountant.

The structure of this accounting system will consist of two clearly distinguishable characteristics:

1. The system must have a sound basis in accounting precision providing for reporting on a consistent basis. Supporting evidence for forecasting and projections will be well documented.
2. The management accountant designing the structure must be well versed in the objectives of the system. The outstanding trait here must be deep understanding of business generally and of his firm's business specifically. An analytical mind working from a solid foundation of accounting is necessary to develop a structure of managerial accounting.

The Frame of Reference

The managerial accountant must develop a frame of reference quite in contrast to that used by the financial accountant. Consider the following data characteristics to witness what is required by managerial accounting and what is provided by financial accounting.

Description. Financial accounting is primarily concerned with the dollar consequence of operations. However, the managerial accountant is quick to recognize that not all economic events are readily convertible into the dollar terms. Consider the changes in economic values and equities. Appreciation in value of property for example may have great significance where management is contemplating a sale. Lacking some required qualifications or conversion, these data do not become processed in financial records. This distinction may be recognized profitably in

classifying decisional premises as segregated from those considerations that are fixed in business events reflecting the dollar consequences of those events.

The consideration of time. The financial accountant is concerned with past happenings; the reporting of where the business has been and is in time. The managerial accountant has a view of the future. Historical events are useful only in retrospect. The future however is the object of managerial effort. Business decisions are forward looking; they are made to influence the future. It is the future not the past that challenges a forward looking management team. An accounting for the future demands a break-away from historical (financial) accounting characteristics—an adaptation of many available considerations to the *specific* requirements of each issue encountered. Managerial accounting here requires skill in recognizing appropriate data to apply and facility in manipulating the information to produce the needed conclusion.

The concept of realization. Financial accounting has its focus on actual events. Managerial accounting requires focus on potential, on opportunities. Where resources are in scarce supply their commitment to one course of action instead of others precludes the advantages that could have accrued from some other choice. These lost benefits are just as real and significant a cost as actual expenditures. The managerial accountant in this instance will take the position that it may be just as important and possibly more so to know what the organization is not doing as compared to what it is actually doing. The significance here is one of distinction—between those events rooted in accomplished fact and those which are, or were, mere possibility.

The quantitative unit. Monetary values are provided by financial accounting, whereas statistical data is the requirement from managerial accounting in this category. The latter is not as restricted to the double-entry system as financial accounting and hence relies on statistical evidence very frequently. Forecasting makes free use of statistics, and while monetary units may result, there is no dominance of dollar information found in financial accounting.

Rigidity of format. The operating statements and supporting schedules of financial accounting all present great masses of data in an aggregate format. The proper choice of the titles contained in the ledger, as well as the chart of accounts, all commit one to a rigid format. These items may or may not be homogeneous. Managerial accounting often concentrates on details. A specific problem is the focal point. The data used in these circumstances is pertinent to the problem with other elements outside of the parameters of consideration. These elements may provide reference points for evaluation, but the emphasis is on specific data related directly to the issue under study.

The concept of reality. Those events in a business which have not yet reached the stage of completion and which will not permit reasonable identification of their consequences do not normally become a part of the financial accounting statements. Financial accounting is objective in nature while managerial accounting is subjective. Managerial decisions rely heavily upon subjective evidence. The matter of judgment as opposed to measurement is a characteristic of management.

Conclusion

The intent of this paper has been to demonstrate the relationship of financial and managerial accounting to the realm of decisional premises used by management. It has sought to point out the differences between the areas and the consequent limitations of each of them.

It is not intended or suggested that attempts be made in including data regarding future events within the framework of traditional financial accounting. A loss of objectivity would certainly result. The demonstrable accuracy so highly sought would likewise suffer. The usefulness of managerial accounting is in recognizing the needs of management beyond the formal statements.

The employment of accounting skills and accuracy by participating in the decision making and planning processes is the role of the managerial accountant. The shaping of the future, of planning for change—these are the marks of the managerial accountant. His final products are analysis, projection and conclusion. His tools are the observed data, statistical measurement, mathematical treatment, non-numerical evaluation and deduction. He combines these factors with a personality that is forward seeking for both himself and his company. His confidence will be well fortified by a deep understanding of his chosen field of endeavor, that of accountancy, and by a firm grasp of total management responsibility.

To perceive and meet this challenge requires one's concentration and fortitude over the span of a career. Constant alertness to self-improvement and advanced learning must be maintained. Never before in our economy has opportunity for the accountant been more widely demonstrated than at the present. Our educational institutions offer vastly improved formal preparation over that available to our predecessors. With a challenge so apparent, with the means to achieve it so much within grasp, we submit accounting will take on an even greater stature in the conduct of business.

September 1962 *NAA* BULLETIN

Award Paper
NAA Research Essay Contest

Choosing Accounting Practices for Reporting to Management*

By CHARLES T. HORNGREN

I. OBJECTIVES OF MANAGEMENT ACCOUNTING

Management Accounting—Its Distinctive Purposes

THE ACCOUNTING SYSTEM is the major formal information system in almost every organization. An effective accounting system provides information for three broad purposes: (1) external reporting to stockholders, government, and other outside parties, (2) internal reporting to managers for planning and controlling current operations, and (3) internal reporting to managers for making special decisions and formulating long-range plans.

Management (internal parties) and external parties share an interest in all three important purposes, but the

CHARLES T. HORNGREN, *Chicago Chapter, 1960, C.P.A., is Associate Professor of Accounting at the Graduate School of Business of the University of Chicago. Author of a number of articles which have appeared in accounting periodicals, Mr. Horngren is likewise author of "Cost Accounting: A Managerial Emphasis" published by Prentice-Hall earlier this year and, with J. A. Leer, of "CPA Problems and Approaches to Solutions," which the same publisher issued in 1959. A graduate of Marquette University, Mr. Horngren received an M.B.A. degree from Harvard Graduate School of Business and a Ph.D. from the University of Chicago.*

emphasis of financial accounting and management accounting differs. Financial accounting has been mainly concerned with the first purpose and has traditionally been oriented toward the historical, stewardship aspects of external reporting. The distinguishing feature of management accounting is its emphasis on the second and third purposes.

The job of serving both internal and external demands can be an imposing one. Conventional accounting systems have tended to grow primarily in response to external forces. Management accounting, on the other hand, attempts to implement a more balanced, multi-goaled perspective. The widespread problem that management accountants must face has been aptly described as follows:

"Very few people in business have had the opportunity to reflect on the way in which the accounting model developed, particularly on how an instrument well adapted to detect fraud and measure tax liability has gradually been used as a general information source. Having become accustomed to information presented in this form, business people have adapted their concepts and patterns of thought and communication to it rather than adapting the information to the job or

*I am indebted to the members of the Workshop in Accounting Research, Institute of Professional Accountancy, Graduate School of Business, University of Chicago—especially Professors Sidney Davidson, David Green, Jr., Richard Lindhe, and George H. Sorter—for constructive criticism.

person. When one suggests the reverse process, as now seems not only logical but well within economic limits, he must expect a real reluctance to abandon a pattern of behavior that has a long history of working apparently quite well."[1]

A management accounting planning and control system should be designed to spur and help executives in searching for and selecting short-run and long-run goals, formulating plans for attaining those goals, implementing plans, appraising performance and pin-pointing deviations from plans, investigating reasons for deviations, re-selecting goals, etc. Management accounting is concerned with accumulating, classifying, and interpreting costs and other information that induce and aid individual executives in fulfilling organizational objectives as revealed explicitly or implicitly by top management.

Types of Information Supplied by Management Accounting

What information should the management accountant supply? The types of information needed have been neatly described by Simon et. al. as a result of their study of seven large companies with geographically dispersed operations. The approach of the Simon research team would probably be fruitful in any company:

"By observation of the actual decision-making process, specific types of data needs were identified at particular organizational levels — the vice presidential level, the level of the factory manager, and the level of the factory head, for example—each involving quite distinct problems of communication for the accounting department."[2]

The research team found that three types of information, each serving a different purpose, often at various management levels, raise and help answer three basic questions:

1. Score-card questions: "Am I doing well or badly?"
2. Attention-directing questions: "What problems should I look into?"
3. Problem-solving questions: "Of the several ways of doing the job, which is the best?"

Score-card and attention-directing uses of data are closely related. The same data may serve a score-card function for a foreman and an attention-directing function for his superior. For example, many accounting systems provide performance reports through which actual results are compared to predetermined budgets or standards. Such a performance report often helps answer score-card questions and attention-directing questions simultaneously.

Furthermore, the "actual results" collected can help fulfill not only control purposes but also the traditional needs of financial accounting. The answering of score-card questions, which mainly involves collection, classification, and reporting, is the task that has predominated in the day-to-day effort of the accounting function.

Problem-solving data may be used to help in special nonrecurring decisions and long-range planning. Examples include make-or-buy, equipment replacement, adding or dropping products, etc. These decisions often require expert advice from specialists such as industrial engineers, budgetary accountants, statisticians, and others.

Management Accounting and the Overall Information System

These three uses of data may be related to the broad purposes of the accounting system. The business information system of the future should be a single, multi-purpose system

[1] William R. Fair, "The Next Step in Management Controls," in Donald G. Malcom and Alan J. Rowe (ed.), *Management Control Systems* (New York: John Wiley & Sons, Inc., 1960), pp. 229-230.

[2] H. A. Simon, *Administrative Behavior* (2nd ed.; New York: The Macmillan Company, 1957), p. 20. For the complete study see H. A. Simon, H. Guetzkow, G. Kozmetsky, and G. Tyndall, *Centralization vs. Decentralization in Organizing the Controller's Department* (New York: Controllership Foundation, Inc. 1954). This perceptive study is much broader than its title implies.

with a highly-selective reporting scheme. It will be tightly integrated and will serve three main purposes: (1) routine reporting on financial results, oriented primarily for external parties (score-keeping); (2) routine reporting to management, primarily for planning and controlling current operations (score-keeping and attention-directing); and (3) special reporting to management, primarily for long-range planning and nonrecurring decisions (problem-solving). Although such a system can probably be designed in a self-contained, integrated manner to serve routine purposes simultaneously, its special decision function will always entail much data that will not lie within the system.

Uses of Data and Organization of the Accountant's Work

The Simon study also emphasized that ideally the management accountant's staff should have its three distinct functions manned by full-time accountants: (1) score-keepers, who compile routine data and keep the information system running smoothly; (2) attention-directors, who attempt to understand operating management's viewpoint most fully and who spotlight, interpret, and explain those operating areas that are most in need of attention; and (3) problem-solvers, who search for alternatives, study the probable consequences, and help management follow an objective approach to special decisions.

If one accountant bears responsibility for more than one of these three functions, his energies are prone to be directed to (1), then to (2), and finally to (3). If this occurs, his two foremost values, as far as management is concerned, are likely to be dissipated.[3]

II. GUIDES TO SELECTION OF MANAGEMENT ACCOUNTING PRACTICES

II-A. RELEVANT INFORMATION—THE BASIC NEED

The National Association of Ac-

[3]Simon, et al., op. cit., p. 5.

countants' Research Planning Committee has stated: "Guides are needed by the management accountant to aid him in selecting practices from among the many alternatives. These guides provide assurance that practices chosen will yield data *relevant to the recipient's purposes.* [Emphasis supplied]" Any guide, therefore, must be concerned with the concept of relevancy, because the assembly and interpretation of relevant data is the management accountant's fundamental task.

Relevant data may be defined broadly as that data which will lead to an optimum decision. The distinction between *relevancy* and *accuracy* should be kept in mind. Ideally management accounting data should be relevant (valid, pertinent) and accurate (precise). However, figures can be precise but irrelevant, or imprecise but relevant. But relevancy is basic to management accounting. Although accuracy is always desirable and often extremely important, it is really a subobjective in any conceptual approach to gathering data for planning and control.

Some executives have implied that many accountants have a twisted orientation regarding accuracy and relevancy. That is, many accountants are preoccupied with accuracy and are little concerned with relevancy. This is a reflection of the product costing and income determination goal of industrial accounting that so often overrides other important goals. What may be accurate with respect to the product costing goal may be entirely irrelevant with respect to management decisions. For example, scrupulous determinations of bases for overhead allocation may yield seemingly "accurate" results for product costing purposes but may be wholly misleading for planning and control purposes. Reverence for accuracy, while admirable, may narrow the horizons and usefulness of the industrial accountant.

Now we shall examine the meaning of relevancy as it bears on the two broad purposes of management accounting.

II-B. OBJECTIVE OF PLANNING AND CONTROLLING OPERATIONS

The Key Questions

The directing of attention, the providing of clues, the raising of pertinent questions, the inducing of desired behavior—these are the principal tasks of accounting for planning and controlling operations. The accountant's role here includes score-keeping and attention-directing.

Some guides to management accounting practice in this area have been described profusely in the accounting literature. For example, it has become almost self-evident that appropriate budgets and standards have wide usefulness in the execution of the accountant's attention-directing function. Much of the literature on standard costs[4] gives the impression that they are always based on sound engineering studies and rigorous specifications. Although this approach is often useful, it should be stressed that less scientific standards provide a forceful way of presenting information in order to stimulate corrective action. An accounting system is effective when it automatically calls management's attention to the areas that most sorely need investigation. Accuracy of standards, while desirable, is not as basic to successful management accounting as the more fundamental notion—that of the relevancy of using some predetermined targets as a means of implementing management by exception.

Another example of an obvious guide is the frequent need to sacrifice precision for promptness in reporting. The need for timely data is so acute in many cases that it should be fulfilled promptly in a flash report, even if the wanted data ordinarily are only part of a more complete formal report. Thus, an effective management accounting system is designed to supply reports on a highly selective basis; relevancy often overrides accuracy in these score-keeping and attention-directing areas. That is, highly accurate but stale data are irrelevant, because they have no bearing on the decisions then facing the recipient.

This notion of relevancy provides the cornerstone in constructing guides for the purpose of planning and controlling current operations. The logical questions to be asked are:

1. What are the objectives of the organization as a whole?
2. Who are the executives who are expected to seek such objectives? What are their spheres of responsibility?
3. What data can be provided to help them toward making individual decisions that will harmonize with and spur them toward overall company objectives?

Assuming that the answers to question (1) are available[5], we turn to the questions under (2).

Tailoring the System to the Organization—Responsibility Accounting

Our initial guide is as follows: *Focus the basic design of the accounting system upon the responsibility centers of individual managers.* The accounting system must cohesively reflect the plans and actions of all responsibility centers in the organization—from the smallest to the biggest. This basic idea is being implemented on a wide scale in the form of so-called *responsibility accounting, profitability accounting,* or *activity accounting* systems.[6]

---

[4]Consider the definition by the 1951 Committee on Cost Concepts, American Accounting Association, *The Accounting Review,* (April, 1952), p. 177, "Standard costs are *scientifically* predetermined costs." (Emphasis supplied.)

[5]Profitability is generally regarded as the prime objective. A discussion of organizational objectives, such as profitability, growth, power, or social service, is beyond the scope of this paper. See Wm. Travers Jerome III, *Executive Control—The Catalyst* (New York: John Wiley & Sons, Inc., 1961), Chapters 4 and 14.

[6]Martin N. Kellogg, "Fundamentals of Responsibility Accounting," *N.A.A. Bulletin* (April, 1962), pp. 5-16. John A. Higgins, "Responsibility Accounting," *The Arthur Andersen Chronicle* (April, 1952). The term *activity accounting* is used by Eric Kohler and may be used interchangeably with *responsibility accounting.* See Kohler, *A Dictionary for Accountants* (2nd ed.; New York: Prentice-Hall, Inc., 1957), pp. 22-23.

Ideally, particular revenues and costs would be recorded and automatically traced to the one individual in the organization who shoulders primary responsibility for the item. He is in the best position to evaluate and to influence a situation. For example:

"The sales department requests a rush production. The plant scheduler argues that it will disrupt his production and cost a substantial though not clearly determined amount of money. The answer coming from sales is: 'Do you want to take the responsibility of losing the X Company as a customer?' Of course, the production scheduler does not want to take such a responsibility, and he gives up, but not before a heavy exchange of arguments and the accumulation of a substantial backlog of ill feeling.

Analysis of the payroll in the assembly department, determining the costs involved in getting out rush orders, eliminated the cause of the argument. Henceforth, any rush order was accepted with a smile by the production scheduler, who made sure that the extra cost would be duly recorded and charged to the sales department—'no questions asked.' As a result, the tension created by rush orders disappeared completely; and, somehow, the number of rush orders requested by the sales department was reduced to an insignificant level."[7]

Practically, the diffusion of control throughout the organization complicates the task of collecting relevant data by responsibility centers.[8] The organizational networks, the communication patterns, and the decision-making processes are complex—far too complex to yield either pat answers or *the* ideal management accounting system.[9]

Harmony of Objectives

Our next guide is: *Study and delineate individual manager needs in relation to his sphere of responsibility and the objectives of the organization as a whole.*

This sweeping guide has many subguides in the area of planning and controlling current operations. We have already seen that the individual manager requires score-card and attention-directing data. But what data are relevant? To be relevant, the data should impel the manager toward decisions that will harmonize with top management objectives. It follows that the management accountant must evaluate the influence of the accounting system on the motivations of individuals. The example of rush orders cited above shows how the accounting system can affect management behavior.

The trouble here is that conflicts arise between individual goals and top management goals. We all know of instances where a manager's attempt to "look good" on a performance report resulted in action detrimental to the best interests of the organization as a whole. Examples include tinkering with scrap and usage reports, encouraging false timekeeping on the part of subordinates, reducing costs by lowering quality or by causing higher costs in other departments and, in general, doing "a little monkey business to come out right."

These examples do not necessarily imply nefarious behavior on the part of the individual manager. Often it is merely a matter of faulty cost analysis that is engendered by the accounting system. For example, the use of *net* assets as an investment base

[7]Raymond Villers, "Control and Freedom in a Decentralized Company," *Harvard Business Review*, Vol. XXXII, No. 2, p. 95.

[8]One of the major difficulties here is that the organization structure itself is often only vaguely understood. Problems of organization are discussed in many management texts. See Pfiffner and Sherwood, *Administrative Organization* (Englewood Cliffs, N. J.: Prentice-Hall, Inc., 1960); March and Simon, *Organizations* (New York: John Wiley & Sons, 1958).

[9]Any thorough study of an information system is likely to disclose points of strength and weakness in the organization. No management accounting system by itself can cure basic weaknesses in executive talent or organization structure. However, it can pinpoint areas that demand attention.

for judging managerial efficiency may encourage incorrect decisions by divisional management. If assets are replaced or scrapped before they are fully depreciated, the division may have to show a loss. Even though such a loss is irrelevant to replacement decisions (except for its impact on the timing of future income tax outlays), it does affect the division's immediate profit and could wrongly influence the division manager's decision.[10]

The successful use of budgets, standards, and various other measuring sticks is largely dependent on their value as motivating devices—as mechanisms that will influence managers and subordinates to act in accordance with the desires of top management. For example, different types of motivation may result when maintenance costs are charged to a responsibility center on the basis of (1) a rate per maintenance labor hour, (2) a rate per job, or (3) a single amount per month.[11] Anthony has commented on the motivational approach as follows:

"The usefulness of such a motivational approach becomes apparent when the concepts are applied to a practical control problem. Without such an approach, one can easily become immersed in pointless arguments on such matters as whether rent should be allocated on the basis of square footage or cubit footage. There is no sound way of settling such disputes. With the notion of motivation, the problem comes into clear focus. What cost constructions are most likely to induce people to take the action that management desires? Answering this question in a specific situation is difficult. . . ."[12]

Although the views on these matters are far from settled,[13] most accountants and executives probably would agree with the following summary observations on costs for motivation:

"Interview results show that a particular figure does not operate as a norm, in either a score-card or attention-directing sense, simply because the controller's department calls it a standard. It operates as a norm only to the extent that the executives and supervisors, whose activity it measures, accept it as a fair and attainable yardstick of their performance. Generally, operating executives were inclined to accept a standard to the extent that they were satisfied that the data were *accurately recorded,* that the standard level was *reasonably attainable,* and the variables it measured were *controllable* by them."[14]

The above quotation centers on three guides that are basic to the management accountant's work in this area:

1. Score-keeping data should be *accurate.*

2. Budgets or standards should be *understood* and *accepted* as reasonably attainable goals.

3. The items used to judge performance must be *controllable* by the recipient.

Importance of Accuracy: The Score-keeping Function

The success of the score-keeping function in management accounting depends heavily on accuracy. Earlier we saw that relevancy and accuracy were both important but that accuracy was a subobjective in any con-

[10]For an interesting discussion of how division managers' interests can conflict with the interests of the company as a whole, see John Dearden, "Problem in Decentralized Profit Responsibility," *Harvard Business Review* (May-June, 1960), pp. 79-86.

[11]Report of the 1955 Committee on Cost Concepts, American Accounting Association, *The Accounting Review* (April, 1956), p. 189. Also see Norton M. Bedford, "Cost Accounting as a Motivation Technique," *N.A.(C.)A. Bulletin* (June, 1957), pp. 1250-1257.

[12]Robert N. Anthony, "Cost Concepts for Control," *Accounting Review* (April, 1957), p. 234. Anthony has suggested that a control technique can be judged in two ways: by the *direction* and by the *strength* of its motivation. See his *Management Accounting* (rev. ed.; Homewood, Ill.: Richard D. Irwin, Inc., 1960), p. 317.

[13]For a provocative view, see Andrew Stedry, *Budget Control and Cost Behavior* (Englewood Cliffs, N. J.: Prentice-Hall, Inc., 1960).

[14]Simon *et. al., op. cit.,* p. 29.

ceptual approach to management accounting. This in no way meant that accuracy was unimportant. An accounting system will not mean much to management if the score-keeping function is haphazard. This problem of having source documents reflect physical realities is immense and pervasive.

For example, Scharff[15] had a study made of the accuracy of time reporting in the shops of a large steel and alloy plate fabricator. Each workman reported his own time. The findings revealed that the time reported against any job could vary as much as 15 or 20 percent from actual time without this circumstance being detected by the foreman's checking of time cards at the end of the day or by other checks, such as comparing estimated with actual hours, etc. The two most glaring sources of error were, first, inadvertently charging time to the wrong job and, second, willfully charging time to the wrong job when it was obvious that a given job was running over the estimated hours. In all, some twenty-five sources of error were identified. Scharff believes that the average accountant should be more sensitive to possible errors, more aware of the futility of trying to get time reported accurately in small increments, and more conscious of the natural tendency of individuals to report their activities so as to minimize their individual bother and maximize their personal showing.

Understanding the Acceptance of Goals: The Attention-Directing or Interpretative Function

Score-keeping is essential for cost accumulation, but attention-directing is the key to augmenting management's appreciation of the accounting function. The accountant's "staff" role includes being an attention-director (interpreter and analyst) and a score-keeper (cost accumulation and reporter—a policeman of sorts). However, these two roles often clash. Therefore, as mentioned earlier, the

accounting department should divorce attention-directing from score-keeping. Otherwise, the day-to-day routine, the unending deadlines, and the insidious pressures of cost accumulation will shunt attention-directing (with the accompanying frequent contacts between accountants and operating people) into the background and, most likely, into oblivion.

The attention-directing roles (for example, explaining variances) should be occupied by capable, experienced accountants who, at least to some degree, can talk the line manager's language. Indeed, the attention-directors are the individuals who will largely establish the status of the controller's department in the company. Close, direct, active contacts between accountants and operating managers strengthen understanding and acceptability of the standards, budgets, and reports that are the measuring devices of performance.[16]

Controllability of Items: The Importance of Cost Behavior Patterns

Management accountants are increasingly aware of the desirability of distinguishing between controllable and uncontrollable items on a performance report. From the viewpoint of planning and controlling operations, little is accomplished by mixing controllable and uncontrollable items in the same report; in fact the indiscriminate listing of such costs often leads to confusion and discouragement on the part of the departmental manager. Again, the motivational impact should provide the guide here. For example, some top managements assign central research costs and facilities to divisions, not because the resulting divisional rates of return can be defended but because the division manager's resentment sparks an interest in central research activities. On the other hand, many accountants confine performance reports to controllable items only.

This fundamental idea that individuals should be charged only with costs subject to their control is con-

---

[15]Sam E. Scharff, "The Industrial Engineer and the Cost Accountant," *N.A.A. Bulletin* (March, 1961), pp. 17-18.

[16]Simon *et. al., op. cit.,* pp. 45-56.

ceptually appealing. Practically, however, there is still much to be learned about interpreting and using the following guides:

"There are few, if any, elements of cost that are the sole responsibility of one person. Some guides in deciding the appropriate costs to be charged to a person (responsibility center) are as follows:

(a) If the person has authority over both the acquisition and the use of the services, he should be charged with the cost of such services.

(b) If the person can significantly influence the amount of cost through his own action, he may be charged with such costs.

(c) Even if the person cannot significantly influence the amount of cost through his own action, he may be charged with those elements with which the management desires him to be concerned, so that he will help to influence those who are responsible."[17]

II-C. Objective of Long-Range Planning and Special Decisions

Need for a General Approach

Management accounting has a clear need for a general approach to accounting for special decision-making purposes. Existing literature and practice are characterized by diversity of general approaches and by disjointed efforts to meet very specific needs. Managerial economists, operations researchers, and statistical decision theorists perhaps have made more progress than accountants in attempting to formulate general quantitative approaches to special decisions. The rise of operations research

as a distinct field may indicate that not enough practicing accountants have responded to the management need for aid in tackling these business problems.

The area of long-range planning and special decisions offers very imposing problems for executives. Management accountants need to keep abreast of the growing body of knowledge and standards concerning the decision-making process. For example, the general superiority of discounted cash flow approaches in capital budgeting decisions is being increasingly acknowledged.[18] The correct application of relevant cost analysis, discounted cash flow techniques, and possibly statistical probability theory will help management toward intelligent decision-making. All of these techniques can easily be deemed to fall within the province of the management accountant's problem-solving function.

At the same time, the need for a team approach to these decisions is well recognized. The effective management accountant knows when to call upon appropriate specialists such as mathematicians, statisticians, industrial engineers, and others.[19]

There are two joint guides for the accountant in this area: (1) an awareness of what constitutes relevant data for special decisions and (2) a recognition of the conflicts existing between certain accounting concepts and purposes.

Relevant Data for Special Decisions

The isolation and measurement of *relevant* revenue and cost factors are by far the most challenging chores in the area of special decisions. Business decision-making entails choosing between alternative courses of action. The alternative actions take place in

---

[17]Report of 1955 Committee on Cost Concepts, *op. cit.*, p. 189.

[18]N.A.A. Research Report No. 35, *Return on Capital as a Guide to Managerial Decisions* (New York: National Association of Accountants, 1959).

[19]Although the electronic computer has enlarged the accountant's opportunities, it has also accelerated a challenge—the threat

of other quantitative specialists. The management accountant should view accounting broadly and learn how allied disciplines pertain to his job. Otherwise, the management scientists, the statisticians, and the operations researchers may nibble away at his job and gradually devour it—leaving for the accountants only the routine duty of score-keeping for income statements and balance sheets.

the future, whether it be five seconds or many years ahead; hence, the decision will be influenced by the expected results under the various alternatives. The financial ingredients of the forecast must necessarily be based on expected future data. Consequently, to be relevant for these purposes, all data must be expected future data.

But *all* future data are not necessarily relevant to a given decision; only those data that will be *different* under alternatives are relevant. For example, relevant costs for special decisions are those *future* costs that will be *different* under available alternatives. The key question in determining relevancy is, "What difference will it make?"

For example, assume that a company is thinking of rearranging its plant facilities. Accounting records show that past direct labor costs were $2.00 per unit. No wage rate changes are expected, but the rearrangement is expected to reduce direct labor usage by 25 percent. Direct material costs of $6.00 per unit will not change under either alternative. An analysis follows:

Relevant costs per unit

	Do not rearrange	Rearrange
Direct labor	$2.00	$1.50

The cost comparison above is one of *expected future costs* that will *differ* under alternatives. The $2.00 direct labor charge may be the same as in the past, and the past records may have been extremely helpful in preparing the $2.00 forecast. The trouble is that most accountants and managers view the $2.00 past cost as the future cost. But the crucial point is that the $2.00 is an expected future cost, not a past cost. *Historical costs in themselves are irrelevant though they may be the best available basis for estimating future costs.*

The direct material costs of $6.00 per unit are expected future costs, not historical costs. Yet these future costs are irrelevant because they will not differ under alternatives. There may be no harm in preparing a comparative analysis that includes both

the relevant direct labor cost forecast and the irrelevant direct material cost forecast:

Cost comparison per unit

	Do not rearrange	Rearrange
Direct material	$6.00	$6.00
Direct labor	2.00	1.50

However, note that we can safely ignore the direct material cost, because it is not an element of difference between the alternatives. The point is that irrelevant costs may be included in cost comparisons for decisions, provided that they are included properly and do not mislead the decision-maker. A corollary point is that concentrating solely on relevant costs may eliminate cluttersome irrelevancies and may sharpen both the accountant's and the manager's thinking regarding costs for decision-making.

In summary, Exhibit 1 shows that relevant costs for decisions are expected future costs that will differ under alternatives. Historical costs, while helpful in predicting relevant costs, are always irrelevant costs *per se*.

The basic approach to relevant cost analysis provides a common thread among all special decisions. The accountant or executive who develops an understanding of the concept of relevancy has taken a giant stride toward being able to analyze properly the quantitative aspects of any special decision, whether it be make or buy, the special order, buy or rent, equipment replacement, and so forth.

Note, too, that the area of special decisions again demonstrates the contrast between relevancy and accuracy. For example, the conventional ledgers amass data that are, in varying degrees, considered accurate or at least objectively determinable. Yet in long-range planning and special decisions, all the key data employed are necessarily expected future data. No general ledger system yet devised can possibly produce such data *per se*. Admittedly, much historical ("accurate") data may be helpful in predicting the appropriate future (relevant) data. But, in exercising his problem-solving function, the man-

| Past costs | | Expected future costs | | |
(often used as a guide for prediction)		Do not rearrange	Rearrange	
Direct material	$6.00	$6.00*	$6.00*	
				Second line of demarcation
Direct labor	2.00	2.00	1.50	

First line
of
demarcation in a conceptual
approach to distinction between
"relevant" and "irrelevant"

* Although these are expected future costs, they are irrelevant because they are the same for both alternatives. Thus, the second line of demarcation is drawn between those costs that are the same for the alternatives under consideration and those that differ; *only* the latter are relevant costs *as defined here.*

EXHIBIT 1

agement accountant looks at the future first. He then selects the forecasting procedure that seems best under the circumstances.

Here we see that management accounting's scope is not limited by whatever accounting system design is used for routine data compilation, no matter how impressive and responsive the system may be. The problems of management accounting are too broad and too deep to be jammed into a single systems design, even if it is attuned to multi-purpose uses.

Conflict of Concepts and Purposes

Heavy spending on capital assets since World War II has been accompanied by a hearty interest on the part of economists, financial analysts, and accountants in management approaches to these capital budgeting decisions. Space does not permit an expanded discussion of the technical issues here.

Much of the uproar has arisen because conventional accounting practices have not been aimed at the needs of the specific decision-making process. Regarding the relative merits of capital budgeting techniques, N.A.A.

Research Report No. 35 rightly favors the discounted cash flow technique. The discounted cash flow method is more objective because its answer is not directly influenced by decisions as to depreciation methods, capitalization versus expense decisions, and conservatism. Erratic flows of revenue and expenses over a project's life are directly considered under discounted cash flow but are "averaged" under the financial statement (conventional) method. "The financial statement method utilizes concepts of capital and income which were originally designed for the quite different purpose of accounting for periodic income and financial position."[20]

II-D. Cost Behavior and Overall Reporting

The need for knowledge of cost behavior patterns pervades all functions of management accounting. For example, we have already seen the need for distinguishing between controllable and uncontrollable costs. In addition, so-called *breakeven analysis* cannot be conducted effectively with-

[20]*Ibid.*, p. 64.

The Relevant Costing Approach: Model Income Statement by Segments* (In thousands of Dollars)

	Company as a whole	Company breakdown into two divisions		Possible breakdown of Division B only				
		Division A	Division B	Not allocated	Product 1	Product 2	Product 3	Product 4
Net sales	1,500	500	1,000	0	300	200	100	400
Variable manufacturing cost of sales	780	200	580	0	120	155	45	260
Manufacturing contribution margin	720	300	420	0	180	45	55	140
Variable selling and administrative costs	220	100	120	0	60	15	25	20
(1) Contribution margin	500	200	300	0	120 (40%)	30 (15%)	30 (30%)	120 (30%)
Fixed expenses directly identifiable with divisions:								
Programmed** fixed costs (certain advertising, sales promotion, engineering, research, management consulting, and supervision costs)	190	110	80	45***	10	6	4	15
(2) Performance margin	310	90	220	(45)	110	24	26	105
Other fixed costs (generally uncontrollable, such as depreciation, property taxes, insurance, and perhaps the division manager's salary)	70	20	50	20	3	15	4	8
(3) Segment margin	240	70	170	(65)	107	9	22	97
Joint fixed costs (not clearly or practically allocable to any segment except by some questionable allocation base)	135	45	90	(no allocations attempted beyond Divisions A and B)				
(4) Net income before income taxes	105	25	80					

* There are two different types of segments illustrated here: divisions and products. A segment is any line of activity or subdivision of the business for which separate determination of costs and sales is wanted. Examples might be divisions, products, customers, plants, territories, and so forth.

** Programmed costs are those relatively fixed costs arising from policy decisions of management; they may have no particular relation to any base of activity. These are controllable at least when they are planned.

*** Only those costs clearly identifiable with particular products within a division should be allocated.

EXHIBIT 2

SEPTEMBER 1962

out assurance that the cost-volume-profit relationships depicted are valid and reasonably accurate. So, while he recognizes the importance of cost accounting for compiling costs of product, the management accountant is also concerned with a host of other cost concepts. He realizes that no single cost concept is pertinent for all purposes. He has what may be called a *relevant costing* viewpoint.

Accounting reports should be designed to highlight the relevant data approach that has been supported here. For example, as a minimum, the income statement should be designed to facilitate its possible use for many purposes, not just one. As Exhibit 2 demonstrates, the income statement for management use should no longer aim at producing one income figure. Modern needs have made a singular concept of income obsolete.

The model income statement focuses on the appropriate data for overall appraisals of current performance. Also, special decisions such as pricing, dropping or adding products, advertising and promoting specific products, and selecting distribution channels are more likely to be based on relevant information. The conventional income statement often fails to distinguish between fixed and variable costs; controllable and uncontrollable costs; and joint (common) and separable costs. These distinctions are vital for judging performance and for various marketing, manufacturing, and financial decisions.

Examples of how different figures in Exhibit 2 may be relevant for various purposes follow (numbers refer to those at left of exhibit):

(1) Contribution margin: This is particularly helpful in selecting which products to push and in quickly estimating the changes in profits that will ensue from fluctuations in volume or product mix.[21]

(2) Performance margin: This version of income is probably most appropriate for judging per-

---

[21]For a number of examples of the usefulness of the contribution margin see N.A.A. Research Report 37, *Current Application of Direct Costing*, 1961.

formance by division managers or product managers. It is superior to the contribution margin for this purpose because these managers can influence certain fixed costs, which are sometimes called *programmed* or *managed* costs. (Note that while certain programmed costs, such as salesmen's salaries, may be easily traced to divisions, they may not be directly traceable to products.)

(3) Segment margin: This is computed after deducting the directly identifiable fixed costs that are generally considered uncontrollable in the short run. Although this figure may be helpful as a crude indicator of long-run segment profitability, it should ordinarily not influence appraisals of current performance.

(4) Net income before income taxes: This may sometimes be a helpful gauge of the long-run earning power of a whole company. However, the attempt to refine this ultimate measure by breaking it into segments (and still have the whole equal the sum of the parts) seldom can yield meaningful results. Here again, we see where relevancy is a more fundamental concept than accuracy. It is difficult to see how segment performance can be judged on the basis of net income after deductions for a "fair" share of general company costs over which the segment manager exerts no influence. Examples of such costs would be central research and central administrative costs. Despite the example of allocation to Divisions A and B, unless the general company costs are clearly separable, the usefulness of such allocation is questionable.

III. RESPONSIBILITY FOR SELECTING MANAGEMENT ACCOUNTING PRACTICES

An enlightened chief management accountant, working with top management and qualified internal or external consultants, should bear primary responsibility for selecting company management accounting practices. He should tap all resources, including the industry trade associations, the professional accounting bodies, outside auditors, government agencies, friends in the industry, and the growing literature on management and management accounting.

The biggest danger here is probably the temptation to superimpose a sample management accounting system on a company without making a tough-minded appraisal of the underlying needs of the organization and its individual executives.

Despite the obvious need for the tailor-making of management accounting systems, outside groups have an opportunity to propel the progress of management accounting. There is a continuing need for research and education, such as that conducted by the N.A.A., to describe current practices that are effective for specified purposes. Most important, there is a burgeoning mass of fundamental knowledge that should be conveyed by the N.A.A., other associations, and educational institutions if management accounting is to thrive.[22]

IV. CONCLUSION

An understanding of the overall purposes and functions of the accounting system is basic to choosing effective accounting practices for reporting to management. The business information system of the future should be a multi-purpose system with a highly selective reporting scheme. It will be highly integrated and will serve three main purposes: (1) routine reporting on financial results, oriented primarily for external parties (score-keeping); (2) routine reporting to management, primarily for

planning and controlling current operations (score-keeping and attention-directing); and (3) special reporting to management, primarily for long-range planning and non-recurring decisions (problem-solving).

Any guide to management accounting must aim at supplying relevant information—the basic need. Relevant data may be defined broadly as that data which will lead to an optimum decision, a decision that will best aid individuals toward overall organizational objectives.

With regard to the objective of planning and controlling operations, some of the more important guides center about responsibility accounting, accounting techniques for motivation in harmony with organizational goals, accurate score-keeping, full-fledged attention-directing, and careful classifying of controllable items.

With regard to long-range planning and special decisions, there is an evident need for a general, future-oriented approach that de-emphasizes historical revenues and costs, and there is a need for recognizing the conflict between the purposes and methods of conventional accounting and management accounting.

The accounting reports themselves should be structured to highlight relevant data. The need for knowledge of cost behavior patterns pervades all functions of management accounting. Reports at various management levels should distinguish between controllable and uncontrollable costs, variable and fixed costs, and joint (common) and separable costs.

The chief management accountant, working with top management and qualified internal or external consultants, should bear primary responsibility for the selection of company management accounting practices. In order to execute this responsibility, he needs to keep abreast of the growing body of fundamental knowledge in management accounting. Moreover, he must see that his staff receives training and experience in attention-directing and problem-solving as well as score-keeping, if the role of management accounting is to flourish in the organizations of tomorrow.

---

[22]Critics of conventional education in accountancy basically maintain that too much effort is given to preparing score-keepers and not enough to educating attention-directors and problem-solvers. See Herbert F. Taggart, "Cost Accounting Versus Cost Bookkeeping," *Accounting Review* (April, 1951), pp. 141-151.

Published Forecasts and Internal Budgets

Leopold Schachner, CPA, Ph.D.

LEOPOLD SCHACH-NER, CPA, Ph.D., is Associate Professor of Accountancy at Baruch College, City University of New York, and a member of the American Accounting Association, American Finance Association, and American Association of University Professors. He has published in many professional journals.

Published forecasts are in the news, and practitioners who may be required to review them are looking into the prospect of deriving forecasts from internal budgets. The author discusses relations between the two, similarities, dissimilarities, and problems that will be encountered.

The announcement by the Securities and Exchange Commission, in February 1973, that it planned to permit the publication of earnings forecasts by registrants, marked a sharp turn in SEC policy.[1] Previously the SEC had not permitted the inclusion of forecasts in filings by listed companies under the federal securities laws.

Briefly, under the new SEC position, publication of financial forecasts and projections is generally voluntary. The Commission does not allow any statement of certification or verification by a third party at this time. The projection should be of sales and earnings, expressed as a reasonably definite figure, and the underlying assumptions should be set forth. Filed projections should be updated regularly, and also whenever the issuer materially changes its projection. The SEC proposals contain also a provision for comparison of the forecast with actual results.

Why the Change in Policy?

There is a dictum of conservatism to the effect that *if it is not necessary to change, then it is necessary not to change.* Both those who favor the new policy and those who oppose it appear to agree with this dictum. Those who favor the new policy point out that change is necessary because we must face the reality that de facto public forecasts are a part of the reporting environment. Corporations are making earnings projections available to selected security analysts, or they comment on forecasts prepared by analysts. The SEC's announcement may therefore be viewed as an attempt to make information on forecasts available on a regulated, and hence more equitable, basis.

Forecasts, it is argued, are needed; and they can be provided with a fair degree of quality. Investors are indeed concerned with expectations about the future: the future economic outlook of the company and its industry, and the expected future growth in sales and earnings. It is widely believed that predictions of future earnings are the primary factor in the valuation of common stocks.

There are also significant arguments against published forecasts; and they were presented at the lengthy SEC hearings held late in 1972. Fear of liability for inaccurate projections emerged as a major deterrent, and there are many others. One of those arguing against was Harvey E. Kapnick, Chairman and Chief Executive of Arthur Andersen & Co. An extensive statement of his views may be found in his article "Will Financial Forecasts Really Help Investors?" published in August 1972 in the *Financial Executive*. A major contention of his is that forecasting—a prediction about an uncertain future—is a function of the investor and not of management.

The position of the AICPA at the SEC hearings was that publication of forecasts be permitted for a trial period.[2] The AICPA representative declared:

> We believe that after establishing suitable guidelines, the Commission should permit publication of forecasts for a trial period, during which time it could encourage companies to disclose forecasts. This should provide the experience necessary to form a sound basis for reaching a decision as to whether prohibition or permissive or mandatory publication would best serve the public interest in the long run.

A step toward published forecasts is a rather drastic move. When change of such magnitude is introduced, one must be prepared to deal with the numerous problems brought about by that change. We have to look at the implications of the new procedures. Solutions must be found first, or change may have to come only on some gradual basis. Problems must be worked out so that

---

[1] Securities and Exchange Commission, *Statement by the Commission on the Disclosure of Projections of Future Economic Performance*, February 2, 1973.

[2] "Trial Period Suggested for Publication of Forecasts," *The Journal of Accountancy*, January 1973, pp. 9-12.

JANUARY 1975

corporate management is satisfied that they will be able to perform their function while publishing forecasts.

Did the SEC, by merely permitting voluntary published forecasts, largely meet the AICPA suggestion that publication of forecasts be permitted for a trial period? Perhaps so, but it may work out in practice differently: under pressure from security analysts and some stockholders, corporations may commence the publication of forecasts whether or not they are in a position to do so.

What Is a Financial or Earnings Forecast?

A forecast is a prediction, a projection. The SEC announcement of February 1973 uses the terms *projection* and *projection information*. At the SEC hearings, the AICPA representative distinguished the forecast from a budget.[3] He said:

> Our comments are not directed to the type of forecasts which are intended purely for management purposes and may be deliberately overstated as goals for corporate personnel. Such forecasts are commonly referred to as budgets.... For purposes of our discussion, we intend to use the term *forecasts* to mean financial summaries of the best possible estimates of future expectations.

The emphasis on the *best possible estimates of future expectations* is a recurring theme in the discussions on published forecasts. Thus, the MAS task force of the AICPA, in its exposure draft, "Standards for Systems for the Preparation of Financial Forecasts," lists the following as the first standard:[4]

> A financial forecasting system should provide a means for management to determine what it considers to be the single most probable forecasted result.

While a published forecast should be one that is highly probable of achievement, in the final analysis it is derived from the same basic data as the internal budget. The information used in preparing both must reflect the plans of the company. Thus, publishing a forecast would in many, perhaps most, cases result in dual budgeting, where both the internal budget and the published forecast are based on the same set of data.

The reason for the emphasis on the best estimate of expected performance is, of course, that investors would rely on published forecasts when making investment decisions. It may be noted that the forecast could also be usefully expressed as a range rather than a point estimate in terms of specific figures. This would communicate the probabilistic nature of the forecast. However, range presentation, to be helpful to investors, would have to include the related probabilities for the range interval.[5] In a study prepared for the Financial Executives Institute (the "FEI Study"), only a small percentage of companies were found to express their internal budgets in terms of ranges.[6]

The Role of Internal Budgets

The internal budget that we are concerned with here is the one that is usually referred to as the "profit budget" or "master budget." An essential management tool, it is an annual profit plan constructed by responsibility centers to aid in coordinating operations. It summarizes the objectives of all subunits of the enterprise and quantifies the expectations regarding future revenues, expenses, cash flows, and financial position.

It is clear that the published forecast cannot simply be an abridged version of the budget, for the budget is a most versatile tool. In addition to planning and coordinating activities, it is also used, among others, for motivation, evaluation of performance, and control of decentralized operations. The content and the amount of detail presented in a budget varies greatly among companies.

Budgets are necessarily imprecise, even though scientific techniques may be used in their preparation. The relative weights to be attached to variables, in assessing a company's future prospects, are largely a matter of judgment. A budget is always based on assumptions.

Disclosure of Underlying Assumptions

The SEC's preliminary statement on published forecasts requires that the underlying assumptions be set forth. That need is perceived by virtually every writer on the subject. Yet the SEC does not indicate the *extent* to which the disclosure of the underlying assumptions should help evaluate a forecast. It merely provides that investors should be in a position to evaluate their assessment of a company's future performance in the light of assumptions made. But, first, what is an assumption?

Examples of Assumptions

1. The United States economy will experience a moderate recession (i.e., no increase in gross national product) in the next fiscal year.

[3] Ibid.

[4] "MAS Panel Drafts Forecast Guidelines," *The Journal of Accountancy*, June 1974, pp. 8-10.

[5] Similarly, if the forecast is given in terms of specific figures for expected values, it was suggested that variances (S^2) should be computed and attached to indicate the variability in the expected values. See John J. Clark and Pieter Elgers, "Forecasted Income Statements: An Investor Perspective," *The Accounting Review*, October 1973, pp. 668-678.

[6] A. T. Kearney, Inc. and Sidley & Austin, *Public Disclosure of Business Forecasts* (Financial Executives Research Foundation, 1972), p. 13.

2. There will be no material change in bases and rates of taxation. Enactment of an excess profits tax is not expected.

3. International exchange rates or import duties will not change materially.

4. New labor agreements to be negotiated next year will be negotiated without work stoppages and on terms satisfactory to the company. The new contracts are expected to meet the federal guideline of 5½ percent.

5. The total debt will be reduced by approximately $25,000,000 by the end of next fiscal year. Interest rates are not expected to change materially.

6. Our new plant at location X will be completed by the end of the second quarter and production will begin immediately.

It may be noted that most of the above assumptions, which are not meant to be representative, are predictions about the future. However, some reflect corporate planning: namely, debt reduction and the use of new production facilities. Furthermore, assumption No. 1 carries an implied assertion that the gross national product is a relevant macroeconomic variable for predicting the company's sales and earnings. An example of a common assumption representing an assertion is the one stating, expressly or implicitly, that the accounting principles used in the preparation of the forecast are consistent with those used in the financial statements. Thus, an assumption may be an assertion, a prediction, or a plan of action, and it may be expressed or implied.

Incidentally, in situations where most of the crucial assumptions are predictions, the financial forecast is then a prediction about the future, based largely on some prior predictions agreed to beforehand. This may not be ignored when evaluating the reliability of a given financial forecast. The distinction between a prediction and a plan of action may, of course, become blurred if there is considerable uncertainty in the execution of the plan.

Generally, assumptions underlying internal budgets may include: such macroeconomic considerations as gross national product and aggregate disposable income; policies and legislative programs in the U.S. and in foreign countries; company strategy; assessment of competition from within the industry and from other industries; availability of resources, such as raw materials and labor; prospective product demand; labor relations; wage and price estimates; development of new products; research and development programs; completion of facilities; and many others.

While the list of assumptions can be quite long and their documentation quite voluminous, the important question is how much of it should be disclosed in a published forecast, and to what depth. In an article in which John C. Burton, Chief Accountant of the SEC, is the coauthor it was suggested that "the statement of assumptions should include quantitative information as to the sensitivity of the forecast to each assumption."[7] This is a demanding requirement indeed. On the other hand, there is a report of general agreement, at a distinguished conference, that there should be only "limited disclosure of the underlying assumptions."[8] There was also agreement at that conference "to await the SEC's rules, which are expected to set forth guides." Is there really a question as to what the rules are going to be, if promulgated, despite the fact that there are no perfect solutions because the task is simply very difficult?

The investor-analyst, in order to be able to translate his own assessment of the assumptions into revised earnings figures, would require a level of disclosure on a product line, or line-of-business, basis that is virtually unprecedented. So far the SEC has not put forth such requirements for *historical* financial statements. The external analyst, to do independent recomputations, would have to know a great deal about a company's cost structure by line of business.

Knowledge of a company's cost structure is associated with contribution margin reporting. The costs and expenses specific to individual business segments have to be analyzed into three categories: variable, discretionary, and fixed. Since these three types of cost behave differently as conditions change, a change in a segment's sales volume tends to produce a disproportionate change in its earnings. Corporate management has not been receptive to detailed external reporting that spells out these relations.

A financial forecast is, in effect, a commitment that plans will be executed and that management will take all necessary steps to achieve the planned level of operations in terms of the contemplated costs and revenues. Now, if competitors and other adversary parties, like major suppliers and labor unions, have detailed knowledge of expectations, strategies, and specific plans, they could counteract and preclude occurrence of the anticipated events, thereby nullifying the substance of the forecast. Also, an assumption could be a novel idea, or a relation first perceived by management. By disclosing original concepts or insights in detail, management is putting its business acumen on display for others to share.

Assumption No. 4 in the above example is a case in point. In that assumption, there is a wishful prediction that the new labor contract will be negotiated without work stoppages and on terms satisfactory to the company. (This assumption was included in a published forecast for fiscal

[7] Henry B. Reiling and John C. Burton, "Financial Statements: Signposts as Well as Milestones," *Harvard Business Review,* November-December 1972, p. 53.

[8] "SEC Dispels Misinterpretations of Forecasting Policy," *The Journal of Accountancy,* May 1973, pp. 22-24.

year 1974, in conjunction with a proposed takeover.) It is a kind of assumption that one might be inclined to look at with a critical eye. There is a common awareness that management must be circumspect here in the phrasing of its expectations, in order not to jeopardize its bargaining position or its credibility. Similar considerations apply to the disclosure of the expected outcome of negotiations with major suppliers.

It appears, therefore, that the SEC would have to opt for limited disclosure of the underlying assumptions. However, in that case the question would arise whether the game is worth the candle. The reason for seeking extensive disclosure of assumptions is usefulness. A low level of detail could render a forecast worthless to the investing public. If assumptions are disguised in such a way that they have little value to adversary parties, they may be of dubious utility to investors as well.[9]

Deviation of Actual from Forecast

The degree of detail presented in a published forecast has implications also for the analysis of deviations of actual results from the forecast. The SEC proposal contains a requirement for a comparison of the forecast with actual results and an explanation of variances. The article coauthored by John C. Burton noted that "presumably, explanations of variances between budget and actual data often will be presented in terms of crucial assumptions gone wrong."[10] The more detailed the assumptions, the greater the potential and aroused interest for such explanations, which could, however, get quite voluminous and complex. Assumption No. 1 in the examples of assumptions provides a fitting illustration:

1. The United States economy will experience a moderate recession (i.e., no increase in gross national product) in the next fiscal year.

With respect to this assumption alone, an unfavorable variation of actual sales from forecast could be due to at least three factors: (1) inaccuracy in the assumed effect of GNP upon industry and firm sales; (2) incorrect prediction of GNP; and (3) poor operating control, that is, the sales department somehow failed to translate opportunities into achievements. The third factor may then require further analysis. The third factor, reflecting management's resourcefulness and vigor in operating the business and executing plans, is generally considered to be more important than the first two factors, which reflect merely on management's forecasting ability.

Failure to achieve a sales forecast would then have to be translated into an earnings variance. It should be realized, however, that the forecasting method for sales would typically employ more than one independent variable. Furthermore, aside from the sales variance, the path from sales to earnings may lead through a host of complex assumptions. Consequently, the explanation of variances could become quite voluminous.

SEC guidelines on the extent of explanations would be most essential. It could, for instance, set control limits defining a variance range inside which explanations would not be required. The technique involved could be similar to that used in statistical quality control. Such control limits would assure management a certain latitude, which would be beneficial behaviorally.

Yet a published forecast would generate expectations that only performance within some defined limits of accuracy could fulfill. The quest for accuracy could perhaps be mitigated by comprehensive product-line disclosure in conjunction with the underlying detailed assumptions. In that case, the external analyst could substitute his own judgment and projections for those of management and might be less concerned with accuracy. But that is not likely to happen.

Unable to substitute his own projections for those of management, the investor will demand reasonable accuracy. He will expect forecasts to be substantially fulfilled, because he will rely on them in making his buy and sell decisions. There are already suggestions in the literature on methods for the construction of indexes of accuracy and precision.[11] These would help evaluate a company's forecasting record by measuring differences for a particular year, as well as the trend in differences over time.

This one-dimensional emphasis on accuracy is a unique feature of published forecasts. With internal budgets, analysis of performance is also intended as a soul-searching activity. If actual results do not meet budgeted expectations, the unfavorable variance may be interpreted as a signal for lowering goals in the preparation of next year's budget.

---

[9] There are legal implications here which the SEC would presumably endeavor to work out by means of appropriate rules. For by putting down vague assumptions, the company could be sued for omitting the statement of a material fact. The courts have been applying increasingly higher standards of performance. In the case concerning Douglas Aircraft Corp. [*Beecher* v. *Able*, CCH Fed. Sec. L. Rep. ¶94,450 (S.D.N.Y., 1974)], the federal district court said: "Moreover, any assumptions underlying the projection must be disclosed if their validity is sufficiently in doubt that a reasonably prudent investor, if he knew of the underlying assumptions, might be deterred from crediting the forecast. Disclosure of such underlying assumptions is '. . . necessary to make . . . [the forecast] . . . not misleading . . .'" 15 U.S.C. §77k(a).

See "SEC Undismayed by Adverse Court Ruling on Forecasts," *The Journal of Accountancy*, June 1974, pp. 16-19.

[10] Reiling and Burton, *op. cit.*, p. 53.

[11] R. Austin Daily, "The Feasibility of Reporting Forecasted Information," *The Accounting Review*, October 1971, pp. 686-692.

As noted earlier, the emphasis on preparing financial forecasts that are highly probable of achievement would in many, perhaps most, cases result in dual budgeting.

Dual Budgeting

Dual budgeting is not really uncommon. Companies that engage in motivational budgeting may, and perhaps should, operate a dual budgeting system. This is so because budgets designed to motivate should be tight enough to offer a challenge.[12] In fact, they should be so tight that there is a real risk they will not be fully met. Now, such a budget could not be used for coordinating corporate activities. Bottlenecks would develop. Accordingly, there is precedent for dual budgeting and the two systems are, apparently, *not* mutually destructive.

The problem with dual budgeting here is that the financial forecast, being a published document, enters the public domain. The following comment is taken from the FEI Study (pp. 110-111) mentioned earlier:

> Some companies would contemplate the institution of a "dual forecasting" system—one for publication and a second for internal use.... Apart from the drain on corporate resources of such a system, it is difficult to imagine a more satisfactory situation from the standpoint of counsel representing a selling share-holder than the discovery that, in addition to the public "conservative" forecast upon which his client relied in deciding to sell, there was an "internal" forecast which predicted the far better results actually achieved—for whatever reason.

Dual or multi-budgeting systems, then, though sometimes used internally, have some legal implications if the output of only one of the systems is being published.

But there is still another problem associated with the quest for forecast accuracy that should be considered. This problem arises whether or not the company uses a dual budgeting system. It relates to the possibility that a published forecast will tend to encourage middle management to create slack in the budget. A perceived need for built-in slack may be caused by the pressure on corporate management to meet published forecasts, which would be transmitted down the organization. The budgeting task is usually assigned to line managers at various levels, subject to review. Budget staff merely provides technical assistance.

Slack in Budgets

It was reported, on the basis of an empirical study, that "there is a positive relationship between a control system

that stresses heavily the attainment of departmental budgets and middle managers' need to create slack, to be safe."[13] In other words, "budgetary slack is created as a result of pressure," which is quite plausible.

Budgetary slack is intentionally planted by managers bargaining for understated revenues and overstated costs.[14] The expense categories in which slack accumulates are the same as those that become targets for cost reduction programs when business conditions deteriorate. The size of the potential cost reduction will depend on the amount of slack built into the system.

This is how it works. During the bargaining process for next year's budget, a middle manager, say a divisional manager, succeeds in having top management agree on a budget. In it, he underestimates sales volume and over-estimates certain expenses, say, the need to hire additional administrative staff. Come next year, if earnings do not meet expectations, he can tap the sales volume held in reserve, which can easily be obtained; or he can simply fail to hire the additional staff.

Generally, when the divisional manager wishes to utilize slack after the budget is approved, he will consider what effect this will have on his ability to put slack into the following year's budget. In any event, if the slack is not recovered, it is lost, and the company's earnings will be less than optimum. Thus, suppose that the budgeted year's earnings do meet expectations, then the divisional manager might not bother to tap the sales volume held in reserve; and he probably would hire the additional administrative staff that he could really do without.

Budgetary slack, then, should be distinguished from a conservative forecast prepared by corporate management. A conservative forecast, everything being equal, does not reduce actual profits. It may merely produce a favorable variance between actual and budget. On the other hand, budgetary slack, if not utilized, decreases actual earnings. Incidentally, a company with a fluctuating pattern of earnings will have better slack utilization than a company exhibiting steady growth. The level of accumulated slack would tend to be larger in the latter.

Corporate management must depend on estimates submitted by lower levels of management. (There is no such thing as one big brain.) It finds it difficult to determine the amount of slack, due to peculiarities in each division. Earnings are affected by many variables. Also, a great number of alternative courses of action may be open. It

[12] G. H. Hofstede, "The Game of Budget Control," in Robert N. Anthony, John Dearden, and Richard F. Vancil, *Management Control Systems, Text, Cases, and Readings* (Richard D. Irwin, Inc., Homewood, Ill., 1972), pp. 561-571.

[13] Mohamed Onsi, "Factor Analysis of Behavioral Variables Affecting Budgetary Slack," *The Accounting Review*, July 1973, pp. 535-548.

[14] Michael Schiff and Arie Y. Lewin, "Where Traditional Budgeting Fails," *Financial Executive*, May 1968, pp. 51-62; "The Impact of People on Budgets," *The Accounting Review*, April 1970, pp. 259-268.

may be difficult, therefore, to set satisfactory goals and to decide objectively on the amount of earnings to expect from a given division or other profit center. Accounting performance reports and analyses of variances do not isolate slack, so that top management cannot objectively determine its level. If the SEC should decide to implement its proposal on published forecasts, corporate management may have to devise means to deal effectively with budgetary slack.

A Final Word

The SEC proposal for published forecasts poses difficult problems. Its successful implementation requires that solutions be found in a number of areas, including report content, extent of disclosure of assumptions, explanation of variances, dual budgeting implications, and budgetary slack.

The proposal states that certification or verification of forecasts by third parties will not be required at this time. However, it may be expected that CPAs would eventually get involved, with or without attestation. The FEI Study (p. 17) reports that the companies surveyed did not utilize external auditor assistance in the preparation of budgets or forecasts. This would most likely change if the SEC proposal should be implemented. After all, public accountants are specialists on disclosure. □

lease-or-buy decisions

by Gordon B. Harwood and Roger H. Hermanson

The net present value method recognizes the time value of money, resulting in a decision that maximizes the present value of net cash inflows.

The manager of a small client calls you with a problem. This client is a corporation that operates a public golf club for profit. The problem concerns the company's fleet of 40 golf carts. The old battery-powered carts that were purchased as a fleet about five years ago, and that are now fully depreciated, are going to have to be replaced. The immediate question is whether to purchase the new carts or to lease them. A salesman has offered to sell the club 40 new gasoline powered carts for $1,600 each. If purchased, the new carts are expected to have a salvage value of $200 each at the end of five years. Another salesman representing a different company has proposed to lease the carts to the club for $400 per year over a period of five years (payable at the end of each year). In either case, the out-of-pocket operating costs (gas, oil and maintenance) are expected to be $300 per year per cart. The annual revenue produced by the fleet of carts is expected to be $60,000. The corporation has been offered $150 cash for each of the old carts, regardless of whether it leases or buys the new ones. How should you advise a client to make a fixed asset acquisition decision such as this?

All applicable factors should be taken into consideration—both nonquantifiable and quantifiable. Nonquantifiable factors include such items as the possible effect of a decision on employee morale, employee safety, possible alternative uses of the facilities after acquisition and so on. As to the quantifiable factors, many businessmen attempt to use the payback method for arriving at fixed asset acquisition decisions. The payback method involves dividing the initial outlay by the annual net cash benefits. Generally, the shorter the payback period, the better the alternative is considered to be. Of course, no alternative would be given further consideration if the payback period is calculated to be longer than the expected life of the asset. But there are several problems with using the payback method. The most obvious is that it cannot be used in situations such as that just described, because the lease alternative has no initial outlay. Other less obvious weaknesses are that it does not consider the time value of money and that it ignores returns received after the end of the payback

Gordon B. Harwood, *CPA, Ph.D., is assistant professor of accounting at Georgia State University, Atlanta. A member of the American Accounting Association, the National Association of Accountants, the Georgia Society of CPAs and the American Institute of CPAs, he is coauthor of "Optimizing Organizational Goals in Assigning Faculty Teaching Schedules," which appeared in* Decision Sciences, *July 1975.* **Roger H. Hermanson,** *CPA, Ph.D., is research professor of accounting at Georgia State University. Hermanson is coauthor of several books and articles on accounting and is a member of the American Accounting Association, the Financial Executives Institute, the Georgia Society of CPAs and the AICPA.*

Exhibit I

Summary of information needed for using the net present value method

Transaction	Time frame	Amount of effect	Direction: decrease — increase +
A *Financing effects on cash flow*			
1 Initial outlay (out-of-pocket costs) to acquire the asset (net of any investment tax credit)	Immediate if purchase	Full amount	—
2 Proceeds from selling old asset	Time of sale (usually immediate)	Full amount	+
3 Tax effect of gain or loss on disposal of old asset	Time of disposal (usually immediate)	Amount of loss or gain × tax rate	+ if loss — if gain
4 Proceeds from sale of new asset at end of life	Time of sale	Full amount	+
B *Operating effects on cash flow*			
1 Annual cash inflow (after taxes) from utilizing the asset—that is, cash generated	Annually over life	Amount of inflow (1 — tax rate)	+
2 Annual cash outflow (after taxes) from utilizing the asset—that is, operating and maintenance cash outflow	Annually over life	Amount of outflow (1 — tax rate)	—
3 Tax shield from deducting depreciation on tax return	Annually over life	Annual depreciation × tax rate	+
4 Depreciation tax shield on old asset disposed of*	Annually over life	Annual depreciation × tax rate	—

C *The decision*—Select the alternative which has the highest present value of the net cash inflows (or lowest present value of the net cash outflows).

---

* This should be considered only in cases where one of the alternatives is to retain and use the old asset and there is book value remaining to be depreciated. It is included here only so this model can be used for a broader range of these decisions.

---

period. Thus the payback method can lead to erroneous capital expenditure decisions.

Accounting and finance textbooks commonly recommend that the net present value method (or some variation thereof) be used to deal with the quantifiable factors in arriving at decisions of this kind. A dollar in hand today is worth more than a dollar to be received two years from now because the dollar in hand can begin earning a return immediately. The net present value method takes the time value of money into consideration. The alternative to be selected will always be the one which results in the highest present value of the net cash inflows.[1]

---

[1] These decisions can be phrased in such a way that the alternative with the lowest present value of the net cash outflows will be selected. For instance, if there are two ways to accomplish the same goal, it would be desirable to select the one that involves the least cost (measured in terms of the lowest present value of the net cash outflow).

At the practical level, clients often have trouble implementing the net present value method in concrete situations because of the potential for confusion in identifying certain information needed to use this kind of decision model, namely, (1) the transactions that will give rise to a change in the funds flow of the concern, (2) the time frame in which the effect is felt, (3) the amount by which the flow of funds is affected after considering taxes and (4) the direction of the effect (whether a decrease or an increase). The chart in Exhibit I, this page, presents a summary of these points, which can be used in making the fixed asset acquisition decisions clients often face.

Exhibit II, page 85, illustrates the application of the checklist given in Exhibit I to the situation of the public golf club considering the purchase

Exhibit II

Illustration of the application of the checklist

Alternatives

Transaction	Purchase new carts		Lease new carts	
A *Financing effects on cash flow*				
1 Initial outlay (out-of-pocket costs) to acquire the asset	$1,600 $\times$ 40 carts = (see footnote 3 on page 86 for mention of the effect of any investment tax credit)	$-64,000	Not applicable	
2 Proceeds from selling old asset	$150 $\times$ 40 carts =	+6,000	$150 $\times$ 40 carts =	$+6,000
3 Tax effect of gain or loss on disposal of old asset	$6,000 gain $\times$ .22 =	-1,320	$6,000 gain $\times$ .22 =	-1,320
4 Proceeds from sale of new asset at end of life	$8,000 $\times$ .567 =	+4,536	Not applicable	
B *Operating effects on cash flow*				
1 Cash inflows (after taxes) from utilizing the asset	$60,000 (1 - .22) $\times$ 3.605 =	+168,714	$60,000 (1 - .22) $\times$ 3.605 =	+168,714
2 Cash outflows (after taxes) from utilizing the asset	$12,000 (1 - .22) $\times$ 3.605 =	-33,743	$28,000 (1 - .22) $\times$ 3.605 =	-78,733
3 Depreciation tax shield from utilizing new asset	$\dfrac{\$64,000 - \$8,000}{5 \text{ yrs.}} = \$11,200$ per yr. $11,200 $\times$ .22 $\times$ 3.605 =	+8,883	Not applicable	
4 Depreciation tax shield on old asset	Not applicable since continued use of old asset is not an alternative.		Not applicable since continued use of old asset is not an alternative.	
Net present value—(Select the alternative with the highest net present value)		+$89,070		+$94,661

and lease alternatives for obtaining its golf carts. (An item-by-item discussion of the solution follows below.) This client requires a return of 12 percent on investments because this is the rate it must pay to borrow funds at the bank.[2] The client's aftertax income is such that the marginal tax effects of this investment are in the 22 percent category.

Discussion of Exhibit II

Each of the items contained in Exhibit II will be discussed and the reasoning behind each calculation given.

Financing transactions

All cash flow effects of acquiring or disposing of the capital assets are included among these transactions.

1 *Initial outlay to acquire the asset*—To purchase the carts an initial outlay of $64,000 is required.[3] No initial outlay is required to lease the carts.

2 *Proceeds from selling old asset*—Under either alternative $6,000 will be received immediately from selling the old carts.

3 *Tax effect of gain or loss on disposal of old asset* —Since the old carts were fully depreciated, there will be a gain of $6,000 from the sale of the old carts (40 carts × $150 each). When this gain is reported for income tax purposes it will result in increasing the amount of income taxes paid by $1,320 under either alternative. To keep the example simple, it was assumed this impact would be immediate rather than delayed by a year.

4 *Proceeds from sale of new asset at end of life*— Under the purchase alternative $8,000 will be received from the sale of the new asset at the end of five years (40 carts × $200 each). Since the amount is to be received five years from the point of decision, the amount must be discounted to its present value. To do this you would consult Table 1, this page, which shows the present value of $1 to be received in so many periods given a certain interest (or discount) rate. The table shows that the present value of $1 to be received five years from now, assuming a discount rate of 12 percent (which the client has specified in the example given), is .567, or $.567. Therefore, the present value of $8,000 to be received five years

from now assuming a 12 percent discount rate is $8,000 × .567, or $4,536.

This transaction does not apply to the lease alternative. Ownership has not been obtained, so the client will not be selling the new carts at the end of their useful life if leased.

Table 1

Present value of a lump sum

Periods	8%	10%	12%	14%	16%	18%	20%
1	0.926	0.909	0.893	0.877	0.862	0.847	0.833
2	0.857	0.826	0.797	0.769	0.743	0.718	0.694
3	0.794	0.751	0.712	0.675	0.641	0.609	0.579
4	0.735	0.683	0.636	0.592	0.552	0.516	0.482
5	0.681	0.621	0.567	0.519	0.476	0.437	0.402

Operating transactions

All cash flows resulting from the use of the assets in operations are included among these transactions.

1 *Cash inflows (after taxes) from utilizing the asset* —Under either alternative revenue of $60,000 per year would be received from renting the carts to golfers. The receipts would be taxable, and therefore the aftertax receipts (cash residue) would be equal to $60,000 (1 − tax rate) or $60,000 (1 − .22). This would leave $60,000 × .78 or $46,800 after taxes each year for five years. To find the present value of this stream of cash inflow (called an annuity since it is constant in amount), it is necessary to use Table 2, page 87.

Again we would use the 12 percent column and the five period row to find the present value factor of 3.605. This factor literally means that if one were to invest $3.60 at 12 percent, he would be able to withdraw $1 at the end of each of the next five years and would then have a zero balance in the investment. Alternatively, it is possible to state that the present value (or the value at the present point in time) of an annuity of $1 to be received at the end of each of the next five years is $3.60. Therefore, the present value of the annuity of $46,800 cash inflow (after taxes) to be received at the end of each of the next five years is $46,800 × 3.605 = $168,714.

2 *Cash outflows (after taxes) from utilizing the asset.* Under the purchase alternative there would be the $12,000 yearly operating costs ($300 × 40 carts). Since these are deductible for tax purposes, the aftertax cost would be $12,000 (1 − tax rate) or $12,000 (1 − .22). Thus, $12,000 × .78 = $9,360 annual cash outflow after taxes. To find the present value of this annuity it is necessary to refer again to Table 2 and use the same 3.605 used above (the number in the 12 percent column

---

[2] Although this does not conform with theoretical concepts of the cost of capital, it is a rate that can be readily and objectively identified by the manager of a small business. Its use can be supported on practical grounds.

[3] To the extent that an investment tax credit can be taken, the initial outlay is reduced by the amount of that credit. The rules regarding applicability of such a credit should be checked in each instance of an asset acquisition. The percentage rate is changed periodically by Congress to stimulate or dampen the economy.

and five period row). Therefore the present value of this annuity is $9,360 \times 3.605 = $33,743.

Under the lease alternative the outflow from operations is $28,000. This is made up of $12,000 yearly operating expenses plus $16,000 annual lease payments ($400 $\times$ 40 carts). The annual outflow after taxes is $28,000 (1 – tax rate) or $28,000 (1 – .22). Thus $28,000 $\times$ .78 = $21,840 annual cash outflow. The present value of this annuity is $21,840 $\times$ 3.605 = $78,733.

Table 2

Present value of an annuity

Periods	8%	10%	12%	14%	16%	18%	20%
1	0.926	0.909	0.893	0.877	0.862	0.847	0.833
2	1.783	1.736	1.690	1.647	1.605	1.566	1.528
3	2.577	2.487	2.402	2.322	2.246	2.174	2.106
4	3.312	3.170	3.037	2.914	2.798	2.690	2.589
5	3.993	3.791	(3.605)	3.433	3.274	3.127	2.991

---

3 *Depreciation tax shield from utilizing new asset* —The cost less salvage value of the new asset can be depreciated over the useful life of the asset. This item is deductible for tax purposes, and, since the tax rate is 22 percent, each dollar of depreciation taken reduces income taxes by $.22. Assuming straight-line depreciation is used, the annual depreciation is

$$\frac{\text{cost-salvage}}{\text{useful life}} = \frac{\$64,000-\$8,000}{5 \text{ years}} = \$11,200 \text{ per year}$$

The reduction in income taxes each year resulting from the depreciation deduction is equal to $11,200 $\times$ .22 or $2,464. The present value of this reduction in income taxes is found as follows: $2,464 $\times$ 3.605 = $8,883, using the same present value factor as before.

4 *Depreciation tax shield on old asset*—This was not applicable in the illustration given. It is applicable in a case, for example, where a company is deciding between continuing the use of a presently owned asset that has a remaining useful life of a number of years or acquiring a new asset to take its place. If the new asset is acquired, depreciation will no longer be taken on the old asset. This amounts to the loss of the tax shield resulting from depreciation on the presently owned asset and the substitution of a new depreciation tax shield as treated in paragraph 3 above.

The loss of this depreciation tax shield needs to be considered in such cases; the lost tax shield has the effect of partially offsetting the depreciation tax shield created by the acquisition of the new asset.

The decision

As Exhibit II shows, the lease alternative results in a total increase in cash inflows (at their present value) of $94,661. The purchase alternative results in a total increase of $89,070. Thus, on the basis of the quantifiable factors in this situation, the client would elect the alternative of leasing the golf carts.

Conclusion

Smaller clients often sense that mere intuition is inadequate for making capital expenditure decisions but are baffled as to what specific approach to use. The net present value method is a decision method that is recommended by many authorities for weighing the quantifiable factors surrounding these kinds of decisions. This method is recommended because it recognizes the time value of money and results in a decision that maximizes the present value of the client's net cash inflows (or minimizes the present value of the client's net cash outflows). A checklist summary of the net present value method is given in Exhibit I of this article, and an example of the application of the checklist is shown in Exhibit II. Both of these exhibits may be retained for use by clients as a guide in applying the method as the occasional need arises. ∎

human resource accounting as a management tool

by Thomas W. McRae

Measuring client personnel development costs for management planning and control is an aspect of human resource accounting (HRA), a topic that encompasses several approaches to measuring and accounting for the cost or value of an organization's human resources. HRA ranges from proposals to account for the costs of recruiting, hiring, training and developing employees as capital investments for management planning and control purposes to proposals to account for the value of an organization's human resources as capital assets for financial reporting purposes.

HRA describes the process of measuring the cost or value of an organization's personnel and recognizing those amounts as capital investments. The objectives of HRA are to provide

☐ Quantitative information on an organization's human resources that management and investors can use in their decision-making processes.

☐ Methods of evaluating management's utilization of human resources—for example, monetary measures of turnover costs.

☐ A theory to explain the nature and determi-

nants of the value of people to formal organizations, to identify relevant variables and to develop an ideal model for the management of human resources.

Advocates of the various proposals to measure and report the cost or value of human resources as capital investments claim that the information enables management to make hiring, training, development and replacement decisions on the basis of realistic cost-benefit analysis and provides investors with an improved basis to assess the value of an enterprise and to make better investment decisions.

Measuring personnel development costs and accounting for those costs as assets for management planning and control form the central focus of this article. Other aspects of HRA are peripheral.

Research and experimentation in HRA are particularly suited to the public accounting profession. The public accountant, by virtue of his professional relationship with clients and his knowledge of the need for objective information that can be audited and then accepted by management, is in a strategic position to experiment with HRA and to develop its potential as a useful management tool. A system to measure the costs of developing personnel and to account for those costs as deferred charges, or amortizable assets, is among the most feasible and least controversial of HRA proposals

Thomas W. McRae, *CPA, is a research administrator in the AICPA's technical research division. He is a member of the AICPA, the American Accounting Association and the National Association of Black Accountants.*

The Journal of Accountancy, August 1974

A system to measure the costs of developing client personnel would add a new dimension to the management advisory services that public accountants now provide.

and would be most useful for management planning and control. The necessary measurement techniques would not differ substantially from those in current use in accounting. Moreover, the development of the system would add a significant new dimension to the management advisory services that public accountants now provide. One writer states:

"A new way of thinking about the human resource is emerging. It is apparent that the reconceptualization of the only vital factor of production will have a profound impact on the way managers manage. The new set of concepts is coming as an outgrowth of the design of accounting systems adequate to measure the costs of human resources and to report manpower as a capital asset. Though of itself the revised accounting system will not improve the management of [people], it will provide substantive evidence of [their] value and, therefore, act to emphasize that [each person] *is a unique entity requiring individualized consideration.*"[1]

An HRA proposal, even one with limited objectives, must address the following:

□ The conceptual justification for capitalizing the specified aspect (cost or value) of human resources.

□ The types of costs to be measured and the methods of measuring them.

□ The method of accumulating costs. Should cost be accumulated for all employees, for classes of employees or for individual employees?

□ The assignment of common costs to classes or individuals.

□ The cutoff between costs to be capitalized and costs to be included in current expenses.

□ The method and period of amortization.

□ The disposition of unamortized costs related to a terminated employee.

□ The uses of the data for management planning and control.

Each of the foregoing topics is discussed in this article, but, to provide perspective, a project being conducted by the Human Resource Laboratory of American Telephone and Telegraph Company (AT&T) will be described first.

The Bell system project

The Human Resource Laboratory of AT&T is conducting an HRA project—"Force-Loss Cost Analysis"—designed to measure the costs of employing and developing toll directory and assistance operators. The project, according to H. W.

---

[1] Robert Wright, "Managing Man as a Capital Asset," *Personnel Journal*, April 1970, p. 290.

Gustafson, who directs it, is designed to develop "a cost-data collection system in which employee-replacement costs are treated as capital investments—not operating expenses," so that "by amortizing the investment—taking into account tenure and employee's increased productive capability due to job experience—it is possible to cal-

> The human resources of an enterprise are not recognized as assets under GAAP, although those resources clearly have substantial economic value to the enterprise.

culate recovery or loss on investment if an employee leaves prematurely."[2]

The decision to limit the project to the job of operator was based on the need for objective data that could be audited. Other factors that influenced the company to select the job of operator were (1) the uniformity of the training and the job experience, (2) the high turnover rate among operators and (3) the relative significance of operators in its work force.

The company recognizes as an investment for management planning and control purposes the costs of hiring, training and developing an operator to the level of normal productivity. In analyzing those costs in internal "force-loss analysis reports," the company classifies as separate cost components (1) employment costs, (2) training costs, (3) efficiency recovery costs and (4) extra supervision costs.

Employment costs represent the total cost of hiring an individual. The costs of recruiting, processing and selecting an individual are accumulated as they are incurred, and the additional hiring costs that apply to applicants for all types of employment are allocated on the basis of the percentage of applicants for operator positions to all applicants.

Training costs represent the costs incurred in the company's initial training program for operators and the costs incurred for supplemental training during the first month of employment. These costs include the wages of both the new operator and the instructor.

Efficiency recovery costs are the portions of the wages of newly trained operators for work that does not meet the normal or expected level of pro-

ductivity and, thus, represent the total cost of increasing the productivity of new operators from the level attained in the initial training program to the expected level. For example, if after initial training an operator is only 60 percent as efficient as the norm, 40 percent of the operator's wages is recorded as efficiency recovery costs.

The costs of extra supervision consist of the wages of service assistants who provide this supervision during the period necessary for new operators to develop a level of normal productivity. The amount of extra supervision is measured by the number of discussions between an operator and the supervisor.

The accumulated costs are amortized on a straight-line basis, and the amount of amortization is adjusted monthly for increases in the expected tenure of an operator. Expected tenure is actuarially determined and increases with the length of employment. Thus, during the early months of employment, when efficiency recovery costs are recorded, the adjustment to the investment is the net of the amount amortized and the amount deferred as efficiency recovery costs.

The total investment is the amount expended on an employee by the time the employee resigns or is dismissed. The amount of the investment amortized during the period of employment represents the portion of the investment recovered; the remainder represents the portion of the investment lost. The total costs of employees who leave the company within the first two weeks after employment represent short-tenure losses.

Force-loss cost analysis is used entirely for management planning and control. The director of the project contends that, by comparing costs incurred for employee development, management can determine the payoff on a specific personnel program or evaluate alternative programs in terms of their impacts on the loss of employees and the related costs and, in turn, on future earnings. Also, local offices are claimed to be more cost-conscious because the information is available.

Justifying deferral of costs

APB Statement No. 4 (para. 132) defines assets as economic resources that are recognized and measured under generally accepted accounting principles (GAAP). The human resources of an enterprise are not recognized as assets under GAAP, although those resources clearly have substantial economic value to the enterprise. Ownership of an economic resource is a criterion for recognizing the resource as an asset under GAAP. Since an enterprise acquires only a contractual right to the services of its human resources, the enterprise acquires the benefit of those services at the time they are performed. Thus, neither the cost

[2] Florence Stone, "Investment in Human Resources at AT&T," *Management Review*, October 1972, pp. 23-27. Most of the information in this section is based on this article and on a "Force-Loss Cost Analysis Report" made available to the author.

nor the value of human resources is recognized as an asset in financial accounting.

The matching concept, however, requires costs to be associated with related revenue in measuring the periodic net income of an enterprise. Under that concept, costs incurred in one period that benefit later periods are deferred and allocated to the periods that receive the benefit.

". . . The essential criterion for determining whether a cost is an 'asset' or an 'expense' relates to the notion of future service potential. Thus human resource costs, which are sacrifices incurred by the firm in obtaining services with the objective of deriving future benefits, can be classified as either assets or expenses. They should be treated as expenses in the periods in which benefits result. If these benefits relate to a future time period they should be treated as assets."[3]

A large part of the costs of human resources (wages and salaries of employees and related costs) in manufacturing enterprises is allocated directly or indirectly to products and is deferred as product costs to be recorded as an expense at the time the products are sold. The costs incurred to recruit, hire, train and develop human resources, however, cannot be related to products. Yet, the costs are clearly intended to benefit several periods and are similar to other preproduction costs. Deferring those costs as intangible assets and amortizing them over the periods which they benefit are thus justifiable under GAAP.

Justifying the deferral of the costs of developing human resources under GAAP is not necessary, however, to justify that practice for management planning and control. For that purpose, demonstrating the usefulness of the information is all that is necessary.

Personnel development costs

The costs of developing personnel that probably should be considered for possible deferral are generally similar to those identified in the Bell system project: employment costs, training costs, efficiency recovery costs and extra supervision costs. However, those designations and the methods of measuring the different types of costs may not be appropriate in other industries. For example, identifying and measuring the costs of developing managerial and professional personnel may involve special problems that relate particularly to the elaborateness of most training and development programs and the long period required to develop the full potential of managers and professional staff.

Employment costs. The employment costs in all

industries include the expenditures required to attract, screen and select an employee. These costs include expenditures for advertising, college recruiting, preemployment screening and interviewing, preemployment visits and plant tours, testing, medical examinations, checking personal references and other investigations. The costs of operating a recruiting department, an allocated portion of the costs of operating a personnel department and an appropriate share of general overhead costs are also part of employment costs.

Training costs. The nature, significance and timing of training costs vary from industry to industry and for different types of personnel. But training costs always include the cost of the training programs required before an employee is assigned to productive work and also the cost of on-the-job training. Training costs also include the costs of all training programs after employees are assigned to full-time productive work, whether the programs are conducted inside or outside of the organization. For example, continuing education programs are essential for the development of managerial and professional personnel. The direct costs of training programs are all of the costs of operating the programs, including the wages and salaries of trainees and instructors. Indirect training costs include an appropriate share of general overhead costs and a portion of the costs of operating facilities, such as professional libraries, which

> The problem of determining the unit for costs accumulation and amortization is analogous to the problem of determining the appropriate depreciable base for physical assets. Essentially, the question is: What is the most appropriate unit for accumulating personnel development costs for management planning and control?

are maintained to support training programs and for other purposes.

Efficiency recovery costs. Efficiency recovery costs represent the costs incurred to develop an employee from the time he is assigned to a regular job until he reaches the normal or expected level of efficiency. Costs designated "extra supervision costs" in the Bell system project should probably be a part of efficiency recovery costs. Measuring efficiency recovery costs requires the development of norms and methods of measuring actual performance against those norms. Levels of normal efficiency and procedures for measuring efficiency

3 R. Lee Brummet, Eric G. Flamholtz and William C. Pyle, "Human Resource Measurement—A Challenge for Accountants," *The Accounting Review*, April 1968, p. 218.

would generally vary from organization to organization and for different types of personnel. The efficiency-recovery component of personnel development costs is probably the most difficult to measure, and the measurements would probably be less objective than the measurement for other components.

Other costs. Another element of the costs of developing personnel, although not identified in the Bell system project, is the cost of maintaining the personnel of an organization in a state of readiness to perform their intended functions. Costs of that nature may relate to fully trained, fully efficient employees and include, for example, wages of a staff member of a public accounting firm who is unassigned because an appropriate assignment is not available.

Costs accumulation and amortization

The problem of determining the unit for costs accumulation and amortization is analogous to the problem of determining the appropriate depreciable base for physical assets. Essentially, the question is: What is the most appropriate unit for accumulating personnel development costs for management planning and control? Most informed individuals would agree that the value or utility of an efficient combination of individuals into a functioning organization is greater than the sum of the value or utility of all of the individual employees of the organization. That type of reasoning may seem to suggest that costs to develop personnel should be accumulated in a single account for all personnel. However, that form of reasoning is not sound. The combination of physical assets into an efficient production unit also creates a unit that is worth more than the sum of the value of its individual parts, but the costs of physical assets are not recorded in a single account. So the reasoning does not provide sufficient support for the view that costs of developing personnel should be recorded in a single account. The unit for cost accumulation must be determined by the information needs of management.

Accumulating costs for each employee probably provides the most information, although this requires subjective allocations of common costs. Subjective allocations are common in accounting and should not destroy the usefulness of the information produced. Moreover, management would have the total information and could analyze the information in different ways for different purposes.

Allocating costs to employees

As suggested in the preceding section, many of the costs of developing personnel cannot be assigned to individuals directly but must be allocated on some systematic and rational basis. Allocation methods would obviously vary with the nature of the organization and the type of costs to be allocated. For example, an organization may normally attract, screen and evaluate many individuals for a few positions. The total cost of that effort may be allocated ratably to the number of people hired.

Cutoff for deferring costs

The cutoff for deferring costs in the Bell system project is the time in which an operator attains the normal level of productivity. The cutoff may not be as clear in other organizations with different types of personnel. For example, professional development in public accounting continues throughout the professional life of an individual. In some organizations realistic cutoffs may be determinable, but in others no reasonable cutoffs can be determined. Those circumstances should not normally cause an insurmountable problem so long as the types of costs to be deferred are specified clearly.

Method and period of amortization

Amortization of the amount invested in an individual employee begins in the Bell system project before the total investment has been accumulated and is based on a straight-line method designed to spread the cost over the expected tenure of the employee. Tenure is actuarially determined and adjusted monthly. Other methods of amortization, such as reverse sum-of-the-digits, have been suggested in the literature.[4] The reverse sum-of-the-digits method is supported by the appealing argument that an employee becomes more valuable to an organization the longer he remains with the organization. That argument points up a perplexing dilemma—if the argument is carried to extremes, no amortization would be recorded. Deferral of the costs of developing personnel seems to require some method of systematic and rational amortization, somewhat like accounting for intangible assets or prepaid expenses.

One writer contends, "Human resources, then, should be accounted for much like the intangible prepaid expenses and deferred charges which represent costs awaiting assignment to future revenues —the future benefit is in the form of services rather than physically divisible units.[5]"

Determining estimated "useful life" is another difficult problem that most organizations can resolve only on a subjective basis. Determining expected tenure on an actuarial basis is unlikely to be appropriate for organizations with diverse personnel, e.g., the background of personnel in a public accounting firm as contrasted with the background of telephone operators would make it difficult to

4 Marvin Weiss, "Accounting for Human Resources," *The Magazine of Bank Administration.* December 1972, p. 15.
5 Sandra E. Peterson, "Accounting for Human Resources," *Management Accounting,* June 1972. p. 19.

use actuarial methods. Although the problem cannot be solved satisfactorily in concept, a practical and satisfactory solution is possible. One possible method is to assume that each employee will spend his entire working life as a member of the organization. A possible justification for that method is the notion that the position that an individual fills is permanent even though his occupancy of the position is not. That method of determining the estimated "useful life" of an employee coupled with some form of increasing amortization, such as the reverse sum-of-the-digits method, would recognize that an employee becomes more valuable to an organization the longer he remains a member of it.

> The unamortized costs of training and developing an employee are recognized as a loss in the Bell system project if the employee resigns or is dismissed. On the surface, that seems an entirely reasonable method of determining and accounting for the costs of turnover. The method, however, deserves closer examination.

But to mention the working life of an employee as the maximum possible life is not to endorse it as a practical basis for amortization. The problem is complex and can be solved only by informed judgment in specific circumstances. The following comments suggest some of the complexities:

". . . these assets can be amortized over their expected useful lives. . . . the expected remaining service life of employees may lengthen as well as shorten; however, conventional amortization procedures have been modified to allow book values to move up or down to reflect underlying changes in the value of human resources. For example, an employee may be more valuable after he has completed one year on the job because his expected remaining tenure is much greater than when he was first hired."[6]

"Amortization should be computed, as in the case of physical assets, based upon the life expectancy of the investments. This requires that each outlay be related to its expected economic benefit and amortized over the period during which the benefit is being enjoyed. The procedure, in theory, is again no different from that of depreciation of physical assets, but, as a practical matter, it may take some different turns. Investments in

recruiting and acquisition provide benefits during the total time the individual remains with the firm, so 'expected life' with the firm is a reasonable base. Investments in special skill training such as computer programing using FORTRAN may have a more limited life and thus should be amortized over the useful expectancy for the skill."[7]

Another writer,[8] in discussing accounting for the costs of developing human resources in public accounting firms, describes two possible methods of costs accumulation and amortization. Under the first method, costs are accumulated and amortized by type of resource (professional development, on-the-job training, and so on). The author explains:

"There is a subjective problem in determining the period of amortization for each classification. . . . it is first necessary to decide the upper (maximum) limit of amortization. Since the staff turnover rate for most companies [public accounting firms] is three years, there does not appear to be any justification for an amortization rate of more than three years. Within that limit, then, recruiting and self-professional development . . . should be amortized over the entire three-year period. . . . professional development is amortized over two years, and on-the-job training . . . over two years."[9]

Under the second method described, the individual is the unit for costs accumulation and the costs are amortized over a period no longer than 10 years—the mean length of time for an individual to become a partner. In the words of the author:

"In this model, there is no amortization for the first three years of employment. After the third year, amortization is begun, using the straight-line method, over the remaining seven years. The asset is thus hung up for three years—the average length of time it takes to become a senior—because until this time there is no return on the investment of the accountant."[10]

Disposition of unamortized costs

The unamortized costs of training and developing an employee are recognized as a loss in the Bell system project if the employee resigns or is dismissed. On the surface, that seems an entirely reasonable method of determining and accounting for the costs of turnover. The method, however, deserves closer examination.

Most discussions of turnover costs assume that the costs are losses that an organization should attempt to avoid. That view is not entirely supportable. A reasonable level of turnover is necessary and desirable in most organizations. In fact, most personnel managers plan for a level of turnover

---

[6] William C. Pyle, "Human Resource Accounting," *Financial Analysts Journal*, September-October 1970, p. 70.

[7] R. Lee Brummet, "Accounting for Human Resources," JofA, Dec.70, p.64.
[8] Peterson, *op. cit.*, p. 21.
[9] *Ibid.*
[10] *Ibid.*

considered desirable to maintain a viable organization. To them, planned turnover serves the same purpose as pruning a tree to get rid of deadwood and to provide a healthy environment for new growth. To the extent that a certain level of turnover is planned or desirable, recognizing as losses all the unamortized costs accumulated for employees who leave an organization may not be reasonable. At least, other possible methods of disposing of unamortized costs should be explored. One

> After considering some of the significant problems in measuring personnel development costs, the conclusion that public accounting firms should conduct experiments in HRA seems inescapable.

feasible suggestion is to recognize the costs of abnormal turnover as losses and to allocate the costs of normal turnover to the remaining employees. In many respects, the costs of normal turnover are similar to the expected costs of unsuccessful recruiting efforts.

Uses of data

Devising and testing a new system of accounting for the costs of developing personnel would not be justified unless the information produced by the system proved useful for management planning and control. The increasing volume of HRA literature contains some persuasive arguments demonstrating that management can use the information produced by a system of HRA in several ways.[11] Suggested uses range from the relatively mundane determination of the costs of turnover through improving capital budgeting decisions and return-on-investment calculations to relatively complex behavioral changes.

The information produced by a system of accounting for the costs of developing personnel may assist management to

☐ Evaluate the cost and effectiveness of recruiting efforts and to change those efforts, if necessary, to optimize their effectiveness.

☐ Determine the amount of training costs required and prepare realistic budgets for those costs.

☐ Evaluate the effectiveness of training programs and adjust the programs, if necessary, to optimize the benefits.

☐ Determine turnover costs and the desirable level of turnover.

☐ Determine net short-term layoff costs—the net savings or net costs from reduced manpower as compared to the loss of experienced employees, rehiring and retraining former employees or hiring and training new employees.

☐ Determine the cost of developing new skills, and the expected payoff from those skills, by comparing the cost of developing new skills with alternative investments in other assets such as machinery, equipment or business acquisitions—in short, capital budgeting.

☐ Determine return on investment more precisely for both decision-making and management accountability.

HRA in public accounting firms

After considering some of the significant problems in measuring personnel development costs, the conclusion that public accounting firms should conduct experiments in HRA seems inescapable.

Public accounting firms are ideal organizations to experiment with HRA for several reasons. Some of these follow:

☐ Services of public accounting firms are derived exclusively and directly from human resources.

☐ Public accounting firms have available the expertise to develop complex programs and systems to account for the costs of human resources.

☐ Some public accounting firms now engage in experiments to account for human resources.[12]

☐ Public accounting firms would develop a new expertise to offer to their clients.

But before initiating experiments in public accounting firms, the profession should unambiguously specify objectives and develop a standard set of guidelines. The types of costs to be accumulated should be specified. Procedures for accumulating and allocating costs to individuals should be set out in detail. A method of amortization should be selected based on the judgment and experience of practicing accountants. An acceptable method of handling the unamortized costs of an employee who leaves the firm should be agreed on. Also, the possible uses of the information should be determined. Undoubtedly, the experiments will suggest additional uses and will indicate that some of the expected uses are impractical. ∎

---

[11] See, for example: Brummet, Flamholtz and Pyle, *op. cit.*, pp. 217-24, and Wright, *op. cit.*, pp. 290-97.

[12] Touche Ross & Co. has developed a system of accounting for investments in people and has used the system in an office in Canada with a staff of 120. The firm has also found that some clients are interested in the system. Michael O. Alexander reports on several aspects of the system in "Investments in People," *Canadian Chartered Accountant*, July 1971, pp. 38-45. Eric Flamholtz reports in "Human Resources Accounting: A Review of Theory and Research" (a paper presented to the Organization Behavior Division of the Academy of Management at the 1972 annual meeting of the Academy) that he is engaged in research to develop a valid, reliable and practical system of accounting for the value of human resources in Lester Witte & Company.

The Accounting Review

VOL. XLIII   APRIL 1968   No. 2

Human Resource Measurement— A Challenge for Accountants

R. Lee Brummet, Eric G. Flamholtz and William C. Pyle

A FAVORITE cliché for the president's letter in corporate annual reports is "Our employees are our most important—our most valuable—asset." Turning from the president's letter and looking to the remainder of the report, one might ask, "where is this human asset on these statements which serve as reports on the firm's resources and earnings?" What is the value of this "most important" or "most valuable" asset? Is it increasing, decreasing, or remaining unchanged? What return, if any, is the firm earning on its human assets? Is the firm allocating its human assets in the most profitable way? No answers are to be found.

INADEQUACY OF CONVENTIONAL PRACTICE

Although financial reports do not presently provide the information necessary to answer such questions, a growing number of corporate managers are showing concern that their accounting systems are not adequate. They are questioning why they cannot get information relating to the condition of their firm's human resources and how they are changing. The accountant faces a challenge which he cannot reasonably sidestep. The authors of this paper are engaged in research to assist in meeting this challenge.

As corporate managers make expenditures which they justify as investments in human resources, accountants reflect them as immediate charges to income without considering the timing of expected benefits. This treatment is elected because

R. Lee Brummet is Professor of Accounting in the Graduate School of Business Administration; Eric G. Flamholtz and William C. Pyle are Assistant Project Directors in the Institute of Social Research and are doctoral candidates in the Graduate School of Business Administration, University of Michigan.

The Accounting Review, April 1968

investments in people seem more tenuous than investments in machines, and because there are special difficulties involved in distinguishing between the future benefits of such expenditures and the portion consumed currently. We also have difficulty thinking of people individually as assets since they are not legally owned by the firm and because of cultural constraints or taboos on the notion of valuing an individual in monetary terms.

Reflecting conservative doctrine, accountants have elected to treat expenditures made for recruiting, hiring, training, and developing people as "expenses" rather than attempting to formulate rules to distinguish between their asset and expense components. A few infrequent exceptions to this general treatment may be found where future benefits are readily identifiable. Prepaid wages and salaries are, for example, treated as assets, but these are exceptions to general practice afforded human resource costs.

It is becoming increasingly clear that although outlays for human resources have been traditionally treated as "consumption" rather than "capital" by economists, and as "expenses" rather than "assets" by accountants, these treatments are the result of conventional boundaries of the concept of an asset, and not because of the real nature and timing of benefits that result. The essential criterion for determining whether a cost is an "asset" or an "expense" relates to the notion of future service potential. Thus human resource costs, which are sacrifices incurred by the firm in obtaining services with the objective of deriving future benefits, can be classified as either assets or expenses. They should be treated as expenses in the periods in which benefits result. If these benefits relate to a future time period they should be treated as assets.

NEED FOR HUMAN RESOURCE ACCOUNTING

Human resource information is essential for each of the several phases of management's planning and control functions. These phases and their interrelationships, as suggested in the American Accounting Association's *A Statement of Basic Accounting—Theory*, are shown in Figure 1. The accounting function typically has an important role to play in phases 1, 3, and 5, and a limited role in the other two functions. Let us examine how accounting for human assets can be useful in each of these phases.

Measurements of human resources should assist in *recognizing and defining problems*. Trends in the ratio of investments in human assets to total assets (the human asset investment ratio) may be a useful predictor of future profit performance. There is some evidence to indicate a degree of meaningful correlation between profitability of organizations and their expenditures on acquisition, training, and retention of human resources. This suggests that firms with a high human asset investment ratio will ultimately generate high profits, while firms with a low ratio may experience profit declines.

Another problem area which can be recognized and defined with information about human resources involves personnel turnover. Although it is generally recognized that turnover is costly to the firm, managers do not have adequate measurements of the magnitude of such losses. It has been estimated that the insurance industry, for example, experiences a 100% turnover of agents in about 5 years; yet the amount of associated cost is unknown. Measurements of these costs could be useful in deciding on remedial action and the assessment of results.

Some   organizational   psychologists,

Brummet, Flamholtz and Pyle: Human Resource Measurement

FIGURE 1

THE MANAGEMENT PLANNING AND CONTROL CYCLE.

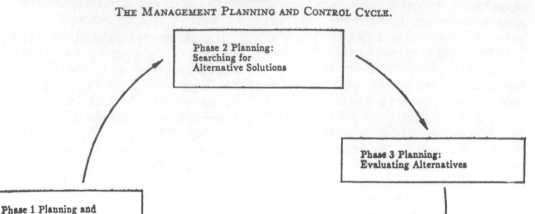

Source: The American Accounting Association, *A Statement of Basic Accounting Theory*, 1966.

notably Rensis Likert of The University of Michigan's Institute for Social Research, believe that certain managerial leadership styles result in the long-run liquidation of human assets while showing immediate increases in earnings. Likert believes that managers are sometimes encouraged to put pressures on employees for cost reduction which result in immediate increases in current net income as measured by conventional practice but which also result in unmeasured deterioration of employee attitudes, motivation, and other psychological variables that will determine the level of profits in *future* periods. If the accounting system provided measurements of the value of the firm's human resources and their changes over time, the "net income" (as conventionally defined) might be adjusted to reflect changes in the value of human resources, in order to avoid the illusion of reporting of "profits" derived from the liquidation of human resources. A net income figure adjusted for changes in the value of human resources would thus give a more realistic measurement of managerial effectiveness. Trends in this "adjusted" net income figure should provide an improved basis for projection of future earnings possibilities.

The process of *searching for alternative solutions* requires imagination and systematic thought based on an awareness of the critical nature of all human resources. The availability, on a routine basis, of

The Accounting Review, April 1968

assessments of human resources should produce a conscious recognition of this factor in the development of alternatives.

Human resource accounting information is critical in the *evaluation of alternatives*. It can be useful in capital budgeting decisions involving human resources, where the impact of decisions on human assets is typically considered to be a "qualitative" factor and, accordingly, is ignored. It can also be used to evaluate investments in human capital.

At present, rather sophisticated tools are used to evaluate alternatives in capital budgeting decisions. Yet the effects of decisions on human assets are generally ignored, or considered to be nil. Further, human assets are not included in the asset base used to calculate rates of return on investment. Accordingly, human assets are implicitly assumed to be a free good— one without cost. But since human as well as physical assets have an opportunity cost associated with their use, this cost should be quantified and considered in evaluating alternatives.[1]

Human resource accounting should make it possible to evaluate investments in human assets themselves. Many firms invest heavily in training programs without evaluating the expected payoff or return on such investments. Similarly, it is currently in vogue for firms to send their managers to a variety of executive development programs. The value of such training and development programs is essentially taken on faith, with such expenditures treated as a luxury that the firm can afford only when its profits are high. It is suggested that a systematic attempt should be made to evaluate the yield or return on these investments over time.

In the process of *selecting among the evaluated alternatives*, the addition of information about human resources and predicted changes in the value of human resources over time will tend to alter the decision models used. Accounting for human resources will tend to move "the human factor" from a qualitative factor that is typically held constant or ignored to a quantitative one which may be an integral part of decision models. For example, in a choice among alternative locations for a new plant, where present employees will be requested to relocate, the firm may survey its employees to determine their attitudes toward the alternative locations being considered, and attempt to determine the expected turnover associated with each location. An "expected cost" of turnover can thus be calculated. This factor could be critical to selection among the various alternatives.

Human resource accounting should also be useful in *reporting on actions taken and results achieved* in relation to objectives and goals. Information about the composition of investments in human resources can be analyzed to determine standard costs of recruiting, hiring, training, and developing individuals in order to bring them up to their present level of technical competence and familiarity required for a given position. In addition to providing a cost control mechanism, these data should be useful to estimate replacement costs to acquire people for various positions. Replacement costs can be used to budget investments in manpower planning and development. The result is a standard cost accounting system for human resource costs similar to that for manufacturing costs.

---

[1] This suggestion is not without precedent. The tax courts, for example, have set legal precedent in certain defense contracts that return on investment might take into account the prior expense of gathering certain kinds of engineering talent in estimating their rate base. Utilities have also begun investigating the possibilities of including human assets in calculating their rate base. Similarly, in the sale of insurance companies the sales force is usually treated as an asset whose value is equal to the present value of future earnings.

Brummet, Flamholtz and Pyle: Human Resource Measurement

RESEARCH IN HUMAN RESOURCE ACCOUNTING

This brief sketch of the role of human resource information in the process of managerial planning and control suggests some of the practical potential of human resource accounting. At present, the authors are involved in extensive research in human resource accounting which is focused upon three broad objectives:

1. the development of human resource accounting systems in a number of corporations,
2. the formulation of a body of generalizations about the ways in which information provided by a human resource accounting system should be used in planning and controlling within a firm, and
3. a set of generalizations about the behavioral impact of a human resource accounting system on people.

The initial stage of research involves the development of a human resource accounting system itself. Since October 1966, the authors have worked with a top management group of the R. G. Barry Corporation[2] in the development of what is believed to be the first human resource accounting system actually in use. The work at Barry has focused first upon developing a human resource accounting system for managerial personnel. Later the concepts may be applied to the firm's other human resources, including lower levels of the organization and customers.

The elements of this system can be outlined briefly. First, an attempt has been made to identify human resource costs and separate them from other costs of the firm. Techniques and procedures have been formulated to distinguish between the asset and expense components of human resource costs. The resulting human assets are then classified into functional categories such as recruiting, hiring, training, development, and familiarization. Amounts in the functional asset accounts are then allocated to "personal-

ized asset accounts" for individual managers. Rules and procedures for recording expirations in assets over their expected useful life have been formulated. A manual containing instruments for the collection of the system's primary data has also been designed. A generalized model of the flow of data through the system is shown in Figure 2.

The human resource accounting system for managers of the R. G. Barry Corporation was put into operation on January 1, 1968. This system includes some 90 members of management. Beginning balances for their personalized asset accounts were entered as account balances with a credit to a category designated as "Capital Invested in Human Resources." Thus the stage has been set for study and refinement of the system and the beginning of phases 2 and 3 of the project carried on with this corporation. Other organizations will be brought into this study during 1968.

MULTIPLE MEASURES OF HUMAN RESOURCES

In developing human resource accounting, it has been decided to utilize multiple measurements of human resources to increase the utility of the information communicated. Specifically, an attempt is being made to measure human resources in terms of their acquisition cost, replacement cost, and economic value. *Acquisition cost* refers to the conventional accounting concept of historical cost which is derived from transactions data. It provides a basis for determining the firm's cost to acquire its

[2] The management group from R. G. Barry actively engaged in this research effort include Gordon Zacks, President, Robert L. Woodruff, Jr., Vice President, Personnel, Edward Stan, Treasurer, Richard Burrell, Controller, and Peter Seldin, Personnel Assistant. This project is being conducted under the auspices of the Center for Research on the Utilization of Scientific Knowledge of the Institute for Social Research at the University of Michigan.

The Accounting Review, April 1968

FIGURE 2

GENERALIZED MODEL OF HUMAN RESOURCE ACCOUNTING SYSTEM FOR
INVESTMENTS IN MANAGERS

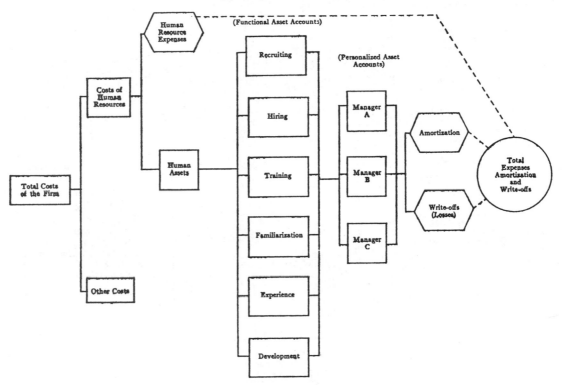

human resources and thus the magnitude of its investment in human resources. *Replacement cost* is a measure of the cost to replace the firm's existing human resources. It should indicate what it would cost the firm to recruit, hire, train, and develop people to their present level of technical proficiency and familiarity with the organization and its operations. The concept of the *economic value* of human resources is the present value of the portion of the firm's future earnings attributable to human resources. The use of these multiple concepts should contribute to the objective of developing useful approximations of the unknown value of human resources and the changes taking place in this value.

While there are some special problems associated with acquisition and replacement cost measurements of human resources, the basic approach is similar to those related to other assets. Problems of estimating *value* in a more direct way present some interesting possibilities. Earnings in excess of the average within an industry may be translated into "goodwill," which may be allocated to human resources in terms of the ratio of human assets to total assets.

An even more direct approach is to estimate the contribution of human resources to the total economic value of the firm. This involves forecasting future earnings, discounting them to determine the firm's present value, and allocating a portion to human resources based on their relative contribution. This is the approach

Brummet, Flamholtz and Pyle: Human Resource Measurement

FIGURE 3

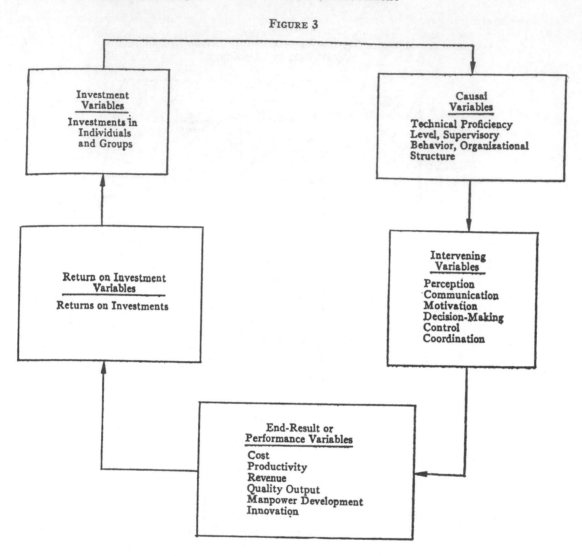

used to value sales forces in the insurance industry at the time of acquisition or sale of firms.

Another approach involves the utilization of studies now being conducted by the Institute for Social Research at The University of Michigan. Periodic measurements are being made of the behavior of managers and supervisors and their level of technical proficiency, the resulting motivations, loyalties, and behavior of subordinates, and the communication, decision-making, and control processes of

the divisions or profit centers. Statistical analysis of variations in leadership styles, technical proficiency levels, motivational, attitudinal, behavioral, and performance variables may establish relationships which are hypothesized to exist among such variables. If, for example, a meaningful relationship is established between changes in leadership styles (causal variables) which result in changes in subordinate attitudes, motivations, and behavior (intervening variables), which produce changes in productivity, innovation, and

The Accounting Review, April 1968

manpower development (end result variables), then trends in earnings can be predicted. Forecasts of predicted earnings can be discounted to determine the present value of the firm and its human resources. A simplified illustration of these concepts and their interrelationships is shown in Figure 3. The underlying theory which is the basis for this approach is presented in Likert's *The Human Organization: Its Management and Value*. It is important to note that although evidence exists that there are definite meaningful relationships among these variables, little has been done to apply these findings to the problem of valuing human resources.

After human resource accounting systems have been designed and installed in a number of organizations, the second phase of the research may be undertaken. This phase will involve monitoring the way in which the system is being used in order to increase knowledge of the application of the system. Although a number of potential uses of the system are presently anticipated, more will be learned about the specific ways in which human resource information may be used in decision-models. The technique of simulation will be utilized to determine whether decisions involving people will be modified if information about human resources is used in decision-models.

The third phase of the research will be aimed at developing a body of generalizations about the impact of human resource accounting on people. The basic thrust will be to determine how people react to being viewed as assets or resources of an organization with a monetary figure designated as the firm's investment in them; whether knowledge of the firm's investment in an individual will affect the individual's attitude toward the organization or his motivation and productivity; and the ways in which knowledge of differential investments in people will affect relationships among peers and between superiors and subordinates.

It is significant to note that many of the concepts and much of the terminology being used in developing human resource accounting are being adopted from conventional accounting. They are merely being applied to a problem that has been relatively ignored. Although familiar accounting concepts and terminology are being used, human resource accounting is not being designed for use in published financial statements. It is intended as a managerial tool. It is designed to satisfy information needs presently faced by operating management. It aims to provide management with relevant, timely, quantifiable, and verifiable information about human resources to encourage informed judgments and decisions. It is future oriented, and thus deals not only with transactions data as conventional accounting, but also with measurements of replacement cost and economic value. Since human resource accounting is intended as a managerial tool, it need not be constrained by accounting conventions, legal restrictions, or tax laws.

The relevance of human resource data for management decisions can hardly be denied. Although the reliability of measurements in the field are not yet fully established, a start has been made and businessmen are reacting with understandable enthusiasm.

INTERNAL ACCOUNTING CONTROL: A MATTER OF LAW

The Foreign Corrupt Practices Act has made the internal accounting controls of public companies a matter of law.

by J. Michael Cook and Thomas P. Kelley

Traditionally, independent auditors have been concerned with internal accounting control as a basis for determining the scope of their examinations of financial statements. Authoritative literature discusses the auditor's approach to the study and evaluation of internal accounting control and defines material weaknesses in those controls in this limited context, that is, in terms of errors or irregularities that could be material to the financial statements being audited.

When there are material weaknesses in internal accounting control, auditors are usually able to satisfy themselves that the financial statements are presented fairly in conformity with generally accepted accounting principles by modifying the nature, timing and extent of other auditing procedures. Material weaknesses may not have been corrected because, exercising business judgment, management has decided that cost/benefit considerations do not justify a change; that is, the cost of the added control would exceed the benefit to be derived. Management is expected to make such judgments and has been doing so without significant challenge for years.

However, times have changed. In December 1977, President Carter signed the Foreign Corrupt Practices Act of 1977. The act

makes internal accounting control a matter of law for all U.S. companies that are registered or file reports with the Securities and Exchange Commission under the Securities Exchange Act of 1934. The accounting standards section of the act amends the Securities Exchange Act of 1934 to require those companies ("public companies"), among other things, to

☐ Devise and maintain a system of internal accounting controls sufficient to provide reasonable assurances that

i Transactions are executed in accordance with management's general or specific authorization.

ii Transactions are recorded as necessary (I) to permit preparation of financial statements in conformity with generally accepted accounting principles or any other criteria applicable to such statements; and (II) to maintain accountability for assets.

iii Access to assets is permitted only in accordance with management's general or specific authorization.

iv The recorded accountability for assets is compared with the existing assets at reasonable intervals and appropriate action is taken with respect to any differences.

The purpose of this article is to present the authors' views on the scope and effect of the act and on the recommendations for management action contained in the *Tentative Report of the* [American Institute of CPAs] *Special Advisory Committee on Internal Accounting Control* (September 15, 1978). The article also outlines some of the changes in reporting practices that may come

J. MICHAEL COOK, CPA, is a partner of Deloitte Haskins & Sells and is presently the assistant to the managing partner of the firm. Mr. Cook has recently completed three years of service as a member of the AICPA auditing standards executive committee. Among other things he was chairman of the AudSEC task force on reports on internal control. **THOMAS P. KELLEY,** CPA, is the AICPA managing director–technical. His duties have included providing staff support to the AICPA special advisory committee on internal accounting control, whose tentative report was issued on September 15, 1978.

The Journal of Accountancy, January 1979

about as a result of the act and that may have an effect on nonpublic companies.

Background

During the course of the investigations that took place after Watergate, it became clear that many corporations had made questionable or illegal payments. These payments included domestic political contributions and payments to foreign officials to obtain or maintain business or for other purposes deemed corrupt. In many instances, these payments were hidden by falsifying records and maintaining off-the-books accounts. Congress intended the accounting standards section of the act—which also includes a requirement for accurate books and records—as a means of increasing corporate accountability, thereby making it more difficult to conceal illegal payments.

Recognition of congressional intent can be helpful in deciding on the actions that should be taken to provide management and the board with reasonable assurance of compliance with the accounting standards section of the act. The act specifically adopts existing concepts of internal accounting control, and its legislative history gives recognition to the need for judgment in applying those concepts. For example, the internal accounting control provision of the act is taken verbatim from section 320.28 of Statement on Auditing Standards no. 1, *Codification of Auditing Standards and Procedures*. Also, in discussing the requirement for accurate books and records, the 1976 *Report of the Senate Committee on Banking, Housing, and Urban Affairs* (Senate Report no. 94-1031) stated that accuracy ". . . does not mean exact precision as measured by some abstract principle. Rather, it means that an issuer's records should reflect transactions in conformity with generally accepted accounting principles. . . ."

Essentially, then, the act codifies existing concepts and existing good practices. However, codification in the law of existing standards may result in those standards and compliance with them being interpreted by the courts. Prudent managements will take steps to review their existing internal accounting controls, the documentation that exists with respect to those controls and the procedures in effect to provide reasonable assurance of compliance with them.

As noted above, the internal accounting control provision of the act was taken verbatim from sec. 320.28 of SAS no. 1. This was

not done without due consideration. For example, in March 1976, Senator William Proxmire (D-Wis.) introduced legislation (S.3133) that would have required the SEC to issue rules or regulations concerning a company's obligation "to maintain accurate books, records, or accounts of all transactions." On May 12, 1976, the SEC issued its *Report on Questionable and Illegal Corporate Payments and Practices*. That report clearly implied that the rules and regulations contemplated by S.3133 were not necessary because

"The concept of internal accounting controls is not new. It has been recognized by the accounting profession as being an important responsibility of management. Because the accounting profession has defined the objectives of a system of accounting control, the Commission has taken the definition of the objectives of such a system contained in our proposed legislation [introduced by Senator Proxmire as S.3418 in May 1978, 17 months before the date of the act] from the authoritative accounting literature."

The legislative history of the act also gives appropriate recognition to other aspects of authoritative literature, particularly the cost/

"Prudent managements will take steps to review their existing internal accounting controls. . . ."

benefit relationship in deciding whether "reasonable assurance" has been achieved and the need for judgment. For example, the *Report of the Senate Committee on Banking, Housing, and Urban Affairs* states that

"While management should observe every reasonable prudence in satisfying the objectives called for in new paragraph (2) of section 13(b), the committee recognizes that management must necessarily estimate and evaluate the cost/benefit relationships of the steps to be taken in fulfillment of its responsibilities under this paragraph. The accounting profession will be expected to use their professional judgment in evaluating the systems maintained by issuers. The size of the business, diversity of operations, degree of centralization of financial and operating management, amount of contact by top management with day-to-day operations, and numerous other circumstances are factors which management must consider in establishing and maintaining an internal accounting controls system."

The Scope of the Internal Accounting Control Provision of the Act

In considering the implications of the act, it is particularly important to recognize that it deals with internal *accounting* controls. Nowhere in the act or in the legislative history is there any reference to administrative controls. The distinction between accounting controls and administrative controls is established in authoritative auditing literature. SAS no. 1, sec. 320.27—.28, defines these two types of controls as follows:

☐ *Administrative control* includes, but is not limited to, the plan of organization and the procedures and records that are concerned with the decision processes leading to management's authorization of transactions. Such authorization is a management function directly associated with the responsibility for achieving the objectives of the organization and is the starting point for establishing accounting control of transactions.

☐ *Accounting control* comprises the plan of organization and the procedures and records that are concerned with the safeguarding of assets and the reliability of financial records and consequently is designed to provide reasonable assurance that [the objectives in the act are met]. . . .

Notwithstanding the emphasis in the act, in the legislative history and in authoritative literature on internal *accounting* controls, some accountants continue to believe that compliance with the accounting standards section of the act cannot be evaluated without considering the full range of a company's internal controls, whether accounting or administrative. They argue that it is a misstatement of management's responsibility for safeguarding the company's assets to restrict that responsibility to losses arising from intentional and unintentional errors in processing transactions and handling assets. In addition, they argue that there are few administrative controls that are not also accounting controls.

We do not dispute the argument that management's control concerns extend to controls over all aspects of the business. Investors expect management to institute controls that, for example, promote efficient and effective operations. But such controls are not accounting controls under the act. They have not been made a matter of law. If the full range of all internal controls were comprehended by the act, then selling a product at a price that proves to be unprofitable might be construed to be an illegal act. Similarly, decisions to incur expenditures for equipment that proves to be unnecessary or inefficient, for materials that prove to be unsatisfactory in production, for merchandise that proves to be unsalable, for research that proves to be unproductive, for advertising that proves to be ineffective, might all be construed to be illegal acts. Surely this was not the intent of Congress when it framed the internal accounting control provision of the act!

It is true that many controls serve both administrative and accounting control purposes. Sec. 320 of SAS no. 1 recognizes this. However, that does not mean the distinction between the two types of controls is not valid. In deciding whether a control is administrative or accounting in nature, careful consideration should be given to the definition and explanatory discussions in the SAS from which, as previously noted, the internal accounting control provisions of the act have been taken. In that connection, sec. 320.19 of SAS no. 1 makes it quite clear that asset safeguarding in the context of internal accounting control relates to protection from loss arising from intentional and unintentional errors in processing transactions and handling the related asset. The authors believe this is the way in which the act should be interpreted. Indeed, we believe it is the only reasonable way in which the act could be interpreted.

The definition of accounting control in the SAS emphasizes reliability of *financial records* as an overriding objective. This is consistent with the objective in sec. 320.28-(b) that "transactions are recorded as necessary (1) to permit preparation of financial statements in conformity with [GAAP]. . . ." Sec. 320.38 explains that "this objective is expressed in terms of permitting, rather than assuring, the preparation of financial statements in conformity with generally accepted accounting principles or any other applicable criteria. This distinction recognizes that, beyond the necessary recording of transactions, management's judgment is required in making estimates and other decisions required in the preparation of such statements."

The tentative report of the special advisory committee states that

"The committee believes that management cannot limit its internal accounting control concerns to the financial records or even to the financial statements themselves. The committee believes that companies should have accounting controls that extend to the external reporting of historical financial information. External reports of historical financial information include the financial statements and related notes, other accounting or financial information included elsewhere in a document containing financial statements (such as a registration statement, proxy statement, or annual report), and other forms of financial reporting to the public, such as interim reports and earnings releases. . . ."

Clearly, that conclusion is an extension of the traditional boundaries of internal accounting control in two respects:

1 From concern over the preparation of financial statements to concern over all external reporting of historical financial information.

2 From concern over the reliability of financial records for purposes of maintaining accountability for assets and permitting the preparation of financial statements from those records to concern over controls to assure reliable financial reports.

The traditional boundaries recognize the practical limitations of accounting control procedures and techniques. The committee's tentative report only partially acknowledges those limitations when it observes that

"Management should also recognize that the control procedures over external financial reporting typically involve subjective judgments to a greater extent than control procedures over processing routine transactions, some of which may be relatively mechanical."

Management clearly is responsible for "external reporting of historical financial information." We certainly do not disagree with the recommendation that managements should review their controls over the financial reporting process. But an argument can be made that such controls are not required by the act itself.

Many highly subjective judgments are required in the preparation of financial statements. For example, the disclosure of contingencies requires an estimation of the possible outcome and effect of a future event. If it is subsequently determined that management's judgment in this regard was incorrect and a contingency should have been disclosed but was not, would this be indicative of an absence of internal accounting controls and, therefore, a possible violation of the accounting standards section of the act? If so, what controls over a decision which requires the knowledge of persons at the highest level of management are required to establish that a violation has not occurred?

This article has emphasized the definition and scope of internal accounting control because the authors believe it to be of prime importance. Public companies should carefully define the scope of their internal accounting control concerns in order to be in the best position to respond to a challenge as to compliance with the internal accounting control provisions of the act.

Recommendations for Management Action by the Special Advisory Committee

The special advisory committee on internal accounting control was formed in August 1977 to develop criteria for evaluating internal accounting control "in reasonable detail and susceptible to objective application." The AICPA recognized that the broad guidance in authoritative auditing literature had been developed for a limited purpose and that there was a need to provide guidance that would be helpful to management. The committee consists principally of financial executives, internal auditors and CPAs engaged in management advisory services.

The Foreign Corrupt Practices Act of 1977 became law after the committee had begun its work. Although the committee was not formed because of the act, its final report is expected to be useful to management and boards of directors in considering whether their companies comply with the internal accounting control provision of the act. On September 15, 1978, the committee issued a tentative report for public comment.

The committee's conclusions are summarized in one paragraph of the tentative report:

"The committee believes that management should initiate a preliminary assessment of the internal accounting control environment and of the appropriateness and effectiveness of existing accounting control procedures and techniques based on its overall knowledge of the company. On the basis of that preliminary assessment, management should plan the manner, extent, and timing of other procedures deemed appropriate. Those procedures should relate to

"**a** A reexamination of the accounting control procedures in place and the ongoing process of evaluating them.

"**b** A consideration of the need for a shift toward more explicit documentation of those control procedures and the process of evaluating them."

Those recommendations are a reasonable, measured response to present regulatory and legislative initiatives. In considering the recommendations, it is important to bear

"... documentation of important policies and of control procedures facilitates compliance with internal accounting controls and would be important if it becomes necessary to demonstrate compliance with the act."

in mind that the committee has defined the term "management" to include the board of directors and committees thereof, where their involvement would be appropriate. The authors believe that board involvement is appropriate, as a minimum, in establishing the proper internal accounting control environment and in exercising an oversight role over the development, review, evaluation and monitoring of control procedures and techniques.

The tentative report places great emphasis on the "internal accounting control environment," a term that may be new to many readers. The report does not specifically define the environment. Rather, it describes the environment by discussing the significant factors that shape it. They are identified as

☐ *Organizational structure.* An appropriate framework for planning, direction and control is likely to strengthen the control procedures in place.

☐ *Personnel.* Competent and honest people are essential to the effective operation of control procedures.

☐ *Delegation and communication of responsibility and authority.* To create a network of personnel who are specifically authorized to approve or disapprove designated transactions and who are prohibited from engaging in or approving other specified transactions.

☐ *Budgets and financial reports.* To enable managers to receive direction, know what is expected of them and perform in a complementary, unified manner.

☐ *Organizational checks and balances.* These are carried out to an important extent by the financial control function and by internal auditing.

☐ *EDP considerations.* These may influence a company's organizational structure and its control procedures and techniques.

The committee believes that a strong control environment results in an appropriate and necessary level of control consciousness. If the necessary level of control consciousness is not present, control procedures may be inoperative because, the committee points out, individuals would hesitate to challenge a management override of a specific control.

Although the tentative report does not suggest that a corporate code of conduct or written policies and procedures are mandatory, it observes that formal policies and procedures, including policies on "adherence to appropriate standards for ethical behavior, including compliance with applicable laws and regulations," are helpful if controls are "to be understood and to operate effectively."

It seems clear to the authors that documentation of important policies and of control procedures facilitates compliance with internal accounting controls and would be important if it becomes necessary to demonstrate compliance with the act.

As stated above, the committee recommends that management make a preliminary assessment of its control environment and procedures and techniques as a basis for determining the "manner, extent, and timing of other procedures deemed appropriate." In making a preliminary assessment, management would be likely to use its general knowledge of the control environment and the accounting system; existing documentation with respect to the environment, the accounting system and accounting control procedures and techniques; recent reports from internal and external auditors; and current discussions with such auditors. The tentative report lists several matters that management might consider in its preliminary assessment, such as the extent to which internal audits are used and internal control weaknesses that have come to management's attention.

The "other procedures deemed appropriate" relate to deciding on an appropriate approach to evaluating specific control procedures and techniques, obtaining an understanding of the flow of transactions and of the accounting control procedures in place, concluding whether the control procedures in place meet the objectives in the act, and monitoring compliance to obtain reasonable assurance that such controls continue to function properly.

The committee recognized that the approach a company might take to evaluate its controls would vary depending on its specific circumstances. For example, the tentative report suggests grouping transactions into "cycles" (revenue, expenditures, production or conversion, financing, and external financial reporting). However, it recognizes that some companies might study their transactions in other ways, for example, by function or by operating unit.

The committee has also suggested criteria (and examples of selected control procedures and techniques intended to clarify and illustrate the criteria) that, when met, will provide management with reasonable assurance that the broad objectives of internal accounting control have been achieved. The committee specifically requested comments on the adequacy and usefulness of its suggested criteria.

However, the tentative report states that "the suggested criteria have been developed from the perspective of a hypothetical manufacturing entity and, therefore, some businesses may have to develop additional criteria to recognize their special characteristics. Also, some of the criteria may not be applicable to some companies because of the absence of the specific transactions." Furthermore, the tentative report notes that "the wide range in the size of the over ten thousand publicly held companies in the United States, in their operating style, in the complexity of their transactions, in the diversity of their products and services, and in the geographical dispersion of their operations clearly makes it impossible to enumerate specific controls that will answer every question and meet all the needs of all companies."

At this time, it is not clear whether the committee's final report will indicate that its suggested criteria are effectively a set of minimum standards for the largest possible number of public companies or that they are merely intended to illustrate an approach to an evaluation of internal accounting control or something in between.

Some believe that no attempt should be made to specify criteria that can be used by management in its evaluation of internal accounting control and that, if met, can provide reasonable assurance of compliance with the internal accounting control provision of the act.We suspect that those who hold that view are concerned that any criteria developed by the committee will soon be incorporated into regulations by the SEC or, perhaps, by the new auditing standards board, without appropriate recognition of the need for flexibility in their application.

Although the SEC has made it clear that it welcomes the initiative of the AICPA in establishing the special advisory committee, it must necessarily be guided by congressional intent. As discussed earlier, the *Report of the Senate Committee on Banking, Housing, and Urban Affairs* has made it clear that cost/benefit considerations and professional audit judgments are essential to an evaluation of internal accounting control. This would not seem to indicate a need for inflexible regulatory requirements. And, as auditors are well aware, the AICPA auditing standards executive committee recognized that there is a need for flexibility in the wide variety of circumstances encountered in business operations. There is no reason to believe that the auditing standards board will take a different position.

Possible Changes in Reporting Practices

Space does not permit a detailed analysis of possible developments in reporting on internal accounting controls by management and auditors. However, changes may come as a direct result of action on one of the key reasons underlying the formation of the special advisory committee. That was the recommendation of the Commission on Auditors' Responsibilities (the Cohen commission) that there be a report by management on the financial statements and that it present "management's assessment of the company's accounting system and the controls over it. . . ."

Harold M. Williams, chairman of the SEC, stated in a speech before the American Accounting Association on August 22, 1978, that

"A management report dealing with the issuer's internal controls is something to which the Commission will give serious attention in the relatively near future. And, some degree of auditor involvement with that report is a corollary we will have to consider in light of the traditional familiarity and expertise in this area of the accounting profession."

The days when changes of such magnitude took years to effect are long past. Many managements are considering what is needed to support a representation on internal accounting controls. (Some companies have already made public representations.) An SEC requirement for such a representation seems likely for 1979 annual reports. And the significant issues of public reporting by auditors on internal accounting controls are the subject of one of a high priority project of the auditing standards board.

But what about private companies? Since they are not subject to SEC requirements, what has all of this to do with them? The concept of "an audit is an audit" causes a potential problem for private companies. If an auditor is required to report publicly on the internal accounting controls of a public company, there may be CPAs who will hold the view that a similar requirement should apply to audits of private companies. It's too early to guess what the decision will be on this issue. Clearly, however, the decision will be of vital importance to private companies and their CPAs.

Summary

The Foreign Corrupt Practices Act of 1977 has made the internal accounting controls of public companies a matter of law, and the effects of the act may ultimately reach nonpublic companies. Yet there are several areas where views differ, for example, the definition and scope of internal accounting controls and the criteria appropriate for an evaluation of those controls. Also, there are important areas requiring further study, for example, cost/benefit analysis and issues related to public reporting on internal accounting control. The tentative report of the AICPA special advisory committee on internal accounting control (its final report is expected to be issued in spring 1979) includes views and recommendations that should receive the careful attention of all persons interested in the subject. ■

October 1963 *NAA* BULLETIN

Give Consideration to Direct
Costing for External Reporting

By JOHN R. E. PARKER

DIRECT COSTING has earned the acceptance of many accountants and businessmen, particularly those in industry. Nevertheless, the status of the method as to general acceptance is clouded with uncertainty. Financial statements that include inventories valued at direct cost may be subject to qualification by external auditors if the valuation differs materially from what it would be under absorption costing. Furthermore, direct costing is not likely to be recognized for tax purposes. Because of these uncertainties, direct costing is often confined to purposes of internal reporting. In these cases, external financial statements prepared from accounts based on direct costing are converted to an absorption cost basis. However, the adjustments that restore the applicable amount of fixed overhead to inventory are neither involved nor difficult.

On the other hand, some accountants believe that direct costing procedures, in addition to aiding management, yield more useful results to external users of financial data. Upwards of forty percent of the companies that use direct costing internally also use the method in external financial statements.[1] Moreover, among the remaining companies that use direct costing—despite the ready adjustment referred to above—there is a strong preference for external reports that are in agreement with the internal financial statements.

Distinguishing Marks of
Direct Costing

The separation of fixed and variable costs has been stressed as the principal characteristic of direct costing. However, this is almost mandatory for many managerial purposes. Such segregation is basic to direct costing but not exclusive to it. In other words,

---

[1] Wilmer Wright, *Direct Standard Costs for Decision Making and Control*, McGraw-Hill, 1962, p. 214.

JOHN R. E. PARKER, *Member-at-Large 1961, C.A., is an Associate Professor at Queen's University, Kingston, Ontario, having previously taught at McGill University and the University of Saskatchewan. Formerly Director of Staff Training with Riddell, Stead, Graham & Hutchison, Chartered Accountants, Montreal, Quebec, Mr. Parker, a graduate of the University of Washington and Dalhousie University, has been a frequent contributor to professional journals in Canada.*

OCTOBER 1963

the separation of costs can be useful in absorption costing, although not basic to the method. The point to be emphasized is that direct costing incorporates the separation of costs in the recording phase of the accounting process. Through redesign of the income statement, the separation of fixed and variable costs becomes the basis of the direct cost reporting system.

But direct costing also limits inventory valuation to variable costs. Herein lies the fundamental difference between direct and absorption costing for financial statement purposes. Conventional procedures of absorption costing exclude selling, general and administrative expenses, interest and similar items from inventory value. They may also omit variations from standard cost which represent inefficiencies in the use of materials, manpower and plant. To these exclusions from inventory valuation direct costing adds all fixed manufacturing costs.

In general terms, absorption costing emphasizes the distinction between production costs and all other costs. On the other hand, direct costing emphasizes the distinction between fixed and variable costs. Each values inventory accordingly. Absorption costing, with a balance-sheet emphasis, includes all costs believed to add to inventory value, and therefore applies fixed manufacturing costs to inventory. Direct costing, with an income-statement emphasis, excludes from inventories these fixed manufacturing costs as having been applied against income of the period. These costs are value added from an absorption costing viewpoint. From a direct costing viewpoint, they are costs which cannot properly be deferred.

Theoretical Support for Direct Costing

Direct costing claims theoretical support by virtue of the generally accepted accounting concept that pe-

riod cost should be recognized in the income account of the period in which they are incurred. Only these costs which are a function of output should be deferred as inventory costs and matched against future revenue. The proponents of direct costing suggest that the individual product does not incur fixed overhead; fixed manufacturing costs are incurred on a time basis, regardless of the volume of production or sales. The question to be answered concerns the nature of fixed overhead: Are fixed costs really period costs?

Those who favor direct costing claim that the fixed portion of manufacturing overhead is not really a cost of production but only a standby cost which facilitates production, and which must be incurred regardless of the level of production or sales. In theory, direct costing views the fixed overhead of a business as a constant quantity that is incurred during a period of time. When the time period expires, the fixed costs incurred expire with it. Accordingly, the whole of the fixed overhead must be allocated to what has been sold in the period, as this is the only source of revenue from which the fixed costs can be recovered. The next accounting period will incur its own fixed overhead; therefore, it is regarded as irrational to defer in the inventory account any portion of the previous period's fixed costs. Moreover, fixed costs are the result of a special kind of management decision; hence it is reasonable to accord a different accounting treatment to the fixed and variable portions of manufacturing overhead.

Attempts have also been made to justify direct costing on the basis of what is termed "contribution theory." Each sales dollar is said to consist of two parts: (1) a reimbursement of total variable costs and (2) the remainder of the sales dollar which contributes to the coverage of fixed costs and profits. As applied to the measurement of income, this accords with the economists' concept of the margin which clearly demonstrates that profit does not accrue on a unit basis. No profit, regardless of price, is realized until fixed costs are fully recovered.

Profit, then, accrues in a manner that is not revealed by the margin between selling price and full unit costs, fixed and variable. The difference between the aggregate value of sales and the aggregate variable cost of the products sold provides a fund of contribution from which to discharge the fixed costs and provide for the profits of the entity. After fixed costs have been recovered, the sale of an additional unit of product results in an addition to total revenue which, in the final analysis, increases net profit by an amount equal to the difference between the selling price and the unit's variable cost.

Direct Costing and General Acceptance

Is direct costing a generally accepted method of accounting? This question can be answered with no more authority than an informed opinion.

At the outset, it must be recognized that a compendium of generally accepted accounting principles does not exist. As a result, many accounting practices have simply evolved on an *ad hoc* basis. This is significant because, in audit reports, the profession is committed to the existence of generally accepted accounting principles. However, it is not clear to whom accounting principles must be acceptable or to what extent acceptance is necessary. Furthermore, the process of accepting alternative practices is so uncertain that one may question how improvements can be made, if such improvements are not permissible until generally accepted![2]

As they presently exist, generally accepted accounting principles are incomplete in terms of fulfilling the need for an integrated and comprehensive structure of accounting theory. The bulletins of the American Institute of Certified Public Accountants, together with the various releases of other professional accounting organizations, probably represent the best evidence of general acceptance. However, such statements lack the absolute authority to be binding on all accountants under all conditions. Moreover, these bulletins and other pronouncements have been directed more to accounting practices than to the underlying principles. Therefore, they generally lag behind the problems they purport to solve.

In this case, there is a minimum of help to be gained from "official" pronouncements. Organizations of professional accountants in North America have maintained silence with respect to direct costing. There is nothing in the bulletins of the American Institute of Certified Public Accountants that can be used with any degree of certainty to either support or reject the use of direct costing in external financial statements. The same can be said of the bulletins issued by the Canadian Institute of Chartered Accountants.

However, a 1957 pronouncement by the Committee on Concept and Standards of the American Accounting Association states that "the cost of a manufactured product is the sum of the acquisition costs reasonably traceable to that product and should include both direct and indirect factors. *The omission of any element of manufacturing cost is not acceptable.*"[3] Although this statement implies a lack of acceptability to direct costing for external purposes, inasmuch as published financial statements were under

---

[2] George R. Catlett, "Relation of Acceptance to Accounting Principles," *The Journal of Accountancy*, March 1960, pp. 34 and 35.

[3] American Accounting Association, "Accounting and Reporting Standards for Corporate Financial Statements, 1957 Revision," *The Accounting Review*, October 1957, p. 539 (emphasis provided).

OCTOBER 1963

discussion, it is significant that two of the seven members who comprised the committee dissented from the majority position. Their published dissent expressed the opinion that "direct costing is at least as acceptable in accounting theory as is the conventional 'full costing' concept."[4]

Favorable implications from official statements are tenuous at best. In Accounting Research Bulletin No. 43, which superseded all previous bulletins, the American Institute of Certified Public Accountants does not speak of direct costing but states that "the exclusion of all overheads from inventory costs does not constitute an accepted accounting procedure."[5] Although certainly not intended as such, this statement has been interpreted in terms favorable to direct costing. While admitting that it is not proper to exclude all overheads from inventory costs, proponents of direct costing contend that it is proper to exclude fixed overhead. There is also the statement of the Committee on Accounting and Auditing Research of the Canadian Institute of Chartered Accountants in its Bulletin No. 5:[6]

> Sometimes certain costs are excluded in determining inventory values. Usually expenditures arising out of abnormal circumstances, such as rehandling of goods and idle facilities, are not included. *Similarly, in some cases, fixed overhead is excluded where its inclusion would distort the profit for the year by reason of fluctuating volume of production.*

It is possible to read into this statement an implication of acceptability for direct costing. However, Bulletin No. 5 does not mention direct costing; as a result, the position of the Institute is not clear.

A somewhat more positive expression comes from across the water. Statement on Accounting Principles N 22, issued by the Institute of Chartered Accountants in England and Wales, recognizes the acceptability of direct costing as follows:[7]

> Where, however, the levels (of production or sales) are subject to material fluctuation and are not kept in balance, it may be decided to exclude these (period) expenses from stock on the ground that, as they would be incurred whatever the levels of production or sales, their inclusion in stock has the effect of relieving the profit and loss account in the period when they are incurred of expenses which it should fairly bear and of charging these expenses in a later period to which they do not properly relate.

The above position is based on the premise that no one method of accounting for manufacturing overhead is suitable for all businesses. It should be recognized that British philosophy supports maximum freedom in accountancy, together with consistency in the application of accounting principles or full disclosure of departures from consistent application where the effect of the departure is material. This philosophy is in contrast with what seems to prevail in North America, where there is evidence of a desire for greater uniformity and comparability in financial reporting, narrowing the areas of difference and inconsistency.

Basic Accounting Theory and Direct Costing

From a practical point of view, all costs incurred by a business entity are intended to produce revenue. In strict

---

[4] *Ibid.*, p. 545.

[5] Committee on Accounting Procedure. *Restatement and Revision of Accounting Research Bulletins, ARB No. 43,* American Institute of Certified Public Accountants, 1953, p. 29.

[6] Committee on Accounting and Auditing Research. *The Meaning of the Term Cost as Used in Inventory Valuation Bulletin No. 5,* Canadian Institute of Chartered Accountants, 1950, p. 2 (emphasis provided).

[7] Council. *Treatment of Stock-in-Trade and Work in Progress in Financial Accounts, Accounting Principles N 22,* Institute of Chartered Accountants in England and Wales, 1960, p. 3.

theory, therefore, all costs attach to the product or service that provides the source of revenue from which costs are recoverable. However, as pointed out by Professors Paton and Littleton, "Not all costs attach in a discernible manner, and this fact forces the accountant to fall back upon a time-period as the unit for associating certain expenses with certain revenues."[8]

The concept of period costs is well established in accounting practice, even though the same authors further state that "time periods are a convenience, a substitute, but the fundamental concept (remains) unchanged."[9] Accounting is an art that is generally regarded as being utilitarian by nature. Therefore, accounting principles are closely related to the way in which accountants do their work in practice. This close relationship between use and principle serves to explain the recognition of period costs in accounting theory. Here is an example of conflict where the practical difficulties of cost allocation override what appears to be sound accounting theory.

The adoption of the fiscal year as a convenient period for financial reporting is basic to the accounting process. The related concept of period costs is primarily the result of a practical need to minimize the incidence of cost allocation. Accounting theory recognizes that there is no practical solution other than period-cost treatment in the case of selling and administrative costs. If period-cost treatment is sound for certain costs that have a closer affinity to time than to activity, it is sound for all such costs, regardless of the functional relationships that may exist. The fact that fixed manufacturing overhead is essential to production does not neces-

sitate allocating this cost to each unit of output.

Fixed costs, by definition, relate to the capacity and organization provided, which is not necessarily the same as the normal level of activity. As a result, a joint-cost situation arises under absorption costing, in that fixed manufacturing overhead can consist of product-cost and period-cost components. Conventional procedures of absorption costing frequently involve the problem of separating the cost of product from the cost of unused capacity. Period-cost treatment of idle capacity is widely recognized in accounting theory. Therefore, it is not difficult to agree with Raymond P. Marple that it takes "a considerable amount of stretching to jump to the conclusion that costs which are charged against the period when the capacity is not used can . . . be transferred into effective and deferrable product costs when management decides to use, as compared with not use, the provided capacity."[10]

The test to be applied in deciding whether an item of cost is a proper period charge involves determining that the item represents an expenditure from which only the current period will benefit. The concept of future benefit is widely accepted by accountants in explaining the nature of an asset.[11] Referring to asset expiration, the Committee on Concepts and Standards of the American Accounting Association states: "Expired costs are those having no discernible benefit to future operations."[12]

Future benefit is a useful criterion

[8] W. A. Paton and A. C. Littleton, *An Introduction to Corporate Accounting Standards*, American Accounting Association, 1940, p. 15.

[9] *Ibid.*

[10] Raymond P. Marple, "There is a Fundamental Error in Absorption Costing," *The Controller*, July 1961, correspondence, p. 318.

[11] For a more complete treatment of future benefit and cost obviation, see David Green, Jr., "A Moral to the Direct Costing Controversy," *Journal of Business*, July 1960, pp. 222-223; and Charles T. Horngren and George H. Sorter, "Direct Costing for External Reporting," *The Accounting Review*, January 1961, pp. 84-93.

[12] American Accounting Association, *op. cit.*, p. 541.

for determining those costs that should be treated as product costs. Under the going-concern or continuity postulate, inventory valuation is, by nature, much more a process of cost deferral than a process of valuation. To the extent of variable manufacturing costs, inventory produced but unsold in one accounting period relieves subsequent periods of further outlays. Thus, the future benefit of cost obviation clearly exists in the case of variable manufacturing costs.

Since the fixed costs incurred during one accounting period have no bearing on reincurring the same kind of fixed costs in subsequent periods, the cost obviation test for future benefit fails when applied to fixed manufacturing overhead. Also, it is difficult to explain why the production of an additional unit necessitates charging to that unit a normal share of costs which are incurred even if the unit is not produced. Assuming that capacity is available, the decision to produce an additional unit does not increase fixed costs, nor does it reduce the costs of subsequent periods. The only logical conclusion is that fixed manufacturing costs are irrelevant in such circumstances and, therefore, do not represent asset values under the going-concern concept.

It must also be recognized that potential future revenue is implicit in the recognition of assets. In the absence of revenue-producing potential, an item of cost that might otherwise represent an asset cannot benefit future operations and, therefore, becomes an expired cost. On the other hand, in circumstances where potential future revenue exists, this fact is nothing more than *per se* evidence that an asset exists. It is still necessary to determine the value that should be assigned to that asset.

There is, of course, an inevitable lag between the production of goods and their ultimate sale. The resulting delay in revenue recognition means different things to different people.

Those who favor absorption costing believe that the matching process necessitates that full costs, fixed and variable, be matched with the recognition of revenue at the time of sale. Under direct costing, fixed manufacturing overhead of prior periods is not considered a proper charge against future revenue. In the opinion of Louis H. Jordan, "the matching process degenerates into mere subtraction: from revenues for the period determined in a variety of ways are subtracted expenses also determined in a variety of ways." [13]

Direct costing procedures produce a concept of inventory valuation that is at least as acceptable in accounting theory as the conventional absorption cost concept. Inventories valued on the basis of variable costs reflect the amount of working capital tied up in unsold products. Under the going-concern assumption, such a concept is consistent with a deferred-cost interpretation of inventory and fully recognizes the nature of assets as "service-potentials available for or beneficial to expected operations." [14]

The Duple Motor Bodies Case

The House of Lords decision in the case of Duple Motor Bodies vs. Ostime ranks as an interesting and authoritative treatment that, in substance, rejects absorption costing in the circumstances that prevailed. A tax case, the decision establishes that the inclusion of overhead in inventory results in a disallowance of deductible expenditures in the period in which they are incurred. However, their Lordships also recognize the importance of consistency and the fact that no change in the method of inventory valuation is justified unless there is a good reason, such as a change in circumstances.

[13] Louis H. Jordan, "A Discussion of the Usefulness and Theory of Direct Costing," *NAA Bulletin*, March 1962, p. 60.
[14] American Accounting Association, *op. cit.*, p. 538.

It is interesting to note that Lord Simonds found the absorption cost method undesirable because it could lead to absurd conclusions. In an article that appeared in the Canadian Tax Journal, Gwyneth McGregor states, "In arriving at the cost of work in progress it was 'undesirable to indulge in what is no better than guesswork': and a large part of the (absorption cost) method appeared to the learned judge to involve 'the wildest guesswork.'" [15]

Further Inquiry Needed

The central issue in the direct costing controversy involves the process of matching costs with revenue, particularly in terms of timing the release of fixed manufacturing costs to expense. Under absorption costing, fixed overhead is matched with revenue when the products to which the fixed costs relate are sold. Direct costing writes off the fixed portion of overhead to revenue on a time basis as incurred. Considered from a more fundamental point of view, the direct costing controversy revolves around the definition of an asset and the costs that should be included as such in the balance sheet. As a corollary, the nature of expense is also involved.

The uncertainty that exists with respect to direct costing makes it impossible to conclude that the method conforms with generally accepted accounting principles. In fact, the majority of informed opinion may hold the opposite view. However, the theo-

retical structure of direct costing appears to be sound. Furthermore, the statements of professional accounting organizations do not clearly rule out the acceptability of direct costing.

In the context of financial reporting, public accountants do not object to the use of direct costing where the external financial statements are adjusted to reflect the applicable portion of fixed costs in inventory or where the effect is not so material as to require adjustment of the statements for external reporting. Moreover, there is still sufficient doubt concerning the acceptability of direct costing that qualification may not result even in circumstances where inventories are materially different from what they would be under absorption costing. The decision to adopt direct costing for external reporting is likely to result in a consistency qualification in the year of change, because it cannot be stated that accounting principles have been applied on a basis consistent with the preceding year.

It is apparent that direct costing and absorption costing involve two different concepts of inventory valuation. Two methods of inventory valuation, one of which omits a significant portion of the cost included in the other, cannot both be recognized as conforming with generally accepted accounting principles. One method or the other has to be the proper practice to follow. In the long run, no useful purpose is served by ignoring this fact. However, further research and experience are required in order to develop the insight needed to resolve the direct costing controversy.

[15] Gwyneth McGregor, "Accountancy in the Lords," *Canadian Tax Journal*, July-August 1961, p. 269.

OCTOBER 1963

Is Financial Reporting Influencing Internal Decision Making?

If managers do not reduce the impact of external financial reporting on strategic planning, they may be substituting short-term profits for the long-term survival and growth of the organization.

By Stephen F. Jablonsky and Mark W. Dirsmith

Stephen F. Jablonsky is assistant professor of accounting and management information systems at Pennsylvania State University. He holds a Ph.D. degree from the University of Illinois and is a member of Central Pennsylvania Chapter, through which this article was submitted.

The discounted cash flow (DCF) technique has long been suggested as a mechanism appropriate for making capital investment decisions and evaluating performance. Empirical evidence has suggested, however, that this model has not been as widely adopted by the business community as might be expected.

Issues related to the dysfunctional consequences of performance evaluation have long been recognized. In a pioneering article, Ridgway[1] sought to examine the construction and use of performance measures at all levels of the organization, including the evaluation of profit centers in decentralized companies. Ridgway concluded that if a certain type of information is collected and disseminated to organizational members, it may be interpreted by these individuals as defining important aspects of organizational activity and would, therefore, tend to influence their behavior, although not necessarily as intended.

Financial accounting information is collected and disseminated to the financial community where it is used in the evaluation of organizational activity. One, therefore, must ask, "Does this information wrongly influence decision making *within* the organization?"

Accrual Numbers vs. Cash Flows

The proponents of the DCF method for making capital budgeting decisions and evaluating subunit performance have long heralded its characteristics. Given the advantages of the DCF approach it seems logical to assume that it would have been quickly adopted by the business community. However, such has not been the case.

In a 1965 study, Robichek and McDonald[2] found that of 163 firms selected for examination from the *Fortune 500* list of companies, less than half employed the DCF technique in making capital budgeting decisions. Similarly, in a 1966 study concerned with examining the approaches taken to evaluate divisional performance, Mauriel and Anthony[3] found that approximately 60% of the firms participating in their mail survey employed an accounting return on investment (ROI) criterion in evaluating divisional performance. Furthermore, it was found that generally accepted accounting principles tended to influence the methods used in calculating the profit and investment base of the division.

Consistent with earlier studies, Fremgen[4] in 1973 found that ROI and payback benchmark techniques are still widely used in companies having large annual capital budgets. Indeed, it was

MANAGEMENT ACCOUNTING/JULY 1979

found that for companies having capital budgets in excess of $100 million, 72% used payback benchmarks and 60% used an ROI criterion in making decisions. For these same companies, 31% thought that the accounting return on investment criteria was the most important technique employed in making capital budgeting decisions, second only to the discounted rate of return method. Curiously, Fremgen found that nonuse of DCF is most prevalent in organizations having the largest capital budgets where one would expect to have the most expertise available to understand and use DCF. Similarly, in a 1977 study, Gitman and Forrester[5] found that 53.6% of the high stock price growth firms in their study primarily used a discounted rate of return method (a DCF technique) in making capital budgeting decisions, but 25% of the firms indicated that the accounting return on investment was the primary method employed.

Some reasons for the continued importance of the payback benchmark and ROI techniques in making capital investment decisions include: (1) a lack of understanding of the DCF approach by corporate management; (2) an inability to predict specific cash flows associated with a capital asset or division more than a few years into the future; and (3) a preference for payback benchmarks by risk adverse corporate managers with strong liquidity preferences.

In a classic article, Lerner and Rappaport[6] thought that the explanation lay elsewhere. Reasoning that external decision makers use financial accounting information to evaluate organizational performance, they concluded that corporate managers may be motivated to optimize accrual performance measures rather than unreported, but perhaps more relevant, projected cash flows. For example, in making capital investment decisions, management would be motivated to select those projects which would cause externally reported earnings figures to grow at a steady rate rather than those projects which would produce erratic earnings figures, even though they may have a more desirable cash flow associated with them. It is important to underscore the Lerner and Rappaport conclusion that the conflict between organizational objectives and external performance evaluation criteria is resolved in favor of the external performance evaluation criteria.

The use of ROI in making capital budgeting decisions may be a reflection of this conflict, but it cannot be attributed to it alone. More recently, Rappaport[7], basing many of his remarks on a *Business Week* survey, indicated that bonuses as compared to executive salaries are becoming an increasingly important component of the compensation package. These bonuses, at least at the divisional level, are generally determined by divisional profits or ROI, increases in divisional profits over

time, divisional profits as compared to other entities in the industry, and achievement of a stated profit or ROI target. Thus, companies may be formally biased in the direction of using accrual accounting numbers in internal decision making.

A similar conclusion is implied in a discussion of accounting information by Stern.[8] Stern reasoned that the use of financial accounting information, or more specifically earnings per share (EPS), will result in misguided investment decisions and that sophisticated investors are able to sort out distortions created by accounting data by means of using additional information about the organization. This process of searching for and using additional information results in relevant information about the company's activities and prospects of security prices, thus inducing these prices to fully reflect all publicly available information. Stern indicated that sophisticated investors gather additional information in order to discount expected future earnings, less the amount of new capital needed to generate future earnings, to arrive at a free cash flow (FCF) amount which, in turn, will affect security prices. Stern's FCF model focuses on the existing organization and on the organization as a changing entity by emphasizing the following: net operating income, the amount of and expected rate of return on new capital investments, the time frame of the investment streams and related returns, the risk of established organizational activity as perceived by investors, and cash flows associated with the sources of financing. Thus, it would appear that from the perspective of external performance evaluation, DCF techniques which are being applied to estimate free cash flows are being used by sophisticated investors, as well as sophisticated management in assessing the organization's fitness for the future. If this perspective does represent the true state of the world, then why do the accounting return on investment and payback techniques play a dominant role in capital budgeting decisions in a large number of companies? To answer this question, we must consider the form versus substance issue in financial reporting.

Reported Earnings—Are They Understood?

The effects of alternative accounting practices are often debated with respect to their impact on reported earnings. The current controversy surrounding the accounting treatment for the oil industry's exploration and development activities is a case in point. Briefly, opponents of the successful efforts method of accounting, the treatment recommended in FAS No. 19, have predicted a series of dire economic consequences for the oil industry if this statement is allowed to stand because of its impact on reported earnings. At the base of the argument against the successful efforts method is the position that the accounting treat-

Mark W. Dirsmith is assistant professor of accounting and management information systems at Pennsylvania State University. He holds a Ph.D. degree from Northwestern University.

ment used for external financial reporting will influence decisions made within oil companies, such as reducing future efforts to explore and develop new oil fields.

Horngren[9], however, indicated that such a position is predicated upon the mistaken belief that investors in the aggregate can be fooled by the accounting treatments used in preparing financial statements. Evidence in support of efficient capital markets suggests that the market is not fooled. That is, the market does not react to changes in earnings figures that are merely a result of changes in accounting treatments which are devoid of economic substance, for example, a change from one accounting treatment to another that reveals no new information about the economic activity of the organization. Thus, Horngren underscores a critical difference between form and substance—investors are not influenced by variations in the form in which financial information is presented but *are* influenced by the substantive economic activity of the organization.

Given an efficient capital market, it would seem naive for managers to believe in the "bottom line mentality" of investors. Carrying Horngren's argument one step further, managers should not be influenced in their own decision-making activity by variations in accounting numbers where these variations are *not* attributable to substantive economic events. Indeed, research findings related to the income smoothing hypothesis seem to support this contention. Basically, the income smoothing hypothesis states that changes in the generally accepted accounting principles used to generate financial statements may be manipulated so that reported income streams are not widely fluctuating. The evidence obtained to date generally rejects this hypothesis. Thus, it would seem that management does not believe that investors can be fooled by variations in form.

Concerning the distinction between form and substance, two empirical studies which examine the effect of external financial reporting on internal decision making appear to be especially germane to the current discussion. The first may be described as focusing on change in the form of financial information. The second is concerned with changes in the substance of the firm activity. The first study, conducted by Arnold and Keller[10], examined the extent to which the financial reporting system influences internal decision making. This inquiry investigated if the accounting method adopted for the investment tax credit affected the investment patterns in plant and equipment by major companies in various industries. The two accounting treatments considered were flow-through and deferral methods. Arnold and Keller reasoned that because the investment tax credit treatment affects externally reported earnings, decisions made within the organization should be

> *The market does not react to "cosmetic" changes in earnings figures.*

influenced if managers are in fact concerned with reported earnings. They hypothesized that the investment tax credit accounting method adopted by major companies has affected their acquisition of plant and equipment. A matched sample consisting of eight pairs of for-profit, nonfinancial organizations in eight industries was selected with both accounting methods represented in each pair. Results indicated that the method used did not influence internally made plant and equipment acquisition decisions.

Following Horngren's position, this variation in form of treating the investment tax credit is devoid of substance and should, therefore, have no impact on investor decision-making behavior. If investors are not influenced in their decision making, it would seem that management would in turn not be influenced by changes in reported earnings generated by differences in accounting treatment in making capital investment decisions. Thus, the results obtained by Arnold and Keller are to be expected. But what if changes in reported earnings involve substantive events?

The second study conducted by Dirsmith[11] was designed to determine whether externally reported financial information had a differential impact on internal decision making when a firm was faced with a disruption in the supply of raw materials. Decision makers could react to the disruption with one of three basic responses corresponding to Anthony's[12] decision-making typology. That is, they could consider the disruption as an operating control, management control, or strategic planning problem and employ the related decision strategy. According to Anthony, as the progression is made from operating control to management control to strategic planning, the underlying decision processes become more complex, ill-defined, externally oriented and creative; the time frame becomes longer; the appraisal of organizational performance becomes more difficult; and solutions to problems cannot be dealt with via programmable decision models.

The question addressed was whether this progression resulted in greater or reduced importance of externally reported financial information. Dirsmith reasoned that increased importance would be placed on financial statement information when the disruption was considered at a strategic level because the potential is more likely for major changes in the goals and objectives of the firm. When significant changes in organizational goals and objectives are contemplated, a major point of reference that both investors and managers can turn to is financial information reported in published financial statements. It was hypothesized that as the progression is made from operating control to management control to strategic planning decisions, the external impact on financial statements becomes a more important consideration for management personnel in their decision-making activity.

Not only is there consideration given to financial statement impact after the decision is made, but its consideration pervades the decision process itself. It was further hypothesized that as the progression is made from operating control to management control to strategic planning decisions, financial accounting information per se is more actively used by management in its decision-making processes.

These hypotheses were tested by distributing a questionnaire to corporate managers and independent auditors which described a hypothetical organization dealing with the shortage in raw material. Three responses to this raw material shortage, corresponding to Anthony's classification, were described in the questionnaire. Study participants were asked to indicate the role played by financial accounting information in formulating these responses. The results obtained strongly indicated that both hypotheses be accepted. Thus, it was inferred that externally reported accounting information does influence decision making within the firm and, more specifically, that it had its greatest effect when strategic planning decisions are involved.

Dirsmith concluded that a paradox appears to exist with respect to the use of historically-based financial accounting information by investors and managers. At a time when a firm must explore new and uncertain activities to insure organizational growth and survival, historical cost financial statements which reflect the status quo are a principal point of reference in the strategic planning decision process. Financial reporting, therefore, acts as a constraint to formulating strategies and, thus, externally reported accounting information does influence internally-made decisions when this information involves issues of economic substance.

Factors that Influence Financial Reporting and Strategic Planning

The implication that the financial reporting system influences strategic planning was discussed with both corporate managers and independent auditors in numerous informal meetings by the researchers. Many individuals indicated that such an influence quite probably does exist and that there are many factors which condition this relationship. Some of these factors include: the distance between management and investors—the more closely associated these groups are, the weaker the influence on strategic planning, probably because there are additional, viable communication channels available in such contexts; the mix between short- and long-term investors—the greater the proportion of long-term investors to short-term investors, the weaker the influence,

probably because such individuals are more interested in the long-term survival and growth of the company and are, therefore, more willing to tolerate reported earnings fluctuations caused by the implementation of strategic plans; and the nature of understandings between management and individuals supplying capital—the greater the flows of funds are bound by contractual agreements or long established understandings, the stronger the influence. Another factor is the stability of the company or industry. If the activities of a company/industry are very stable, the stronger the influence will be in comparison with companies/industries that are changing rapidly—probably because sophisticated investors become attuned to looking for major changes in organizational activity if there is a precedent for such change.

Some of these views are supported by the Gitman and Forrester and the Fremgen studies, although some considerable leaps of faith are required. First, concerning the closeness between management and investors, Fremgen found that the use of ROI was greater for companies having large capital budgets. If the size of capital budgets is roughly determined by the size of the company, and if large companies have a larger, more diverse group of investors with perhaps a weaker communication linkage, then one would expect to find internal decision making constrained by financial statement impact.

Second, concerning the nature of understanding between management and suppliers of capital, Fremgen found that the most important external factor influencing internal decision making, such as capital rationing, concerned a limit placed upon new debt by some agreement with outside parties (for example, bond indenture). The second and third most important internal factors concerned management's desire to maintain a regular dividend policy, thus restricting funds available for new investment, and their desire to maintain some specific earnings per share or price-earnings ratio thereby restricting the ability of the organization to issue additional shares of common stock.

Third, concerning the stability of the company/industry, Fremgen found that the second most important nonfinancial factor which influences capital investment decisions within the organization involves a perceived necessity by management to maintain existing programs or product lines. Indeed, fully 79% of the firms participating in this study thought that this was an important consideration. This finding strongly supports the contention that strategic planning, one aspect of which deeply involves redefining product lines, is influenced by concerns other than discounted cash flows, such as the impact on financial statements. In a similar vein, Gitman and Forrester found that for the companies examined in their study, which included only high stock price growth or-

Dirsmith shows that financial reporting can act as a constraint on corporate strategy.

ganizations, accounting rate of return played a less important role in the capital budgeting process than for companies in the Fremgen study which did not use the stock price screening mechanism. Gitman and Forrester found that only 25% of the companies responding to their questionnaire perceived accounting return on investment to be the primary means by which capital investment decisions were made (internal rate of return amounted to 53.6%), as compared with Fremgen's study in which 31% viewed accounting returns on investment as the most important means by which these decisions are made for companies having large capital expenditures (time adjusted rate of return amounted to 34%). These results would be consistent with the view expressed here that the financial reporting system would not have as great an impact on internal decision making for companies that can be characterized as changing rapidly—if it can be assumed that high stock price growth companies are those that are dynamic rather than stable.

Implications for Management

We conclude that the financial reporting system does have an impact on internal decision making. When large capital expenditures are involved or when a strategic decision of major economic consequence is made, managers tend to emphasize financial accounting information in making their decisions. To the extent that internal decision making is wrongly influenced by the external financial reporting system, we believe that the process of financial accounting policy formulation by the Financial Accounting Standards Board and other bodies should be made sensitive to the needs of reporting entities.

But, does reporting entity involvement influence standards setting? In the case of FAS No. 14, reporting entities were strongly opposed to the exposure draft suggestion that intersegment transfers be accounted for using *market related* transfer prices, regardless of transfer prices used for internal purposes. Companies responding were influential in having this suggestion dropped in the final pronouncement in favor of using transfer prices employed within the organization, thereby allowing a congruity between internal and external information and evaluation[13]. Simply stated, corporate management can affect financial reporting policy pronouncements and should become even more involved in responding to suggested changes in financial reporting.

The nature of policy issues to be addressed should not be constrained to the rather mundane level of selecting between various methods of accounting treatment, such as LIFO vs. FIFO inventory treatment, or flow through vs. deferral treatment of income tax credits. Nor should the issues addressed be totally concerned with pro-

nouncements made by the FASB. The issues that must be addressed concern more aggressive, forward-looking forms of financial reporting. For example, more use could be made of providing forecast information in 10K Reports filed with the SEC as allowed on a voluntary basis according to an amendment to rule 14a-9 of the Securities Exchange Act of 1934. This channel of communication could reflect the financial statement effect of strategic plans and explain any interruptions in earnings data. The increased use of this channel might be an especially valuable device for stable firms in that it might be used as a forum for discussing new organizational directions.

Additionally, the business community should support the conclusions of the Advisory Committee on Corporate Disclosure to the SEC which recommended that reporting entities be encouraged to experiment with disclosing *soft* information by the institution of *safe harbor* rules. This soft information would include such items as: changes in such critical expenditures as R&D; the explanation of earnings variations; earnings projections; and planned capital expenditures. Obviously, such disclosure could reduce significantly the constraints imposed on strategic planning by the *current* financial reporting system.

Finally, management could reduce the impact of financial reporting on internal decision making at the divisional level by altering the methods used to evaluate the performance of divisional managers. Rappaport suggests three approaches to integrating management incentives and strategic planning. First, the period over which performance is evaluated should be extended to fall more in line with the strategic planning time frame. Second, multiple criteria such as market share, productivity levels, product quality measures, product development measures, and personnel development measures should be used to evaluate managers. Third, accrual accounting numbers such as ROI could be adjusted to be more consistent with the DCF model, that is DCF could be used subject to an earning's constraint. □

> To reduce adverse effects, management should alter methods of measuring division manager performance.

[1] V. F. Ridgway, "Dysfunctional Consequences of Performance Measurements," *Administrative Science Quarterly*, September 1956.
[2] Alexander A. Robichek and John G. McDonald, *Financial Management in Transition*, Stanford Research Institute, Menlo Park, California, 1965.
[3] John J. Mauriel and Robert N. Anthony, "Misevaluation of Investment Center Performance," *Harvard Business Review*, March-April 1966.
[4] James N. Fremgen, "Capital Budgeting Practices: A Survey," MANAGEMENT ACCOUNTING, May 1973.
[5] Lawrence J. Gitman and John R. Forrester, Jr., "A Survey of Capital Budgeting Techniques Used by Major U.S. Firms," *Financial Management*, Fall 1977.
[6] Eugene E. Lerner and Alfred Rappaport, "Limited DCF in Capital Budgeting," *Harvard Business Review*, September-October 1968.
[7] Alfred Rappaport, "Executive Incentives vs. Corporate Growth," *Harvard Business Review*, July-August 1978.
[8] Joel M. Stern, "Earnings Per Share Don't Count," *Financial Analysts Journal*, July-August 1974.
[9] Charles T. Horngren, "Oil Accounts Should Be Uniform," *The Wall Street Journal*, March 31, 1978.
[10] Jerry L. Arnold and Earl C. Keller, "The Influence of External Reporting Methods Upon the Internal Decision-Making Process: An Empirical Analysis," presented at the national American Accounting Association meetings, August 1975.
[11] Mark W. Dirsmith, "Accountability and Decision Making: A Systems Perspective," The Pennsylvania State University, AMIS Working Paper 78-1.
[12] Robert N. Anthony, *Planning and Control Systems: A Framework for Analysis*, Harvard University, Boston, Mass., 1965.
[13] Lawrence A. Klein, "The Influence of Outside Parties on the Financial Accounting Standards Board: An Analysis of Responses to the Exposure Draft on Segment Reporting," unpublished Ph.D. dissertation, The Pennsylvania State University, 1978.

A "unique view" of one of the most accomplished
U.S. Presidents may be obtained from
an examination of his financial records.

THOMAS JEFFERSON: MANAGEMENT ACCOUNTANT

BY WILLIAM G. SHENKIR, GLENN A. WELSCH AND JAMES A. BEAR, JR.

THE *Concise Dictionary of American Biography* describes Thomas Jefferson as a "statesman, diplomat, author, scientist, architect, apostle of freedom and enlightenment."[1] The historian, Dumas Malone, in the introduction to the first of his projected six-volume biography of Thomas Jefferson, refers to the "trinity of American immortals"—Washington, Lincoln and Jefferson—and states:

> Others may deserve to stand beside them, but the supreme eminence of these three is practically unchallenged at the present time. Washington is the major symbol of the independent Republic itself, Lincoln of the preserved Union, but Jefferson surpassed both of them in the rich diversity of his achievements. No historic American, except possibly Benjamin Franklin, played so notable a part in so many important fields of activity and thought; government, law, religion, education, agriculture, architecture, science, philosophy.[2]

To the many facets of Thomas Jefferson's life one can add yet another: accountant. Jefferson was a meticulous record-keeper and personally maintained an unending series of Account Books for 59 years as well as other specific financial records for shorter periods of time.[3] This article discusses Jefferson's financial records. In the discussion which follows, the pervasive contribution of financial records to the historian again comes into sharp focus.

Primarily, the records discussed are the Account Books which contain entries made from August 18, 1767 (when Jefferson was 24 years of age), until one week before his death on July 4, 1826 (at age 83), a Ledger Book, the manufacturing records of his nail factory, and the Fee Book and Miscellaneous Accounts.[4]

A point of departure in discussing Jefferson's financial records is to ask: What motivated him to personally maintain meticulous financial records, and what was the source of his apparent knowledge of accounting? Several noteworthy insights are provided in Malone's biography of Jefferson. Peter Jefferson, the father of Thomas, who had amassed substantial property in Virginia by the time of his death (when Thomas Jefferson was only 14 years of age), "kept his accounts methodically," and young Thomas undoubtedly observed the record-keeping activities of his father.[5] Also, Jefferson's father was a well-known surveyor and has been described as a "mathematical man."[6] Thomas Jefferson apparently acquired his father's interest in mathematics for it was always one of his favorite subjects.[7] In his study

---

[1] *Concise Dictionary of American Biography* (Charles Scribner's Sons, 1964), p. 492.

[2] Dumas Malone, *Jefferson and His Time*, Volume I, *Jefferson the Virginian* (Little, Brown and Company, 1948), pp. vii-viii.

[3] In addition to the various financial records, Jefferson maintained a Farm Book, Garden Book, Case Book (a record of 939 law cases), and a Weather Memorandum Book.

[4] A complete typescript and photostat of the Account Books are in the Alderman Library at the University of Virginia; the originals are to be found in numerous repositories. For locational information of the originals see: Dumas Malone, *Jefferson and His Time*, Volumes I, II, III and IV. Photostats of the manufacturing records of the nail factory which are found in the Farm Book as well as the Nailery Manufacturing Account are also in the Alderman Library, as is a photostat of the Fee Book and Miscellaneous Accounts. The original Ledger Book is deposited in the Alderman Library. The materials in the Alderman Library were used in developing this article.

[5] *Jefferson the Virginian*, Volume I, pp. 20 and 32.

[6] *Ibid.*, p. 33.

[7] *Ibid.*, p. 54.

of mathematics at the College of William and Mary (Williamsburg, Virginia), Jefferson probably read of the art of bookkeeping since in those times it frequently was included in treatises on mathematics.[8]

Another explanation for Jefferson's maintaining extensive financial records was that it was a "fairly usual custom" of plantation owners of that day to keep accounts of cash receipts and disbursements. Mr. Jefferson, in addition to an "insatiable intellectual curiosity," appeared to have a natural aptitude and an orderly discipline essential to keeping records.[9] On this point, Malone comments as follows: "A decade before he became important as a draftsman of state papers he showed that he was particularly good at keeping accounts, and at any sort of paper work in which diligence, accuracy and neatness were required."[10] Further, record-keeping was "a part of the business of life which he took seriously and attended to with care."[11] Because he was such an excellent keeper of records, he left a rich storehouse of documents which few men of his eminence have matched.

---

[8] Jefferson's library contained numerous works on mathematics. See E. Millicent Sowerby, *Catalogue of the Library of Thomas Jefferson*, Volume IV (Washington, The Library of Congress, 1955), p. 4ff.

[9] Helen Duprey Bullock, "The Papers of Thomas Jefferson," in Constance E. Thurlow and Frances L. Berkeley, Jr., *The Jefferson Papers of the University of Virginia* (University of Virginia Library, 1950), p. 280.

[10] *Jefferson the Virginian*, Volume I, p. 116.

[11] *Ibid.*, p. 127.

In assessing Jefferson's accounting knowledge, special recognition should be accorded the training in finance and administration provided by the plantation economy of that time. The plantation was an early and unique school of management.[12] Elaborating on the "unique schooling in management" provided by the plantation system, Julian Boyd, editor of *The Papers of Thomas Jefferson*, stated:

> Neither law, merchandising, nor commerce could equal that system in the range and depth of experience that it afforded as a training ground for managers. A knowledge of all these was in some degree necessary for the planter, to say nothing of other skills not demanded of the merchant or shipper.[13]

Plantation owners, such as Washington and Jefferson, were engaged not only in supervising the slaves but with their total sustenance. Additionally, there was the task of planning the crops and marketing the products as well as overseeing the many artisans that might have been employed on the plantation. The daily tasks confronting the plantation owner were no less difficult managerial problems than those that confront the modern-day businessman. For example,

> In his extraordinary effort to breed mules for carriage and farm uses Washington was prompted by one of the elementary concerns of an administrator: that of obtaining a more efficient, cheap, and dependable source of power than that afforded by horses and oxen. Jefferson, in making endless estimates of the time required for a particular task by a given number and kind of slaves—for example, the quantity of nails that a boy might reasonably be expected to produce in a day—was also a manager engaged in calculating efficiency and in adapting the labor force of different sexes and varying degrees of maturity and strength to appropriate tasks.[14]

Without denying the grave defects in the plantation system, "the plantation school of administrative experience was nevertheless an excellent preparation for office. Washington and Jefferson were the two most conspicuous examples of those who mastered its hard lessons."[15]

THE ACCOUNT BOOKS

Though the historians have labeled them Account Books, in a stricter sense they may be more appropriately characterized as a diary or day book. (Jefferson alluded to them as his Memorandum Books.)

---

[12] The authors are indebted to Julian P. Boyd, editor of *The Papers of Thomas Jefferson*, for reading the manuscript and contributing this idea.

[13] Julian P. Boyd (editor), *The Papers of Thomas Jefferson*, Volume 17 (Princeton, 1965), p. 345.

[14] *Ibid.*, p. 346.

[15] *Ibid.*

The notations in them comprise carefully dated statements distinguished by their conciseness. In addition to entries for cash receipts and disbursements, the Account Books include a wide range of items such as personal events, quotations and Latin phrases, an occasional inventory of the wine cellar, measurements for a new canal, and agricultural and architectural notes. In the early years of developing these records, Jefferson was practicing law and much of the information pertained to his law practice. The legal memorandums generally are crossed out, evidently done when each case was closed, or when a particular action called for in the entry had been completed. Though the Account Books are informal and express few philosophical impressions, they do provide an incomparable record of Jefferson's daily activities.[16] Jefferson apparently carried small pocket slates ("ivory books") on which items were jotted down for later entry in the Account Books. Several of his pocket slates are exhibited today in his home, Monticello, near Charlottesville, Virginia.

These financial records have been of immeasurable value to historians in their biographical work on Jefferson. In his four-volume biography on Thomas Jefferson, Dumas Malone makes numerous references to these records, as do other biographers.[17] The use of these financial records as an invaluable resource in the writing of history can be observed by juxtaposing the historian's writings with the entries in the Account Books. As an example, consider the following passage describing one of Jefferson's trips in 1775 to Philadelphia to attend the sessions of the Continental Congress as a delegate from the Colony of Virginia:

> On the day before he left Williamsburg he received from the Treasurer of the Colony £315 for the use of the Virginia delegates. The expenses of the various delegations were borne locally and continued to be until the Constitution of 1787 went into effect. As paymasters the individual colonies, not Congress, called the tune. In Virginia these funds were raised by subscription, and Jefferson himself had made a contribution. He could well afford to do so, and he was in a generous frame of mind. The future champion of democracy traveled impressively. By the time he reached Philadelphia he had four horses. One of these, an animal named General, sired by the noted Janus and six years old, he purchased for £50 in Fredericksburg, where he remained three days and also bought harness, a postilion's whip, and swingletrees. He had at least two servants: Jesse, who rode postilion, and Richard, apparently a body servant.
>
> After he crossed the Potomac and came into another "country," he began to keep his records in Maryland currency, the exchange fortunately being favorable to Virginia. He may have been struck by the difficulties and annoyances arising from the lack of a uniform intercolonial medium but the problem was not serious the rest of the way, since the currency of Pennsylvania and Delaware was on a par with that of Maryland. This sort of information he invariably jotted down. In Annapolis he stopped long enough to have the pole of his phaeton mended; he visited the seat of government, as he had done nine years before; also, he availed himself of the opportunity to purchase books. Beyond Wilmington, not being sure of his way, he hired a guide and horse at no small cost. The total distance from Williamsburg to Philadelphia by the common route was approximately 325 miles, but because of his stops he took ten days to cover it. This was a slow-moving age, and he never lived to see a fast one.[18]

Though the historian had other sources of evidence to write the above passage, the Account Books were footnoted since they supplied much of the data as indicated by the following entries for this trip (1775).

June 10. recd. of Treasurer for use of myself & other delegates of Congress £315.

June 11. set out from Wmsburgh. for Philadelphia
  pd. ferrge., breakfast, dinner &c. at Ruffin's ferry 13/8
  gave ferrymen 1/

  12. pd. breakfast &c. at K. Wm. Ct. House 7/6
  pd. Farleigh's store books for servt. 5/
  pd. dinner &c. at Aylett's 3/

  13. pd. in Fredsburgh. for a hair-bag 4/

  14. pd. Alexr. Spotswood for a horse (The General) £25. & gave him an order on H. Skipwith for £25. more, the balance. He was got by Janus & is 6. years old.
  pd. for postillion whip 1/6
  pd. Green for harness £3-10-6
  pd. for box lock 1/6
  gave Richd. to pay for washing 1/3

  15. pd. for swingle trees 24/
  pd. for horse doctor 6/
  borrowed of Weedon 13/6
  pd. Weedon £3-8-1 1/2
  pd. ferrge. & ferrymen Fredsbgh. 3/9
  pd. guide 1/6
  pd. ferrge. at Howe's 20/
  ferrymen 1/6

Maryland. The following articles in Maryland currency, where coins are as follows pistereen 1/4 —English shilling 1/8—Dollar 7/6—Guinea 35/ half do. £3
Note the true difference of exchange with Virginia is 100 = 125.

June 16. pd. at Mrs. Halkirson's Port Tobacco for

---

[16] *Jefferson the Virginian*, Volume I, p. 118.

[17] For example, see: Nathan Schachner, *Thomas Jefferson: A Biography* (Thomas Yoseloff, 1951).

---

[18] *Jefferson the Virginian*, Volume I, p. 202.

dinner & lodging &c. £1-3-10.
servt. at do. 1/4

17. pd. at Mrs. Gibson's Upper Marlborough
 for breakfst. dinner, Lodging &c. 30/2
servts. at do. 2/2
pd. ferrge. & ferrymen at London town
 7/6
pd. Aikman, bookseller at Annapolis for
 books 31/
gave Richd. to buy comb 10d.
pd. a smith for mending pole at Phaeton
 2/
pd. for shewing apartment in State house
 3/9
pd. for mending umbrella 2/

18. pd. for breakfast, dinner, lodging, breakfast &c. at Middleton £2-2-8 servts. 1/8
pd. ferrge. from Annapolis to Rockhall £3.
gave ferryman 5/2 1/2

19. pd. at Greentree's at Rockhall lodging &c.
 18/4
gave servt. at do. 10d.
pd. for breakfast, dinner &c. at Down's
 10/8

Pennsylvania & Delaware counties, currency same as Maryland, only that
English shillings are true difference
of exchange same as Maryland, i.e.
100 = 125

June 20. pd. Scurrie at Middletown or Wither-
 spoon's lodging &c. 17/11

servt. at do. 6d.
pd. at Wilmington for mending whip 1/
pd. Marshall at do. for breakfast &c. 4/11
pd. Mrs. Withey at Chester for dinner &c.
 8/
arrived in Philadelphia.
pd. for horse & guide from Wilmington to
 Philadelphia 28/

Another interesting example of the use of the financial records by historians is found in a description of Jefferson's activities on July 4, 1776. The author of the Declaration of Independence "on his way to or from the State House . . . paid for a thermometer," and noting that Jefferson's thoughts were not entirely on the weather or the events in Philadelphia, the passage goes on to say: "on that day he also paid for seven pairs of women's gloves, destined for Monticello."[19]

The entries in the Account Books for July 4, 1776, read as follows:

July 4. pd. Sparhawk for a thermometer £3-15
 pd. for 7 pr. women's gloves 27/
 gave in charity 1/6
 [On this July 4th, he also recorded the
 temperature several times.]

[19] Ibid., p. 229.

Students of history are always pleased to find in Jefferson's financial records entries reflecting the early activities of notable personalities of the Revolution. For example, one entry in the Ledger Book reads: "Nov. 10, 1769 rec'd of Patrick Henry clerk 2-10-0." Other entries reveal transactions between Jefferson and James Monroe and James Madison.

THE LEDGER BOOK

While the Account Books contain valuable information about Jefferson's daily activities, they do not directly reveal much of his knowledge of accounting. In contrast, the Ledger Book provides important insights into his familiarity with accounting. For reasons unknown, the Ledger Book encompasses only the first three years of his long period of financial record-keeping. Significantly, Jefferson recognized the need for a ledger-type classification to supplement the chronological record of the Account Books.

The Ledger Book now available is a handsome leather-bound book with the early pages labeled "Paiments" (on the left facing page) and "Receipts" (on the right facing page). Written in his impeccable handwriting, it is a masterpiece in neatness and penmanship. Exhibit I, page 37, in Jefferson's handwriting, reveals that his first Ledger Book entry on the cash receipts page for August 18, 1767, was "Cash in hand 4-13-4." On the next line is the entry "recd of Wm. Bowan 10/9," which is the posting of the first cash item in the Account Books which reads "Aug. 18 recd. of W. Bowan for law fund 10/9." (See first line of Exhibit II, page 38, Account Books.) The first entry on the "paiments" page of the Ledger Book was on August 19, 1767, and reads "paid J. Madison senr. club in punch at Staunton 0-1-6," which is the posting of the item entered in the Account Books as "pd. Mr. Madison for clube in punch 1/6."

Similarly, for the first three years all cash receipts and payments in the Account Books can be readily traced to the Ledger Book.[20] Since payments were more numerous, that page of the Ledger Book was usually filled first, in which case totals were computed for the payments and the opposite receipts page. Since there was some unused space on the receipt page, a diagonal line was drawn from the last entry on the page to just above the line on which the total was entered. The totals for cash payments and receipts were then carried forward to the next pair

[20] To indicate the transfer of an item from the Account Books to the Ledger Book, Jefferson entered an "X" in the left margin of the Account Books. A check ("∨") or an occasional "posted" was used to indicate a transfer to the receivable/payable accounts discussed later and which are found in the Fee Book and Miscellaneous Accounts.

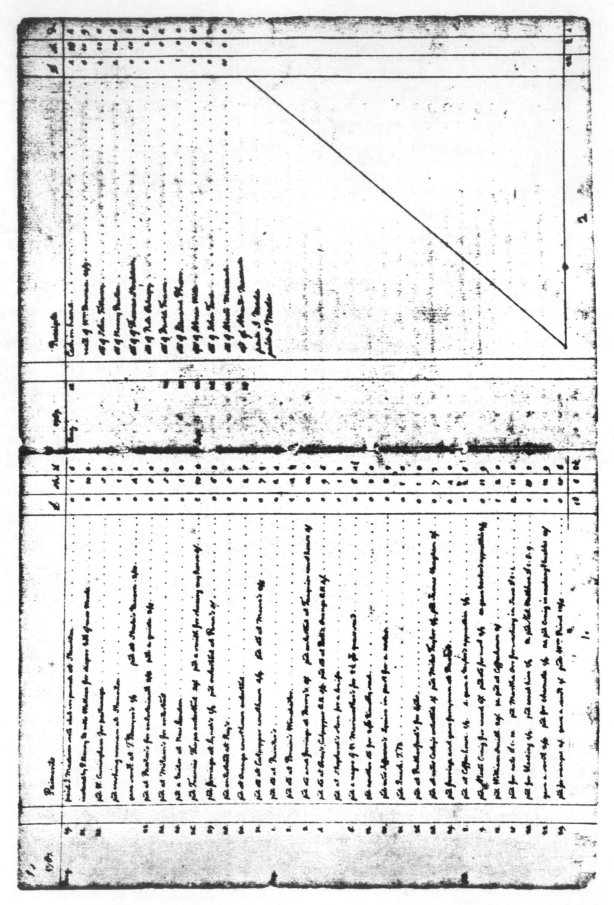

EXHIBIT I First Two Facing Pages of Ledger Book (1767).
(Source: Ledger Book. Reprinted by permission of the owner, J. Randolph Kean.)

EXHIBIT II First Page of Account Books (August-September 1767). (Source: Account Books. Original deposited in the Library of Congress. Reprinted by permission of the owner, J. Randolph Kean.)

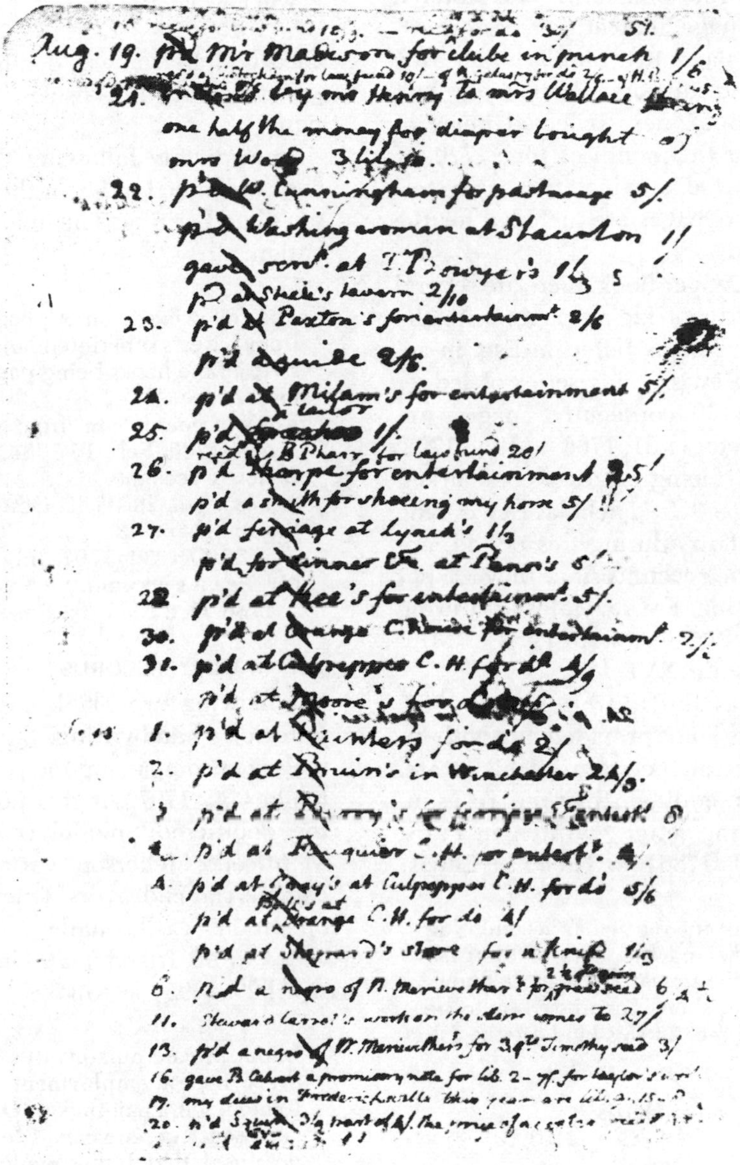
Aug. 19. pd Mr Madison for clube in punch 1/6
22. pd ... Cunningham for pasturage 5/.
pd washing woman at Staunton 1/
gave servt. at T. Bowyer's 1/3
pd at Steele's tavern 2/10
23. pd at Paxton's for entertainmt. 2/6
pd a guide 2/6.
24. pd at Mifam's for entertainment 5/.
26. pd ... for entertainment 2/5
pd a smith for shoeing my horse 5/
27. pd ferriage at Lynch's 1/3
28 pd at Kee's for entertainmt. 5/.
1. pd at Printers for do. 2/
2. pd at Irwin's in Winchester 21/3.
4. pd at Fauquier C.H. for entert.
pd at Orange C.H. for do. 2/
pd at Sheppard's store for a knife 1/3

of pages; thus, the first items on the succeeding pair of pages read "paiments brought forward" and "receipts brought forward."

On the fourth page of payments and receipts, near the middle of the page, Jefferson totaled the receipts and disbursements at May 31, 1768.[21] He counted the cash on hand on that date and entered the amount in the disbursements column as "cash in hand." He then totaled the disbursements page and drew double lines across the date, notation and money columns. On the opposite page, the total receipts computed did not equal the total disbursements on the preceding page; therefore, an item was entered for "omissions" sufficient to balance the two pages (a cash overage). Again, the diagonal and double lines were drawn. In the middle of the page, he began a new accounting period. The date is June 1, 1768, and the first item for receipts is the balance of cash on hand which had been entered previously on the disbursements page for balancing purposes.

21 In starting a new ledger page on May 22, 1768 (and thereafter), Jefferson used "disbursements" instead of "paiments."

One year later on May 31, 1769, Jefferson again balanced receipts and disbursements by counting the cash on hand and entering the amount on the disbursements page. To balance receipts with disbursements, an entry for "omissions" was entered on the disbursements page, indicating a cash shortage (see Exhibit III, page 40). Similarly, on May 31, 1770, receipts and disbursements were balanced. The Ledger Book next reflected items of disbursements only for the month of June 1770, of the new accounting period, at which time it mysteriously ends. No receipts pages are included for the new accounting period.

At this point in the Ledger Book, there are several blank pages, then a pair of facing pages with the heading "The Est. of Thomas Jefferson Esq. in account with Nicholas Lewis." This series of ledger accounts, comprising 79 consecutive pages, reflected entries from October 31, 1786, to June 1792. Significantly, the left facing pages were marked "Dr." and the right pages "Cr." Nicholas Lewis, who managed Jefferson's affairs during this period, apparently maintained the accounts since they are not in Jefferson's handwriting. For several years during this period of time, Jefferson was in Paris as Minister to the Court of Louis XVI.

Though Jefferson was abroad from 1784 to 1789, those who managed his lands provided him with interpretative summaries of the status of his estate. Significantly, Jefferson "audited" their reports as indicated in the following letter (written in Paris, France, December 19, 1786) to Nicholas Lewis:

> I am obliged to you for the particular account you give me of my affairs, and the state of the cash account made out by the steward. His articles however were generally so shortly expressed as to be quite unintelligible to me. Of this kind are the following.
>
> To James Foster & Benjamin Harris
> pr. Carter Braxton.   £131.10
> To Richard James & Wm. Clark
> for cash.   20.
> To Joseph Ashlin & C. Stone for
> cash at different times   74.10.2
> To Vincent Markham & Richd. James
> pr. Doctr. Gilmer.   385.0
> To Tandy Rice & Charles Rice
> for cash.   69.18.8 1/2
> To David Mullings & Henry Mullings
> for cash.   31.15
> To Carter Braxton pr. settlemt by
> Colo Lewis   119.12.8
> To do for cash.   11.17.4
>
> The steward intended this account for my information, but mentioning only names & sums without saying in some general way why those sums were paid to those names, leaves me uninformed. However the account having passed under your eye leaves me also without a doubt that the articles are

right. I suppose, in the 1st article for instance, that Carter Braxton (to whom I was indebted for a doz. bottles of oil only) stands in the place of some person to whom I owed £131.10, and so of the rest, as you give me reason to hope that all other debts will now be paid off.[22]

Clearly, Jefferson was dealing with the present-day principles of "full-disclosure" and "fair presentation."

Immediately following the Lewis accounts one finds a detailed index in the Ledger Book in Jefferson's handwriting. The index begins with the explanation:

> The following is an Alphabet to all the accounts from J. Key's superintendance to Mr. Lewis's inclusive, all the books being pages in one series, as follows:[23]
> Key's accounts are from pa. 1-24.
>   date 1783. Feb. 15-1784. Dec. 25.
> Ballow's accounts .... 25-237. ....
>   1785. Jan. 20.-1786. Oct. 27.
> the smith's books .... 238-569. ....
>   1786. Oct. 30.-1791. July 25.
> Mr. Lewis's accounts .... 570-659. ....
>   1786. Oct. 31.-1792. June 23.

THE NAILERY RECORDS

Following two blank pages, one finds again, in Jefferson's handwriting, the ledger records for the nailery encompassing the period May 31, 1794-September 30, 1797. At this point in time, the use of the debit-credit model is clearly discernible. At Monticello, Jefferson variously operated several commercial endeavors. One of the most interesting operations was his nailery. In this respect Jefferson wrote to his friend Jean-Nicholas DeMeunier (on April 29, 1795) as follows:

> In our private pursuits it is a great advantage that every honest employment is deemed honorable. I am myself a nail-maker. On returning home after an absence of ten years, I found my farms so much deranged that I saw evidently they would be a burden to me instead of a support till I could regenerate them; & consequently that it was necessary for me to find some other resource in the meantime. I thought for a while of taking up the manufacture of pot-ash, which requires but small advances of money. I concluded at length, however, to begin a manufacture of nails, which needs little or no capital, & I now employ a dozen little boys from 10 to 16 years of age, overlooking all the details of their business myself drawing from it a profit on which I can get along till I can put my farms into a course of yielding profit. My new trade of nail-making is to

---

[22] Paul Leicester Ford (editor), *The Writings of Thomas Jefferson*, Volume IV (New York: G. P. Putnam's Sons, 1894), pp. 340-341.

[23] Only the accounts of Mr. Lewis have been preserved.

EXHIBIT III Balancing Technique in Ledger Book (May 31, 1769).
(Source: Ledger Book. Reprinted by permission.)

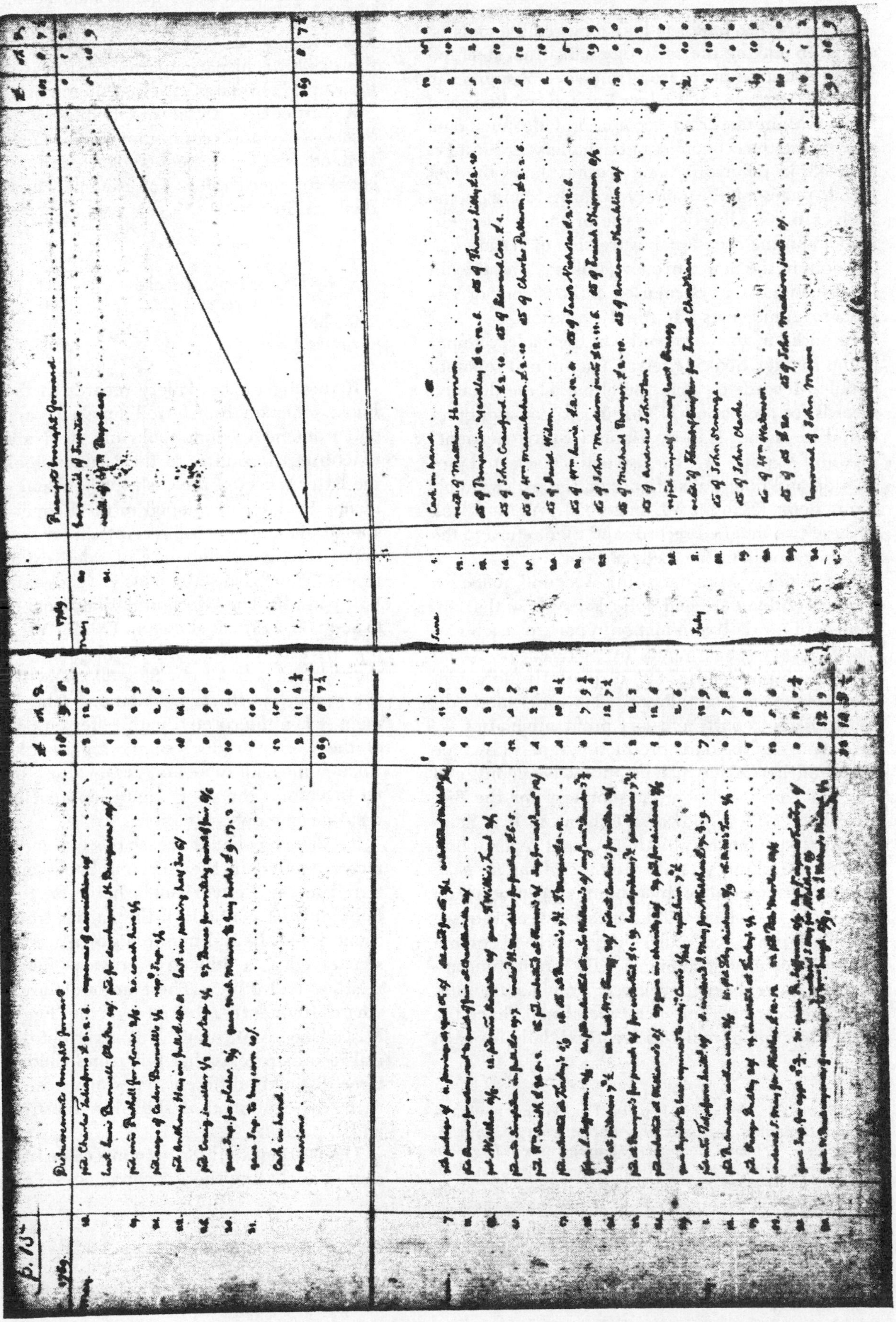

me in this country what an additional title of nobility or the ensigns of a new order are in Europe.[24]

In his travels, Jefferson had acquired the tools essential to making the early-day nails from steel rod which could be purchased from several sources in the new country. The Ledger Book, Farm Book and Nailery Manufacturing Account provide much data concerning the economics of the nailery. Exhibit IV, page 43, in Jefferson's handwriting, shows the first facing pages of the nailery records found in the Ledger Book. Observe his use of the debit-credit model and the occasional expression of certain values both in the new currency (dollars) and the old English monetary system used in the Colony of Virginia for some years after the Revolution.

In addition to the records on the nailery found in the Ledger Book, Jefferson maintained separate detailed records on that operation. These detailed records for the period 1796-1800 are commonly referred to as the "Nailery Manufacturing Account" (Exhibit V, page 44). He also entered selected production and financial statistics on the nailery in his Farm Book (Exhibit VI, page 45). We will look at these two detailed records and then return to the nailery records in the Ledger Book.

The "Nailery Manufacturing Account" reflects a very carefully designed job-cost system that included (1) a daily production report for each employee (specifying inputs of material—iron—and units of output—nails), (2) a quarterly statement of profit for each employee, (3) work standards, (4) spoilage reports and (5) profit summaries.

One page of the daily production report (by type of nail, such as XII, which meant twelve penny, and by employee) and a profit summary for the first quarter of 1796 is shown in Exhibit V. It is noteworthy that Jefferson's quarterly profit report (bottom left of Exhibit V) reflected *in total and for each employee*: materials used (column 1), production (column 2), spoilage (difference between the two columns), profit (column 3), days worked (column 4), and daily profit (column 5). The profit value appears to have been developed from actual sales price and cost data for each type of nail. Since the output by type of nail was recorded daily for each

employee, a profit allocation was feasible. Exhibit VI from his Farm Book reflects such a computation, in Jefferson's handwriting, for the autumn of 1794. The data on "wastes" by each worker reflected in this exhibit is of particular interest as is the use of the words "estimate . . . actual" in the title.

A particularly significant feature of Jefferson's cost system was his continuing development and use of standards. This aspect is reflected in his learning curve for piece rates. For example, in the Farm Book we find:[25]

	nails
a boy after 6 months makes	500 (per day)
" 1 year "	800
the best	884
a hired hand	1,000

Returning to the nailery records in the Ledger Book, Jefferson transferred (posted) appropriate data from the Account Books and the "Nailery Manufacturing Accounts" to the Ledger Book so that the latter reflected the cash receipts and disbursements. He later developed in the Ledger Book an annual summary of cash receipts and disbursements and a three-year summary of sales, expenses and profits. These two statements are shown in Exhibit VII, page 46. The "Recapitulations from May 1794 to Sept. 30, 1797" as shown in Exhibit VII is revealing. After this analysis observe the statement: "Note the nail rod was all out Sep. 30. 97. which makes it a proper epoch for calculation." This last statement, when interpreted with Jefferson's earlier use of the word "profits." shows remarkable insight. Though the nailery records are on a cash basis, with no inventory, the profit figure approaches an accrual income determination.

It will be recalled that cash receipts and disbursements entered in the Account Books were transferred to the Ledger Book; however, the Ledger Book did not contain all the entries from the Account Books. In addition to his own account Jefferson served as a fiduciary (trustee) for numerous relatives and others. These accounts are found in what is frequently referred to as the "Fee Book and Miscellaneous Accounts."[26] A review of these financial records reveals that Jefferson included at least three distinctly different types of items. Typically, each was captioned as shown in Illustrations 1, 2 and 3, page 42.

The postings to these accounts came from several sources including the Account Books. Periodically,

[24] Ford, *op. cit.*, Volume VII, p. 14. For general, nonfinancial information on the nailery operation see: James A. Bear, Jr., "Thomas Jefferson—Manufacturer." *The Iron Worker*, Autumn 1961, pp. 1-11; James A. Bear, Jr., "Mr. Jefferson's Nails." *The Magazine of Albemarle County History*, Vol. XVI (1957-58), pp. 47-52; Dumas Malone, *Jefferson and His Time*, Volume II, *Jefferson and the Ordeal of Liberty* (Little, Brown and Company, 1962), pp. 217-220; Edwin Morris Betts (editor), *Thomas Jefferson's Farm Book* (Princeton University Press, 1953), pp. 426-453.

[25] Farm Book, p. 110.
[26] The original "Fee Book and Miscellaneous Accounts" is owned by The Henry E. Huntington Library and Art Gallery, San Marino, California.

ILLUSTRATION 1—Estate Accounts

Left facing page

"The estate of Peter Jefferson dec.
   in Acct Dr."

Right facing page

"With Th. Jefferson   Cr."

ILLUSTRATION 2—Debt Accounts

Left facing page

"Balance Account for Sep. 30, 1791.
   to inst Debts.

Date of Feb 2	Principal	Interest	Total	Proceed. subseq to Sep. 30. 91"

Right facing page

"Credits

Date of Feb 8	Principal	Interest	Total	Proceed. subseq to Sep. 30. 91"

ILLUSTRATION 3—

Balances due between Jefferson and individuals (including certain employees)

Left facing page

"Will Beck (name)   Dr. £ ς ∂"

Right facing page

"Cr.   £ ς ∂"

---

each of the above accounts was balanced and ruled in the modern-day manner. These accounts reflect the comprehensiveness of his accounting system and include cash, receivables and payables and, significantly, interest accruals.

The author of the Declaration of Independence quietly died at Monticello on July 4, 1826, precisely 50 years after formally signing it. Very possibly his last written words were in the final entry in his Account Books on June 28, 1826, only six days prior to his death at age 83. The entry simply stated: "Isaacs for cheese 4.84."

FINANCES OF THE NEW GOVERNMENT

Jefferson's long involvement in maintaining personal financial records appears to have significantly influenced some of his views as a public servant. First as Secretary of State for President Washington, next as Vice President with John Adams, and finally as President for eight years, Jefferson was intensely interested in the evolving financial procedures being developed by the new government. For government, he insisted on forthright and orderly accounting just as he did in private life. Thus, we find him writing to James Madison, on March 6, 1796, as follows:

The accounts of the US ought to be, and may be made as simple as those of a common farmer, and capable of being understood by common farmers.[27]

Reflecting the political issues of the day and his increasing concern about the approach to fiscal responsibility being developed in the government, President Jefferson (in 1802) wrote to his Secretary of the Treasury, Albert Gallatin, as follows:

I think it an object of great importance, to be kept in view and to be undertaken at a fit season, to simplify our system of finance, and bring it within the comprehension of every member of Congress. Hamilton set out on a different plan. In order that he might have the entire government of his machine, he determined so to complicate it as that neither the President or Congress should be able to understand it, or to control him. He succeeded in doing this, not only beyond their reach, but so that he at length could not unravel it himself.

Continuing his concern for fiscal responsibility, Jefferson stated in the letter:

If . . . [there] can be added a simplification of the form of accounts in the treasury department, and in

---

[27] Ford, *op. cit.*, Volume VII, pp. 61-62.

EXHIBIT IV First Two Facing Ledger Pages of Nailery (May–December 1794).
(Source: Ledger Book. Reprinted by permission.)

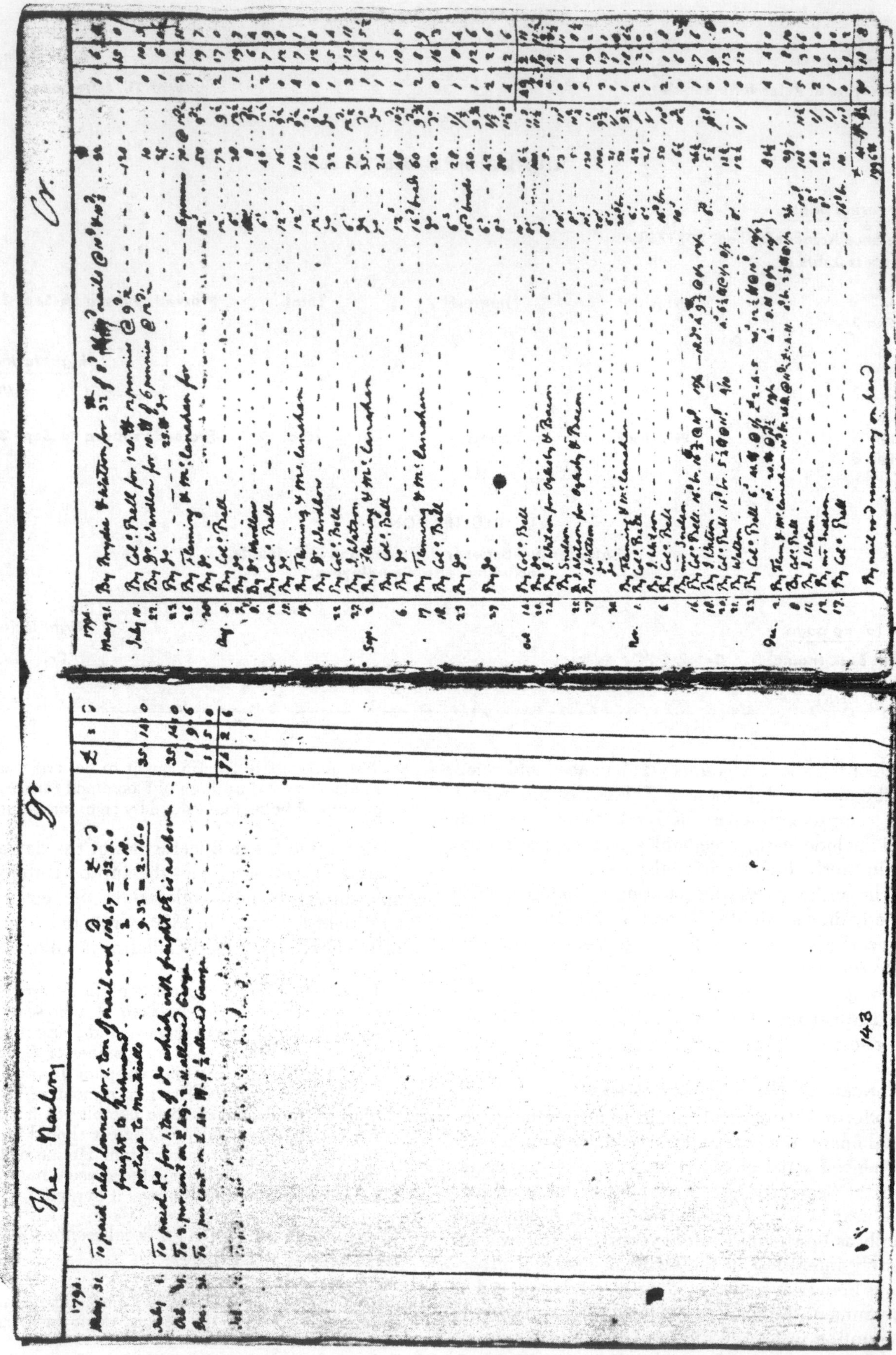

EXHIBIT V Quarterly Profit Report of Nailery (January 1-March 31, 1796).
(Source: Nailery Manufacturing Account. Reprinted by permission of owner, The William Andrews Clark Memorial Library, University of California, Los Angeles.)

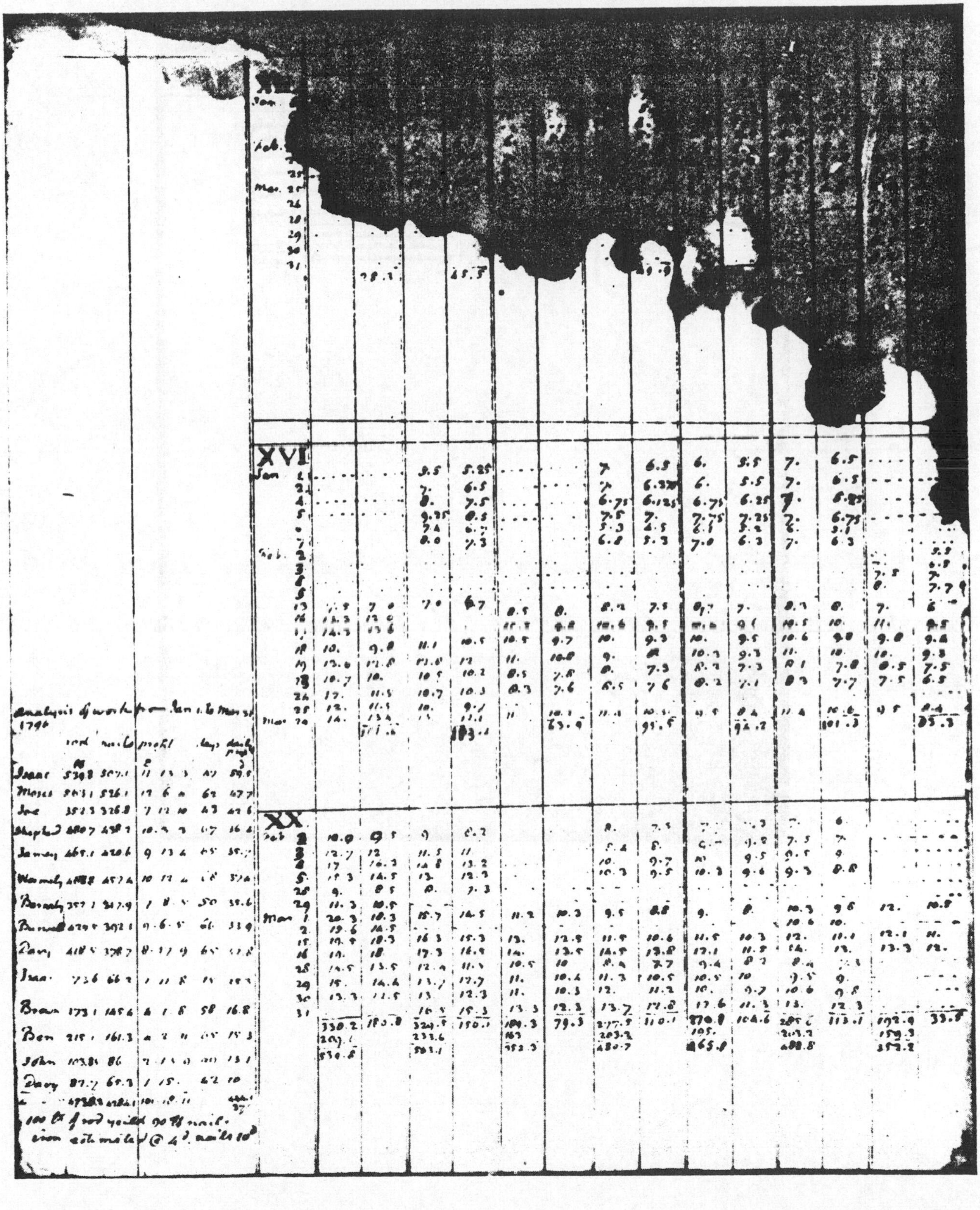

Analysis of work from Jan. 1 to Mar. 31 1796

	rod	nails	profit	days	daily profit
	lb		£		d
Isaac	539.8	507.1	11 13 3	47	59.8
Moses	565.1	526.1	12 6 4	62	47.7
Joe	352.3	326.8	7 12 10	43	42.6
Shepherd	480.7	458.2	10.3.3	67	36.6
Jamey	465.1	420.6	9 13 4	65	35.7
Wormeley	488.8	457.4	10 12 4	68	37.4
Barnaby	357.1	317.9	7 8 5	50	35.6
Burwell	429.5	392.1	9.6.5	66	33.9
Davy	418.5	378.7	8.17.9	65	32.8
Isaac	73.6	66.2	1 11 8	15	25.3
Bran	173.1	145.6	4 1 8	58	16.8
Ben	215.1	161.3	4 2 11	65	15.3
John	103.8	86	2 1 3 0	40	13.1
Davy	87.7	65.3	1 15.	42	10
	4738.8	4284.1	101 10 11		aver. 37

100 lb of rod yield 90 lb nails.
iron estimated @ 4d. nails 10d

EXHIBIT VI Estimates of Nailery Scrap, Costs and Profits (Autumn 1794). (Source: Farm Book, p. 111. Reprinted by permission of the owner, The Massachusetts Historical Society.)

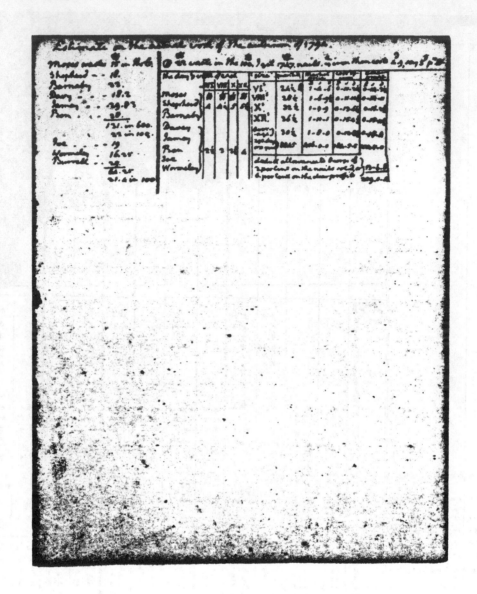

EXHIBIT VII Statement of Cash Receipts, Disbursements and Profits for the Nailery (1794-1797). (Source: Ledger Book. Reprinted by permission.)

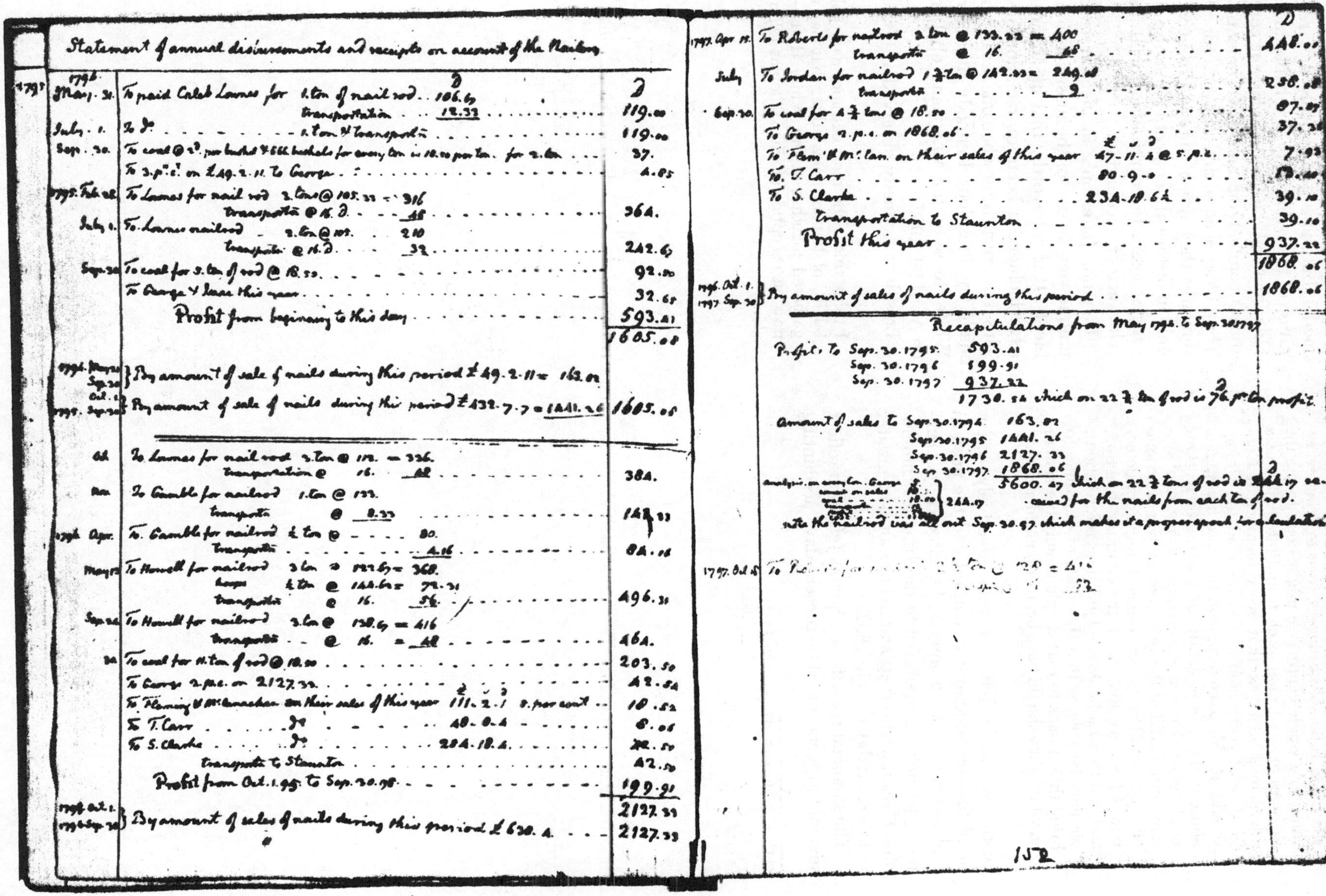
Statement of annual disbursements and receipts on account of the Nailery

1794 May. 31.	To paid Caleb Lownes for 1. ton of nail rod 106.67, transportation 12.33	119.00
July. 1.	To do. 1. ton & transportn	119.00
Sep. 30.	To coal @ 2d. per bushel & 66 bushels for every ton is 18.00 per ton. for 2. ton	37.
	To 3. pr. ct. on £49.2.11. to George	4.85
1795. Feb.	To Lownes for nail rod 2. tons @ 108.33 = 316, transportn @ 16. D. 48	364.
July 1.	To Lownes nailrod 2. ton @ 105. 210, transportn @ 16. D. 32	242.67
Sep. 30	To coal for 5. ton of rod @ 18.50	92.50
	To George & Isaac this year	32.68
	Profit from beginning to this day	593.41
		1605.08
1794. May 31 Sep. 30	By amount of sale of nails during this period £49.2.11 = 163.82	
Oct. 1 1795. Sep. 30	By amount of sale of nails during this period £432.7.7 = 1441.26	1605.08
	To Lownes for nail rod 2. ton @ 112. = 336. transportation @ 16. 48	384.
	To Gamble for nailrod 1. ton @ 133. transportn @ 8.33	142.33
1796 Apr.	To Gamble for nailrod ton @ 80. transportn 4.16	84.16
May	To Howell for nailrod 3 ton @ 122.67 = 368. hoops ton @ 144.64 = 72.31, transportn @ 16. 56.	496.31
Sep. 30	To Howell for nailrod 3. ton @ 138.67 = 416, transportn @ 16. = 48	464.
30	To coal for 11. ton of rod @ 18.50	203.50
	To George 2. pr. c. on 2127.33	42.54
	To Fleming & McLanahan on their sales of this year £111.2.1 5. per cent	18.52
	To T. Carr do. 48.0.4	8.08
	To S. Clarke do. 204.18.4	32.50
	transportn to Staunton	42.50
	Profit from Oct. 1. 95. to Sep. 30. 96.	199.91
		2127.33
1795 Oct. 1. 1796 Sep. 30	By amount of sales of nails during this period £638.4	2127.33
1797. Apr. 15.	To Roberts for nailrod 3. ton @ 133.33 = 400, transportn @ 16. 48	448.00
July	To Jordan for nailrod 1 3/4 ton @ 142.33 = 249.08, transportn 9	258.08
Sep. 30.	To coal for 4 3/4 tons @ 18.50	87.87
	To George 2. p. c. on 1868.06	37.36
	To Flem. & McLan. on their sales of this year £47.11.4 @ 5. p. c.	7.93
	To T. Carr 80.9.0	13.40
	To S. Clarke 234.18.6 1/2	39.10
	Transportation to Staunton	39.10
	Profit this year	937.22
		1868.06
1796. Oct. 1. 1797 Sep. 30	By amount of sales of nails during this period	1868.06

Recapitulations from May 1794. to Sep. 30. 1797

Profit. to Sep. 30. 1795.	593.41	
Sep. 30. 1796	199.91	
Sep. 30. 1797	937.22	
	1730.54	which on 22 3/4 ton of rod is 76 pr. ton profit.
Amount of sales to Sep. 30. 1794.	163.82	
Sep. 30. 1795	1441.26	
Sep. 30. 1796	2127.33	
Sep. 30. 1797.	1868.06	
	5600.47	which on 22 3/4 tons of rod is 246.17 received for the nails from each ton of rod.

note the nailrod was all out Sep. 30. 97. which makes it a proper epoch for a calculation.

1797. Oct. 5 To Roberts for [illegible]

152

the organization of its officers, so as to bring everything to a single centre, we might hope to see the finances of the Union as clear and intelligible as a merchant's books, so that every member of Congress, and every man of any mind in the Union, should be able to comprehend them, to investigate abuses, and consequently to control them. Our predecessors have endeavored by intricacies of system, and shuffling the investigator over from one officer to another, to cover everything from detection. I hope we shall go in the contrary direction, and that by your honest and judicious reformations, we may be able, within the limits of our time, to bring things back to that simple intelligible system on which they should have been organized at first.[28]

In this statement Jefferson very effectively articulated the fundamentals of control and the need in government, as in commerce, for effective yet simple approaches responsive to the broader community. His suggestions appear to have an even greater relevance today than in 1802.

The financial records of Thomas Jefferson reflect several aspects of the present-day accounting

[28] *Ibid.*, Volume VIII, pp. 139-141.

model, but more perceptively they reveal a recognition of the essentiality of reliable and understandable financial data in the efficient conduct of personal, commercial and governmental endeavors. They have been a rich resource for the historian; similarly they are of interest to accountants, not only in historical perspective but also because they suggest again the continuing social and economic relevance of accounting.

In sum, Jefferson's financial records afford a unique view of one of the most accomplished Presidents. It is noteworthy that his breadth of knowledge included a keen appreciation of accounting. This is not surprising when one recalls the statement made by President Kennedy at a dinner in the White House for the American Nobel Prize winners on April 29, 1962.

President Kennedy observed:

I think this is the most extraordinary collection of talent, of human knowledge, that has ever been gathered together at the White House—with the possible exception of when Thomas Jefferson dined alone.

SECTION VIII

Outlook for the Future

When studying accounting in an academic environment, it is important to recognize that the future will quickly become the present as one moves from classroom to the world of business. While not all students of accounting will become practitioners, all of us will, on a daily basis, utilize accounting information and contribute to the data base of accounting reports.

Obviously, the developing accountant has a vested interest in the future of the profession. Equally important, however, is the interest of the user of accounting information. As the profession changes, so will change its informational output which will have a direct impact on all in the business environment.

This section, which specifically deals with the future dimensions of the profession, is divided into three parts addressing projected changes in accounting practice and organization, career opportunities for individuals in the profession, and the ever present impact of electronic data processing and computers.

The future dimensions of accounting focus not only on the profession but on the accountability of other types of organizations such as government. Likewise, government intervention of the accounting process holds a spectre of dimensional complexity for statement preparer and user alike.

Many sources are available which speak to the future of the profession in particular and the business community in general. These readings are not exhaustive but provide a sampling of views from individuals willing to face this future, comment on it today, and work toward responses to the implications thereof.

Charles Chazen, CPA

The Profession Today— and Tomorrow

In this article the author, a widely-known practitioner of many years, discusses the profession's present problems and the future developments he sees as likely.

Charles Chazen, CPA, a partner in the Los Angeles office of Laventhol & Horwath, serves as national director of the Accounting and Auditing Department. A member of AICPA Council, he also serves on ACSEC and is a former member of Audsec. A former director of the California CPA Society, Mr. Chazen has been widely published in professional journals and has been active in the National Arbitration Association.

I wonder at times if we give enough serious thought to the impressions we create as public accountants and auditors. We are all too familiar with the often-quoted description now 70 years outdated (we hope):

The typical auditor is a man past middle age, spare, wrinkled, intelligent, cold, passive, noncommittal, with eyes like a codfish, polite in contact, but at the same time, unresponsive, cold; calm and damnably composed as a concrete post or a plaster-of-paris cast; a human pertrification with a heart of feldspar and without charm of the friendly germ, minus bowels, passion, or a sense of humor. Happily, they never reproduce and all of them finally go to Hell.

Just as the image of the public accountant has changed over the years so has the nature of public accounting. Many of us are old enough to remember when accounting was more of an art, when the profession had broad rules and guidelines as the basis for application of judgment to specific situations. Unfortunately, this is no longer true. In the last 10 or 15 years accounting has changed from an art to an accumulation of cookbook-type rules to be followed literally and almost blindly. This change resulted from the need to respond to problems the profession and the business environment have faced in recent years.

Problems of the Profession

The manner in which public accounting is practiced today is governed principally by two factors. One is the existing economic and business conditions and the related accounting rules which are continually updated by regulatory bodies and by our profession. The second is the demands and expectations of the users of the statement. These users include just about everybody—management, investors, creditors—all the way down to the active consumers who are always on the alert for material to use as a basis for a class action suit.

The continuous criticism we face is basically the result of alleged failures in meeting demands from both of these sectors. We are told that today's public accounting and auditing in many respects do not meet the requirements of today's economic and business conditions or the needs of all financial statement users.

The impression has grown over the years that the financial statements reported on by CPAs not only imply accuracy, but absolute precision. Balance sheets balance, related financial statements and exhibits dovetail, and amounts shown are usually in precise dollars, sometimes even in precise pennies. Many of our problems come about when statement users discover that the inference of absolute precision is not borne out.

Some of our troubles stem from trying to please everybody with general purpose financial statements aimed at every conceivable user, from the most sophisticated to the least informed. With it all, or maybe because of it, some critics say that we have failed to meet the needs of statement users.

In the decade of the 1960s, the accounting profession grew dramatically. Our rate of growth was among the greatest, if not the greatest, of any industry during that time span. As a result, quality control lagged, some of our existing rules were rubbed a little thin, and creative accounting was applied to newly developed or expanding economic phenomena, like business combinations and lease transactions.

Over the years, users of financial statements have become skeptical about the meaning of an

THE **CPA** JOURNAL / MAY 1978

accountant's report. First of all, the statement user may not completely understand the terms used in this report. Furthermore, he may not believe the CPA's opinion.

The inability of our profession to maintain credibility was in no small part caused by significant reporting deficiencies, which according to the FASB (in its Conceptual Framework Discussion Memorandum) were principally the result of the following failures:

• Acceptability of two or more methods of accounting for the same facts;
• Switches to less conservative accounting methods;
• Front-ending of income;
• Use of reserves of artifically smooth earnings fluctuations;
• Failure of financial statements to warn of impending liquidity crunches;
• Deferrals followed by "big bath" write-offs;
• Unjustified optimism in estimates of recoverability;
• Off-balance sheet financing;
• Use of the excuse of immateriality to justify omission of unfavorable information or departures from standards.

Self-protection has been a major factor in both the development and lack of development of our profession. Critics from within, like Abe Briloff, critics from without, like Abe Pomerantz and the courts, and regulatory bodies, such as the SEC, have had a beneficial effect on the quality of audit work. They have caused us to improve our standards and our work. But they may well have also stifled the development of pure accounting. We have not been able to work in a free, uninhibited atmosphere in which legitimate ideas could be advanced and acted on for the sake of the pure art. Practically everything that the profession has done or been a party to in the decade of the 70s has been affected, to some extent, by the element of fear.

The self-preservation need to carefully follow all of the rules also has lead to criticism of the profession. We wear belts, suspenders, and anything else available to hold up our statements. As a result, statements sometime

become precisely correct and completely useless.

Conceptual Frameworks and Developed Rules

The FASB says that a conceptual framework for accounting and reporting has never been articulated authoritatively. While individuals, organizations and committees have developed their own ideas of a conceptual framework, no framework yet has been accepted as a standard. Earlier attempts include Accounting Research Studies No. 1 and 3, "The Basic Postulates of Accounting" and "A Tentative Set of Broad Accounting Principles for Business Enterprises." More recently, the APB issued its Statement No. 4, "Basic Concepts and Accounting Principles Underlying Financial Statements of Business Enterprises." According to the FASB, this statement describes the way things are but does not describe how things should be. We cannot take those postulates and lay them on a situation not covered by the statement and arrive at a reliable answer.

The rules that the profession has developed over the years for the most part have been reactions—they were designed to put out fires, to answer emergencies. We have seldom planned ahead. The result is that our body of rules consists of single-purpose regulations created to solve specific problems, rather than an umbrella framework that we can look to to solve any problem that comes up.

One of the allegations of the Metcalf study, and others, charges that business economics are affected by accountants' rules rather than accounting rules reflecting economics. University professors, in cooperation with the FASB, recently agreed to undertake studies of the effects that specific accounting standards may have on management in their business decision and on investors and creditors in their assessments of companies and their securities.

Specifically, the studies will include an attempt to ascertain if reinsurance practices or operating procedures have changed as a result of the issuance of FASB

Statement No. 5, "Accounting for Contingencies" and whether the issuance of FASB Statement No. 8, "Accounting for the Translation of Foreign Currency Transactions and Foreign Currency Financial Statements," had any impact on the market price of common stock of companies with significant foreign operations.

Reviews of the Profession and of Principles

The present state of affairs has led to a close examination of the accounting profession from several different angles. Congressional committees are trying to decide what's best for us. The Cohen Commission has studied the role and responsibilities of independent auditors. The SEC appointed an Advisory Committee on Corporate Disclosure to study what types of reporting companies should use to communicate financial information to various users, and also to determine the form and organization of that information.

The FASB has embarked on a major project to develop a conceptual framework for financial accounting and reporting. Its expressed goal is to achieve a framework which will:

• Act as a guide for establishing accounting standards;
• Provide a frame of reference for resolving accounting questions in the absence of a specific standard;
• Determine bounds for judgment in preparing financial statements;
• Increase users' understanding of and confidence in financial statements;
• Improve comparability.

The concepts considered in the FASB's conceptual framework discussion memorandum are very deep, highly complex and extremely theoretical. Whether a pragmatic foundation can be developed and, if developed, whether it will serve the intended purpose remain to be seen. It is obvious, though, that we have to stand back, take a long, hard look and create something which will replace the patchwork we are presently working with and serve as a model against which to match future events and transactions that presently cannot be anticipated or contemplated.

There are some things that we *can* expect as a result of the FASB study, either directly or indirectly. Let us examine some of these.

Current Value Accounting

When the future of accounting is discussed by a group of accountants, invariably one of the first ideas that pops up is current value accounting. Should we be accounting in some fashion that will somehow equate the balance sheet with current reality, whether it be fair value accounting, inflation accounting, measuring variable buying power by means of general price level accounting or some other form? A criticism often leveled against us in our failure to recognize that a balance sheet is not really a statement of financial position. Except for LIFO, accelerated depreciation and maybe a few other practices, historical cost reporting does not accommodate changing prices or changing values. In the eyes of many, historical cost financial statements are based on an archaic concept and have lost credibility.

It is questionable whether traditional financial statements tell the full story. Other countries have mandated some form of current value accounting, recognizing that in inflationary periods, capital-intensive businesses under-report actual costs, and money-intensive businesses fail to report significant economic facts under the historical cost method of accounting.

In this country, the comment is often made that investors, creditors and business management are being penalized by the failure of our profession to recognize that business capital is leaking away through income taxes based on illusory earnings that fail to tell the effect of inflation. In a recently published monograph entitled "Accounting in an Inflationary Environment," prepared for our firm by Professor Lawrence Revsine of Northwestern University, the author concluded that continual reliance on traditional historical cost accounting procedures can result in

serious profit overstatements in our present environment. This, he said, can lead to erroneous dividend decisions, taxation of capital and the misallocation of resources.

I think there is a lot of merit to the complaints of these critics. Historical costs have proved to be of value in the past, but there are obvious signs that this value is diminishing. The concept of current value is recognized as more appropriate in more and more financial presentations and is being requested with increasing frequency by lenders, by creditors and by others. One of the most important purposes of the conceptual framework project is the determination of the desirability of the use of some form of current value accounting as a standard. I am convinced that the FASB will recommend current value accounting for fair and comprehensive reporting. At first, this may take the form of data supplementing the basic financial statements. Ultimately, it will become a part of the basic statements.

Forecasting

Another change that I am confident we will soon see is the addition of some form of forecast information in published annual reports. The Trueblood Committee, in its 1973 report, encouraged the use of financial forecasts in financial reports. The SEC's Advisory Committee on Corporate Disclosure has recommended that companies should be encouraged to disclose, on a voluntary basis and under a safe harbor rule, projections of future economic performance. The SEC has made various attempts to determine the feasibility of the inclusion of forecast information in annual reports, and at the present time, permits inclusion on a voluntary basis.

Investors and others interested in the operations and growth of a company are not particularly concerned with the past. They care about what is going to happen in the future. They care about the anticipated progress of the company so that they can make better informed investment decisions. The

SEC staff has conducted in-depth interviews with a number of analysts and members of management of large corporations to get their views on the desirability of the inclusion of projections of earnings. Most of the corporate executives and some of the analysts indicated that earnings forecasts are not key concerns.

I can understand management's lack of interest, although obviously they prepare forecasts for internal management purposes, but I cannot understand why an analyst would not be concerned about the future. Maybe this survey only indicates that analysts prefer to receive earnings forecasts in *unpublished* form so as to have a greater impact in their business counseling. If forecasts were published, maybe the analysts feel that a major portion of their services would not be required by the investor.

In this era of enlightenment, where the consumer is king, management's future plans and concepts of future earnings must not be kept from those who need this information to make decisions. The inclusion of forecast financial information in financial reports will become a standard procedure in the not too distant future.

Readability of Financial Statements

The readability of financial statements and annual reports is in desperate need of improvement. As a means of communication, they leave much to be desired. The expansion of required disclosures has generally resulted in confused rather then enlightened readers. Even CPAs sometimes are bewildered by the long, complicated, technical, rambling notes found in published reports. The statements themselves, in an effort to be fully and completely explanatory, have become so technical and cluttered that they are meaningless to many investors, maybe most of them.

The FASB's exposure draft on "Accounting and Reporting by Defined Benefit Plans" is a typical example. The principal users of statements issued by pension plans will be the participants in the plan. I think it fair to assume that employee-participants, as a class,

THE CPA JOURNAL / MAY 1978

are not among the most sophisticated statement readers. The financial statements proposed by the FASB include all of the information, both financial and disclosure, that the FASB considers necessary for participants to be in a position to assess the benefit security that is provided by the plan assets.

If participants are furnished with financial statements similar to the model statements included in the appendix to the exposure draft, I believe the average employee will not be in a position to assess the benefits security provided by the plan assets and that he'll probably toss the statements away with a sense of confusion, bewilderment and even frustration.

Financial statements are a form of communication. Communication, to be effective, must be expressed in such a manner that the understanding of the reader coincides with the intent of the writer. We must develop and refine our language to be more explicit and less technical.

On the other hand, the user of statements has a responsibility to learn what it is we do and what we mean in financial language so that he or she can understand the significance of what we say. As the FASB points out, financial statement users will have to make the requisite effort to understand the conceptual framework when it is developed. That is a major expectation. To even hope to achieve it, the framework will have to be published in the simplest of terms and most comprehensible form.

Basic Conceptual Views

In its discussion of elements of financial statements, the conceptual framework discussion memorandum proposes two alternative conceptual views of earnings, *the asset and liability view* under which earnings are determined as a measure of change in the economic resources of a business for a period, and the *revenue and expense view* under which earnings are a direct measure of the effectiveness of an enterprise in using its inputs to obtain and sell outputs. Whichever concept is adopted, the result will still be a general purpose financial statement, and this seems to be the heart of

some of our major problems.

Audience of Financial Reporting

A financial statement which tries to be all things to all users frequently misses its mark with some users. The chairman of the SEC's Advisory Committee on Corporate Disclosure has said the financial statements and disclosures should be designed for sophisticated investors. In a recent court decision, however, a federal judge said that financial statements should be understandable to the "untutored eye" of the unsophisticated investor.

I don't know who's going to win that battle, but my crystal ball tells me that in addition to general purpose financial statements that will be structured to match the ultimate conceptual framework, we will see a trend toward simplified financial statements for other than SEC and sophisticated users, to meet the general public's need for less complex and more understandable reporting.

We will probably find more statements restricted to specific purposes. The interests of sophisticated users, the SEC, security analysts and money managers will be met by financial statements containing those elements which the FASB decides should be present in full, comprehensive statements. The general public, however, will have difficulty in coping with these complicated concepts and the accounting profession will probably explore approaches to simplified statements presenting only the most relevant information for average shareholders.

We face serious problems today concerning reporting by small and closely-held companies. The still unanswered question is whether the accounting rules and professional standards should include some flexibility to recognize the special problems of such companies. I do not think we will see the development of two sets of GAAP, but rather a new dimension in determining materiality. The concept of *qualitative* materiality is going to emerge as a significant factor in alleviating the problems of accounting for the small and closely-held companies.

The SEC rules and our own professional literature now contain specific requirements which are selective as to size and type of company. Part 2 of APB Opinion 28, "Interim Financial Reporting," applies only to publicly-held companies. The SEC's Accounting Series Release No. 190 on replacement cost accounting applies only to companies that exceed a specified size. It would not be unreasonable to extend this sort of philosophy to smaller companies. However "small" is defined, it may be decided, for example, that deferred tax computations, imputed interest provisions, statements of changes of financial position and other technical requirements may not be particularly relevant.

The Cohen Commission has recognized the concept of qualitative materiality. In the discussion of illegal acts in the report of its tentative conclusions, the commission said, "Conventional concepts of materiality, based principally on quantitative considerations, are inapplicable to known illegal or questionable acts." To me, this is an invitation to consider making qualitative distinctions in other areas of reporting as well.

I don't view this as a deterioration into two sets of GAAP, one for the big and one for the small. I see this as recognizing that the needs of investors, financial analysts and the SEC for financial data and disclosures may be different than the needs of management and the local bank. Small and closely-held companies are in a completely different environment than large and public companies.

The conceptual framework discussion memorandum seems to perpetuate, or at least it does not diminish, the problems of big GAAP/little GAAP. However, in spite of this failing of the memorandum, or maybe because of it, I foresee a swing to a qualitative materiality concept and a loosening of some of the rules for smaller companies.

Who Will Set Standards?

There remains the question of who will be in charge of standard-setting in the future. All the signs indicate that the FASB expects to

THE PROFESSION TODAY—AND TOMORROW /

remain in business. The various stages of the conceptual framework project will take some time. Furthermore, if they were not to add another subject to their agenda, the projects that they have scheduled will take years to complete.

On the other hand, members of Congress and others are clamoring for the government to take over the job of developing accounting standards. While the SEC and the CASB have no interest in taking it over, politics and politicians being what they are, they may have no choice.

SEC chairman Harold Williams, in his testimony before the Metcalf Committee, recommended that the profession be given another year to straighten itself out. That year will expire in June 1978. What will happen then remains to be seen. I have a hunch that the clamor and furor raised in recent months have convinced the FASB, the AICPA and the profession in general that we had better put our house in order, and fast. I doubt that all of the progress expected of us can take place by next summer, but evidence of legitimate attempts should buy us more time. I believe that ultimately our efforts will allow us to continue to set our own standards.

If we continue to be masters of our own fate, we must remember that the development of accounting concepts is a never-ending process. The conceptual framework created by the FASB must be flexible enough to accommodate economic and technological changes and it should be strong enough to prevent the dulling of good accounting concepts by the application of marginal methods of compliance. If it doesn't work, we've got to be ready to jump right in with some new ideas. Maybe my predictions are a form of wishful thinking because I think they represent significant professional progress. But in the final analysis, it is not only the rules that are going to determine the success of our future, it is also how you and I follow them—how we practice accounting. If we learn from today, I'm convinced there will a better tomorrow. Ω

A Woman CPA Looks at Public Accounting

One principal in a public accounting firm talks about her career and offers advice for women entering the accounting field today.

No longer satisfied with supporting roles, women have made it clear for some time now that they want to be in the front lines of business. Unprecedented numbers of women are entering the work force, and some of them, especially those who have been in business for several years, are beginning to land coveted top management positions. In the professions, too, more women are realizing their fullest potential.

Stephanie M. Shern, a principal with Arthur Young & Co. in New York, gave us her views on women in accounting from the perspective of one who began her career with a Big 8 firm right after college ten years ago. There are three women partners and eight women principals at AY. She asked a female colleague, senior accountant Deborah Daly, to interview her so the questions would reflect areas of interest to the current crop of young women entering the field today.

Mrs. Shern received a B.S. degree in accounting from Pennsylvania State University in 1969. She joined the New York office of Arthur Young & Co. in that year and is now a principal. She received her CPA certificate in New York and was named to Arthur Young's National Retail Industry Group. Mrs. Shern is Chairman of the New York State Society of CPAs' Retail Accounting Committee, for which she has conducted various seminars, and is a newly elected member of the board of directors of the Metropolitan (New York) Retail Financial Ex-

ecutives Assn. She is also a member of the National Retail Merchants Assn., the National Mass Retailing Institute, and the American Institute of CPAs.

Ten years ago, the accounting profession was dominated by men. What changes for women have you noticed in the accounting profession since then?

The major change I have seen over the ten year period is that there are definitely more women in accounting—and in business— than when I started. When I was in college, I was the only woman in most of my classes at Penn State University. Today, I understand that at times 50% of the students in those classes are women. When I started with Arthur Young, I began with a group of about 120, which included about eight or ten women. Today Arthur Young & Co.'s new recruits consist of approximately 33% to 50% women, so there is a big difference in the numbers of women who are going through the accounting schools and the numbers of women who are being hired.

At upper levels of management, though, I have not seen that kind of increase. There are still very few women in positions of authority at upper management levels. I work with only one client that has a woman as its controller, and it's not one of Arthur Young's larger clients. I think this is a function of the fact that it takes time to gain a

0025-1690/80/6108-0001/$01.00/0

position of authority, and since there were fewer women in the graduating classes in the late '60s and the early '70s, it is just going to take time for us to gain these positions.

Why did you choose the accounting profession, and why have you remained in public accounting, particularly at Arthur Young & Co.? Do you feel that accounting is a valuable long-term career for a woman?

I had no clear career objective in mind when I began my collegiate studies. I though I might want to become a buyer, so I began in a merchandising curriculum. But I found out that it was a long, hard haul for anybody to become successful quickly. While I was in that curriculum, however, I also had to take an accounting course. Accounting was easy for me, I maintained good grades, and I thought, why not pursue that? So, I switched my major and as I continued in that major, I realized that while I liked accounting, I really wasn't sure what I was going to do with my accounting degree once I got it. I learned that the best route to pursue if you weren't clear about your career objective was to try public accounting because at least you would get exposure to a lot of different companies. So, that's how I ended up in public accounting.

I stayed because I realized, not too long after I began, that public accounting offers a very diverse atmosphere. There are very few industries or companies that can hold your interest and challenge you over a long period of time unless you just happen to luck into a really dynamic industry and a very dynamic position. In public accounting you are constantly exposed to new ideas, new clients, new people.

It has continued to be very challenging for me. I stayed with Arthur Young & Co. because it allowed me to get exposure to a lot of different industries and clients. In all my years with Arthur Young, I have never been held back from any particular engagement. I've taken midnight fuel inventories, climbed oil tanks, and run around airports after fuel trucks; I've worked on engagements for large clients and I've worked with small clients. Recently, I've also been getting involved with Arthur Young's practice development efforts. You might ask, well, couldn't I have done all this someplace else. Maybe yes, maybe no; I've just decided that I like it here, so why try elsewhere?

As to whether I think accounting is a good long-term career for a woman, I guess I would have to say, it really depends on the woman. It is definitely a challenging job for either a woman or a man. It takes a lot of hard work, it requires making some major decisions as far as lifestyle goes, but I think the key issue here, as in any other profession, is whether or not you want the

It is difficult for a man to accept his wife's career, especially if the husband does not work a lot of overtime.

career. Most career-oriented people spend about 75% of their waking hours at their jobs. You can't have both an active social life and an active career. You also have to have determination and drive. And if you have that, whether you are a woman or a man, you'll be successful.

What major decisions have you made along the way?

I've decided all along that my social life in general is not as important to me as my professional life. I decided some time ago that my professional career was more important than many other things, such as playing tennis, reading, and the like. That's not to say I don't do these things; it's just that I don't have hours to linger on a shopping spree or to spend in a health spa. And then I made the decision not to have a family because, the way I see it, I don't have the time for both a career as a working woman and as a mother.

The general public seems to retain the view that the life of the CPA is staid and uniform, that the CPA's life has only to do with books of numbers, and that he or she looks at them only between the hours of 9 and 5.

Oh yes, public accounting is more than just bookkeeping or verifying figures. We serve our clients as business advisors to a great extent, and we get involved in economics, politics, professional developments. My role is a very challenging one and very demanding, and it's always changing, and I like that.

At any time in your career did you feel you received preferential treatment from Arthur Young because you are a member of a minority? Did the firm help you in any way in terms of setting a path for you?

I'd have to answer that, most definitely not, it did not give me preferential treatment. It did not, because I am a woman, sit down with me and say, okay, Stephanie, we want you to be our next woman partner and this is the career path we see for you to get there. I've been told by some of my peers and partners from other public accounting firms that if I were with their firms, that would have been done for me. But at Arthur Young & Co., the partners believe that a woman, a man, a black, an oriental—anyone and everyone has to perform and to meet the standards that have been set by the partners and must be judged on the objective merits of that performance. I would like to have thought that being a woman would be helpful to me, and I'm not naive enough to say that it has not been, but I would have to say that I have definitely not been given preferential treatment.

Is that a contradiction? How is it that being a

woman has helped you, yet hasn't meant that you've received preferential treatment?

Arthur Young hasn't given me preferential treatment, but the climate of the times is such that socio-business conditions are favorable—and sometimes preferential—to women. I'm glad I'm a woman in a business profession at this time. Of course, my future success will be based on my credentials, technical skills, and competence—and not on the fact that I'm a woman.

Do you feel that you have to exert more effort to gain more respect than your male peers do when dealing with executives?

Yes. Men walk into a room and walk into a situation, and whether they are dressed properly or not, they have an element of respect. When a woman walks in, there is a little bit of testing that goes on. Now, it's not necessarily blatant testing, but then there is always that degree of uneasiness. Questions might be asked or statements might be made such as, perhaps you could double-check with partner so-and-so, or maybe you could just let partner so-and-so know, or what do you think partner so-and-so would say?

How do you handle that?

I just say that I'd be happy to let partner so-and-so know, but I don't think the partners would disagree with me and I think that this is the way we should proceed. And then I might come back and say to the partners I work for, look, this fellow is testing me, and this is what I told him. Most often, the partner agrees with how I've handled the situation and the client's apprehension goes away once we've dealt with each other.

Do you think that the way you dress to work influences the way your peers and your superiors react to you? Do you feel they respect you more when you dress in a more professional manner?

Most definitely, yes. Your attire can make you or break you on that first contact. It affects the way your peers, people above you, and your clients perceive you. I've seen women—including women who have come to work for me—walk into a room wearing completely inappropriate clothing—for example, clothes that were too casual for the circumstances or ridiculous accessories—and it completely turns me off, and I know it turns off the other individuals who might be with me. A man doesn't have that problem. A man walks into a room with a suit and tie on, and even if his suit and tie are not the most fashionable, he passes in his uniform.

I, myself, feel better if I am dressed right for the occasion. You may have read Molloy's *The Woman's Dress for Success Book*. I am not so sure I want to dress as conservatively as he suggests, but he's definitely right in general. A suit or a conservatively-styled dress is the way to present a successful image, and it is the way to represent your firm or company.

You are saying that women sometimes make bad judgments about clothes or presentation of themselves, whereas men, whether or not they have good taste, at least always seem to know the code. Why?

I think it's *because* men have a dress code, to begin with. And women don't. Women don't have a "uniform," as men do. And maybe they should. Women don't have an example to look to, either. Girls, when they're growing up, had usually only teachers or nurses to look to as professional examples, or if a woman went to work, she often wasn't at a high enough professional level to worry about what she wore to work. Your father, though, even if he wasn't at a high professional level, if he had a white collar job at all, he wore a suit and tie.

On the engagements that you have worked, do you feel that clients are more receptive to you because you are a woman?

I would have to say that, in the ten years I have been with Arthur Young & Co., it's worked both for me and against me to be a woman. I think it was more of an advantage in my earlier years with Arthur Young than it is now. At the level I am now, when I deal with the men who have responsible positions in client operations, at times they're not really sure of my position because I'm operating on their level. Yet when I first started, it was very simple for clients to accept the fact that I was there doing the job that I was sent to do because I was working at a lower level—and the client person was above me. I was no challenge to his or her authority. I was there to get an audit done—but I was not then dealing one-on-one.

Would you say that accounting takes women more seriously than do other professions?

I really don't think there is any profession that takes women more or less seriously than any other. There are professions that have more women in them than men, but most professions, such as law or medicine, have the same evolution going on that we have in accounting. Increasing numbers of women are entering the professions. And as more women get involved, women will be taken more seriously. A key point to be made is that this is an evolutionary process. It's not going to happen overnight. It's probably going to take 10 or 20 years for everything to shake itself out.

Do you think that in 20 years or so women will truly be considered with the same equanimity in the business and professional world as are men?

Yes, in the United States, anyway. In 20 years, maybe, I think women will be taken as seriously

I've taken midnight fuel inventories, climbed oil tanks, and run around airports after fuel trucks.

as men and it will not be that unusual for a woman to opt to have a career permanently because there are more and more women who are coming out of school and are doing that, and as more and more women do it, it will just become accepted.

In other countries, it will take longer, and who knows whether in some countries it will ever happen. For example, the international business scene still presents a problem for women today. Many foreign countries are reluctant to accept women in responsible positions—even some of the more progressive countries. And in the Middle East, Japan, and other parts of the Orient, for example, business careers are nonexistent for women.

Your attire can make you or break you on that first contact ... A man doesn't have that problem.

You have a secretary and she is a woman, and you've implied there are other accountant-professional women you've hired to work with you or for you in one capacity or another. Does the fact that you are a "woman boss" ever present any problems?

The first time I had to hire a secretary, it was really difficult. I had no idea what a secretary should do or what I wanted her to do. I say "she" because no men applied. I think I ended up hiring somebody without any thought as to credentials or technical skills. I had several secretaries before I figured out how I wanted a secretary to operate.

As far as professional staff people go, I guess I've interviewed people from after the first year I was hired. The way we're set up, the firm gives you one day to talk to new recruits or new hires—they want new people or prospective people to talk to people at all levels—so I've been in an interviewing position almost as long as I've been here. But I'd have to say that was difficult, too. It was difficult to figure out what the firm was looking for—and at that point I didn't know very much about the audit process.

Now I am much more knowledgeable about what is needed. I guess in both instances, I'd have to say, "Experience helps."

Did you ever fire anyone, say, a secretary, in your early years?

Yes, it was awful.

But what about the reaction to you as a woman, just on that basis?

In both cases, people wonder what you're going to be like because you're a woman. I had one experience—a professional audit senior said he refused to work with me because I was a woman. But other than that, the general reaction is that people just wonder what it's going to be like because I'm a woman.

How do you manage a family life as well as a full-time career?

At some point you make a decision as to what you want to do with your life, or which direction you want it to take. For the first couple of years that I was in public accounting I was single, and it was easy to accommodate my job because my social life was whatever I made it when I got home from work. After I got married, the next couple of years were not easy because no man really understands or appreciates what it's like to be married to a woman with a career. It is difficult for a man to accept his wife's career, especially if the husband does not work a lot of overtime. It's hard to balance working, maintaining a house, and socializing. But then, as I said earlier, at some point you sort out your priorities and if you have a fairly good relationship with your spouse, you can work things out.

How do you accommodate the day-to-day household chores?

It's not easy to take care of the cleaning, cooking, just the running of a household. I don't think men quite realize that. I don't think my husband quite understands that. All he knows is, it works. The house is always clean and we always have a full refrigerator.

How do you manage that?

(Laughs) That's a good question. I don't have any outside help. Since we have a home now, I've thought about it more, but I've never had the time to try to find someone who could do it (the household work) the way I want it. But I'm pretty organized. My husband goes crazy sometimes with my lists. I have a list for everything. Actually, I'm very organized, and I can clean my house very quickly if I have to, so it works.

Have you ever asked your husband to share in the household chores?

No. When we first got married, he did some of those things because he had been a bachelor for a number of years and had had his own apartment before then. He had cooked, he had cleaned, he had done his own food shopping and all that kind of thing. But then we just sort of got away from that. Men don't usually want to take that extra step to make sure the house is just perfect ...

And you do, so you will do it fairly cheerfully? (Laughs) Yes.

Would you say this works well because of individual temperament between you and your husband? I take it he is not an accountant?

No, he works more in a service line. He is not a financial person. But he's very independent, too (as I am), and he does not rely on his home life for every satisfaction in life or every interest. He likes his own interests, his own hobbies. And I think that's what makes my career very palatable to him because I don't think he would like a very dependent person for a wife. I don't think he would be able to handle a relationship with a more dependent woman, someone who needed to have him home every night. So it's worked out well for us that I'm independent too.

In what ways do the demands of the professional life infringe on your normal life? When you have pressure and stress at work, do you feel that you take it home with you or do you try not to?

I think everybody says that he or she tries not to take it home, but I don't manage that easily. I might not realize it, but my husband can always tell when I've had a bad day or I've had a problem at work. I think it's difficult to separate the stress you have at work from your home life.

What are your feelings about a woman making more money than her husband? Do you think it creates problems? Also, do you think at times there is competition between husbands and wives?

I think this is a very timely and very appropriate question to ask because I'm sure a lot of women are facing this now. It takes a very strong man to be able to handle this situation. I have not really had the problem with my husband in terms of competition or making more money. We are involved in two completely different professions. He has chosen his work style—what he likes to do—and I have chosen mine. He would not like to work all the overtime I do, and he would not be particularly enthused about the travel that most of us at Arthur Young do.

The way we view income is that it is a total pool and the pool is used for various purposes. It's not "my money" and "your money." That philosophy has worked very successfully for us.

Of course, there are other pressures created outside your marriage.

What kinds of outside pressures?

Well, some of my husband's associates who are providing the sole income for their families—wife and children—can be envious of my husband or might tell him, well, you can afford this and that because your wife works. Or, my husband wonders whether someone else competing with him for a promotion who had a family and needed the raise, would get a promotion rather than himself.

So, in general, how has your husband reacted to your overtime, your travel, and your success?

My husband understands that overtime is part of the job. Travel, he understands, is also part of the responsibilities of my position. In fact, my husband enjoys my travel because if I am going to a fairly interesting place, he sometimes joins me at the end of my trip and so we have been able to visit many places. His reaction and the rest of my family's reaction to my success have been positive.

Do you think women will rise faster in the professions, say medicine, than in business? That is, do you think it will be easier for a woman to achieve high status in the professions than to reach a high level in a corporate hierarchy? Why or why not?

Well, that's a little hard to answer. I think women have been in the medical profession for awhile; they have been doctors for awhile. I would say it will take some time for more women to gain top corporate spots because they need to develop a broader perspective on business, more business savvy, and the "network" which men have. □

The way we view income is that it is a total pool ... It's not "my money" and "your money."

Portrait of the Divisional Controller

"Cost accounting is where the action is," controllers say.

By Paul A. Janell and Raymond M. Kinnunen

Although divisional controllers are the nerve centers in a company's accounting control and reporting system, little has been written about this essential function. We conducted a research project to gain information concerning the educational backgrounds and career paths of present divisional controllers.

In addition, we sought the perceptions of divisional controllers with regard to factors other than formal education that were important to their position. The controllers sampled also were asked to furnish advice as to the type of formal education and job-related experiences that they would recommend to individuals aspiring to a position of divisional controller in the future.

The sample consisted of 245 divisional controllers in *Fortune* 500 companies. We received replies from 180 divisional controllers for a total response rate of 73.5%. This relatively high response rate apparently indicates considerable interest in the issues addressed by the questionnaire. Table 1 provides data on relative size in terms of divisional sales for the division controllers participating in the survey.

What Is a Controller's Career Path?

In the initial part of the survey, we examined the careers of the divisional controllers in terms of their five most recent positions and the number of years they had occupied each position. We selected five most recent positions because we felt they would encompass the majority of meaningful job experiences for most of the respondents.

Table 2 provides a profile of the years of work experience for the divisional controllers replying to the questionnaire. An analysis of the data disclosed that, on the average, divisional controllers have a total of approximately 15 years of experience and that they tend to spend an average of slightly fewer than three years in each position as they progress through the organization. Although the divisional controllers have spent an average of three-and-a-half years in their current position, more than one-half (60.9%) have been in their current position for fewer than three years, and approximately one-fourth (26.8%) have been in their current position for one year or less. A further indication of rapid progression is that approximately 90% of the respondents had occupied their previous position for five years or less. Moreover, divisional controllers have achieved their present position by moving up through the ranks within their own company as opposed to "job-hopping." The survey results indicate that more than 90% of the divisional controllers had been promoted to their current positions from within.

An analysis of the respondents' five most recent positions revealed that most of their work experience was in accounting and finance-related positions. Additionally, 22% had some public ac-

Paul A. Janell is an associate professor of accounting at Northeastern University. He holds a Ph.D. degree from Michigan State University. He is a member of the Boston Chapter through which this article was submitted.

Raymond M. Kinnunen is an associate professor of business administration at Northeastern University. He holds a DBA degree from Louisiana State University.

0025-1690/80/6112-2746/$01.00/0

counting experience and 15% had some experience in internal auditing. Only 9% of the respondents indicated that at least one of their last five positions was a line position. Another 11% indicated that they performed in a staff position not directly related to accounting, finance or controllership functions such as administrative assistant to the president or manager of data processing. Table 3 shows sample profiles of two respondents in terms of job titles and years' experience per position.

We also asked the respondents if they had attained any professional certificates. Thirty-nine of the respondents indicated that they were CPAs (Certified Public Accountants), two individuals were CIAs (Certified Internal Auditors), and one individual had attained the CMA (Certificate in Management Accounting). The Certificate in Management Accounting program was established by NAA in early 1972 to provide recognition of educational attainment and competence in the field of management accounting.[1]

What Is a Controller's Educational Background?

We also wanted to find out about the formal educational background of controllers and to get their suggestions concerning formal education for future divisional controllers. Table 4 shows that formal education was almost universal among controllers sampled. Of the sample of 180 controllers, 95% had obtained a minimum of a bachelor's degree, with 83% holding a bachelor's degree in business administration. Of the remainder, 9% held bachelor's degrees in liberal arts, and 3% in engineering. Of the total sample, approximately one out of every three divisional controllers held a master of business administration degree (MBA). Given this educational profile, it is not surprising that all controllers recommended the minimum of a bachelor's degree and 88% recommended a graduate degree. A large percentage (70.5%) recommended the MBA (see Table 5).

The implication is that a graduate degree, especially the MBA degree, is now an important part of a controller's education and will be even more important in the future. The fact that an extremely large percentage (83%) of the divisional controllers held their bachelor's degrees in business and recommended (88%) a minimum of that same degree to others aspiring to become controllers indicates a need for a technical or specialist background in the business area. On the other hand, approximately 12% of our sample held baccalaureate degrees in areas other than business, 6% recommended a baccalaureate in liberal arts with an MBA, and 6% recommended an engineering degree with an MBA. Although these percentages are relatively low, they do imply that one can succeed as a divisional controller without a bachelor's degree in either accounting or business as long as one has an MBA at the minimum in terms of formal business education.

Other Skills Are Necessary

The individual controllers also mentioned factors other than formal education that they considered important in attaining their present positions (see Table 6). From the 92.2% of controllers responding to this question and out of the more than 350 responses, we developed four major categories: managerial ability, communication and interpersonal skills; personal characteristics; experience, and knowledge of the company.

As shown in Table 6, over one-third of the responses were grouped in the category that includes managerial ability, communication skills and interpersonal skills. Examples of these responses included: "motivating people," "working well with others," "human relations," "ability to motivate and supervise people," "communication skills," "ability to interact with superiors and subordinates," and so on. The second largest number of responses were categorized as personal characteristics, which included such items as: "initiative," "willingness to accept responsibility," "aggressiveness," "flexibility," "analytical ability," and so on. The next highest choice related to gen-

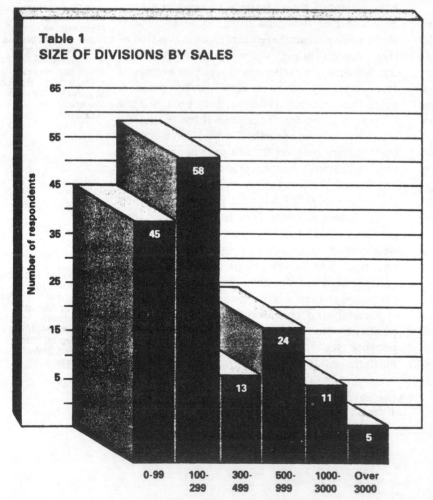

Table 1
SIZE OF DIVISIONS BY SALES

Number of respondents (y-axis: 5, 15, 25, 35, 45, 55, 65)

Values: 0-99: 45; 100-299: 58; 300-499: 13; 500-999: 24; 1000-3000: 11; Over 3000: 5

Sales revenue (millions)

eral experience, with approximately one-third of these respondents citing accounting. Other responses referred to practical experience in general, general business experience, general management experience, and so on. Finally, 16.4% of the responses were grouped in the category of knowledge of the company. Examples of responses in this category included: "orientation to the business—not just finance," "knowledge of products and markets," "broad knowledge of business functional relationships," "knowledge of other divisional operations," "familiarity with the industry," "functional knowledge of operations within your division," and so on.

From the responses to this question, one could infer that the controller's job in large divisionalized organizations extends far beyond accounting. The responses overwhelmingly indicate that a broad experience and knowledge base is important.

The data indicate that controllers possess managerial capabilities and require experience and knowledge of the total company that could characterize them as "generalists" rather than "specialists."[2]

The findings in our study are consistent with a recent survey in which chief executive officers suggested how accountants could increase their value to their organizations. Among the responses cited were:

> "Accountants should obtain a broad knowledge so as to understand non-accounting aspects of problems which they encounter."
> "Accountants should learn and understand the company's business."
> "Accountants should become better acquainted with the people, conditions, and equipment that are represented by the figures they work with."[3]

Job Experiences Related to the Divisional Controllers

In this part of the survey, we asked the divisional controllers to tell us what job experience would be important to individuals aspiring to be divisional controllers. We asked them to rank the functional areas they considered important with a rank of 1 = most important, 2 = next most important, and so on. A summary of the results appears in Table 7.

Cost accounting was ranked number one by 36.7% of the respondents, followed by general accounting, public accounting, and finance, which were ranked number one by 24.4%, 21.7%, and 12.8% of the respondents respectively. To further analyze the importance attributed to each area, we listed the number of times an area was ranked as one, two, three or four, as well as the total number of times the area was ranked in the top four. Thus,

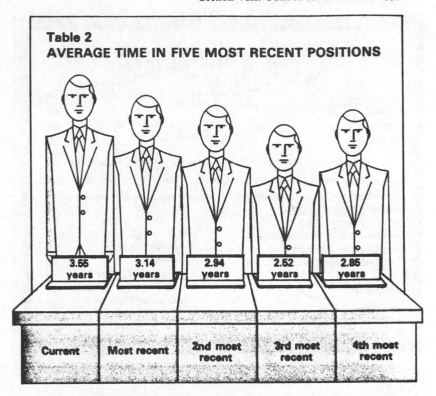

Table 2
AVERAGE TIME IN FIVE MOST RECENT POSITIONS

3.55 years	3.14 years	2.94 years	2.52 years	2.85 years
Current	Most recent	2nd most recent	3rd most recent	4th most recent

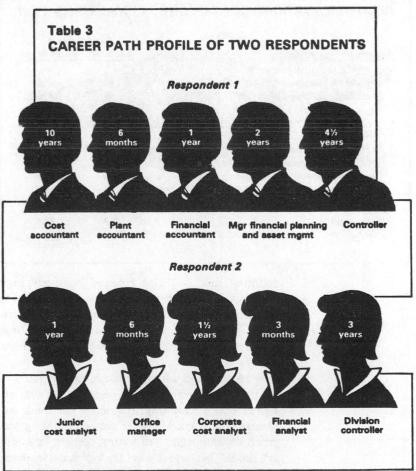

Table 3
CAREER PATH PROFILE OF TWO RESPONDENTS

Respondent 1

10 years	6 months	1 year	2 years	4½ years
Cost accountant	Plant accountant	Financial accountant	Mgr financial planning and asset mgmt	Controller

Respondent 2

1 year	6 months	1½ years	3 months	3 years
Junior cost analyst	Office manager	Corporate cost analyst	Financial analyst	Division controller

while cost accounting was ranked number one the most often, general accounting made the top four an equal number of times.

The job experiences related to accounting generally received the highest rankings. Finance, which in many ways is closely related to the ac-

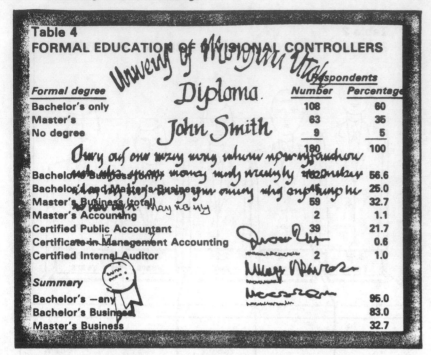

Table 4
FORMAL EDUCATION OF CORPORATE CONTROLLERS

Formal degree	Respondents	
	Number	Percentage
Bachelor's only	108	60
Master's	63	35
No degree	9	5
	180	100
Bachelor's Business		56.6
Bachelor's and Master's Business (total)		25.0
Master's Business (total)	59	32.7
Master's Accounting	2	1.1
Certified Public Accountant	39	21.7
Certificate in Management Accounting		0.6
Certified Internal Auditor	2	1.0
Summary		
Bachelor's —any		95.0
Bachelor's Business		83.0
Master's Business		32.7

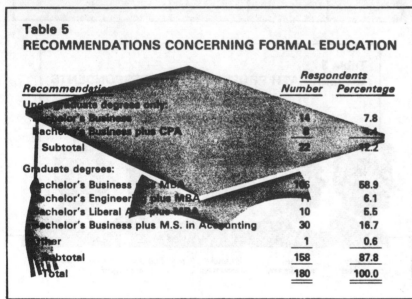

Table 5
RECOMMENDATIONS CONCERNING FORMAL EDUCATION

Recommendation	Respondents	
	Number	Percentage
Undergraduate degrees only:		
Bachelor's Business	14	7.8
Bachelor's Business plus CPA	8	7.4
Subtotal	22	12.2
Graduate degrees:		
Bachelor's Business plus MBA	106	58.9
Bachelor's Engineering plus MBA	11	6.1
Bachelor's Liberal Arts plus MBA	10	5.5
Bachelor's Business plus M.S. in Accounting	30	16.7
Other	1	0.6
Subtotal	158	87.8
Total	180	100.0

counting function, also received relatively high rankings. Data processing received high marks for the third and fourth most important job experiences. The other functional areas—marketing, production, and engineering—were farther down the list.

We also asked why individuals ranked particular items number one. The respondents who assigned cost accounting a number one rank explained that a knowledge of cost acccounting was especially important "to control costs in inflationary times," because it was "the key in determining profit margins for making decisions regarding customers and markets, managing product mix," and it was "the key to proper pricing, cost control, and budgets."

Others commented that cost accounting is "where the action is—current and future business decisions are based on good cost accounting . . .,"

"complete accurate cost information is (one of) . . . the most important ways to improve profitability," and "the most dynamic function . . . encompasses reality of . . . price-cost relationships."

Those individuals ranking general accounting as the number one job experience did so primarily because of the relationship of general accounting to financial reporting. Note the following comments: "determines the transactions involved in actual operating profit," "compliance with regulations of IRS and SEC," "backbone of all financial reporting," and "a good foundation of basic principles and policies coupled with a total system understanding is essential in producing meaningful management reports."

An analysis of the respondents ranking public accounting number one reveals that CPAs get broad experience in a relatively short time and increase their maturity and professionalism. These perceptions are reflected by the following sample responses: "broadest experience in shortest time due to exposure to a wide variety of companies and accounting systems," "allows for an exposure to all systems cycles," "widest possible experience in a short time frame," "diversified experience gives valuable insights into various systems and methods of solving accounting and reporting problems," "best experience because very quickly you relate to the executives of each client," "exposure and experience with corporate vice presidents gave a broader exposure faster and required an 'executive' approach to accounting and financial matters," and "excellent interface with other business systems and environments." Of the 39 CPAs in the sample, 22 ranked public accounting as the most important job experience.

The respondents who ranked finance as number one emphasized the importance of financial analysis and the ability to evaluate various alternatives in the decision-making process. Their responses included: "(It is) the foundation for a businessman controller, a functioning member of the management team," "must have knowledge (of finance) to evaluate alternative business opportunities in view of long- and short-term impact on company's financial position," and "analysis of manufacturing, marketing, and economic questions (is) of primary interest to (the) success of the business."

The responses to ranking internal audit as the number one job experience were similar to the responses about public accounting in that a broad exposure was stressed, but the focus was on one company as opposed to many companies or business in general. This fact is shown by the following comments: "best overall exposure to company in shortest time," "provides a knowledge of company, operations, practices and people," " a comprehensive exposure to all areas of accounting . . . to a variety of successful management people," and "gives a wide exposure to many areas of the corporation."

From the data on job experiences one can see that having a sound accounting background is crucial to the division controllership function. Many respondents also pointed out the need to be familiar with other aspects of the company, finance and data processing in particular, as well as to the company and business in general. Data in the educational background section supported the notion that a strong business education was important to the position. Also, the controller's job in a large divisionalized organization involves much more than just accounting; it requires "people skills," managerial ability, and a broad exposure to business.

Controller: the Total Picture

As we said, we wanted to develop a divisional controller's profile in terms of education and career path and to gather advice concerning education and job experience from individuals who had embarked on a career path that led to the controller position. The information we present here indicates a number of important factors for students and other individuals aspiring to become divisional controllers: the MBA degree will be more prevalent in the future, acquiring general management characteristics is important, progression will take approximately 12 years, and a sound management accounting background is extremely advantageous. Students also should take courses such as business policy and strategy, marketing management, and production management to get an overall view of the company.

Because most undergraduates are offered only a small sampling of these courses, they may want to pursue an MBA. The data obtained from our survey tend to support this idea. The fact that most of the controllers surveyed (80%) had no experience outside the accounting-finance-controllership area, that 33% had MBAs, and that 71% recommended the MBA degree indicate that the MBA degree is compensating for a partial weakness in undergraduate programs concerning broader aspects of education related to managing the total corporation. One could infer that obtaining an understanding of the entire operation of a company and its relationship to its environment is difficult at the undergraduate level. Because the functioning of the control system requires an understanding of the operations of the total firm, it may be that graduate courses provide a more in-depth view. This would be true of business policy courses that focus on the firm in relation to its environment and include management control as a major vehicle for implementing corporate strategy.[4]

The "total picture" view also is supported by the notion that the higher one goes in the controller ranks and the larger the organization, the less a controller would have to do with strictly "number crunching" and the more he or she would have to do with advising divisional management and administering the day-to-day functioning of the management control system. For example, some of the major tasks performed by divisional controllers should include:

1. Meeting the requirements described for the company-wide management control system as designed by the corporate controller;
2. Adapting the management control system (MCS) as it pertains to responsibility centers *within* the division to meet the particular needs of divisional management;
3. Informing the corporate controller of possible improvements in the overall MCS;
4. Providing analytical assistance to divisional management in the form of developing plans and budgets, reviewing performance and formulating appropriate corrective action, and meeting the requests of top management for explanations associated with the first two jobs;
5. Educating management personnel as to the proper use of the MCS, including its limitations and the proper role for the controller with respect to management control;
6. Cooperating with the corporate controller within his legitimate sphere of "functional supervision."[5]

Table 6
FACTORS IMPORTANT TO ATTAINING THE POSITION OF DIVISIONAL CONTROLLER

Category	Responses	
	Number	Percentage
Managerial ability, communication and interpersonal skills	123	33.6
Personal characteristics	99	27.1
Experience in general	84	22.9
Knowledge of the company	60	16.4
	366	100.0

Table 7
EXPERIENCE IMPORTANT TO DIVISION CONTROLLERSHIP FUNCTION

Area	Times ranked				
	#1	#2	#3	#4	In top #4
Cost accounting	66	48	20	11	145
General accounting	44	66	21	14	145
Public accounting	39	12	11	15	77
Finance	23	18	33	21	95
Internal audit	7	20	27	23	77
Data processing	2	14	32	47	95
Marketing	5	10	13	16	44
Production	3	8	16	17	44
Engineering	2	0	4	2	8

PORTRAIT OF THE DIVISIONAL CONTROLLER

In our research, we found that divisional controllers play an extremely important management and accounting role in large divisionalized corporations. From a management or internal reporting point of view, the role is broad, reaching beyond the traditional accounting function. Individuals aspiring to become divisional controllers and educators teaching them should be made aware of this trend. A broader preparation must be made available to students, and appropriate guidance offered them in preparing for a career as a divisional controller.   □

---

[1] At this time, certificates have been awarded to over 1,300 people. For more information, see the section "Institute of Management Accounting," MANAGEMENT ACCOUNTING, March 1979.
[2] See, for example, Hugo E.R. Uyterhoweven, "General Managers in the Middle," *Harvard Business Review*, March-April 1972.
[3] F. Don Stoddard, "The Accountant's Role in Management," MANAGEMENT ACCOUNTING, July 1978.
[4] For a discussion of management control from a total company point of view see, Raymond M. Kinnunen and Robert H. Caplan, III, "The Domain of Management Control," *University of Michigan Business Review*, May 1978.
[5] Robert H. Caplan, III, *Management Control Systems*, copyright 1967 by the President and Fellows of Harvard College (unpublished).

Professional

Special report—AICPA survey reveals rapid increase in use of EDP by CPA firms

A 1978 survey by the American Institute of CPAs has revealed a rapid increase in the use of electronic data processing by CPA firms.

More than 28,000 CPA firms received questionnaires regarding the use of in-house computers, timesharing, service centers and tax return preparation services in the management of an accounting practice. Approximately 8,200 firms responded to the survey (see exhibit 1, page 10).

In-house computers

Firms using in-house computers rose to 3,246 from 675 reported in the 1974 AICPA EDP survey (see JofA, July75, p.81).

Of the firms with in-house computers, the most prevalent vendors are Burroughs (801), IBM (798), Litton/Sweda (298), DEC (251), NCR (124), Wang (117) and Warrex Centurian (60).

Compared with the 24 hardware vendors reported in the 1974 survey, the number of vendors supplying the in-house computers used by CPA firms has increased to 85. Of these, 8 have each supplied more than 50 CPA firm installations as compared with 4 in the 1974 survey. And nearly one-third of the in-house installations are in sole practitioners' offices.

Personal computers are also having an impact on CPA firms. For example, over 30 firms in the

Exhibit 1

1978 EDP survey

Tabulation of the 8,213 responses

	Yes	No	No reply
Does your firm currently			
Use a tax return preparation service?	6,179	2,005	29
Have an in-house computer?	3,246	4,917	50
Write its own programs?	1,172	6,919	122
Use a service bureau?	4,351	3,749	113
Use timesharing?	647	7,413	153
Use nonhardware vendor software?	2,205	5,804	204
Use a computer audit software package?	161	7,885	167
Specialize in particular industries?	921	5,986	1,306

survey reported using Radio Shack's TRS-80, APPLE or SOL hardware.

Timesharing

Twenty-two timesharing services were used by 647 of the 8,213 responding firms (197 in 1974).

Predominant vendors are COM-SHARE (164), General Electric (123) and TYMSHARE (114). The remaining 19 services were each used by less than 20 firms.

Tax planning and statistical sampling, applications that work well in the real-time environment that timesharing offers, were—as in 1974—the most popular timesharing applications.

Tax return preparation

Seventy-five percent of the responding firms (6,179) indicated that they used a tax return preparation service.

Major vendors are COMPU-TAX (2,559), DYNATAX (916), FAST-TAX (355), TACS (283), UNITAX (273), DIGITAX (267) and SCS (218).

With the exception of COMPUTAX, DYNATAX and FAST-TAX, most services tended to be geographically oriented, with one or two states accounting for the majority of their users.

EDP applications

EDP uses in the CPA firm remained relatively unchanged from the 1974 survey. Client accounting (most notably, general ledger) and practice management continue

to be major applications.

The types of applications and how they are implemented are summarized in exhibit 2, below.

Accounting and audit software

According to the survey, 1,172 firms use their own personnel to write computer programs. The most common programming languages include RPG (421), BA-SIC (365) and COBOL (155).

Over 2,200 firms reported using software packages purchased from someone other than their hardware vendors.

Only 161 firms indicated that they use an audit software package. The most widely used packages include AUDITAPE (26), CARS 3 (10) and STRATA (9).

Sharing data

When asked if they would be willing, on an informal basis, to share their knowledge and experiences with other practitioners, 6,324 firms said they would.

These responses were used by the AICPA to build a file, which can be employed to answer requests from Institute members such as the following: "I'd like to talk to someone who has had experience in running inventory applications on a Wombat Model 12."

Conclusion

Survey results indicate that CPA firms are increasingly relying on EDP to support their practices. This is evident by the number of

Exhibit 2

EDP applications

	In-house computer	Service centers	Timesharing
Taxes			
Return preparation	502	141	38
Planning	288	186	203
Maintenance of client tax data	252	142	40
Client accounting			
Depreciation	1,268	724	108
General ledger	2,524	2,693	173
Accounts receivable	1,229	679	54
Accounts payable	678	400	32
Payroll	1,791	1,544	86
Customer billing	867	343	27
Inventory	336	236	19
Budgeting	681	341	79
Report preparation	2,012	1,755	136
Audit assistance			
Statistical sampling	220	117	208
Compliance testing	61	48	61
Substantive testing	70	48	61
Practice management			
Time and billing	1,427	849	80
Internal accounting	1,342	572	53
Staff scheduling	249	60	14

installations, which grew by almost 400 percent from 1974 to 1978.

While the rate of growth may slow down, it is not unreasonable to predict that 10,000 CPA firms will have in-house computer facilities by 1982.

—Alan Frotman
Manager, AICPA
computer services division